Visions of the Heart

CANADIAN ABORIGINAL ISSUES

Second Edition

DAVID LONG
Associate Professor
The King's University College
Edmonton

OLIVE PATRICIA DICKASON
Adjunct Professor
University of Ottawa

Harcourt
Canada

Harcourt Canada

Toronto Montreal Fort Worth New York Orlando
Philadelphia San Diego London Sydney Tokyo

Copyright © 2000 Harcourt Canada, Ltd.

All rights reserved. No part of this publication may be reproduced or transmitted in any form or by any means, electronic or mechanical, including photocopy, recording, or any information storage and retrieval system, without permission in writing from the publisher. Reproducing passages from this book without such written permission is an infringement of copyright law.

Requests for permission to photocopy any part of this work should be sent in writing to: College Licensing Officer, CANCOPY, 1 Yonge Street, 19th Floor, Toronto, ON, M5E 1E5. Fax: (416) 868-1621. All other inquiries should be directed to the publisher.

Every reasonable effort has been made to acquire permission for copyright material used in this text, and to acknowledge such indebtedness accurately. Any errors or omissions called to the publisher's attention will be corrected in future printings.

Canadian Cataloguing in Publication Data

Main entry under title:

Visions of the heart: Canadian aboriginal issues

2nd ed.
Includes index.
ISBN 0-7747-3635-6

1. Native peoples — Canada.* I. Long, David Alan, 1958- .
II. Dickason, Olive Patricia, 1920- .

E78.C2V58 2000   971'.00497   C99-931284-7

Acquisitions Editor: Megan Mueller
Developmental Editor: Lise Dupont
Production Editor: Stephanie Fysh
Production Coordinator: Cheryl Tiongson

Copy Editor: Claudia Kutchukian
Permissions Editor: Cindy Howard
Cover Design: Sonya V. Thursby, Opus House Incorporated
Interior Design: Dave Peters, revised by Sonya V. Thursby, Opus House Incorporated
Typesetting and Assembly: Carolyn Hutchings Sebestyen
Printing and Binding: Kromar Printing Ltd.

Cover art: *We Walk Together* by Daphne Odjig. Acrylic on canvas: 38" by 30". Copyright © Daphne Odjig. All rights reserved. Image provided by Gallery Gevik.

Born 1919 on the Wikmemikong Reserve on Manitoulin Island, Daphne Odjig is a member elect of the Royal Canadian Academy and has been exhibited widely across North America.

Statistics Canada information is used with the permission of the Minister of Industry, as Minister responsible for Statistics Canada. Information on the availability of the wide range of data from Statistics Canada can be obtained from Statistics Canada's Regional Offices, its World Wide Web site at http://www.statcan.ca, and its toll-free access number 1-800-263-1136.

Harcourt Canada
55 Horner Avenue, Toronto, ON, Canada M8Z 4X6
Customer Service
Toll-Free Tel.: 1-800-387-7278
Toll-Free Fax: 1-800-665-7307

This book was printed in Canada.
1 2 3 4 5   04 03 02 01 00

PREFACE

The postcolonial age in which we live is a fundamental turning point in human history. The hallmark of this age is the movement throughout the world of diverse peoples seeking to challenge the basic ethnocentric tenet of colonialism — that one people's way of thinking and acting is *the* way for all peoples. As the research and writing contained in this second edition of *Visions of the Heart* suggests, proper scholarly understanding of this age depends on critical, interdisciplinary analysis of socio-structural, historical, geographical, anthropological, psychological, literary, aesthetic, interpersonal, and spiritual dimensions of human life. Our descriptions and analyses of relations between Aboriginal and non-Aboriginal peoples in Canada testify to the complex, sometimes apparently contradictory, character of postcolonial processes, circumstances, and structures. Collectively they also capture a central and quite striking feature of this time in history, namely the slow, sometimes painful, and some would argue inexorable, movement toward just relations between diverse people. The liberating vision embodied in postcolonial thought and activity is that the fundamental values of human freedom and dignity ought to be protected, cultivated, and celebrated. As we examine the experiences, thoughts, and activities of Aboriginal and non-Aboriginal people committed to these values, we see numerous signs of hope. One of the most significant of these is that an increasing number of people seem to be committed to realizing a shared, postcolonial vision.

This is not to gloss over or diminish the many experiences of pain, anger, confusion, and fear, for contributors to *Visions of the Heart* acknowledge (in some instances as a consequence of their own lived experience) that the experience of and response to colonial oppression are profoundly real and not easily captured in academic writing. Neither do we mean to give the impression that identifying some "central" aspect of postcolonialism will automatically result in people thinking or acting in more just and humane ways. Indeed, suspicion toward the word "central" is basic to postcolonial theorizing and activity. The self-conscious deconstruction of an imposed centre and the simultaneous reconstruction of one's personal or a people's identity undergirds many a postcolonial experience and project. The importance of postcolonial scholarship is thus that it seeks to give voice to the authentic experiences and perspectives of those who live oppressed, marginal lives, as well as to name and deconstruct the circumstances and unjust human actions that contribute to the centring of certain people and the marginalizing of others. Consequently, our analyses of the honourable as well as ignoble aspects of this country's history are informed both by Aboriginal people's experiences as well as by the healing- and justice-informed visions of their hearts.

An experience shared by a number of people during the summer of 1997 illustrates that impassioned pleas for justice, guidance, and critical understanding can indeed unify and bring hope to people with very different backgrounds and experiences. It occurred in the living room of two non-Aboriginal people who have loved and served the Stoney people of Morley, Alberta, for more than 30 years. In the room with Warren and Mary Anna were my partner Karen and I, along with a Stoney mother and her daughter. Together we opened ourselves to the stories of these two Stoney women as they graciously and vulnerably shared their feelings of anger, sadness, frustration, and hope. As we communed with these two sacred storytellers, aspects of their stories brought us to tears, while others made us laugh and opened small cracks of hope in our hearts and minds. Although everyone in the room knew that the physical and social conditions experienced by the majority of people living on the Stoney reserve would remain unchanged that night, we also sensed that the healing experienced that evening in the relationship between a mother and her daughter was more than emotional and spiritual. We all recognized more deeply than before that inward and outward healing will occur to the extent that people are willing and able to listen to and honour the healing- and justice-informed visions of their hearts.

Some people assert that as we near the third millennium, there is a woeful lack of vision in Canada. This perspective is not shared by contributors to *Visions of the Heart,* for it seems to us that it is precisely Aboriginal people's commitment to the visions of their hearts that has long animated their willingness and ability to seek personal and social justice, healing, and reconciliation. Our contribution to dialogue and healing in this edition of *Visions of the Heart* is therefore twofold: to critically examine past and present sources of oppression of Aboriginal life in Canada and to explore ways in which Aboriginal people in Canada continue in their efforts to realize the visions of their hearts. The contributors to this collection also agree that as we approach the new millennium, academic and non-academic writers must take seriously our role as storytellers. We recognize that just as storytellers of the past gave expression to a myriad of experiences, the invitation of difference into academic and non-academic conversations is the lifeblood of genuine, visionary dialogue. In *Visions of the Heart* we thus invite readers into our accounts and analyses of Aboriginal people's struggles to attain their visions. Our continued hope is that readers will appreciate that even though it may take but a brief historical moment for a nation to fall, genuine visions that seek justice, healing, and reconciliation are difficult if not impossible to eradicate.

ACKNOWLEDGEMENTS

Editing *Visions of the Heart* has once again been a rewarding experience, due in large part to those I worked and lived with who helped bring it to fruition. Undoubtedly, my editorial task would have been much more difficult had not Lise Dupont from Harcourt Brace shared my enthusiasm for this book and with gentle firmness encouraged me to "encourage" contributors to give this book the priority that she believed it deserved. Moreover, much that is positive about the paths this book takes in relation to contemporary Aboriginal issues reflects the skill and effort of its writers. Consequently, I once again want to acknowledge my appreciation for the insights, commitment, and passion for justice and healing that the contributing authors brought to their work. I also continue to be grateful for my colleagues at The King's University College, who contributed to this book through their willingness to listen to my ideas and challenge me to wrestle with the many dimensions of human social life often glossed over or ignored by mainstream sociology.

On a more personal note, I am privileged to receive support, encouragement, and joy from my partner Karen, and from our children, Jennica, Bethany, Sarah, and Kathryn. Karen's enduring love and support continue to surprise and amaze me, and though my dedication of this book to her pales in comparison to the dedication she brings to our relationship, I nonetheless wish to offer this book to her today (in lieu of flowers). I am also thankful for John, Michelle, Erin, and Nathan, who as part of my family continue to bring everyday challenges, renewal, and hope into my life. Finally, although there are many signs of hope in the lives of Aboriginal people in Canada, it is an understatement to say that it is unfortunate that many of the issues addressed in this book continue to be a part of Canadian life. I therefore feel greatly indebted to the many courageous and trusting Aboriginal people who disclosed their personal thoughts and experiences to those of us committed to listening to their stories and to giving them an academic voice. Without their contributions, it would be impossible to even begin to understand and address aspects of relations between Aboriginal and non-Aboriginal people in a manner that promises healing and delivers hope.

David Long

A Note from the Publisher

Thank you for selecting *Visions of the Heart: Canadian Aboriginal Issues*, Second Edition, by David Long and Olive Patricia Dickason. The authors and publisher have devoted considerable time to the careful development of this book. We appreciate your recognition of this effort and accomplishment.

We want to hear what you think about the second edition of *Visions of the Heart*. Please take a few minutes to fill in the stamped reply card at the back of the book. Your comments, suggestions, and criticisms will be valuable to us as we prepare new editions and other books.

CONTENTS

INTRODUCTION

The legitimate claims of Aboriginal peoples challenge Canada's sense of justice and its capacity to accommodate both multinational citizenship and universal respect for human rights. More effective Aboriginal participation in Canadian institutions should be supplemented by legitimate Aboriginal institutions, thus combining self-rule with shared rule. The Commission's proposals are not concerned with multi-cultural policy but with a vision of a just multinational federation that recognizes historical nations as an integral part of Canadian identity and the Canadian political fabric. (RCAP, 1996b, p. xxiv)

Contributors to *Visions of the Heart* agree that Canada will flourish to the extent that Aboriginal and non-Aboriginal people share a just and healing vision for this country. We also recognize, along with the Royal Commission on Aboriginal Peoples (RCAP) organizers and contributors, that there is great value in honouring people's experiences, perspectives, and visions that have long been communicated through stories passed across generations and between diverse peoples, stories that have been spoken and conveyed symbolically in countless contexts. Humans have chiselled their stories into stone tablets, etched them with ochre onto papyrus leaves, woven them into wampum belts, inscribed them in ornate, highly formalized manuscripts, drawn them with bright crayons on construction paper, and conveyed them through an array of electronic media. People have also expressed and commemorated their heartfelt visions in a vast number of ways, from Hebrew priests slaughtering sacrificial lambs during Passover to signify cleansing, to Plains Amerindian males engaging in self-mutilation to induce personal and communal visions in their version of the Sun Dance, to Muslims expressing their desire for purification through fasting during Ramadan, to celebrations by gays and lesbians in their adaptations of Canada Day parades. Regardless of how they are embodied, genuine communal visions invite a people to contemplate, lament, and celebrate the vagaries of human experience. Moreover, shared vision cultivates hope by enabling a people to articulate their path toward a common future. The contributors to this book acknowledge that Aboriginal people in Canada have long expressed such heartfelt visions, or, as we call them, *Visions of the Heart*.

Unfortunately, not all visions of the heart seek peace, justice, healing, and harmony among different peoples. A disquieting message from much of human history is that shared visions that leave a path of human misery and destruction in their wake can and do flourish. For example, roughly 500 years ago European explorers from France and Great Britain sought to discover lands and possibly peoples suitable for colonizing. By and large their colonizing vision was informed by a perspective that regarded Aboriginal inhabitants of any lands they "discovered" as inferior. Consequently, whether colonizers used the language of assimilation or extermination in relation to Aboriginal peoples, their vision of a "New World" rarely if ever included indigenous ways of thinking and acting. Woven throughout the pages of this book are pictures of the multifaceted relationship between European colonization and the physical, cultural, and structural aspects of Aboriginal life in this country. The result, depending on one's perspective, is a collection of somewhat less than pretty sociohistorical pictures.

Since the early 1960s, there have been significant changes in the experiences of Aboriginal peoples in Canada and in writing by and about them. Prior to that time, a number of theoretical perspectives assumed that social disorganization, cultural conflict, and feelings of inferiority experienced by racial and ethnic minority group members reflected their inability or unwillingness to adjust to rapid social and cultural change. Anthropologists, including Franz Boas, acknowledged the distortions that ethnocentrism can bring to understanding various societies, though these writers were, for the most part, blind to the pervasiveness and effects of colonialism. What undergirded the perspectives of those who were blind to their own ethnocentrism before the 1960s was their assumption of the superiority of dominant individuals, groups, and societies. Consequently, Aboriginal and other marginalized peoples living in Canada and elsewhere were often blamed for having inadequate skills, for lacking understanding of European ways, and for their general unwillingness to commit themselves to alleviating their personal and social problems. Scholars, government officials, and others found apparent support for these theoretical perspectives in Aboriginal peoples' high rates of physical and mental illness, family violence, suicide, homicide, incarceration, and unemployment, and in their relatively impoverished standards of living. They further assumed that little could be done to help Aboriginal people in Canada, since not only did they regard Aboriginal people as being responsible for their own problems, they also viewed them as lacking the adequate technical and interpersonal skills and commitment necessary to address their problems in constructive ways.

During the 1960s, a different set of theoretical assumptions emerged in relation to the personal and social problems experienced by Aboriginal people in Canada. According to those writing out of this emergent post-colonial perspective, colonized social structures and processes needed to be examined in light of the experiences and perspectives of marginalized people. These analysts further drew attention to the fact that colonization operates at different levels and in a multitude of contexts. At the structural level, all aspects of indigenous life are formally reorganized through the enforcement of policies and legislation that reflect a colonial perspective and that primarily serve the economic, political, legal, and cultural interests of settlers. At the intergroup and interpersonal levels, the homogenizing, imperialist cultural ways and means of colonialism gradually displace the diverse experiences, perspectives, and expressions of Aboriginal and other marginalized peoples. According to postcolonial analysis, colonization thus represents a "totalizing" phenomenon in that it leaves no area of social life or individual experience untainted.

Although contributors to *Visions of the Heart* agree with the major assumptions underlying postcolonial analysis, we also recognize that human beings are creative social agents who experience, interpret, and adapt to social life in many different ways and for many different reasons. According to critics of Native residential schools, for example, the violent and oppressive character of these institutions was directly responsible for the personal, familial, cultural, and economic problems experienced by the Aboriginal people who attended them. While acknowledging that the residential school system had many personally and socially destructive consequences, some point out that many Aboriginal people benefited personally and socially from attending these schools. Jan Hare and Jean Barman note in their analysis that understanding the past and present significance of residential schooling means much more than critiquing the personal and cultural experiences of students and their extended families, tallying up how many Aboriginal people were negatively or positively affected, or exploring the evolution of educational policies and practices. They assert that we understand residential schooling and other social phenomena to the extent that we listen to those who offer a variety of perspectives on their historical, structural, cultural, and interpersonal dimensions. Readers should thus keep in mind that while postcolonial perspectives provide us with a certain direction and focus, like any other perspective on human life they provide us with only a partial understanding.

In this second edition of *Visions of the Heart*, we again want to invite readers to explore and reflect critically on the relationships between European colonization and a wide variety of issues involving Aboriginal peoples in Canada, including changes in the roles of Aboriginal elders, emerging issues for Aboriginal women, changes in the organization of Aboriginal government, the grouping of Aboriginal people into different categories with different rights and responsibilities, the pervasiveness of violence and the fragmentation of healing and health-related services and provisions in Aboriginal communities, the establishment of reserves and residential schools, the experiences of Aboriginal children and related healing initiatives, culturally oppressive practices and policies that comprise the corrections system in Canada, the structure and dynamics of coalition support for the Lubicon First Nation and other Aboriginal peoples in Canada, and the contributions of Aboriginal and other peoples toward a more holistic economic development perspective. As you read and think about these and other issues, we again ask that you attempt to walk in the shoes of those who have benefited from colonization as well as those who have not.

Continuing in the spirit of the first edition, our hope is that readers of this second edition will once again be challenged and enabled to put their own understandings and perspectives about Aboriginal life in Canada to the test. To encourage dialogue beyond this book, questions specific to each contribution are included at the end of each chapter. Beyond these specific questions, we want to encourage readers to reflect on the more general questions of who should be responsible for addressing current aspects of Aboriginal life and how those who are responsible for bringing about healing changes should go about their tasks. The Glossary included in this edition is intended to provide readers with a more clear sense of how contributors to this book understand key terms, while the Further Readings section at the end of each chapter suggests directions that readers might take should they decide to pursue an area in more depth. *Visions of the Heart* is therefore intended as more than a collection of articles by individuals writing on a common theme in their areas of expertise. Together, these chapters illustrate the value of discussion involving people with different experiences and perspectives. The chapters also support the view that unifying dialogue does not imply sameness of experience and oneness of voice. Regardless of whether contributors have painted relatively abstract, generalized pictures or intimate, highly detailed portraits of Aboriginal–non-Aboriginal relations, we agree that meaningful academic discourse on Canadian Aboriginal issues should embody and cultivate respect for differences in experience and perspective. The diverse character of this collection thus represents our way of attempting to be inclusive in our dialogue and to challenge those who esteem unity of literary or methodological style and oneness of voice.

In the first edition, contributors agreed that before 1996 there had been relatively few comprehensive examinations of Canadian Aboriginal issues. We acknowledged that a large number of national and provincial task forces, non-governmental organizations, and individual researchers had examined many different areas of Aboriginal life in Canada but qualified this with the comment that studies offering a "big-picture" perspective on contemporary Aboriginal issues in this country had until that time been few and far between. That, of course, was just prior to the release in 1996 of the five-volume *Report of the Royal Commission on Aboriginal Peoples*. The original mandate of the RCAP was published in 1991, and was followed by four years of public hearings throughout Canada involving thousands of intervenors sharing their experiences, thoughts, and research findings. The final report is thus a comprehensive historical document that places the experiences of Aboriginal peoples and the issues they face in a broad socio-historical context. It contains a wealth of descriptive information, stories, commentary, analysis, and recommendations for change. As a compilation of individual and collective stories, questions, experiences, and insights the document is an invaluable source for Aboriginal and non-Aboriginal leaders, researchers, policy-makers, lawyers, and community activists, to name a few. And while the RCAP final report contains a wealth of information, thoughtful recommendations, and many valuable insights, in an important respect it embodies something that is much more significant than the words, statistics, and ideas printed on its pages: fundamentally, the RCAP is a watershed of hope for Aboriginal and non-Aboriginal peoples throughout Canada, since it represents the commitment of many people to work together in realizing a postcolonial vision for this country.

The Royal Commission on Aboriginal Peoples can be regarded as a watershed for a number of reasons. First, it involved hundreds of thousands of people across Canada expressing their commitment to the idea that all Canadians need to hear the stories of Aboriginal peoples. In part this meant providing a safe and open opportunity for commission intervenors to tell others how they experience and understand the history, place, and experiences of Aboriginal people in Canada. Those who attended the hearings thus had an opportunity to hear a great many voices and many more stories that were drawn from every province and territory of Canada; agonizing laments of circumstances involving lost individuals, abusive experiences, and destroyed families and communities; analyses of the social structures, processes, and decisions that built and served to perpetuate colonial rule over Aboriginal people for the past 500 years in North America; and resurrected stories and lessons that somehow survived the onslaught of colonial oppression. Second, the RCAP as a symbol of hope testifies to the resourcefulness, courage, strength, understanding, wisdom, and vision of Aboriginal and non-Aboriginal peoples in Canada. By inviting people from all over Canada to share their insights and understanding, the RCAP provided a concrete opportunity for diverse people to begin building a shared vision for this country. The final report is thus a humbling document, for it offers both a penetrating analysis and an invitation to bring justice, healing, and hope to historically colonized relations involving Aboriginal and non-Aboriginal peoples in Canada. Its notably "post" postcolonial character is evident in comments and accounts that suggest that healing and reconciliation are not only possible, but have already happened or are in the process of being experienced by diverse people in countless contexts. If a key character of postcolonial critique and analysis is that all vestiges of colonization ought to be scrutinized in light of the experiences and perspectives of marginalized people, then the RCAP foreshadows an age that will follow our postcolonial times. As noted in the final report (1996a, p. 611):

> Equating Aboriginal peoples with racial and cultural minorities is a fundamentally flawed conception. People came to Canada from other countries in large numbers, over a period of several hundred years, and they came as immigrants — that is, for the most part they chose to leave their homelands as individuals and families and to settle in an already established country. Aboriginal people are not immigrants. They are the original inhabitants of the land and have lived here from time immemorial.

The RCAP foreshadows a time after our postcolonial age by embodying the efforts of diverse people challenging and enabling one another to "look" honestly and critically at all of their lives together. As Fox and Long note in their chapter on violence and healing, it is in some respects a sign of healing that Aboriginal people across Canada are publicly voicing the internal conflicts and lack of consensus in their communities. Such temporary, albeit painful, paths of healing are necessary if Aboriginal people are to experience the physical, social, emotional, and spiritual harmony and vitality that characterize healthy individuals and societies. Finally, the RCAP embodies hope, since it seeks to develop ways and means through which the revitalization of Aboriginal people's confidence in themselves, their communities, and their cultures can be cultivated and realized in their daily lives (RCAP, 1996b, p. 12). As Chief Gordon Peters noted, "Some call it healing; some call it regeneration. No matter what it is called, it is the same process — people taking control over their individual lives" (RCAP, 1996c, p. 14).

Contributors to *Visions of the Heart* recognize that the means by which people take control over their lives are numerous. We also share the hope that knowledge gained from our research and writing on paths and obstacles to healing will contribute to critical, informed dialogue and meaningful opportunities for personal and social change. Toward that end, research in *Visions* generated as well as drew upon a significant amount of quantitative data, notably in the work of Norris, Wall, Hare and Barman, Peters, Monture-Angus, Brascoupé, and Long. Their data come from a large number and variety of sources, including submissions to the RCAP; national, provincial, and territorial task forces; data from federal and provincial ministries; non-governmental studies; and numerous other reports and discussion papers. Nonetheless, contributors recognize that social scientists and others can easily make the mistake of generalizing from aggregate data that has been drawn from regions, cities, reserves, and settlements with vastly different historical and social characteristics. Even Mary Jane Norris, who uses national-level data in her detailed demographic analysis, cautions against the temptation to quickly generalize from such data to all First Nation, non-status, Métis, or Inuit people in this country.

While generalized pictures of Aboriginal life are important, qualitative research that explores individual experiences and stories fleshes out our understanding of human life. The qualitative approach to research is well represented throughout *Visions of the Heart*. Indeed, the contributions of Couture, Fox, Long, Peters, Hare and Barman, and Brascoupé illustrate that giving voice to the uniqueness of Aboriginal and non-Aboriginal people's experiences and perspectives deepens our understanding of individual and collective aspects of life in Canada. Moreover, research that honours the diverse and subtle character of human experience challenges readers to reflect critically on the role of all storytellers and the validity of their stories.

Contributors to this second edition recognize that all analyses of Aboriginal social issues are highly interpretive. Moreover, we all continue to support the healing and social justice perspective that informs *Visions of the Heart*, a perspective that maintains that academics should do more than just describe social circumstances and name particular visions that legitimize oppression. Our goal is to challenge and enable readers to think beneath and beyond social scientific descriptions; to ask informed, critical questions; and to engage in humble, visionary dialogue in relation to Canadian Aboriginal issues. Together, the chapters highlight a number of significant issues in research involving Aboriginal peoples. Perhaps the most basic of these is that much contemporary social science provides a rather impersonal, detached approach to understanding social life in Canada. We recognize that writers and readers hold a variety of views on the relationship between researchers and researched, and that we undoubtedly have different reasons for viewing the relationship the way we do. Constructive dialogue therefore depends on having a sense of how and why we view the relationship in particular ways. This does not necessarily require having to tell our own personal story every time we speak or write. Rather, it means honestly reflecting on certain fundamental methodological and theoretical issues in research that involve human subjects. The issues that the contributors to *Visions of the Heart* reflected on included (1) the benefits and drawbacks of using certain types of data (ethnographic, oral history, interview, survey, archival, etc.); (2) the dilemmas confronted in attempting to convey the inner workings of societies based on oral traditions to mass audiences; (3) the general challenges in doing cross-cultural research; (4) the different experiences, concerns, and perspectives of Aboriginal and non-Aboriginal people in relation to the lives of Aboriginal peoples, perhaps also including differences among Aboriginal (or non-Aboriginal) people; and (5) the politically charged issues surrounding voice appropriation, all of which are fundamentally a question of the appropriateness and validity of telling another's story. Although not all contributors articulate their position on all of these methodological and theoretical issues, there is agreement that the different styles of writing as well as the various methodological and theoretical approaches to exploring Canadian Aboriginal issues that are represented throughout *Visions of the Heart* are a strength of this collection.

One major theme that runs throughout the book concerns the relationship between past experiences and present circumstances involving Aboriginal people in Canada. All contributors in this edition place the development of issues and activities involving Aboriginal peoples in a historical context. Furthermore, Voyageur, Fleras, Wall, and Long all underscore that Canadian Aboriginal issues do not merely involve high-profile Aboriginal and non-Aboriginal leaders, and that there are a multitude of interactions through which diverse actors support or oppose one another in interpersonal, communal, national, and international contexts. Along with providing a sense of socio-historical context, a number of contributors invite readers to reflect on the everyday, grass-roots experiences and perspectives of Aboriginal and other peoples. Couture's account of the re-emergence of Aboriginal elders and Fox and Long's oral historical account of violence and healing in Stoney Country illustrate particularly well that certain perspectives on life can only be gained from experience. Also, Peters's vision of the role of Aboriginal people in urban areas, Fournier and Crey's call to recognize the important place and future role of Aboriginal children, Monture-Angus's analysis of Aboriginal (in)justice, Brascoupé's drawing together of a number of indigenous and spiritual insights into a more holistic vision of economic development, and Long's examination of coalition support for the Lubicon First Nation all demonstrate that meaningful dialogue and constructive social change depend on people's openness to different experiences, perspectives, and visions. Unlike most social-scientific accounts of Aboriginal life in Canada, these chapters seek to highlight the importance of readers asking how Aboriginal people themselves might interpret the lives and experiences of Aboriginal people in Canada. Although not all of the chapters were written by Aboriginal authors, by attempting to break down the socially constructed barriers between researchers and researched these writers offer an alternative and more personal view of social science. Indeed, each chapter in *Visions of the Heart* shows in its own way that the contribution of Aboriginal people to the formation of modern Canada has been both much greater and more multifaceted than has ever been generally acknowledged, and that Aboriginal people continue to actively contribute to Canadian society today. Authors in this collection share the conviction and hope that in taking up the challenge to understand the place and experience of Aboriginal people in Canada, academics and non-academics alike will contribute to justice, healing, and reconciliation in relations among and between Aboriginal and non-Aboriginal peoples in Canada.

REFERENCES

Royal Commission on Aboriginal Peoples (RCAP). 1996a. *Gathering Strength.* Ottawa: Supply and Services.
————. 1996b. *Looking Forward, Looking Back.* Ottawa: Supply and Services.
————. 1996c. *Restructuring the Relationship.* Ottawa: Supply and Services.

CHAPTER 1

Toward a Larger View of Canada's History: The Native Factor[1]

Olive Patricia Dickason

A major lesson of the Oka confrontation of 1990 for most Canadians was the startling realization of how little they knew about their own history. For many, it was a revelation to learn that the conflict, far from being a flash in the pan, had roots that go deep into our national past — easily to the first meetings between Amerindians[2] and Europeans, and by extension even beyond, if the attitudes that both sides brought with them are included. Nothing in our standard national histories prepared Canadians for this. The accepted historical approach, at least until recently, has been to begin with the voyages of Jacques Cartier, give a brief summary of his relations with the Amerindians of the St. Lawrence Valley, go on to discuss the fur trade and missionary activity that were described as radically altering the Amerindian way of life, and perhaps to include something about the role of Amerindians in the colonial wars of the seventeenth and eighteenth centuries. Once launched into the political and constitutional development of our country, historians have habitually left the Amerindians far behind as picturesque but irrelevant relics of the past. Not even mentioned are the numbered treaties of the west and north, by which the federal government acquired enormous areas of Amerindian lands for white settlement and industrial development, paving the way for the creation of the Canadian confederacy. Until well into the twentieth century, Canadian historians habitually depicted Natives as barbarians much in need of the civilizing influence of whites. There was little, if any, serious attempt to examine the Amerindian side of the story.[3]

HISTORY AS DEFINED IN THE WESTERN WORLD

History as developed in the Western world during the nineteenth century is based upon written documentation, particularly when derived from official sources (Dickason, 1997, p. xi). Oral tradition was not considered reliable (or even pertinent) for historical purposes, and so was categorically dismissed. Further, until the past few decades, the emphasis was almost exclusively on public affairs, where the powerful and important dominated; not only were the rank and file who made up the bulk of society largely excluded, but preliterate or tribal societies were almost completely ignored. Such societies were labelled prehistoric or perhaps protohistoric; the best they could hope for was to become historic by extension, when they came into contact with literate societies. Since this meant that history began with the arrival of Europeans, Canadians considered theirs a young country, a land of much geography and little history.[4] As H.H. Trevor-Roper, Regius Professor of Modern History at Oxford University, maintained when discussing Africa, the period before the arrival of Europeans "is largely darkness, like the history of pre-European, pre-Columbian America. And darkness is not a subject of history" (*The Rise of Christian Europe*, cited in Krech, 1991, p. 345).

In the case of Canada, the meeting of the French and Amerindians on the North Atlantic Coast in the sixteenth century was very poorly documented, because with few exceptions (principally Jacques Cartier, who made three official voyages during 1534–42), early visitors came over on their own initiative, attracted by the profits to be made from fishing and whaling. Keeping records was not a concern, except perhaps for commercial reasons, and the survival rate of those records has reflected their low official importance. It should also be remembered that these meetings were not a first, either for the French or for the Natives. The French had been trading with Amerindians in Brazil for nearly a century before they began seriously to develop the northern fur trade toward the end of the sixteenth century. By that time, northern Amerindians and Inuit had been dealing with Basque and Breton fishermen for almost as long, and before that may have encountered Norse. The earliest accounts we have indicate prior familiarity on both sides (except perhaps for the Norse); nowhere in the documented Canadian experience do we find Amerindians reacting toward Europeans as they did in the Caribbean toward the Spanish, whom they at first regarded as returning spirits. The closest approximation of this that has been recorded for Canada was Cartier's reception by the people upriver on the St. Lawrence above Stadacona (today's Quebec City), especially at Hochelaga (today's Montreal). There is some indication that they regarded Cartier as a shaman, with curing powers; however, their joy seems to have been mainly inspired by the French breach of Stadacona's control of the river and the consequent prospect of direct trade with the new arrivals. Known documentary sources about these contacts, patchy as they are, in most cases have not been thoroughly searched by historians with Native history in mind. Surviving records, early published material, and Native traditions all need to be re-examined with this in view. A point to remember is that written accounts, no matter how apparently objective they may seem, are always influenced by the attitudes and beliefs (not to mention the cultural outlook) of the writer. It is not unusual for these reports to differ, sometimes widely, even when dealing with the same event. This can be a particular problem with printed material, when texts have not only been edited differently in various editions, but have also been changed from the original manuscript. To complicate the matter even further, many of these manuscripts are now lost. Sorting out the biases and misinformation from facts is rarely simple, no matter what the source.

TOWARD A BROADER CONCEPTION

Despite such difficulties, this century has seen a move toward a broader view of history, a move that has meant that, among other things, historians have begun to pay more attention to tribal nations. Because those nations were oral, rather than literate, peoples (even those who did possess a form of writing had not developed it into a widely shared form of communication), reconstructing their precontact history in the Western sense of the term is a daunting task. The inadequacy of written sources means that researching such a history calls for an interdisciplinary approach, one that draws from geology, archaeology, anthropology, linguistics, oral traditions, and the arts. Each provides insights that when pieced together with whatever documentary evidence exists help to fill in the picture. A principal problem for this approach has been the development of critical techniques to evaluate the information; cross-checking can be difficult, if possible at all. On top of that, the type of information provided by oral history does not necessarily fit the requirements of Western-style history.[5]

Before delving into research methods, two questions should be answered: why is an understanding of prehistory important, and why should historians concern themselves about first contacts if the information is so difficult to come by? To begin with the second question, first contacts set the pattern for what was to follow in Amerindian–white relationships. The first impression of Europeans—that Amerindians were "a remarkably strange and savage people, without faith, without law, without religion" (Thevet, 1878, p. 135)—crystallized into attitudes that determined patterns of relationships, which in turn influenced policies.

It is comparatively simple to trace out this sequence in today's some-times problematic relations between First Nations and mainstream soci-ety. Two clear examples of this are the confrontation at Oka in 1990 over land that the Mohawk claim to be theirs since time immemorial and Jus-tice Allan McEachern's rejection in 1991 of the Gitksan and Wet'-suwet'en claim to 58 000 square kilometres of traditional lands in north-ern British Columbia, a resource-rich area about the size of Nova Scotia. Justice McEachern denied the existence of Aboriginal rights of ownership and jurisdiction,[6] drawing on arguments that had been developed origi-nally from the sixteenth through the eighteenth centuries to justify the European takeover of Aboriginal lands. According to these arguments, a sedentary lifestyle based on farming within a nation-state is a prerequisite for proprietary and sovereign rights; since hunter–gatherers changed their abodes with the seasons, they had no legitimate claims to either. The Mo-hawk are facing the added challenge of proving that they were the first, and continuous, occupants of the lands they are claiming. From these ex-amples it should be clear why it is important to understand the nature and history of precontact societies in Canada, at least as far as we are able. As Renaissance Europe had debated, were these fully formed societies, al-though of models very different from those of Europe? Or were they liv-ing according to nature, and thus with no more property rights (or rights of any kind, for that matter) than panthers or bears, to use a nineteenth-century journalistic expression?

WHAT GEOLOGY HAS TO SAY

Geology is included among the disciplines that contribute to our knowl-edge about our First Nations, because it tells us what the ecological con-ditions were, and so when and where humans could survive. Since Cana-da was largely icebound until about 14 000 to 10 000 years ago, human habitation appears to have been first confined to the few areas that es-caped glaciation, such as the Yukon. In regions south of the glaciers, it has been estimated that ecological conditions have been suitable for human habitation for about 50 000 years or more. It is widely believed by schol-ars (although passionately disputed by many Natives) that Amerindians first crossed over from Siberia on foot during periods when intensification of the glaciation lowered the sea level, transforming the Bering Strait into a grassy strip some 2000 kilometres wide, dotted with clumps of birch, heath, and willow ("What the Stone Tools Tell Us," cited in Dickason, 1997, p. 3). Geologists inform us that this land bridge, called Beringia, emerged several times during the late Pleistocene geological age (the Wisconsin stage) between about 75 000 and 14 000 years ago (Young, 1988). It provided a rich habitat for such animals as mammoth, mastodon, giant bison, saiga antelope, and the predators that preyed upon them. That the herds attracted human hunters is a reasonable assumption that is supported by archaeological evidence from both sides of the Bering Strait.

However, the presence of land game does not necessarily imply that the rich marine life off the coasts was ignored. Nor did the convenience of the pedestrian route mean that it was the only one that was used. In fact, the evidence is to the contrary; early campsites tend to be by sea coasts and waterways, probably because of the comparative ease of harvesting marine resources, not to mention that of water travel. This is supported by mounting archaeological evidence indicating the use of coastal water routes. As well, the Japanese Current, sweeping straight eastward across the Pacific to the Americas, provided a natural aquatic highway that would not have presented any great problems. We know that sea voyages were being undertaken as early as 50 000 years ago, as that was the time that humans reached the island continent of Australia. The argument that Arctic conditions were too dangerous for early sea-going technology is tenuous at best; the sea-going Beothuk canoe, for example, was well adapted for use among the ice floes.

ARCHAEOLOGY LENDS A HAND

Archaeology has been history's principal ally in tracing out the first settling of the Americas. But here also difficulties abound. Because bones do not preserve well in New World soils, the evidence of very early human presence has been based on artifacts rather than skeletal remains, a situation unique to the Americas (Dillehay, 1991, p. 13). Rather than providing sure answers, dates established so far for human habitation have given rise to more questions, as the oldest ones have come out of unglaciated South America, and the most recent ones for precontact migration have come from the icebound Arctic. This, of course, argues for first arrival by sea. Attempts to prove an American genesis for modern Amerindians on archaeological evidence have not been successful.[7] For most Amerindians, this is not important, because scientific evidence is not needed to convince them that this is the land of their origin.

Archaeology has been described as "simply another process for understanding the past" (Devine, 1991, p. 21). No more than other types of knowledge does it give us final answers; what it does do is provide fresh insights as new data and new dating and interpretive techniques become available, which they are doing at an increasing rate (Trigger, 1985, p. 52). Dating and, especially, interpretation have always been particular problems for archaeologists, who even under the best of circumstances must work with non-perishable material remains, a tiny percentage of the data that would have been available from the site when it was active. It is extremely rare for sites to be preserved as they were used—Pompeii, buried under a volcanic eruption in A.D. 79, is probably the best known; in the Americas, there is Ozette, a Makah village on the Olympic Peninsula in the state of Washington, that was buried under a mud slide about 500 years before Columbus. Since Makah still live in the area, archaeologists have been able to work with the people to reconstruct the village's lifestyle. More often there is little, if any, apparent connection between ancient sites and present-day inhabitants. The best that can usually be hoped for is to be able to deduce the broad outlines of the social dynamics of the communities that once occupied them. As Bruce Trigger has observed (1985, p. 52), archaeology studies what humans made or used; while such data can sometimes suggest what people thought and did, they are inadequate for fleshing out the intricacies of social interactions. Nor, where writing is absent, can archaeology pinpoint languages, except perhaps in very general terms. Even where writing, in whatever form, is present, unlocking its information can offer formidable challenges. Such has been the case with the hieroglyphs of the Maya of Central America, which only recently have begun to yield to long-standing and persistent efforts to reveal their secrets.

In spite of these difficulties, archaeology is still our main source of information about the distant past; for one thing, it can reveal much about trade patterns by tracing the sources of non-local plants, as well as non-local materials used in the manufacture of such items as tools. For another, it can tell us much about the tools themselves. Tools as such do not reveal methods or systems of use, but as archaeologists learned when they began to involve Native communities in their projects, knowledge of these ancient technological systems has not entirely disappeared. An example of what can happen through such co-operation was recently illustrated when archaeologists and villagers of the Koani Pampa in the Bolivian altiplano co-operated to reconstruct and put into practice ancient agricultural techniques for growing potatoes and were rewarded with a dramatic increase in yields.[8] In this case, recovering an ancient technology brought material benefits to the natives concerned, and satisfaction to the archaeologists for having proved a point. In Canada as well, co-operation between archaeologists and the Native communities affected by their work has already brought benefits, not the least of which is a much wider and deeper understanding of the complexity and creativity of our Aboriginal societies and, consequently, of ourselves as a multicultural nation.

ANTHROPOLOGY'S CONTRIBUTION

Anthropology, as a discipline, is closely connected to both archaeology and history. In the widest sense, anthropology is the science of humans in their myriad diversities. Where history looks for its evidence principally in documents, and archaeology to artifacts and material remains, anthropology relies mainly on direct observation of living societies; it is the study of humans in terms of their time and place. History and archaeology are concerned with the past, anthropology with the present, although within the framework of what went before. Physical anthropology illustrates one type of linkage with both history and archaeology. Since physical characteristics are influenced by cultural behaviour, skeletal remains can tell us something about ways of life: height, for instance, can be influenced by nutrition, diet can affect jaw conformity and the condition of teeth, diseases can affect bones, and injuries can point to occupational hazards or war.

Each of these approaches to the study of humans is supplementary to the other, as was demonstrated above in the case of archaeology. Historians are capitalizing more and more upon anthropology as they look for information to help them understand Native behaviour as reported in the documents. Some call this partnership between anthropology and history "ethnohistory," but the term is not universally accepted; history is history, say some historians, even if in some cases they have to turn to other than documentary evidence. The term "ethnohistory" came into use in the fifties, following a proposal by anthropologist William N. Fenton to the Institute of Early American History and Culture that ethnologists and historians get together on the "common ground" of Indian–white relations to enhance our understanding of the past (Merrell, 1989, p. 94). That historians were slow to respond reflected, at least in part, hesitancies about entering unknown territory.

LANGUAGE, ORAL TRADITION, AND THE ARTS

Still another discipline that contributes to this holistic approach is that of language. Studies have shown that prehistorically unglaciated North

America contained by far the greatest number of languages, 93 percent, along with a higher degree of differentiation than did the glaciated areas (Dickason, 1997, p. 5). The two most widely diffused languages in the prehistoric Americas were Cree in the once-glaciated north and Inuktitut in the icebound Arctic. The latter still shows clear traces of its Asiatic connections. Of the 500 or so languages spoken in North America, the greatest concentrations were in California and on the coast of the Gulf of Mexico; in South America, the number totalled more than 1500. It has been proposed that such a wealth of languages was more likely to have evolved in many localities over a very long span of time, rather than to have been brought in by separate migrations (Gruhn, 1988, pp. 77–79). It has even been theorized that all Amerindian languages, except for Na-Dene (Athapaskan) and Eskimo-Aleut, developed from a single prototype called Amerind. This highly controversial hypothesis postulates three founding migrations, the first of which brought Amerind, by far the largest, most widespread, and most diversified of the three proposed basic groups (Greenberg, 1987, pp. 331–37). Such theorizing has received some support from recent genetic studies, which suggest that Amerindians have all descended from four primary maternal lineages, although this is vigorously disputed by advocates of a multiplicity of migrations (Schurr et al., 1990).[9]

As Europeans initially saw it, these riches of languages were not parallelled by systems of writing. While Amerindians did not have alphabetic script, they had other means of recording information, such as by using drawings, symbols, glyphs, and knotted, coloured strings. Eighteen of these systems have now been identified as being in use when the Spaniards arrived. As pictographic symbolism and various types of glyphs are slowly being better understood, the distinction between oral and written traditions is becoming less and less clear. Such forms of communication were also once widely used in Canada. A modern expression of this is the syllabic script developed by Methodist missionary James Evans (1801–46) at Norway House, Manitoba, which was quickly adopted across the Cree-speaking north. Evans drew on symbols already used by the Cree as well as shorthand to create the script, which was soon adapted to other Aboriginal languages as well. Today it is in wide use across the north, both by Amerindians and Inuit, and is taught in schools. A still earlier example was that of Abbé Pierre-Simon Maillard (c1710–62), who by building on the work begun by earlier missionaries adapted Mi'kmaq symbols to develop a hieroglyphic script for that language (Dickason, 1997, p. 214).

As understanding develops, so does acceptance by ethnohistorians of oral history as a source of evidence, particularly for the recent past. More controversial is such evidence for the distant past, particularly when there are different versions of the same event. In that case, independent confirmation is needed. Myths are in another realm; with their different conception of time and nature, they deal with the interconnecting patterns of the spiritual and material worlds, whereas history deals with humans within the time and space of the material world. Myths tell us about a people's view of themselves and how they relate to the world around them; history records the actions by which humans work out their destiny. Mythic descriptions of how humans came to be here are many and varied, abounding in metaphors; what these stories have in common is their emphasis on and confirmation of the peoples' place in the web of the universe as well as their fundamental attachment to the land. Their underlying message is clear: however and whenever Amerindians came to be here, this is their homeland; they have no bonds with any other.

Besides myths and storytelling, rituals and the visual arts also have roles in explicating and recording these relationships. Orally and visually, they are all part of the dialogue by which peoples create their cultural contexts and thus define themselves.

POINTS OF DEPARTURE

Obviously, undertaking a history of Canada's Aboriginal peoples is not a simple matter. Two points of departure suggest themselves. First, despite the rich variety of their cultures, there is an underlying commonality in Amerindian worldviews that is evident in their myths.[10] Central to the myths, wherever they are found, is the concept of the interconnectedness of all living things, all of whom are "people" and some of whom are human. Humans are seen as part of the world system, with some advantages, but also with responsibilities, rather than as the dominating force, as in the European view. These underlying assumptions meant that Amerindians and Europeans each shared a basic civilization, even though it was expressed in a multitude of ways. The "formidable originality" of Amerindian civilizations has led some scholars to place them on a par with those of the Old World, the Han, the Gupta, and the Hellenistic age (Needham and Gwei-Djen, 1985, p. 64). Canada was in the northern zone of a hemispheric civilization, just as the American hemisphere would later be on the western periphery of European civilization.

Second, it is important to keep in mind the fundamental importance of the early encounters between Europeans and Amerindians. As already noted, these set the pattern for Amerindian–white relationships that has influenced policies to this day. The general sixteenth-century European impression that Amerindians were "sans foi, sans loi, sans roi" stemmed from first reports that New World people lacked churches and market-places and lived according to nature "like beasts in the woods." Columbus, for one, could not see that Amerindians had government, as in warm latitudes they wore little, if any, clothing. When he spoke with an elder-ly chief "who seemed respectable enough although he wore no clothes," Columbus was surprised to observe "sound judgment in a man who went naked" (Anghiera, 1912, vol. 1, pp. 102–3). Leading European thinkers concluded that Aristotle's doctrine "that some men are by nature free and others servile" applied to Amerindians; in other words, that they were not yet fully developed as human beings, although capable of becoming so, like children. The custom of referring to Amerindians as children, or even worse as "savages," would endure until well into the second half of the twentieth century. Such a people were obviously not qualified to run their own affairs; besides, the rights of Christians had priority over those of non-Christians. On both these counts, Europeans had no doubts about their right to claim New World lands for themselves. As we learn more about Amerindian societies, it becomes clearer all the time how wrong these European impressions were; New World societies met individual and community needs very well and had worked out solutions to problems of living that are still viable today.

Lack of official documentation for the early contact period, at least as far as Canada is concerned, is offset to some extent by the publicity to which the discoveries gave rise. Columbus's letter making his sensational announcement was disseminated with unheard-of speed, thanks to the printing press. This heralded new fashions in literature: cosmographies, particularly popular during the last half of the sixteenth and first part of the seventeenth centuries, and travel tales, much in vogue during the sev-enteenth into the eighteenth centuries until they were overtaken by ex-plorers' accounts, which hit their stride during the eighteenth and con-tinued through to the early twentieth century. Cosmographers, as their name indicates, set themselves the task of describing the whole world and everything in it, particularly its peoples and their societies; travel ac-counts concentrated more on adventure, while explorers' accounts devel-oped a scientific bent, particularly during the nineteenth and twentieth centuries. Not to be overlooked are the accounts written for special pur-poses, such as promoting colonization and its attendant commercial prospects. This varied literature is invaluable for the researcher, because it opens a window onto the type of information that was being dissemi-nated, as well as reactions to the wonders of worlds previously unknown to Europeans. For the student of Amerindian–white relations, this literature is in some ways more useful than official records, as it reflects more clearly the general level of knowledge and the interests of the time. As always, however, caution must be exercised, particularly when generalizing.

EARLY INTERACTIONS

What this literature reveals, although not always directly, is the highly charged nature that so often characterized early interactions. Far from overwhelming simple savages, Europeans often found themselves in complex and difficult negotiations from which they did not always emerge the winners. Recollet friar Gabriel "Theodat" Sagard (fl. 1614–36) tells of one such confrontation at Tadoussac, which occurred when a chief felt himself to be insulted by inappropriate gifts offered by the French during pretrade ceremonies. He told his people to help themselves to whatever French trade goods they wanted, paying what they wished. Although the French were not in a position to resist, the Amerindians, on thinking the matter over, later brought extra furs to make up the value of what had been taken. Both sides agreed to forget the incident and "to continue always in their old friendship." As Sagard saw it, the French were more concerned about offending the Amerindians than the Amerindians were of antagonizing the French (Sagard, 1939, pp. 45–46; Dickason, 1997, p. 82). Both the seventeenth-century entrepreneur Nicholas Denys (1598–1688) and the eighteenth-century Jesuit historian Pierre-François de Charlevoix (1682–1761) reported that some sagamores took a haughty tone when dealing with the French; in the words of Charlevoix, they made it clear "they were honoring the Great Sagamo of the French by treating him as an equal" (Denys, 1908, pp. 195–96; Charlevoix, 1744, part I, p. 128).

An important factor that has been all too often overlooked by historians was the role of religion in these early encounters. Ritual was traditionally very important to Amerindians, whose most respected leaders were also shamans. A major factor in the success of the French with their Amerindian alliances was their identification of the centrality of religion in Amerindian leadership and their enlistment of these sentiments in their favour. This was of considerable consequence to the role of the missionaries, who besides functioning in their evangelical capacity also operated as agents of the state. In this, the French conformed to Amerindian political reality; as one eighteenth-century colonial governor observed, "It is only these men [the missionaries] who can control the Savages in their duty to God and the King."[11] Without an appreciation of how spiritual sensibilities shaped Amerindian politics, it is not possible to understand Native behaviour in relation to Europeans or, for that matter, in any other field of action. Treaties illustrate this, as well as the roles of reciprocity and the principle of family connections.

THE ROLE OF TREATIES[12]

The importance of treaties would be difficult, if not impossible, to overestimate; as long as people have lived in organized societies, treaties have been fundamental to intergroup relationships. Among Amerindians, as with tribal societies in general, treaties were major instruments for stabilizing intergroup relations. Without treaties and their resulting alliances, the situation was one of latent, if not outright, hostility. Accords were worked out on the basis of kinship and reciprocity. Fictive kinships were established through the use of family terminology to delineate relationships, and gift exchanges — "I give to you that you might give to me" — symbolized the obligations incurred, which usually had social and political ramifications beyond the immediate purpose of the treaty. For the treaty to be effective, the basic exchanges had to be equal. Rituals, often both extensive and elaborate and always with spiritual ramifications, ceremonially sealed the commitments. Both rituals and exchanges had to be repeated from time to time if the treaty was to be kept alive, a recognition that changing circumstances could affect the agreements. This did not mean that treaties were by their nature short-lived; quite the contrary, some endured through the generations so that the resulting alliances came to be considered traditional.

   With the arrival of Europeans, two approaches developed for negotiating treaties: to follow the Amerindian custom or to rely upon written agreements, which were supposed to be binding without further ado once they were signed. The French, armed with a century of experience in trading with Brazilian natives, favoured the former, while the later-arriving English, with less experience in dealing with Amerindians, favoured the latter. As the French saw it, negotiating within the framework of Aboriginal custom more effectively engaged the loyalty of the Natives, for which written texts were unnecessary; in the British view, the written texts were a legal confirmation. The British treaties habitually included an Amerindian acknowledgement that they were now subjects of His Britannic Majesty, a provision not likely to have had its counterpart in the Amerindian-style treaties entered into by the French.[13] Whether written or unwritten, for the Amerindians the treaties were ritualized compacts that established the reciprocal balance within which relations with Europeans could evolve in harmony (Friesen, 1986, p. 51). For the Western-trained historian, the Aboriginal approach has meant considering treaties by their results rather than by their actual terms, since these agreements were unwritten and usually unrecorded. Still, their historical importance is beyond question, as the Amerindian role in the colonial wars makes abundantly clear.

Another point for the historian to consider is the nature of the treaties themselves. All of those entered into with the French can be classified as "peace and friendship" treaties, as can those entered into by the British until the Proclamation of 1763. They reflected the need for peaceful relations to carry on commercial activities such as trade and fisheries, as well as for European settlement. Land was negotiated for as needed, on an individual basis — a procedure, however, that soon led to disputes, augmented by the fact that Amerindians had no concept of outright individual ownership. The Proclamation, issued after the defeat of the French in North America, sought to remedy this by reserving to the British government the right to acquire Amerindian lands. This shifted the emphasis of treaties from peace and friendship and acknowledgement of British suzerainty, although they were still present, to negotiating terms by which lands were freed for increased European settlement. In effect, treaties became real-estate deals, but with a difference: because of reserving to itself the sole right to acquire Amerindian lands, the British government in effect put itself in a fiduciary position toward Amerindians. In other words, the British had implicitly accepted the responsibility of ensuring that Amerindians were fairly dealt with.

Here, another dichotomy of views quickly revealed itself. The British now looked upon the treaties as a tool for extinguishing Aboriginal land rights once and for all. Ironically, they resorted to Amerindian-style metaphors to express the binding nature of the obligations incurred by these surrenders: the phrase "as long as the sun shines and the rivers flow" first appears in a written treaty in 1794, and it was used by the British to assure the Mi'kmaq signers that they would always be provided for (Wildsmith 1985, p. 200). Amerindians, for their part, looked upon the treaties as reciprocal arrangements by which they agreed to allow the British to share their lands in return for a guarantee that their rights would be protected. For them, the treaties provided leeway to adapt, within the framework of their own traditions, to the demands of a changing world. Consequently, in those areas where European settlement was expanding, most of the pressure for treaties came from the Amerindians themselves. The government, for its part, only entered into treaties when the lands involved were foreseen as being needed either for settlement or for industrial development. Post-Proclamation treaties were first signed in southern Ontario, beginning in 1764.

In all, close to 500 treaties and agreements have been negotiated between Canada and more than half of its Aboriginal peoples. Negotiations are ongoing; an outstanding agreement that came into effect on 1 April 1999 resulted in the creation of Nunavut, which was carved out of the Northwest Territories. This new territory has a population of 25 000, of which 80 percent are Inuit. Its first premier is Paul Okalik, an Inuit lawyer who represents Iqaluit West in the legislature. Agreements entered into in the recent past are those of the Western Arctic (with the Inuvialuit, 1984) and the James Bay Agreement of 1975. Land claims are flourishing across Canada, particularly in those regions not covered by treaty, but in other areas as well, such as those where the government is charged with not honouring its treaty obligations. These claims have been given a collective boost through the 1998 decision of the Supreme Court of Canada allowing oral history and tradition as legal evidence. The Supreme Court ruled that the oral history of the Gitskan Wet'suwet'en bands supporting their claim to having inhabited their British Columbia lands since time immemorial had not been given proper weight when their claim was rejected in 1991. This decision signals a fundamental change in attitude from the long-standing position of the courts that oral history and tradition were hearsay and therefore not acceptable as evidence. The implications of this shift are profound not only for the courts, but also for historians. They will take years to unfold.

SOME CONCLUDING REMARKS

Recent confrontations between Amerindians and the dominant society, of which Oka is but the most spectacular example, and the rise of Amerindian participation in the constitutional debates give witness to the continuing strength of Native cultures. In treating the Native factor within a narrow focus and dismissing it as a relic of the past, historians have impoverished Canada's history. However, when reassessing the evidence, particularly for the early period, historians will have to do more than just keep the Native factor in mind: they will have to make the effort to understand Native concerns and above all to appreciate Native perceptions, and internalize these as part of Canadian history. The Native contribution to the formation of modern Canada has been both much greater and more multifaceted than has ever been acknowledged. Native peoples are still an active element in our society today. As just one example, Amerindians have been in the forefront of the environmental movement. Canada's First Nations are a vital part of our national persona, both present and future. The challenge that faces historians is to take a broader and deeper view of Canada's past, which will not only change our understanding of our history, but will enormously enrich it. Because our sense of history is fundamental to our sense of ourselves, both as individuals and as a nation, it arms us for the formidable task of working out solutions for the social and political problems that are developing not only as a result of our rapidly evolving technology, but also from our changing ideological position. As the ante rises, so does the importance of history.

NOTES

1. An earlier version of this paper appeared in Riewe and Oakes (1993, pp. 1–10), and some of its material is drawn from Dickason (1997, particularly Chapter 1).
2. I use the term "Amerindian" as it is more specific than "Indian." The term "Indian," of course, originated in a case of mistaken identity.
3. See James W. St. G. Walker's pioneer study, "The Indian in Canadian Historical Writing" (1971). See also his follow-up article, "The Indian in Canadian Historical Writing, 1971–1981" (1983).
4. On 18 June 1936, William Lyon Mackenzie King, Liberal prime minister of Canada 1921–26, 1926–30, and 1935–48, observed in the House of Commons "that if some countries have too much history, we have too much geography" (Colombo, 1974, p. 306).
5. Some of these problems are described by Rowley (1993).
6. "Land Claim Dismissed," *The Edmonton Journal*, 8 March 1991; "Judge Heard 100 Witnesses Read 10 000 Documents," *The Edmonton Journal*, 8 March 1991; "Natives Hit Another Dead End," *The Edmonton Journal*, 17 March 1991; "A Stunning Blow to Native Rights," *The Gazette*, Montreal, 13 March 1991.
7. See, for example, Goodman (1981). Some of the various approaches to the study of early man in the Americas are found in Laughlin and Harper (1979).
8. "Archaeology Makes Edible Impact," *The Christian Science Monitor*, 9 October 1991, p. 12. Not only did potato yields rise from 2.5 tons to 70 tons per acre, but weather damage to crops was minimized. All of this was achieved without the use of fertilizers or large infusions of capital.
9. For a different interpretation of the evidence, see Milford H. Wolpoff's article "From the Middle to the Upper Paleolithic: Transition or Convergence?" in Trinkaus (1989).
10. Claude Lévi-Strauss (1988; 1981) is particularly strong on this point.

11. National Archives of Canada, Archives des Colonies, C11B 12:37v, Saint-Ovide à Maurepas, 25 novembre 1731.
12. This section is reworked from materials published elsewhere.
13. During the colonial wars, the French repeatedly denied responsibility for the actions of the Amerindian allies on the grounds that they were independent. The Indians enthusiastically endorsed this; for example, the Abenaki in 1715 declared that the French monarch was not their king, as they already had their own natural leaders (letter of Michel Bégon, cited in Dickason, 1976, p. 13).

DISCUSSION QUESTIONS

1. Outline the attitudes that have given rise to the saying that Canada is a young country of much geography and little history.
2. Why were the first meetings of Europeans with Canada's Aboriginal peoples so poorly documented?
3. Describe the role of archaeology in tracing Canada's early history.
4. How important were first impressions in the development of European attitudes toward Amerindians? What was the effect on subsequent policies?
5. What can geology tell us about the presence of early peoples in the Americas?
6. What is "ethnohistory"? Would you put it in a separate category from standard history? Why or why not?
7. How do written and unwritten treaties compare with each other?
8. Discuss the effect of the Proclamation of 1763 on treaties.

FURTHER READINGS

Calloway, Colin. 1997. *New Worlds for All: Indians, Europeans, and the Remaking of Early America*. Baltimore: The Johns Hopkins University Press. Europeans sought to remake the Americas in the image of their Old World civilization, but what emerged was a multiplicity of new American nation-states, each with its own distinctive identity. They have all been marked by the Aboriginal civilizations that were overrun.

Chiappelli, Fred, ed. 1976. *First Images of America*. 2 vols. Berkeley, Calif.: University of California Press. A wide-ranging collection of essays on first contacts between Europeans and Amerindians throughout the Americas.

Honour, Hugh. 1975. *The European Vision of America*. Cleveland: The Cleveland Museum of Art. A catalogue of European reactions to the Americas expressed in visual representations from the days of first meetings through to the late nineteenth century.

Josephy, Jr., Alvin M. 1992. *American in 1492*. New York: Alfred A. Knopf. This hemispheric-wide survey brings into sharp focus the high level of achievement and rich variety of New World cultures on the eve of the European arrival.

McGhee, Robert. 1989. *Ancient Canada*. Ottawa: Canadian Museum of Civilization. Archaeologist McGhee reconstructs selected scenes from Canadian precontact history and in the process examines some unsolved mysteries. Why was an adolescent buried with such ceremony on the Labrador coast 7000 years ago? And what is the explanation for those hilltop fortresses in British Columbia? Answers are still being sought.

Ray, Arthur J. 1996. *I Have Lived Here Since the World Began*. Toronto: Lester Publishing. This overview of 12 000 years of Canadian Aboriginal history until today interweaves Native legends and perceptions with chronological history. Beautifully illustrated, it is at its best when dealing with the West.

Weatherford, Jack. 1991. *Native Roots*. New York: Crown Publishers. Exploring the inability (or unwillingness) of sixteenth-century Europeans to appreciate, or even to see, the civilizations of the Americas, Weatherford concludes that modern North American cultural roots lie buried in ancient archaeological sites. Although he deals specifically with the United States, his observations also apply to Canada.

REFERENCES

Anghiera, Pietro Martire d'. 1912. *De Orbe Novo*. 2 vols. Tr. Francis Augustus MacNutt. New York: Putnam's.
Charlevoix, Pierre-François. 1744. *Histoire et description générale de la Nouvelle France*, 3 vols. Paris: Giffart.

Colombo, John Robert, ed. 1974. *Colombo's Canadian Quotations*. Edmonton: Hurtig.

Denys, Nicolas. 1908. *The Description and Natural History of the Coasts of North America* (Acadia), ed. William F. Ganong. Toronto: Champlain Society.

Devine, Heather, 1991. "The Role of Archeology in Teaching the Native Past: Ideology or Pedagogy?" *Canadian Journal of Native Education* 18(1): pp. 11–22.

Dickason, Olive Patricia. 1976. "Louisbourg and the Indians: A Study in Imperial Race Relations, 1713–1760." *History and Archaeology* 6: 1–206.

———. 1997. *Canada's First Nations: A History of Founding Peoples*. Second Edition. Toronto: Oxford University Press.

Dillehay, Tom D. 1991. "The Great Debate on the First Americans." *Anthropology Today* 7(4): pp. 12–13.

Friesen, Jean. 1986. "Magnificent Gifts: The Treaties of Canada with the Indians of the Northwest 1869–70." *Transactions of the Royal Society of Canada*, ser. 5(1): pp. 41–51.

Goodman, Jeffrey. 1981. *American Genesis*. New York: Summit Books.

Greenberg, Joseph H. 1987. *Language in the Americas*. Stanford, CA: Stanford University Press.

Gruhn, Ruth. 1988. "Linguistic Evidence in Support of the Coastal Route of Earliest Entry into the New World." *Man* (n.s.) 23(2): pp. 77–100.

Krech, Shepart, III. 1991. "The State of Ethnohistory." *Annual Review of Anthropology* 20: pp. 345–75.

Laughlin, William S. and Albert B. Harper, eds. 1979. *The First Americans: Origins, Affinities, and Adaptations*. New York: Gustav Fischer.

Lévi-Strauss, Claude. 1981. *The Naked Man*, tr. J. and D. Weightman. New York: Harper and Row.

———. 1988. *The Jealous Potter*, tr. Bénédicte Chorier. Chicago: University of Chicago Press.

Merrell, James H. 1989. "Some Thoughts on Colonial Historians and American Indians." *William and Mary Quarterly* (3rd ser.) 46(1): pp. 94–119.

Needham, Joseph and Lu Gwei-Djen. 1985. *Trans-Pacific Echoes and Resonances: Listening Once Again*. Philadelphia: World Scientific.

Riewe, Rick and Jill Oakes, eds. 1993. *Human Ecology Issues in the North*, vol. 2. Edmonton: Canadian Circumpolar Institute.

Rowley, Susan. 1993. "Frobisher Miksanut: Inuit Accounts of the Frobisher Voyages." Pp. 27–40 in *Archaeology of the Frobisher Voyages*, ed. William W. Fitzhugh and Jacqueline S. Olin. Washington, DC: Smithsonian Institution Press.

Sagard, Gabriel. 1939. *The Long Journey to the Country of the Hurons*, tr. H.H. Langton. Toronto: Champlain Society.

Schurr, Theodore G. et al. 1990. "Amerindian Mitochrondrial DNA Have Rare Asian Mutations at High Frequencies, Suggesting They Derived from Four Primary Maternal Lineages." *American Journal of Human Genetics* 46: pp. 613–23.

Thevet, André. 1878. *Les singularitez de la France Antarctique*, ed. Paul Gaffarel. Paris: Maisonneuve. (Reprint of 1558 edition.)

Trigger, Bruce G. 1985. *Natives and Newcomers: Canada's Heroic Age Reconsidered.* Kingston: McGill-Queen's University Press.

Trinkaus, Erik, ed. 1989. *Emergence of Humans: Biocultural Adaptations in the Late Pleistocene*. Cambridge, UK: Cambridge University Press.

Walker, James W. St. G. 1971. "The Indian in Canadian Historical Writing." *Canadian Historical Association Historical Papers* 1971: pp. 21–51.

———. 1983. "The Indian in Canadian Historical Writing, 1971–1981." Pp. 340–61 in *As Long as the Sun Shines and Water Flows*, ed. Ian A.L. Getty and Antoine S. Lussier. Vancouver: University of British Columbia Press.

Wildsmith, Bruce H. 1985. "Pre-Confederation Treaties." P. 200 in *Aboriginal Peoples and the Law*, ed. Bradford W. Morse. Ottawa: Carleton University Press.

Young, Steven B. 1988. "Beringian: An Ice-Age View." Pp. 106–10 in *Crossroads of Continents: Cultures of Siberia and Alaska*, ed. William W. Fitzhugh and Aaron Crowell. Washington, DC: Smithsonian Institution.

CHAPTER 2

The Role of Native Elders: Emergent Issues

Joseph E. Couture[1]

Shorn of the various surface features from different cultures, Coyote and his kin represent the sheerly spontaneous in life, the pure creative spark that is our birthright as human beings and that defies fixed roles or behavior. He not only represents some primordial creativity from our earlier days, but he reminds us that such celebration of life goes on today, and he calls us to join him in the frenzy. In an ordered world of objects and labels, he represents the potency of nothingness of chaos, of freedom — a nothingness that makes something of itself. (Erdoes and Ortiz, 1984, p. 39)

In discussing the relationship of humankind to the Earth, we must understand the basic difference between the Navajo view of Mother Earth, and what the Western European or contemporary American mind means when it tosses around poetic metaphors like "mother nature," or "mother earth."

The contemporary American means that the earth and all of nature is like his natural mother. But the Navajo (and other American Indians) means that his natural mother is the closest thing he will ever know that is like his real mother — The Earth. (Begay, 1979, p. 28)

There are those who say that the Native Way holds a key, if not *the* key, to the future survival of mankind. They say that it is in the nature of the Native's relationship to the cosmos, the land, to all life-forms, to himself, manifest in ritual and ceremony. They say that to learn the "how and why" of the traditional Native stance is to find the key, to discover a "saving grace" of insights and a creative power beyond any rationality, all crucial to human continuance (see Berry, 1987a–d; Brumble, 1980; Steinmetz, 1984). If that is so, as I know it to be, then, central to this discovery, and primary to the Native existential positioning, is the presence and function of Elders. This chapter is dedicated as a tribute to their contemporary emergence.

To that end, comments to situate somewhat my experience with Elders and some of the difficulties in writing about them are presented, some events are highlighted and interpreted, the importance of a number of

Elder teachings are underscored, and the relevance of Elder inner and outer behaviours is set forth. A discussion of several other Elder-related issues leads to a conclusion to this chapter.

INTRODUCTORY REMARKS

I agree with Brumble (1980, p. 34), who says that Elders have become the focus of a "cultural dialectic." Involved are Elders in treaty and non-treaty communities, as well as Natives and non-Natives. Included are social scientists of all stripes pushing to observe and analyze, striving for their syntheses, as well as increasing numbers of Natives engaged in a return to their roots. Both tend to look indiscriminately to Elders, wherever they can be found, for insights and guidance (see Brown, 1982b, p. 119, for similar views). Both experience difficulties in this endeavour, the former hardly aware that what they expect to observe is restricted by the conditions necessary for their presence as observers (Carter in Rothman, 1987, p. 71) and the latter confused by the rarity of top or true Elders and by the relative immaturity and unsteadiness of younger spiritual teachers and ceremonialists.

It is true, in my view, that Elders themselves, of whatever type and development, form an unusual phenomenon. Like all other Natives, they too have been influenced by the forces and consequences of "Contact." Early on, they were, so to speak, hammered back into the woodwork. Long proscribed and banned by governments and churches, now barely emerged from decades of withdrawn, underground activity, they are perceived, not as harbingers of a lost Eden, but as the oral historians, guardians of the Secrets, as interpreters of the Life of the People, as unusual teachers and way showers to the People.

In the late 1960s, triggered by a sudden, strong wave of seekers, Elders, although flattered and grateful, were initially flustered and were forced initially to rethink and redefine themselves and their roles. They were faced with dire and unsettling questions about identity and survival, and with the basic paradoxes regarding the nature of the Native world and the fundamental issues about the world in which humans live.

My views on Elders derive in general from experiences with a number of true Elders over the years since 1971, and particularly from apprenticeship with several Medicine Elders initiated that same year.

Use of the term "Native" herein connotes inclusivity. It refers to all Original Peoples in Canada. In the context of this kind of discussion, by choice I favour this broad connotation since Elders themselves of all

Tribes stress Native identity as being a state of mind, as it were, centred in the heart. The late Abe Burnstick's frequent reply to "Who is an Indian?" was to exclaim, with finger stabbing his heart area, "An Indeeyin is Indeeyin rawt heah!"[2]

A difficulty confronting Native writers is to write for print-literate readers, especially of social science and professional education perspectives, as though these readers will somehow respond as to an oral literature.

To so write, for one thing, requires keeping in hand an immense oral "reference bibliography," that is, the stories, legends, prophecies, ceremonies, songs, dance, language, and customs of the People. To so write also requires that the qualitative dimensions of these sources be expressed and conveyed with integrity, for example, the non-verbal expressions and gestures of the storyteller and the ceremonialist—and that is virtually impossible. And, although Elders have declared that the "time has come to share the secrets," its achievement remains most awkward, if not painful.

Nonetheless, in my view and that of Brumble, the task of written sharing and communication must resolutely begin at this time in our history (Brumble, 1980, p. 42; see also Buller, 1980; Gould, 1988; Lincoln, 1980). There is a need in the contemporary Native world to articulate traditional views, and to transmit with discernment and discretion to the extent possible, something of the fullness of the Traditional Experience and Story—as embodied in the highest, most evolved Elders—in its intricacies, beauties, and ineffabilities. Further, in the view of Berry and others, there is a worldwide human need to survive to which Native North Americans have something significant to contribute (see Fox, 1972, 1983; Hausman, 1986; Steinmetz, 1984).

There is therefore a challenge, and the tentative solution followed here is to write as a storyteller as much as possible, from a general, social science perspective. In other words, as I now proceed, the best I can, with the expression and sharing of my thoughts and feelings regarding my experience with Elders, my endeavour attempts to circumscribe that experience and amplify it to some extent by deliberate association with Western social science and education constructs.[3]

In so doing, the hope is to avoid what someone has called the "barbarism of reflection," the overrefinement that is unable to sustain the poetic wisdom and imagination that establishes and sustains true Elders and, better yet, to suggest something of how normal and natural it is for Elders to think and behave a certain way.

My proposition assumes that traditional values are dynamic[4] and can be and are being re-expressed in new forms, and that these are being brought about by Elders now at grips with an ever-increasing flow of Natives and non-Natives seeking advice and counsel, healing and inspiration, interpretation of the past and present, in their apprehension and concern over future survival.

SOME HISTORY

The late 1960s and early 1970s witnessed the political emergence of Native organizations in Alberta. The opening round of activity by both political and service leaders and organizers, initially enthusiastic, climaxed in early 1969 in much discouragement and deep, angry frustration. Both deliberate and unwitting obstacles to program development were formidable. In negotiations, mutual distrust predominated. Confrontation was required and frequently resorted to, and conflict became a working condition in the drive to break open bureaucratic and political doors. It was a time also when programs were exceedingly difficult to start and maintain, largely for lack of adequate core and development monies, and partly for lack of skill and insight on both sides. In the midst of this period of dismaying hurt and resentment, a major shift in consciousness, nonetheless, slowly dawned. It started that same year with Native leaders seeking out Elders, and continued subsequently when others also began the trek back to the Elders of their Tribes.

Amazingly and concurrently, virtually everywhere in North America signs of revitalization appeared. However, because past and current efforts to resolve the enormous cultural, socio-economic, and political difficulties were stark, they were unsettling failures.

So began a period of intense introspection, induced by a sharp perception of disheartening results and encouraged by an intuitive sense that Natives, through a return to cultural origins, might allay their profound consternation and anger and find answers to the basic question of "How can we change the direction of the destructive currents? The white man doesn't have any answers. What can we do for our children and our children's children? Maybe if we talked to some old people. ..." That incipient awareness became the theme of the beginning struggles, a theme soon variously played across the country.

A second event, parallelled also subsequently in other areas of the continent, such as the Smallboy and Mackinaw camps in the Alberta Rockies and the Rolling Thunder camp in Nevada, occurred in the fall of 1972. It is most noteworthy for it presents clear, milestone evidence of ominous stirrings within Native consciousness.

Elders from six different tribes in Alberta gathered for twelve days on the West Coast of Vancouver Island under the leadership of the Indian Association of Alberta. After two days of discussion on education-related issues, in substance, the following was declared:

> In order to survive in the 20th century, we must really come to grips with the White man's culture and with White ways. We must stop lamenting the past. The White man has many good things. Borrow. Master and use his technology. Discover and define the harmonies between the two general Cultures, between the basic values of the Indian Way and those of Western civilization — and thereby forge a new and stronger sense of identity. For, to be fully Indian today, we must become bilingual and bicultural. We have never had to do this before. In so doing we will survive as Indians, true to our past. We have always survived. Our history tells us so.[5]

In discussion of that statement, the following comment was made by an Elder:

> On a given day, if you ask me where you might go to find a moose, I will say "if you go that way you won't find a moose. But, if you go that way, you will." So now, you younger ones, think about all that. Come back once in a while and show us what you've got. And, we'll tell you if what you think you have found is a moose.[6]

Because of its obvious, singular importance, one particular event has been underscored. However, and once again, that one incident is to be understood within a continental context of similar contemporaneous events throughout "Indian Country." Since that era, and understandably, attention to Elders continues to accrue, especially to both their role and function, and to the relevance of their teachings to contemporary Native identity and survival.

SOME TEACHINGS

A few recurring sayings reveal characteristic simplicity, range, and richness. For example:

> "Don't worry. Take it easy. Do your best. It will all work out. Respect life. Respect your Elders. It's up to you. You have all the answers within you."

> "Listen to what Mother Earth tells you. Speak with her. She will speak to you."

"What is Life but a journey into the Light? At the centre of Life is the Light."

"Soon I will cross the River, go up the Mountain, into the Light."

These typical sentences set forth a deep, strong, moral, and spiritual vision and understanding. These interrelated principles are corollaries or facets of a unitary, primary traditional insight that is variously stated. For example:

The centred and quartered Circle is the sign of wholeness, of inclusiveness of all reality, of life, of balance and harmony between man and culture. (Traditional saying)

There are only two things you have to know about being Indian. One is that everything is alive, and two is that we're all related. (Anonymous Indian)

Comment

One sees here the classical themes of holism and personalism, of relationality, of an environment and cosmos that are alive. A broad characteristic goal of traditional education has always been that the whole person in the whole of his/her life be addressed. In the traditional setting, one effectively learns how to become and be a unique expression of human potential. These same traditional processes, in the context of extended family and community Elders, describe a strong sense of responsibility both toward self and toward the community.

Such statements also, in my view, provide reference points to the seeker in his/her journey "back," suggest something of the richness of the spirit of Tradition, and provide as well "memory-bank data," as it were, for Elder reinterpretations, of which the 1972 Declaration is a prime example.

The 1972 statement is several-fold in its importance. For example, for the first time since the signing of the Western treaties, top Elders responded in assembly as the historians of their tribes, as philosophers and teachers of Tradition. They expressed anew for the people the meaning of their history, in light of present conditions, and pointed out a saving and safe direction to pursue so that the People's History could be sustained and forwarded.

Also crucial is that to describe the behaviour needed, Elders focussed on needed connections between the two general cultures, urging discerning openness and selectivity over distrusting and closed defensiveness. A further declaration emphasis is the redefinition of Native identity—a landmark moment—for to become bicultural is designated a positive, warranted, existential act. At that meeting, it was clearly understood that to be bilingual would always be "better" and "richer," but what the Elders affirmed is that bilingualism is not essential for a core sense of self as Native, keeping open thereby the possibility of authentic Nativeness to those large numbers of Natives who, for whatever reason, do not speak a Native language.

Thus, criteria were defined whereby the survival movement could judge whether or not it has found a "moose." That day Elder mediation, empowered, sanctioned, and formalized, redirected the struggling emergence of the People.

Grown men cried that day.

Traditional Native holism and personalism as a culturally shaped human process of being/becoming is rooted in a relationship with Father Sky, the cosmos, and with Mother Earth, the land — a characteristic that has led comparative religionists to rank Native American religion as a fifth classical world religion. These experts point to the centrality of land in Native spiritual and religious experience as its distinctive dimension (see Hultkranz in Capps, 1976, pp. 86–106; see also Berry, 1987; Fox, 1972, 1983). This relationship with the land/cosmos is personalized and personal, and marked by a trust and a respect that stems from a direct and sustained experience of the oneness of all reality, of the livingness of the land.

The richness of this holism and personalism extends further. When one looks beyond or behind the externals of local and regional custom, language, and history, more of the core dynamic of the Native Way of life is revealed. In the West, classical existentialism stresses the utter validity of subjectivity, that is, of the feeling, reflective subject who has the freedom to make choices and thus to determine his/her life. Therefore, what one does is of keystone importance. The doing that characterizes the Native Way is a doing that concerns itself with being and becoming a unique person, one fully responsible for one's own life and actions within family and community. Finding one's path and following it is a characteristic Native enterprise that leads to or makes for the attainment of inner and outer balance. This is in marked contrast with general Western doing, which tends and strains toward having, objectifying, manipulating, "thingifying" everyone and everything it touches (see Couture, 1987, pp. 180–82).

Behavioural Features

The exemplars of such a way of living, relating, and perceiving, of course, are the most evolved, or "true," Elders. The preceding references to typical sayings may now be usefully supplemented by a description of a number of Elders' behaviours.

It is no simple matter to describe Elder behaviour because of the deep interconnectedness of all facets of their behaviour. The observations that follow are not rigorously organized in pyramidal fashion, but rather as one link leading to the next, in cyclical fashion up and around a same conceptual axis — Elders.

Comment

I am of the opinion that true Elders are superb embodiments of highly developed human potential. They exemplify the kind of person that a traditional, culturally based learning environment can and does form and mould. Elders also are evidence that Natives know a way to high human development, to a degree greater than generally suspected. Their qualities of mind (intuition, intellect, memory, imagination) and emotion, their profound and refined moral sense manifest in an exquisite sense of humour, in a sense of caring and communication finesse in teaching and counselling, together with a high level of spiritual and psychic attainment, are perceived as clear behavioural indicators deserving careful attention, if not compelling emulation.

To relate to Elders, to observe and listen carefully, and to come to understand the what, why, and how of such behaviours, grounds or enroots one, so to speak, in the living earth of Native Tradition.

It is not possible to study and examine Elders in the conventional sense simply because that is not the "way." One learns about Elders by learning from them over a long period of time, by becoming comfortable with a learning-by-doing model. Their counselling and teaching focus on learning from one's experience. Thus, through respectful and patient observation, evidence of remarkable, incisive intellect, of tested wisdom, of sharp and comprehensive ability, allied with excellent memory recall and well-developed discursive ability, is eventually perceived.

Further signs of Elderhood are found in their level of trust of both life itself and of their own experiences, by being into true feelings (i.e., into the spiritual side of feelings, without sentimentality); by the art of being still, quiet, unafraid of darkness and nothingness; by the ability to laugh at one another, as well as at self. All that is so because they are trained in the lessons of how the very nature of our being is in at-one-ment with the cosmo-genesis. And so they hold to the land, ceremony, medicine, linked to the past, in Spirit (see Cordova, 1938, pp. 23–24; Buller, 1980, p. 166).

What is the "secret," if any, behind those admirable multibehaviours? My experience suggests that it is their knowledge of and skill in "primordial experience."[7] Primal experience for true Elders, in my view, is centred in the pervasive, encompassing reality of the Life-Force, manifest in "laws"—the Laws of Nature, the Laws of Energy, or the Laws of Light (Couture, 1989, pp. 22–23). In other words, true Elders are familiar with Energy on a vast scale, in multiple modes—energy as healing, creative, lifegiving, sustaining. Both the experience and perception of such manifestations, the manifestations themselves, reveal that all is one, is natural, and is the realm of creative Spirit—the mysterious "Life-Force" (the Wakan-Tanka of the Sioux). There is no "between" between the God-Creator, Source and Sustainer-of-Life, and the Cosmos, the environment, all life forms, and Native soul (see Couture, 1989).

Such outstanding qualities and levels of insight and skill testify to an inner and personal, fundamental, consistent, and unchanging process, to a capacity to respond to life as its conditions invariably change. "We have always survived. Our history tells us so."

Elders are an invitation to taste existence within the functioning of the natural world, to experience the mystique of the land. They are, Berry says, in "fascination with the grandeur of the North American continent" (Berry, 1987a, p. 185). They acquire knowledge and insight into the nature of the universe. For centuries, they have wondered over the revelation of the universe.

It strikes me that their "wisdom" is rooted in Immanence and Transcendence, that this wisdom is attuned to the Immanent in time and space, in the dimensions and seasonal rhythm of the universe, and to the Transcendent, the Above of the confines of historical space and time. This timeless positioning makes for the Story, as carried down through the ages to its being retold and reshaped presently, leading to the discovery of new forms needed to transform current conditions of Native individuals and groups, and thereby of humankind.

Elders hold the secrets of the dynamics of the New Vision. They are propelled by the past, are drawn absolutely to the future. Theirs is a bioconcentric Vision, a vision of earth and community—an ecological vision of an enduring Mother Earth and the People, a relationship intertwined in a single destiny. In other words, Elders hold a depth insight into the structure, functioning, and manifestation of the entire ecological process (Berry, 1987a, p. 185).

The powerful and awesome beauty of Elder vision and experience includes the contemporary state of the ecology—a deep point of agony, for Mother Earth and Father Sky are in a worldwide, unprecedented state of ecological devastation and disintegration.[8]

Elders have what Berry calls "an earth response to an earth problem" (Berry, 1987a, p. 186). "We need only to listen to what Mother Earth is telling us," the Elders repeatedly utter. Their "earth response" is the Story that has never ceased, that carries the dream of the earth as our way into the future. In a sense, this Story holds the "genetic and psychic encoding" needed by humankind for survival.[9] Their "earth response" is processive through and through, and the only immutable reality is the Life-Force itself.

True Elders are so, and do what they do, because they have shamanic personalities—a non-romantic, brilliant sensitivity to the dimensions and patterns of manifestations of the natural world in its most challenging demands and delights. As humans, as one of the earth's life-forms, they are capable of relations so that all others can equally flourish. Their power and personality hold the ability to shake us and lead us out of the current global cultural pathology and bring us along into and through a healing and restructuring at a most basic level. They facilitate healing because they have sensitivity to the larger patterns of nature, in its harsh and deadly aspects as well as in its life-giving powers, always in balance with all life-forms.[10]

More can be said about Elder perception. Once again, their perceived world is radically and entirely relational, that is, all realities are constituents of that perception. These are what Fontinell (1988, p. 138) calls "fields" of being and what Fox refers to as "isness."[11] Therefore their "faith," if that is an appropriate term, or their "knowledge" and "wisdom," is of these "fields." Theirs is a "faith" founded in what they experience. Characteristically, their "faith" is a fundamental mode of experience rather than an intellectual grasp and understanding of concepts. It is also perforcedly a "knowing" that is ongoing, an open-ended task because, for one grounded in Nature, there can be no once and for all determination of just what is authentic (as opposed to that which is apparent, absolute revelation).

Elders should not be considered as concerned, therefore, with a Western sense of "belief"—a going beyond that for which there is evidence at the present moment—but as having "faith"—experiential knowing, an integrating experience "whereby all modes of experience are brought together in a relatively cohesive whole which is expressed in the life of the person, thus rendering human life meaningful" (Fontinell, 1988, p. 140).

I suspect that the traditional Elder capacity to accommodate change, upon contact with Western Christianity forms, readily led them to become Christian, but in a way that allowed not only transformation of perception but sustained a full continuity with the faith of the People.[12] My hypothesis is that conversion was a simple instance of new growing out of the old, forming a new syncretism congruent with their "faith."

SUMMARY

I concur with Gravely, who says that a true Elder is not classifiable as a "passive informant on the traditional past," but as "a creative theologian, open to the possibilities of his situation, to new ideas and symbols, and to a dialogue between the traditions" (Gravely, 1987, p. 11). Elders manifest consistency in the life process and in relationship to several worlds, moving in and out as shamans are wont to do, with seriousness and humour, with persistent attention and awareness.

Elders possess keys to a classical journey of human and earth ecological transformation. In this era, they are being called upon to reinterpret and to apply the Tradition, the Story, in a new way. There is urgency to this for Mother Earth is no longer looking after herself naturally, but is an earth looked after, and badly, by humanity. Elders are now so engaged.

SOME ISSUES

Every turn in this chapter raises questions, or issues, that deserve more extensive exploration, but which an overview description such as this precludes. Nonetheless, in this last section, aspects of either a practical or academic concern are reviewed.

The rapid decrease in numbers of true Elders is most alarming. Who is to replace them? For some decades now, significant numbers of communities across Canada have lost all their traditional Elders. Many individuals, forced to seek out Elders in other tribal traditions, initially encounter some difficulty because of differences in ways. This is a two-way pressure on both Elder and seeker.

The range of kinds of Elders also is bothersome. An Elder's prediction states that these times of emergence are to be marked by chaos and confusion before changing into a time of light and peace. Certainly a significant part of this difficult phase is attributable to "instant" Elders, overnight wonders who, with limited ceremonies and an abundance of clichés, confuse and stall many in their personal journey. The mantle will fall to those spiritual people, less evolved, of less ability and knowledge. "True" Elders are those who have gone through painful encounter with spiritual realities and who become thereby, in the perception of the People, intermediaries between their respective cultural communities and the spiritual forces of the universe and defenders of the community's psychic integrity. They are those who have enacted and sustained a personal relationship with Nature.

Elders are a national issue because of their qualities and rarity (see Phillips, Troff, and Whitecalf, 1976; Phillips and Troff, 1977). The needs of the People require guiding wisdom as assurance of a continuing, living Native presence in Canada, and for during the time needed to acquire a "faith" about the real possibility of survival.

The practical requirements of establishing and maintaining a relationship with Elders are not readily perceived. First of all, at the level of individual need and change, much time and patience are required. There are no shortcuts to attitudinal and spiritual change, no possible end-runs around phases of inner change. A complete and enduring commitment is required. Secondly, the "return" is not only to "primal roots," to the living core of the Tradition itself, but is conditional on personal achievement so as to arrive at presenting to the world an authentic mode of living (see Berry in Hausman, 1986, p. 7). And that is not an easy matter.

The "knowing" of Elders is problematic to those who, for a range of reasons, were not schooled in oral tradition. Elders as "knowers" know intimately, directly, and are non-dualistic in their perceptions and understandings. Western-trained people are inherently scholastic and dualistic in perception and thinking. True, the sense of identity of Elders is marked by an ordered consciousness. However, at the same time, it is unbounded by space and time, all the while remaining in direct consideration of both dimensions of historical time and space. Again, attainment to that state of development is a basic challenge.

Problematic also, and for that same kind of mind, is that Elders have consistency, continuity, and clarity of insight and skill regarding paradigmatic alteration (i.e., reinterpreting the Story) that, in my view, as Grim declares, "germinates understanding of the creative role of imagination and intuition in human history" (Grim, 1987, p. 235). Elders are positioned, I would suggest, to contribute to facilitating what Wilson (1985, p. 55) calls "quantum leaps" in developing new models of thought.

It would seem that presently there are growing numbers of Western academic approaches hinting at hitherto unknown possible amenability with Native mind. Keutzer, commenting on the work of such physicists as Bohm, Einstein, and Capra, suggests that such physicists are becoming students of consciousness itself (see Keutzer, 1984). Their concepts of "flow" and "hologram," for example, and statements that "everything is alive" are very suggestive. To Keutzer's list, I would add the names of such theologians and historians as Fox and Berry and of the physicist-philosopher Swimme.

A corollary to the issue of "knowing" is that of mysticism (currently a much abused and misapplied concept, in my view). From a Native spiritual standpoint, as I see it, mysticism is a question of becoming/being rooted or grounded in relationships with all constituents or dimensions of reality. I like Fox's description of mysticism because it is congruent with my understanding of Native spiritual experience. He holds that "the essence of the mystical experience is the way we are altered to see everything from its life-filled axis, to feel the mysteries of life as they are present within and around us" (Fox, 1972, p. 77). That's Indian!

To arrive at a direct experiential understanding of that definition is a primary learning task. To discover how ceremonies, for example, mediate helping energy and teaching takes some doing. Prayer, ritual, and ceremony ground one in life, for "It's all deah, in de sereemonees!"[13]

To acquire an awareness of all earth forms as having a life of their own, to become aware of all as Spirit-bearing, as Spirit-expressing, takes some doing. To become steeped in, adept in, Native mysticism is to enter into the beautiful, the truth, the Oneness, in balance against all negativity and absence. It is to activate and sustain personal discovery that leads to a true sense of self-understanding, to a sense of future time through awareness of the past — which leads to learning how to intuit the close relationship between one's culture and one's genetic impulses.

Elders have teaching challenges to deal with. One is with regard to non-Natives. They are aware of the currently unfolding prophecy that "The White brother will come to the Red brother for teaching." There is acceptance of the non-Natives who come to them. However, they find themselves struggling with a different mind-set and affectivity, as well as with language barriers. Also, because of the knowledge level of both Native and non-Native seekers, so many are not grounded in a sense of the real but mysterious power of nature in mountains, rivers, lakes, rocks, life-forms, all as enmeshed in the web of the universe. So, the legends and stories require pedagogical adaptation. The stories have to be retold, reshaped, and refitted to meet contemporary seekers' changed and changing needs.

Such encounters are but necessary moments in the retelling and reshaping of the Story, as in the case of the 1972 Declaration. New legends as well as the retelling of ancient stories are forthcoming across the continent, sparked by Medicine Elders' dreams and visions. Tradition through Elders is converged on the present, revealing forgotten depths of perception and understanding.

Present Elder endeavour is in a tensional context. Elders are aware of the tensional exchange between the Story of the People and the need for a new direction, as we have seen. They are aware of the tensional exchange between immanent direction within living matter itself and the transcendent source of the creative impulse. They are aware of the tensional character of awakening, of the inner dynamics of spiritual and socio-political life.

Conclusion

We look to Elders for the way words are used, for the structural devices they employ, for the teaching and counselling approaches they utilize, for the philosophical and spiritual perspectives of the world, experienced and envisioned. We look to them to show us the "the archetypal essences appearing in animal forms" as Brown says (1982a, p. 7). In other words, to show us the Way.

We look to them to tell us about the "moose."

Daniel Deschinney, a Navajo Blessingway singer, explains how a Navajo experiences the sacred mountains' inner forms:

> When a Navajo experiences the sacred mountains' inner forms kindling new strength within himself, he says "I am invincible. I am beautified." To be invincible is masculine. To be beautified is feminine. These two concepts together are a powerful entity. There is no strength from only one. Power comes from the interaction between them. When you have strength, you recognize your opportunity, you know what you must do, and you have the grace to do it. (Quoted by Johnson, 1988, p. 47)

Notes

1. The author is an Alberta Métis of Cree ancestry. His PhD training and experience are in the areas of Native development, psychology, and education at all levels. His work experience includes teaching, addictions counselling, community development, and research. He has been apprenticed to Elders since 1971.
2. The late Elder Abe Burnstick, Stoney Nation, Paul's Band, Duffield, Alberta, was a pre-eminent orator and teacher.
3. This position I take regarding the difficult issue of oral-literate mind versus print-literate mind finds support in the views of Geertz and Jules-Rosette, for example. Geertz holds that the main task in interpreting cultures is one of "explicating explications" (Geertz, 1973, p. 18). In other words, it is imper-

ative to acquire the feel for the "homely in homely context," for to fail to do so is a failure to place common-sense thought within context of its use. The development of the "thickest descriptions" possible becomes therefore both an ideal and necessary objective.

It also means, as Jules-Rosette points out, dealing frontally with the problems of subjective interpretation (1978, p. 563). The "veil of objectivity" masks an inability to grasp another interpretive system or style of perception. Objectivity has "totally falsified our concept of truth" (Polanyi in Jules-Rosette, 1978, p. 289) — the "veil of objectivity" is a protective shield of one's own oracular structure. It covers what Wilson calls "profound parasitic lay assumptions" (1987, p. 118). This difficulty is illustrated by the case of Casteneda. His construct of reality was so impenetrable that drugs were needed to forcefully assault it to allow him to receive spiritual insight.

4. For more detail about the creative capacity of Native culture, see Couture (1987, pp. 180–84).
5. Declaration rendered by Elder Louis Crier, Cree Nation, Ermineskin Band, Hobbema, Alberta.
6. Observation made by the late Elder Charlie Blackman, Chipewyan Nation, Cold Lake Band, Cold Lake, Alberta.
7. Huston (1953, p. 276) claims that "there is, first, a Reality that is everywhere and always the same; and second, that human beings always and everywhere have access to it."
8. See *Akwesasne Notes*. This internationally established Iroquois journal of social comment has for over two decades now reported on ecological deterioration abundantly and consistently. With special attention to Aboriginal regions worldwide, its regular columns, in cause–effect terms, describe the autistic relationship between the ecological vision and the industrial vision.
9. See Berry (1987b) for a provocative, insightful discussion of this concept.
10. See Berry (1987b, pp. 211–12) and Kelsey (1978) for more detail on shamanic personality and qualities.
11. "Isness" as a term is frequent in all of Fox's writings.
12. See Gravely (1987) for discussion of the adaptability of Black Elk.
13. Elder Abe Burnstick.

DISCUSSION QUESTIONS

1. Why were elders so important to Native communities in the past, and what contributed to the waning of their roles?
2. How would you explain the re-emergence of different types of elders within and outside Native communities?
3. In what respects have elders become the focus of a cultural dialectic? What difficulties do you think this might pose for elders and the communities in which they live?

4. Do you know someone who is a true elder? If you do, how is this person similar to and different from the ideal, true elder outlined in this chapter?

5. In what respects might the bio-centric vision of elders benefit humanity in the future? Can you think of other ways of thinking and doing that could hinder the continued re-emergence of elders?

FURTHER READING

Bouchard, Dave (text) and Roy Henry Vickers (images). 1990. *The Elders Are Watching.* Vancouver: Raincoast Books. Combined images and texts that convey lessons from Native elders past and present. A call to reflect and dream, to imagine and envision the meaning and hope that can be drawn from the wisdom of all of our elders.

Brown, Joseph Epes. 1964. *The Spiritual Legacy of the American Indian.* Wallington, Pa.: Pendle Hill Publications. Brown asserts that ignoring or denying the spiritual legacy offered by Native Americans contributes to the impoverishment of all peoples. He invites readers to appreciate the ways in which the living religions of Native Americans can inform and enrich our everyday lives, our cultural sensibilities, and our social, economic, legal, and political structures.

Cardinal, Douglas and Jeanette Armstrong. 1991. *The Native Creative Process.* Penticton, B.C.: Theytus Books. Cardinal and Armstrong share their understanding and vision of "our Native way" by blending conversational commentary with striking images.

Patt, Neal, ed. 1991. *Place Where the Spirit Lives: Stories from the Archaeology and History of Manitoba.* Winnipeg: Pemmican Publications. Seven stories of Native people in Manitoba based on the writings of archaeologists are combined with seven teachings from Native elders and teachers. An example of the way in which legend and science can complement and enrich each other.

Wolfe, Alexander. 1989. *Earth Elder Stories: The Pinayzitt Path.* Saskatoon: Fifth House. Stories belonging to the descendants of Pinayzitt that tell of how Earth Elder and his people survived sickness, participated in treaty-signing, obtained the grass dance, and lived in relation to Indian agents and other non-Native people. Invites the reader into a mystical encounter with history and a historical encounter with mysticism.

REFERENCES

Begay, I. 1979. "The Relationship between the People and the Land." *Akwesasne Notes* (Summer): pp. 28–30.

Berry, T. 1987a. "Creative Energy." *Cross Currents* (Summer/Fall): pp. 179–86.

———. 1987b. "The Dream of the Earth: Our Way into the Future." *Cross Currents* (Summer/Fall): pp. 200–15.

———. 1987c. "The New Story: Comment on the Origin, Identification and Transmission of Values." *Cross Currents* (Summer/Fall): pp. 187–99.

———. 1987d. "Twelve Principles for Reflecting on the Universe." *Cross Currents* (Summer/Fall): pp. 216–17.

Brown, J.E. 1982a. "The Bison and the Moth: Lakota Correspondences." *Parabola* 8(2): pp. 6–13.

———. 1982b. *The Spiritual Legacy of the American Indian*. New York: Crossroad.

Brumble, D. 1980. "Anthropologists, Novelists and Indian Sacred Material." *Canadian Review of American Studies* 11 (Spring): pp. 31–48.

Buller, G. 1980. "New Interpretations of Native American Literature: A Survival Technique." *American Indian Cultural Research Journal* 4(1 and 2): pp. 165–77.

Capps, W., ed. 1976. *Seeing with a Native Eye*. New York: Harper and Row.

Cordova, Viola. 1938. *Philosophy and the Native American: The People before Columbus*. Albuquerque, N.M.: Southwest Indian Student Coalition, University of New Mexico.

Couture, J. 1987. "What Is Fundamental to Native Education? Some Thoughts on the Relationship between Thinking, Feeling, and Learning." Pp. 178–91 in *Contemporary Educational Issues: The Canadian Mosaic*, ed. L. Stewin and S. McCann. Toronto: Copp Clark Pitman.

———. 1989. "Native and Non-Native Encounter: A Personal Experience." Pp. 123–54 in *Challenging the Conventional: Essays in Honor of Ed Newsberry*, ed. W. Cragg. Burlington, Ont.: Trinity Press.

Erdoes, R. and A. Ortiz, eds. 1984. *American Indian Myths and Legends*. New York: Pantheon Books.

Fontinell, E. 1988. "Faith and Metaphysics Revisited." *Cross Currents* (Summer): pp. 129–45.

Fox, M. 1972. *On Becoming a Musical, Mystical Bear: Spirituality American Style*. New York: Paulist Press.

———. 1983. *Meditation with Meister Eckhart*. Sante Fe, N.M.: Bear and Co.

Fox, M. and B. Swimme. 1982. *Manifesto for a Global Civilization*. Santa Fe, N.M.: Bear and Co.

Geertz, C. 1973. *The Interpretation of Cultures: Selected Essays*. New York: Basic Books.

Gould, Janice. 1988. "A Review of Louise Erdrich's 'Jacklight.'" Pp. 11–14 in *The People before Columbus*. Albuquerque, N.M.: Southwest Indian Coalition, University of New Mexico.

Gravely, W. 1987. "New Perspectives on Nicholas Black Elk, Oglala Sioux Holy Man." *The Illif Review* 44 (Winter): pp. 1–19.

Grim, J. 1987. "Time, History, Historians in Thomas Berry's Vision." *Cross Currents* (Summer/Fall): pp. 225–39.

Hausman, G. 1986. *Meditation with Animals*. Albuquerque, N.M.: Bear and Co.

Huston, S. 1953. "Philosophy, Theology, and the Primordial Claim." *Cross Currents* 28(3): pp. 276–88.

Johnson, T. 1988. "The Four Sacred Mountains of the Navajos." *Parabola* (Winter): pp. 40–47.

Jules-Rosette, Benetta. 1978. "The Veil of Objectivity: Prophecy, Divination, and Social Inquiry." *American Anthropology* 80 (September): pp. 549–70.

Kelsey, M. 1978. "The Modern Shaman and Christian Belief." *Transcend* 22: pp. 1–6.

Keutzer, C. 1984. "The Power of Meaning: From Quantum Mechanics to Synchronicity." *Journal of Human Psychology* 24 (Winter): pp. 80–94.

Lincoln, K. 1980. "Trans — to the Other Side of, Over, Across." *American Indian Cultural and Research Journal* 4(1 and 2): pp. 1–17.

Philips, Donna and R. Troff, eds. 1977. *Enewuk*. Saskatoon: Saskatchewan Indian Cultural College.

Philips, Donna, R. Troff, and H. Whitecalf, eds. 1976. *Kataayuk: Saskatchewan Indian Elders*. Saskatoon: Saskatchewan Indian Cultural College.

Rothman, T. 1987. "A What You See Is What You Beget Theory." *Discovery* (May): pp. 90–96, 98–99.

Steinmetz, P. 1984. *Meditation with Native Americans: Lakota Spirituality*. Santa Fe, N.M.: Bear and Co.

Wilson, G. 1987. "What Is Effective Intercultural Communication?" *Canadian Ethnic Studies* 18(1): pp. 118–23.

Wilson, R.A. 1985. "Quantum Leaps." *New Age* (June): pp. 52–55, 80.

CHAPTER 3

Aboriginal Leadership

Peter McFarlane

At the time of contact with Europeans, the First Nations of Canada had developed finely tuned political institutions that were remarkably successful in keeping order, respecting individuals, and promoting social harmony. As in all other aspects of Native cultural, economic, and political life, however, Native political institutions were as varied as the 50 or so peoples who make up the First Nations.

The semi-settled Iroquois differed significantly from woodland peoples, who in turn were very different from the Plains Indians and the fisher peoples of the West Coast. Each group — indeed, each nation — had developed its own distinct institutions to serve its specific needs.

The arrival of the Europeans posed an unprecedented challenge to Native societies and, by extension, to Native leadership. As European power began to gain greater control over larger and larger areas of North America, Native societies were subjected to — in a relatively short time — the aggressive evangelism of the Christian churches, successive plagues of deadly new diseases, and the gradually engulfing wave of European settlement. From contact to the arrival of the settlers, Native leaders were faced with the challenge of trying to prevent, or at least to slow, the European onslaught. After traditional Indian lands were settled and the colonial powers were exerting effective control over First Nations territory, the challenge became one of preserving First Nations sovereignty and seeking redress on the land question. That struggle continues today.

In this chapter, we will look at how individual Indian leaders, from traditional leaders like Big Bear to modern organizers like George Manuel, fought first to hold onto their peoples' sovereignty and later struggled to win it back from a Canadian state that was determined to undermine their efforts with an array of political, legislative, and, in some cases, military manoeuvres.

TRADITIONAL NATIVE LEADERSHIP

Although the differences among Native societies at contact were considerable, there were a number of broad similarities in both the style and the role of Native leadership within their communities. Most cultures, for example, had some system of hereditary or life-chiefs, with built-in checks and balances to ensure that the successor represented the interests of the people and that the serving chief did not abuse his powers.

Part of the success of the hereditary chief system can be attributed to the fact that the next in line for the position generally was trained in his role from a very early age by the elders in the community.[1] In the case of the Plains Cree, for example, the young hereditary chief was examined closely in his youth to make sure that he displayed the qualities of industriousness, courage, and self-control needed to carry out his future responsibilities (Mandelbaum, 1979, p. 106).

Like other Native political institutions, the process for anointing leaders drew much of its strength from its flexibility. If the youth showed that he did not have the mettle for the job, he could be passed over and someone else would be found to fill the role. Similarly, in most societies, if a hereditary or any chief showed incompetence, lack of self-control, or antisocial behaviour, or if he pursued policies that a significant number of people in the community opposed, the dissidents could simply drift away and informally coalesce around someone they thought a more worthy leader.

In some cultures, this practice occasionally led to a band's having two or more chiefs, who were recognized as such, serving with a minimum of friction between them (Mandelbaum, 1979, p. 108). At other times, a serving chief would step aside and make room for the more successful rival. Clinging to power was extremely difficult, if not impossible, since the people could refuse to co-operate, even with a hereditary or life-chief.

The fact that the people could withdraw their support from a leader at any time made it essential that the chief not only serve the people's will, but also try to ensure that rifts did not develop in the community on important issues. Consensus politics was not merely a shared value but an integral part of the Native political system.

A successful chief would have to master the art of building a consensus not only among his immediate followers, but also within the community as a whole. Along with earning the respect of the people, the chief had to retain the support of various other individuals representing separate centres of influence. In woodland hunting societies, these centres of influence tended to be unofficial. For example, certain individuals would be recognized as spiritual leaders, and their counsel, as well as that of the elders, would be weighed along with the chief's. The most successful hunters would also be recognized as community leaders, and together the elders, spiritual leaders, and leading hunters would be given favoured places around the council fire and their words special consideration.

In semi-settled and plains hunting societies, the chief's power was more formally diluted by the separate centres of power that controlled policing, war-making, hunting strategies, and religious observances. These institutions often included a young men's or warriors' society and a women's society, as well as recognized community officials like a village crier and messenger, a religious leader, an elder who led the marches to and from the seasonal camping areas, and a war chief who generally assumed complete control of the band during times of crisis. The head of each institution was accorded his or her measure of respect while performing well-defined roles in the life of the community.

In both the wandering and semi-settled societies, this often meant that the chief's main responsibilities were guiding meetings toward consensus, managing trade, negotiating treaties with the leaders of neighbouring nations, preserving group harmony, sponsoring ceremonies, and ensuring that the basic economic needs of the people were being met.

It was in this latter role of ensuring the distribution of wealth within a society that chiefs were often judged by their own people (Manuel and Posluns, 1974, p. 95). If a family was hungry, it was primarily the chief's responsibility to ensure that they were fed. When guests visited the community, the chief was expected to feed and house them. During ceremonies, he was expected to contribute more than anyone to the communal feast. In some societies, when there was a dispute between two members of the band, the chief would sometimes be compelled to settle it by paying restitution to the injured party from his own goods in order to preserve group harmony (Mandelbaum, 1979, p. 107).

This exceptional material generosity expected of the chief extended also to the spirit. In some groups, like those of the Plains Indians, even if one of the chief's relatives were murdered, the chief was expected to forego the blood vengeance that would be the right, or in some cases even the duty, of one of his fellow band members.

The local chief's need to promote harmony and political consensus was also felt at the tribal or national level. On issues like treaties with other First Nations, which required the agreement of the national council, the ranking chief faced the same constraints as the local chiefs. Important decisions could be taken only after a consensus had been reached — often after days of discussion. As Bruce Trigger pointed out in his study of the Huron people, "not even the smallest units were required to surrender any of their rights. No headman could rely on officially sanctioned power to see that his decisions were enforced" (Trigger, 1987, p. 54). At the national as well as the local level, the chief's influence on any issue rested on the personal trust he had earned over time and on his ability to marshal convincing arguments for or against an issue at council meetings. Even when the council came to a decision, there was no formal way to compel a dissenting band or community chief to join in the agreement.

Once a consensus had been reached, it was the ranking chief's role to sit down with his counterpart to discuss the treaty terms and to strike a final deal, which would be followed by ceremonial gift-giving and community celebrations. The gift-giving and celebrations were an essential part of the process, since most treaties were less business arrangements than genuine testaments of friendship between peoples, which the parties were assumed to have entered into in a spirit of mutual generosity.

Among the First Nations in Canada, as in the rest of North America, the natural function and style of leadership was interrupted by the arrival of the Europeans. During the period of the explorers and traders, however, those challenges often came in the form of new economic opportunities. Most Native societies already had long-standing trade relations with neighbouring peoples, so the arrival of European traders simply offered them new partners with new products to exchange. The roles of Native leaders in both inter–First Nations and European trade were also similar. They tried to maximize the economic benefits for their people by playing off local suppliers against each other or by making an exclusive arrangement with one supplier in exchange for special price considerations.

Although the early trade between the First Nations and the Europeans tended to be beneficial to all parties, including the Native societies that acted as intermediaries in the trade between the Europeans and their neighbours, the arrival of the Christian missionaries was more problematic. The conversion of part of a band or nation was a strain on the harmony of the group that was aggravated by the missionaries' systematic attacks on Native culture.

Still, it was by the arrival of the European settlers and their governments, with their vast claims on First Nations territory, that traditional Native societies were most seriously undermined. In trying to settle the European land claims, the leaders of the First Nations faced a technologically powerful force operating on a set of unfamiliar values that viewed Native societies as either opportunities to be exploited or obstacles to be shoved aside.

EUROPEAN APPROACH TO NATIVE LEADERSHIP

The British system for transferring the ownership of much of the North American continent to European hands was a deceptively simple one. After the Royal Proclamation of 1763 acknowledged the existence of Aboriginal title (Smith, 1975, pp. 2–3), the British set out to extinguish it, piece by piece, by signing formal treaties with the First Nations. Native leaders were thus an essential element in the whole process, since it was their signatures on the documents that conferred legitimacy on the territorial annexations.

In general, treaties were not initiated by the British until they required a specific piece of land for settlement. Only then would a government agent be sent out to arrange a meeting with the Native group in the area. The agent generally was someone, like a missionary or a former trader, whom the local chiefs knew personally, and his job was to announce the date and the place of the treaty talks.

Although some of the trappings remained, like the exchange of gifts, the whole tenor of the treaty process changed when the chiefs were confronted by the representatives of the European settlers. Unlike disputes between rival First Nations, which could involve conflict over a particular hunting ground or the need to secure safe passage through territories, the settlers' representatives would arrive demanding that the First Nations cede virtually all of their national territory to the colonizing power.

The difficulties in addressing such drastic demands were greatly increased by the fact that most chiefs were asked to sign treaties that had been unilaterally drawn up by a group of legislators and bureaucrats operating out of a far-off capital, long before the emissary arrived for the negotiations. The Native leaders would rarely be given a chance to discuss the terms with the actual framers of the treaties in London or Ottawa, and the government agent, even when he was sympathetic to the Native position, would have little leeway in renegotiating them.

More often than not, while the treaty talks were being undertaken, the colonial government was already operating a series of fortified military posts in the region and parts of the land under question were already being cleared and settled.

If Native leaders resisted signing the treaty, it would generally be made clear during the negotiations that, whether they signed or not, settlers would come and the First Nations would be left with no guarantee of having any payment or any land reserved for them in the future. In the end, most Native leaders signed the British and later Canadian treaties with a greater or lesser degree of reluctance, while they continued to protest the terms of the treaties and seek renegotiation.

This British pattern was followed most faithfully in Upper Canada between 1764 and 1854. The results were the so-called lettered treaties with the Mississaugas, Chippewas, and Mohawks.[2] These pre-Confederation treaties involved an initial gift or cash payment and small annuities to the members of the tribe or band (GBC, 1913, pp. 472–74).

When the Dominion government formally took over from the British in 1867, it continued the well-established British practice with its so-called numbered treaties. In the early years of Confederation, the priority was western expansion, so the focus of treaties 1 to 8 was to gain control of First Nations lands on the prairies. This meant expropriating both Indian and Métis lands and subjugating their peoples to the power of the Dominion.

In negotiating the numbered treaties, Ottawa had a significant liability: the prairie Indians were aware that the signing of the British treaties contributed to certain social problems for Indians living in Ontario. This liability would be offset in the West, however, by the very real fears of the Plains peoples in the 1870s that the rapidly disappearing buffalo could leave them facing starvation.

The extinction of the buffalo was a determining factor in Canada's successful push into the region. The massive herds had been the heart and soul of the Plains Indians' economy. The buffalo was their main food source and its hides provided not only clothing and shelter, but also their primary source of income in the buffalo hide trade. By the 1870s, an estimated 160 000 Canadian buffalo a year were being slaughtered by American hide hunters moving up from the south and by the large, well-organized Métis hunting parties moving west from Manitoba and Saskatchewan. The Chippewa and Plains Cree, and later the Blackfoot people, watched with alarm as the foundation of their way of life, their culture, and their very existence was being destroyed.

It was at the moment when the Plains Indians were staring into the face of hunger that the Canadian government agents arrived on the scene with their treaty proposals. In dealing with the Dominion government, Native leaders were faced with three unacceptable alternatives. They could submit to the unilaterally drawn-up treaty terms. They could refuse to sign and try to pursue their traditional life with the knowledge that their lifeblood, the buffalo, was disappearing and that the settlers would continue arriving. Or they could stand and fight and risk the destruction of their people at the hands of the superior military force the settlers had at their disposal. As we will see in the rest of this chapter, during the settlement and development of Canada, and up to the present day, Native leaders have at various times exercised all three options.

In Manitoba and parts of Saskatchewan, where settlement was most concentrated and where the buffalo were the first to disappear, the local Cree and Chippewa accepted the treaty terms. Treaty Number 1 was signed at Stony Fort in Manitoba in 1871 and gave the First Nations small reserves, agricultural implements, and an annuity of $3 per head in exchange for an enormous tract of land in southern Manitoba (GBC, 1913, p. 474). During the next five years, the Canadian state followed the disappearing buffalo westward with treaties 2 to 5.

If all of the leaders of the Plains Indians had faced the collapse of the herd in the same way — by submitting to the government's treaty terms — we might conclude that Ottawa was simply a hard, if rather heartless, bargainer with the First Nations. But when it came time to sign Treaty Number 6, the government ran into a stone wall in the form of a short, wily, single-minded Plains Cree leader called Big Bear, who refused to sign a unilaterally determined treaty that would surrender title to traditional Cree lands and lead to the destruction of his people's way of life.

The resistance of Chief Big Bear, and later of his war chief Wandering Spirit, not only brought to light the extreme pressures the Native leaders in Canada were operating under during the early years of Confederation, but also showed how determined the settlers' government was to crush all resistance. In the short and medium terms, the failure of Big Bear's resistance validated the decision of the Indian leaders who signed the treaties and accepted the allotted reserve lands — if only to ward off military conflict or starvation. But in the longer term, Big Bear's actions have lived on as a symbol of First Nations resistance to the unjust terms of the treaties and as an inspiration to generations of Native leaders who followed.

BIG BEAR, WANDERING SPIRIT, AND THE PATH OF RESISTANCE

The first official Canadian government contact with the Plains Cree chief Big Bear came in 1875, when Ottawa sent a number of agents to the West to prepare for treaty meetings at Fort Pitt and Carlton House for the following August.

George McDougall, a Protestant missionary who had some experience with the Plains Indians, had been sent to Big Bear's camp bearing the usual gifts — knives, ammunition, tea, sugar, and tobacco — to announce the meetings.

At the time, the situation was becoming increasingly difficult for Big Bear and his people. By 1875, only remnants of the once great buffalo herds could be found on the plains, and each year the numbers continued to decline. New settlers were continuing to arrive on Cree lands that were ceded under treaties 1 to 5, and the North West Mounted Police were installing themselves in a series of forts across the vast section of the prairie that still belonged to Big Bear's people.

As the alarm grew among the interior Plains Cree, more and more Cree were turning to Big Bear for spiritual as well as political leadership. Among his people, Big Bear's medicine bundle was said to give him the power to become invisible, and he had demonstrated in his youth a certain ability to see into the future when he had a vision of "the coming of the white man, his purchase of the land," and the gradual weakening of the Cree people (Dempsey, 1984, p. 17).

As a leader, Big Bear dedicated his life to trying to ensure that his vision would not be fulfilled, and by 1875 Big Bear's direct following had swelled into the hundreds as the Cree of the central plain looked to him to preserve their freedom.

It was not surprising, then, that when George McDougall arrived to speak about Treaty Number 6, he was given a chilly reception. In fact, Big Bear even refused his gifts.

"We want none of the Queen's presents," he told the government agent. "When we set a fox trap we scatter pieces of meat all around but when the fox gets into the trap we knock him on the head. We want no baits! Let your Chiefs come and talk like men with us" (Dempsey, 1984, p. 63).

His last statement, "Let your Chiefs come," was a call Big Bear would make at numerous times, to numerous interlocutors, in the continuing hope that, if he could negotiate chief to chief with the head of the white government, he could strike a deal that he and his people could live with.

But Big Bear's call to meet with the non-Native leaders would remain unanswered. Canada had already incorporated the lands of the Plains Indians into its maps and it was not about to recognize what it saw as a competing claim to Dominion sovereignty. Big Bear would be given ample opportunity to talk to government agents, but they would be people who had no authority to negotiate any of the fundamentals of the treaties (Dempsey, 1984, p. 63).

The Dominion's attitude toward the Cree leader was reflected in McDougall's report of their initial meeting. Rather than advising Ottawa to try to work to win Big Bear's support for the treaty, McDougall suggested it simply by-pass his objections. The reason was that Big Bear was half Ojibwa. As McDougall put it, Big Bear was "a Soto [Ojibwa] trying to take the lead in their Council." Big Bear, he added, "for years has been regarded as a troublesome fellow. These Sotos are mischief makers through all this Western country and some of them are shrewd men" (Dempsey, 1984, p. 63).

Big Bear showed how troublesome he could be by spending the next year meeting with other Cree chiefs and trying to build a common front against the treaty. His biographer, Hugh Dempsey, estimates that by the summer of 1876, Big Bear had won support for his stand against the treaty from the majority of the chiefs of the central plain.

In response, the government sought to isolate him and his followers by making separate deals with the more co-operative leaders in the region. When the Carlton House and Fort Pitt meetings were set to take place in August 1876, government emissaries ensured that only the more accommodating chiefs—particularly the Christian chiefs who were being strongly urged by the missionaries to accept the government's offer—were present.

When the provisions of Treaty Number 6 were announced to the assembled chiefs that summer, they were similar to the previous five treaties, but with a slight increase in the cash settlement. In exchange for the Plains Cree ceding to the Dominion 120 000 square miles of Cree land, or more than twice the combined area of the three Maritime provinces, the government was offering $12 per person as a signing bonus, an annuity of $5 per head, and a promise to help the Cree get started in agriculture (GBC, 1913, pp. 473–74).

Word travelled quickly on the Prairies, however, and the assembled chiefs knew from the example of the more eastern Cree that what was being offered amounted to a very bleak future for their people. But with the devastation of the buffalo herd, they also knew that the decision was between accepting the thin gruel of the government treaty and having their people face widespread famine with the disappearing buffalo.[3]

After two days of painful discussions and vain attempts to have the terms of the treaty improved, the assembled Cree leaders resigned themselves to their fate and signed.

Big Bear had heard about the meeting while he was out on the plains with his followers, and he rushed to Fort Pitt to try to take part in the negotiations, but he arrived too late—the signatures were already on the document. When some of the chiefs tried to convince him to add his signature to theirs, Big Bear reacted angrily. "Stop, stop, my friends. I have never seen the Government before; I have seen [the government agent] many times. I heard the Government was to come and I said I shall see him. When I see him, I will make a request that he will save me from what I most dread; that is, the rope to be about my neck" (Dempsey, 1984, p. 74).

Big Bear continued to insist that Indian land "isn't a piece of pemmican that can be cut off and given back to us," and he set out to win support for his position from Indians across the prairie (Manuel, 1972). He was, however, acutely aware that he was walking a fine line in refusing to bend to Canadian power. His refusal to sign, he knew, would not make the whites go away, and he was concerned that it might cause the Canadian government to dispense with the discussions altogether and send the military after his people. The fear was expressed in a vision Big Bear had after the Fort Pitt meeting.

"I saw a spring shooting up out of the ground," he recounted, "I covered it with my hand, trying to smother it, but it spurted up between my fingers and ran over the back of my hand. It was a spring of blood" (Dempsey, 1984, p. 45). With the vision, Big Bear feared — as it turned out correctly — that continued agitation would lead to war.

Despite these concerns, Big Bear could not bring himself to surrender his people to the constrictive terms of Treaty Number 6. So he began an eight-year odyssey of almost Homeric proportions, leading his people across the plains searching for the rapidly disappearing buffalo and trying to find a way to preserve Cree independence from the encroaching Canadian state.

By the late 1870s, the thunderous herds of buffalo of only two decades earlier had been reduced to a few small, isolated groups. By the early 1880s, starvation began to stalk the very old and very young of Big Bear's band. Several times during this period, Big Bear approached government forts to ask for emergency rations for his people, but he was essentially told to sign or starve.

Under such extreme pressure, the consensus that Big Bear had built among his followers against signing the treaty document began to slip away. Facing what appeared to be the starvation of their children, small groups began to break away from Big Bear's band and head to the Canadian forts in search of food. Under the authority of the Canadian state, the local official would acknowledge one of the band members as chief and, in exchange for regular rations, the newly appointed chief would offer his signature to Treaty Number 6. The band would be allotted reserve lands and the cash payment called for under the treaty, and the newly created chief would renounce his people's right to the traditional Cree homeland.

By 1882, even members of Big Bear's family were beginning to abandon him. So he led his bedraggled band to Fort Walsh, where the local Indian agent was doling out treaty moneys. The sight of Big Bear and his hungry people was a surprise to the agent, but he was even more surprised when the by-then famous holdout chief said he would sign Treaty Number 6 in exchange for food.

Big Bear's apparent capitulation was front-page news throughout Canada. But if the Indian Affairs officials thought this was the end of Big Bear's resistance, they were mistaken. Big Bear delayed his people's departure to their reserve as long as he could while they fed on Canadian rations. When he finally set out, he did not go to the appointed lands. He began wandering again, while he carried on a drawn-out, long-distance negotiation with the authorities on the location and size of his people's reserve. As it turned out, he would never lead his people onto that or any reserve.

In 1884, Big Bear made a final attempt to have the treaty provisions overturned. He called a mass meeting of all of the Plains chiefs on Chief Poundmaker's reserve in Alberta in the hope that, if they stood together, the Plains Indians could negotiate a new deal with the government.

The turnout of disaffected treaty Indians was remarkable, with thousands of Prairie Indians gathering together to discuss how they might work together to have the treaties renegotiated. The meeting started with the Plains chiefs appointing Big Bear as their spokesman. The plan was to have Big Bear travel to Ottawa and try to find someone who would not only listen, but who had the power to make changes to the treaties they had signed under duress.

It was a crucial moment in Canadian history. Despite all of the forces ranged against them, the Prairie Indians had managed to make a last stand around a leader who had the strength, the vision, and the oratorical skills to make their case to the foreign powers. There is no way of knowing whether or not Big Bear's journey to Ottawa would have slowed the Canadian move onto Indian land, but there is no doubt that Big Bear's arrival in Ottawa at that crucial moment in time would have offered the Plains Indians a historic opportunity to state their case to the country at large. At the very least, such an intercession by Big Bear could have avoided the bloodshed that was to follow.

Big Bear, however, would not get his chance to confront the lawmakers in the Canadian government. After the meetings on Poundmaker's reserve were over, the chiefs and thousands of Plains Indians held a traditional thirst dance. While the ceremony was taking place, a scuffle broke out between a Cree man and a non-Native shopkeeper in the nearby village. A contingent of North West Mounted Police officers, which had been strategically stationed in the vicinity, quickly moved in to make an arrest. What followed was an indication of just how explosive things were becoming on the prairie.

As soon as the Cree warriors saw the redcoats moving in, they took to their mounts and began to circle the police, challenging them to fire the first shot. Greatly outnumbered, the police held their fire, but from the moment the warriors went into action, Big Bear was no longer in control of the camp. According to the Cree tradition, when hostilities were imminent, the war chief, in this case Wandering Spirit, assumed full authority.

Wandering Spirit remained in command of Big Bear's band after the camp broke and the other Cree returned to their reserves. But after the terrible suffering of his people during the previous eight years, Wandering Spirit was no longer trying to avoid confrontation; he was seeking it. And he found it the following year when Louis Riel electrified the plains with his Métis uprising.

Wandering Spirit was one of the few Cree leaders to openly align himself with the Métis forces. As soon as he heard that the Métis had taken up arms, he led his warriors into the settlement of Frog Lake and took the local whites hostage. The situation escalated dramatically when the local Indian agent, Thomas Quinn, refused Wandering Spirit's order to accompany him to the Cree camp. In a fit of rage, Wandering Spirit raised his rifle and shot Quinn in the head. A killing spree followed; minutes later, nine whites were dead.

The massacre at Frog Lake and the eventual crushing of the second Riel Rebellion were the end of any hope Big Bear had of negotiating with the Dominion government. Canadian troops, bolstered by volunteers from the East, swept onto the plains and seized military control of the territory.

Big Bear's band was hunted down along with the Métis rebels. Wandering Spirit and seven of his Cree followers were sent to the gallows for the Frog Lake killings. Big Bear was spared that fate when the white witnesses to the massacre testified that he had tried vainly to get his war chief and warriors to stop the killing. But on his arrest, Big Bear, along with other leaders involved even obliquely in the rebellion, was stripped of his hereditary chief's position by the governor of Indian Affairs. Big Bear was released after three years in custody, but by then he was a tired, sick old man and he died shortly after. The remainder of his band was scattered throughout Cree communities on the prairie, never to be reunited.

Henceforth, the prairie would be under Canadian control. Native leaders would no longer face the challenge of negotiating a fair deal with the settler government, but rather the more difficult task of freeing themselves from the sophisticated system of social and political control that the Canadian state gradually brought into force. Isolating, and then undercutting, the Native leadership would become a key element of Ottawa's strategy of overcoming Native resistance.

DESKAHEH AND THE IROQUOIS RESURGENCE

As a traditional leader operating outside the Canadian-backed band council system, Big Bear was part of a disappearing breed. In fact, even while Big Bear was being approached by McDougall in 1875, Ottawa was moving quickly to put Native leaders under the direct control of the Department of Indian Affairs.

At Confederation, the Dominion government had awarded itself all powers "over Indians and Lands reserved for the Indians" in section 24 of the British North America Act. A year later, in 1868, the government gave itself the power to decide who and who would not be recognized as chief. According to the 1868 legislation, the governor of the Indian Affairs branch could move into any band, remove the chief, and order government-sponsored elections to take place to decide on a candidate who passed the government's criteria for honesty, temperance, morality, and, later, the catch-all category of "competency."

Along with giving the governor of the Department of Indian Affairs (DIA) the right to depose serving chiefs, the Indian Act defined the chiefs' role in a way that eviscerated their powers. Under the act, the chief was given the authority only over regulations pertaining to public health, the observance of "order and decorum" at meetings, the repression of intemperance and profligacy, and the maintenance of roads and public buildings.

This reduction of the chief's areas of influence continued in 1880 when measures were introduced to suppress the potlatch, traditional dance ceremonies, and other important Native religious practices. As a result, the chiefs who played a central role in these cultural events lost even more of their influence in the community.

Over the next 25 years, Ottawa also saw that most of the remaining traditional chiefs were replaced by the government-controlled band council chiefs who served under Ottawa's direction. By World War I, most chiefs were elected under the DIA system, and there was no doubt about whose interests they were expected to serve. As the last numbered treaty, Treaty Number 11, put it, chiefs were to be "responsible to His

Majesty for the faithful performance by their respective bands" (Smith, 1975, p. 208). From representing largely self-governing bands within independent Native nations, the Indian leaders had been reduced, in legal terms, to servants of His Majesty.

It is not surprising, then, that the two most prominent Native leaders during the first half of the twentieth century, Deskaheh and Andy Paull, were not band chiefs elected under the government-controlled system.

Andy Paull rose to national prominence through the newly formed, and generally regionally based, Indian organizations that began to take shape before World War I and grew significantly during the 1920s.

Deskaheh, on the other hand, was a traditional chief from the Iroquois Longhouse who was able to use the unique historic position of his people —as allies of the British during the French and American wars—to push his case for international recognition of the Iroquois nation.

The upsurge in Iroquois resistance in the 1920s was linked to the fact that the Iroquois had preserved a large measure of their traditional political structures, their constitution (the Great Law of Peace), and the superstructure of the Iroquois Confederacy. Iroquois history was also recorded on the wampum belts, and this allowed successive generations of Iroquois people to keep traditional values alive.

Deskaheh was the strongest leader who emerged to challenge the Dominion government during the period. Born on the Six Nations reserve in 1873, Deskaheh (whose Christian name was Levi General) had been brought up within the Longhouse. As a relatively young man, his leadership skills were recognized when he was given the important post of Longhouse speaker.

Initially, Deskaheh's main concerns were cultural. He was determined that his people would not lose their language and traditions under the unrelenting Anglo-American cultural onslaught. But during World War I, Deskaheh began to move into the political arena. The issue that led him there was conscription. When Ottawa announced that members of the First Nations would be drafted to serve in the Canadian military, Deskaheh and a group of his supporters immediately went to Ottawa to argue that the Canadian government had no jurisdiction over their people.

Eventually, the Dominion government acknowledged that, since Native people were not technically citizens of Canada (they lacked the right to vote or serve in professions), they should be exempt from the draft.

The admission was seen as a significant victory by the First Nations in gaining acknowledgement of their separate status from other Canadians. In 1921, Deskaheh tried to expand on that wartime victory by travelling to London to lobby the Colonial Office for recognition of the Iroquois claim to independence. Deskaheh travelled on his own Iroquois passport and tried to impress upon the British that the treaties recognizing Iroquois sovereignty that his people had signed with the representatives of George III must be recognized by the current monarch, George V.

The British were dismissive. They told Deskaheh they had already turned the whole Indian question over to the Dominion government, so he should go back home and address his plea to Ottawa. In 1922, the Dominion government responded to the Iroquois petition by agreeing to set up a three-person arbitration panel to decide the question of Iroquois sovereignty (Six Nations, 1976, pp. 7–8).

The initial hopes of the Iroquois were dampened when it became known that Ottawa wanted the panel members to be drawn from the Supreme Court of Ontario—part of the very group of Canadians responsible for administering the laws underpinning the territorial and jurisdictional claims of the settler society. When the Iroquois asked that the panel be made up instead of international jurists, the Dominion government refused, offering as a concession only that one member of the panel could be selected by the Iroquois, but that he or she had to be a "British subject."

What Ottawa was offering, the Mohawks suspected, was a bit of political theatre, where Mohawks would be invited to speak their minds, their words would be duly recorded, and then the government-appointed panel would summarily dismiss their case.

Deskaheh, therefore, decided to seek a higher authority to hear the Iroquois plea: the League of Nations. The League had made the protection of small nations from the aggression of the bigger powers one of its cornerstones. In 1923, Deskaheh, still travelling on his Iroquois passport, headed off to Geneva to put his case directly to the nations of the world. After months of diligent lobbying, Deskaheh managed to have four members of the league—Ireland, Panama, Persia, and Estonia—agree to jointly put the case for Iroquois sovereignty on the international order paper. As a preliminary step, the League of Nations invited both the Iroquois nation and Canada to submit their case to a special hearing.

The Dominion government reacted with a mixture of surprise and alarm at the news from Geneva. Duncan Campbell Scott, deputy minister of Indian Affairs, indicated in a private letter that the Dominion government would not stand idly by while the Iroquois went abroad to campaign for sovereignty. As he put it, "The Indians concerned are taking this course at their own risk and with the full knowledge of the facts and I fear must suffer the consequences" (Six Nations, 1976, p. 4).

Ottawa's first move was to undermine Deskaheh diplomatically by asking for British help in scuttling the hearings. All the British could do was to get a delay, but, as it turned out, that was all that the Dominion government needed. While Deskaheh was continuing to win support for the Iroquois cause (Norway, the Netherlands, and Albania joined the original four states backing it), Ottawa moved against his Longhouse supporters in Canada by force.

Using the powers the government had given itself in the 1880 amendment to the Indian Act, the minister responsible for Indian Affairs dissolved the Longhouse government and ordered DIA-sponsored elections be held in the Six Nations community. Immediately after the announcement, RCMP officers were sent onto the reserve to confiscate the Iroquois papers and symbolic articles, like the historic wampum belts.

The move against the Longhouse in Canada was used by Ottawa to isolate Deskaheh abroad. While the Iroquois leader was still trying to drum up support in Geneva, Canadian and British delegates were informing the international community that Deskaheh was no longer the legal representative of his people. With his political base effectively cut out from underneath him, Deskaheh was forced to leave Europe in defeat.

Deskaheh went into exile in the United States, where he continued to agitate for Iroquois sovereignty. In 1925, he made a radio broadcast from Rochester, New York, in which he accused the Canadian government of genocide against his people. Ottawa, he said, was trying "to punish us for trying to preserve our rights. The Canadian Government has now pretended to abolish our government by Royal Proclamation, and has pretended to set up a Canadian-made government over us, composed of the few traitors among us who are willing to accept pay from Ottawa and do its bidding" (Six Nations, 1976, p. 16).

Deskaheh died later that same year. But the Longhouse and Mohawk traditions have proven remarkably resilient. Even today, many decades after the DIA-backed band chiefs were installed in all Mohawk communities, a sizable portion of the people in each community continue to reject Canadian citizenship, with the leadership insisting their people are part of the independent Iroquois nation that Deskaheh fought for.

The persistence of the Longhouse went a long way in preserving at least part of the traditional Iroquois polity, but in other areas of the country, the Canadian drive to replace the traditional Native leadership with the band council system was more complete. The Department of Indian Affairs' control of the councils, however, only led to the emergence of new Indian organizations and what might be called independent "Indian populists," in an attempt to find new mechanisms to put First Nations grievances forward.

ALLIED TRIBES AND ANDY PAULL

While many Iroquois, particularly Mohawks, continued to look to the by-then largely underground Longhouse for leadership, Native activists in other parts of Canada were busy building Indian organizations that would allow them to take their case to Ottawa, outside the controls of the Department of Indian Affairs' band council system.

Most of those organizations were regional in nature, and they were founded by local activists who travelled from reserve to reserve to build new local alliances. This type of organizing was greatly hampered by the fact that, in some parts of the country, Indians were required to get permission from the Indian agents even to leave their communities. Organizing often had to be carried out in semi-secrecy, and the only funding came from passing the hat at community meetings.

One of the largest and most important of the new regional organizations was the Allied Tribes of British Columbia. The Allied Tribes had been founded in 1916 at a meeting of 16 B.C. chiefs at Spences Bridge sponsored by James Teit, a sympathetic anthropologist. What made it such a significant concern to Ottawa was that its main focus was the so-called B.C. land question, which stemmed from the fact that most B.C. natives had never signed a treaty ceding their lands to British or Canadian authorities.[4]

This was due not so much to resistance on their part as to the fact that the governors of British Columbia had never bothered to negotiate treaties with the First Nations of most of the colony. After the province entered Confederation in 1871, the matter of treaties was simply brushed aside and forgotten.

The Allied Tribes' main strategy was to put together a legal case to take to the Privy Council in Britain to argue for their unextinguished Aboriginal title to the land. At the same time, the organization was also active at the community level, with organizers travelling to Indian communities across the province to win support for its goals and to urge people on to acts of resistance in their daily lives.

In 1926, the Allied Tribes sent a delegation to London to look into the possibility of Privy Council hearings on the B.C. land question. The leadership stated its case frankly in a petition to the king that read in part: "We Indians want our Native titles to our Native lands, and all our land contains, as we are the original people of Canada. We Indians want our consent before laws are made upon our possessions."[5]

The British gave the Allied Tribes delegation the same response they had given Deskaheh five years earlier: they told it to go home and take the matter up with the Dominion government. And once again, Ottawa agreed to hold a special hearing on the issue. But, as was the case with the Mohawks five years earlier, Ottawa was not about to have its control of Aboriginal lands seriously questioned.

In the government's view, such recognition would mean that not only B.C. Natives, but also First Nations in Quebec, northern Ontario, and the Yukon and Northwest Territories would have similar rights, since few treaties had been signed in those areas either. As the deputy minister of Indian Affairs, Duncan Campbell Scott, put it, recognition of the B.C. land claim would "smash confederation" (Canada, 1961, p. 583).

When the Allied Tribes leaders assembled in Ottawa for the 27 March 1927 hearing, the deck had already been stacked against them. The committee was made up largely of B.C. senators and MPs who were not prepared to give an inch of their province's territory to the First Nations. The only concession the politicians would make was to give B.C. Indians $100 000 a year in compensation for the fact that they were not receiving treaty money. (On a per-person basis, this amounted to roughly the same $5 annuity the signatories of Treaty Number 6 had received 50 years earlier.)

While the government was rushing to close the door on the B.C. claim and on the claims of Aboriginal title to the other unceded parts of the country, it was also working on a more ambitious plan to shut down the young Indian organizations. Three days before the Allied Tribes hearings began, the federal government passed legislation making it illegal for anyone to collect money from Indian band members for the purpose of pursuing a land claim.

The new clause was inserted into the Indian Act under section 149a, which stated that "every person who solicits or requests from any Indian any payment or contribution or promise of any payment or contribution for the purpose of raising a fund for the prosecution of any claim" would be liable to fines or imprisonment (Manuel and Posluns, 1974, p. 95).

As a justification, the Department of Indian Affairs argued that the measure would protect First Nations people against unscrupulous lawyers. To the leaders of the Allied Tribes and other organizations, however, the legislation appeared to be directed at their attempts to contest their claims of Aboriginal title in the courts. The 1927 legislation was so broadly written that it could also be interpreted to make groups like the Allied Tribes—which focussed on the land issue and were funded directly by Indian people—illegal.

Indian leaders have referred to section 149a as "the darkest hour in the history of the Parliament of Canada" (Manuel and Posluns, 1974, p. 95).

In retrospect, the draconian measure shows not only the lengths that the Dominion government would go to in trying to subvert First Nations claims to their homelands, but also how nervous the government was about its own legal title to the land.[6]

While the 1927 proscriptions were an immediate and serious blow to the Indian movement, they did not completely crush First Nations resistance. In the short term, they sank organizations like the Allied Tribes, but similar Indian organizations survived by shifting their focus away from the question of Aboriginal title toward more local concerns.

This period also saw the rise of what can be termed "Indian populists" — individual activists who emerged to fill the gap left by the more aggressive land claim organizations like the Allied Tribes. Probably the most influential of these populists was the B.C. Squamish leader Andy Paull.

Andy Paull had, in fact, been one of the leaders of the Allied Tribes. He attended the organization's first meeting at Spences Bridge in 1916, and he had travelled to Ottawa five times as an Allied Tribes spokesman to promote the B.C. Indians' claims. After the collapse of the Allied Tribes, Paull continued to pursue the issue with his informal network of contacts. In a sense, he served as a living link to the small isolated Indian organizations across the country. When Paull took the train to Ottawa, he would get off at numerous places along the way to visit local Indian communities and meet with activists. On his way back, he would stop again to report on how his meetings had gone and on his future plans. For the scattered Native organizations and community-based activists, Andy Paull became the personification of the wider struggle.

During the late 1920s and through the 1930s, Andy Paull also served as a much-needed beacon of hope. With the Depression, most bands were once again finding themselves stalked by hunger. The government refused to give the people the same amount of relief it gave to whites, under the pretext that Indians could get most of their food from hunting and fishing. At the same time, a web of legislation had been enacted restricting Indian fishing and hunting rights and the ability of farm-based Native economies to sell their produce in the open market.

While the economic situation deteriorated, the physical health of the people began to fail. A new scourge, tuberculosis, was moving through the reserves, claiming hundreds and even thousands of lives each year — with the annual body count perfunctorily listed in Parliament during the Department of Indian Affairs budget debates.

Politically, the communities were more tightly controlled during this period than they had ever been before or since. The local Indian agents, who were often retired military men, held sway over everything, from the number of days a band member could hunt and fish to when and how long individuals could leave the reserve, and even how many hours a day a band member could spend in a pool hall.

In those difficult days, it was individual leaders like Andy Paull who demonstrated that resistance was still possible. In Paull's case, he would suddenly arrive in a community in worn-out country clothes and urge the people to stand up to the local Indian agent and the priests who ran the residential schools and demand their right to fair treatment and Depression-era financial assistance. As he told his followers: "White people have not yet paid for this country. They must treat us in decent way, not wield dictatorial powers over us" (Paull, 1951, p. 14).

Andy Paull also continued to use every opportunity to travel to Ottawa to press the Native case. Part of his effectiveness in dealing with the parliamentarians came from the legal training he had received in a Vancouver law office. As a young man, he had served as a legal assistant for four years and had acquired enough experience to be called to the bar. But Paull was ineligible because status Indians were considered minors before the law (Dunlop, 1989, p. 40).

Virtually all professions during this period were closed to status Indians. The only way they could be admitted was to renounce their Indianness and became "enfranchised" as full Canadians. It was a route that a small number took, but Paull refused. Instead, he became known by the then-oxymoron of an "Indian lawyer."

When he was in Ottawa, Andy Paull changed his country clothes for some of the flashiest suits in the capital and went toe to toe with the MPs and bureaucrats in debate. As a leader, he was particularly effective in shaming the government into honouring its meagre treaty commitments and in giving emergency aid to communities that required it.

In the 1940s, World War II opened up new avenues for furthering the Native cause. The conscription issue again offered both a threat and an opportunity for reaffirming First Nations sovereignty. Like Deskaheh before him, Paull fought hard against the threatened Native draft, and once again Ottawa backed down. But Paull was never satisfied with small victories. As the war drew to its obvious conclusion, he began arguing that the First Nations of Canada should be given a separate place at the peace negotiating table with the other self-governing members of the empire like Australia and New Zealand.

Paull's radical-sounding demand for self-governing status surprised even many of his fellow Indian leaders. As might have been expected, Ottawa ignored the request, but the postwar period did offer the Native movement a considerable opening. Partly as a result of the surge in postwar liberalism, Ottawa pledged to undertake a major revision of the Indian Act in 1949–50, which led to the lifting of the restrictions on Indian organizing.

By then, Andy Paull was building a new and much more ambitious organization: the North American Indian Brotherhood. With this vehicle, Paull was aiming at nothing less than organizing all of the First Nations peoples on the continent for redress of historic grievances.

His plan was probably too ambitious, at least for the times. As one Mohawk activist put it, "the train can't run until the track has been laid,"[7] and in the 1940s, the track that would allow the First Nations to build a national organization was still decades from being laid.

Still, Andy Paull was able to elucidate a vision that those who followed could put into practice. George Manuel, one of Paull's protégés, described Andy Paull as the last of the "one-man shows," but he was also "the inspiration and the spark" that ignited the modern Indian movement.

In his face-to-face lobbying of parliamentarians, Andy Paull was also fulfilling the goal Big Bear had set for himself half a century earlier: getting an opportunity to stand before the people who held the power to put forward the First Nations case.

Big Bear had hoped that if he explained the position of the Cree nation, he could convince the settlers' government to respect the Cree's way of life, their Aboriginal title to the land, and their right to govern themselves. By Andy Paull's time, it was clear that simply stating the First Nations case would not be enough. It would take not only the efforts of many other far-seeing leaders like Big Bear, Deskaheh, and Andy Paull, but also the efforts of hundreds, even thousands, of activists working to build a movement that was strong enough to force Ottawa to respond to the First Nations' historical demands.

THE NEW GENERATION: GEORGE MANUEL AND THE NATIONAL INDIAN MOVEMENT

Building the national Indian movement was a long and arduous task that involved Native leaders from across the country slowly building up local and regional organizations.

The first boost to the effort came when the proscriptions on Indian organizing were lifted in the 1951 revision of the Indian Act (see Smith, 1975, pp. 154–96). But the movement was also aided by the postwar economic boom, which offered employment opportunities for the members of many bands. It was a time when more Native families were able to

afford a car, and this fact was not inconsiderable in allowing Indian activists to travel easily to surrounding communities, and across their
provinces, to carry out organizing activities.

There was also a general improvement in health in the communities.
Although First Nations people continued to lag far behind other Canadians in health (as in wealth, employment, etc.), the plague of tuberculosis,
which killed thousands of Native people a year in the 1930s and 1940s,
was subsiding in most Native communities.[8]

The small-scale but persistent organizing efforts of the previous generation were also beginning to pay off. Natives in the prairie provinces, in
particular, had managed to create increasingly effective provincial organizations that, by the end of the 1960s, were led by a trio of strong and very
politically adept leaders—Harold Cardinal in Alberta, Walter Deiter in
Saskatchewan, and Dave Courchene in Manitoba—each of whom played
a key role in launching the first national status Indian organization.

The final organizing drive was inadvertently spurred on by the Department of Indian Affairs itself, when measures were introduced to de-
volve certain additional powers to the band chiefs to make them something like village reeves rather than mere departmental factotums.[9]

The small but real increase in powers for the chiefs helped raise their
status in the community, where in some places their subservient position
to the Indian agents had made them objects of ridicule. As the chiefs and
their band councils gradually assumed more power, the office began to attract men and women who saw the position as a way to challenge Ottawa
on an array of local issues.

The same sort of unintended effect occurred from 1965 to 1968 when
the Department of Indian Affairs brought together representatives of the
various Indian organizations into the National Indian Advisory Board,
which was given the mandate of reviewing the Indian Act.

On the face of it, it looked like a progressive move by the department.
But the Indian "advisers" soon discovered that what the department was
looking for from the board was a stamp of approval for its plan to abolish
not only the Indian Act, but also virtually all First Nations rights, including their rights to their reserve lands.

The department's plans would be made public in the summer of 1969
in the Indian policy statement, known as the White Paper, presented by
the Minister of Indian Affairs, Jean Chrétien. But in the late 1960s, the
National Indian Advisory Board itself was used by the Native leaders
as an important organizing tool. The official meetings, under the co-
chairmanship of the Department of Indian Affairs deputy minister, Robert
Battle, and the Shuswap Indian leader, George Manuel, were characterized

by push-and-pull debates between department officials and Native representatives. But as George Manuel and the other Native leaders saw it, the real meetings took place in the hotel rooms afterward, where Native leaders, who had been brought together from across the country, quietly planned the founding of a national Indian organization.

That organization, the National Indian Brotherhood (NIB), was launched in December 1968 under the provisional leadership of Walter Deiter of Saskatchewan. The NIB was a major breakthrough in Indian politics. It gave a single voice to status Indians across the country with a membership in the hundreds of thousands, rather than the mere hundreds of people represented by most band chiefs. George Manuel replaced Deiter as the president of the National Indian Brotherhood a short time later, and went on to dominate Native politics in Canada for the next decade.

George Manuel had grown up on the Neskonlith reserve in the interior of British Columbia and came from a family active in the First Nations struggle. His true mentor, however, was Andy Paull. Manuel's first contact with Paull came in his youth when Paull visited Neskonlith on his frequent trips through the B.C. interior. As a young boom man on the South Thompson River, Manuel became directly involved with Paull when he was fighting a ruling that required gainfully employed Indians to pay their own medical costs. Manuel had contacted Paull about the issue, and soon after George Manuel became a local organizer for Andy Paull in the B.C. interior. On Paull's death in 1959, George Manuel emerged as the most prominent Indian leader in British Columbia, and then in the entire country.

George Manuel was elected president of the newly formed National Indian Brotherhood in 1970. At the time, the NIB was largely a paper organization without an office, funding, or a clear political direction. During his six years of leadership, Manuel transformed it into the largest lobbying organization in Ottawa, with a mandate to pursue self-government for all of the 50-some First Nations in Canada. Under George Manuel's leadership, the rather bureaucratic structure required to run an organization like the National Indian Brotherhood was set within the larger framework of Native consensus politics. He insisted, for example, that anyone working in the Native movement should always "consult the people, politicize the people and never get too far ahead of them, because when all is said and done, they are your masters" (cited in McFarlane, 1993, p. 226).

It was also during George Manuel's tenure that the modern ideology of the movement began to take shape. In the early 1970s, the NIB was caught up in the general swirl of extra-parliamentary opposition activities that shaped the period. The Native movement was influenced by the Black Power movement in the United States and by the Third World anticolonialist ideology that had developed during the African wars of liberation. Young Indian activists began to speak of "Red Power" and incorporate a certain Marxist perspective into their worldview.

After George Manuel set up the National Indian Brotherhood headquarters in Ottawa, he used his first year in the capital to acquaint himself with the local power structure and to meet with representatives of the generally leftist Third World countries of Africa. His contacts with the Tanzania High Commission led him to tour the African country at the end of 1971, where he met and became friends with one of the architects of African liberation, Julius Nyerere.

From Deskaheh's time to Manuel's, looking beyond Canada's borders for allies in the First Nations drive toward self-government had become, if not commonplace, at least a frequent tactic used by First Nations leaders. George Manuel took it further and launched the U.N.-affiliated World Council of Indigenous Peoples in 1975 at a Port Alberni, British Columbia, conference that included indigenous peoples from North, Central, and South America, Eurasia, and the Arctic — and even a delegation of Sami reindeer herders from northern Scandinavia.

Within Canada, George Manuel had the task of directing a movement and an organization that were peopled by strong regional figures. He could call on the political expertise of the prairie leaders who had helped put him in power, as well as people like the Mohawk chief Andrew Delisle, a strong force in Quebec, and Phillip Paul, a close Manuel ally from British Columbia. Most of these leaders had decades of experience in Native politics and had built and run organizations of their own.

One area of political development where George Manuel played a significant role was in making room for more women in the mainstream of the movement. As an organizer in the B.C. interior, one of his strongest allies had been Genevieve Mussel, who at the time was one of the few female band chiefs in Canada. During the 1950s, most Native women political activists were sequestered off in the Homemaker's Association and played primarily a supporting role to the largely male-staffed organizations. When George Manuel took over as president of the NIB, he hired Marie Smallface Marule, a Blackfoot Indian who had spent three years working in Africa, as his executive director. Marie Marule was given almost complete power over the organization when George Manuel was absent, and he relied on her as a primary source of political advice. With Marie Marule in charge, a number of other very talented Native women were attracted to the organization and filled many of its most important posts.

During the early 1970s, however, the number of powerful regional figures in the Native movement and their often conflicting interests made the National Indian Brotherhood a difficult horse to ride. Within the provincial organizations, rivalries and suspicions still existed between different tribal groups, and nationally, the treaty and non-treaty Indians often saw issues differently. A nationwide consensus on any issue was always a challenge, and generally at least a few bands would withdraw their support from a national initiative they could not agree with.

Yet, given the broad historical and cultural differences among the First Nations, a surprising degree of unity was attained in a relatively short time. Much of the NIB's early success can be attributed to the sheer force of Manuel's personality, which combined Andy Paull–type charisma with the organizational skills needed to build a national movement. At the core of Manuel's leadership style was his traditional background. He had been raised in the B.C. interior by his grandfather, who had grown up before widespread settlement in the area, and George Manuel had inherited much of his grandfather's traditional worldview and an understanding of the special relationship between the Native community and its leaders.

For Manuel, this understanding translated into a step-by-step approach to leadership. In the early 1970s, he worked on specific issues that could mobilize and radicalize the people in the communities. He first drew the battle lines over Indian control of education. His immediate goal was to have the right to educate Indian children returned to Indian communities. But in the longer view, he was trying to use the schools issue as a model for similar battles — over control of economic development, Native justice, and culture — that the movement would undertake in the future.

Another of the ramparts Manuel frequently attacked was the Department of Indian Affairs itself. Instead of a frontal assault, however, he used a tactic that department had so often used against Native leadership in the past — trying to isolate it with a view to undercutting its influence.

In this case, Manuel successfully lobbied the Prime Minister's Office for the creation of a joint NIB–cabinet committee. The first meeting in 1972 was a historic one, as George Manuel managed to sit down with what Big Bear personified as "the Government" to make the First Nations case for self-government and justice on the land question. By the early 1970s, the Native movement had clearly set out on the road to regaining lost lands and liberty, but reaching its destination would require a long and difficult struggle.

In the short term, the joint NIB–cabinet committee allowed Indian leaders to circumvent to some degree the Department of Indian Affairs bureaucracy and speak directly to the various ministers. For example, the NIB was able to address the minister responsible for housing about the need for better housing on reserves, or the health minister about the need for more clinics in isolated communities. In this way, the stranglehold the Department of Indian Affairs had held over the First Nations was loosened and the national Native leadership was able to play one department off another to get the best deal possible for their people.

The activists in Ottawa were also greatly aided by a new restiveness in Native communities that was causing concern in Ottawa, where fears were being expressed that the Canadian Indians might take the militant path of the Black Panthers in the United States. To be fair, under the Liberal regimes of Lester B. Pearson and Pierre Trudeau, there was also a new willingness in Ottawa to at least address Native concerns. Taken together, the surge in activism from below and a new willingness to listen in Ottawa presented George Manuel and his team of activists with a number of important opportunities for furthering the First Nations cause.

While George Manuel made significant progress on most fronts during his six years in Ottawa, the one area where he and his organization ran into a stone wall was the recognition of their people's Aboriginal right to the land. The bitterest defeat came with the signing of the James Bay agreement between Quebec and the Cree and Inuit in the province in 1975.

The James Bay agreement was described as the first "modern" treaty, but the final result and the process leading up to it were remarkably similar to the unilateralism of the numbered treaties of the nineteenth century. Quebec waited until it was already moving bulldozers onto Cree territory before it entered into negotiations with the Cree leaders, and throughout the discussions, officials from the Quebec government and the James Bay Corporation let it be known that if the Crees refused to sign, the hydroelectric project would be built anyway. "Sign or starve" had been replaced by "sign or you get nothing."

George Manuel's term as NIB president ended in 1976, but instead of retiring, he returned to British Columbia to launch and lead what he described as his "peoples' movement." Manuel later explained that his experience in Ottawa, and especially during the "gun-to-the-head" negotiations leading up to the James Bay agreement, had taught him that governments and their agencies respond only to shows of power.

Since the indigenous peoples in North America were small minorities in their homelands, Manuel believed that the ballot box was insufficient to give them power over their lives. What he proposed was an Indian movement that would not only lobby the government through organizations like the NIB, but also have at its base a strong activist grass-roots organization that could back up the self-government demands by the other means available in a democratic society, including public protests, direct action, and civil disobedience.

George Manuel spent the next three years building such a movement in British Columbia. In 1980, he had an opportunity to put it to work on the national stage. And the issue was one that would dominate the Native movement, and the political life of the whole country, for much of the next decade: the Constitution.

When Prime Minister Trudeau introduced his constitutional repatriation package in 1978, George Manuel and other Native leaders realized that some of its provisions, especially the Charter of Rights and Freedoms, could override protections of First Nations hunting and fishing rights and their right to collectively possess their reserve lands. For Indian leaders, the constitutional battles ahead would be important in their own right, but they would also serve as important symbolic issues to be used to radicalize people in the communities and to win acceptance of broader First Nations powers within Canada from the public at large.

From his B.C. base, George Manuel launched a court case to block the Trudeau package and mobilized his peoples' movement in a so-called constitutional express of 1000 activists who travelled to Ottawa by train to protest against any constitutional changes at the expense of First Nations rights.

Manuel led the Native protesters to the steps of Parliament and managed to win public sympathy for the Native cause, while sending fears of a widespread Indian insurrection through the government. Largely as a result of his efforts, the formal recognition of Aboriginal rights was inserted into the Constitution, with a mandated set of negotiations between the federal and provincial governments and the Native organizations over the exact content of those rights.

George Manuel would not be part of those negotiations. While in Ottawa fighting on the Constitution issue, he suffered the first of a series of debilitating heart attacks, and he was forced to withdraw from most of his political activities. The breach would be filled by a new generation of leaders who would draw their inspiration from men like Big Bear, Deskaheh, Andy Paull, and George Manuel while they searched for new ways to carry the struggle forward.

NATIVE LEADERSHIP TODAY

When George Manuel stepped down as the head of the National Indian Brotherhood and returned to British Columbia in 1976, he was replaced by a Saskatchewan Cree, Noel Starblanket, who served only two years and was followed by Del Riley. In 1982, the NIB changed its structure and its name to the Assembly of First Nations (AFN). Instead of being based on provincial organizations, the new Assembly of First Nations would be made up directly of the bands. This solved some of the tensions that had grown up within the provincial organizations, which in places like British Columbia often forced the organization to speak with one voice for radically different groups like the coastal and interior Indians. Henceforth, the national organization's membership would be composed of the 600 or so band chiefs, each of whom would have an equal voice in the assembly.

The change from the provincially based NIB to the constituent assembly model of the AFN was completed under the leadership of the Saskatchewan Cree leader David Ahenikew. But it was the young Dene leader George Erasmus, who took over as national chief in 1984, who represented the status Indians during the negotiations with the federal and provincial governments on the nature of the treaty and Aboriginal rights that were to be included in the Constitution. Erasmus remained the national chief for six years and proved to be the most effective leader since George Manuel in promoting unity in the First Nations movement. Erasmus was able to use the ongoing constitutional negotiations with the federal and provincial governments as a focal point for discussion and planning on self-government issues.

The constitutional negotiations ultimately broke down, but the 1980s saw significant gains for the movement as Native leaders were able to use the national profile of the negotiations to win broad (although not necessarily deep) support from the Canadian people for their self-government demands. During the negotiation of the Charlottetown Accord in the early 1990s, the growing public support was reflected in the fact that the new leader of the Assembly of First Nations, Ovide Mercredi, as well as the leaders of the non-status Indian and Inuit organizations were invited to the table with the prime minister and premiers to discuss Canada's constitutional future.

In the end, the Charlottetown Accord was defeated in a national referendum, but the federal and provincial governments had acknowledged that the First Nations of Canada had an "inherent right" to govern themselves.

If such an acknowledgement had come a century or so earlier, it would have gone a long way to addressing the concerns of Native leaders like

Big Bear. But by the 1990s, it was seen as just another small step on a very long road. The Native leaders of today have set themselves the task not only of winning constitutional recognition of their status as nations, but also of rebuilding those nations in the modern world. That task will not be an easy one.

Many decades of assimilationist policies, like the residential school system, have taken their toll on Native cultures and languages. The challenge will not be simply restoring lost political rights, but reviving Native cultures and economies. Although the national leadership has tended to focus on the political battles, there are perhaps even more far-ranging changes going on at the local level, where activists have been trying to envision and, to a certain extent, put in place the form of self-government that would best serve the interest of their individual nations. And just as the movement saw a rapid growth in provincial organizations in the 1960s as a prelude to building the national organization, the 1980s saw the growth of so-called tribal councils as the beginning of new Indian governments.

It was a natural evolution. Native leaders were basing their right to govern themselves on the fact that their people, whether Cree, Shuswap, or Haida, had been governing themselves for thousands of years. In the hunting societies, the people had spent much of the year in relatively small bands, but generally they had come together at least twice a year, in the fall and the spring, to hold religious festivals, arrange marriages, and convene national councils where treaty-making and other tribal issues would be discussed. Today, the tribal councils are the forum where the individual First Nations work to preserve and promote their culture, language, and historical values, and where the drive for sovereignty is often most strongly expressed. The challenge for the national leader of the Assembly of First Nations, by both necessity and tradition, has become very much a matter of building a broad consensus within the constituent First Nations for any national initiatives he or she might want to take.

In this sense, the rise of the tribal councils has made the task of the national leadership more difficult, as power and influence in the movement become more dispersed across the country. A powerful Cree leader, Matthew Coon Come in Quebec, for example, often eclipses his AFN counterpart, Ovide Mercredi, on the national and even international stage. The national leader has to win not only the consensus of 600 or so isolated band chiefs, but also the support of the new and often powerful tribal leaders. In the need for consensus-building among strong and largely independent groups, it seems that the future will call for more, not less, of the traditional style of leadership.

As in the past, the basis of unity will likely be found in the fact that the ultimate goals that Native leaders across Canada have pursued have changed little since the days Big Bear was roaming the prairie. Big Bear's demand to speak to "the Government" is little different from today's demands for nation-to-nation negotiations between the leaders of the First Nations and the Canadian state. Then, as now, Native leaders have been preoccupied with obtaining a new deal on the ownership and use of their traditional lands and with gaining recognition, in fact and in law, of the First Nations' right to govern themselves.

NOTES

1. "His" is used in this instance because women were not traditionally chiefs, although in a number of societies, like the Iroquois, heredity passed from mother to child, and women, specifically the clan mothers, were given the job of choosing chiefs.
2. They were called "lettered treaties" because the British referred to the treaties simply as A, B, C, etc. After Confederation, the Dominion government listed the treaties by number: Treaty Number 1, Treaty Number 2, etc.
3. As Dempsey (1984) points out, a number of Cree spokespeople at the meeting made a direct connection between signing the document and receiving emergency rations from the government in times of mass starvation.
4. The idea of "Aboriginal title" has long existed in the British tradition. By definition, indigenous peoples can be said to have Aboriginal title to an area if they can show long-term, continuous use of that area before the Europeans arrived, as long as that title has not been extinguished by a treaty. Most courts, however, have suggested that, at most, Aboriginal title confers on the First Nations the right to carry on traditional hunting and fishing activities in the area. Native leaders, on the other hand, assert that Aboriginal title confers at least as much ownership right as the Europeans acquired by simply arriving on the shores of North America, planting their flag, and claiming the territory as part of their own national territory.
5. The petition is in the Shuswap Nation Archives, Kamloops, British Columbia.
6. At the time, Ottawa had some basis for its concern about the Allied Tribes' attempt to take the case of the B.C. Indians to the Privy Council in London. In 1921, the Privy Council had ruled that the indigenous peoples of Nigeria still held Aboriginal title to their land because the colonial authorities had never "extinguished" that title through the treaty process.
7. Bill Badcock interview.
8. The exceptions were in the isolated communities of the far north, where tuberculosis continued to take a deadly toll for decades.

9. One of the main reasons behind the devolution of powers during the period was to prepare for the DIA's plan to remove special status from Indian lands. The reserves, as part of the national territory of the First Nations, would cease to exist, and Indian communities would be transformed into simple municipalities under the control of the provinces.

DISCUSSION QUESTIONS

1. Virtually all of modern Canada was part of the territory of one of the First Nations. What was the main Native nation in your region?
2. How did the colonial authorities address the question of Aboriginal title for that nation? Were treaties signed? If so, what were the terms? If not, why not?
3. What was the role of Native leaders in the treaty process during the time of the numbered treaties?
4. What was the main role of Native leaders after the last numbered treaty was signed in 1921?
5. What are the main challenges that Native leaders face today?

FURTHER READING

Churchill, Ward. 1993. *Struggle for the Land.* Monroe, Me.: Common Courage Press. Individual lands claims are looked at from the perspective of the overall struggle for Native rights in North America.

Manuel, George and Michael Posluns. 1974. *The Fourth World: An Indian Reality.* Toronto: Collier Macmillan. Covers George Manuel's life before his election as the president of the National Indian Brotherhood.

McFarlane, Peter. 1993. *From Brotherhood to Nationhood: George Manuel and the Modern Indian Movement.* Toronto: Between the Lines. Covers George Manuel's role in building the modern Indian movement from the 1950s to the 1980s.

McGhee, Robert. 1941. *Ancient Canada.* Ottawa: Canadian Museum of Civilization. Archaeologist McGhee reconstructs selected scenes from Canadian precontact history, and in the process examines some unsolved mysteries. Why, for example, was an adolescent buried with great ceremony on the Labrador coast 7000 years ago? And what is the explanation for those hilltop fortresses in British Columbia? Answers are still being sought.

REFERENCES

Canada. 1961. *Proceedings of the Joint Senate–House of Commons Committee on Indian Affairs*. May 25. Ottawa: Supply and Services.

Dempsey, Hugh A. 1984. *Big Bear: End of Freedom*. Vancouver: Douglas & McIntyre.

Dunlop, Herbert Francis. 1989. *Andy Paull: As I Knew Him*. Vancouver: Standard Press.

Geographic Board, Canada (GBC). 1913. *Handbook of Indians of Canada*. Ottawa: GBC.

Mandelbaum, David G. 1979. *The Plains Cree: An Ethnographic History and Comparative Study*. Regina: Canadian Plains Research Centre, University of Regina.

Manuel, George. 1972. Speech to the UBCIC annual meeting. November.

Manuel, George and Michael Posluns. 1974. *The Fourth World: An Indian Reality*. Toronto: Collier Macmillan.

McFarlane, Peter. 1993. *Brotherhood to Nationhood: George Manuel and the Modern Indian Movement*. Toronto: Between the Lines.

Paull, Andy. 1951. In *The Native Voice* (October): p. 14.

Six Nations Museum Series. 1976. "Deskaheh: Iroquois Statesman and Patriot." *Akwesasne Notes*.

Smith, Derek G., ed. 1975. *Canadian Indians and the Law: Selected Documents 1663–1972*. Toronto: McClelland & Stewart.

Trigger, Bruce G. 1987. *The Children of Aataentsic: A History of the Huron People to 1660*. Montreal: McGill-Queen's University Press.

CHAPTER 4

Contemporary Aboriginal[1] Women in Canada

Cora J. Voyageur

INTRODUCTION

> Indian people must wake up! They are asleep! ... We were in touch but
> now we are not. Part of this waking up means replacing women to their
> rightful place in society. It's been less than one hundred years that men lost
> touch with reality. There's no power or medicine that has all force unless
> it's balanced. The woman must be there also, but she has been left out!
> When we still had our culture, we had the balance. The women made cer-
> emonies, and she was recognized as being united with the moon, the earth
> and all the forces on it. Men have taken over. Most feel threatened by holy
> women. They must stop and remember, remember the loving power of their
> grandmothers and mothers.[2] (Rose Auger, Cree Elder, Alberta)

Wake up! This statement has been repeated by First Nations women
across Canada for the past 25 years. They have been trying to get the attention of First Nations men, their chiefs and band councillors, the federal government, and mainstream society. They want to create awareness
of, and subsequently change, their circumstances in the reserve setting, in
urban areas, and within Canadian society in general. According to a Department of Indian Affairs demographic profile, First Nations women
rank among the most severely disadvantaged groups in Canadian society.
They are worse off economically than both non–First Nations people and
First Nations men (Canada, 1979, p. 31).

Change for First Nations people began after World War II. They vol-
unteered for duty, fought for Canada, and played an important role in
Canada's war effort. But when they returned, they were relegated to their
subordinate position in Canadian society.

In 1969, the Liberal government's White Paper on Indian policy
(Canada, 1969) united First Nations people. The government attempted
to renege on its treaty obligations and dissolve the reserve system. This
move drew a storm of protests from First Nations people across the nation.

The White Paper was subsequently withdrawn, but not before it served as a catalyst for First Nations political organization.

First Nations women organized lobby groups such as Indian Rights for Indian Women and the Tobique Indian Women's Group. They forced women's issues and concerns onto the agendas of tribal administration and the government. They had grown increasingly frustrated with the economic, social, and political situations in their communities and had decided that they must attempt to equalize the gender biases prevalent in their communities and in Canadian law.

The gender bias in the First Nations community and in Canadian legislation has a long history. Since contact with Europeans, First Nations women have been placed in a precarious situation by governments, both foreign and domestic. In the 500 years since the Indians "discovered" Columbus, the traditional role and status of First Nations women has changed dramatically. In many communities, they were removed from their roles as advisers and respected community members by adopted foreign ideologies. Native academic Paula Gunn Allen states that Indian women and their egalitarian system were replaced by a male-dominated, hierarchical system at the behest of Jesuit missionaries (Gunn Allen, 1992, pp. 40–41). In return, Indian men were given authority and social standing. Patricia Albers, editor of *The Hidden Half: Studies of Plains Indian Women*, states that Indian women are ancillary to the male-dominated universe of Native diplomacy, warfare, and hunting featured in books, scholarly articles, and movies (Albers and Medicine, 1983, p. 2).

Women were also subjugated in the spirit world. Gunn Allen states that tribes systematically replaced female deities with male deities after European contact. For example, the Hopi goddess Spider Woman was replaced by Tawa, the Cherokee goddess River Foam was replaced by Thunder, and the Iroquois divinity Sky Woman now gets her ideas and power from her dead father (Gunn Allen, 1992, p. 41).

Despite all the changes endured by indigenous peoples, many aspects of the traditional Native women's role have remained constant. Women are still responsible for maintaining culture, stabilizing the community, and caring for future generations. They still play an influential yet unrecognized and unappreciated role in the community.

Contemporary First Nations women share many of the concerns of women in general — children, family, social issues, economics, education, employment, and political rights. In addition, First Nations women find themselves in a unique political and social situation. In a submission to the Royal Commission on Aboriginal Peoples, the Manitoba Indigenous Women's Collective wrote:

As Aboriginal women, we face discrimination and racism because we are Aboriginal and because we are women. We lack access to jobs, to support, to training programs, and to positions of influence and authority. (Green, 1993, p. 111)

Aboriginal women are in a worse economic situation than non-Aboriginal women and Aboriginal men. They generally hold fewer jobs and have a lower life expectancy. An Indian and Northern Affairs study showed that First Nations women constituted 26 percent of the First Nations labour force compared with 43 percent for non-Aboriginal women. This same study showed that a 50-year-old Aboriginal woman's life expectancy was two years less than that of a non-Aboriginal woman (Canada, 1979, p. 20).

First Nations women have a much tougher battle to fight in their pursuit of social and political recognition and equality. They have many adversaries: government, mainstream society, and, at times, their own people. Sociologist Linda Gerber calls the situation of contemporary First Nations women a "multiple jeopardy" (1990, p. 69), stating:

[N]ative females suffer multiple jeopardy on the basis of a number of objective indicators of social and economic well being. The fact that Indians as a group are disadvantaged and Indian females in particular suffer the greatest disadvantage suggests that Indian status, with its historical trappings of colonial dependency, does indeed create additional barriers to economic and social health. The position of Indian women, with respect to labour force participation and income, suggests that they are the most severely handicapped in their exchange relations with employers. (1990, p. 72)

This chapter examines the roles and concerns of First Nations women in contemporary Canadian society. It argues that specific events such as the creation of the Indian Act in 1869 and the passing of Bill C-31 in 1985 have had a great impact on First Nations women.[3] To fully understand the present social, political, and economic position of First Nations women in Canada, one must first look at Aboriginal women in a historical context. It is certain that past events laid the foundation for the current situation.

REGAINING ABORIGINAL WOMEN'S VOICE

Since the early 1970s, Aboriginal women have organized and found their own political voice. Aboriginal women had had their voices appropriated by others and thus were essentially silenced. Métis academic Emma

LaRocque, in her preface to *Writing the Circle: Native Women of Western Canada*, states that Native women were "wordless," that their words were literally and politically negated (1990, p. xv). Their concerns and needs were determined and articulated by their husbands and fathers, missionaries, and government agents. This has changed; Aboriginal women are no longer relying on the government or male-dominated Native political organizations to determine their fate. They are speaking for themselves collectively for the first time since European contact. Kenneth Lincoln, author of *Native American Renaissance*, refers to this articulation as a "rebirth" (Lincoln, 1983, p. 13).

The tenacity and relentless efforts of Aboriginal women such as Sandra Lovelace, Yvonne Bédard, and the late Jenny Margetts have won them recognition as worthy adversaries. However, this political activity has also brought them scorn and resentment. Nellie Carlson, an activist with Indian Rights for Indian Women, states:

> Indian women worked so hard to have Bill C-31 passed. We had no money; our lives were threatened, we were followed everywhere we went, our phones were tapped — that's how Indian women were treated for speaking out.[4]

She further states that Indian Rights for Indian Women fought for sixteen years to regain status for First Nations women. Their hard work brought some victories, such as the passing of Bill C-31 in 1985. Bill C-31 attempted to eliminate the sex discrimination in the Indian Act by reinstating Indian status to women who married non-Indian men and others who lost their status for a variety of reasons.

It has been a long struggle for Aboriginal women to tell their own story. Women have emerged from the purely domestic roles to share in rebuilding their communities. Their concern for community improvement has made them tireless workers and enduring advocates. However, Aboriginal women still encounter many obstacles in their pursuit of a better community.

Aboriginal women must contend with many archaic notions that date as far back as contact with Europeans. Racism and stereotyping of Aboriginal women illustrate this. American Aboriginal lawyer and scholar Rebecca Tsosie speaks of the myth of Aboriginal women in the bifurcated role of either "Pocahontas" or the "squaw," as illustrated in a series of Hollywood movies (Tsosie, 1988, p. 2). Although these stereotypes have faded over time, the legacy of past attitudes is still being felt by Aboriginal women today.

FACTORS LEADING TO THE PRESENT SITUATION

Many factors have led to the lower social, economic, and political status experienced by most Aboriginal women. These factors include the European hegemonic view of the New World, the historical unimportance of women in European society, ethnocentric practices that misinterpreted or ignored women's issues, the subjugation of Aboriginal people, and the adoption of European values and governing systems by Aboriginal men in the community.

European Hegemony

European expansion marked the transition to modern times; with colonization, the Europeans brought a self-imposed burden of "civilizing the barbarians" (Clough and Rapp, 1975, pp. 125, 139).

Upon contact, Europeans had established opinions of cultural, intellectual, and structural[5] supremacy over those encountered in the new land. European ideology stated that their civilization was superior to all others,[6] Indians were savages, and women were socially and politically invisible; individualism and patriarchy[7] prevailed. These attitudes caused the Europeans to "fix" unacceptable social conditions. They also affected the recording and writing of history dominated by men. Europeans viewed men, the holders of power and privilege, as the creators of civilization: analytical, logical, and inherently superior to women (Chalus, 1990, p. 32).

The Historical Unimportance of Women

History was, and some may argue still is, a man's world. With the exception of the likes of Cleopatra, Joan of Arc, Queen Elizabeth I, or Queen Victoria, few women have been viewed as significant to the course of history. In public affairs, women were invisible, viewed as chattels owned by men. They were not given political or social rights; thus, European women had little or no political or economic power.

European men set standards for women's decorum, which stated how a cultured woman should conduct herself. Restraint, modesty, submission, compliance, and piety all combined to create a gender role for women (Chalus, 1990, p. 38). Women were seen as being psychologically unstable, physically fragile, and morally susceptible. It is not surprising that these attitudes and standards were transported to the New World and imposed upon Native women by European men.

Prior to colonization, women were a strong force in many Aboriginal societies.[8] Legal scholar Robert Williams states that in a number of North American Indian tribes, women traditionally selected male chiefs as political leaders and could also remove them (1990, p. 1034). Also, in many tribes, women owned substantial property, including the marital home, and exercised exclusive dominion over the means of production and the products of major subsistence activities such as farming (Williams, 1990, p. 1034). Women in many tribes held the power to initiate or call off war.

The Iroquois Confederacy operated on a matriarchal system prior to the arrival of the Europeans (Native Women's Association of Canada, 1992, p. 2). This system was based on the concept of equality between the genders. Iroquois women played a profound role in the political and economic life of the community as nurturers, educators, and providers.

Ethnocentric Historical Records

Since the written word is considered the "true medium" of historical accuracy, history was left to the discretion of the literate. Those with the ability and opportunity to write had their own agendas to promote. Early accounts of the position of women in the colonial cultures were written by male European fur traders and missionaries. These early accounts tell us as much about the ideological perspectives of the authors as they do about the subject at hand. Explorers and traders were part of the patriarchal and hierarchical structure that dominated women. As a result, they did not acknowledge the contributions made by women to everyday life. Patricia Albers writes that journalistic accounts ignore or trivialize women's activities and experiences by dealing with and writing about Indian men (Albers and Medicine, 1983, p. 3). Much of the early literature on Aboriginal women contradicted what was to come later. The early ethnographic record supplies ample evidence of a variety of roles for females. For example, anthropologist Judith Brown states that older women in the Wabanaki, Algonquin, Delaware, Powhatan, and Iroquois tribes had authority over kinsmen and had the right to exert power over them and extract labour (Brown, 1982, p. 144). Females in the Wabanaki tribe achieved positions of leadership in both religious and political spheres when they reached middle age (Ezzo, 1988, p. 141).

Despite evidence from some early descriptions of women's authority, it is clear that reporting of Indian activities has often been based on purely ethnocentric interpretations. Anthropologist Alice Kehoe states that at the turn of the century, ethnographers were frustrated in their quest for data by the traditions of their discipline (1983, p. 53). However, because they viewed Indians as a "dying breed," it became important that details of Indian life be collected for posterity. As a result, there was a big push for ethnographic information related to Indians.

Encounters between recorder and subject were limited in duration and frequency. The resulting data were sometimes inaccurate and contained both gender and ethnocentric biases. One example of misinterpretation is the explanation of why a woman walked behind her husband. The assumption of the female's inferior status clouds the real reason the man walked in front of his wife: it was the man's responsibility to protect his wife because she was the giver of life and more powerful than he.

Data collection was guided by conventions that did not allow for accurate depictions of either the roles or the contributions of women. Ingrained biases were prevalent in all aspects of information gathering. One reason is that anthropologists were predominantly male. Their scholarly custom was to speak exclusively to male subjects. Common practice dictated that the ethnographer and his male assistant interview a limited number of middle-aged and elderly Indian men about life in the community. If and when Indian women were interviewed, the situation was uncomfortable for the women, who were accustomed to being insulted by European men. In addition, it was culturally inappropriate for Indian women to discuss "women's roles and practices" with males (Kehoe, 1983, p. 54).

The hegemonic ideals of European traders and missionaries supplanted the indigenous perspective on Indian women. In contrast to what was written about Indian women, indigenous customs held women in high regard; they were powerful within their communities.

Subjugation of Indigenous People

One of the primary reasons for the situation of Aboriginal women today is that indigenous people, in general, were subjugated by the immigrant European society. The subjugation was based on the myth of the savage Indian, who could not own land; Europeans viewed the land as vacant and therefore free for the taking (Cumming and Mickenberg, 1972, p. 18).

Missionary and government ideology held that the only way for Indians to survive was to give up everything that defined them as a people: religion, language, lifestyle, and identity. For example, residential schools were created to convert Indian children from "savages" to "civilized" citizens for the betterment of the Indian and society as a whole (Voyageur, 1993, p. 2).

Duncan Campbell Scott, assistant deputy superintendent of Indian Affairs, implemented an assimilation policy to rid Canadians and the government of the "Indian problem" (McDonald, 1987, p. 30). The Parliamentary Subcommittee on Indian Women and the Indian Act (1982) noted:

Between 1913 and 1930 the administration of Indian Affairs followed a rigid policy of forced assimilation. Traditional practices such as the Sundance and the Potlatch were prohibited and traditional languages were suppressed. Duncan Campbell Scott in explaining the rationale for changes to the legislation in 1920 said, "Our object is to continue until there is not a single Indian in Canada that has not been absorbed into the body politic. This is the whole object of this Bill." (McDonald, 1987, p. 30)

The elimination of the Indian would occur through education and religious training in European customs and values. Separate legal Indian status was conceived as a stopgap measure by white legislators, who expected that Indians would gradually abandon their Native identity in order to enjoy the privilege of full Canadian citizenship—a state to which all would and should aspire (Francis, 1993, p. 201).

When Indians met the minimal requirements for citizenship—literacy, education, and "acceptable" moral character—they were allowed the rights of full citizenship through voluntary enfranchisement. They would be allowed to vote, purchase alcohol, and obtain land under the homestead system, and would no longer have to live under the aegis of the repressive Indian Act. It is ironic that enfranchisement, the right of full citizenship, was used as both a reward and a punishment. It was a reward if the First Nations person obtained a university degree, joined the military, or became a minister. But enfranchisement was a punishment if the First Nations person was caught in possession of alcohol or raised the ire of the Indian agent, who had the discretion to strike anybody from the band list for whatever reason.

The Indian Act

The British North America Act of 1867 gave the power of legislative control over Indians and their lands to the federal government. Thus empowered, the Canadian Parliament began drafting provisions for what was to become the Indian Act. The Indian Act was, and perhaps still is, the most oppressive legislation in Canadian history. Prior to this act, the statutory definition of Indians was all persons of Indian blood, their spouses, and their descendants. This definition was to be applied when determining the right to possess or occupy lands. However, in 1869,[9] the government passed an act aimed at the gradual enfranchisement of Indians. The act determined the scope of government responsibilities with those who entered into treaties.

The first Indian Act to bear the official title the Indian Act was passed in 1876. This act redefined Indian as

Firstly: any male person of Indian blood reputed to belong to a particular band;
Secondly: any child of such person;
Thirdly: any woman who is or was lawfully married to such a person. (Paul, 1993, p. 19)

The Indian Act encompassed virtually every aspect of Indian life. It was primarily social legislation, but it had a broad scope, with provisions for liquor control, agriculture, education, by-laws, mining, Indian lands, and band membership (Paul, 1993, p. 13).

Impact of the Indian Act on Aboriginal Women

The Indian Act of 1876 consolidated legislation that was already in place. The measure depriving an Indian woman of her status when she married a non-Indian was first legislated in the 1869 Indian Act (Jamieson, 1978, p. 72). This act was also the first legislation that officially discriminated against women by assigning them fewer fundamental rights than men. Gender-based, discriminatory provisions within the Indian Act limited women's social and political rights.

The enactment of discriminatory legislation aimed at women through the Indian Act placed women in a subordinate position to men. This contributed to cultural changes in many tribes that had previously acknowledged the political power of women. For example, the treaty process required that "official" representatives be elected. This practice eliminated women from local and national politics, while men were legally given more political power than they possessed under traditional politics.

Until 1951, the Indian Act denied women the right to vote in band elections, to hold elected office, and to participate in public meetings that decided band business (Fiske, 1990, p. 122). The few administrative and political decisions allowed by the Indian Act were to be made by Indian men. Thus, women's traditional social and political powers were also legislated to Indian men.

The 1869 Indian Act determined legal status by patrilineal affiliation. Indian women were not legal entities and had virtually no rights. The political status accorded them was that of chattel of their husbands, much like the political status accorded to European women in their patriarchal society. If an Indian man was enfranchised, his wife and minor children were automatically enfranchised. At the time, it was thought by Euro-Canadians that enfranchisement as Canadian citizens was the most desirable goal for Indians to attain.

If a woman married a man from another reserve, she became a member of her husband's band. The act stated that a woman must follow her husband, so if her husband died or she divorced him, she could not return to her reserve. There were provisions stating that upon the death of an Indian man, his estate passed to his children, not to his wife.

The most troublesome portion of the 1869 Indian Act for women was section 12(1)(b). This section further illustrates the male bias in the Indian Act. It pertained specifically to a woman losing her status by marrying a non-Indian man.

> 12. (1) The following persons are not entitled to be registered, namely ...
> (b) a woman who married a person who is not an Indian, unless that woman is subsequently the wife or widow of a person described in Section 11.[10] (Jamieson, 1978, p. 8)

If an Indian woman married a non-Indian man, she then became a non-Indian in the eyes of the government: she became one with her husband, who became in effect her owner under the patriarchal legislation. She was stripped of her Indian status and not able to live on the reserve with her extended family. Many Indian women who married out had no idea that they had lost their Indian status until they attempted to return to their reserve following the break-up of their marriage.

What made this section so discriminatory was that if an Indian man married a non-Indian woman, he did not lose his status. To add insult to injury, a non-Indian woman who married an Indian man became an Indian in the eyes of the law, was given band membership, and was able to live on the reserve. Non-Indian women did not lose their newfound Indian status when they were divorced or widowed; they and their children maintained band membership.

Under the Indian Act, Indian women lost their independence, were not legal entities unto themselves, and had no legal recourse to remedy the situation.

THE BEGINNING OF CHANGE

Legislative Changes

The 1960s brought a number of legislative changes that greatly affected the political position of First Nations people. As political organizations formed, they fought for and achieved many needed changes. As demands for Aboriginal and treaty rights grew, so too did demands for equality by First Nations women.

The discriminatory treatment of First Nations women was chipped away by a number of legislative changes. The most significant were the

Bill of Rights in 1960, the Charter of Rights and Freedoms in 1982, and Bill C-31 in 1985.

The Bill of Rights

The Bill of Rights was enacted by the federal government in 1960. Unlike the United States, which added a Bill of Rights almost immediately to its Constitution, the Bill of Rights was omitted from Canada's Constitution Act of 1867. It was not until after World War II that Canada, like most developed countries, saw the need to protect civil liberties (Hogg, 1992, p. 779). Section 1 of the Bill of Rights guaranteed equality to all under the law, regardless of race or sex. Section 2 provided that any federal statutes or regulations that infringed any of the rights listed in the bill would be brought to Parliament's attention. However, there was a legal debate about the effect of this provision: did section 2 render the infringing laws null and void, or was it merely to be used as a guide? This was not settled until the Drybones case.

Court challenges, dealing with a variety of issues, contributed to amendments to the Indian Act. The first important Indian challenge to the Bill of Rights was the Drybones case in 1969. Drybones was an Indian man charged with possession of alcohol. Under the Indian Act, Indians were not permitted to possess alcohol (Hogg, 1992, p. 669). Since this rule did not apply to non-Indians, the basis for the legal argument was that the law discriminated against Indians. The Drybones case successfully argued that Indians and non-Indians were not treated equally under the law. This case also saw the Supreme Court of Canada decide the effect of section 2 of the Bill of Rights. It held that any federal law that infringed the Bill of Rights would be inoperative; thus, section 2 was more than just a guide.

The Lavell and Bédard cases dealt more specifically with Indian women. These were the first cases to attempt to gain Indian women recognition as "full persons" with the same rights and status as Indian men (Atcheson, 1984, p. 12). Jeanette Corbière Lavell was an Ojibwa woman who lost her status after marrying a non-Indian man. She challenged the band administration's decision to strike her name from the band list (Atcheson, 1984, p. 12). Yvonne Bédard, a Six Nations woman, tried to return to her reserve to live in a house that was left to her in her mother's will. Because she had married a non-Indian, her name was taken off the band list and she and her children were ordered to leave the reserve (Atcheson, 1984, p. 12).

Lavell and Bédard argued that section 12(1)(b) of the Indian Act discriminated on the basis of sex, which contravened the Canadian

Bill of Rights. The two cases were heard together before the Supreme Court of Canada, which affirmed a lower court's decision upholding the validity of section 12(1)(b). The decision stated that the Canadian Bill of Rights meant equality only in the administration and enforcement of the law. The actual substance of the law could discriminate between men and women as long as the law was applied by its administrator in an even-handed way (Atcheson, 1984, p. 12). Thus, the Supreme Court of Canada backtracked from the Drybones case by refusing to declare a discriminatory section of the Indian Act inoperative.

The Lovelace case of 1981 was another important case to challenge section 12(1)(b) of the Indian Act. Sandra Lovelace, a Maliseet woman, lost her status and band membership when she married a non-Indian man. She took the Canadian government to an international court, the United Nations Committee on Human Rights, because her rights as an Indian woman were denied by section 12(1)(b) (Stacey-Moore, 1993, p. 22). She won her case and brought international shame on the Canadian government. The Human Rights Committee found the government of Canada in breach of the International Covenant on Civil and Political Rights to freedom from sexual discrimination (Silman, 1987, p. 251). However, the government of Canada delayed amending this discriminatory legislation for four years. Meanwhile, other Indian women's groups were lobbying the government, national Native organizations, and local band administrations to deal with their concerns. For example, 200 Tobique women and children marched from their New Brunswick reserve to Ottawa, a seven-day trek, to protest housing conditions (Silman, 1987, p. 149).

The Charter of Rights and Freedoms

The Bill of Rights lost most of its significance with the adoption of the Charter of Rights and Freedoms in 1982, which was part of the Canadian Constitution Act. This act ended the United Kingdom's imperial authority over Canada. The Charter protects certain fundamental rights and freedoms, one of which is equality before the law. Indian organizations had to do some effective lobbying of Canadian Parliament to get Aboriginal and treaty rights entrenched in the Constitution for the paternalistic attitude of the Canadian government to end.

Section 15(1) of the Charter states:

> Every individual is equal before and under the law and has the right to the equal protection and equal benefit of the law without discrimination

and, in particular, without discrimination based on race, national or ethnic origin, colour, religion, sex, age or mental or physical disability.

In addition, section 28 states:

Notwithstanding anything in this Charter, the rights and freedoms referred to in it are guaranteed equally to male and female persons.

Although both sections stated that discrimination on the basis of sex and race would contravene the Charter of Rights and Freedoms, the Indian Act continued to do exactly that. It was not until three years later that the discriminatory provisions of the Indian Act were amended.

Although section 35 of the Charter guarantees Aboriginal and treaty rights to Indian people and section 27 states that these rights apply equally to men and women, Native women were not assured that governments and Aboriginal leaders would speak to their concerns. The Native Women's Association of Canada wrote the following about the process of entrenching Aboriginal rights into the Constitution: "These arrangements are required to provide an arrangement that gives Native women and their children a destiny that they can participate in full and directly themselves" (Stacey-Moore, 1993, p. 21).

The entrenchment of Aboriginal and treaty rights in the Charter of Rights was a major step toward ensuring the rights of Native women and would assist them in fighting against gender-based discrimination.

Bill C-31

Bill C-31 came into effect on 17 April 1985 to rectify the infamous section 12(1)(b) of the Indian Act. Bill C-31 was also meant to restore Indian status to people who had been enfranchised. Some have argued that Bill C-31 is an Indian issue rather than solely an Indian women's issue, since enfranchisement occurred for a number of reasons: obtaining a university degree, joining the military or the clergy, or voluntary enfranchisement (Sanders, 1984, p. 38). However, it should be seen primarily as a women's issue because women were affected the most by involuntarily losing their status for marrying non-Indian men. Joan Holmes, researcher for the Canadian Advisory Council on the Status of Women, states that 12 305 of 16 980 losses of status, or 72.5 percent, were to women because of marriage to non-Indians (1987, p. 9). A United Nations Human Rights Committee report states that in Canada for the period 1965 to 1978, there were 510 marriages between Indian women and non-Indian men and 448 marriages between Indian men and non-Indian women (McDonald, 1987, p. 28). However, only the Indian women who married non-Indian men lost their Indian status.

The Indian Act requires that Indians be registered in a central registry and that applicants apply for Indian status to the registrar (Paul, 1993, p. 6). Bill C-31 states that those eligible to be registered as status Indians include

1. women who lost status as a result of marriage to non-status men;
2. individuals who lost status or were denied status under other discriminatory provisions of the Indian Act;
3. individuals who lost status through enfranchisement, a process under the old act whereby persons could voluntarily give up status; and
4. children of persons in any of the above categories. (Paul, 1993, p. 6)

In addition, Bill C-31 gave individual bands the authority to determine their own band membership. In other words, only First Nations should be able to decide who their members are and what their rights and responsibilities are to those members. This is where much of the present-day contention lies.

Although Bill C-31 was meant to rectify the past injustices of the Indian Act, it appears to have created new problems. For example, the bill allows for a separation of status and band membership.[11] The federal government determines status, while the individual First Nation's administration (chief and council in most cases) determines band membership. Band councils, made up primarily of men, determine whether women who marry out can regain band membership. Therefore, Bill C-31 has created new problems by stratifying Indian status into three possible scenarios: Indian status (determined by Indian Affairs in Ottawa), band membership (determined by chief and council), and both status and band membership (chief and council accept Indian Affairs' decision to confer Indian status to an individual and subsequently confer band membership).

CONTEMPORARY FIRST NATIONS WOMEN'S CONCERNS

Anthropologist Joanne Fiske studied the link between political and social life on a British Columbia Indian reserve. She writes that Indian women's domestic responsibilities are undifferentiated from community obligations (1991, p. 127): women are expected to share their surplus food, assist young people, and intervene in domestic disputes in an effort to restore harmony. Fiske concludes that Indian women cannot fulfill their domestic goals without political action (Fiske, 1991, p. 136).

The Indian world is a political world; there is no getting around it. As Karen Ilinik states, "If you don't want to get involved, you really have to work at it" (1990, p. 37). Women of the New Brunswick Tobique Reserve took some radical steps to improve their economic and political situation. They were desperate for housing, many of them finding themselves and their children out on the street with no place to go. Some women had been kicked out of their houses by their husbands.[12] Since the Indian Act gave men sole ownership of the family house through a certificate of possession, their wives had no housing rights and no legal recourse (Silman, 1987, p. 11). They took action by marching on Ottawa to protest their situation.

Indian women found themselves at the mercy of their husbands, the chief and council, and the federal government. This situation of male domination in the Indian community[13] was brought about by many factors.

Adoption of European Values

There is a discrepancy between the traditional respect accorded to Indian women and the reality of gender tensions generated within the community (Fiske, 1990, p. 130).

In a submission to the First Nations Circle on the Constitution, Mary Stanaicia addresses the adoption of non-traditional leadership principles by Indians:

> The Indian Act imposed upon us a patriarchal system and laws, which favored men. By 1971, this patriarchal system was so ingrained the "patriarchy" was seen as a "traditional trait." Even the memory of our matriarchal forms of government and descent was forgotten or unacknowledged. How can our Aboriginal leaders argue a case for traditional laws and customs when they continue to exclude women? Recognizing the inherent right to self-government does not mean recognizing and blessing the patriarchy created in our communities by foreign governments. (Canada, 1992, p. 34)

It appears that First Nations men have adopted the attitude that First Nations women are dispensable. This has likely resulted from their indoctrination in residential schools, the practices legislated by the Indian Act, and Euro-Canadian control of the socialization process of society in general. A submission to the First Nations Circle on the Constitution echoes the impact of the Indian Act on Indian government:

> Contrary to our traditional systems, the Indian Act system provides a political voice only to elected chiefs and councilors, normally residents

on reserve and usually male. The Indian Act silences the voice of the Elders, women, and youth. We believe that true Aboriginal government must reflect the values on which our traditional governments were based. (Canada, 1992, p. 34)

First Nations leaders — that is, First Nations men — must loosen their grasp on the power given to them by the Department of Indian Affairs and other government departments. They must remember that they are there to serve all the people. Men must be re-educated about the nature of their responsibilities in our efforts to abolish the subjugation of women in our communities (Monture-Okanee, 1992, p. 260). First Nations women have suffered from the lack of respect and validity shown to them by those who were traditionally their protectors.

Community Conflict over Legislative Change

Another reason for the contemporary situation is the conflict raised in the communities over the legislative changes described above. Challenges by Native women to the non-status issue were attacked by male-dominated Indian organizations, the largest being the National Indian Brotherhood (which later became the Assembly of First Nations, or AFN). They feared that if the Indian Act was struck down on the basis of discrimination, Indian people generally might lose certain special rights under the Indian Act. They also felt that the Indian Act should be kept intact for use as a bargaining tool with the federal government (Paul, 1993, p. 31). The National Indian Brotherhood and other organizations lobbied the government to allow bands to deny women their full status. They wanted the authority to determine band membership. Noel Starblanket, president of the National Indian Brotherhood, stated:

> The Canadian Government cannot change one section of the Indian Act without looking at the effect those changes will have on the Indian people of our communities. We feel the wrong being done to Indian women and their offspring cannot be undone by imposing further hardship on the rest of Indian people. (Paul, 1993, p. 31)

There was a general fear that the success of any equality argument would undermine the Indian Act's special protections and that the white paper's policy could succeed through court decisions, even though it had been defeated politically. Chiefs and councillors are primarily concerned about the long-range cultural and economic impact in their community (Opekokiw, 1986, p. 16).

There has been much conflict between those Indians recognized under Bill C-31 and band members over the distribution of already scarce resources. Housing has been the source of one such conflict (Silman, 1987, p. 11). Reserves usually have a long waiting list for housing, and the people already on the waiting list grew resentful of the perceived "special status" given to new Indians who wanted to move back to the reserve (Paul, 1993, p. 68). There was a belief that Bill C-31 Indians did not have to wait as long for houses or were placed at the top of the waiting list.

Some bands have not given band membership to people given status by the federal government because they do not have the resources or the land base to do so. Most reserves are already overcrowded, and many feel that conditions will worsen if a rush of reinstated Indians want to return to the reserve. Pamela Paul, in her study of the impact of Bill C-31 on First Nations people, states that many reinstated people say that they are not interested in returning to the reserve because they are established off the reserve, and the reserve has nothing to offer them in terms of housing or employment. They are more interested in health and education benefits (Paul, 1993, p. 108).

There is a great deal of tension between reinstated members and band councils. In some cases, such as the Sawridge Band in Alberta, discriminatory practices have continued, as the band has developed a rigorous and prying membership code so that few, if any, can qualify for membership.[14]

Indian women have not been welcomed back with open arms and warm hearts, which is the custom. Patriarchy cannot be solely blamed for this situation, which can be viewed more as an economic guarding of scarce resources by the band. However, continued discrimination by band administrations has left many Indian women sceptical about whether male-dominated organizations and band councils will ensure their political rights.

Reinstated Indians are referred to as "C-31s" and sometimes scornfully called "paper Indians" or "new Indians" (Paul, 1993, p. 94). Bill C-31 has further divided the Indian community and given rise to negative attitudes toward reinstated members. It seems that C-31 Indians are being blamed for creating or exacerbating social problems that are occurring on the reserves. One band administrator stated that the influx of C-31 people is bringing changes in culture and ideas into the community. He also blames them for increased drug, alcohol, and child abuse problems, and even for a decrease in church attendance[15] (Paul, 1993, p. 97). But this band administrator ignores the fact that Indian culture may or may not be retained when non-Indian women have children. According to Kathleen Jamieson, a researcher for the Advisory Council on the Status of Women/Indian Rights for Indian Women, during the period from 1965 to 1976, the ratio of Indian men marrying non-Indian women to Indian women marrying non-Indian men was 0.8:1 (1978, p. 66). These data also show a constant increase in the number of Indian men marrying non-Indian women, from 258 in 1965 to 611 in 1976. It is sad that Indian men feel obliged to protect their non-Indian wives' newly found Indian status at the expense of the status of their own mothers, sisters, and aunts.

The fear of an influx of reinstated Indians to reserves has been unfounded to date. Gail Stacey-Moore, spokesperson for the Native Women's Association of Canada, states that of the 70 000 reinstated Indians, only 1400 (2 percent) have moved back to the reserve (1993, p. 22).

Political Inequality

A third factor of concern to Indian women is political inequality. Most of the elected leaders in the Indian community are male. Although traditionally many leaders in the First Nations community were male, women's input was sought in decision making. This practice stopped when Indian agents and other Indian Affairs officials chose to deal exclusively with men. Locally elected individuals are placed in the position of intermediary between the Department of Indian Affairs and the people. The Department of Indian Affairs makes all the important and fiscal decisions. Sometimes the band in question is informed and consulted, and sometimes it is not. The band administration simply carries out initiatives or decisions given to them by the department.

The chief and council are the allocators of the scarce resources to band members. Joanne Fiske calls them "power brokers" (1990, p. 123). They determine which band members receive limited band employment opportunities, education funding, occupational training, housing, housing repairs, and other band-administered services. This power, however limited, has a great impact on the day-to-day lives of band members. In some respects, the chief and council have taken over the powerful role of Indian agent as intermediary between the government and the people. It is therefore in the best interest of the band members to stay in the favour of the allocators.

Although women make up about 50 percent of the population, they do not make up 50 percent of the leadership. There are only a handful of women chiefs.[16] There is no guarantee that the concerns of women, such as child care, housing, education, family violence, and social programs, will be heard and acted upon. A very high percentage of Aboriginal Indian women are single parents (Statistics Canada, 1998), which may lessen their influence with the male-dominated council. Single mothers may have less political influence in the community or less time to deal with community issues. The inability to muster political power can also cause a person to be disregarded.

Women hold many of the administrative positions[17] but few of the decision-making positions. They do the preparatory work and must receive approval from a superior, usually a man. However, this situation may change over time because more Aboriginal women than men are getting a postsecondary education (Ponting and Voyageur, 1998). If women speak out against inequality and injustices to the reserve administration, they are labelled as troublemakers and can face barriers in subsequent encounters with the band. Glenna Perley summed up the political climate when she stated, "The chief treated us like we were invisible," after she and other women exposed the treatment they had received at the hands of the chief and council to the media (Silman, 1987, p. 124).

SPEAKING WITH OUR OWN VOICES

Indian women have taken the initiative to protect their own rights and interests, since the past has shown that Aboriginal men do not always act in the best interest of Aboriginal women. Bold moves on the part of Aboriginal women have ruffled a few feathers in the community. For example, the Native Women's Association of Canada attempted to block the national referendum on the Constitution because they were excluded from constitutional negotiations. They charged that the consultation process used by male leaders infringed upon their right to freedom of expression (Stacey-Moore, 1993, p. 21). Aboriginal women demanded a seat at the constitutional table to ensure that their issues would be addressed and demanded a portion of the funding given to male-dominated political organizations.

This action pitted First Nations males against First Nations females. The Native Women's Association was accused of placing individual rights over the rights of the collective and of going against tradition. It is ironic that the men who made these accusations live under the untraditional Indian Act. Women were also pitted against women, because the NWAC was seen as dividing the First Nations community and wiping out the image of a "united front" put forth by the Assembly of First Nations.

By speaking on their own behalf, Indian women can pursue their own priorities and concerns, a major one being family violence. Since women and children are usually the victims of this violence and men are usually the perpetrators, women believe that male-dominated organizations and band councils will not give this issue priority. It is seen as a woman's problem and not a general societal problem. If the Indian communities cannot address Indian women's concerns, then women must advocate on their own behalf.

Conclusion

It appears that the tension between Aboriginal women and male-dominated organizations began when women decided that they would stand up for their rights as individuals.

Aboriginal women have reached a point in their political and individual growth where they will not sit helplessly by while others negotiate their future, because this has not worked for them in the past. They have gained their own voice and can now articulate their own needs and concerns. They must work against adversity, because some leaders are not prepared to relinquish power.

The women are moving ahead. Women as the workers and caregivers feel a responsibility to the children and grandchildren in the community. They initiate and sustain many community programs and services and are prepared to deal with societal problems such as family violence, child abuse, unemployment, and alcohol abuse. They do not want these issues to be swept under the rug. Elder Joyce Leask states:

> There are lots of times that people have things to say that hurt us, but that's what life is all about: a lot of frank statements that must be made. We must be strong enough to be honest. (Canada, 1992, p. 56)

Aboriginal women are playing a greater part in the education of their children and in promoting health, training, and recreational programs in their communities.[18] They are concerned about the loss of cultural identity and the decrease in language retention in the youth because of pressures from the dominant society.

First Nations women are bringing about social, educational, and economic change through their relentless efforts and unwavering commitment to their communities. Some were in desperate situations and felt they had nothing to lose because their children's welfare and their cultural identity as First Nations women were at stake.

In many respects, Aboriginal women still play the traditional role they played before European contact; they are still the care-givers, the transmitters of culture, and the nurturers. They are ultimately responsible for the future of the community — only time and the conditions have changed. Although they are no longer the social and political equals of men that they once were, Aboriginal women demand the respect and recognition of Aboriginal men.

NOTES

1. I decided to change the title of this chapter after being encouraged to by an acquaintance I met one day. She told me that she had studied this chapter as part of a Women's Studies course. She said she liked the article but consensus in the group was that I should "get with the program since the word 'Indian' was politically incorrect and that nobody called themselves Indian anymore." This encounter caused me to rethink the issue. In rewriting this chapter, I have used the term Aboriginal as a collective term that includes status, non-status, Métis, and Inuit and the term First Nations to refer to those with legal Indian status. I still use the term Indian in quotations, to refer to specific policies, and in the historical sense.
2. Excerpt from Rose Auger's chapter in Meili (1991), p. 25.
3. The perspectives put forth in this chapter are based on the author's personal experiences as a Native woman, conversations with other Native women, and a survey of existing literature.
4. Personal interview with Nellie Carlson, activist and founding member of Indian Rights for Indian Women in Edmonton, 4 April 1993.
5. Structural supremacy means the hierarchical structure of European society at the time of contact.
6. This ethnocentric view may be shared by all people, but we are dealing specifically with the European view of Indian people and the results of that view.
7. According to *Webster's Ninth New Collegiate Dictionary*, patriarchy is a social system marked by the supremacy of the father and the legal dependence of wives and children and by the reckoning of descent and inheritance in the male line.
8. It must be understood that there is no "pan-Indian" form of social structure or hierarchy with regard to the treatment of women. Tribes were individual in their customs and values and must not be viewed as a homogeneous group. The practice of viewing all Indians in the same light is one that exists to this day and that must be resisted.
9. The Gradual Enfranchisement Act of 1869 was the first legislation to deal with Indians after Confederation, but there had been earlier acts. The Act for the Gradual Civilization of the Indian Tribes of Canada was passed in 1857.
10. Section 11 states:
   11(1) Subject to Section 12, a person is entitled to be registered if that person

(a) on the 26th day of May 1874 was, for the purposes of An Act providing for the organization of the Department of the Secretary of State of Canada, and for the management of Indian and Ordinance Lands, being chapter 42 of the Statutes of Canada, 1868 as amended by section 6 of chapter 6 of the Statutes of Canada, 1869, and section 8 of chapter 21 of the Statutes of Canada, 1874, considered to be entitled to hold, use or enjoy the lands and other immovable property belonging to or appropriated to the use of the various bands or bodies of Indians in Canada;

(b) is a member of a band

(i) for whose use and benefit, in common, lands have been set apart or since the 26th of May 1874 have been agreed by treaty to be set apart, or

(ii) that has been declared by the Governor in Council to be a band for the purpose of the Act;

(c) is a male person who is a direct descendent in the male line of the male person described in paragraph (a) or (b);

(d) is the legitimate child of

(i) a male person described in paragraph (a) or (b), or

(ii) a person described in paragraph (c);

(e) is the illegitimate child of a female person described in paragraph (a), (b) or (c);

(f) is the wife or widow of a person who is entitled to be registered by virtue of paragraph (a), (b), (c), (d) or (e).

11. Status means registration on the Main or Central Indian Registry in Ottawa. Band membership means that the band accepts and recognizes a person as a member.

12. On the Tobique Reserve, some men kicked their wives and children out of their family homes and moved their girlfriends in. The women resorted to living in abandoned shacks or tents.

13. Community means the reserve and the urban area.

14. The long-time chief of the Sawridge First Nation, Walter Twinn, passed away in 1997. His sister, the only Bill C-31 applicant able to regain Sawridge band membership, is now the chief.

15. It is interesting that church attendance is viewed as a measure of tradition in a reserve community, especially since traditional religious rituals do not occur in a church.

16. Currently in Alberta, 4 of 44 chiefs are female. There are a number of reasons for this situation. For example, females running for chief may not have sufficient community support to attain the office. In addition, women may choose not to venture into a primarily male domain until there are more females holding the post.

17. Administrative means secretarial and support staff.

18. The author drew this conclusion after attending a number of conferences dealing with Native women's issues.

DISCUSSION QUESTIONS

1. How did European society subjugate its women?
2. How was the Canadian government responsible for the current situation of First Nations women?
3. What was the impetus for First Nations women to organize?
4. Why is it in First Nations men's best interest to maintain the status quo?
5. What are some of the benefits and some of the drawbacks of Bill C-31 status?
6. Will First Nations women's social, economic, and political position ever equal First Nations men's? Why or why not?

FURTHER READINGS

Green, Joyce. 1993. "Constitutionalizing the Patriarchy: Aboriginal Women and Aboriginal Government." *Constitutional Forum* 4(4): pp. 110–19. This article details the political jockeying between the Native Women's Association of Canada (NWAC) and male-dominated political organizations during the constitutional negotiations in 1992 and explains NWAC's position.

Holmes, Joan. 1987. *Bill C-31 Equality or Disparity: The Effects of the New Indian Act on Native Women.* Ottawa: Canadian Advisory Council on the Status of Women. This background paper was commissioned by the Canadian Advisory Council on the Status of Women to gauge the impact of Bill C-31 on Indian women. It clearly explains sections of the Indian Act that discriminated against Indian women.

Jamieson, Kathleen. 1978. *Indian Women and the Law in Canada: Citizens Minus.* Ottawa: Minister of Supply and Services Canada. This classic was commissioned by the Canadian Advisory Council on the Status of Women and Indian Rights for Indian Women. It laid the foundation for social and political arguments that are still cited almost twenty years later.

Paul, Pamela Marie. 1993. "The Trojan Horse: An Analysis of the Social, Economic and Political Reaction of First Nations People as a Result of Bill C-31." Unpublished Master's thesis, University of New Brunswick. This thesis analyzes the social, economic, political, and cultural complexities as viewed by the people affected by Bill C-31. It is a candid review of the internal and external conflicts caused by this policy, which was intended to correct past wrongs.

Silman, Janet. 1987. *Enough Is Enough: Aboriginal Women Speak Out.* Toronto: Women's Press. This book details the struggles of the Tobique women of New Brunswick in their fight for political and social rights and their part in the implementation of Bill C-31. It contains memoirs of the women involved — their ongoing struggles with fellow reserve members, band administrators, and government officials.

Stacey-Moore, Gail. 1993. "In Our Own Voice." *Herizons: Women's News and Feminist Views* 6(4): pp. 21–23. Stacey-Moore speaks to the recent reclaiming of Indian women's social and political voice. Indian women have begun to articulate their own issues and concerns and have confronted male-dominated Indian organizations with those same issues.

REFERENCES

Albers, Patricia and Beatrice Medicine, eds. 1983. *The Hidden Half: Studies of Plains Indian Women.* New York: University Press of America.

Atcheson, M. Elizabeth. 1984. *Women and Legal Action: Precedents, Resources and Strategies for the Future.* Ottawa: Canadian Advisory Council on the Status of Women.

Brown, Judith. 1982. "Cross Cultural Perspectives on Middle-Aged Women." *Current Anthropology* 23: pp. 143–53.

Canada, Department of Indian Affairs and Northern Development (DIAND). 1969. *Statement on Indian Policy 1969* (The White Paper). Ottawa: Supply and Services.

Canada, First Nations Circle on the Constitution (FNCC). *To the Source: Commissioners' Report.* Ottawa: Assembly of First Nations.

Canada, Indian and Inuit Affairs Program, Research Branch. 1979. *A Demographic Profile of Registered Indian Women.* Ottawa: Research Branch, Indian and Inuit Affairs Program.

———. 1998. Information on female chiefs received from Roxzanne Hilton, Edmonton.

Chalus, Elaine H. 1990. "Gender and Social Change in the Fur Trade: The Hargrave Correspondence, 1823–1850." Unpublished Master's thesis, University of Alberta.

Clough, Shepard and Richard T. Rapp. 1975. *European Economic History: The Economic Development of Western Civilization.* New York: McGraw-Hill.

Cumming, Peter A. and Neil H. Mickenberg. 1972. *Native Rights in Canada.* Toronto: Indian–Eskimo Association of Canada and General Publishing.

Ezzo, David A. 1988. "Female Status and the Life Cycle: A Cross Cultural Perspective from Native North America." Pp. 137–44 in *Papers of the Nineteenth Algonquian Conference.* Ottawa: Carleton University.

Fiske, Joanne. 1990. "Native Women in Reserve Politics: Strategies and Struggles." *Journal of Legal Pluralism* 30: pp. 121–37.

Francis, Daniel. 1993. *The Imaginary Indian.* Vancouver: Arsenal Pulp Press.

Gerber, Linda M. 1990. "Multiple Jeopardy: A Socio-Economic Comparison of Men and Women among the Indian, Métis and Inuit Peoples of Canada." *Canadian Ethnic Studies* 22: pp. 69–80.

Green, Joyce. 1993. "Constitutionalizing the Patriarchy: Aboriginal Women and Aboriginal Government." *Constitutional Forum* 4(4): pp. 110–19.

Gunn Allen, Paula. 1992. *The Sacred Hoop: Recovering the Feminine in American Indian Traditions.* Boston: Beacon Press.

Hogg, Peter W. 1992. *Constitutional Law of Canada.* Scarborough, Ont.: Carswell Thomson Professional Publishing.

Holmes, Joan. 1987. *Bill C-31 Equality or Disparity: The Effects of the New Indian Act on Native Women.* Ottawa: Canadian Advisory Council on the Status of Women.

Ilinik, Karen. 1990. "Breaking Trail." *Arctic Circle* 1(3): pp. 36–41.

Jamieson, Kathleen. 1978. *Indian Women and the Law in Canada: Citizens Minus.* Ottawa: Minister of Supply and Services Canada.

Kehoe, Alice. 1983. "The Shackles of Tradition." Pp. 53–76 in *The Hidden Half: Studies of Plains Indian Women,* ed. Patricia Albers and Beatrice Medicine. New York: University Press of America.

LaRocque, Emma. 1990. "Here Are Our Voices — Who Will Hear?" Pp. xv–xxix in *Writing the Circle: Native Women of Western Canada,* ed. Jeanne Perreault and Sylvia Vance. Edmonton: NeWest Publishers.

Lincoln, Kenneth. 1983. *Native American Renaissance.* Berkeley: University of California Press.

McDonald, Michael. 1987. "Indian Status: Colonialism or Sexism?" *Canadian Community Law Journal* 9: pp. 23–48.

Meili, Diane. 1991. *Those Who Know: Profiles of Alberta's Native Elders.* Edmonton: NeWest Publishers.

Monture-Okanee, Patricia A. 1992. "The Roles and Responsibilities of Aboriginal Women: Reclaiming Justice." *Saskatchewan Law Review* 56: pp. 237–66.

Native Women's Association of Canada. 1992. *Native Women and the Charter: A Discussion Paper.* Ottawa: Native Women's Association of Canada.

Opekokiw, Delia. 1986. "Self Identification and Cultural Preservations: A Commentary on Recent Indian Act Amendments." *Canadian Native Law Reporter* 2: pp. 1–25.

Paul, Pamela Marie. 1993. "The Trojan Horse: An Analysis of the Social, Economic and Political Reaction of First Nations People as a Result of Bill C-31." Unpublished Master's thesis, University of New Brunswick.

Ponting, J. Rick and Cora J. Voyageur. (Forthcoming). *Challenging the Deficit Paradigm: Grounds for Optimism in the Situation of First Nations in Canada.*

Silman, Janet. 1987. *Enough Is Enough: Aboriginal Women Speak Out.* Toronto: Women's Press.

Stacey-Moore, Gail. 1993. "In Our Own Voice." *Herizons: Women's News and Feminist Views* 6(4): pp. 21–23.

Statistics Canada. 1998. *The Daily.* 13 January, Cat. no. 11-001.

Tsosie, Rebecca. 1988. "Changing Women: The Cross Currents of American Indian Feminine Identity." *American Indian Culture and Research Journal* 12(1): pp. 1–31.

Voyageur, Cora J. 1993. "An Analysis of the University of Alberta's Transition Year Program, 1985–1992." Master's thesis, University of Alberta.

Williams, Robert. 1990. "Gendered Checks and Balances: Understanding the Legacy of White Patriarchy in an American Indian Cultural Context." *Georgia Law Review* 24: pp. 1019–44.

CHAPTER 5

The Politics of Jurisdiction:
Pathway or Predicament?

Augie Fleras

INTRODUCTION: RECALIBRATING RELATIONSHIPS

Indigenous peoples throughout the world are casting about for ways to postcolonize from within (Fleras and Elliott, 1992; Stasiulis and Yuval-Davis, 1995; Havemann, 1999). Energies are focussed on reconstitution-alizing their relationship with society in a manner that sharply curtails state jurisdictions while confirming indigenous models of self-determination as a basis for renewal and reform (see Alfred, 1995). The emergence of in-digeneity ("aboriginality") as a theory and practice has proven pivotal in the reconstruction process. Indigeneity as a principle not only challenges the legitimacy of the sovereign state as the paramount authority in deter-mining who controls what and why (Maaka and Fleras, 1997), but also provides the catalyst for advancing innovative patterns of belonging that reflect and reinforce the notion of a "nation" as a shared sovereignty. De-mands for indigenous self-determination are not about separation or non-interference in specific jurisdictions. Emphasis is focussed instead on es-tablishing non-dominating relations of relative autonomy between fundamentally autonomous peoples by constructively engaging with dif-ferences in a spirit of give-and-take (Scott, 1996).

There is much to commend in relying on jurisdictions as a basis for sorting out state–indigenous peoples relations (Jull and Craig, 1997). Yet recourse to jurisdictions as policy agenda may prove double-edged (McHugh, 1998). The postcolonizing of indigenous peoples–state rela-tions is appreciably diminished when the disengagement process is per-vaded by competitive power struggles over who gets what. An adversari-al relationship is fostered that inadvertently reinforces the very colonialism under challenge. A preoccupation with "cutting deals" in the absence of a clear vision or firm principles may also have the effect of glossing over the key element in any productive interaction: namely, the re-engaging of a relationship in the spirit of co-operative co-existence rather than the letter of the law (McHugh, 1998). The paradoxes of jurisdiction are especially glaring when sorting through treaty-making claims. The state is drawn into the most contentious of all relations — namely, the competition between co-sovereign political communities, with each claiming intrinsic authority over separate spheres of jurisdiction without relinquishing what they share in common (Asch, 1997). Proposed instead of a competitive claims-making process is a commitment to constructive engagement as one way of circumventing the interactional gridlock created by "jurisdictions by jurisprudence." Inasmuch as jurisdictions through constructive engagement may culminate in innovative patterns of living together with differences, the likelihood of forging a partnership between peoples on a government-to-government basis is enhanced.

A parallel situation exists in Canada where the politics of jurisdictions complicates debates over who controls what and why. Canada's Aboriginal peoples have taken the initiative in exploring the jurisdictional implications of recent federal decisions to uphold their status as peoples with an inherent right to self-government. Consider only the Delgamuukw ruling in late 1997: Delgamuukw acknowledged the validity of Aboriginal claims to lands, together with the associated powers that had never been ceded by treaty or agreement. Such an admission confirms Aboriginal perceptions of aboriginality (indigeneity) as one of three orders of government in Canada, alongside the provincial and federal, each of which is sovereign within its own jurisdiction yet shares in the jurisdiction of Canada as a whole (RCAP, 1996). The refracting of Aboriginal peoples–state relations through the prism of multiple yet interlocking jurisdictions should come as no surprise. Canadian politics at federal–provincial levels have long entailed jurisdictional disputes over who controls what and why — especially in Quebec, where struggles over jurisdiction are central to all interaction. A similar logic can be applied to Aboriginal peoples–state relations, where the restructuring process is aimed at sorting out what is "mine," what is "yours," and what is "ours." Yet efforts to shape an appropriate working agenda continue to be marred by state miscalculation of aboriginality as discourse and transformation. Current efforts to circumvent this potential impasse by redefining Aboriginal peoples–state relations on a jurisdiction-by-jurisdiction basis are fraught with ambiguities and contradictions. Any shift to constructively re-engage these relations without rethinking the constitutional principles upon which Canada is governed will remain mired in paradigm muddles that resist any resolution without a radical rethinking of an agenda for belonging together with shared yet separate jurisdictions (Fleras and Maaka, 1998).

This paper argues that current developments in Aboriginal peoples–state relations in Canada are animated by the politics of jurisdictions. Federal and Aboriginal authorities appear to be grid-locked in a power struggle over a proposed realignment of who controls what and why, and no amount of coaxing will resolve the issue without a rethinking of the underlying constitutional principles. The paper also argues that debates over jurisdiction are inextricably linked with issues around Aboriginal models of inherent self-government structures. The animating logic behind Aboriginal peoples–state relations is not about Aboriginal rights per se, nor is it ultimately concerned with the resolution of historical greivances by way of regional agreements — at least no more so than provocations between Quebec and Ottawa are about language or culture, but rather are a jockeying for jurisdiction within a provincial–federal matrix. At the core of this emergent framework for Aboriginal peoples–state relations is the crafting of a new political order. Aboriginal leaders are pursuing a national political agenda that focuses on wresting jurisdiction away from federal and provincial authorities while reaffirming Aboriginal peoples as fundamentally autonomous political communities, both sovereign in their own right yet sharing in the sovereignty of society by way of multiple yet overlapping jurisdictions (see Ponting, 1997; Asch 1997). Equally important is the need to discard colonialist constitutionalisms ("first principles") that privilege Crown priorities and replace them with constitutional principles that concede the legitimacy of Aboriginal models of self-determination over jurisdictions pertaining to land, identity, and political voice. No assurances exist as to when state responsiveness for constructively engaging with aboriginality will congeal in any substantial sense, given the magnitude of the task in reversing colonizing trends that demeaned Aboriginal peoples–state relations. Much ultimately depends on how adroitly "national interests" can absorb a paradigm shift that invokes the reality of aboriginality as a catalyst for working through differences in a postsovereign Canada.

This paper is organized around the theme of aboriginality in challenging the jurisdictional grounds of Aboriginal peoples–state relations. The paper begins by exploring the principles and practices of aboriginality in advancing indigenous models of self-determination over internal jurisdictions. The highly contested link between aboriginality and sovereignty is also discussed: a sharing of sovereignty through a jurisdictional division of authority may facilitate the process for working together rather than standing apart, of building bridges rather than erecting walls, and of belonging together with differences rather than creating stifling conformity. Attention then turns to Canada, where the politics of jurisdiction are transforming the policy dimensions of Aboriginal peoples–state relations. Historical policy agendas that attempted to whittle away Aboriginal jurisdiction are being replaced by policy initiatives that are meant to restore Aboriginal autonomy—albeit within the framework established by central authorities. Of particular note throughout the restructuring process is the privileging of Aboriginal models of inherent self-government as a precondition for a new constitutional relationship. But the adversarial nature of stand-alone regional (claims-making) agreements in advancing self-government draws attention to the dangers of any restructuring without a visionary constitution to absorb the impending shocks. The paper concludes by exploring the possibilities of constructive engagement as a working model for reconstitutionalizing Aboriginal peoples–state relations along postcolonizing lines. To the extent that Aboriginal peoples–state relations appear to be caught in a time warp between old and new is unsettling, to be sure, but unlikely to deter the inexorable march toward postcolonizing from within.

Several caveats are in order. First a word on terminology: the terms "indigenous peoples" and "Aboriginal peoples" as well as "indigeneity" and "aboriginality" are employed interchangeably (technically they do not mean the same thing) but consistently within a given context. Hence, the terms "indigenous peoples" and "indigeneity" refer to peoples of the Fourth World in general, whereas references to "Aboriginal peoples" and "aboriginality" will be restricted to the Canadian context (references to "Aboriginal" have a derogatory connotation in New Zealand and Australia). Second, references to "first nations" need some clarification. Used in the lower case, the expression refers to the original occupants in the white settler dominions. An upper-case designation, "First Nations," entails a political–legal designation applied to status Indians in Canada. Third is the issue of voice appropriation. I do not pretend to speak for Aboriginal peoples in Canada or those in New Zealand or Australia. Nor do I intend to give an account of Aboriginal experiences either in the past or at present. Such a presumptuous act would be inappropriate and arrogant; it would also have the consequence of reinforcing the very colonialisms that both the book and this chapter are seeking to challenge and transform. By the same token, however, it is essential for any student of indigeneity to engage with indigenous perspectives as a way of understanding the policy interface that occupies the social, political, and economic dimensions of Aboriginal peoples–state relations. The growing volume of literature by indigenous authors, academics, and critics has made it that much easier to deconstruct the colonialisms that continue to obstruct our visions of a postcolonial Canada (see also Chesterman and Galligan, 1997).

INDIGENEITY AND THE POLITICS OF JURISDICTION

White settler dominions such as Canada, Australia, and New Zealand share much in common, structurally speaking (Reynolds, 1996; Durie, 1998). In these white settler dominions, indigenous peoples continue to be embedded within and constrained by colonial constitutionalisms that have the effect of denying or excluding. Consolidation of settlement and colonialist capitalism in each of these dominions continue to be constructed around the dispossession and disempowerment of indigenous peoples (Fleras, 1999). Constitutional principles were unilaterally imposed that bolstered "westocentric" agendas and priorities while ignoring or dismissing indigenous values and perspectives as irrelevant or inferior. Only in recent years have settler colonies taken the initiative in re-engaging with the dispossessed by deconstructing the colonialist assumptions and capitalist priorities at the core of dominion society-building.

Indigenous peoples in these postcolonizing dominions have also become increasingly politicized in the hope of reconstitutionalizing their relationship with society at large. The now encapsulated descendants of the original occupants insist on the following demands as a minimum for atonement and reform: (a) a special relationship ("nation to nation") with the state; (b) repossession of land and resources unless explicitly ceded by treaty, Parliament, or conquest; (c) acknowledgement that legitimacy rests with the consent of the people rather than with state authority; (d) recognition of indigenous peoples as sovereign for the purposes of entitlement and engagement; and (e) espousal of new patterns of belonging in which the rights of sovereignty are shared with society at large (Stea and Wisner, 1984; Morse, 1992; Fleras and Elliott, 1992; Havemann, 1999). To date, only the most egregious aspects of colonialism have been dismantled by central authorities; left unexplained or explored are the more systemic forms of colonialism that continue to privilege the state as absolute authority (Fleras and Spoonley, 1999).

Of particular note in the re-engagement process are indigenous demands for recognition of a special kind of jurisdiction by virtue of their constitutional status as "original occupants." Claims to indigeneity stand in sharp contrast with the concerns of immigrant minorities in a multi- or binational society (Gutmann, 1996). A multinational society consists of two or more culturally distinct peoples that international law has decreed constitute nations with inherent rights of self-determination to freely pursue their political status by virtue of (a) original occupancy of a territory, (b) a degree of institutional completeness, and (c) a common language, culture, and identity (Kymlicka, 1995; Hall, 1996). Each of these peoples aspires to maximize autonomy to bolster their distinctiveness and inde-pendence as a people or nation. In contrast to multicultural minorities, whose members are willing to share society by building bridges rather than erecting walls, indigenous peoples in multinational states do not necessarily feel obligated to "share" society with another nationality, since they have the option of withdrawing into nationhood (Gutmann, 1996). Moreover, unlike refugee or immigrant groups who are looking to "put down roots" or "play by the rules," national minorities assume the politically self-conscious stance of a "nation" when they go beyond cul-tural concerns and physical survival (Fleras and Elliott, 1992). The addi-tional step consists of asserting that they possess a special relationship with the state, along with a corresponding set of collective entitlements that flow from inherency and original occupancy. The logic behind multi-nationalism is anchored in establishing an appropriate relationship of sovereignty, one that entails accommodation with other nationalities by establishing semi-autonomous jurisdictions — from separate territories to parallel institutions — within an overarching framework (Gutmann, 1996). For in the final analysis, references to indigeneity or sovereignty or to autonomy or self-determination are not about separation or even non-interference. Central to each of these are the notions of control and con-sent: control over decisions pertaining to land, identity, and political voice; and consent in terms of appropriate relations with the state (Pritchard, 1998).

Indigeneity as Discourse and Transformation

Indigeneity as a concept can be defined as the "politicized awareness of original occupancy as basis for entitlement and engagement" (Maaka and Fleras, 1998). Reference to indigeneity represents a subset of ethnicity: just as ethnicity consists of a shared awareness of traditional differences as the basis for belonging or benefits, so too indigeneity entails the recognition of original occupany in sorting out who gets what (Fleras and Elliott, 1996). As a discourse, indigeneity embraces the once-novel notion of indigenous peoples as "First Nations" whose customary rights to self-determination over jurisdictions pertaining to land, identity, and political voice have never been extinguished but remain undisturbed as a framework for distri-bution. Emergence of indigeneity as transformation connotes a fundamen-tal challenge to the prevailing social and political order. Institutional structures that once colonized the "nations within" are no longer accept-able in a postcolonizing order; proposed instead are indigenous models of self-determination that confirm indigenous rights as a basis for belonging and development while sharply curtailing state jurisdiction (Alfred, 1995).

References to indigeneity go beyond the simple expediency of creating cultural space or social equity. Their scope transcends a commitment to official multiculturalism, with its focus on removal of discriminatory (both cultural and structural) barriers within the existing institutional framework. Indigeneity is not about secession or independence through non-interference in internal jurisdictions; instead, it is about relationships of non-dominance involving interdependent people who work through differences in a non-coercive spirit of relative yet relational autonomy (Scott, 1996). Nor is the focus of indigeneity on the restitution of historical grievances or the restoration of indigenous rights per se. Indigeneity as principle and practice is ultimately concerned with reshaping the interactional grounds of indigenous peoples–state relations in hopes of crafting a legitimate political order for exploring the idea of *multiple yet interlocking jurisdictions* as an innovative framework for belonging (Kymlicka, 1995; Tully, 1995; Chartrand, 1996; Webber, 1994). For example, the Nisga'a agreement (see Appendix), in principle, is constructed around the constitutional principle of exclusive federal and provincial jurisdiction, exclusive tribal jurisdiction, and shared jurisdictions (Gosnell, 1999). Inasmuch as indigeneity challenges the dominance of the state as the final arbiter of jurisdictional control and absolute authority, the principle of indigeneity is indeed "subversive." In its willingness to work within the system rather than outside of it, primarily by exploring the possibility of belonging together with fundamental differences, indigeneity is consistent with postcolonial constitutionalism (Maaka and Fleras, forthcoming).

Indigeneity as Sovereignty

Indigenous challenges to the legitimacy of white settler dominions have eroded political conventions that once proscribed indigenous peoples–state relations. In consisting of claims that simultaneously deny yet affirm the reality of a sovereign state, indigeneity assumes a political framework that is inherently contradictory of settler state sovereignty (Havemann, 1999). As far as indigenous peoples are concerned, they *are* sovereign for the purposes of entitlement and status regardless of formal recognition since they never explicitly consented to surrender this sovereignty, even in the face of European invaders and expropriation of land and resources. Indigenous claims to sovereignty are aimed at securing self-determination over jurisdictions of meaning and relevance, without necessarily advocating secession. Sovereignty as self-determination goes beyond the idea of secession or even non-interference in jurisdictional domains except in conditions of grave oppression or a society in deterioration (RCAP, 1996). Implied instead is the concept of people existing in relationship with one another in a state of relative yet relational autonomy (Scott, 1996).

Several models of self-determination as sovereignty can be discerned (see Table 5.1) (also O'Regan, 1994). At one end of the continuum are references to absolute sovereignty (statehood), with complete independence and control over internal and external jurisdictions. In-between are models of "de facto" sovereignty (nationhood) and "nested" sovereignty ("communityhood") that do not entail any explicit separation ("sovereignty without secession"), but are limited only by interaction with similar bodies and higher political jurisdictions. Indigeneity as practice can co-exist with the principle of a multiple yet interlocking sovereignty at this level as long as jurisdictions are defined and divided accordingly. At the opposite pole are sovereignties in name only (nominal sovereignties), that is, a "soft" sovereign option with residual powers of self-determination within existing institutional frameworks. Table 5.1 provides a somewhat ideal-typical overview of different types of indigenous sovereignty models.

The distinction between the right of sovereignty versus the right to sovereignty is critical (Chartrand, 1993). Indigenous peoples possess sovereignty by virtue of original occupancy, have the status of fundamentally autonomous political communities whose sovereign rights were never extinguished, and define themselves as sovereign for purposes of entitlement or engagement (Cassidy, 1991). But the right to self-determination does not entitle indigenous peoples to separate or secede, at least not according to U.N. dictates on the primacy of state sovereignty and territorial integrity. Distinctions of this sort confirm that references to indigenous sovereignty below the level of statehood are provisional: that is, a people retain the right of self-determination over those jurisdictions that are of direct relevance to them, but not without taking into account the legitimate concerns of bordering jurisdictions (Clark and Williams, 1996).

ABORIGINAL POLICY: CONTESTING JURISDICTIONS

To what extent has the state contributed to or detracted from Aboriginal aspirations for control of jurisdictions? Do state initiatives facilitate the achievement of Aboriginal claims to self-determination and innovative patterns of belonging, or do they have the effect of blocking or undermining Aboriginal jurisdictions over land, identity, and political voice (Spoonley, 1993)? The role of state policy and administration in the dis-

TABLE 5.1

Levels of Sovereignty as Self-Determination

Statehood	Nationhood
• absolute (de jure) sovereignty	• de facto sovereignty
• internal and external jurisdiction	• self-determining control over multiple yet interlinked jurisdiction within framework of shared sovereignty
• complete independence with no external interference	• nations within

Community	Institutional
• "nested" sovereignty	• nominal sovereignty
• community-based autonomy	• decision-making power through institutional inclusiveness
• internal jurisdictions limited only by interaction with similar bodies and higher political authorities	

possession of indigenous peoples has been well documented. Little can be gleaned by rehashing the negative consequences of even well-intentioned actions by Indian Affairs officials, who are often more interested in careerism and empire-building than in fostering Aboriginal empowerment (Ponting and Gibbins, 1980; Ponting, 1986; also Shkilnyk, 1985). What more can be added to the sorry legacy of official indigenous policy, with its focus on promoting "national interest" rather than on protecting Aboriginal concerns? Yet the verdict in assessing state performance may be more accurately described as ambivalent. The state is capable of progressive policies that enhance indigenous rights; it is equally capable of regressive measures that exclude, deny, or exploit (Spoonley, 1993). Policies of disempowerment tend to dictate and delimit the actions and options of indigenous peoples; by contrast, enabling policies provide a window of opportunity for empowerment (Johnston et al., 1997). Moves to expand jurisdiction may inadvertently yet simultaneously close space because of unforeseen circumstances.

A similar assessment can be applied to Canada where Aboriginal relations with the state have long been mediated by legislation, policy, and administration (Frideres, 1993/98). Aboriginal affairs policy can be seen as evolving through a series of overlapping stages, with their focus never wavering from a fundamental commitment to Aboriginal self-sufficiency. An initial period of co-operation and accommodation gave way to a largely misguided and paternalistic policy of assimilation, a policy driven by racist assumptions of white superiority as the basis for control and coercion. The treatment of Aboriginal peoples as captive "wards" was intended to facilitate the eventual absorption of Aboriginal peoples into the mainstream — but had little success. A shift from assimilation through residential segregation toward integration and ordinary citizenship gathered momentum after the late 1940s. Integrationist policies and programs sought to "normalize" relations with Aboriginal peoples by terminating their relationship with the Crown. Yet federal efforts to integrate by "mainstreaming" Aboriginal peoples had the catalytic effect of mobilizing Aboriginal peoples in protest against the ill-fated White Paper of 1969, which was a government attempt to back out of its treaty obligations and the reserve system (Weaver, 1981). Federal policy discourses shifted toward the principle of devolution from the 1970s onwards, in part to acknowledge Aboriginal jurisdiction over land, identity, and political voice, in part to confirm the legitimacy of Aboriginal rights as a basis for belonging, rewards, and relations, and in still other part to defuse mounting resentment and international disapproval. Both government and Aboriginal initiatives continued to explore the implications of the self-governing autonomy model by focussing on the jurisdictional possibilities involving Aboriginal peoples as "peoples" with an "inherent" right to self-government.

Eroding Aboriginality: Jurisdictions Lost/Jurisdictions Reclaimed

Aboriginal policy in the broadest sense began with the Royal Proclamation of 1763, which sought to establish the principle if not the practice of Crown sovereignty over the unexplored interior of "Turtle Island." The Proclamation designated as Aboriginal hunting grounds those vast tracts of land encircled by the Thirteen Colonies, Rupert's Land, and the Mississippi River. To ensure orderly settlement, these lands were closed to European trespass or individual purchase without the express consent of the Crown (Rotman, 1997). The vision of a working partnership was clearly articulated: the Proclamation not only recognized Aboriginal land title under traditional use and ancestral occupancy, it also established the basis for mutually exclusive political systems, each of which was autonomous and self-governing. The Supreme Court of Canada has ruled to this effect, arguing that British protectorate status did not extinguish Aboriginal rights or Aboriginal orders of government, but reinforced Aboriginal people's status as distinct political communities with exclusive and shared jurisdictional authority.

Once the British assumed dominance as the major European power in Canada, any pretext at sovereign co-existence began to unravel (Allen, 1993). The end of the War of 1812 with the United States eliminated the need for Aboriginal allies, thus rendering them expendable and subject to expedient actions. Crown commitments and responsibilities that had been incurred through interaction or treaties were now displaced by a growing interest in land, minerals, and settlement at the expense of Aboriginal peoples. The Crown unilaterally asserted sovereignty over people and lands; Aboriginal consent was simply assumed or deemed irrelevant. Aboriginal tribes may have had "natural title" to the land by virtue of prior occupancy, but their "uncivilized" status enabled the British to rationalize moral and legal justifications for dispossessing them in the name of civilization, Christianity, and "progress" (Allen, 1993). The post-1815 era was subsequently dominated by a commitment to pacify Aboriginal tribes through conquest-oriented acculturation and to displace them into increasingly remote areas. The 1867 Constitution Act confirmed state responsibility for Aboriginal peoples by conferring federal jurisdiction over Aboriginal lands and affairs (Ponting and Gibbins, 1980; Kulchyski, 1994). Confirmation of federal jurisdiction over Aboriginal affairs was abetted by the establishment of the Indian Affairs branch under the Secretary of State (Ponting and Gibbins, 1980). Canadian federalism tended to dismiss any thought of Aboriginal peoples as political communities, preferring instead to see them as wards of the state with limited civil rights but fully entitled to federal custodial care (a trust relationship that was transformed into a fiduciary responsibility in the 1980s) (Jhappan, 1995). The concept of guardianship reinforced the stereotype of Aboriginal peoples as child-like wards of the state who were deemed too incompetent to look after themselves except under the tutelage of Crown-appointed guardians (Ponting and Gibbins, 1980; Ponting, 1986). Aboriginal languages, cultures, and identity were suppressed — ruthlessly at times — while band communities were locked into patterns of dependency and despondency, with little opportunity for development or dignity. The signing of eleven numbered treaties and Williams treaties between 1871 and 1923 established a system of reserves, thereby allowing the Crown to simultaneously open land for settlement and advance the cause of assimilation.

Legislation served as an important tool in controlling Aboriginal peoples and their resources (Rotman, 1997). Passage of the 1876 Indian Act bestowed sweeping state powers to invade and regulate the most minute aspect of reserve life — even to the point of curbing constitutional and citizenship rights (Ponting, 1997). The Indian Act defined who came under its provisions, what each status Indian was entitled to under the government's fiduciary obligations, who could qualify for enfranchisement, what could be done with reserve lands and resources, and how local communities were to be ruled. Traditional leadership was stripped of its authority, at least in its official sense, then discredited as a legitimate political voice (Dickason, 1992). Local governance took the form of elected band councils, many of which were perceived as extensions of central authority, with limited powers and subject to Ottawa's priorities or approvals (Webber, 1994). Even economic opportunities were curtailed. Under the Indian Act, Aboriginal people could not possess direct title to land or private property; they were also denied access to revenue from the sale of leases or band property. Punitive restrictions not only foreclosed Aboriginal property improvements, they also forestalled the accumulation of economic development capital for investment or growth — especially since Aboriginal land held in Crown trust was immune to mortgage, collateral, or legal seizure (Eckholm, 1994). In that the Indian Act was an essentially repressive instrument of containment and control, its role in usurping Aboriginal authority and replacing it with federal jurisdiction could not have been more forcefully articulated.

Nevertheless, neither assimilation as policy nor the reserve system as practice brought about the goal of "no more Indians" (Smith, 1993). Rather, this grand experiment in social engineering proved disastrous in seeking to erode the social and cultural foundations of Aboriginal society as the price of admittance to society (Frideres, 1998). Failure to bring about the intended results exerted pressure to rethink the Aboriginal affairs policy agenda, especially after World War II, when the contradiction of fighting for freedom overseas clashed with a host of domestic human rights violations. An official commitment to assimilation merged with the principles of integration as a blueprint for reform. Strategies to desegregate once-isolated Aboriginal enclaves by reintegrating them into the mainstream proved increasingly attractive for political and economic reasons. Aboriginal services were costly to maintain; they were also seen as an international embarrassment to Canada. A discussion paper to do away with the "Indian problem" by doing away with Aboriginal peoples as a legal construct was tabled by then Minister of Indian Affairs, Jean Chrétien. The White Paper proposed to terminate the special relationship between Aboriginal peoples and the Crown, thus eliminating the status of Aboriginal peoples as a collective entity (Weaver, 1981). Federal responsibility over Aboriginal peoples would be transferred to the provinces. Both the Indian Act and the Department of Indian Affairs were to be dismantled, while Aboriginal assets (including lands) would be divided on a per-capita basis for "disposal" as individual owners saw fit. Also recommended was the eventual abolition of Aboriginal treaty privileges and special status, as a precondition for "normalizing" entry into Canadian society.

But the White Paper badly miscalculated Aboriginal aspirations. What policy officials endorsed as progressive and widely desired was roundly condemned as regressive by Aboriginal elites and leaders. The White Paper was accused of everything from cultural genocide to callous expediency in offloading federal costs and reneging on Crown responsbilities. Aboriginal peoples possessed a special, one-of-a-kind relationship with the Crown in Canada, Aboriginal leaders argued, and they could not afford to sever this legally obligatory ("fiduciary") relation for the uncertainties of provincial jurisdiction (Rotman, 1997). Aboriginal groups galvanized into protest action, including establishing the first national body of status Indians, the National Indian Brotherhood, in hopes of shelving the White Paper in exchange for a new "Indian" agenda (Allen, 1993). This collective show of strength chastened central authorities; they were left with no option but to cobble together a policy agenda that embraced Aboriginal demands for control of their destiny and lands without risking Canada's integrity as a united and prosperous society in the process.

A general commitment to the principle of devolution eventually replenished the policy vacuum created by the White Paper void. This shift was preceded by a period of impasse — even paralysis — as government response lurched from crisis to crisis with little vision of how to bridge the gap of misunderstanding across a cultural divide. The Calder decision in 1973, with its qualified support for the idea of Aboriginal rights and title, proved a starting point for reassessment. Two trends eventuated from this ruling. On the one hand were Aboriginal moves to transform the federal policy agenda in a way that enhanced Aboriginal autonomy over land, identity, and political voice. This focus on self-determination through self-government became increasingly politicized and geared toward the constitutional entrenchment of collective Aboriginal rights. On the other hand were government initiatives to expand Aboriginal jurisdictions over domains of relevance to Aboriginal peoples. A program of community self-government negotiations in line with Cabinet-approved guidelines for community self-sufficiency, but outside any federally imposed blueprint, was announced by central authorities in 1986 as a practical, albeit interim, alternative to be pursued on a band-to-band basis and in conjunction with negotiations for constitutional entrenchment of self-governance. The Sechelt of British Columbia were the first to take advantage of this opening by establishing municipal-level governing structures beyond the scope of the Indian Act and the Indian Affairs Department. Currently, thirteen First Nations in Ontario, B.C., Alberta, and Saskatchewan have negotiated self-government arrangements, and another 350 communities are currently engaged in discussions.

A revised social–political contract involving Aboriginal jurisdiction over local affairs both reflected and reinforced developments within the federal Department of Indian Affairs and Northern Development. The department had moved away from a control-and-deliver mentality that had prevailed as the blueprint since 1876. The reorganization of the department into a decentralized service delivery through direct band involvement drew its inspiration from three assumptions: first, the need to establish Aboriginal rather than federal control over community affairs; second, a perception that properly resourced communities were better equipped to solve local problems; and, third, a suspicion that centralized structures are ineffective for problem solving when dealing with a geographically dispersed and culturally diverse people. The shift toward devolution resulted in the establishment of community-based control over local jurisdictions related to Aboriginal administration of departmental programs, local decision making, and mutual accountability (Canada, 1993). Service delivery on a program-by-program basis was replaced by more flexible funding arrangements to improve management of service delivery, develop long-term expenditure plans, reduce administrative burdens, and emphasize local responsibility for good program management. The department also endorsed the goal of Aboriginal self-government and greater autonomy of Aboriginal peoples through the resolution of comprehensive land claims (Allen, 1993). In short, DIAND repositioned itself as a developmental and advisory agency for the transfer of federal funds to self-government structures in the same way that provinces receive federal block funding for programs and services.

Recent developments have further redefined the relational status of Aboriginal peoples within the constitutional framework of Canadian society. The commitment to self-governing autonomy revolves around four policy pillars introduced by Prime Minister Mulroney to ostensibly defuse the Oka crisis: accelerated land claims settlement, improved socioeconomic status on reserves, reconstruction of Aboriginal–government relations, and fulfilment of Aboriginal concerns. By mid-1991, Ottawa had officially endorsed a parallel Aboriginal constitutional process that promised Aboriginal peoples the historic right to negotiate on a government-to-government basis, that is, as a distinct tier of government with corresponding rights, to sit with Canada's First Ministers and debate constitutional reform. Terms of the failed Charlottetown Accord agreement included constitutional entrenchment of Aboriginal self-government both inherent in nature and sovereign in sphere, but circumscribed in extent by virtue of the Canadian Constitution and Charter of Rights (no external sovereignty). Even the notion of inherent self-government proved palatable as long as inherency was not used to declare independence or undermine Canadian sovereignty. In short, a threshold in restructuring Aboriginal peoples–state relations had been scaled; this baseline would henceforth represent the minimum base point for future negotiations, and the Liberal government took advantage of this momentum by eventually accepting Aboriginal peoples as having an inherent right to self-government as the basis for a new partnership (Canada, 1994).

To sum up, the politics of jurisdiction have proven pivotal in understanding the development of Aboriginal affairs policy and administration. Aboriginal policy can be described historically as a series of contested and evolving sites involving a struggle between competing forces over jurisdictions pertaining to power and possessions. Overt policies of integration and assimilation have been shelved in favour of recognizing Aboriginal rights for the purposes of entitlement and engagement. Sections 25 and 35 of the 1982 Constitution Act have opened and expanded areas of jurisdiction that the colonialist era denied or constrained. The emergence of a partnership commitment to self-determining self-government represents the latest initiative to expand Aboriginal control and consent by sharply curtailing state jurisdiction.

Many applaud government decisions to recognize inherent self-government arrangements as an existing treaty right, with or without constitutional backing. Others are less confident about these initiatives and have expressed grave concerns over process and outcome. Government promises about Aboriginal rights are vague and unenforceable, as are the terms of reference and means of implementation, thus allowing room to wriggle out of commitments if realities outstrip expectations (*Wataway News*, 7 April 1994). Some see Aboriginal self-government as a "recipe" for social disaster and disunity, others query the soundness of a system based on race and separate status, and still others are worried about the implementation, costs, and jurisdictions. The principle of Aboriginal self-government is criticized as a simplistic solution to a complex problem espoused primarily by Aboriginal elites who are out of touch with urban realities and needs (*The Globe and Mail*, 22 January 1998). The dangers of a new Aboriginal bureaucracy and increased dependence on federal transfers is also raised (Mulgrew, 1996). Critics have also attacked government initiatives as little more than political expediency to amplify the eighteenth-century role of Aboriginal peoples as allies (or pawns) in a constitutional cat-and-mouse game between Quebec and Ottawa. Finally, divisions have appeared within Aboriginal communities as well. Aboriginal women are concerned about the protection of individual equality provisions under self-government arrangements, even to the point of rejecting the legitimacy of self-government itself. Self-governance may also prove irrelevant to those who are distanced from traditional institutions of a reserve-based government and legislation (Ponting, 1997). Solutions to these jurisdiction conundrums will take more than money or experts — the question is whether implementing inherent rights to Aboriginal self-government will secure the basis for renewal and reform.

RECLAIMING JURISDICTION: ABORIGINAL SELF-GOVERNMENT

> Jurisdiction is the central crux of self-government. (Wally McKay, Presentation to the Royal Commission on Aboriginal Peoples [Criminal Justice], 1995)

Canada is struggling to recast its relationship with Aboriginal peoples in response to massive disparities, mounting resentment, and emerging political realities. The interplay of racism, paternalism, and disempowerment has inflicted a serious toll in terms of social, health, economic, and cultural costs. Many Aboriginal people have lost their language and identity as well, and this spiritual loss is compounded by skyrocketing rates of alcoholism, substance abuse, domestic violence, suicide, diabetes, and heart disease (Rotman, 1997). The need for structural change is broadly acknowledged by Aboriginal and non-Aboriginal leaders alike, but they disagree on how to hasten this transformation from colonized subjects to self-determining peoples (Fontaine, 1998). Central to most proposals for restructuring is establishing Aboriginal self-government as a basis for healing.

Few should be surprised that debates over Aboriginal peoples–state relations are channelled into how Aboriginal peoples want to be governed. Making federalism the preferred discourse for couching political relationships is quintessentially Canadian. Canada itself is a territoriality based on an intricate allocation of separate yet overlapping jurisdictions, and this division of jurisdictions between Ottawa and the provinces is being played out at the level of Aboriginal self-government. Yet jurisdictional wrangles continue to plague the different orders of government. Federal and provincial authorities are locked in battle over who has what responsibility for which of Canada's Aboriginal peoples. Federal authorities are reluctant to extend jurisdiction and fiduciary responsibility beyond status Indians on reserves. Provinces that have long sought more jurisdiction over social policy are equally dismayed by the prospect of assuming additional costs, arguing for an extension of federal jurisdiction for even off-reserve status Indians. Aboriginal peoples are no less hesitant to disturb the status quo; any shift toward giving authority to cash-strapped provinces would not only constitute a breach of federal fiduciary responsibility, it could well erode the jurisdictional authority of existing Aboriginal governments.

Neither constitutional nor judicial developments have proved helpful in sorting out jurisdictions. Constitutional entrenchment of Aboriginal rights in 1982 was long on principle but short on specifics. Subsequent conferences and court decisions have not removed the uncertainty over what these rights mean, where they apply, and how they are to be implemented, despite years of intensive litigation ("Self-Government Alone," 1997). Nevertheless, guidelines are beginning to fall into place. According to the Royal Commission on Aboriginal Peoples (1996), section 35 of the Constitution Act confirms the status of Aboriginal peoples as equal partners in Canada. Aboriginal governments should be recognized as one of three distinct orders, each of which is internally sovereign by virtue of inherent (rather than delegated) constitutional status, yet shares in the sovereign powers of Canada by way of overlapping and exclusive jurisdictions. Moreover, Aboriginal peoples define themselves as fundamentally autonomous political communities whose sovereignty has an independent source. Failure to restore Aboriginal self-governing rights to their rightful constitutional status cannot be tolerated much longer, given the magnitude of the problem that confronts Aboriginal peoples:

> The systematic, sustained denial of this reality, manifest through the violation of agreements, the suppression of cultures and institutions, the refusal to live up to legal obligations is the core of the problem. We cannot escape the fact that we have built a great liberal democracy, in part through the dispossession of aboriginal people and the imposition of our cultural norms. (RCAP, 1996)

This commitment to Aboriginal self-government invariably raises questions about feasibility, costs, and options. Questions also arise over the degree to which contemporary initiatives for self-government are consistent with traditional patterns of governance.

Traditional Aboriginal Governments

Aboriginal history did not begin with the Constitution Act of 1867 or the landing of European explorers (Mercredi and Turpel, 1993). The First Nations were established and functioning political communities prior to European contact, with unique means of decision making, various leadership styles, and varied power-sharing arrangements bestowed by the Creator and rooted in history and culture (Clark, 1990). Aboriginal governments ranged in scope from small-scale foraging bands to complex chiefdoms along the east and west coasts, and included complicated Iroquoian confederacies that acknowledged tribal autonomy over local interests yet allocated authority over external matters to a grand council (Dickason, 1992; Allen, 1993). Yet certain principles prevailed. Aboriginal communities possessed self-governance in the sense of territorial jurisdiction; they also had the freedom to regulate their affairs without external interference (Frideres, 1998). These political systems were organized around extended kinship groups and traditional leaders, whose duties and relations were defined by custom and supported by a communal culture (Boldt, 1993). Political processes were not necessarily formalized into specific institutions or mandatory divisions of jurisdiction. Lacking in general were a body politic, explicit political machinery, and formal hierarchy of authority. Members of the community constituted the government in a way that blurred any rigid distinction between ruler and ruled. Power and authority were rarely differentiated into formal offices or specialized institutional structures, but were dispersed and diffused. The absence of coercive power or wealth to compel compliance meant traditional leadership had to be earned—in large measure by acting as the servant of the people in conjunction with collective dictates. Power and authority were vested in the group rather than a specific individual or structure; accordingly, decision making was largely communal, consensual, and consultative. Other political functions within the tribe were also performed in an undifferentiated style. In all respects, then, Aboriginal governments were equivalent to a government by the people, for the people, and of the people.

The practice of Aboriginal self-government remained undisturbed during the early colonial era (Clark, 1990). Little was done to challenge Aboriginal jurisdictions over internal domains; with few exceptions, Aboriginal peoples were left largely to their own political devices on land that rightfully belonged to them or was reserved for their use. Pockets of Aboriginal jurisdiction under Crown supervision persisted even with the Constitution Act of 1867 and the Indian Act of 1876, which assumed absolute jurisdiction over Aboriginal peoples and their lands (Clark, 1990). The imposition of a colonial system of government proved the undoing of

Aboriginal peoples: conventional philosophies and norms were replaced with an alien system of delegated authority. Band councils did not serve as true governments in the sense of inherent authority, popular consent, or independent jurisdiction. Many were perceived as extensions of the administrative arm of central authorities (Prince, 1994). The introduction of a co-opted hierarchical authority in effect severed the link between culture and politics. This imposed government became the antithesis of self-government — more of an "other-government" — with a corresponding loss of jurisdiction over land, culture, and destiny (Mercredi and Turpel, 1993).

Inherent Rights to Aboriginal Self-Government

Current government objectives are aimed at exploring the implications and parameters of inherent Aboriginal self-government rights. Such recognition signifies a remarkable departure from even the immediate past, when governments were resolutely opposed to any concessions that might encourage international recognition of peoplehood, self-determination, or sovereignty. Much of the impetus for this push into the unknown stemmed from Conservative government proposals in 1990 to (a) accelerate land claims settlement, (b) improve socio-economic status on reserves, (c) rebuild Aboriginal–government relations, and (d) address Aboriginal concerns. The Liberal government continued on this path by expanding its commitment to the principle of inherent Aboriginal self-government rights. In the words of former Minister of Indian Affairs Ronald Irwin:

> The federal government is committed to building a new partnership with Aboriginal people, a partnership based on mutual respect and trust. Working steadily towards the implementation of *the inherent right of self-government is the cornerstone of that relation.* (Canada, 1994; emphasis added)

Jane Stewart, Minister of Indian Affairs in 1999, is also committed to the principle of inherent Aboriginal self-government. She is equally insistent on "restoring jurisdiction" as a touchstone for progress and renewal (Barnsley, 1997). Restrictions still apply: Aboriginal inherent self-government rights are "contingent" rather than sovereign rights, according to the *1995 Federal Policy Guide on Self-Government*; they are also intended to be based on practical, negotiated arrangements rather than through the Constitution or courts. It is worth noting that Canada's representatives to the Third Session of the U.N. Human Rights Working Group (Pritchard, 1998) have confirmed this country's commitment to

Aboriginal self-government over a broad range of jurisdictions as long as this recognition does not impair the territorial integrity or political unity of Canada, is consistent with the Charter of Rights and Freedoms, and does not interfere with the participation of Aboriginal peoples in Canadian society.

The principle of Aboriginal self-government has evolved into a contested site (Cassidy, 1991). If viewed from the vantage point of the Canadian state that claims absolute sovereignty, Frank Cassidy writes, then Aboriginal self-government is compartmentalized inside a division of power that reflects Crown supremacy. If, however, Aboriginal self-government asserts the collective and inherent rights of aboriginality as equivalent to those of existing governments, a new structural arrangement is required. This latter assertion rejects the legitimacy of existing political relations and colonial institutions as a framework for attaining Aboriginal goals. Proposed instead is the restoration of an Aboriginal-based model of governance as a third order of government both independent of and related to the provincial and federal levels. Conferral of a third tier of governance is seen as enabling First Nations to conduct relations on a nation-to-nation basis, with jurisdictional control over internal spheres. Ovide Mercredi and Mary Ellen Turpel (1993, p. 123) concede as much:

> No one should get the impression that we are not talking about sovereignty for our people and lands. We are talking about a sovereign order of government within Canada. We are talking about exclusive jurisdiction for that order ... just like the provincial governments are sovereign.

References to inherent rights to self-government are paramount (Little Bear et al., 1984; Cassidy, 1991). Inherency suggests that the legitimacy of law, authority, and governance do not derive from external sources such as the Crown, Parliament, or Constitution. Legitimacy stems instead from original occupancy, consent of the people, founding people status, treaties, international law, and cultural minority rights (Macklem, 1993; Hall, 1996). The origins of inherent self-governing rights reside with Aboriginal peoples as autonomous political and cultural entities; they also reflect Aboriginal possession of their territories and customary political rights prior to European contact. In other words, self-governing rights are inherent and inalienable, implying that Aboriginal rights can never be extinguished without explicit consent, as vigorously noted by Elijah Harper (RCAP, 1996, p. 19):

> Self-government is not [something] that can be given away by any government, but rather ... flows from Creator. Self-government ... is taking

control and managing our own affairs, being able to determine our own future and destiny. ... It has never been up to the governments to give self-government. It has never been theirs to give.

Self-government models will vary, with differences being contextual rather than categorical, that is, in accordance with community needs and local circumstances. Some will reflect a government model, others will reflect an Aboriginal model, and still others will combine elements of both. Many will seek reforms or integration within the existing federal framework, in part because they lack any viable indigenous political alternatives. A few want a fundamental restructuring of their relationship within a truly confederal Canada (Alfred, 1995). Jurisdictional matters are expected to vary from band to band; nevertheless, they are likely to include (a) control over the delivery of social services such as policing, education, and health and welfare (institutional autonomy); (b) control over resources and use of land for economic regeneration; (c) control over the means to protect and promote distinct cultural values and language systems; (d) control over band membership and entitlements; and (e) control over federal expenditures according to Aboriginal priorities rather than those of the government or bureaucracy. This is not to say that all Aboriginal communities possess the jurisdictional capacity to fully engage in self-government, given the associated costs and responsibilities; but many do, and they are casting about for ways to establish arrangements that will exchange all vestiges of internal colonialism for political self-determination.

Questions of jurisdiction will pervade the politics of self-government. Aboriginal peoples are seeking to expand their control over internal matters in the same way the Québécois are seeking internal sovereignty as a basis for protecting what they see as theirs. Patterns of jurisdiction are open to negotiation, ranging from shared arrangements on the one hand, to exclusive tribal control over land ownership and membership — up to and including autonomous political structures (inherent self-government) and cultural sovereignty — on the other, as long as these reflect a community-derived legitimacy and consent of the people. The notion of multiple yet overlapping jurisidictions is contingent on a distinction between core and periphery jurisidictions (RCAP, 1996). Core jurisdictions entail those matters of vital political, economic, cultural, and social concern to Aboriginal peoples; do not have a major impact on adjacent jurisdictions; and can be exercised without federal or provincial input. Peripheral jurisdictions include those realms that have an impact on adjacent jurisdiction or attract federal or provincial interest. A substantial degree of co-ordination and compromise may be required in promoting an arrangement in which each order is sovereign yet shares in the sovereignty of Canada. Implementation of self-governing rights will also require a high threshold of immunity from federal law in deciding "mine" from "yours" and "ours," except in cases where federal legislation can be justified under strict constitutional standards, serve a compelling need, and not imperil the Crown's fiduciary obligations to Aboriginal peoples.

The range and scope of self-governing jurisdictions will be varied. It is also anticipated that the right to self-government will be vested in Aboriginal nations rather than communities, that is, a sizable body of Aboriginal peoples with a shared sense of national identity that constitutes a predominant population in a certain territory (RCAP, 1996). Between 60 and 80 historically based Aboriginal nations can be discerned from the 1000 or so Aboriginal communities, based on economies of scale and natural ties, thus reviving the nation-way in which Aboriginal peoples were once organized. Four self-governance possibilities exist as noted earlier: (a) statehood with complete political independence, both internal and external; (b) nationhood, with retention of authority and jurisdiction over all internal matters; (c) municipality, with control over delivery of services by way of parallel institutions; and (d) institutional, with meaningful decision making through representation and involvement in mainstream institutions. Generally speaking, Aboriginal claims for self-government are consistent with the model of "domestic dependent nations" in the United States. American First Nations do not possess external sovereignty (for example, they cannot raise an army); nevertheless, these domestic dependent nations retain considerable control over internal sovereignty, subject to certain restrictions at the federal and state levels. To date, the Canadian government has offered a level of self-government with powers that go beyond a municipal jurisdiction but encompass less than a provincal jurisdiction. Aboriginal leaders publicly endorse a model somewhere between provincial and federal authority, but appear willing to compromise.

Putting Self-Government in Perspective

An inherent right to Aboriginal self-government is widely endorsed within Aboriginal circles. The rationale for support reflects several lines of reasoning, including (a) all Aboriginal peoples have the right to control their destiny by virtue of original occupancy; (b) international law (to which Canada was a signatory in 1967) stipulates the right of all peoples to self-determination; and (c) treaty rights affirm rather than deny Aboriginal self-government. References to Aboriginal self-government raise the spectre of separation, but contrary to popular belief, most Aboriginal proposals are not intended to make a total break with Canadian society. With few exceptions, Aboriginal demands for self-governing sovereignty rarely extend to calls for political independence or territorial autonomy. Proposed instead is a relationship of relative and relational autonomy within a non-coercive context of co-operative co-existence. This excerpt from the Royal Commission on Aboriginal Affairs (1996, p. xi) is typical and should allay alarmist fears:

> To say that Aboriginal peoples are nations is not to say that they are nation-states seeking independence from Canada. They are collectivities with a long shared history, a right to govern themselves and, in general, a strong desire to do it in partnership with Canada.

In other words, inherent self-government is not the same as secession or absolute sovereignty. What is entailed is a *functional* sovereignty where First Nations are treated as sovereign for the purposes of entitlement and engagement. The intent is not to demolish Canada or overturn its sovereignty — in fact, that would not be seen in the best interests of Aboriginal peoples — but only to dismantle that part of the "house" that has precluded them from their rightful place as the original occupants and the nominally sovereign co-founders of Canada (Borrows and Rotman, 1997). By the same token, Aboriginal leaders categorically reject the view of themselves as individual Canadian citizens who happen to live on reserves. No less dismissive is the labelling of Aboriginal peoples as yet another ethnic or immigrant minority. Aboriginal peoples define themselves as a de facto sovereign political community whose collective rights to self-government are guaranteed by virtue of indigeneity (ancestral occupation) rather than because of need, disadvantage, or compensation. Admittedly, the attainment of status as a nation will require a reversal of assimilationist assumptions that historically have moulded Aboriginal realities. It will also have to overcome a hardening of Canadian attitudes toward First Nations, together with a public perception of Canada as essentially sound and beyond the need of a major overhaul (Monti, 1997).

FROM CUTTING DEALS TO CONSTRUCTIVE ENGAGEMENT

Aboriginal struggles to sever the bonds of colonialist dependency and underdevelopment appear to be gathering momentum. Several innovative routes have been explored for improving Aboriginal peoples–state relations, including constitutional reform, indigenization of policy and administration, comprehensive and specific land claims, constitutional reform, Indian Act amendments, devolution of power, decentralization of service delivery structures, and, of course, self-government arrangements (Prince, 1994). The distributive ideals associated with aboriginality are varied, as might be expected in light of diverse constituencies and varied histories, but typically involve demands for Aboriginal jurisdiction over land, resources, culture, and identity. Yet the politics of jurisdiction are not without its costs and consequences, which inadvertently may be reinforcing the very colonialisms that Aboriginal peoples are seeking to escape. Reliance on confrontational models for allocating jurisdictions are self-defeating if the debate over jurisdictions lacks a unifying vision or set of principles. That makes it doubly important to revisit jurisdictions as the solution and the problem.

Jurisdictions by Jurisprudence

One of the more striking developments in Aboriginal peoples–state relations is a growing reliance on restitutional claims-making ("regional agreements" or "comprehensive land settlements") for sorting out who controls what and why (McHugh, 1998). The logic behind a claims-making approach is relatively straightforward: in an effort to right historical wrongs by settling outstanding complaints against the state for breaches of indigenous rights, the government offers a compensation package of cash, land, services, and controlling rights to specific indigenous claimants in exchange for "full and final" settlements of treaty-based grievances. In Canada these regional agreements, from the James Bay Cree Settlement Agreement of 1975 to the Nunavut Agreement in 1993, involve extinguishing Aboriginal title to a region in exchange for a package of perpetual Aboriginal rights to various categories of land, co-management and planning in various socio-economic and environmental issues, hefty compensation payouts to foster Aboriginal economic developments and political infrastructures, and various self-management and self-government entities (Jull and Craig, 1997).

Governments have taken to regional agreements as one way of establishing jurisdictional certainty in land titles and access to potentially lucrative resource extraction (Jull and Craig, 1997). They also are endorsed as a case of restorative justice in compensating historically disadvantaged peoples for unwarranted confiscation of land, while offsetting corresponding social and cultural dislocations. Yet critics and supporters disagree on whether regional agreements are a catalyst for crafting a new political order or little more than an administrative quick fix to make the "Indian problem" go away. Supporters point to regional agreements as an innovative, even unprecedented, process by which two peoples negotiate the basis by which they will share territories, public revenues, decision making, and economic development through a mix of pragmatism, recognition, accommodation, and tolerance (Jull and Craig, 1997). Critics point to the uninintended consequences of agreements that impart a new meaning to the Canadianism "Two nations warring in the bosom of a single state" (Fleras and Maaka, 1998). A claims-making approach for reconstituting state–indigenous peoples relations embraces an underlying agenda, the sum total of which has transformed the challenge of working through differences into a zero-sum game of winners and losers. However unintended, the consequences of the claims-making process foster an adversarial mentality: disputants are drawn into a protracted struggle between opposing interest groups over "mine," "yours," and "ours" that concedes as little as possible. Issues, in turn, become occluded inside a rigid format that complicates the process of securing a compromise without losing face. Levels of rhetoric under a claims-making model are stretched to the breaking point as each party attempts to manoeuvre itself for maximum effect. Rhetoric tends to get blown out of proportion to enhance the number of media "hits." The claims-making game compels indigenous peoples to articulate their aspirations in the language of the protagonist, with the result that indigenous aspirations are distorted to fit a "westocentric" framework.

Difficulties are also further heightened when central authorities and indigenous peoples operate at cross-purposes in the claims-making process (Minogue, 1998). Governments prefer a full and final settlement of past injustices, if only to eliminate uncertainty from any further governance or development (Graham, 1997). Such pragmatism misreads indigenous perceptions of settlements as a precondition for constructing relationships that secure cultural survival, recognition as a people, and sufficient resources to bolster the prospect of self-determintion (Coates and McHugh, 1998). For indigenous peoples, the resolution of claims provides a means to this end (including the acquisition of administrative powers, financial compensation, and control of traditional lands and resources) — not an end in itself, but one stage in an evolving and ongoing relationship between partners over time. Or as Peter Jull (Jull and Craig, 1997) puts it when arguing for the primacy of relationship rather than results, albeit in a different context, attainment of indigenous autonomy is not so much a farewell, but the beginning of a new relationship; indigenous models of self-determination are not about separation from society, but the beginning of full participation in national life.

Re-engaging Constructively

A restitutional claims-making policy environment has proven to be a double-edged success. Claims-making resolutions are undeniably important as part of a broader exercise in relations-repair but, on its own and divorced from the bigger picture of rethinking state–indigenous peoples relations, such a preoccupation is fraught with hidden messages and underlying contradictions (Rotman, 1997). Reliance on claims-making as an exclusive platform for indigenous affairs policy may accentuate competitive opposition and power-conflict models that reinforce the very colonialism that is being contested. Grievances remain grievances no matter how much money is being exchanged, without a corresponding state commitment to restore the relationship in a generous and unquibbling fashion (see Milroy, 1997). A preoccupation with contesting claims to the exclusion of engagement has also had the effect of glossing over the central element in any partnered interaction: namely, the managing of a relation in the spirit of co-operative co-existence and relational autonomy (McHugh, 1998).

Pressure is mounting to transcend claims-making as an exclusive model for defining state–indigenous peoples relations. Proposed instead is a more flexible approach that emphasizes engagement over entitlement, relationships over rights, interdependence over opposition, co-operation over competition, reconciliation over restitution, and power-sharing over power conflict (Fleras and Maaka, 1998). Advocated, too, is a policy framework that acknowledges the importance of working together rather than standing apart — even if a degree of "autonomy" may be inescapable in the constructive "partnering" of indigenous relations with the state. The emergence of a "constructive engagement" model of interaction to replace the claims-oriented "contestation" model may provide a respite from the interminable bickering over who owns what, while brokering a tentative blueprint for working together by standing apart.

At the crux of a constructive engagement policy model is the recognition of aboriginality as a basis for reconstructing state–Aboriginal peoples relations. This commitment to aboriginality as a framework for renewal and reconciliation entails a fundamental shift in mindset. Among the key planks in engaging with aboriginality in a constructive manner are the following preconditions:

1. Indigenous peoples do not aspire to sovereignty per se. Strictly speaking, they already *have* sovereignty by virtue of original occupancy, never having relinquished this independence by explicit agreement. The fact that indigenous peoples *are* sovereign for the purposes of en-

titlement or engagement would imply only the creation of appropriate structures for its practical expression.

2. Aboriginal peoples are not looking to separate or become independent. Except for a few ideologues, appeals to sovereignty and Aboriginal models of self-determination are discourses about relationships of
relative autonomy within the context of non-domination between
interconnected peoples (Scott, 1996). Relations-repair is the key
rather than throwing money at the problem.

3. Indigenous peoples are neither a problem for solution nor a need to
be met. They are a people with inherent rights to benefits, recognition, relations, and identity. Nor should they be considered a competitor to be jousted with but a partner with whom to work through
differences in a spirit of co-operative co-existence. In acknowledging
that "we are all in this together for the long haul," is there any other
option except to shift from the trap of competing sovereignties to the
primacy of relations between partners (McHugh, 1998)?

4. The fundamental autonomy of Aboriginal peoples as a political community is critical in crafting a new political order (Chartrand, 1996).
The rights of Aboriginal peoples as original occupants must be accepted as having their own independent sources rather than being
shaped for the convenience of the political majority or subject to uni-
lateral override (Asch, 1997).

5. Power-sharing is pivotal in advancing co-operative engagement and
co-existence. All internally divided societies that have attained some
degree of stability entail a level of governance that connotes a sharing of power (Linden, 1994). Precise arrangements for rearranging
power distributions are varied, of course, but predicated on some degree of relative autonomy for operationalizing indigenous models of
self-determination over shared yet separate jurisdictions.

6. Innovative patterns of belonging are integral to constructive engagement. Indigenous proposals for belonging to society are anchored in
primary affiliation with the ethnicity or tribe rather than as individual citizens, thus implying that peoples can belong in different ways
to society without necessarily rejecting a sense of citizenship or loyalty to the whole. This would suggest a dual citizenship, that is, to society as well as to the indigenous nation (RCAP, 1996).

7. Placing constructive engagement at the centre of a relationship entails
a fundamental rethinking of how to go about deciding who controls
what. Parties must enter into negotiations over allocating multiple yet
interlocked jurisdictions not on the basis of jurisprudence but on the
grounds of justice, not by cutting deals but by formulating a clear vision.

8. Constructive engagement also goes beyond the dualities that polarize and provoke. Dualisms establish a confrontation between two entities: a choice must be made in terms of this opposition, thus disallowing the possibility that each of the opposing terms requires and draws upon a supposed opposite (Fay, 1996). A dialectical mode of thinking is proposed instead, in which differences are not perceived as absolute or antagonistic, but as deeply interconnected and existing in a state of creative tension with potential opportunity.

To sum up, an adherence to constructive engagement is shown to transcend the legalistic (abstract rights) or restitutional (reparations), however important these concerns are in identity building and resource mobilization. Increasing reliance on contractual relations as a basis for sorting out ownership may have elevated litigation to a preferred level in resolving differences (Spoonley, 1993), yet this reliance on the legalities of rights and reparations tends to emphasize continuities with the past at the expense of social changes and evolving circumstances. By contrast, a constructive engagement policy orientation goes beyond the idea of restitution as an excuse to cut deals. It is focussed on advancing a relationship on an ongoing basis by taking into account shifting social realities in sorting out who controls what in a spirit of give-and-take. Policy outcomes with respect to jurisdiction cannot be viewed as final or authoritative, any more than they can be preoccupied with "taking" or "finalizing," but must be situated in the context of "sharing" and "extending." Wisdom and justice must precede power, in other words, rather than vice versa (Cassidy, 1994).

REMAKING CANADA: MUDDLING THROUGH MODELS

> Canada is a test case for a grand notion — the notion that dissimilar people can share lands, resources, power, and dreams while respecting and sustaining their differences. (RCAP, 1996, p. ix)

In the space of just over two decades, Aboriginal peoples have recoiled from the brink of dependence and disappearance to resume a pivotal role in the reconstruction of Canadian society. Such a reversal originated and gained legitimacy when the "costs" of excluding Aboriginal peoples from the national agenda proved unacceptably high in social, political, and economic terms (Fleras and Krahn, 1992). The start of a new millennium may well see Canada on the threshold of an Aboriginal paradigm shift. To be sure, the condition of Aboriginal peoples continues to represent Canada's great moral failure, of a people both demoralized and dispossessed by a division of wealth in the land that has passed them by. Yet the recognition of Aboriginal peoples as having an inherent right to self-government rather than being wards of a guardian state holds the promise of a new beginning. Governments have accepted the idea that Aboriginal peoples (a) are a distinct society, (b) possess a threatened culture and society, (c) depend on government trust responsibilities for survival, (d) desire more control in line with local priorities, and (e) prefer to achieve their goals in partnership with central authorities. Government acknowledgement of aboriginality as a government-to-government relation is a positive sign (Fontaine, 1998), as is the promise to treat Aboriginal peoples as equal partners in all relevant constitutional talks. And the courts continue to provide an expansive view of Aboriginal and treaty rights, including the precedent-setting Delgamuukw ruling of 1997 (but see Rotman, 1997).

The rhetoric of revolution may be compelling but premature, despite the collapse of egregious colonialist structures. Aboriginal efforts to redefine their relationship with the people of Canada are fraught with ambiguity and deception in light of competing paradigms and entrenched interests (Fleras and Elliott, 1992). The politics of restructuring often conceal hidden agendas and contested realities between the "two solitudes." The government continues to call the shots regarding what is acceptable and desirable, while Aboriginal values and aspirations continue to be overwhelmed by the majority "whitestream" (Denis, 1996). The fundamental objective of Aboriginal affairs policy agendas—to eliminate the Aboriginal "problem" through local self-sufficiency—has scarcely budged with the passage of time (Ponting and Gibbins, 1980) and is repeated again in the 1995 Federal Policy Guideline. Only the means have changed, with crude assimilationist strategies conceding ground to more sophisticated channels that not only co-opt aspects of Aboriginal discourse for self-serving purposes, but also have the effect—however inadvertent or unintended—of advancing a corporatist agenda. There remains considerable resistance to creating indigenous models of self-determination that involve fundamentally separate structures with distinctive power bases and parallel institutions. As principle or practice, aboriginality poses an unprecedented challenge to the balancing act in any society constructed around a series of compromises. Central authorities prefer instead a benign arrangement that compartmentalizes aboriginality into packages of institutional flexibility and delegated responsibility. Inasmuch as the intent is to simply rearrange the furniture without altering the floor plan of a house in distress, the government's Aboriginal agenda prefers to focus on appearances rather than on substance.

Aboriginal peoples–state relations in Canada are currently under re-assessment at the policy and administration levels. A proposed paradigm shift is gathering momentum — partly in response to escalating Aboriginal pressure and prolonged public criticism, and partly to deflect a growing crisis in state legitimacy. But the widely heralded realignment of jurisdictions is riddled with inconsistencies and contradictions as competing interests clash over a new Aboriginal agenda. On one side, the contestation paradigm with its roots in the "old rules of the game" appears to be drawing to a close, but not without a struggle (Borrows and Rotman, 1997, p. 31). On the other side, a new decolonizing paradigm based on empowerment and renewal through constructive engagement has not yet taken hold, in spite of its lofty ideals to promote national reconciliation through "justice," "adaptation," and "workable inter-cultural relations" (Weaver, 1991, p. 15). Instead of a paradigm shift, in other words, what we appear to be witnessing is a paradigm "muddle." Aboriginal–state relations are imbued with an air of ambivalence as colonialist paradigms grind up against new realities, as the old (contestation) collides with the new (constructive engagement) without displacing the other. Metaphors borrowed from plate tectonics and continental drift suggest diverse viewpoints on a collision course as perspectives slide into each other, past each other, around each other, and over or under each other. Each of the "plates" tends to talk past the other by using the same words but speaking a different language. Central authorities perceive Aboriginal jurisdictions in terms of municipal-level, self-governing, administrative structures under provincial jurisdiction. By contrast, Aboriginal views of self-government and autonomy are defended on grounds other than Crown authority, as self-contained and inherent rather than delegated, with claims over jurisdictions pertaining to land, identity, and political voice (Cassidy, 1994). Neither paradigm is strong enough to dislodge its conceptual opponent, with the result that the renewal process is enlivened by discordant amalgams of progressive and traditional. Such a state of tension and conflict is likely to persist until such time conventional thinking accepts a unifying "vision" of Canada as an assymmetrical pluralism of three founding peoples — Aboriginal, French, and English — each sovereign in their own right, yet sharing in the recalibrating of a postcolonizing Canada.

DISCUSSION QUESTIONS

1. Explain how the politics of jurisdiction (that is, who controls what and why) are central to many of the issues that animate Aboriginal peoples–state relations in Canada.

2. What is meant by the concept of indigeneity as discourse and transformation? Indicate why political authorities have had such difficulty in coping with the demands of indigeneity.

3. The indigenization of Aboriginal policy and administration is perceived as critical in decolonizing the Aboriginal agenda. Describe briefly the indigenizing of Aboriginal policy and administration from 1867 to the present.

4. Expand on the notion and implications of Aboriginal peoples in Canada as peoples with an inherent right to self-government.

5. To what extent can traditional Aboriginal governance provide a model for contemporary models of Aboriginal self-government?

6. The use of regional settlements as a basis for renewal and reform are fraught with ambiguity and confrontation if conducted without a clear vision and firm set of principles. Indicate how and why this is so.

7. What are the key components of a constructive engagement approach in the restructuring of Aboriginal peoples–state relations?

FURTHER READINGS

Deputies Council for Change. 1991. *Towards Managing Diversity: A Study of Systematic Discrimination at DIAND*. Ottawa: Deputies Council for Change. A personal favourite in terms of capturing the degree of bureaucratization within the Department of Indian Affairs. This superb case study of DIAND reveals how efforts to restructure Aboriginal–state relations by "indigenizing" the bureaucracy have fallen short of the mark because of systemic institutional barriers. A must-read for anyone who still thinks that organizational change is a straightforward process.

Dickason, Olive Patricia. 1992. *Canada's First Nations: A History of Founding Peoples from the Earliest Times*. Toronto: McClelland & Stewart. For those interested in a history of the First Nations, this book is a model of artful historical reconstruction with a relatively balanced account of Aboriginal–white relations from the past to the contemporary present.

Fleras, Augie and Jean Leonard Elliott. 1992. *The Nations Within: Aboriginal–State Relations in Canada, the United States, and New Zealand*. Toronto: Oxford University Press. This book not only traces the evolution of Aboriginal policy and administration in three white settler colonies, it also explores the resurgence of Aboriginal consciousness and the importance of traditional structures as a basis for renewal. The authors conclude that Canada may offer the greatest potential for national conciliation and Aboriginal healing.

Weaver, Sally. 1981. *Making Canadian Indian Policy: The Hidden Agenda 1968–1970.* Toronto: University of Toronto Press. This book provides an insider's account of the politics behind the ill-fated White Paper of 1969, followed by its subsequent demise. It also points out how Aboriginal reaction to the White Paper culminated in the gradual overhaul of Aboriginal–state relations. The Social Science Council selected this book as one of Canada's 20 best social scientific works over the past 50 years.

Wotherspoon, Terry and Vic Satzewich. 1993. *First Nations: Race, Class, and Gender Relations.* Scarborough, Ont.: Nelson. Unlike many books in the field of Aboriginal–state relations, this one is organized around an explicit theoretical framework. The authors contend that an understanding of Aboriginal issues must be located within the context and dynamics of capitalist societies. The use of a "political economy" perspective may not appeal to everyone, and the authors' attempts to be inclusive of race and gender do not always match the rhetoric, but this text adds fresh insights to an already crowded field.

REFERENCES

Alfred, Gerald Robert. 1995. *Heeding the Voices of Our Ancestors: Kahnawake Mohawk Politics and the Rise of Native Nationalism in Canada.* Toronto: Oxford University Press.

Allen, Robert S. 1993. *His Majesty's Indian Allies: British Indian Policy in the Defence of Canada, 1774–1815.* Toronto: Dundurn Press.

Asch, Michael, ed. 1997. *Aboriginal and Treaty Rights in Canada: Essays on Law, Equity, and Respect for Difference.* Vancouver: University of British Columbia Press.

Barnsley, Paul. 1997. "Minister Anticipates Changes in Department." *Windspeaker* (December).

Boldt, Menno. 1993. *Surviving as Indians: The Challenge of Self-Government.* Toronto: University of Toronto Press.

Borrows, John and Leonard I. Rotman. 1997. "The Sui Generis Nature of Aboriginal Rights: Does It Make a Difference?" *Alberta Law Review* 36: 9–45.

Canada, Department of Indian Affairs and Northern Development (DIAND). 1969. *Statement on Indian Policy 1969* (The White Paper). Ottawa: Supply and Services.

————. 1993. *DIAND's Evolution from Direct Service Delivery to a Funding Agency.* Ottawa: Department of Indian Affairs and Northern Development.

————. 1994. "Federal Government Begins Discussions on Aboriginal Self-Government." News Release 1-9354.

Cassidy, Frank. 1991. "Introduction." Pp. 1–16 in *Aboriginal Self-Determination,* ed. F. Cassidy. Lantzville, B.C., and Montreal: Oolichan Books and the Institute for Research on Public Policy.

————. 1994. "British Columbia and Aboriginal Peoples: The Prospects for the Treaty Process." *Policy Options* (March): pp. 10–13.

Chartrand, Paul L.A.H. 1993. "Aboriginal Self-Government: The Two Sides of Legitimacy." Pp. 231–56 in *How Ottawa Spends: A More Democratic Canada,* ed. S.D. Phillips. Ottawa: Carleton University Press.

————. 1996. "Self-Determination without a Discrete Territorial Base?" Pp. 302–12 in *Self-Determination: International Perspectives,* ed. D. Clark and R. Williamson. Toronto: Macmillan.

Chesterman, John and Brian Galligan. 1997. *Citizens without Rights: Aborigines and Australian Citizenship.* London: Cambridge University Press.

Clark, Bruce. 1990. *Native Liberty, Crown Sovereignty: The Existing Aboriginal Right of Self-Government in Canada.* Kingston, Ont.: McGill-Queen's University Press.

Clark, Donald and Robert Williamson, eds. 1996. *Self-Determination: International Perspectives.* Toronto: Macmillan.

Coates, Ken and Paul McHugh. 1998. *Living Relationships. Kokiri Ngatahi. The Treaty of Waitangi in the New Millennium.* Wellington, N.Z.: Victoria University Press.

Denis, Claude. 1996. *We Are Not You: First Nations and Canadian Modernity.* Peterborough, Ont.: Broadview Press.

Dickason, Olive Patricia. 1992. *Canada's First Nations: A History of Founding Peoples from Earliest Times.* Toronto: McClelland & Stewart.

Durie, Mason. 1998. *Te Mana, Te Kawanatanga: The Politics of Maori Self-Determination.* Auckland, N.Z.: Oxford University Press.

Eckholm, Erik. 1994. "The Native and Not-So Native American Way." *New York Times Magazine* (27 February): pp. 45–52.

Fay, Brian. 1996. *Contemporary Philosophy of the Social Science.* London: Blackwell.

Fleras, Augie. 1999. "Comparing Ethnopolitics in Australia, Canada, and Aotearoa." Pp. 187–234 in *New Frontiers: First Nation Rights in Settler Dominions in Canada, Australia, and New Zealand,* ed. Paul Havemann. Auckland, N.Z.: Oxford University Press.

Fleras, Augie and Jean Leonard Elliott. 1992. *The Nations Within: Aboriginal–State Relations in Canada, the United States, and New Zealand.* Toronto: Oxford University Press.

————. 1996. *Unequal Relations: An Introduction to Race, Ethnic, and Aboriginal Dynamics in Canada.* Scarborough, Ont.: Prentice-Hall.

Fleras, Augie and Vic Krahn. 1992. "From Community Development to Inherent Self-Government. Restructuring Aboriginal–State Relations in Canada." Paper presented at the Annual Meetings of Learned Societies, Charlottetown, P.E.I. (June).

Fleras, Augie and Roger Maaka. 1998. "Rethinking Claims-Making as Maori Affairs Policy." *He Pukenga Korero* 4(1): 34–49.

Fleras, Augie and Paul Spoonley. 1999. *Recalling Aotearoa: Indigenous Politics and Ethnic Relations in New Zealand.* Auckland, N.Z.: Oxford University Press.

Fontaine, Phil. 1998. "Shared Visions for the Future." *Time* (January 9, Canadian edition): 48.

Frideres, James S. 1998. *Native Peoples in Canada: Contemporary Conflicts,* 5th ed. Scarborough, Ont.: Prentice-Hall.

Gosnell, Joseph. 1999. "Nisga'a Rights." Letter to *The Globe and Mail* (January 20): A18.

Graham, Douglas. 1997. *Trick or Treaty?* Wellington, N.Z.: Victoria University Institute of Public Policy.

Gutmann, Amy. 1996. "Challenges of Multiculturalism in a Democratic State." Pp. 156–82 in *Public Education in a Multicultural Society,* ed. Robert K. Fullinwider. New York: Cambridge University Press.

Hall, Tony. 1993. "The Politics of Aboriginality." *Canadian Dimension* (January–February): 6–8.

———. 1996. "Peoples in Captivity." *Canadian Forum* (November).

Havemann, Paul, ed. 1999. *New Frontiers.* Auckland, N.Z.: Oxford University Press.

Johnston, Elliott, Martin Hinton, and Daryle Rigney, eds. 1997. *Indigenous Australians and the Law.* Sydney, Australia: Cavendish Press.

Jull, Peter and Donna Craig. 1997. "Reflections on Regional Agreements: Yesterday, Today, and Tomorrow." *Australian Indigenous Law Reporter* 2(4): 475–93.

Kulchyski, Peter, ed. 1994. *Unjust Relations: Aboriginal Rights in Canadian Courts.* Toronto: Oxford University Press.

Kymlicka, Will. 1995. "Misunderstanding Nationalism." *Dissent* (Winter): 131–37.

Linden, Wilf. 1994. *Swiss Democracy.* New York: St. Martin's Press.

Little Bear, L., Menno Boldt, and J. Anthony Long, eds. 1984. *Pathways to Self-Determination: Canadian Indians and the Canadian State.* Toronto: University of Toronto Press.

Maaka, Roger and Augie Fleras. 1997. "Politicizing Customary Rights: Tino Rangatiratanga as Post-Colonizing Engagement." *Sites* 35: 20–43.

———. 1998. "Indigeneity at the Millennium." Paper presented to the New Zealand Sociological Association Annual Meetings. Napier, N.Z. (November 26).

———. (Forthcoming). *Indigeneity at the Millennium: Indigeneous Peoples–Crown Relations in Canada, New Zealand, and Australia.* Auckland, N.Z.: Oxford University Press.

Macklem, Patrick. 1993. "Ethnonationalism, Aboriginal Identities, and the Law."
Pp. 9–28 in *Ethnicity and Aboriginality: Case Studies in Ethnonationalism*, ed.
Michael D. Levin. Toronto: University of Toronto Press.

McHugh, Paul. 1998. "Aboriginal Identity and Relations—Models of State Practice and Law in North America and Australasia." Pp. 84–121 in *Living Relationships. Kokiri Ngatahi. The Treaty of Waitangi in the New Millennium*, ed. Ken
Coates and Paul McHugh. Wellington, N.Z.: Victoria University Press.

Mercredi, Ovide and Mary Ellen Turpel. 1993. *In the Rapids: Navigating the Future
of First Nations*. Toronto: Penguin Books.

Milroy, Stephanie T. 1997. "Maori Issues." *New Zealand Law Review* Part 2:
247–73.

Minogue, Kenneth. 1998. *The Treaty of Waitangi: Morality or Reality?* Wellington,
N.Z.: Business Roundtable.

Monti, Lorne. 1997. "Mercredi's Legacy." *New Federation* (October/November):
12–14.

Morse, Bradford W. 1992. "Comparative Assessment of Indigenous Peoples in
Quebec, Canada, and Abroad." Report prepared for la Commission d'étude sur
toute offre d'un nouveau partenarlat de nature constitutionelle, Ottawa
(April).

Mulgrew, Ian. 1996. "B.C. Unfinished Business." *BCB* (September): 36–45.

O'Regan, Tipene. 1994. "Indigenous Governance. Country Study—New
Zealand." Paper prepared for the Royal Commission on Aboriginal Peoples,
Ottawa.

Ponting, J. Rick, ed. 1986. *Arduous Journey: Canadian Indians and Decolonization.*
Toronto: McClelland & Stewart.

———. 1997. *First Nations in Canada: Perspectives on Opportunity, Empowerment,
and Self-Determination*. Toronto: McGraw-Hill.

Ponting, J. Rick and Roger Gibbins. 1980. *Out of Irrelevance: A Socio-Political Introduction to Indian Affairs in Canada*. Toronto: Butterworths.

Prince, Michael J. 1994. "Federal Expenditures and First Nations Experience."
Pp. 261–300 in *How Ottawa Spends, 1994–95: Making Changes*, ed. Susan D.
Phillips. Ottawa: Carleton University Press.

Pritchard, Susan. 1998. "Human Rights Working Group—Third Session, 27 October to 7 November 1997." *Indigneous Law Bulletin* 4(10): 4–11.

Reynolds, Henry. 1996. *Aboriginal Sovereignty*. Sydney, Australia: Allen &
Unwin.

Rotman, Leonard I. 1997. "Creating a Still-Life Out of Dynamic Objects: Rights
Reductionism at the Supreme Court of Canada." *Alberta Law Review* 36: 1–8.

Royal Commission on Aboriginal Peoples (RCAP). 1996. *Report of the Royal
Commission on Aboriginal Peoples*. Vol. 1. *Looking Forward, Looking Back*. Ottawa: RCAP.

Scott, Craig. 1996. "Indigenous Self-Determination and the Decolonization of
the International Imagination." *Human Rights Quarterly* 18: 815–20.

Sharp, Andrew. 1997. *Justice and the Maori*, 2nd ed. Auckland, N.Z.: Oxford University Press.

Shkilnyk, Anastasia. 1985. *A Poison Stronger Than Love*. New Haven, Conn.: Yale University Press.

Smith, Dan. 1993. *The Seventh Fire: The Struggle for Aboriginal Government*. Toronto: Key Porter Books.

Spoonley, Paul. 1993. *Racism and Ethnicity*. Auckland, N.Z.: Oxford University Press.

Stasiulis, Daiva and Nira Yuval-Davis. 1995. "Introduction: Beyond Dichotomies — Gender, Race, Ethnicity, and Class in Settler Societies." Pp. 1–38 in *Unsettling Settler Societies*, ed. D. Stasiulis and N. Yuval-Davis. Thousand Oaks, Calif.: Sage.

Stea, David and Ben Wisner, eds. 1984. "The Fourth World: A Geography of Indigenous Struggles." *Antipodes: A Radical Journal of Geography* 16(2).

Tully, James. 1995. *Strange Multiplicity: Constitutionalism in an Age of Diversity*. Cambridge: Oxford University Press.

Weaver, Sally M. 1981. *Making Canadian Indian Policy: The Hidden Agenda, 1968–1970*. Toronto: University of Toronto Press.

———. 1991. "A New Paradigm in Canadian Indian Policy for the 1990s." *Canadian Ethnic Studies* 22(3): 8–18.

Webber, Jeremy. 1994. *Reimaging Canada: Language, Culture, Community, and the Canadian Constitution*. Montreal and Kingston: McGill-Queen's University Press.

CHAPTER 6

Aboriginal Self-Government in Canada: The Cases of Nunavut and the Alberta Métis Settlements

Denis Wall

INTRODUCTION

From the moment of organized European appearances in North America, negotiation has been a central characteristic of relationships between Aboriginal residents and newcomers. It is a characteristic that has been evident in treaty-making throughout Canada for more than 300 years, and it continues to be the order of the day in modern treaties, claims, and agreements being negotiated with First Nations,[1] Inuit, and Métis across Canada.[2]

One of the central issues in the negotiations over the past three decades has been the question of Aboriginal self-government, which has taken second place only to comprehensive land claims negotiations in areas where no treaties have been signed to date.

THE MEANINGS OF ABORIGINAL SELF-GOVERNMENT

Aboriginal statements reveal some of the expectations behind demands for self-government. For example, the Dene Declaration (Dene Nation, c1976, no page) states: "What we seek then is independence and self-determination within the country of Canada. This is what we mean when we call for a just land settlement for the Dene Nation."[3]

While this may seem clear enough, the Declaration does recognize that "the challenge to the Dene and the world is to find the way for the recognition of the Dene Nation" (Dene Nation, c1976, back cover). The Dene were quite clear, however, in their descriptions of the principles that should underpin negotiations for self-government. Here is a sample of those principles, which are echoed in many statements today, including the report of the Royal Commission on Aboriginal Peoples (RCAP):

> 5. The Dene have the right to practice and preserve their languages, traditions, customs and values.
> 6. The Dene have the right to develop their own institutions and enjoy their rights as a People in the framework of their own institutions.
> 7. There will therefore be within Confederation, a Dene government with jurisdiction over the geographical area and over subject matters now within the jurisdiction of either the Government of Canada or the Government of the Northwest Territories.
> ...
> 10. Dene will be compensated for past use of Dene land by non-Dene. (Dene Nation, c1976, n.p.)

Underlying themes in the Dene Declaration are not new, and they are described equally well elsewhere. An example on the international scene is the United Nations call for the protection of the cultural, political, and economic rights of independent peoples in the U.N. International Bill of Human Rights. The opening sentence in Part 1 of Article 1, item 1, reads: "All peoples have the right of self-determination" (United Nations, 1983, p. 10).

In British Columbia in 1978 the Union of British Columbia Indian Chiefs produced a publication for the tenth Annual Assembly based on the ideas of George Manuel, the president at the time. It states, "We must be masters in our own house, in order to survive as Indian people. There is no basis in the laws of Canada to restrict the recovery of our Aboriginal rights because we have never given up our rights to control our own lives and means to live" (Union of B.C. Indian Chiefs, 1978, p. 4).

During the negotiations leading to the Constitution Act, 1982, self-government was a topic of discussion, but a definition was not written into the Charter of Rights. Although attempts were again made in 1992, the Charlottetown Accord did not become a Canadian reality. The Métis Nation Accord (1992, pp. 2–3), which could have become part of the Constitution Act had the Charlottetown Accord been approved in 1992, provides some of the detail about self-government for the Métis.

> 3. Self-Government Negotiations
> a) ... the representatives of the Métis Nation and the Provinces agree to negotiate in good faith the implementation of the right of self-government, including issues of
> i) jurisdiction; and
> ii) economic and fiscal arrangements, with the objective of concluding tripartite self-government agreements elaborating the relationship among the Métis Nation, Canada and the Provinces.

b) For the purposes of the Northwest Territories, negotiations will be conducted through comprehensive land claims, treaty or self-government negotiations and will include both Métis and Indians as parties.

4. Land and Resources

Within the context of self-government negotiations,

a) Canada and the Provinces agree, where appropriate, to provide access to lands and resources to Métis and Métis self-governing institutions.

The Accord recognized that Alberta had established a land base and governing institutions for the Métis on the Métis settlements.

Up to 1995, a question remained as to whether any Canadian government considered Aboriginal self-government an inherent right that predated European contact. Eventually, when he was Minister of Indian Affairs, Ron Irwin stated it was the policy of the Liberal government that self-government is an "inherent right [and] is an existing Aboriginal right under the Canadian Constitution" (INAC, 1995). The right has not been written into the Constitution, but it is intended to cover Inuit and Métis, as well as First Nations peoples.

Prior governments had apparently committed to negotiate community-based self-government and constitutional change to recognize the Aboriginal right (INAC, 1988, 1987). A federal statement of 1988 (INAC, 1988, pp. 2–3) first notes, as does the 1995 policy mentioned above, that "[i]t is important to note that this self-government policy does not involve increasing the level of program funding to Indian communities," and continues by stating:

> The process of developing and negotiating self-government arrangements for Indian communities requires a great deal of commitment on the part of communities and government alike. ... The department stands ready to work with those communities to further the development of Indian self-government in Canada.

In any event, the federal Liberal government has stated again in its response to the *Report of the Royal Commission on Aboriginal Peoples, Gathering Strength: Canada's Aboriginal Action Plan* that it continues to supports negotiations for self-government:

> The Government of Canada will consult with Aboriginal organizations and the provinces and territories on appropriate instruments to recognize Aboriginal governments and to provide a framework on principles to guide jurisdictional and inter-governmental relations. (INAC, 1997, p. 15)

Aside from these recent statements about political rights for Aboriginal peoples, historically, during the negotiations of Canada's treaties with Indians in the 1800s, the goals of the Indian negotiators were "[t]o affirm the on-going cultural and spiritual survival as distinct Indian tribes and nations, by preserving distinctive traditions and institutions" (Price, 1991, p. 48).

RENEWING THE RELATIONSHIP

One of the central themes of the *Report of the Royal Commission on Aboriginal Peoples* (RCAP, 1996) and of the federal government response is the need to develop a renewed relationship among the federal, provincial, and territorial governments and Aboriginal peoples.

That theme has been a steady refrain in Canadian government policy historically as well. Many of the treaties of the 1800s did create "new relationships." In the 1930s, one example of a renewed relationship with the Métis is contained in the report of the Ewing Commission (Ewing, 1936) of Alberta. By the mid-twentieth century, the Special Joint Committee on the Indian Act, a Senate and House of Commons Committee, held hearings that led to the rewriting of the Indian Act. The committee heard about the need for a different relationship. One famous submission (Canada, 1947, p. 310) was by Diamond Jenness, a senior Canadian government bureaucrat, on 25 March 1947, in which he read into the record his personal "Plan for Liquidating Canada's Indian Problem within 25 Years." His plan curiously presaged the Trudeau government's White Paper, "Statement of the Government of Canada on Indian Policy" (Canada, 1969), which called for a "restructured" relationship, essentially the elimination of the relationship, between Indians and the federal government.

The Report of the Special Joint Committee of the Senate and the House of Commons (Canada, 1984), The Penner Report, called for a renewed relationship. Any number of government, civil, and Aboriginal agency reports have called for renewing, revising, and restructuring Aboriginal–non-Aboriginal relations in Canada. Much of the commentary accepts, seemingly uncritically, that the one major hope of a more positive relationship lies in Aboriginal self-government.

Today, descriptions of Aboriginal self-government vary from the ideal of parity among Aboriginal, provincial, and federal legislative and financial authority to descriptions of Aboriginal communities simply taking administrative control after governments have made the important policy and financial decisions. The former is a far cry from the kinds of colonial controls governments have exhibited.[4] A common sentiment is that colonial controls and the resulting abuses heaped on Aboriginal people for more than a century must be rejected. The latter, a commonly held vision of self-government, is exemplified by Geoffrey York (1989, p. 269), who puts great store in more involvement by Aboriginal peoples in decision-making processes that affect them:

> Cultural revival among Aboriginal people is just one step toward regaining what has been lost. Self-government is the other key to the future of native people. When they are permitted to gain influence over the central institutions in their communities — the schools, the justice system, the child welfare system — Indian and Métis people have already demonstrated that they can repair the damage caused by centuries of racism and neglect.

Today federal and provincial governments are attempting to find ways for Aboriginal peoples to be more involved in decisions that affect their destiny, an involvement that is usually controlled, however, by current provincial and federal authorities.

Those who are critical of many current forms of Aboriginal self-government view them as little more than convenient arrangements that allow Aboriginal people administrative responsibility for services that are ultimately controlled by the federal or provincial government.[5] They argue that self-government is essentially glorified municipal government, which is far from the ideal of a third level of government that is equal in legislative and financial authority to the federal and provincial governments.[6]

Among academics, political leaders, and government representatives, differences of opinion about Aboriginal self-government abound: differences about the most beneficial structure of self-government, about who controls what, about when self-government should be implemented, and about whether or not true self-government can ever be achieved.

Another complicating factor is that Aboriginal self-government has no universal standard. That is, its structure can change from community to community. The Royal Commission on Aboriginal Peoples recognized this and has said, "It lies with each group to determine the character and timing of any moves to enhance its own autonomy" (RCAP, 1993, p. 41). Federal government policy statements also have stated this, such as a 1988 policy statement on self-government (INAC, 1988) that clearly expressed that self-government would be negotiated community by community.

Self-government proposals also have their critics among the very people within the communities for whom they are intended. For example, Inuit women have objected to many parts of the Nunavut agreement partly because of concerns about an emphasis on conventional southern Canadian notions of resource management that they argue have emphasized the economic, social, and political roles of men at the expense of those of women (Inuit Women's Association, 1993).

Another example of conflict within communities, this time in Alberta, is the response of the Métis of the Paddle Prairie Settlement in Northern Alberta to a realignment of the relations between the Métis settlements in Alberta and the provincial government. The concerns of that settlement's Council managed to threaten the negotiation of governance restructuring. On 14 November 1989, the Paddle Prairie Settlement Council, whose land was among the most oil rich of all the settlements, indicated it would leave the negotiation because the Council felt, among other things, that land ownership should remain with individual settlements and not, as indicated in the agreement, with a General Council that would administer all eight settlements (*Windspeaker*, 1989).

That said, the following sections of this chapter describe two cases of self-government, the Métis settlements in Alberta and those in Nunavut. I would like to look briefly at the Alberta Métis Settlements Accord and agreements of the late 1980s and then turn to Nunavut. Although these two contemporary forms of self-government differ, their similarities are striking. Both sets of negotiation with government began in the mid-1970s and ended in the early 1990s. The new governance structures of the settlements and the Nunavut government are circumscribed by more than one piece of legislation. Both sets of negotiation used referenda to seek the approval of residents of the area. Both agreements are being implemented using transition commissions, involved distributing financial compensation over extended periods of time, and set aside Aboriginal-owned lands, which are constitutionally protected. Both agreements were negotiated under the threat of legal action, claimed outright land and resource ownership, and demanded compensation for the loss of land and resource revenues.

One major difference between these two forms of Aboriginal self-government (and described by Asch [1993], who has used other Aboriginal examples) is that the Alberta Métis Settlements Councils are clear examples of "ethnic governments" that are elected and operated by members of a particular "ethnic" group. Nunavut, on the other hand, is an example of a public government in which anyone who meets residence requirements, regardless of ethnicity, can participate in electing the government.

MÉTIS SETTLEMENTS: THE PROVINCIAL EXAMPLE

The Métis Settlements Accord led to Royal Assent of four pieces of Alberta legislation in November 1990. These established land ownership rights (of 1.28 million acres) and a reorganized form of governance for the Métis of the eight Alberta settlements. The Alberta government agreed to pay $310 million over seventeen years. A Transition Commission, membership tribunal, revenue trust fund, and other working groups, with provincial government and settlement representatives, were established to assist in implementation and maintenance.[7]

The final agreements were driven by land claims disputes of the 1970s. During this time the Federation of Métis Settlements sued the provincial government for misappropriated resource revenues. After the implementation of the agreements, the suit was "stayed" and will not be reactivated unless there are significant changes to the agreements that negatively affect Métis land ownership.

The Management Model

The management model used to structure the renewed form of Métis settlement governance fits well with contemporary government management rhetoric, the central features of which are accountability, responsiveness, co-operative management, local responsibility, flexibility, self-reliance, cost effectiveness, and efficiency. These features are described in the book *Reinventing Government* by Osborne and Gaebler (1992).[8]

Peter Lougheed, the Alberta premier who began these negotiations to restructure the relationship between the province and one group of Métis in Alberta, wanted a made-in-Alberta solution to Aboriginal self-reliance.[9] Resolution 18, which Lougheed introduced in the provincial legislature in 1982, was a commitment made by the government that led to the Métis Settlements Accord.[10]

Currently, the Métis in Alberta operate their settlements much like municipal governments: a General Council is responsible for eight settlements, each of which has its own local council. As with municipal councils, the Métis settlements are ultimately responsible to a Minister of the Crown. The very basic advisory role for the Métis suggested in the 1936 Ewing Commission Report has evolved into municipal-style governance today, although the responsibility of the provincial minister has not changed.[11]

Some argue that the current relationship between the Alberta government and the Métis settlements has changed fundamentally from pre-1990 relations and is as close to the ideal of self-government as can be expected. Bell (1994, p. 83) seems to feel this way with her insistence that "The Métis settlements legislation represents a significant accomplishment in the resolution of historical grievances ... ." Recent changes to the legislative regime have set the stage for structural changes within the settlements that in turn may result in more participation in decision making by settlement residents. The Aboriginal Affairs Branch of the provincial government and the settlements are now working more closely together than ever before: both are represented on the Transition Commission, on the membership tribunal, and elsewhere. Thus, there continues to be significant opportunity for provincial involvement and influence in running the Métis settlements.

In the final analysis, the financing of the settlements (housing, roads, social services, job training, and so on) still very much depends on the provincial government; as well, the development and implementation of legislation that restructured land ownership and governance have depended on the good will of government.

Some significant changes in the relationship from the pre-1990 period have taken place: land ownership has been secured, revenue sources have been adjusted, and decision-making involvement has been refined, clarified, and expanded at the settlement level.

NUNAVUT: THE FEDERAL EXAMPLE

With the introduction of land claims policies of the federal government and the Trudeau government's acceptance of the notion of Aboriginal rights following the Nisga'a case of 1973, Canadian comprehensive land claims began in earnest.[12] Since then, specific and comprehensive claims have piled up on the federal doorstep by the hundreds. One of these claims was the 1976 Inuit claim over eastern Arctic lands. That claim's settlement resulted in Nunavut, Canada's third territory stretching from Hudson Bay to the northernmost parts of Ellesmere Island. Under the terms of the settlement, the government of Nunavut will have powers like those of other territorial governments, established and maintained in the context of a very close working relationship with the federal government in Ottawa. There is nothing new in this close working relationship. The Nunavut Development Timeline (see Table 6.1) identifies major events on the road to Nunavut, including a good deal of federal involvement. Figure 6.1 on page 155 is a map of Nunavut.

The signing of the Nunavut agreement took place on 25 May 1993, and the Nunavut Land Claims Agreement Act was given Royal Assent on 10 June 1993.[13] This agreement not only settled the comprehensive land claim to the eastern Arctic but enabled the establishment of the new territory of Nunavut as well. A separate political accord establishes the

TABLE 6.1

Nunavut Development Timeline

1875   The Northwest Territories Act passed.

1875   The District of Keewatin established.

1877   District of Keewatin reduced in size because of Manitoba's expansion.

1898   Yukon Territory Act.

1905   Provinces of Alberta and Saskatchewan established on 1 September 1905.

1912   Boundaries of Manitoba, Ontario, and Quebec extended north.

1921   NWT Council enlarged to six members.

1922   Indian Act changed to include administration of Inuit.

1951   A new Indian Act passed protecting Indian lands from alienation and Indian property from depredation, as well as providing for a form of local government.

1960   Aboriginal people given the right to vote in federal elections.

1963   Full-time Commissioner of NWT appointed.

1966   (Aug. 30) Carrothers Commission advises against partition of the NWT for ten years. Two federal constituencies created.

1969   Nisga'a of British Columbia go to court for a declaration of their title to land.

1969   Federal government White Paper on Indian Policy, "A Statement of the Government of Canada on Indian Policy," recommends repeal of Indian Act and abolition of all legal distinctions between Natives and non-Natives.

1969   (Dec.) Indian Claims Commissioner appointed to receive and study Indian grievances and claims and recommend measures to resolve them.

1970   (Sept.) The Committee for Original Peoples' Entitlement (COPE) incorporated.

1970   India Brotherhood of the NWT established to deal with concerns about Treaties 8 and 11.

1971   (Aug.) The Inuit Tapirisat of Canada (ITC) established.

1972   The Métis and Non-Status Native Association of the NWT incorporated.

1973   Nisga'a case (*Calder v. Attorney-General of B.C.*) decided by the Supreme Court of Canada, and later the federal government reversed its position on Aboriginal title.

1974   The Office of Native Claims established within the Department of Indian Affairs and Northern Developmnet (DIAND) to evaluate and negotiate comprehensive and specific Indian land claims.

1974   Milton Freeman's "Inuit Land Use and Occupancy Project" identifies boundaries of Inuit land use in Kitikmeot, Keewatin, and Baffin. Adopted in 1979 as Nunavut boundaries.

(*continued*)

TABLE 6.1 (Continued)

1975   The first fully elected NWT Assembly.

1975 (Nov.) Inuit Tapirisat of Canada authorized by voting delegates to begin land claims negotiations.

1975   The James Bay and Northern Quebec Agreement signed between the Grand Council of the Crees, Northern Quebec Inuit Association, the Government of Quebec, the James Bay Energy Corporation, the James Bay Development Corporation, the Quebec Hydro-Electric Commission (Hydro-Quebec), and the Government of Canada. It was the first modern treaty, a comprehensive claim, between Canada and Aboriginal peoples.

1976 (Feb. 27) Inuit Tapirisat of Canada (ITC) proposes division of the NWT and creation of a new territory Nunavut (Our Land). The Nunavut proposal includes the Inuvialuit.

1976   Inuvialuit split from ITC to settle their claim independently.

1977   The Committee for Original Peoples' Entitlement (COPE) presents "Inuvialuit Nunangat" proposal for an agreement-in-principle.

1978 (Oct. 31) COPE signs the "Inuvialuit Land Rights Settlement Agreement-in-Principle" with the federal government.

1979   NWT divided into two federal electoral districts: Nunatsiaq and the Western Arctic.

1980 (Jan.) The Drury Report (*Report of the Special Representative on Constitutional Development in the Northwest Territories*) recommends that the NWT remain a single political unit and that residents be responsible for political change.

1980 (Oct.) ITC resolution calling for the creation of Nunavut.

1981 (May) The NWT Legislative Assembly approves plebiscite on the creation of Nunavut.

1982 (Feb.) Several members of the Legislative Assembly, the ITC, the Dene Nation, the Métis Nation of the NWT, and COPE unite to form the Constitutional Alliance (CA).

1982 (Apr. 14) Plebiscite held on the question "Do you think the Northwest Territories should be divided? YES or NO." Division supported.

1982 (Apr. 17) Constitution Act, Charter of Rights and Freedoms signed.

1982 (Nov. 26) Minister of DIAND states government intention to support division of NWT in principle.

1982   The Tungavik Federation of Nunavut (TFN) established as a political arm of the ITC to negotiate land claims.

1984 (Jan.) The Council of Yukon Indians signs an agreement-in-principle to settle their land claims with the federal government.

1984 (June 5) (Inuvialuit) Western Arctic Claim signed. This is the first modern treaty or comprehensive land claims settlement north of the 60th parallel in Canada.

(continued)

TABLE 6.1 (*Continued*)

1985   Federal task force reviewing comprehensive claims policy issues its
       report *Living Treaties: Lasting Agreements: The Coolican Report.*
1987   The federal government issues *Comprehensive Land Claims Policy,*
       which modifies policy by allowing federal officials to consider specific
       options or alternatives in a claims settlement that does not formally
       extinguish Aboriginal title.
1988   DIAND releases *A Northern Political and Economic Framework,* which
       supports establishing a northern government, settling land claims,
       and promoting economic development.
1989   (Dec. 7–8) Federal government and TFN agreement on final elements
       of agreement-in-principle on Nunavut land claim.
1990   (Mar. 31) Comprehensive Land Claim Umbrella Final Agreement
       among the Government of Canada, the Council for Yukon Indians,
       and the Government of the Yukon initialled.
1990   (Apr. 30) Agreement-in-principle between the Inuit (TFN) and the
       federal government signed.
1990   (Oct. 19) Government of NWT and TFN sign agreement-in-principle
       regarding division.
1991   (Apr.) Former NWT Commissioner John Parker appointed adviser to
       resolve the boundary dispute between the TFN and Dene/Métis of
       the NWT. The Parker Line is established as the boundary of
       Nunavut.
1991   (July) The Gwich'in (Kutchin) of the Mackenzie Delta reach a land
       claims settlement with the federal government based on April 1990
       agreement rejected by NWT Dene/Métis.
1991   (Dec. 7) Council of Yukon Indians accepts the final land claims
       agreement.
1992   (Jan.) TFN accepts the land claims agreement "Agreement between
       the Inuit of the Nunavut Settlement Area and Her Majesty the
       Queen in Right of Canada" and passes a resolution recommending
       that Inuit ratify agreement.
1992   (Apr. 22) The Gwich'in final comprehensive land claim agreement
       signed.
1992   (May 4) NWT–Nunavut boundary plebiscite held and approval
       received.
1992   (Oct.) Nunavut Political Accord signed by TFN and federal and
       territorial governments. Ensures Nunavut government will be a
       reality by April 1999.
1992   (Nov. 3–6) Inuit of the TFN approve the Nunavut land claims
       agreement and authorize its signing.
1993   (Mar. 15) The Nunavut Tungavik Inc. (NTI) formed to help direct
       the transition to Nunavut.

(continued)

TABLE 6.1 (*continued*)

1993 (May 25) In Iqaluit, NWT, the final Agreement between the Inuit of the Nunavut Settlement Area and Her Majesty the Queen in Right of Canada signed.

1993 (June 10) The Nunavut Land Claims Act is given Royal Assent. Nunavut Implementation Commission is instituted.

1993 (July 9) The Nunavut land claims settlement becomes law.

1995 (Dec. 11) Plebiscite held on capital of Nunavut. Iqaluit receives 60.2 percent of vote.

1996 (Apr. 30) Iqaluit officially declared the future capital of Nunavut.

1999 (Apr. 1) Nunavut born with elected legislative assembly, Cabinet, territorial court, and public service.

Source: Adapted in part from E. Simpson, L.N. Seale, and R. Minion. 1994. *Nunavut: An Annotated Biliography*, pp. 7–19. Edmonton: Canadian Circumpolar Institute and the University of Alberta Library.

actual Territory of Nunavut that, as mentioned earlier, has a public government (as opposed to an ethnic, exclusively Inuit government).

"The concept of Nunavut has been part and parcel of the Inuit land claim ever since they first put (it) forward ...," notes Donald Purich. He goes on to say that since 1976 "the Inuit position has always been that before they sign(ed) a land claims agreement they must have a guarantee that Nunavut ... be created" (1992, p. 9).

The creation of the government of Nunavut and the associated land claims settlement are the results of the largest of Canada's modern treaties. After public referenda supported the establishment of Nunavut, the federal government agreed to a compensation package of $1.14 billion to be paid over fourteen years, as well as Inuit ownership of approximately 350 000 square kilometres of land, 36 000 square kilometres of which include mineral rights.

The RCAP (1996) states:

Article 19 of the agreement lays out Inuit rights to land within the new public territory. ... Inuit-owned lands will take one of two forms: fee simple including surface and subsurface rights, and fee simple excluding surface and subsurface rights. ... Title will be owned collectively and vested in a designated Inuit organization (DIO), which is either Tungavik or a designated regional Inuit organization. Inuit title can be transferred only to another DIO, or in the case of land within a municipality, to Canada, the territorial government or a municipal corporation.

FIGURE 6.1

The Nunavut Settlement Area

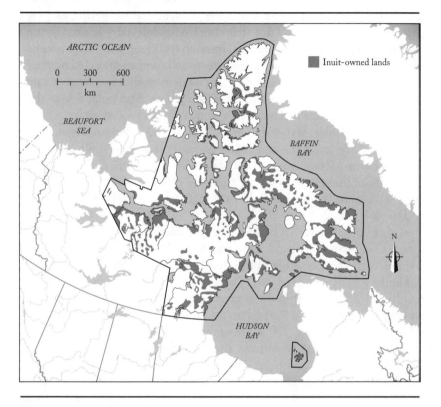

Source: André Légaré. 1996. *Canadian Journal of Native Studies* 16(1):
pp. 139–63.

The settlement stipulates that Inuit (Nunavut Tungavik, Inc.) will participate with the federal government in controlling land-use planning, wildlife harvesting, offshore resources, and environmental protection.

Nunavut does represent a unique form of Aboriginal self-government. Titus Allooloo, a member of the NWT Legislative Assembly, said on 31 October 1989: "We dream of making laws and policies which truly reflect the needs and conditions of Nunavut Territory ..." and, of course, the Inuit. At least one major contradiction is contained in this ideal state: even though Nunavut has a public government, it is seen by many, Inuit and commentators such as Purich (1993) alike, as the "homeland" of the Inuit—a very ethnic notion.

Other Issues

There are a number of other problems associated with the development of the land claim treaty and Nunavut. One problem that has been a sticking point during negotiations of this and other land claims is the demand by the federal government that Aboriginal (Inuit, in this case) title to the land be extinguished in exchange for a signed treaty and compensation. Aboriginal groups are concerned that those who sign modern treaties may be giving up more than they bargained for by relinquishing their Aboriginal title to the land, title thåt obtains as a result of historical use and occupancy.

A second problem is that the Inuit claim area appeared to encroach on the Quebec and Labrador land claims of the Innu and the Inuit as well as on the Dene–Métis claims in the Northwest Territories. Overlapping claims are nothing new, however, and were clearly not reason enough to deny settlement.[14] At the time of writing, these were still being discussed and negotiated.

A third problem is that the public government of Nunavut will represent all Nunavut voters and residents, not only the Inuit. Dacks (1986) has raised the concern that as the non-Inuit population increases, Inuit influence will likely be reduced. There are some minor safeguards to protect Inuit influence within the government of Nunavut: Inuktitut will be an official language of government, and the agreement demands proportional representation of staff in government departments.

A fourth potential problem is the fragmentation of the Aboriginal voice in the north, a consequence of the separation of Nunavut from the Northwest Territories. However, Aboriginal groups have not necessarily spoken with a single united voice in the past, and it is possible that Nunavut could strengthen the Inuit voice by giving it the support of a territorial government.

There is also the question of Nunavut government authority over lands and resources. Ownership of Nunavut lands and resources does not necessarily lie with the Nunavut government, but is in the hands of Nunavut Tungavik Inc. (Inuit-owned lands at 18 percent) and the federal government (Crown lands at 82 percent). As a result, co-management boards, which represent the corporate perspectives of Nunavut Tungavik Inc. and the federal government, are responsible for land management and development. Conflicts are very likely to occur when co-management board decisions are not in line with those of the Nunavut government, which represents individual Inuit and non-Inuit residents.

Another issue is whether the Inuit are properly prepared to take control of government decision-making roles. In order to address this concern, the Nunavut Unified Human Resources Development Strategy, part of the Nunavut implementation plan, has attempted to design policy and strategy to build Inuit management capacity — that is, to train Inuit for management and administrative roles in the government of Nunavut and in Inuit organizations.

The Inuit Women's Association in particular has suggested that the economic development model promoted in the agreements is more in tune with conventional southern approaches to the exploitation of non-renewable resources and, consequently, Inuit benefits may be limited (Inuit Women's Association, 1993). For example, women's work may not be recognized or compensated like men's. Also, there appears to be no guarantee that women will receive equal representation on boards or commissions and, as a result, that the government of Nunavut will represent Inuit women's perspectives on social, political, economic, community, family, or cultural development. Although there may well be income support programs for men whose hunting livelihood is interrupted, the Inuit Women's Association has stated that no such programs for the interruption of women's labour in the harvest are expected.

Finally, there are concerns that the territorial status of Nunavut leaves much to be desired in relation to the question of the autonomy of the Nunavut government. Indeed, many questions and concerns may be raised about the strong influence of the federal government through its involvement in co-management boards, land ownership, and financial compensation.

Whether these and other concerns can be satisfactorily addressed will take time, patience, and clear, objective analysis. Resolutions to issues will also require the political good will of both Inuit leaders and the federal government in the years ahead.

CHANGING RELATIONSHIPS

Nunavut is a political fact, but its essence, which involves a complex set of relationships between the people of Nunavut and the federal government, continues to evolve. The Nunavut development timeline earlier in this chapter (Table 6.1, p. 151) illustrates the long history of relations among the Northwest Territories, the Inuit, and the federal government and suggests that these relationships will continue, develop, and change over time.

Relationships between Aboriginal peoples around the world and the governments that administer their affairs are often characterized as "internal colonial" and highly problematic. Some coincident central elements of these difficult relationships are as follows:

1. One ethnic group or coalition rules the affairs of others living within the state.
2. Subordinate ethnic groups are separated territorially in "homelands," "Native reserves," and the like.
3. Land tenure rights are different from those of members of the dominant group.
4. An internal government within a government is specially created to rule the subject groups.
5. There is a unique legal status in which the subject group and its members are considered to have a corporate status that takes precedence over their individual status. Members of the ruling ethnic groups are considered individuals in the eyes of the state.
6. "Relations of economic inequality in which subject peoples are relegated to positions of dependency and inferiority in the division of labour and the relations of production."[15]

The question, then, is this: Has the treaty between the federal government of Canada and the Inuit substantially altered their historical association?

Taking guidance from the points above to analyze this association, the first indicator of contemporary relations is that while the Inuit have negotiated willingly with the federal government, that negotiation has occurred within a context defined by the federal government and the courts. This fact represents significant control by a "coalition" of ethnic groups (non-Inuit) over a subordinate group (Inuit) and suggests that internal colonialism may continue to exist. Alone, this fact is not a powerful indicator of a state of "internal colonialism" for the Inuit of Nunavut; however, when it is combined with the other indicators discussed immediately below, it can be a strong supporting statement about the existence of a colonial relation.

A second key element of the contemporary relationship is that Inuit lands are segregated from those of the dominant group, and they are indeed considered "homelands." This, according to the criteria listed above, is another indicator of a colonial relationship.

A third part of the relationship is that Inuit land ownership remains different from the land tenure rights of other Canadians. Instead of the federal government holding land in trust, as it has for First Nations, the land is owned outright by the Inuit collectively—not individually. That is, fee simple ownership of land vests with corporations in the name of the Inuit. Land can also be expropriated by appropriate authorities after negotiation and compensation. In this respect, at least, land tenure is somewhat similar to that of other corporations.

The different treatment of Aboriginal peoples in Canada regarding their collective land tenure rights may not be a negative situation when considered on its own. Supernault (1988) and others have suggested that Aboriginal people prefer to be treated collectively rather than individually, since the group is paramount to Aboriginal identity. On the one hand, while this may appear to be reason enough for the different treatment of Aboriginal peoples, it can be argued that such treatment is another essential part of a colonial relationship. On the other hand, collective ownership of land and resources may be starting to provide considerable economic clout for Aboriginal corporate bodies. In this sense, collective Aboriginal ownership of land could be providing a considerable economic benefit.[16] In the meantime, some will nonetheless continue to see little economic benefit coming their way.

A fourth concern about the relationship between the Inuit and the federal government is that there is at least one government within a government for the Inuit. The government of Nunavut and Indian and Northern Affairs Canada will mediate Inuit relations with the federal government, which is the final arbiter in a legislative sense. The federal government is also the major financial contributor to the government of Nunavut, although funds will be going directly to Inuit organizations from resource revenues and other forms of economic development.

The final element of the relationship is that as a result of the historical relationship between the Inuit and Canada, Inuit remain among the poorest of Canadians. There remains the hope that the new relationship will alter this situation substantially, but little change has taken place thus far. Here we see clearly that there are "Relations of economic inequality in which subject peoples [the Inuit in this case] are relegated to positions of dependency and inferiority." As the last element of an internal colonial relationship, this fact is another strong indicator of the existence of a potential colonial relationship between the Inuit and the federal government.

In summary, the contemporary relationship between the federal government and the Inuit of Nunavut matches fairly closely the central elements of a highly problematic internal colonial situation:

1. In Canada, one coalition of ethnic groups (non-Inuit) has considerable influence over the affairs of the Inuit.
2. There is the territorial separation of the Inuit in "homelands."
3. Land tenure rights differ from those of members of the dominant group.
4. There are internal governments within a government especially created to deal with Inuit: Indian and Northern Affairs, Canada, and the

government of Nunavut mediate relations between Inuit and the federal government.

5. There is a unique legal status in which Inuit are considered to have a corporate status that takes precedence over their individual status. Members of the ruling ethnic groups are considered individuals in the eyes of the state.

6. And finally, there exist relations of economic inequality in which Inuit are relegated to positions of dependency and inferiority.

In the final analysis, both the Nunavut government and Inuit organizations are in the position of having to defer to federal influences, because the federal government is supported by legislation and its financial obligations. Changes have been made to the relationship between the Inuit and Canada—land ownership is more certain, and decision-making influence may have increased—but it remains to be seen whether or not these changes are substantial enough that they will lead to a significant reversal of the historical internal colonial relationship.

CONCLUSION

Légaré (1996, p. 160) puts one element of the federal government's influence over Inuit decision making this way:

> According to section 5.3 of the agreement, only the governor-in-council or the Minister of DIAND could veto decisions coming from co-management boards. But they could do so only if a regulation put forward by a public board contradicts some of the articles contained in the final land claims agreement. Thus, the Minister's veto is highly unlikely because he would then contradict the decisions of its own board-member representatives and would politically antagonize the Inuit.

Even with recent changes to administrative and legal frameworks, Aboriginal peoples in Canada continue to live in closely watched, supervised relationships with federal and provincial governments. The locus of authority to implement the legal regimes necessary for these forms of Aboriginal self-government continue to rest in the hands of the federal and provincial governments. In most situations where Aboriginal self-government is being implemented, federal and provincial governments continue to exert strong influences and can constrain Aboriginal decision making through legislative and economic means. However, it is important to note that within the constraining financial and legal boundaries set by the federal and provincial governments in domains such as human resources, education, or social policy, Aboriginal decision making may be relatively unencumbered.

The main question addressed in this chapter is whether the recent implementation of Aboriginal self-government involving the Métis of Alberta and the Inuit of Nunavut represents a fundamentally different relationship between Aboriginal peoples and the federal and provincial governments. We can see that the governance structures for the Métis settlements in Alberta are not really new — they are old structures infused with contemporary management notions and practices.

Although some important differences in the structure and process of Aboriginal self-government are evident in the establishment of Nunavut, it nonetheless appears that the recent changes in the relationship between the federal government and the Inuit have not been substantial: many elements of that historical and problematic relationship are still evident.

NOTES

1. In this chapter the notion of "Aboriginal," as defined in the Constitution Act, 1982, section 35, includes Indian (the term "First Nations" is used throughout the chapter to mean Indian), Inuit, and Métis.
2. Here we can include the early Treaties of Peace and Friendship on the east coast of North America; the treaties in Ontario of the 1700s and 1800s; the Numbered Western Treaties; and the modern treaties and agreements, for example, with the Cree and Inuit in Quebec (1975), with the Inuvialuit of the Western Arctic (1984), with the Eastern Arctic Inuit (Tungavik Federation of Nunavut [TFN], 1993), or with the Métis of Alberta starting in the 1930s and continuing today.
3. The document refers to the Dene as a Fourth World people. This is a concept expanded by George Manuel (Manuel and Posluns, 1974), at one time the president of the Union of B.C. Indian Chiefs.
4. See section 35 (2) of the Charter of Rights and Freedoms of the Constitution Act, 1982, which identifies the Aboriginal people of Canada as Indians, Inuit, and Métis. It is not surprising to find all three groups arguing for similar levels of parity with regard to executive and legislative authority.
5. Wotherspoon and Satzewich (1993, p. 235) go so far as to suggest that there are only two actual examples of First Nations "self-government": the Cree-Naskapi (of Quebec) Act of 1984 and the Sechelt Indian Band Self-Government Act of 1986.
6. In a similarly sceptical vein, Haysom (1992, p. 194) is cautious about whether an agreement between the Labrador Inuit Association and the Newfoundland and federal Governments will support self-government,

arguing that "liberal principles require strong and distinct communities but simultaneously undermine them."

7. These include the package of legislation related to the Métis settlements: The Métis Settlements Land Protection Act, 1990; the Métis Settlements Act, 1990; and the Métis Settlement Accord Implementation Act Alberta, 1990.

8. These management notions are remarkably similar to those used by the Ewing Commission (Ewing, 1936, p. 9) and those articulated in the Royal Commission document *Partners in Confederation* (RCAP, 1993, p. 41).

9. Over the years the Métis in Alberta have forged significant relations with the Alberta government, with the province showing a great willingness to deal with the Métis. For example, it was at the request of Métis leaders that the Ewing Commission (1936) was established. The Commission described the extremely poor living conditions of the Métis and recommended the formation of farm colonies, precursors to the current Métis settlements. Today the settlements are the only reasonably stable land base in Canada for people of Métis heritage.

10. Alberta Premier Don Getty's agreement in 1987 to work with the Métis Nation of Alberta Association led to the implementation of the first of a series of Métis Nation Framework Agreements in 1988.

11. "The final control of these colonies must continue to rest with the Department concerned. The management will be carried out under such superintendents or instructors as may be necessary. As matters develop it may be thought wise to provide for a council to be elected by the members of the colony and to be invested with advisory powers only" (Ewing, 1936, p. 12).

12. See Chapter 5 for a more extensive discussion of the impact of the Nisga'a case and the subsequent change in negotiation strategies by the federal government.

13. Pelly (1993, p. 21) describes the basic land claim settlement as follows:

> The land claim settlement gives the Inuit outright ownership of about 18 percent of the land—353 610 square kilometres, including 36 257 square kilometres of sub surface mineral rights. The remaining 82 percent of Nunavut remains Crown land … . Inuit will keep the right to hunt, fish and trap throughout Nunavut. The settlement also gives them $1.15 billion, which they hope will generate economic and social revival.

14. Take, for example, the British Columbia claims during the late 1990s that were rumoured to cover more than the available territory of B.C., mainly because of such overlapping territories.

15. These points have been adapted from van den Berghe (1984, p. 182).

16. See, for example, the report *Coping with the Cash* by the Sustainable Development Research Group (1989).

DISCUSSION QUESTIONS

1. For many years the federal government has been directly involved in the political development of the Northwest Territories. What five key events do you think may have been most critical?
2. Do you agree that the financial and political (legislative) influences exerted by the federal government are critical to Aboriginal self-government? Why or why not?
3. In what ways are the models of self-government, as formulated for Nunavut and the Métis settlements in Alberta, similar and different?

FURTHER READINGS

Asch, M. 1993. *Home and Native Land: Aboriginal Rights and the Canadian Constitution*. Vancouver: University of British Columbia Press. General text dealing with Canadian government, Aboriginal, and legal perspectives on Aboriginal rights in a liberal democracy. Reviews constitutional relationships with Aboriginal peoples and provides some detail on Nunavut and Northwest Territories Aboriginal self-government.

Dene Nation. (c1975). "Dene Declaration—Statement of Rights." A statement on nationhood and an exploration of the possible relations between the Dene Nation of the Northwest Territories and the federal government.

Manuel, George and M. Posluns. 1974. *The Fourth World: An Indian Reality*. Toronto: Collier Macmillan. Describes personal and community history in mid-twentieth century Canada. Sets out personal ideas about the common colonial treatment of Aboriginal peoples throughout the world as well as their special relationships to the land.

Murphy, Robert F. 1971. *Dialectics of Social Life: Alarms and Excursions in Anthropological Theory*. London: George Allen and Unwin. Provides suggestions by a social anthropologist on how to go about perceiving and describing the world. The book continues to retain its relevance to contemporary social analyses.

REFERENCES

Arctic Institute of North America, Sustainable Development Research Group. 1989. *Coping with the Cash: A Financial Review of Four Northern Land Claims Settlements with a View to Maximizing Economic Opportunities from the Next Generation of Claim Settlements in the Northwest Territories.* Yellowknife: Northwest Territories Legislative Assembly.

Asch, M. 1993. *Home and Native Land: Aboriginal Rights and the Canadian Constitution.* Vancouver: University of British Columbia Press.

Bell, C.E. 1994. *Alberta's Métis Settlements Legislation: An Overview of Ownership and Management of Settlement Lands.* Regina: Canadian Plains Research Centre, University of Regina.

Canada, Department of Indian Affairs and Northern Development (DIAND). 1969. *Statement on Indian Policy 1969.* Ottawa: Supply and Services.

Canada, Special Joint Committee on the Indian Act. 1947. Senate and House of Commons Committee Hearings. Ottawa: 25 March.

Dacks, G. 1986. "The Case against Dividing the Northwest Territories." *Canadian Public Policy* 12(1): 202–13.

Dene Nation. c1976. "The Dene-Land and Unity for the Native People of the Mackenzie Valley: A Statement of Rights." Brampton, Ont.: Charters Publishing.

Ewing, A.F. 1936. "Commission Report to the Lieutenant Governor in Council, Edmonton." Edmonton: Government of Alberta, 15 February.

Haysom, V. 1992. "The Struggle for Recognition: Labrador Inuit Negotiations for Land Rights and Self-Government." *Études/Inuit/Studies* 16(1–2): 179–97.

Indian and Northern Affairs Canada (INAC). 1987. "Aboriginal Self-Government: What It Means." *Information.* Ottawa: INAC.

———. 1988. "Indian Self-Government Community Negotiations." Ottawa: INAC, March.

———. 1995. "Government Launches Process for Negotiating Aboriginal Self-Government." News Release. Document #1-9520. Ottawa: INAC, 10 August.

———. 1997. *Gathering Strength: Canada's Aboriginal Action Plan.* Ottawa: INAC.

Inuit Women's Association. 1993. "A Response to the Articles of the Nunavut Proposal." Copy faxed to author 27 October.

Légaré, A. 1996. "The Process Leading to a Land Claims Agreement and Its Implementation: The Case of the Nunavut Land Claims Settlement." *The Canadian Journal of Native Studies* 16(1): 139–63.

Manuel, George and M. Posluns. 1974. *The Fourth World: An Indian Reality.* Toronto: Collier Macmillan.

The Métis Nation Accord. 1992. An unsigned contract drafted for representatives of Canada, the Provinces of British Columbia, Alberta, Saskatchewan, Manitoba, Ontario and the NWT, and the Métis Nation. 7 October.

Osborne, D. and Ted Gaebler. 1992. *Reinventing Government: How the Entrepreneurial Spirit Is Transforming the Public Sector.* Reading, Mass.: Addison-Wesley.

Pelly, D. 1993. "Dawn of Nunavut." *Canadian Geographic* (March/April): 20–29.

Price, R.T. 1991. *Legacy: Indian Treaty Relationships*. Edmonton: Plains Publishing.

Purich, D. 1992. *The Inuit and Their Land: The Story of Nunavut*. Toronto: James Lorimer.

Royal Commission on Aboriginal Peoples (RCAP). 1993. *Partners in Confederation: Aboriginal Peoples, Self-Government, and the Constitution*. Ottawa: RCAP.

———. 1996. *Report of the Royal Commission on Aboriginal Peoples*. 5 vols. Ottawa: RCAP.

Simpson, E., L.N. Seale, and R. Minion. 1994. *Nunavut: An Annotated Bibliography*. Edmonton: Canadian Circumpolar Institute and the University of Alberta Library.

Supernault, C. 1988. "Helping Communities Move Toward Local Self-Government." Paper presented to the Native education conference "Our People, Our Struggle, Our Spirit," Edmonton, Alberta, 1–3 November.

Union of British Columbia Indian Chiefs (UBCIC). 1978. "Indian Government Today!" Vancouver: UBCIC. Spring.

United Nations General Assembly. 1993. "The International Bill of Human Rights." New York: United Nations.

van den Berghe, P. 1984. "Education, Class and Ethnicity in Southern Peru: Revolutionary Colonialism." Pp. 181–202 in *Education and Colonialism*, vol. 2, P. Altbach and G. Kelly. New York: Longman.

Windspeaker. 1989. "Paddle Prairie Pulls Out of Federation: Disagreement over Self-Government Bills Prompts Move." *Windspeaker* 7 (24 November): 1–2.

Wotherspoon, T. and V. Satzewich. 1993. *First Nations Race, Class, and Gender Relations*. Scarborough, Ont.: Nelson Canada.

York, G. 1989. *The Dispossessed: Life and Death in Native Canada*. Toronto: Lester & Orpen Dennys.

CHAPTER 7

Aboriginal Peoples in Canada: Demographic and Linguistic Perspectives

Mary Jane Norris[1]

INTRODUCTION

This chapter explores some of the ways in which Aboriginal peoples are distinct from the rest of the Canadian population in terms of both demography and language. Underlying these two perspectives is the issue of identity, which both defines the Aboriginal population and bears importantly on language maintenance. An understanding of how Aboriginal populations are shaped by demographic and legislative processes is fundamental to the meaningful analysis of issues and to the development of relevant policies and programs.

Defining Aboriginal populations is complicated and multifaceted and includes such concepts as ancestry and self-identity, Indian Act legislation, First Nation membership, Aboriginal community, culture, and language (Guimond et al., forthcoming). Compounding this conceptual complexity is the fact that the Aboriginal population is demographically distinct from the overall Canadian population. Most notably, it is much younger, and it experiences higher mortality and fertility levels. As a result, some of the issues facing Aboriginal people differ from those for the rest of the population. Demographic information is essential in evaluating the success of various policies and programs and in determining future requirements.

Furthermore, the size and growth of Aboriginal populations are not simply functions of the classic demographic components of growth (fertility, mortality, and migration). Rather, size and growth have become an increasingly complex interplay of classic demographic components combined with legislative components (e.g., revisions to the Indian Act). In addition, as individual awareness and ethnic self-identity changes, so too can the reporting of these affiliations with an Aboriginal group. This phenomenon is known as ethnic mobility.

Although there may be a general awareness of Aboriginal and non-Aboriginal differences, until recently there has been considerably less focus on the demographic and linguistic differences among the different Aboriginal groups themselves. Such a focus is crucial if we are to understand the dynamics and needs of different Aboriginal groups. An important component of such differences is language itself, since language use and presence in the community is viewed as a symbol of identity (Drapeau, 1995) and "is the principal instrument by which culture is transmitted from one generation to another" (RCAP, 1996, Vol. 3, p. 602). There is a general consensus that while some Aboriginal languages remain viable for the moment, many are in danger of disappearing.

This chapter incorporates earlier work (Norris, 1990, pp. 33–59; 1996) that demonstrated significant variation among Aboriginal peoples in their demographic characteristics and updates the picture with more recent statistics and population projections.[2] The chapter also compares demographic characteristics of Aboriginal groups with those of the overall Canadian population and profiles the state of Aboriginal languages in Canada by providing a demographic analysis of language survival.

DEMOGRAPHIC PROFILE

Defining Aboriginal Populations

Canada's Aboriginal population can be classified into four major groups: status Indians, who are registered under the Indian Act of Canada; non-status Indians, who have Aboriginal ancestry but lost or never had status under the Indian Act; Métis, who are of mixed Aboriginal and non-Aboriginal ancestry; and Inuit, who are indigenous to Canada's Arctic and sub-Arctic regions (Yukon, Northwest, and Nunavut Territories, northern Quebec and Labrador). These major groups represent the main origins/identities of Canada's Aboriginal population, in combination with legal status criteria. In the case of both status and non-status Indians, the term "First Nations" refers to the Indian people of Canada, regardless of status (e.g., Cree First Nations, Mohawk, etc.). This term came into common usage in the 1970s and has largely replaced the words "Indian" and "band" in the name of communities.

The concepts of ancestry and identity have been variously used in the Census of Canada to establish the size and composition of Canada's Aboriginal populations. There is, however, no one single definition of Aboriginal peoples — definitions can vary according to ancestry, self-identity, legal definitions such as the Indian Act, community, culture, and language.

> At times, the word Aboriginal may denote either all persons of Indian, Métis or Inuit descent or those holding legal Indian Status. In other instances, the concept of "Aboriginal peoples" can refer to persons who have self-identified as Indian, Métis or Inuit, members of First Nations, persons who speak Aboriginal languages or persons who live in certain specific locations, such as Indian reserves, Métis settlements or Inuit communities. (Guimond et al., forthcoming)

Neither existing legislation nor concepts of ethnicity and identity can completely or consistently define who is an Aboriginal person. The two major pieces of legislation in this context are the Indian Act and the Constitution Act. Goldmann (1993) wrote that "The requirements of the original Indian Act, 1876 and all its subsequent revisions and the Constitution Act have had considerable impact on the classification of Aboriginal people in the census. ... [They] provide the fundamental impetus for the definition of the Aboriginal people to be included in the 1986 and 1991 Censuses." While legislation in the Constitution Act recognizes Aboriginal peoples as Indian, Métis, and Inuit, it does not actually define what constitutes their populations. In contrast, Indian Act legislation provides a definition of an Aboriginal population by setting the legal criteria for a person to be recognized as a status or registered Indian in the Department of Indian and Northern Affairs' (DIAND) Indian Register. Revisions to eligibility criteria in the Indian Act legislation in 1985 affected the size and composition of the registered Indian population. Census measures based on the concepts of ethnicity or identity have taken on different meanings over time, reflecting varying population size and composition based on self-reporting.

Concepts Concerning Aboriginal Ancestry and Identity

The measurement of ancestry and identity is not an easy task, inasmuch as we are dealing with ethnicity. Both ancestry (also referred to as ethnic origin in the census) and identity are elements of ethnicity, with ancestry being based on more objective criteria. Identity tends to be more subjective in the sense that it is an "indicator of an individual's feelings, allegiance or association with a particular ethnic group" (Goldmann, 1994, p. 11). But in measurement terms, both are vulnerable to the subjective interpretations of the respondent. The changing concepts and measures of ethnicity in Canada's censuses since 1871 reflect societal conditions. Before 1981, for example, only one single paternal ancestry was reported, to the exclusion of multiple and matrilineal ethnic origins. Factors such as the rate of intermarriage between ethnic and racial groups can also complicate how ethnicity is determined. Difficulties involved in defining and measuring the size of Canada's Aboriginal populations based on census counts have been well-documented (Boxhill, 1984; Kralt, 1990; Pryor, 1984; Goldmann, 1993).

Ultimately identity, and to some extent ancestry, rests on self-definition — in contrast to the more objective, legal criteria of the Indian Act that establishes Indian status. As noted by Frideres (1993, p. 21) in his discussion of Native identity:

> The identity of the individual lies in his/her conceptualization of self. We can attempt to measure this self-conceptualization in some form, but all it tells us is the degree to which an individual feels Native. It does not identify the defining attributes nor the relative importance of each of these attributes.

Frideres (1993, p. 45) concludes that Native identity has become complex and fragmented (as with any identity), with many meanings, including identity with culture, local group experiences, and legal definition of band membership.

Identity with Origins. Statistics Canada first introduced the concept of Aboriginal identity in the 1986 Census as a complement to the concept of ethnic origin or ancestry. This new concept was designed to improve the enumeration of Canada's Aboriginal populations (Guimond et al., forthcoming). The concept has been used twice since, in the 1991 Aboriginal Postcensal Survey (APS) and in the 1996 Census. In the case of Aboriginal ethnicity, the Aboriginal population has been counted through the question on ethnic origin/ancestry/race for practically all censuses.[3] In the 1996 Census, the Aboriginal population was counted through separate questions on origin and identity, yielding different measures and characteristics. The census shows that a respondent with Aboriginal origins may not necessarily identify as an Aboriginal person. Furthermore, the ancestry population that does not report Aboriginal identity tends to be more similar to the general Canadian population in socio-economic/demographic characteristics, whereas the identity population is more dissimilar. The identity population is thought to more accurately capture the essence of the core Aboriginal population.

Ethnic Mobility. Ethnic mobility is an especially relevant concept for Aboriginal ancestry and identity, and it has three fundamental components: ethnicity, the boundaries defining ethnic groups, and the flows of people between groups. Ethnic mobility can refer to changes in ethnic boundaries and in the declared ethnic affiliation of people over time (Goldmann, 1998; Guimond et al., forthcoming). It can be defined as the virtual movements of people through changes in their group affiliation. These movements may be either the result of changes in how people self-identify, or they may be externally imposed when the definition of a group changes "thereby moving the boundaries to include a different subset of people — imposed ethnic mobility" (Goldmann, 1998). An example of the latter is the 1985 revision of the Indian Act (Bill C-31), which re-sulted in new definitions of registered Indians and, consequently, new de-finitions of the population not eligible for registration.

When respondents change their declarations of ethnic origin or iden-tity from one census to another, the size, and hence the growth, of Abo-riginal populations is affected. The impact of ethnic mobility on popula-tion growth can be likened to migration in that it involves "in-mobility" and "out-mobility" from one group to another. For example, "between 1981 and 1991, a period in which this phenomenon seems to have been fairly significant, transfers from a non-Aboriginal origin to an Aboriginal origin (in-mobility) were much higher than the transfers from an Abo-riginal origin to a non-Aboriginal origin (out-mobility)" (Guimond et al., forthcoming). The recognition of this phenomenon is critical if we are to make a meaningful assessment of the demographic trends in population growth and composition of Aboriginal groups based on census ethnic ori-gin and identity data.

Data Sources, Quality, and Comparability

Analyzing the similarities and differences among Aboriginal groups on the one hand, as well as those between Aboriginal and non-Aboriginal popu-lations on the other, is not an easy task. The data presented in this demo-graphic profile are drawn from a wide variety of studies and sources, in-cluding Census of Canada and Aboriginal Peoples Survey (APS) data from Statistics Canada, Indian Register data from Indian and Northern Affairs Canada (INAC), and Medical Services Branch data from Health Canada. The census (including the APS) is the most comprehensive source of Abo-riginal data and generally the only major source for some Aboriginal groups, especially Métis and non-status Indian, used to examine differentials in age–sex structure, fertility, mobility, and migration between Aboriginal groups as well as in comparison with the overall population. The census also provides historical Aboriginal data. "In censuses previous to 1996 counts of Aboriginal persons were derived primarily from a question which asked respondents about their ancestry" (Statistics Canada, 1998b).

In consultation with Aboriginal organizations, Statistics Canada developed the APS, a postcensal survey of Aboriginal populations in Canada that followed the 1991 census. This survey incorporated the dimensions of ethnic identity and ethnic origin by asking respondents who had reported Aboriginal ancestry in the census to elaborate on their identity, specifically, whether they considered themselves to be an Aboriginal person (North American Indian, Métis, or Inuit) (Statistics Canada, 1993c, p. 11). Like the census, the APS includes those persons who reported registered Indian status under the Indian Act (Statistics Canada, 1993a; 1993c). In 1996, the census asked both an ancestry and an identity question.

Indian Register and medical services data provide information on trends in fertility and mortality for registered Indians, and a population register has been maintained for the Inuit of northern Quebec, but no register exists for Inuit in the Territories or Labrador. Unfortunately, registers have never been established specifically for the Métis and non-status Indian groups; consequently, no data exist with respect to their births and deaths.[4]

The present data sources are limited for a variety of reasons, including undercoverage, incomplete enumeration, and misreporting in the census or APS, or late and underreported births and deaths in the Indian Register. Census and APS data are based on self-reported counts and characteristics. As such, these data can be at variance with other estimates of Aboriginal group populations, especially unofficial estimates of Métis and non-status Indians.[5] In the case of registered Indians, the census and Register populations are different in a number of ways. For example, the Register, which was instituted as a result of legal and administrative requirements, lists those persons who are legally status Indians under the Indian Act, including those outside Canada and in institutions. The census excludes institutional[6] residents (such as prison inmates, chronic-care residents, those in rooming homes and hotels, etc.) from its ethnic data, as well as those who no longer officially reside in Canada. Those persons who are homeless are also likely to be excluded. Furthermore, it is quite possible that respondents who are, in fact, registered Indians may not have reported as such in the census (Statistics Canada, 1993a, p. 28).[7]

Comparability of Ethnic Origin and Identity Data over Censuses

Caution must be used when interpreting census and other data on Aboriginal people, because data are not directly comparable from one census to another. A number of factors affect comparability, including changes in concepts (e.g., single- and multiple-ethnic responses), questionnaire format (e.g., instructions, examples), data quality and coverage (e.g., incomplete enumeration), legislation (e.g., Indian Act),[8] and the sociopolitical and economic environment, which can affect ethnic mobility. For example, 1981 and 1986 census data on ethnic origin are not directly comparable, since multiple-ethnic responses were not actively encouraged until 1986, whereas 1986 and 1991 censuses are relatively more comparable (Statistics Canada, 1993a, p. xii). In 1996, further changes were made to the ethnic origin question, most notably the inclusion of "Canadian" among the examples of sample ethnic origins listed on the census questionnaire. This might well have affected the pattern of responses for Aboriginal ancestry.

Similarly, the populations with Aboriginal identity between 1991 and 1996 are not directly comparable. The identity population in the 1991 APS was selected from persons who had reported Aboriginal ancestry or who were registered Indians in the 1991 census, whereas the identity question in 1996 was asked independently from the ancestry question. As a result, there are some respondents in the 1996 census who reported an Aboriginal identity but who had indicated neither an Aboriginal ancestry nor registered Indian status in the corresponding census. There is also inconsistency among individuals in their responses between Aboriginal origin and identity in both 1996 and 1991 (Statistics Canada, 1993c, p. 6). A respondent who indicated North American Indian ancestry may or may not identify with this origin, and could instead identify as Métis.

Apart from changes to questionnaires and revisions to the Indian Act, which can affect ethnic mobility, the declared identity of a respondent can change over time depending on social and personal aspects, family background, and awareness of ancestral roots. For example, in the 1986 census, about 712 000 people reported Aboriginal origins, compared with just over 1 million in 1991. It is speculated that public attention on Aboriginal issues (such as the Oka crisis in 1990) may have increased the reporting of Aboriginal origins, affecting the social and personal considerations of respondents (Statistics Canada, 1993a, pp. i, xii). Clearly, when counts of populations are based on self-reported measures of ancestry and identity, respondent choice has an important effect.

Components of Growth

The following section examines the various components of growth that affect the size, age–sex structure, and growth of Aboriginal populations. These include the explicit demographic components of fertility, mortality, and migration; the component of ethnic mobility; and the legislative components (reinstatements and status inheritance) related to amendments to the Indian Act. The numbers of births and deaths in any population are a function of fertility and mortality rates, respectively, in combination with the age–sex structure of the population. The difference between the number of births and deaths in a population is called the "natural increase." Thus natural increase can be either positive, negative, or (rarely) neutral. In this context, over the past century Canada's earliest population has experienced the three stages of the Demographic Transition as seen in developing countries, which is basically the movement from a population with high fertility and high mortality to one with low fertility and low mortality. For the Aboriginal population,

> [t]he first stage was characterized by high fertility and high mortality rates during the first half of the 1900s. The second stage, which took place during the 1950s and 1960s, saw continued high fertility, however mortality dropped off rapidly due to advances in sanitation and medicine. The third stage, which took place in the 1970s, saw fertility rates decline as the effects of urbanization and modernization were felt, while mortality rates remained low. (Siggner, 1986a, p. 5; 1986b)

Migration between communities also contributes to the changing size and distribution of the Aboriginal population. Migration flows within Canada[9] by place of residence, such as on-/off-reserve, between rural and urban areas, as well as between province and territory, all contribute to the dynamics of population change.

The impact on growth through the legislative components was effected largely through reinstatements and status inheritance related to the 1985 amendments to the Indian Act. Reinstatement refers to restoring Indian status to those persons who had lost status as a result of provisions in the earlier act, especially as the result of out-marriage of registered women to non-status men. Status inheritance refers to a set of descent rules that establish entitlement to Indian status at birth based on the extent of out-marriage between status and non-status (whether Aboriginal or non-Aboriginal) persons. Reinstatements have a positive effect on the growth of the registered Indian population by adding reinstated persons to the registered count, whereas status inheritance has a negative effect, in that some children born to registered Indians are excluded from the registered population. The effects are predominantly opposite for the non-status Indian population.

Finally, ethnic mobility can have either a positive or a negative effect on the growth of Aboriginal groups, depending on changes in identity, and is clearly a less well-defined factor in determining population size and growth.

The next section reviews the trends, patterns, and group differentials associated with these various components of growth.

Fertility

Overall Trends. Over the past century, Canada's Aboriginal people have undergone a fertility transition. Estimates of crude birth rates (the number of births expressed per 1000 persons in a population) for North American Indians from 1900 to 1976 show that until the 1940s, the birth rate remained relatively stable at around 40 births per 1000 population. After the outbreak of World War II, the rate rose rapidly to a peak of 47 births per 1000 by the early 1960s. To some extent, the registered Indian population experienced a baby boom during the mid-1960s, although several years later than among the general Canadian population (Ponting, 1997, p. 79) and for different reasons (e.g., improvements in infant mortality). This boom in fertility was followed by a sharp downturn (much like that in the population in general), but the rapid rate of decline did not persist beyond the 1970s.

For the Inuit of the Northwest Territories, estimates of crude birth rates from 1931 to 1981 indicate a similar pattern. Rates rose sharply from about 30 births per 1000 in 1941 to a high of 60 per 1000 by the 1960s. The rates dropped off sharply after the mid-1960s, plummeting to 35 births per 1000 by the 1980s (Robitaille and Choinière, 1985).

A number of factors have been considered in assessing the rise and fall in Native fertility. The increase in rates between 1941 and 1961 was due in part to improved health conditions for both mother and child. Moreover, as part of the early stages of modernization, more Native women shifted to bottle feeding, leading to shortened intervals between births, and the natural fertility rate increased (Romaniuc, 1981).

The decline in fertility since the 1960s largely reflected the growing use of contraceptives among the Aboriginal population. Birth control has affected both family size and the timing of childbearing. As was the case for European populations entering the Demographic Transition, family size consideration was the dominant issue for Natives. Census data indicate not only that Native families are getting smaller, but also that Native women are having children later and spacing them farther apart (Romaniuc, 1987). As with the population in general, factors such as a declining marriage rate, later marriage, and increased marital instability play a role in Aboriginal fertility.

Trends in Total Fertility Rates. As shown in Figure 7.1, there has been a declining trend in total fertility rates (TFRs) for both the registered Indian and the Inuit populations over the past three decades. These trends and levels differ from those of the general Canadian population and are more pronounced. The TFR for the Canadian population declined fairly steadily from 3.8 births per woman in 1961, to 1.8 by 1974, to its current (1995) level of 1.64, with some fluctuation between 1.6 in 1987 and 1.7 in 1990 (Statistics Canada, 1994b, p. 7). Over roughly the same period, the Inuit TFR declined from an estimate of 9.2 in 1966 to 4.1 by 1983, and was projected to potentially reach 3.4 by 1991 (Robitaille and Choinière, 1985). In 1968, the TFR of registered Indians was estimated to be about 6.1 (Nault et al., 1993). Recent Department of Indian Affairs and Northern Development (DIAND) data suggest that fertility declined from 3.3 in 1981 to 2.85 by 1991, with a continued decline to 2.7 by 1996 (Loh et al., forthcoming). Between 1968 and 1981, the Indian and Inuit TFR declined at a much faster rate than that for Canadians in general, a drop of 48 percent compared with 32 percent for the total population. These trends suggest a convergence of Native fertility toward the overall Canadian fertility level.

FIGURE 7.1

Total Fertility Rates for Inuit, Registered Indians, and Total Canadian Population, Canada, 1961–1996

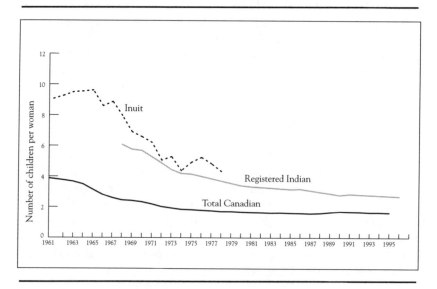

Sources: Total Canadian: Statistics Canada, *Vital Statistics*; Registered Indians: Nault et al., 1993, 1991; 1996 from Norris et al., Loh et al., forthcoming; Inuit: Robitaille and Choinière, 1985, 1991; Norris et al., 1996.

Group Fertility Differentials. Among Aboriginal groups, Inuit fertility rates remain consistently higher than those of registered Indians, which in turn exceed those among the Métis. The lowest rates are found among non-status Indians. Thus TFR estimates based on 1991 census data yield the following ranking: Inuit, 3.4; registered Indians, 2.8; Métis, 2.4; and non-status Indians, 2.0. Overall, fertility levels based on the children/woman ratio for 1991 were higher for the identity population, with a ratio of 510 children aged 0–4 per 1000 women, compared with 470 for the Aboriginal origin population. The lower fertility of the origin-based population is consistent with the observation, noted earlier, that the characteristics of those in the Aboriginal population who do not identify with their origins tend to be more similar to those of the non-Aboriginal population.

Geographic Differentials. Fertility levels have been and continue to be significantly lower in urban than in rural areas and lower off-reserve than on-reserve, with more pronounced differentials among younger women (Norris, 1990, 1996). The TFRs among identity-based registered Indian populations in 1991 are estimated to be 3.7 children per woman on-reserve, 2.4 for women in rural areas, and 2.2 in urban areas. Estimated fertility rates of registered Indians for 1996 are 3.2 on-reserve and 2.4 off-reserve (Loh et al., forthcoming). TFRs for non-status Indians and Métis are also higher in rural than in urban areas (2.4 vs. 1.9 and 2.8 vs. 2.3, respectively). Census data also suggest that the fertility level of Inuit residing in southern Canada is lower than that of Inuit in the North (Robitaille and Choinière, 1985).

Mortality

Mortality Trends. The mortality rates among both the Indian and the Inuit populations have declined significantly over the past century. Registered Indian life expectancy at birth (a measure of mortality not equivalent to average age at death) increased from an estimated 33 years around the turn of the century to about 67 years for males and 74 years for females by 1991 (Table 7.1). Most recent estimates from DIAND suggest continued increases in life expectancy for registered Indians to 68.0 years for males and 75.7 years for females by 1995 (Loh et al., forthcoming). Available estimates for the Inuit of northern Quebec indicate that life expectancy increased by some 30 years, from 35 (for both sexes) in 1940 to the present 1991 estimate of 58 and 69 years for males and females, respectively (Table 7.1). In comparison, the life expectancy of the male and female Canadian population in general

TABLE 7.1

Estimated Life Expectancy at Birth for Registered Indians, Inuit, and Total Canadian Populations, for Selected Periods and Years, Canada, 1900–1995

Year/period	Registered Indians both sexes	Males	Females	Inuit Northern Quebec		Northwest Territories		Total Canadian Year	Males	Females
1900	33			1941–51	35	1941–50	29	1921	58.8	60.6
1940	38			1951–61	39	1951–60	37	1941	63.0	66.3
1960	56			1961–71	59	1963–66	51	1961	68.4	74.2
		Males	Females	1971–81	62	1978–82	66			
1960–64		59.7	63.5							
1965–68		60.5	65.6					1966	68.7	75.2
1976		59.8	66.3					1976	70.2	77.5
1981		62.4	68.9					1981	71.9	79.0
1982–85		64.0	72.8					1984–86	73.0	79.8
1991		66.9	74.0	1991	58M/69F			1991	74.6	80.9
1995		68.0	75.7					1995	75.2	81.4

Sources: Registered Indian life expectancy: 1900, 1940, 1960 from A. Romaniuc, 1981; 1960–64, 1982–85 from Medical Services Branch, Health and Welfare; 1976, 1981 from G. Rowe and M.J. Norris, 1985; 1991 from F. Nault et al., 1993; 1995 from Loh et al., forthcoming. Inuit: N. Robitaille and R. Choinière, 1985; 1991 from E. Létourneau, 1994. Canadian: Statistics Canada, 1995, "Canadian Life Tables," Vital Statistics.

increased by about 12 and 15 years, respectively, over the last 50 years, to 74.6 years for males and 80.9 years for females in 1991 (Table 7.1). By 1995, Canadian life expectancies had increased to 75.2 for males and 81.4 for females. The 1991 discrepancy between male and female life expectancy is greater in both Indian and Inuit populations (7.1 and 11 years, respectively) than in the population in general (6.3 years) (Table 7.1). The 1995 discrepancy between male and female life expectancy is still greater for registered Indians (7.7) than for the population in general (6.2).

Infant Mortality. Infant mortality, which refers to the death of babies aged under one year, is often used as an indicator of a population's standard of living. A large part of the increase in Aboriginal life expectancy is attributable to the rapid decline in infant mortality. At the turn of the century, infant mortality rates (IMRs) of registered Indians were estimated to be some 240 per 1000 live births. This rate declined to about 200 around World War II and to around 30 by the late 1970s (Romaniuc, 1981). Estimates based on adjusted data from the Indian Register indicate a substantial decline in IMRs from 39 per 1000 live births in 1975 to 12 by 1990 (Nault et al., 1993). The most recent DIAND data indicate that the infant mortality rate among registered Indians has since continued its decline to 11.6 by 1995 (Loh et al., forthcoming). Over the same period, Canadian rates decreased much more gradually, from 14.3 in 1975 to 6.8 by 1991 and 6.0 by 1996. These comparisons suggest a convergence of Indian rates toward Canadian levels. The largest discrepancy between Indian and Canadian rates appears to be among post-neonatal deaths — that is, between the ages of 28 days and one year — as opposed to neonatal deaths. The Indian post-neonatal death rate is more than three times the national average: 7.8 per 1000 as compared with 2.1 (Bobet and Dardick, 1995).

Declines in infant mortality of roughly the same magnitude as those of registered Indians have also occurred among the Inuit, although levels of infant mortality remain higher among the latter. In the mid-1960s, Inuit rates were estimated to be about twice as high as Indian rates (Webb, 1973). Since the 1950s, Inuit infant mortality has decreased substantially, from 300 to around 50 per 1000 by 1981 (Robitaille and Choinière, 1985).

Causes of Death. While infant mortality rates of Aboriginal people have dropped significantly, declines in mortality at other ages are much less pronounced. Analysis of age-specific death rates among the registered Indian populations in 1971, 1976, and 1981 indicates little decrease for some ages and, in some cases, even slight increases (Rowe and Norris, 1985). The observed pattern of relatively small declines in mortality at older ages, compared with the great strides made in infant survival, reflects the fact that the major causes of death for registered Indians are associated not with disease but with accidents, poisoning, and violence (Jarvis and Boldt, 1982). Since the 1960s, improvements in health care have resulted in significant decreases in the number of deaths from respiratory conditions, digestive disorders, infection, and parasitic diseases as well as perinatal (around birth) causes. For almost 300 years, tuberculosis was a major threat to Native health and accounted for 30 percent of Indian deaths in the communities around Hudson Bay and James Bay as early as 1885. While the incidence of tuberculosis has declined significantly from about twelve times the national rate in the 1950s (Graham-Cumming, 1967), it is still about seven times higher than the rate for the total Canadian population (Ponting, 1997, p. 85).

Accidents, poisoning, and violence are currently the leading causes of deaths among Indians and Inuit. Rates increased dramatically from 1960 on (Murdock, 1983), such that in 1983 rates were three times those for the Canadian population (Siggner, 1986a). Similarly, injuries and poisoning were the leading causes of death among the Inuit over the 1970–80 period, accounting for a third of deaths in the Northwest Territories compared with only 9 percent among the general Canadian population (Robitaille and Choinière, 1985).[10] Health Canada data for 1992 indicate that injury and poisoning remain the leading causes of death, with motor vehicle accidents and suicide accounting for the two main types of trauma. Indian death rates due to injury continue to be at least three times the Canadian average and, notably, four times higher among males. Death rates for injury, however, have fallen over the 1979–88 period, although they now seem to be levelling off. For example, the 1992 Indian death rates due to injury and poisoning[11] were 169 per 100 000 population, compared with the 1983 rate of 174. The 1992 suicide rate itself is still at least three times the national average, with 40 deaths due to suicide per 100 000 Indian population, compared with 12 for Canadians in general (Bobet and Dardick, 1995).

The predominance of injuries and poisoning as the leading causes of death among Aboriginal people overall also reflects the impact of the high proportion of young adults in the Aboriginal population. The effect of the younger age-structure can be demonstrated by standardizing or controlling for differences in age structure between Aboriginal and non-Aboriginal populations. This technique answers the question, "What would the death rate in a population be if it had the same age structure as another population?" For example, the crude (unstandardized) death rate of the registered Indian population in the mid-1990s was around 5.6 deaths per 1000 population, compared with 6.9 for the overall Canadian population, while its death rate standardized to the age structure of the general Canadian population was much higher at 10.8 (Ponting, 1997). Similarly, causes of death associated mainly with young adults, such as accidents and injuries, are more liable to account for a higher proportion of deaths in the younger Indian population than in the older general population. It is worth noting that when rates by cause from 1978–1986 were standardized according to the older Canadian age structure, diseases of the circulatory system become the leading cause of death among Indians, followed by injuries and poisonings (Harris and McCullough, 1988). This calculation clearly shows the importance of age structure in determining the overall major causes of death in a population. One might expect, therefore, that as the population ages, the leading causes of death overall will shift.

Group Differentials. Mortality among Aboriginal populations in Canada remains much higher than that of the general population. Estimates of life expectancy at birth for registered Indians in the early 1980s and for Inuit as of 1991 are comparable to overall Canadian levels during the 1940s, when life expectancies ranged between 65 and 69 years of age for males and females combined. The current life expectancies of these Aboriginal groups are about ten years less than those of the overall population. In the case of Métis and non-status Indians, direct data on mortality are not available. However, given that these two groups are more urbanized than registered Indians or Inuit, one might speculate that mortality levels of Métis and non-status Indians would be more similar to that of the general population and, hence, lower than those of registered Indians and Inuit. In fact, estimates of life expectancies based on Register and APS data for all four Aboriginal groups reflect this relation.[12] Life expectancies estimated for 1991 are highest for non-status Indians (71 and 78 years for male and females, respectively), the most urbanized identity group, followed by Métis (70 and 77), registered Indians (67 and 74), and Inuit (58 and 69) (Norris et al., 1995).

Geographic Differentials. Life expectancy estimates for the Aboriginal population by place of residence indicate higher life expectancies for urban populations than those for rural or reserve areas. For example, 1991 life expectancy for registered Indians is estimated to be highest in urban areas, at 72.5 and 79 years for males and females, respectively, lower in rural areas (68 and 75), and lowest on reserves (62 and 70) (Norris et al., 1995). Most recent estimates of registered Indian life expectancy, for 1995, by on- and off-reserve are 66.5 and 70.7 for males and 72.4 and 77.3 for females respectively (Loh et al., forthcoming). In a related study assessing the well-being of First Nations (Beaver and Cooke, forthcoming), the authors also demonstrate significant on-/off-reserve differentials in well-being based on selected human development indicators, including mortality, education, and income.

Mobility and Migration

Analyses of census data on mobility and migration suggest that certain patterns and trends in Aboriginal migration[13] have persisted over the past couple of decades (Norris, 1990, 1996). According to data from the past four censuses, 1981 to 1996, Aboriginal people continue to move at a higher rate than the general Canadian population. According to the 1996 census, 53 percent of persons with Aboriginal identity had moved (changed residences) over the past five years (1991–96), compared with 43 percent of all Canadians. Like the rest of Canadians, Aboriginal people are more inclined to move within the same community (defined as non-migrants) than to change communities (defined as migrants). In 1996, 22 percent of the Aboriginal identity populations had moved from one community to another, compared with 20 percent of Canadians. If external migration (from outside Canada) is excluded, then the proportions of movers and migrants in the Canadian population drop 3 percentage points to 40 percent and 17 percent respectively; in contrast, the corresponding proportions for registered Indians remain relatively unchanged at 53 percent and 21 percent respectively, since external migration is a relatively minor component of registered Indian mobility.

Among the four Aboriginal groups (based on identity), total mobility rates (both migrant and non-migrant movers) over the 1991–1996 period were similar for non-status Indians (61 percent), Métis (58 percent), and Inuit (60 percent), but lower for registered Indians overall at 53 percent. Differences in group migration rates (where people changed communities) were more significant, with 27 percent of the more urbanized non-status Indians having migrated, compared with 23 percent of Métis, 21 percent of registered Indians, and only 14 percent of Inuit, the least urbanized of the four groups. While these figures would suggest that registered Indians tend to be less mobile than other Aboriginal populations, an analysis by on- and off-reserve shows that the registered Indian population off-reserve is actually more mobile than both the Métis and non-status Indian populations, as well as the general Canadian population.

By Place of Residence. In general, Aboriginal people who live outside their Aboriginal communities and settlements move to a greater extent than those within their own home communities, and they tend to be more transient than the general population. Census data show that registered Indians living off-reserve tend to move more frequently than either the on-reserve or the general Canadian population (Norris, 1985, 1990, 1996). Higher off-reserve mobility rates suggest a very transient population, perhaps reflecting housing and employment conditions encountered outside Aboriginal communities. This phenomenon is particularly evident among the young. For example, between 1991 and 1996, for every 1000 registered Indian women aged 20–24 living off-reserve, about 840 had moved at some point over the five-year period, compared with about 560 per 1000 among those living on-reserve and 620 for Canadians in general (Figure 7.2). Overall, mobility and migration rates of registered Indians off-reserve (660 and 295 per 1000, respectively) are much greater than the corresponding on-reserve rates (385 and 125) and higher than those for the Canadian population in general (430 and 200), as well as for other Aboriginal groups. The higher mobility and migration rates of the off-reserve Aboriginal population is only partly attributable to movement from reserves and settlements, since they also reflect movement within the same community as well as to and from different communities.

FIGURE 7.2

Age–Sex Specific Mobility Rates for Registered Indians, On- and Off-Reserve, and All Canadians, 1996

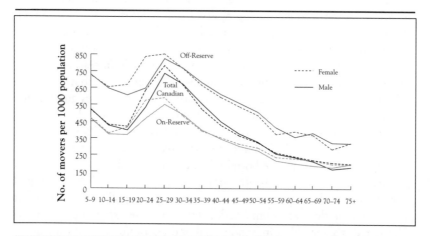

Source: Statistics Canada, *1996 Census,* calculated from unpublished tabulations.

Earlier studies based on 1981 census data (Robitaille and Choinière, 1985; Norris and Pryor, 1984) also showed that in the south, the Inuit and Aboriginal populations in general were more mobile than their counterparts living in northern areas, and at the same time more mobile than non-Aboriginals in the south.

By Age and Sex. Young adults, especially females, tend to be the most mobile in a population, and the Aboriginal population is no different in this respect. Mobility rates follow the standard age pattern for both Aboriginals and all Canadians, decreasing over the school-age years, peaking during the young adult years of 20–29, and then declining fairly steadily thereafter. Young women, particularly those in the 20–24 age group, move and migrate to a greater extent than do their male counterparts (Norris, 1985; 1990; 1996). For example, between 1991 and 1996, among the registered Indian population aged 20–24, 840 per 1000 registered Indian women living off-reserve had moved, compared with 730 for males; similarly, for Canadians, the female rate was higher than that for males (620 versus 510). Some of this gender difference among youth and young adults is attributable to the generally younger ages at marriage of females and their greater participation in and completion of postsecondary education (Tart, 1999), factors that are associated with geographical movement.

One aspect of migration that is characterized by a strong gender differential is the movement to and from reserves. Census data have consistently shown that women predominate in the movement to and from reserves, especially in their out-migration from reserves. The phenomenon of young Indian women leaving reserves to a greater extent than men is similar to, but much more pronounced than, the higher out-migration of women from rural areas among the general population (Norris, 1990). Among youth aged 15–24, 1996 rates of migration from reserve communities are significantly higher for females (125 per 1000) than for males (80). Overall, five-year census out-migration rates for males and females are 70 and 57 per 1000 population on-reserve, respectively.[14]

A number of studies by Gerber (1977), Clatworthy (1980; 1996), and Norris (1985; 1990; 1996) have documented the fact that women are overrepresented in the Aboriginal migrant population, along with younger and female lone-parent families (Clatworthy, 1994). Aboriginal women, especially on reserves, experience push–pull factors in their moves that are different from or additional to those experienced by non-Aboriginal women. Housing and social and economic conditions on reserves are important influences in the decision to migrate. Pre-1985 discrimination against women in the Indian Act would also have been an important factor in on-/off-reserve migration.

Rural/Urban Migration. Aboriginal groups differ not only in their propensity to move or migrate, but also in the types of moves. There are significant differences in rural/urban migration patterns between Aboriginal groups. According to 1991 APS data (data for 1996 still being analyzed), 61 percent of non-status Indian migrants over the 1986–91 period moved between urban areas (63 percent of Canadians in general did so), compared with 36 percent of registered Indians, just half of Métis migrants, and only a quarter of Inuit. In contrast, a third of Inuit migrants had moved between rural communities, compared with only 7 percent of non-status Indians and Métis and 14 percent of registered Indians (for this latter group, reserves are classified as rural for comparison). Migration flows from rural (or reserve) to urban areas accounted for a larger share of registered Indian and Inuit migrants than non-status Indians and Métis. Over the 1986–91 period, both Métis and non-status Indians had relatively small net losses of migrants from urban areas, while registered Indians and Inuit recorded small net gains to urban areas (Norris, 1996).

Migration to and from Reserves. An important aspect of the migration patterns of registered Indians that distinguishes them from other Aboriginal groups is their movement to and from reserves, especially between reserves and cities. Reserves have always been a source of Indian migrants who leave in search of better social or economic opportunities, and since cities are the major destinations of migrants from reserves, they are also the source of the majority of migrants moving to reserves. Between 1991 and 1996, 61 percent of out-migrants from reserves moved to urban areas, while 69 percent of in-migrants to reserves came from urban areas. Over the past five census periods, it appears that both cities and reserves have consistently been the major destinations. Regardless of origin (from reserves or other communities), large cities or urban areas were the major destination for 30 percent of registered Indian migrants in 1996, followed by 28 percent each for reserves and smaller cities, with the remaining 14 percent of migrants moving to non-reserve rural areas (Table 7.2).[15]

Despite the attraction of urban areas, the stream of migration from reserves to cities is smaller compared with the flow from cities to reserves. Overall, nearly three-quarters (73 percent) of registered Indian migrants over the 1991–96 period can be classified into three major flows: urban-to-urban (36 percent), urban-to-reserve (20 percent), and rural-to-urban (13 percent). These proportions are similar to those for the 1986–91

TABLE 7.2

Percentage Distribution of In-Migrants by Place of Destination, Registered Indians, Canada

Place of destination	Selected years				
	1966–71	1976–81	1981–86 (percent)	1986–91	1991–96
Reserve	27	28	30	26	28
Rural	21	16	12	12	14
Urban CMA	26	29	30	35	30
Urban non-CMA	26	27	29	27	28
Urban total	52	56	59	62	57

CMA = census metropolitan area

Source: Statistics Canada, census migration data (1971, 1981, 1986, 1991, 1996), calculated from unpublished tabulations.

period. Flows from reserves to urban areas accounted for only 8 percent of the migration volume. Since the 1970s, registered Indians living on reserves have the lowest rates of out-migration from their communities compared with the registered population in urban and rural areas. Between 1991 and 1996, for every 1000 registered Indians on-reserve, only 64 had migrated out over the five-year period, compared with much higher out-migration rates of registered Indians from small cities or rural communities (about 365 per 1000) and from large urban areas (300 per 1000).

Census data suggest that there has been a consistent net inflow or gain of migrants to reserves, although relatively small in relation to the reserve population. The overall effect of registered Indian migration patterns for the 1991–96 period is a net inflow to reserves of about 13 640[16] migrants and corresponding net outflows or losses of some 5600 migrants from rural areas, 3300 from large cities (urban census metropolitan areas, or CMAs), and 4700 from the smaller cities. Although the major migration flows continue to be between cities and reserves, the impact in terms of net gain or loss of population has been most significant for rural communities and usually least significant for reserves. Rural areas lose registered Indian population largely through migration to urban areas. While small cities have consistently posted small net losses of migrants over the past couple of decades, over the 1991–96 period both small and large cities experienced net losses. Net migration rates by place of residence over the

1991–96 period indicate the extent of the impact of migration on population. The impact was most negative for the rural population, with a net outflow of some 110 migrants per 1000 rural residents, and least negative for large urban metropolitan areas, with a net loss of only 33 migrants per 1000 registered Indians in urban CMAs. For reserves, the only geography experiencing a net inflow of migrants in 1996, the impact was less than rural areas, with a net gain of about 60 migrants per 1000 residents on-reserve (Figure 7.3). Unlike rural and urban areas off-reserve, reserves over the past twenty years have consistently posted net inflows of registered Indian migrants, although relatively small and largely from urban areas (Figure 7.3). Some 40 percent of migrants moving to reserves moved for social or family reasons, and another 25 percent for housing-related reasons (Clatworthy, 1996 and forthcoming). Perhaps the migration of registered Indians from cities to reserves reflects push–pull factors of jobs and housing between cities and reserves, as well as family-related reasons. Unlike most other migrants, especially immigrants, registered Indians usually do have a "home" community, the reserve, to which they can return.

FIGURE 7.3

Five-Year Net Migration Rates by Place of Residence, Registered Indians, Canada, Selected Periods, 1966–71 to 1991–96

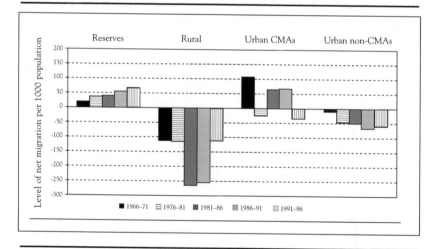

Source: Statistics Canada, census migration data (1981, 1986, 1991 [APS], 1996) calculated from unpublished tabulations; and A.J. Siggner, 1997, "Preliminary Results from a Study of 1966–71 Migration Patterns among Status Indians in Canada," Ottawa: Department of Indian Affairs and Northern Development (1971 census data) (unpublished paper).

Reinstatements and Status Inheritance

The Indian Act's revised legislation (Bill C-31) can affect the population growth of both registered and non-status Indian groups both positively and negatively. Reinstatements have increased the registered Indian population, while decreasing the size of the non-status Indian group, since most of those reinstated are drawn from this latter population (Norris et al., 1996). The second impact of status inheritance on population growth is the set of descent rules, which establish entitlement to Indian status at birth on the basis of out-marriage to non-registered individuals. These rules result in two classes of Indian. In general terms, children born to parents who are both currently registered or entitled to be registered acquire entitlement under section 6(1). Children born to parent combinations involving a parent who is registered or entitled to be registered under section 6(1) and a non-registered parent acquire entitlement under section 6(2). Children of parental combinations involving a non-registered parent and a parent who is registered or entitled to be registered under section 6(2) are not entitled to Indian registration (Clatworthy, 1994, p. 3).

Thus, children who are not entitled to status represent a population loss to the registered Indian group, but a potential gain to the non-status Indian group. However, in terms of the non-status Indian group, it is not certain that all of these persons who are not entitled to registration will necessarily identify with their North American Indian origins in future censuses.

Reinstatements. Close to 105 000 reinstatements of status had occurred by 1996 as a result of the 1985 amendments to the Indian Act. According to the most recent DIAND projections of registered Indians, the annual number of registrants will decline gradually, from about 4000 registrants in 1996 to about 1000 by 2005. The number of registrants is expected to continue to decline to 100 by 2015 and remain constant thereafter for the projection period to 2021 (Loh et al., forthcoming). Consequently, the registered Indian population, through reinstatements, is expected to have gained a grand total of some 128 500 persons by 2016. (Note that the number of potential reinstatements is finite since it is applicable to those persons born prior to April 1985.) It is thought that the non-status Indian population has been and will continue to be the source of most of the reinstated population (Norris et al., 1995; 1996).

Status Inheritance. Bill C-31 births will have a more long-term than immediate impact. The projected impact of Bill C-31 births is based on assumptions about out-marriage and the subsequent assignment of affected births from the registered Indian population directly into the non-status population. The out-marriage rate has a substantial impact on the percentage of people expected to retain status at birth. In the most recent set of DIAND projections, the proportion of births to registered Indian women not entitled to registration, for on- and off-reserve combined, is assumed to increase to 39.5 percent by 2021 (although this could be a high assumption based on more recent data). However, out-marriage rates among the off-reserve population are higher than those on-reserve (57 percent off-reserve compared with 23 percent on-reserve over 1990–95) (Clatworthy, 1997). Correspondingly, the proportion of births not entitled to registration could increase by 2021 to 27.5 percent for the on-reserve population and to 69.1 percent for the off-reserve population (Loh et al., forthcoming).

Ethnic Mobility[17]

Ethnic mobility is the movement of people from one population group to another as a result of changes in ethnic boundaries or changes in the declared ethnic affiliation of people over time. It can be both intragenerational and intergenerational, so that shifts in identity across generations, in addition to fertility and mortality, will affect the future measured growth of Aboriginal groups over the long term.

It can be argued that ethnic mobility is a component of demographic flow and that it can be empirically measured (Goldmann, 1998). Any given population has three dimensions: stock, such as age, sex, size, and composition; location; and flow, generally the result of fertility, mortality, and migration. Populations can be subdivided into groups on the basis of various characteristics (socio-demographic, economic) of the stock. An ethnic group, a type of population group, can be described by its boundaries in relation to other groups at a given point in time.

In the case of Aboriginal groups, boundaries are both externally and internally generated. Internal boundaries are created on the basis of the self-perception of individuals who make up the group, such as Métis or Inuit. The Indian Act creates external boundaries by defining status Indians according to legal criteria, and in the case of the 1985 revisions (Bill C-31), changed those boundaries by redefining who was eligible for registration as a status Indian. The changes in the Indian Act also affect the boundaries of the non-status Indian population. Furthermore, these legally based revisions could affect how individuals self-identify in terms of non-status Indian and Métis.

Analyses of intercensal change by Guimond et al. (forthcoming) demonstrate that changes in Aboriginal populations are due not only to explicit demographic factors such as natural increase but also to ethnic mobility. Consistent with their findings are Aboriginal population projections, which demonstrate that differences between observed (census) and projected populations for 1996 must be due in part to ethnic mobility.

Historical Background

Scholars estimate that at the time of the first European settlement in North America about five centuries ago, the Indian population numbered about 200 000 and the Inuit population numbered about 10 000 (Graham-Cumming, 1967, p. 159). Other estimates (Kroeber, 1939) indicate that before the arrival of Europeans, the total Indian population of North America was about 900 000 people, of whom about 220 000 were in what is now Canada. The advent of the Europeans brought a sharp decline in the Aboriginal population. The effects of war (both international and European), famine (for example, that of 1879–80 on the Prairies [Siggner, 1980, p. 32; 1986b]) and disease (especially tuberculosis) took their toll; by the late 1870s, the Indian population had been reduced to some 80 000 (Graham-Cumming, 1967, p. 159). Other records indicate that shortly after Confederation in 1867, the Indian population was about 102 000 in what is now Canada (Siggner, 1980; 1986b). In the several decades following, the Aboriginal population was relatively stable, fluctuating between that level and about 122 000, which represented from 2.5 to 1.1 percent of the total Canadian population (Siggner, 1980; 1986b).

It was not until the 1940s that the Aboriginal population experienced a significant growth. According to Graham-Cumming (1967), it was around 1940 that Indians were increasing in number at about the same rate as other Canadians, and by the 1960s the Aboriginal population had outstripped other ethnic groups, with a steadily accelerating pace. It reached some 220 000, about the same size as it had been at the beginning of European settlement.

Size and Growth of Aboriginal Populations

In the 1996 census, just over 1.1 million people in Canada reported Aboriginal origins, some 10 percent more than in 1991. About 53 percent of the 1.1 million reported multiple origins — that is, they gave a combination of at least two of the following responses: North American Indian, Métis, Inuit, and non-Aboriginal. About 76 percent (867 200) of respondents with either single or multiple origins reported a North American Indian origin as either the only one (single) or in combination with a non-Aboriginal one, followed by 19 percent (220 700) with Métis origin (single and multiple), and about 4 percent (49 800) with Inuit origin (Table 7.3).

Population counts of Aboriginal groups from 1931 to 1996 censuses based on ethnic origin (ancestry) data are provided in Table 7.3. It should be stressed that the listing of counts for consecutive censuses is not meant to imply comparability from one census to another, and the table provides cautionary notes on their degree of comparability.

For the periods before 1986, a rough assessment of Aboriginal population growth is possible by comparing the 1941 and 1981 censuses, because "both made an explicit attempt to individually enumerate persons of mixed Native (Métis) ancestry" (Statistics Canada, 1983, p. 6). Overall, the Aboriginal population increased by 205 percent during this period, compared with 109 percent for the total Canadian population. Among the different Aboriginal groups, the Inuit had the highest increase (252 percent), followed by the North America Indian population (210 percent) and the Métis (177 percent). Indian Register data also show that between 1971 and 1981 the registered Indian population grew twice as fast as the general population, increasing 27 percent compared with 13 percent for Canada's total population (Perreault et al., 1985). These "relative" growth rates of Aboriginal populations provided by the census data, albeit crude, are corroborated by additional data sources on rates of natural increase of registered Indians and Inuit (Robitaille and Choinière, 1985; Ram and Romaniuc, 1985; Rowe and Norris, 1985). As well, the higher growth rates of Inuit, followed by North American Indian and Métis, tend to reflect the fertility differentials of Aboriginal groups discussed in the earlier section "Components of Growth."

More recent census counts between 1991 and 1996[18] indicate an increase of some 10 percent in the overall population with Aboriginal ancestry, with an increase of only 1.5 percent for single Aboriginal origin responses, compared with a 17 percent increase in multiple responses (Table 7.3). This growth contrasts sharply with the much higher increases observed over the previous 1986–91 intercensal period, which saw the population with Aboriginal origins increase by 41 percent, with increases of 26 and 57 percent, respectively, in single and multiple responses. Clearly, these contrasting rates between two consecutive intercensal periods cannot be explained solely by demographic factors of mortality or fertility, even controlling for differences in incomplete enumeration and undercoverage from one census to another. To some extent, including "Canadian" as an example of an ethnic origin in the 1996 census could have had a dampening effect on the reporting of Aboriginal ancestry and

TABLE 7.3

Census Counts of Aboriginal and Total Canadian Populations, Based on Ancestry, Canada, 1931 to 1996

Census year	Single and multiple responses for Aboriginal ethnic origins	Total Canadian population	Total Aboriginal population	Aboriginal as % of total population	Population of Aboriginal groups		
					North American Indian	Métis	Inuit
1931		10.4	128 900	1.2	n.a.	n.a.	n.a.[3]
1941		11.5	160 900	1.4	118 300	35 400	7 200
1951		14.0	165 600	1.2	155 900	n.a.	9 700
1961		18.2	220 100	1.2	208 300	n.a.	11 800
1971		21.6	312 800	1.5	295 200	n.a.	17 550
1981		24.1	491 500	2.0	367 800	98 300	25 390
1986[1,2]	Single origin	25.3	373 260	1.5	286 230	59 745	27 290
	Multiple origins		338 460[4]	1.3	262 730	91 865	9 180
	Single and multiple combined		711 725[4]	2.8	548 960	151 610	36 470
1991[5]	Single origin	27.3	470 610	1.7	365 375	75 150	30 085
	Multiple origins		532 060[4]	2.0	418 605	137 500	19 165
	Single and multiple combined		1 002 675[4]	3.7	783 980	212 650	49 255
1996[6]	Single origin	28.5	477 630	1.7	394 550	49 800	33 275
	Multiple origins		624 330[4]	2.2	472 670	170 935	16 565
	Single and multiple combined		1 101 960[4]	3.9	867 225	220 740	49 845

(continued)

TABLE 7.3 (*Continued*)

n.a. Not available or not published.

1 Excludes institutional residents.

2 Figures for 1986 exclude population of incompletely enumerated Indian reserves on settlements, estimated at 45 000.

3 Estimate from Robitaille and Choinière (1985) of Inuit population from 1931 census reported to be 6000.

4 Multiple counts by Aboriginal groups include multiple Aboriginal origins, therefore the sum of multiples across Aboriginal groups is greater than total multiples.

5 Figures for 1991 exclude population of incompletely enumerated reserves and settlements estimated at approximately 37 600 (Norris et al., 1995).

6 Figures for 1996 exclude population of incompletely enumerated reserves and settlements estimated at approximately 44 000 (Statistics Canada, *The Daily*, 13 January 1998, cat. no. 11-001).

1931: Includes Native Indian, Inuit, and persons of mixed Native and non-Native ancestry traced on the mother's side.

1941: Includes Native Indian, Inuit, and persons of mixed Native and non-Native ancestry traced on the father's side.

1951, 1961: Includes Native Indian, Inuit, and some persons of mixed Native and non-Native ancestry living on Indian reserves or traced on the father's side.

1971: Includes Native Indian and Inuit only, traced on the father's side.

1981: Includes Native Indian, Inuit, and self-reported Métis, traced through both parents.

1986, 1991, and 1996: Includes North American Indian, Inuit, and Métis, traced through both parents.

Sources: 1931 to 1981: Data and notes from Statistics Canada, 1983, *The Daily*, Table 1, 1 February, cat. no. 11-001; 1986: Statistics Canada, 1987, *1986 Census of Canada — Summary Tabulations of Ethnic and Aboriginal Origins*, Ottawa: Minister of Industry; 1991: Statistics Canada, 1993, *1991 Census*, cat. no. 94-327, Ottawa: Minister of Industry; 1996: Statistics Canada, 1998, *The Daily*, 17 January, cat. no. 11-001; 1996 Census of Population, *The Nation Series*; 1997: *Single Years of Age and Sex*, 29 July, cat. no. 93F0021YDB96000; 1998: *Aboriginal*, 13 June, cat. no. 93F0025XDB96000.

hence growth between 1991 and 1996. However, it seems that ethnic mobility could be a significant component of growth accounting for differentials in intercensal population growth between the 1986–91 and 1991–96 periods. As noted earlier, the sharp increase in the population with Aboriginal ancestry over the 1986–91 period could be related to increased public attention to Aboriginal issues that may have influenced some persons who did not report Aboriginal origins in 1986 to report them in 1991.

Ethnic Mobility Factor in Growth of Aboriginal Ancestry Groups. Among the Aboriginal groups themselves there is significant variation in growth between the two intercensal periods 1986–91 and 1991–96 that again cannot be solely explained by group differentials in fertility and mortality. For example, unadjusted census data suggest that while the growth of the overall Aboriginal population between 1991 and 1996 slowed, the population with multiple Métis origins grew relatively rapidly at 24 percent, compared with a 10 percent increase for North American Indian multiples and a 13 percent decrease for Inuit multiples. In contrast, for single origins, which overall increased by only 1.5 percent, we see that the population with single Métis responses actually declined, while single responses for both the North American Indian and Inuit populations increased by 8 percent and 10 percent, respectively (Table 7.3).

Analyses done by Guimond et al. (forthcoming) that control for various factors[19] affecting comparability among the censuses (1981–86, 1986–91, and 1991–96) demonstrate that explicit demographic forces alone — natural increase and migration — cannot account for the significant variations in growth observed among the three Aboriginal groups. The extraordinary growth in Aboriginal populations observed over the 1981–91 periods "is most likely due to changes in declarations of ethnic origin by individuals," that is, ethnic mobility that the authors suggest "has also contributed to the growth of populations of Aboriginal origin between 1991 and 1996."

The authors suggest that transfers occurred on the part of respondents from a non-Aboriginal origin to an Aboriginal origin, especially over the 1981–91 period. An additional pattern in the phenomenon of ethnic mobility could also be the transfer from one Aboriginal origin to another Aboriginal origin, particularly for the most recent intercensal period. The registered population with North American Indian origins is about 25 percent higher in 1996 than in 1991 and Métis origins about 4 percent higher, whereas the non-status population with North American Indian origins is actually lower by almost 2 percent (Table 7.4). These changes would suggest that the decline in the non-status Indian population along with the increase in Métis multiples noted earlier could be associated with persons who are not registered Indians, perhaps not eligible to be registered, transferring from North American Indian origins in 1991 to Métis origins in 1996.

The following account provides another picture of the size of the Aboriginal groups as defined by Aboriginal identity rather than by ancestry alone.

Aboriginal Identity Population 1986–1991

The identity population represents those persons who consider themselves to be Aboriginal — that is, who identify with one of the major Aboriginal groups (North American Indian, Métis, or Inuit) or who reported themselves as registered under the Indian Act (Statistics Canada, 1993a; 1993c). In 1996 respondents were asked two separate questions, one on ancestry and one on identity. While it might seem intuitive that the Aboriginal identity population would be a subset of the population reporting Aboriginal origins, that is not always the case for various reasons. For example, a respondent might indicate North American Indian and French origins, but indicate Métis identity; or Canadian could be reported as an ethnic origin and North American Indian as an identity; or the respondent is a registered Indian who may or may not have North American Indian ancestry or identity.

Compared with the roughly 1.1 million Canadians who reported Aboriginal origins in 1996, 799 000 persons identified as North American Indian, Métis, or Inuit and/or registered Indian (Table 7.4). (Note that the Aboriginal identity population as defined by Statistics Canada also includes some 19 200 individuals who had no stated identity but were registered Indians or First Nation band members.) Thus for every 100 persons reporting Aboriginal ancestry, there were 73 reporting Aboriginal identity (including registered Indian status and First Nation membership). Of those indicating Aboriginal identity, 97 percent identified with just one Aboriginal group, another 2 percent were either registered Indians or First Nation band members with no identity stated, and about 1 percent identified with more than one Aboriginal group. Identification with more than one Aboriginal group occurred the most among non-status Indians, with about 4 percent identifying with more than one group, followed by 3 percent for Métis. Multiples for both these groups consist of Métis and North American Indian combinations. Perhaps the greater propensity of non-status Indians and Métis to identify with each other's group reflects the fact that Métis can be considered a combination of

TABLE 7.4
Aboriginal Ancestry and Identity Populations by Selected Aboriginal Groups, Canada, 1991 and 1996

Population	North American Indian (NAI)	Registered NAI[1]	Non-status NAI[1]	Métis	Inuit	Other (identity not reported, registered Indian or First Nation member)	Total ancestry and identity
1991	(thousands)						
Ancestry	784.0	357.2	426.8	212.7	49.3	n.a.	1002.7
Identity	460.7	353.0	107.6	135.3	36.2	n.a.	625.7
1996	(thousands)						
Ancestry	867.2	447.9	419.4	220.7	49.8	n.a.	1102.0
Identity	535.1	444.6	90.4	210.2	41.1	19.2	799.0
Registered Indian — Total		488.1					

[1] Data for registered and non-status Indians are based on unadjusted counts derived from 1991 and 1996 census and 1991 APS data. 1991 identity-based counts are from reports on population projections of identity population from Norris et al., 1996; origin-based counts are from unpublished census data on registered and non-status origins, including single and multiple responses. 1996 ancestry- and identity-based counts of registered and non-status Indians are from unpublished census data.

Sources: 1991 published data for North American Indian, Métis, and Inuit: Statistics Canada, 1991 Aboriginal Data, Age and Sex, cat. no. 94-327; 1996 published data: Statistics Canada, 1998, The Daily, 13 January, cat. no. 11-001E.

North American Indian and non-Aboriginal. Also, the degree of inter-marriage with non-Aboriginal persons for non-status Indians and Métis may be greater than that among other Aboriginal groups.

Ethnic Mobility Factor in Growth of Aboriginal Identity Groups. Al-though comparisons between 1991 APS and 1996 census identity popu-lations are limited, the magnitude of the changes suggest, particularly for the Métis and non-status Indians, that ethnic mobility is a major con-tributor to those changes. Between 1991 and 1996 the "comparable Métis population" (1996 identity population with Aboriginal origins) increased dramatically by 38 percent, while the "comparable" non-status population with North American Indian identity decreased by 32 per-cent.[20] This decline in the non-status Indian identity population be-tween 1991 and 1996 could be attributed to a number of factors, espe-cially the reinstatements of non-status Indians to registered Indian, and possibly intercensal changes in identity, perhaps from non-status Indian to either non-Aboriginal or other Aboriginal identity, most likely Métis. Guimond et al. (forthcoming) show that the "adjusted" annual growth rate of the Métis identity population between 1991 and 1996 of 6.7 per-cent exceeds the theoretical (demographic-based) rate of maximum nat-ural increase of 5.5 percent, although the corresponding rate of 2.5 per-cent for the overall identity population was definitely lower. Unlike the Métis, the population with North American Indian identity grew slowly during the 1991–96 period, but well exceeded the theoretical rate of maximum natural increase between 1986 and 1991 (a period of popula-tion explosion). Guimond et al. conclude that people likely changed their declaration of ethnic identity during the 1986–96 period from a non-Aboriginal identity to an Aboriginal identity. It is also possible that per-sons who were not registered Indians may have transferred their identi-ty from North American Indian in 1991 to Métis in 1996. From 1991 to 1996, the lower growth of the overall identity population compared with the high growth of the Métis identity subpopulation suggests that per-haps there is also a shift in ethnic identity within the overall identity population itself from North American Indian to Métis. The Inuit group was the only population with Aboriginal identity that grew at a "demo-graphically" normal rate over the two periods — that is, below the the-oretical maximum rate.

In the case of multiple Aboriginal identities, both the share and size of the adjusted identity population identifying with more than one Aborig-inal group appear to have declined since 1991 from just over 1 percent in 1991 to less than 1 percent in 1996. This could suggest that persons are increasingly inclined to identify with just one Aboriginal group.

Aboriginal Ancestry by Aboriginal Identity. The 1996 census data on Aboriginal ancestry can be cross-classified by the identity respondents reported for registered Indian and non-registered Indian populations separately and combined. The data show while 53 percent of those declaring Métis identity had reported Métis ancestry, 25 percent had indicated North American Indian origins, 12 percent no Aboriginal origins, and the remaining 10 percent multiple Aboriginal ancestry. In contrast, only 5 percent of the non-status population identifying as North American Indian had indicated Métis ancestry. Only 22 percent of some 350 000 non-status persons with a combination of North American Indian and non-Aboriginal ancestries identified with an Aboriginal group or were band members. Among this identity population with mixed Indian and non-Aboriginal ancestry, a significant percentage, nearly 42 percent, identified as Métis, while 58 percent identified as North American Indian. In contrast, 88 percent of registered Indians reporting mixed Indian and non-Aboriginal ancestries indicated North American Indian ancestry, while only 8 percent identified as Métis. The remaining 4 percent did not report an Aboriginal identity. Among 132 000 persons reporting mixed Métis and non-Aboriginal ancestries, close to half (49 percent) reported an Aboriginal identity, with practically all (97 percent) of this identity population indicating a Métis identity. These patterns suggest that persons with North American Indian ancestry who are not registered Indians may be more "fluid" in their identity (in that a significant proportion identify with Métis) compared with registered Indians or persons with Métis ancestry.

Patterns of Identity

The following analysis of Aboriginal origin and identity data suggests that some patterns of identification observed by age and residence are similar between 1991 and 1996, although clearly the ratio of identity to ancestry populations has changed for some Aboriginal groups. Only a basic comparison between origin and identity population can be undertaken here — a more accurate and complete picture would require detailed cross-classification of the identity population by ethnic origin by selected characteristics, such as age and gender, for which the reader is referred to Guimond et al. (forthcoming).

Identity by Aboriginal Group. Some caution is required when comparing and interpreting patterns of identity by Aboriginal group between 1991 and 1996 due to the limitations of comparability noted earlier (especially that identity and ancestry are independent in 1996) and the fact that the census data are unadjusted for incomplete enumeration and undercoverage. Nevertheless, the main purpose here is to assess the basic patterns of identity by selected characteristics and Aboriginal ancestry group, by age, sex, region, and place of residence based on the ratio of the population with Aboriginal identity to the population with Aboriginal ancestry. For example, for Canada in 1996 the population declaring Métis identity was 210 200, while the population reporting Métis ancestry was 220 740, yielding a ratio of 95 persons with Métis identity for every 100 persons with Métis ancestry. Similarly, for 1991 the Métis identity and ancestry populations of 135 300 and 212 700, respectively, yield an identity/ancestry ratio of 64 persons with Métis identity for every 100 persons with Métis ancestry. In the case of a selected characteristic, such as age, identity/ancestry ratios can also be calculated. For example, in 1996 among youth aged 15 to 24, there were 97 persons with Métis identity for every 100 persons with Métis ancestry, compared with 22 persons with North American Indian identity without registered Indian status for every 100 persons, also non-status, reporting North American Indian ancestry. For both 1991 and 1996 those with registered Indian status are automatically included, by definition, in the Aboriginal identity population, mostly in the North American Indian identity category.

The identity/ancestry ratios illustrate not only the variation in Aboriginal groups, but also the dramatic changes in identity between 1991 and 1996, especially for the Métis (Table 7.5), reflecting the effect of ethnic mobility. In 1991 the Inuit group had the highest ratio of identity to origin population, with 74 Inuit persons per 100 persons reporting Inuit ancestry, followed by Métis, with a ratio of 64 Métis per 100 persons reporting Métis ancestry. Census and APS data suggest that identification with Aboriginal ancestry varies by Aboriginal group, such that the Inuit identity population represents the highest proportion (74 percent) of its corresponding origin population, followed by Métis (64 percent) and North American Indian (60 percent). In 1996, while the ratios were higher for both groups, the opposite pattern was observed, with the Métis group showing the highest identity/origin ratio of 95 Métis for every 100 persons reporting Métis ancestry and the Inuit having a corresponding ratio of 82. In the case of the North American Indian group, there was relatively little change between 1991 and 1996. Since those with registered Indian status are automatically included, by definition, in both the 1991 and 1996 identity populations and mostly in the North American Indian category, the identity/ancestry ratios of 60 and 62, respectively, for North American Indians overall would indicate lower ratios among non-status Indians. The estimated ratio of non-status persons with North

TABLE 7.5

Ratio of Aboriginal Identity Population to Aboriginal Origin Population, by Selected Age Groups and Sex, 1991[1] and 1996

Age groups and sex	Total Aboriginal		Total North American Indian		Non-status Indian		Métis		Inuit	
			(number of persons with identity per 100 with ancestry)							
	1991	1996	1991	1996	1991	1996	1991	1996	1991	1996
0–4	66	74	62	65	31	25	65	89	81	85
5–14	65	74	61	65	29	23	66	92	81	85
15–24	64	73	61	63	25	22	62	97	74	83
25–34	59	70	55	60	22	19	64	93	69	80
35–54	57	68	54	56	22	19	61	96	62	77
55+	67	80	65	66	24	24	66	111	71	82
Males	62	73	59	62	25	22	64	96	72	83
Females	63	72	61	61	26	21	63	93	75	82
Both sexes	62	73	60	62	25	21	64	95	74	82

[1] 1991: Ratios reflect adjustments for incomplete enumeration of reserves and settlements in the APS identity population for approximately 20 000 respondents who were enumerated in the 1991 census but not the APS. For comparability, these respondents were removed from the Aboriginal origin population, by age and sex, in order to calculate percentages for the affected populations.

Sources: 1991: Calculated from Statistics Canada, 1991 Aboriginal Data: Age and Sex, cat. no. 94-327, Ottawa: Minister of Industry, Science and Technology, 1993; unpublished 1991 census tabulations for non-status and registered Indians. 1996: 1996 census unpublished tabulations on ancestry and identity.

American Indian identity to the non-status population with North American Indian ancestry was only 25 in 1991 and even lower at 21 in 1996.

As a consequence of these intercensal changes in identity, the composition of the identity population in 1996 has seen an increase in the proportion of Métis and a decrease in the share of North American Indians since 1991, with the Inuit share remaining more or less stable. Also, compared with the ancestry population, the 1996 census data show that the Métis constitute a disproportionately higher share of the identity population at 26 percent compared with 20 percent of ancestry, while the North American Indian share of identity is lower, at 67 percent versus 78 percent.

Identity by Age and Sex. Patterns of identity by age and sex have generally stayed the same between 1991 and 1996, although the ratio of identity populations to ancestry populations has increased. With respect to age, the identity/ancestry ratios tend to be higher in the older (55+) and younger (less than under 25) age groups, and lowest among adults in the 35–54 age groups (Table 7.5). Perhaps the greater propensity of youth and seniors to identify with their Aboriginal origins reflects the current revival among youth in awareness of their Aboriginal origins and the increased and traditional importance of elders as a source of community strength. In terms of gender, there appears to be no overall significant difference between males and females in their identity patterns, although further analysis by age could reveal gender differences.

Identity by Region. The regional comparisons between Aboriginal identity and ancestry populations based on unpublished 1996 census data suggest that persons in western and northern Canada identify with their Aboriginal origins to a greater extent than those in eastern Canada. In 1996 the ratio of identity to ancestry populations was highest, at close to one, in the territories, such that their respective identity and ancestry populations were almost the same. Ratios were also close to one in Saskatchewan (95) and Manitoba (93), with high concentrations of Métis populations, followed by Alberta (79) and British Columbia (76). In eastern Canada, there were just about half as many people with Aboriginal identity compared with persons with Aboriginal ancestry (Ontario, 57; Atlantic, 53; and Quebec, 50). Some of this regional variation may be associated with differences in residential (rural/urban, on- and off-reserve) and Aboriginal group composition and could also be influenced by the size, awareness, and cohesion of regional Aboriginal groups. The higher ratios in the Prairies compared with Ontario could be related to possible differences between

the "historical" Prairie Métis and Métis elsewhere in Canada in identifying with their Aboriginal ancestry.[21] Also, to some extent the way colonization occurred, from east to west, probably affects the regional variations in the ratio of identity to ancestry populations.

Identity by Rural/Urban and On-/Off-Reserve Place of Residence. Data
from the 1991 census and APS and the 1996 census show that identity
with Aboriginal groups overall tends to be higher in reserve and rural
areas than in urban areas, and notably higher on reserves due to the largely registered Indian population that by definition comprises the identity
population. Even those who are not registered but living on-reserve would
be more likely to identify with their Aboriginal origins, a reflection of the
role of largely rural Aboriginal communities in maintaining Aboriginal
identity. In 1996, for every 100 persons with Aboriginal ancestry in rural
areas, there were 68 persons with Aboriginal identity compared with a
corresponding ratio of 63 in urban areas, the contrast being most pronounced for Inuit with corresponding ratios of 91 and 66. However, there
are some variations to this pattern: among the non-status population,
while 21 persons identify with North American Indian origins for every
100 in both rural and urban areas, the corresponding ratio on-reserve is
twice as high at 41. In other words, non-status persons residing on-reserve
are more likely to identify as North American Indians than in off-reserve,
rural, or urban areas. Clearly these patterns of residential identity point to
the role of Aboriginal communities in maintaining Aboriginal identity.

Share and Distribution of Ancestry and Identity Populations

Although Aboriginal populations make up a small proportion of Canada's
total population, those proportions have been steadily increasing (see
Table 7.3, p. 192). The share of population with Aboriginal origins increased from 1.4 percent in 1941, to 2.0 percent in 1981, to 3.7 percent in
1991, to 3.9 percent by 1996, while the population with Aboriginal identity increased from 2.3 percent in 1991 to 2.8 percent in 1996 (based on unadjusted counts).[22] Proportions of provincial or territorial populations that
report Aboriginal ancestry or identity vary considerably across Canada. In
1996, 62 percent of the population in the Northwest Territories and
21 percent of the Yukon population had Aboriginal ancestry, while the
provinces with the highest proportions were Manitoba and Saskatchewan
— around 12 percent — followed by Alberta and British Columbia (5 to
6 percent). In central and eastern Canada, Aboriginal shares were lower
at around 2 to 3 percent, with the exception of Newfoundland (and
Labrador) with 4.5 percent. (Proportions for Aboriginal identity are sim-

ilar to, but lower than, those observed for the Aboriginal ancestry population.)

As in previous censuses, 1981 to 1991, Ontario claimed the largest number of people in 1996 with Aboriginal ancestry, followed by British Columbia and Alberta. Moreover, just over one in five (22 percent) Canadians who reported Aboriginal origins in 1996 resided in Ontario. Together, British Columbia (17 percent) and Alberta (14 percent) accounted for nearly a third of Canada's Aboriginal population, while another 23 percent resided in Manitoba and Saskatchewan combined. Quebec's share was 13 percent, while the Atlantic region had 6 percent, the Northwest Territories 3.6 percent, and the Yukon 0.6 percent. To some extent the regional distribution has shifted from 1991 such that shares of the Aboriginal population for Quebec, Ontario, and Alberta have declined, while those for Atlantic Canada, Manitoba, and Saskatchewan have increased, a reflection in part of the relatively high increase of the population with Métis ancestry.

For both 1991 and 1996, the regional distribution of the identity population differs from that of the origin or ancestry population. Differences in their regional distributions are accounted for by regional variations in Aboriginal group composition and identity. Ontario has the largest shares of both populations; its share of Canada's identity population at 18 percent is smaller than its 22 percent share of the ancestry population. In contrast, Manitoba and Saskatchewan together account for nearly 30 percent of the identity population, compared with just 23 percent of the ancestry population reporting Aboriginal origins. As with the ancestry population, there has been a shift since 1991 in the regional distribution of the identity population such that shares for Ontario, Quebec, and Alberta have declined, while those for the Atlantic region and British Columbia have increased.

Rural/Urban Distribution

A significant proportion of Canada's Aboriginal people continue to reside in rural reserves and settlements for a variety of social, economic, and political reasons. Even though they experience a high degree of geographic mobility, it is not surprising that the concentration of Aboriginal people in rural and urban areas is much different from that of the general population. In 1996, 57 percent of the population with Aboriginal origins lived in urban areas compared with about 78 percent of the nation's population. Moreover, among those who identified with an Aboriginal group, only half (49 percent) resided in urban areas (Table 7.6). (Since figures are not adjusted for incomplete enumeration of reserves and settlements,

TABLE 7.6

Population Distribution and Sex Ratios, by Place of Residence,[1] Aboriginal and Total Canadian Populations, Canada, 1996

Population	Percentage distribution of total population			no. of males per 100 females			Sex ratios
	Reserve	Rural	Urban	Reserve	Rural	Urban	Total
	%	%	%				
Aboriginal							
Origin	22.5	21.0	56.5	106.6	99.4	90.1	95.5
Identity	31.6	19.8	48.6	106.0	100.0	89.4	95.8
Identity population by group							
North American Indian	48.3	12.2	43.4	106.5	93.3	85.9	95.5
Registered Indian	52.6	9.9	37.4	106.4	89.0	82.0	94.8
Non-status Indian	3.6	23.5	72.9	116.1	102.9	96.5	98.6
Métis	n.a.[2]	33.2	66.9	n.a.	105.2	95.9	98.8
Inuit	n.a.[2]	73.4	26.6	n.a.	105.5	88.0	100.3
Other (registered Indian or band member with no identity)	12.1	19.4	68.6	68.1	63.2	68.8	67.6
Total Canadian population	n.a.[2]	22.4	77.6	n.a.[2]	104.8	95.1	97.1

[1] Distribution and ratios based on data not adjusted for undercoverage and incomplete enumeration of reserves and settlements. Percentages of populations residing on-reserve, particularly for registered Indians, are underestimated, and correspondingly, percentages off-reserve are overestimated.

[2] For Métis and Inuit, as well as the general Canadian population, residency on reserves and settlements is classified under rural place of residence. Canadian population in general, Métis and Inuit residents on reserves and settlements, have been classified under rural areas.

Source: Statistics Canada, 1996 census, calculated from unpublished tabulations.

on-reserve percentages are underestimated and off-reserve percentages are overestimated.) Among the groups with Aboriginal identity, the non-status Indian population had the highest proportion, 73 percent, residing in urban rural areas, followed by 69 percent of persons who did not report identity but who were registered Indians or members of an Indian band or First Nation. The majority of Métis (67 percent) also resided in urban areas, compared with only 37 percent of registered Indians and 27 percent of Inuit (see Table 7.6).

On-/Off-Reserve Distribution

An important dimension of the geography of North American Indians, particularly for registered Indians, is the distinction between residence on- and off-reserve. Data from the 1996 census indicate that 48 percent of registered Indians live on-reserve, but this is an underestimate since this figure does not reflect adjustments for undercoverage and incomplete enumeration of reserves and settlements. While adjusted 1996 census data were not available at the time of writing, the real percentage could be closer to 60 percent based on DIAND's 1996 Indian Register and ad-justed 1991 census data.[23] Register data from INAC show a decline in the proportion on reserves since the 1960s (from 85 percent in 1966 to 72 percent by the mid-1970s, stabilizing at around 70 percent during the late 1970s and early 1980s) along with higher proportions of women than men living off-reserve. The share on-reserve dropped to some 60 percent after 1985 due largely to the revision of the Indian Act. Under the amendments to the Indian Act the overwhelming majority (about 84 per-cent) of the close to 105 000 persons who were reinstated between 1985 and 1996 lived off-reserve (Loh et al., forthcoming). Given that the In-dian Act amendments affected mostly non-status Indian women and their children, the reinstated population has been characterized by a majority of women, at least in the early years. In 1987, inclusion of reinstated In-dian women lowered the overall proportion of registered Indian women on-reserve from 69 percent to 62 percent.

Age–Sex Structure

Age Structure

As the contrasting pyramids in Figure 7.4 clearly demonstrate, Canada's Aboriginal ancestry and identity populations have a much younger age structures than the overall Canadian population — a reflection of higher Aboriginal fertility. The Aboriginal population pyramid is much wider at the base, representing the younger ages, and narrower at the middle and old ages, whereas the Canadian pyramid is more rectangular. In 1996, the median age of the Aboriginal identity origin population was 25.5 — 10 years younger than the average of 35.4 years in the general population (Statistics Canada, 1998a). Children under 15 accounted for close to 34 and 35 percent of the overall Aboriginal ancestry and identity populations, respectively, compared with only 21 percent of Canada's total population. In contrast, the proportions of the Aboriginal ancestry and identity Aboriginal populations 55 years of age and over are only 7.5 and 8.3 percent, respectively, compared with 20 percent for the general population. While the age distribution of the identity population is fairly similar to that observed for the Aboriginal ancestry population, the identity population has slightly higher shares of children and seniors, with correspondingly lower shares in the 25–54 age groups.

FIGURE 7.4

Percentage Distribution by Age Group and Sex of Total Canadian, Aboriginal Ancestry, and Aboriginal Identity Populations, Canada, 1996

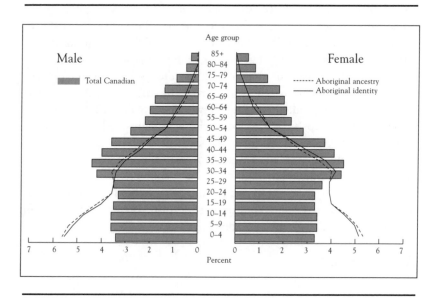

Note: Aboriginal and total Canadian populations have not been adjusted for undercoverage. The Aboriginal populations have not been adjusted for incomplete enumeration of reserves and settlements.

Source: Statistics Canada, 1996 census, calculated from unpublished tabulations.

The differences in age structure among Aboriginal groups reflect their fertility differentials. The Inuit clearly have the youngest age structure, with 41 percent of their identity population under 15, followed by 36 percent for both registered and non-status Indians with North American Indian identity, and only 31 percent of the Métis identity population. It is interesting to note that the registered Indian and band or First Nation members who have no stated identity are a significantly older population than the rest of the identity population, with only 27 percent children.

Given that Aboriginal fertility has been declining, the Aboriginal population is shifting to an older one, although still a younger structure than the Canadian population in general. For example, the rise in median age of DIAND's Register population from 16.5 years in 1971 to 19 in 1981 (Nault et al., 1993), reaching 24 years by 1996 (Loh et al., forthcoming), indicates an aging trend. In comparison, the median age among the total Canadian population rose from 26 in 1971 (Statistics Canada, 1994b, p. 2) to 35 by 1996 (Loh et al., forthcoming). It should also be noted that to some extent ethnic mobility and legislative components can affect aging. For example, status inheritance through intermarriage reduces the proportion of births to registered Indians who are eligible to be registered, thereby lowering the share of children in the population.

Sex Ratios

As with the Canadian population in general, women outnumber men in the Aboriginal population as a whole, with 96 men for every 100 women.[24] However, for the Inuit the opposite is true, although the phenomenon of males outnumbering females has been levelling off with the steady decline in Inuit sex ratios from 105 in 1981 to 100 in 1996 (Table 7.6). The group that exhibited the most atypical sex ratios of only 68 males per 100 females were those registered Indians and First Nation members who did not identify — a group that is also older and mostly urban. Perhaps this disproportionately female population includes those non-Aboriginal women who had earlier gained registered status through intermarriage prior to the 1985 revisions to the Indian Act. Also in 1996 males continue to outnumber females in rural areas for all Aboriginal groups, while the converse is true in urban areas — a phenomenon that occurs among non-Aboriginal populations as well. For registered Indians, the comparison is more pronounced between on-reserve (106) and urban areas (82). Residential differences in sex ratios could be explained by factors such as male–female differentials in migration (e.g., higher rates of female out-migration from reserves) and residential differences in patterns of mortality, fertility, and intermarriage, phenomena that can alter the overall balance between the sexes in the Aboriginal population.

Aboriginal Population Projections

Projections can provide Aboriginal leaders, policy-makers, and program analysts with crucial information on Aboriginal populations: what their future size, growth, group composition, and residential and regional distribution across Canada are likely to be over the next ten or twenty years. Projections represent the future trends that Aboriginal populations are likely to follow if underlying assumptions about growth components and the role they play with respect to demographic (fertility, mortality, migration) and legislative (reinstatements, status inheritance) factors prove to be correct. A critical aspect of projections is that they provide a profile of what the age–sex structure of future Aboriginal populations will look like in 25 years as the population ages. Clearly the reliability of projections of the population with Aboriginal ancestry or identity is vulnerable to future fluctuations in responses to ethnic origin and identity over time, which are difficult to predict. Three sets of Aboriginal projections referenced here that were prepared by Statistics Canada are census- and APS-based projections (1991–2016) for Aboriginal ancestry and identity groups, respectively, and the DIAND projections for registered Indians (1996–2021) based on the Indian Register.[25]

Projected Population Growth and Structure

In terms of future growth, both ancestry and identity projections suggest significant overall increases of about 50 percent (medium assumption) over the 25-year period from 1991 to 2016, a reflection of the still relatively high fertility levels in Aboriginal populations. By 2016 the populations with Aboriginal ancestry and identity are projected to be about 1.6 and 1.1 million, respectively (medium assumption) (Table 7.7). The more recent projections of registered Indians over the 1996–2021 period projected under a medium growth scenario also yield a significantly high increase in population of 46 percent.

Annual growth rates of populations with Aboriginal identity and ancestry are generally projected to decline steadily throughout the projection period, due in large part to declining fertility assumptions. In the case of the registered Indian population, the declining trend can also be attributed to the expected decrease in reinstatements and the negative impact of status inheritance rules (Loh et al., forthcoming).

TABLE 7.7

Total Populations with Aboriginal Identity or Aboriginal Ancestry, by Aboriginal Total and Group, by Selected Projection, Canada, 1991, 1996, 2001, and 2016

	Population projections					
	1991 Ancestry-based			1991 Identity-based		
	Slow growth	Medium growth	Rapid growth	Slow growth	Medium-low growth[1]	Rapid growth
Year			(thousands)			
1991[2]	1084.0	1084.0	1084.0	720.6	720.6	720.6
1996	1186.7	1192.7	1196.8	810.9	811.4	818.4
2001	1274.6	1295.0	1208.9	887.9	890.5	914.4
2016	1515.3	1615.8	1681.1	1071.3	1093.4	1207.1

[1] Current trends with migration.
[2] 1991 base populations of projections have been adjusted for incomplete enumeration and undercoverage.

Source: S. Loh, 1995; M.J. Norris, D. Kerr, and F. Nault, 1996.

Age and Sex Structure

All three sets of projections suggest that after 25 years of population change, the age structure of Aboriginal populations will be quite different, shifting to an older population under the continuation of current trends. For example, for the registered Indian population over the 1996–2021 period, the proportion of young people aged 0–18 will decline from 41 to 28 percent, while both the labour force and the elderly (age 65+) age groups will increase from 55 to 63 percent and from 4 to 9 percent, respectively (Loh et al., forthcoming). In comparison with the 1996 age and sex pyramid of the Aboriginal population in Figure 7.4 (p. 206), the one projected for 2016 in Figure 7.5 is generally narrower at the base and wider at the middle and older ages. The evolution of the age structure from a pyramidal to a rectangular shape reflects the aging process. By 2016, the age structures of both the Aboriginal and total Canadian populations will be quite different, with both populations aging due to declining fertility and mortality levels. But Aboriginal and Canadian populations are experiencing different patterns of aging. The Aboriginal population is aging from youth into the older labour force age groups, so that by 2016 69 percent of the population will be aged 15–64, with most of the growth occurring in the 35–64 age group. The total Canadian population will be aging from working age into the retirement age groups. The median age of the population with Aboriginal identity (around 22 in 1991) is expected to reach 30 by 2016, that of the registered Indian group about 32 by 2021 — still younger than the current (1996) Canadian median age of 34, projected to be 40 by 2016. The age structures of the two populations will still differ by 2016, but not as sharply as for 1991.

Various factors, including aging, higher male mortality in later life, residential migration patterns, status inheritance,[26] and reinstatements, will affect the future sex ratios of Aboriginal populations. For example, the Inuit sex ratio is expected to decline from males outnumbering females at 104 males per 100 females in 1991 to 97 males per 100 females by 2016 (Norris et al., 1995). Sex ratios of registered Indians are also projected to become more balanced on-reserve, declining to 102 by 2021, and increasing off-reserve to 97 (Loh et al., forthcoming).

The comparison of the projected age–sex structure of the Aboriginal population for the year 2016 with the total Canadian populations of 1991 and 1996 (Figure 7.5) provides some perspective on how the future structure of the Aboriginal population will evolve. Its structure in 2016 will be much more similar to that of the Canadian population today than it is now — it will be more rectangular in shape and more concentrated in working age groups. Although the future (2016) age structures of most Aboriginal groups are expected to approach the current (1996) Canadian population, they will still be somewhat younger.

Demography, Ethnic Mobility, and Legislation: Implications for Population Growth

Components of growth are critical in defining and determining not only the current, but also the future, size and composition of Aboriginal populations in Canada. In developing projections of Aboriginal groups, assumptions are usually developed explicitly about the demographic and legislative factors. But ethnic mobility has not been explicitly projected as a component of growth; rather, assumptions have been generally implicit that respondents will be consistent in reporting their origins or identity from one census to another and from one generation to the next. But clearly, ethnic mobility has been a significant component in past intercensal growth and likely will continue to be in the future — and should therefore be a recognized factor in future growth — although to

FIGURE 7.5

Projected Age and Sex Structure of the Population with Aboriginal Identity, 2016, and Current Structure of Total Canadian Population, 1991 and 1996, Canada

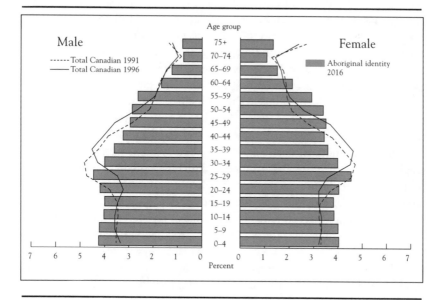

Sources: Aboriginal identity population: M.J. Norris et al., 1996; Total Canadian population: Statistics Canada, 1991 and 1996 census, calculated from unpublished tabulations.

project shifts in declarations of Aboriginal ancestry or identity in future censuses would be difficult.

Impact of Components of Growth Vary by Aboriginal Group

The impact of each component of growth, be it demographic, legislative, or related to ethnic mobility, varies by Aboriginal group such that some groups are more or less affected by a particular component, or even not at all. In analyzing both the past and future size and growth of Aboriginal groups, the impact of each component and its related aspects should be considered. Table 7.8 provides for each Aboriginal group a summary of the different components of growth and four related aspects: measurement, impact on population growth, degree of certainty, and interplay among other components and Aboriginal groups. The aspect of measurement considers whether there are direct or indirect measures of the component or if measurements must be inferred (e.g., fertility is a direct measure for registered Indians, but must be estimated for non-status and Métis groups; the extent of ethnic mobility can only be roughly inferred from demographic analysis). The second aspect refers to the positive or negative impact of that component on population growth of the Aboriginal group (e.g., reinstatements are positive for growth of registered Indians, but negative for non-status Indians). A third consideration is the degree of certainty associated with the component in terms of the actual size of its impact on future or even on past growth. For example, one can be relatively certain about the impact of reinstatements on the future growth of the registered Indian population, but less certain about the extent to which status inheritance will impact on registered Indians, and even less for non-status Indians, particularly the identity population. The demographic impact of status inheritance is difficult to predict because of exogamy and the future identification of children who are offspring of mixed marriages. The fourth aspect is the effect of one component on one Aboriginal group, such as status inheritance of registered Indians, or that same component's impact for other groups, such as Métis and non-status Indians.

A demographic analysis of the projected growth of the population with Aboriginal identity over the 1991–96 period yields basically the same conclusions about ethnic mobility as the analyses of past trends, both unadjusted and adjusted (Guimond et al., forthcoming). A comparison of 1996 projected populations with 1996 census data suggests that factors other than demographic components have affected the projected growth of the Métis and non-status Indian identity groups.[27] The finding that the Métis identity population counts from the census were significantly higher compared with the demographically projected populations for 1996 is also consistent with Guimond et al.'s conclusion concerning the unusually high 1991–96 growth of the Métis. In contrast, the unadjusted 1996 census counts of non-status Indians with North American Indian identity are lower than 1991 census counts and, of course, 1996 projected figures. The large increases in the Métis population along with the sharp decline in the non-status identity population — neither of which were projected — could be associated with the "in-mobility" of transfers to a Métis identity from persons in 1991 with previous non-Aboriginal or non-status Indian identities. Conversely, the decrease in the non-status Indian group could have occurred due to the "out-mobility" of persons transferring from a North American Indian identity to a Métis identity between 1991 and 1996, as well as to an outflow of reinstated persons to the registered population.

TABLE 7.8

Components of Growth Affecting Size and Growth of Aboriginal Groups in Canada: Measurement, Predictability, and Impact on Growth

Components of growth	Aboriginal identity and ancestry groups			
	North American Indian (registered)	North American Indian (non-status)	Métis	Inuit
Demographic				
Fertility Major component. Positive impact of births on growth for all groups. Generally can be projected within reasonable range of certainty.	Direct estimates of fertility available from DIAND Register, with adjustments for late and underreporting of births. Affected negatively by status inheritance (outflow of births from registered Indians not eligible for status).	No direct fertility measures — must be estimated from combined DIAND and census data on fertility (e.g., children ever born data). Could be positively affected by gain of births through status inheritance.	No direct measures — must be estimated from combined DIAND and census data. Possibly affected by status inheritance if non-status descendants of registered Indians identify as Métis.	Direct measures for some regions of Inuit population, but not all. Indirect estimates based on census data. Not affected by legislative component.
Mortality Major component. Negative impact of deaths on growth for all groups. Generally can be projected within reasonable range of certainty.	Direct estimates of mortality available from DIAND Register, with adjustments for late and underreporting of deaths.	No direct measures — must be estimated from combined DIAND and census data (e.g., proxy based on relationship between education and health).	No direct measures — must be estimated from combined DIAND and census data.	Direct measures for some regions of Inuit population, but not all. Indirect estimates based on census data.

(continued)

TABLE 7.8 (*Continued*)

	Aboriginal identity and ancestry groups			
Components of growth	North American Indian (registered)	North American Indian (non-status)	Métis	Inuit
Demographic				
Migration (internal) Direct estimates available for census-based groups. Affects growth either positively or negatively; currently not a major determinant of growth. Can affect age-sex composition by residence. Generally more uncertain to project than fertility or mortality.	Direct estimates from census-based counts of registered Indians — no Register-based counts from DIAND. Trends indicate consistent but small net inflow to reserves. Currently not a major component of growth, on- or off-reserve.	Direct estimates from census-based counts of non-status Indians for identity and ancestry groups. Does not appear currently to be major component of urban/rural growth — can affect regional distribution.	Direct estimates from census-based counts of Métis for identity and ancestry groups. Does not appear currently to be major component of urban/rural growth — can affect regional distribution.	Direct estimates from census-based counts of Inuit for identity and ancestry groups. Can affect regional distribution. Inuit have lowest migration rates of all groups.
Legislative — Indian Act				
Reinstatements Direct estimates available from DIAND. Has been significant component for registered Indians. Can be projected with some certainty.	Direct data from DIAND. Significant component, positive impact of reinstated persons on growth, but future impact expected to decline as number of reinstatements decline. Can be projected with relative certainty for registered Indians.	Impact is negative — most of reinstated come from non-status Indians. But difficult to determine extent of outflow by identity and ancestry for non-status Indians. Future impact will decline.	Impact is minor and negative, but some of the reinstated population has come from the Métis groups. Not significant for future growth.	Reinstatements are not a factor — do not affect growth of Inuit population.

(continued)

TABLE 7.8 (*Continued*)

		Aboriginal identity and ancestry groups		
Components of growth	North American Indian (registered)	North American Indian (non-status)	Métis	Inuit
Legislative — Indian Act				
Status inheritance Estimates for future impact based on assumptions about intermarriage, therefore difficult to predict and not studied. Could be major component, especially off-reserve.	Estimates of impact based on estimates of intermarriage, on- and off-reserve. Expected to have increasing negative impact on population, especially off-reserve, as percentage of births not eligible for status due to intermarriage increases.	Potential impact is positive due to inflow of births to registered Indians not eligible for status. Difficult to project, especially for non-status Indian identity. Depends on future identity declarations of persons ineligible to register.	Possible impact is positive due to inflow of births to registered Indians not eligible for status. Difficult to project impact, especially by identity and ancestry — depends on if any non-status descendants of registered Indians identify as Métis.	Status inheritance is not a factor — does not affect growth of Inuit population.
Ethnic Mobility[1]				
From non-Aboriginal to Aboriginal Change over censuses in individual's declaration of identity and ancestry difficult to measure and anticipate. To some extent can be inferred from demographic analysis. Impact can be positive or negative.	Legal definition changed by revision to Indian Act (Bill C-31), which changed ethnic boundaries for those previously not eligible for status. Perhaps prior to reinstatements some individuals did not declare Aboriginal affiliation.	Ethnic mobility may have been significant factor in past for growth of ancestry group of non-status Indians, especially between 1986 and 1991.	Analyses of census and projection data suggest that ethnic mobility affects growth that cannot be explained by demographic/legislative components alone, suggesting inflows from non-Aboriginal to Métis, 1991–1996 (Guimond et al., forthcoming).	Analyses of census and projection data indicate transfers over the census of respondents' declaration of ancestry/identity from Aboriginal to non-Aboriginal not a factor.

(continued)

TABLE 7.8 (Continued)

Components of growth	North American Indian (registered)	North American Indian (non-status)	Métis	Inuit
		Aboriginal identity and ancestry groups		
Ethnic Mobility[1]				
Between Aboriginal groups Difficult to measure and anticipate. Perhaps some transfer between non-status Indian and Métis identity.	Legal definition changed by revision to Indian Act (Bill C-31), which changed ethnic boundaries for those previously not eligible for status. Perhaps prior to reinstatements some individuals had different Aboriginal affiliation.	In case of identity population, perhaps among non-status Indians there could have been outflow from North American Indian identity to Métis. Possible negative impact on growth.	Analyses of census and projection data suggest ethnic mobility at play — perhaps some inflow from non-status North American Indian identity. Possible positive impact on growth.	Same as above — appears to be no significant transfer from other Aboriginal groups to Inuit.

[1] Aspects of this component are based on analyses from Guimond et al., forthcoming.

In relation to the component of ethnic mobility, it is also important to consider the impact of status inheritance.[28] The identity of those offspring of registered Indians who are not eligible for registered status will become more crucial as their numbers rise. According to the most recent DIAND projections, over the next 25 years (1996–2021) some 83 000 births to registered Indian women will not be entitled to registration. How will these persons who do not have status, but nevertheless are immediate descendants of registered Indians, identify themselves in future censuses? Will they automatically identify with their North American Indian origins? Or will some choose to identify as Métis? Will others not identify at all but only indicate North American Indian ancestry? Clearly, the status inheritance rules and rates of intermarriage have the potential to affect not just the registered Indian population, but also the size and composition of the non-status and Métis populations.

The projection of Aboriginal populations is complex and challenging, involving not only demographic components but also their interplay with components of legislation and ethnic mobility. However, despite the unknowns posed by ethnic mobility and legislation, particularly for non-status Indian and Métis groups, we can be fairly certain about some demographic trends in Aboriginal populations over the next 25 years. These include the fact that the Aboriginal population is aging from the youth age groups into the labour force age groups because of declines in mortality and fertility; as well, although growth rates are relatively high, they will continue to decline. However, the Aboriginal population is growing faster than the Canadian population in general due to higher fertility levels, so the Aboriginal share of the Canadian population will continue to increase, especially among the young, assuming current immigration levels.

LINGUISTIC PROFILE

Aboriginal Languages: Background

Language remains a critical component in maintaining and transmitting Aboriginal culture and identity. Language reflects a unique worldview specific to the culture to which it is linked. While loss of language doesn't necessarily lead to the death of a culture, it can severely handicap transmission of that culture. But language is not only a means of communication — it is also a symbol of group identity to the extent that language and identity are often inseparable.

The variety in Aboriginal culture and identity is reflected in Canada's Aboriginal languages, which are many and diverse. Today, some 50 individual languages belong to 11 Aboriginal language families — 10 First Nations and Inuktitut. Most families consist of separate but related member languages (e.g., the Algonquian language family consists of individual languages such as Cree, Micmac, Blackfoot, and Algonquin). Each individual language can have separate dialects. For example, within the Cree language, there are several dialects, including Swampy Cree, Woods Cree, and Plains Cree.

The range in the size of the eleven Aboriginal language families in Canada is considerable. In terms of mother tongue populations, the largest family by far is the Algonquian language group. According to the 1996 census, there were 147 000 persons in the Algonquian mother tongue population, whereas corresponding counts of the smallest families, such as Haida or Tlingit, contain a few hundred persons or less. In 1996, the three largest families — Algonquian, Inuktitut (28 000), and Athapaskan (20 000) — represented 93 percent of persons with an Aboriginal mother tongue. The other eight language families account for the remaining 7 percent, an indication of their small relative size.

Geography is an important contributor to the diversity, size, and distribution of Aboriginal languages across Canada's regions. For example, the diversity of languages in British Columbia, most of them small in population, are likely the outcome of the province's mountainous geography, which would impose physical barriers to communication. In addition, given plentiful resources, it may not have been as necessary to move for resources, such as for hunting in the case of the more widespread Algonquian and Athapaskan populations. The population bases of the Salish, Tsimshian, Wakashan, Haida, and Kutenai languages in British Columbia were never as widely dispersed as Algonquian and Athapaskan languages that developed in the more open central plains and eastern woodlands (Priest, 1984; Grubb, 1979). The present-day geographic distribution of these languages reflects the different cultural areas of First Nations and Inuit. The languages with the largest numbers of mother tongue population also tend to be widespread, such as the Algonquian family of languages extending from the Atlantic to the Rockies.

Endangered State of Aboriginal Languages

The use and survival of Aboriginal languages are clearly major issues for indigenous people in North America. UNESCO's *Atlas of the World's Languages in Danger of Disappearing* indicates that a large number of Eskimo and Amerindian languages in North America are in danger of disappearing or are moribund: "[T]he fate of the original Indian languages is, with very few exceptions, the worst in the world" (UNESCO, 1996, p. 23). Many of Canada's Aboriginal languages are endangered and have already suffered great losses. At the time of European contact, there were probably many more languages spoken in Canada, as well as in North America in general.[29]

As for any other minority language, the forces of modernization and dominant languages can be erosive. For Aboriginal languages in particular, historical factors such as the discouragement of Aboriginal language use in residential schools served to rupture the transmission of language from one generation to another. Also, the fact that most Aboriginal languages were predominantly oral may have affected their chances of survival.

According to 1996 census data, only a small proportion of the Aboriginal population speaks an Aboriginal language. While in 1996 some 800 000 persons claimed an Aboriginal identity, only 207 000 (26 percent) said an Aboriginal language was their mother tongue (or first language learned). Even fewer, 145 000 (18 percent), used an Aboriginal language in the home, implying that learning an Aboriginal mother tongue does not, in itself, guarantee continued use. On the other hand, some 239 000 (30 percent) had knowledge of an Aboriginal language; that is, they could speak and understand an Aboriginal language well enough to conduct a conversation. Clearly, then, while some people shift from an Aboriginal to another home language, others may be either learning indigenous languages later in life or beginning to use the language later on that they learned in childhood.

Critical Factors and Considerations for Language Survival

Population Size and Intergenerational Transmission. Among Canada's Aboriginal languages, only 3 out of some 50 languages have sufficiently large population bases to ensure survival over the long term, since the more speakers there are the greater the chances of survival. Cree, Inuktitut, and Ojibway, the largest, most widespread, and most flourishing of Aboriginal languages, have significantly large mother tongue populations of 87 600, 25 900, and 27 800, respectively. As well, these languages are highly likely to be passed on to the next generation, as indicated by high continuity indexes that measure the ratio of home language speakers to the population with that particular language as a mother tongue. Inuktitut has a relatively high continuity index of 86 persons speaking Inuktitut at home for every 100 with an Inuktitut mother tongue, followed by continuity indexes of 72 and 55 for Cree and Ojibway, respectively. The state of these three languages can be classified as viable.

In sharp contrast, many of the smaller languages, often with far fewer than 1000 speakers, especially in British Columbia, have very low prospects for continuity and can be considered endangered. For example, as of 1996, there were only 240 persons with a Haida mother tongue, and the continuity index is only 6. Even the larger languages in British Columbia, such as Nishga, with a mother tongue population of 800 persons, have low chances for passing the language on to the next generation, with only 24 persons speaking Nishga at home for every 100 persons with a Nishga mother tongue.

The use of a language at home has important implications for the prospects for transmission to the next generation, and hence for its continuity. A language no longer spoken at home cannot be handed down as a mother tongue to the younger generation. Even with only a few thousand people, some of the smaller languages elsewhere in Canada appear viable when home usage is taken into account. For example, Attikamek in Quebec has a mother tongue population of only 4000 persons, but a continuity index of 97 persons speaking Attikamek at home for every 100 persons with an Attikamek mother tongue. Clearly, the prospects for transmitting Attikamek to the next generation are high.

Thus, even though some languages with some 1000 or more speakers are relatively small, they can be considered viable if their prospects for continuity are high. For example, languages such as Attikamek, Montagnais-Naskapi, Micmac, Dene, and Dogrib are considered viable. These languages tend to be spoken in isolated or well-organized communities with strong self-awareness. In these communities, language is considered one of the important marks of identity (Kinkade, 1991).

Languages with Young Populations. The average age of those who have an Aboriginal mother tongue or speak it as a home language indicates the extent to which the language has been transmitted to the younger generation. The higher the average age, the relatively fewer young people have learned or still understand the language and the older the people who still speak it. If the language is not transmitted to the younger generations, then as these older persons continue to age and then die, so will the language. Viable languages such as Attikamek, Inuktitut, and Dene are characterized by relatively young mother tongue populations (average ages between 22 and 24 years) and corresponding high indexes of continuity (between 86 and 97). In contrast, the endangered languages such as Haida, Kutenai, and Tlingit have typically older mother tongue populations (average ages between 40 and 65) combined with extremely low continuity indexes of 20 or less.

In general, the population with an Aboriginal mother tongue is older than the overall Aboriginal population, so older persons are more likely to have an Aboriginal mother tongue than younger generations. In 1996, only 20 percent of children under 5 had an Aboriginal mother tongue. In comparison, 60 percent of those 85 years and over and 30 percent of those aged 40 to 44 had an Aboriginal mother tongue (Figure 7.6).

Language Erosion during Transition from Youth to Labour Force. Analysis of past census data (1981–96) shows that the use of an Aboriginal language at home relative to the mother tongue population is related to stages in the life cycle. For example, the decline in home language usage is significant as youth leave home and enter the labour force, marry, start families, or move to a larger urban environment. Language loss is most

FIGURE 7.6

Percentage of Aboriginal Population with Aboriginal Mother Tongue by Age Group and Sex, Canada, 1996

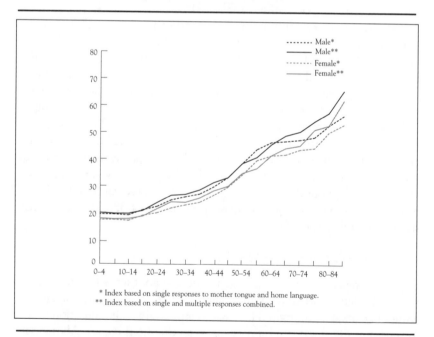

* Index based on single responses to mother tongue and home language.
** Index based on single and multiple responses combined.

Source: 1996 census, unpublished tabulations from M.J. Norris, 1998, "Canada's Aboriginal Languages," *Canadian Social Trends*, 51(Winter). Statistics Canada, Cat. no. 11-008.

pronounced during the labour force years, especially for women. Contributing factors could be the fact that women are more likely than men to leave their reserves and move to other locations where the chances of marrying non-Aboriginals are higher and exposure to the dominant language is much greater (Norris, 1998).

Language and Aboriginal Group Identity

In 1996, practically all (99 percent) of the populations with an Aboriginal mother tongue or home language or knowledge of Aboriginal languages (98 percent) reported an Aboriginal identity. About three out of every four Aboriginal persons with an Aboriginal mother tongue are registered Indians, which is disproportionately higher than their 55 percent share of the identity population. Furthermore, while registered Indians residing on-reserve account for 29 percent of the Aboriginal identity population, their share of the population with an Aboriginal mother tongue is twice that at 58 percent. Similarly, the Inuit represent just 5 percent of the identity population, yet they account for 13 percent of the Aboriginal mother tongue population (Table 7.9).

Clearly, the reserve environment of registered Indians and the northern communities of the Inuit tends to support the maintenance and transmission of Aboriginal languages. In 1996, 52 percent of registered Indians living on-reserve and 67 percent of Inuit (most of whom live in northern communities) reported an Aboriginal mother tongue, compared with only 18 percent of off-reserve registered Indians, 6 percent of non-status Indians, and 7 percent of Métis. Similarly, registered Indians and Inuit have the highest ratio of Aboriginal language use in the home among all groups, with continuity indexes of 80 and 85, respectively. In contrast, non-status Indians and Métis, who tend to live off-reserve and are more scattered throughout urban areas, as well as off-reserve registered Indians, have lower home language–mother tongue ratios of 58, 50, and 40, respectively (Table 7.9).

Language Maintenance and Identity

Language transmission from one generation to another is the major factor in Aboriginal language maintenance. Unlike other minority language groups in Canada, Aboriginal languages cannot rely on immigration flows for maintaining the population of speakers. (While there are Aboriginal languages in the United States, some of which are common to both Canada and the United States, census data show that the flows of Aboriginal people from the United States are not significantly large.) Like other minority languages, Aboriginal languages today are subject to many of the

TABLE 7.9

Aboriginal Identity Population by Aboriginal Group, Aboriginal Mother, and Selected Aboriginal Language Indicators, Canada, 1996

Identity population by Aboriginal group	Total population with Aboriginal identity		Identity population with Aboriginal mother tongue (single and multiple responses)		% of Population with an Aboriginal mother tongue (single and multiple responses)	Index of continuity for home language/ mother tongue (single and multiple responses)
	Population	% Distribution	Population	% Distribution		
Total Aboriginal	799 010		207 280		26	70
Registered Indian	444 645	55	158 655	76	36	70
On-reserve	233 990	29	121 255	58	52	79
Off-reserve	210 660	26	37 395	18	18	39
Non-status Indian	90 435	11	5 120	2	6	58
Métis	210 190	26	14 290	7	7	50
Inuit	41 085	5	27 640	13	67	85
Other identity	19 215	2	2 130	1	11	54
Sum of groups	805 575	100	207 830	100		

Source: Statistics Canada, 1996 census, calculated from unpublished tabulations.

same forces, such as more dominant languages and modernization, that contribute to the decline in their use.

The motivation to maintain or revive an Aboriginal language can be best understood by considering the communicative and symbolic functions of language. In cases where the group may be shifting from its ancestral language to the dominant language, the Aboriginal language may no longer be used as the main form of communication, but it still remains an important symbol of the group's identity. Thus, the loss of a language implies not only the loss of an instrument of communication but also the loss of a symbol of identity. "Hence, the motivation to revive the ancestral language is not communication, since the dominant language fulfils that need, but stems from the desire to revive or protect a tangible emblem of group identity" (RCAP, 1996, p. 612).

Language Maintenance and Revival: Recommendations from RCAP

Language maintenance refers to the steps necessary to ensure that intergenerational transmission can be maintained for those viable languages in communities where the Aboriginal language is still both the mother tongue and the main language of communication.

Revitalization applies to languages that are effectively endangered in communities that are undergoing a shift to the dominant language. To revitalize a language, the capacity to transmit it from one generation to the next must be restored. It is not enough to increase the number of second-language speakers; it is also necessary to increase the number of first-language speakers and to restore the transmission of that language from one generation to the next.

Thus, the transmission of Aboriginal languages from older to younger generations is the critical factor in the evolution of Aboriginal languages. In its recommendations concerning the revitalization of Aboriginal languages, the Royal Commission on Aboriginal Peoples indicated that intergenerational transmission is best effected through use of an Aboriginal language in everyday life in the home and in the community — formal instruction alone is not enough. Once intergenerational transmission is ensured, then language usage can be extended into work, higher education, and government. "[T]he continual exposure to the dominant language and the necessity to use it in every facet of daily life is a powerful catalyst for the decline of the Aboriginal language" (RCAP, 1996, pp. 614–17).

To conclude, Aboriginal languages, whether viable or endangered, serve not only as tools of communication but also remain important symbols of cultural and group identity. Language maintenance and revival are critical if currently viable languages are to continue to be transmitted from one generation to the next and if endangered languages are to survive.

CONCLUSION

This demographic and linguistic profile of Aboriginal people demonstrates that they continue to remain distinct from the rest of the Canadian population. The Aboriginal population continues to be a much younger and faster-growing population, with fertility and mortality levels significantly higher than the overall Canadian levels. Unlike the rest of the Canadian population, the majority of Aboriginal people live in rural or reserve areas. Once off-reserve or away from their own communities, Aboriginal people, especially young adults, move or migrate to a greater extent than Canadians in general. As well, Aboriginal women continue to leave their reserves and rural communities at higher rates than Aboriginal men. Unlike most Canadians, Aboriginal people are confronted with the issue that many of their languages are endangered and nearing extinction, with only one in four Aboriginal-identity persons reporting an Aboriginal language as the mother tongue.

Demographic and linguistic differences also exist among Aboriginal groups themselves. To a large extent, these group differences stem from the extent to which the group's population resides in Aboriginal communities — on reserves or in rural settlements, and in urban areas. Within the Aboriginal population, we see that the extent to which people declare an Aboriginal identity varies across age, sex, region, and residence, as well as by Aboriginal group. Compared with the population with Aboriginal origins, the identity population has higher fertility, is less urbanized, tends to be concentrated more in Aboriginal communities, and accounts for practically all of the population with an Aboriginal mother tongue or home language.

As we move to the future, we can see that issues confronting Aboriginal people will change over the next two decades simply by virtue of changing demographics. Population projections clearly show the impact of declining fertility and mortality levels on the aging of the Aboriginal population overall. The most significant change due to aging is the projected increase in the number of working-age Aboriginal people, which is expected to represent close to 70 percent of the Aboriginal population by 2016. At the same time, while the share of the Aboriginal population aged 65 or older is projected to increase to about 7 percent, this share will be considerably lower than the 16 percent share of seniors projected for the Canadian population by 2016 (Statistics Canada, 1994a). Although both the Aboriginal and Canadian populations are aging, they are experiencing different patterns. The Aboriginal population is aging from youth to working age, while the Canadian population overall is aging into retirement (Frideres, 1993, p. 143).

The implications of aging for the Aboriginal population are most pronounced for the growth of the working-age population and what that suggests in terms of the growing importance of education and job training for the future. Unemployment is already high among the Aboriginal population, and clearly the projected increase of people with Aboriginal identity or ancestry in the labour-force age groups is an issue that must be addressed by Aboriginal leaders and policy-makers alike.

In terms of assessing both current and projected populations of Aboriginal groups, it is clear from the preceding analysis that the size and composition of Aboriginal populations are affected not only by demographic and legislative components but also by the significant factor of ethnic mobility. Demographic analyses of census data and projection data suggest that changes in individuals' declaration of identity and ancestry from one census to another has significantly affected the size and growth of Aboriginal groups, such as the Métis between 1991 and 1996. Thus, today's populations of Aboriginal groups already represent a complex interplay of demographics, legislation, and identity. Both census- and projection-related analyses, as well as Aboriginal identity patterns by ethnic origin, point to some important questions about ethnic mobility, anticipating how and why respondents self-identify in future censuses and how ethnic mobility plays a role in projected growth. Obviously, many factors and implications are associated with the future growth of each Aboriginal group. Not only current demographic differentials but legislation and future patterns of group identity as well will ultimately determine the size and composition of Aboriginal populations over the next few decades.

NOTES

1. The views expressed in this chapter are those of the author and do not necessarily represent the views of Statistics Canada. I would like to acknowledge with thanks the following people from Statistics Canada for their contributions to this paper: to Gerry Ouellete and Lucette Delloso for their technical assistance, to reviewers Gustave Goldmann and Eric Guimond for their valuable comments, and to Robert Riordan for editing parts of this paper. I am also grateful for comments received from the following people in the De-

partment of Indian Affairs and Northern Development: Don Bearon, Victoria de la Ronde, Pierre Gauvin, and Rebecca McPhail.

2. The author gratefully acknowledges Dr. John Flood, director and general editor of Carleton University Press, for permission to use excerpts of this article.

3. In all censuses except 1891, which did not include questions dealing with the ethnic or racial origins of the population (Goldmann, 1993).

4. Canadian vital statistics data on births and deaths are not compiled by ancestry or ethnicity of individuals.

5. Unofficial estimates of Métis and non-status Indians toward the end of the 1970s varied from 350 000 to 1.5 million persons (Kralt, 1990, p. 19).

6. The exclusion of institutional residents from the census count of registered Indians could be a significant factor in relation to the comparability with the Register count, since Aboriginal people represent a disproportionately high share of institutional residents.

7. For example, "[S]ome respondents may not have reported being registered under the Indian Act because of a lack of understanding/familiarity with the wording of a question or because of some objection to its terminology" (Statistics Canada, 1993a, p. 28).

8. "For example, the revisions of the Indian Act in 1924 and 1951 had an impact on how the Aboriginal people were classified in the census" (Goldman, 1993, p. 2).

9. Unlike migration within Canada, which is known as "internal migration," "external migration" (migration to and from Canada) is not considered a significant component of growth for the Aboriginal population.

10. This paragraph is based on Norris (1990).

11. Age–sex standardized to 1981 population of Canada.

12. Estimates of life expectancy for Aboriginal groups by place of residence were developed in relation to previously established registered Indian life expectancy using education — the level of schooling attained — as a proxy (Norris et al., 1995 and 1996).

13. These migration patterns and trends are based on those respondents who self-reported as an Aboriginal person or registered Indian. Excluded from these analyses are the populations of "potential" Aboriginal or registered Indian persons not included in the census for a number of reasons: incomplete enumeration of reserves and settlements, undercoverage, homelessness, institutional residence, or their choice not to report as an Aboriginal or registered Indian, on- or off-reserve.

14. It should be noted that some of the gender differential in census-based out-migration data could also be attributed in part to gender differentials in three areas: undercoverage (missed population) in census (especially in the young adult age groups), since there is higher undercoverage for adult males; population missed in institutions, especially young male Aboriginal offenders; and possibly differences in self-reporting on Aboriginal/registered Indian census questions.

15. Some caution is required in comparing migration data over time, because the population of registered Indians is not directly comparable over census periods in terms of concepts and measurement (see the earlier section on data sources, quality, and comparability). To some extent, the share of in-migrants to reserves may be understated as a destination, particularly for 1986 on, due to the fact that incompletely enumerated reserves are not represented in the current destination, although they are in the origin as place of residence five years ago.

16. If incompletely enumerated reserves and settlements that are not available for the destination (since they were not enumerated) are not removed as place of residence (origin) five years ago, then the calculation of net inflow to reserves decreases to 12 400 (without the inflow to incompletely enumerated reserves).

17. This section draws almost exclusively from Goldmann, 1998.

18. Unadjusted for incomplete enumeration and undercoverage.

19. In their analysis, the authors control for differences in incomplete enumeration and shifting definitions and consider questionnaire changes over the censuses that could affect reporting of Aboriginal origins.

20. For the Métis, Siggner et al. (1998) estimated that the comparable Métis populations, based on the Aboriginal identity populations that have at least some Aboriginal origins, would be 128 500 in 1991 and about 177 565 in 1996 — a significant 38 percent increase. While Siggner and Guimond did not provide similar adjustments for the non-status Indian population, comparable figures can be roughly estimated. The non-status population that identified with North American Indian origins numbered about 90 425, of whom 17 300 did not report Aboriginal ancestry. Comparison with 1991 APS leaves a non-status Indian population of 73 125, significantly lower (32 percent) than the 1991 APS-based (unadjusted) estimate of 107 600 non-status Indians.

21. In his discussion on who is a Native, Frideres notes the distinction made between "historical Métis" and "pan Métis." The historical Métis, who live predominantly in the Prairies, tend to be more established in terms of Aboriginal title, whereas the pan Métis are dispersed throughout Canada without Aboriginal title (Frideres, 1993, p. 43).

22. Adjustments for undercoverage and incomplete enumeration of reserves and settlements would yield slightly higher shares. For example, the 1991 shares of ancestry and origin rise to 3.9 and 2.6 percent, respectively, when so adjusted (adjusted data for 1996 were not available at time of writing).

23. The 1991 census data adjusted for undercoverage and incomplete enumeration indicated that 58 percent of the registered Indian population lived on reserves and settlements, similar to DIAND's Register proportions of about 60 and 58 percent in 1990 and 1996, respectively.

24. The ratio of males to females varies significantly by Aboriginal group and place of residence.

25. Projections of Aboriginal ancestry groups are based on the 1991 census origin data and were prepared for the Employment Equity Data Program (Loh,

1995). Projections of the Aboriginal identity populations are based on the 1991 APS data and were prepared for the Royal Commission on Aboriginal Peoples (Norris et al., 1995 and 1996). Projections of the registered Indian population are based on the Indian Register and were prepared for DIAND (Loh et al., forthcoming). Note that the population bases of registered Indians of the DIAND Register and the census differ — both the identity and Register projections include the component of status inheritance, while the ancestry projections do not.

26. Status inheritance could affect overall sex ratios by altering age structure such that excess male mortality at older ages would be a greater or lesser factor in the overall sex ratio.

27. While the projection and census data are not directly comparable for the same reasons affecting comparability between 1991 and 1996 censuses, they do provide some idea of the impact of non-demographic factors. Comparability with ancestry group projections is somewhat more difficult and not undertaken here due to special definitions making groups mutually exclusive.

28. In the case of the non-status Indian group, it is possible that a greater percentage of reinstatements to the registered population are being sourced from its identity population than projected, such that the size of the identity population decreased more than anticipated due to reinstatements. Also, growth of the non-status Indian group could be overestimated if over the longer term some individuals born to registered Indians but not eligible for registration choose to identify as Métis and not North American Indian as assumed.

29. For example, languages such as Beothuk, Huron, Petun, Neutral, and St. Lawrence Iroquoian have been extinct for well over 100 years. In the past century, other languages have disappeared, including Pentlatch (Salish), Tsetsaut (Athabaskan), Nicola (Athabaskan), and Comox (Salish), the latter having one speaker left by 1990 (Kinkade, 1991).

DISCUSSION QUESTIONS

1. What are your ethnic origins or ancestry? To which ethnic or cultural groups do you trace your ancestry? Do you identify with any or all of your origins? Has your self-identity changed over time, and if so, why?

2. What factors — such as awareness of Aboriginal origins, place of residence (large cities, Aboriginal communities, region), age and gender, use of an Aboriginal language, history and size of an Aboriginal group — do you think play the most significant role in the extent to which people identify with an Aboriginal group? Why?

3. In 1991, half of the Aboriginal population was under the age of 22, while half of the Canadian population in general was under the age

of 34. By 2016, it is expected that half of the Aboriginal population
will be under the age of 30. As the Aboriginal population shifts from
youth into the working-age groups over the next 25 years, what impact do you think this could have on the issues facing Aboriginal people?

4. Aboriginal people, especially youth, who live outside reserves, settlements, or other Aboriginal communities, tend to move or migrate to
a greater extent than the general population, as well as their own
counterparts in Aboriginal communities. Why do you think this is so?

5. Many of Canada's Aboriginal languages, such as Haida, are endan-
gered, while some are still viable, even relatively small ones such as
Montagnais–Naskapi. The three largest and most viable are Cree,
Ojibway, and Inuktitut. What do you think are important factors for
ensuring the survival of Aboriginal languages? What role do you see
Nunavut playing in the future prospects for Inuktitut dialects?

FURTHER READINGS

Beavon, D. and Martin Cooke. Forthcoming, 2000. *Measuring the Well-
Being of First Nation Peoples.* Ottawa: Research and Analysis Directorate, Department of Indian and Northern Affairs. This study assess-
es the well-being of First Nation peoples using the methodology of the
Human Development Index as developed by the United Nations Development Programme. By using the HDI, this study compares Aboriginal peoples to the rest of Canada and to other countries; examines
regional, gender, and on-/off-reserve differences; and examines trends
over time in order to see whether the disparity gap between Aboriginal peoples and the rest of Canada is widening or narrowing.

Clatworthy, S.J. 1997. *Implications of First Nations Demography.* Prepared
by Four Directions Consulting Group, for Research and Analysis Directorate, Department of Indian and Northern Affairs Canada. This
report provides an overview of recent trends in First Nations demography and an assessment of some of the main implications for First Nation communities and populations and the Department of Indian Affairs and Northern Development that are expected to result from
demographic changes in the short (1996–2000) and medium
(2001–10) terms. The study's main findings concern demographic
trends and their implications for health, social welfare, education,
housing, infrastructure, and local economy. As well the study provides

a forward-looking analysis of First Nation membership issues in combination with registered Indian status and the implications for descendants of registered Indians who are neither members of a band nor entitled to be registered.

Clatworthy, S.J. Forthcoming, 2000. "Factors Influencing the Migration of Registered Indians Between On- and Off-Reserve Locations in Canada." Prepared for the Research and Analysis Directorate, Department of Indian and Northern Affairs Canada. Using data collected by the 1991 Aboriginal Peoples Survey and the 1991 and 1996 Censuses of Canada, this study explores several aspects of the migration patterns of registered Indians during the 1986–91 and 1991–96 time periods. The report contains descriptive analyses of census data that document the characteristics of migrants and in-, out-, and net-migration flows for various geographical areas (including provinces, reserves, and rural and urban off-reserve areas) over both time periods. Statistical models based on 1991 APS data explore the contribution of selected factors to registered Indian migration between on- and off-reserve locations. Factors considered in the models include various personal attributes, as well as characteristics of migrant origin and destination communities.

Guimond, E., N. Robitaille, A.J. Siggner, and G. Goldmann. Forthcoming. *Aboriginal Peoples in Canada: A New Demographic Perspective*. Census Monograph Series. Ottawa: Statistics Canada. This analysis focuses on the demography of Aboriginal peoples in Canada, namely Indians, Métis, and Inuit. In order to gain a proper understanding of population change over time, the concepts used to operationally define Aboriginal peoples and collection methods are explored in the various data collection vehicles. The authors provide an extensive review of the terminology that has been used to define Aboriginal peoples. The study looks at all aspects of demographic change, including fertility, mortality, and migration. In addition, "cultural transfer or ethnic mobility" is analyzed, especially in terms of its impact on population change. The study also presents some socio-economic characteristics of Aboriginal peoples.

Kinkade, M. Dale. 1991. "The Decline of Native Languages in Canada." Pp. 157–76 in *Endangered Languages*, ed. Robert H. Robins and Eugenius M. Uhlenbeck. Published with the Authority of the Permanent International Committee of Linguists (CIPL). Oxford: Berg. This article is recommended for a most useful overview of the history and diversity of

Aboriginal languages. It contains a comprehensive documentation of Canada's Aboriginal language families, languages and dialects, and distribution across Canada, and also whether they are found in the United States. The author provides a useful classification system of Aboriginal languages in terms of their viability, ranging from extinct, to near extinction, endangered, viable but with small populations, and viable with large populations.

Loh, S., R. Verma, E. Ng, M.J. Norris, M.V. George, and J. Perreault. Forthcoming. *Population Projections of Registered Indians, 1996–2021.* Ottawa: Population Projections Section, Demography Division, Statistics Canada. This report for the Department of Indian Affairs and Northern Development represents the most recent set of Aboriginal population projections. The report discusses the projection methodology, base populations, assumptions, and results for registered Indians using the Indian Register. Projections are based on adjusted population, birth, death, and reinstatement data from DIAND's Indian Register as well as data from the 1996 census. As well, the projection incorporates the impact of the revised act's inheritance rules on eligibility or entitlement to be registered.

Norris, M.J. 1998. "Canada's Aboriginal Languages." *Canadian Social Trends* 51 (Winter), Statistics Canada, Cat. no. 11-008. This report explores which of Canada's Aboriginal languages are flourishing and which are in danger of disappearing. It incorporates a demographic analysis that examines the factors that differentiate viable languages from endangered ones, such as the average age of speakers and the use of a language in the home. In addition, it compares language use patterns between 1981 and 1996 to understand what happened to Aboriginal languages over the years, and what the future may hold for them in terms of transmission to the next generation. The article uses data from the 1981 to 1996 censuses as well as the 1991 Aboriginal Peoples Survey.

Ponting, J. Rick, ed. 1997. *First Nations in Canada: Perspectives on Opportunity, Empowerment, and Self-Determination.* Toronto: McGraw-Hill Ryerson. This book presents a comprehensive view of the social and political issues that First Nations still encountered in the 1990s as they empowered themselves in their journey toward self-determination. Its contributions represent a diversity of First Nation experiences concerning elders, chiefs, and educators, and the efforts of First Nation women to stop family violence. A wide range of issues is covered, including self-government, Nunavut, healing, residential schools, justice, and racism, along with a discussion of demographic trends. The volume closes with a discussion of the report of the Royal Commission on Aboriginal Peoples.

REFERENCES

Bobet, E. and S. Dardick. 1995. "Overview of 1992 Indian Health Data." Document, Medical Services Branch, Health and Welfare Canada. January.

Boxhill, W. 1984. "Limitations to the Use of Ethnic Origin Data to Quantify Visible Minorities in Canada." Working paper, Housing, Family and Social Statistics Division, Statistics Canada.

Canada, Department of Indian Affairs and Northern Development (DIAND). 1997. *Information: Definitions*. Ottawa: DIAND. November.

Clatworthy, S.J. 1980. "The Demographic Composition and Economic Circumstances of Winnipeg's Native Population." In *Indian Demographic Workshop: Implications for Policy and Planning*. Ottawa: Department of Indian Affairs and Northern Development and Statistics Canada.

———. 1994. "Revised Projection Scenarios Concerning the Population Implications of Section 6 of the Indian Act." Prepared by Four Directions Consulting Group, Winnipeg, for Research and Analysis Directorate, Department of Indian and Northern Affairs, Ottawa.

———. 1996. "The Migration and Mobility Patterns of Canada's Aboriginal Population." Prepared for the Royal Commission on Aboriginal Peoples. Ottawa: Canada Mortgage and Housing Corporation, and the Royal Commission on Aboriginal Peoples.

———. 1997. "Implications of First Nations Demography." Final Report prepared by Four Directions Consulting Group, Winnipeg, Manitoba, for the Department of Indian Affairs and Northern Development.

———. Forthcoming. "Factors Influencing the Migration of Registered Indians Between On- and Off-Reserve Locations in Canada." Prepared for the Research and Analysis Directorate, Department of Indian and Northern Affairs, Canada.

Drapeau, L. 1995. "Perspectives on Aboriginal Language Conservation and Revitalization in Canada." Research study prepared for Royal Commission on Aboriginal Peoples.

Frideres, J.S. 1993. *Native Peoples in Canada: Contemporary Conflicts*. Scarborough, Ont.: Prentice-Hall.

Gerber, L.M. 1977. "Community Characteristics and Out-Migration from Indian Communities: Regional Trends." Paper presented at the Department of Indian Affairs and Northern Development.

———. 1984. "Community Characteristics and Out-Migration from Canadian Indian Reserves: Path Analysis." *Canadian Review of Sociology and Anthropology* 21(2): 145–65.

Goldmann, G. 1993. "The Aboriginal Population and the Census: 120 Years of Information — 1871 to 1991." Paper presented at the 22nd General Population Conference of the International Union for the Scientific Study of Population, Montreal, 24 August–1 September 1993.

———. 1994. "The Shifting of Ethnic Boundaries, Causes, Factors and Effects." Master's thesis. Ottawa: Carleton University.

———. 1998. "Shifts in Ethnic Origins among the Off-spring of Immigrants: Is Ethnic Mobility a Measurable Phenomenon?" *Journal of Canadian Ethnic Studies* 30(3): pp. 121–48.

Graham-Cumming, G. 1967. "Health of the Original Canadians, 1867–1967." *Medical Services Journal Canada* 23(2): pp. 115–66.

Grubb, D. 1979. "Languages of British Columbia." In *The Languages of Canada*, ed. J.K. Chambers. Montreal: Didier.

Guimond, E., A. Siggner, N. Robitaille, and G. Goldmann. Forthcoming. *Aboriginal Peoples in Canada: Demographic Perspectives*. Census Monograph Series. Ottawa: Statistics Canada.

Harris, J. and R. McCullough. 1988. *Health Indicators Derived from Vital Statistics for Status Indian and Canadian Population, 1978–1986*. Ottawa: National Health and Welfare. September.

Jarvis, G.K. and M. Boldt. 1982. "Death Styles among Canada's Indians." *Social Science and Medicine* 16: 1345–52.

Kinkade, M. Dale. 1991. "The Decline of Native Languages in Canada" in *Endangered Languages*, ed. Robert H. Robins and Eugenius M. Uhlenbeck. Published with the Authority of the Permanent International Committee of Linguists (CIPL). Oxford: Berg.

Kralt, J. 1990. "Ethnic Origins in the Canadian Census, 1871–1986." Pp. 13–29 in *Ethnic Demography: Canadian Immigrant, Racial and Cultural Variations*, ed. Shiva S. Halli, Frank Trovato, and Leo Driedger. Ottawa: Carleton University Press.

Kroeber, A.L. 1939. *Cultural and Natural Area of Native America*. Berkeley: University of California Press.

Létourneau, E. 1994. "Projections de la population des Inuit du Québec, 1991–2016." Québec: Bureau de la statistique du Québec.

Loh, S. 1995. "Projections of Canada's Population with Aboriginal Ancestry, 1991–2016." (Revised version of Nault and Jenkins, 1993.) Report prepared by Population Projections Section, Demography Division for Employment Equity Data Program, Housing, Family and Social Statistics Division, Statistics Canada.

Loh, S., R. Verma, E. Ng, M.J. Norris, M.V. George, and J. Perreault. Forthcoming. *Population Projections of Registered Indians, 1996–2021*. Report prepared by the Population Projections Section, Demography Division, Statistics Canada for the Department of Indian Affairs and Northern Development.

Murdock, A.I. 1983. "Mortality Rates in Indian and Inuit Population: Changes in Trends and Recent Experience." Pp. 22–31 in *Proceedings of a Workshop on Indian Demographic Patterns and Trends and Their Implications for Policy and Planning, 20 June 1980*. Ottawa: Department of Indian Affairs and Northern Development, and Statistics Canada.

Nault, F., J. Chen, M.V. George, and M.J. Norris. 1993. "Population Projections of Registered Indians, 1991–2016." Report prepared by the Population Projections Section, Demography Division, Statistics Canada for Indian and Northern Affairs Canada (INAC).

Norris, D.A. and E.T. Pryor. 1984. "Demographic Change in Canada's North." Pp. 117–39 in *Proceedings — International Workshop on Population Issues in Arctic Societies*. Co-sponsored by the Greenland Committee on Northern Population Research, Gilbjerghoved, Gilleleje, Denmark, 2–5 May 1984.

Norris, M.J. 1985. "Migration Patterns of Status Indians in Canada, 1976–1981." Paper presented at the annual meeting of the Canadian Population Society. (June).

———. 1990. "The Demography of Aboriginal People in Canada." In *Ethnic Demography: Canadian Immigrant, Racial and Cultural Variations*, ed. Shiva S. Halli, Frank Trovato, and Leo Driedger. Ottawa: Carleton University Press.

———. 1996. "Contemporary Demography of Aboriginal Peoples in Canada." In *Visions of the Heart: Canadian Aboriginal Issues*, ed. David A. Long and Olive P. Dickason. Toronto: Harcourt Brace and Company.

———. 1998. "Canada's Aboriginal Languages." *Canadian Social Trends* 51 (Winter), Statistics Canada, Cat. no. 11-008.

Norris, M.J., D. Kerr, and F. Nault. 1995. "Technical Report on Projections of the Population with Aboriginal Identity, Canada, 1991–2016." Report prepared by the Population Projection Section, Demography Division, Statistics Canada, for the Royal Commission on Aboriginal Peoples.

———. 1996. "Projections of the Population with Aboriginal Identity in Canada, 1991–2016." Report prepared by the Population Projections Section, Demography Division, Statistics Canada, for the Royal Commission on Aboriginal Peoples. Ottawa: Canada Mortgage and Housing Corporation, and the Royal Commission on Aboriginal Peoples.

Perreault, J., L. Paquette, and M.V. George. 1985. *Population Projections of Registered Indians, 1982–1996*. Ottawa: Indian and Northern Affairs Canada.

Ponting, J. Rick, ed. 1997. *First Nations in Canada: Perspectives on Opportunity, Empowerment, and Self-Determination*. Toronto: McGraw-Hill Ryerson.

Priest, Gordon. 1984. "Aboriginal Languages in Canada." Ottawa: Statistics Canada, Housing, Family and Social Division, Cat. no. CS99-Z-517E.

Pryor, E.T. 1984. *Profile of Native Women: 1981 Census of Canada*. Ottawa: Supply and Services.

Ram, B. and A. Romaniuc. 1985. *Fertility Projections of Registered Indians, 1982 to 1996*. Ottawa: Indian and Northern Affairs Canada.

Robitaille, N. and R. Choinière. 1985. *An Overview of Demographic and Socio-Economic Conditions of the Inuit in Canada*. Ottawa: Indian and Northern Affairs Canada.

Romaniuc, A. 1981. "Increase in Natural Fertility during the Early Stages of Modernization: Canadian Indians Case Study." *Demography* 18(2): pp. 157–72.

———. 1987. "Transition from Traditional High to Modern Low Fertility: Canadian Aboriginals." *Canadian Studies in Population* 14(1): pp. 69–88.

Rowe, G. and M.J. Norris. 1985. *Mortality Projections of Registered Indians, 1982 to 1996.* Ottawa: Indian and Northern Affairs Canada.

Royal Commission on Aboriginal Peoples (RCAP). 1996. *Report of the Royal Commission on Aboriginal Peoples.* Vol. 3. *Gathering Strength.* Ottawa: RCAP.

Siggner, A.J. 1977. "Preliminary Results from a Study of 1966–71 Migration Patterns among Status Indians in Canada." Ottawa: Department of Indian Affairs and Northern Development.

———. 1980. "A Socio-Demographic Profile of Indians in Canada." Pp. 31–65 in *Out of Irrelevance: A Socio-political Introduction to Indian Affairs in Canada,* ed. J.R. Ponting and R. Gibbins. Toronto: Butterworths.

———. 1986a. "The Socio-Demographic Conditions of Registered Indians." *Canadian Social Trends* (Winter), Statistics Canada, Cat. no. 11–008.

———. 1986b. "The Socio-Demographic Conditions of Registered Indians." Pp. 57–83 in *Arduous Journey: Canadian Indians and Decolonization,* ed. J.R. Ponting. Toronto: McClelland & Stewart.

Statistics Canada. 1983. *The Daily* (1 February). Cat. no. 11-001.

———. 1987. *1986 Census of Canada — Summary Tabulations of Ethnic and Aboriginal Origins.* Ottawa: Supply and Services.

———. 1991. *1991 Census of Canada.* Cat. no. 94-327. Ottawa: Minister of Industry.

———. 1993a. *1991 Aboriginal Data: Age and Sex.* Cat. no. 94-327. Ottawa: Minister of Industry, Science and Technology.

———. 1993b. *Mobility and Migration: 1991 Census.* Cat. no. 93-322.

———. 1993c. *Users Guide — 1991 Aboriginal Data.* Ottawa: Supply and Services.

———. 1994a. *Population Projections for Canada, Provinces and Territories, 1993–2016.* Cat. no. 91-520, occasional.

———. 1994b. *Revised Intercensal Population and Family Estimates, July 1, 1971–1991.* Cat. no. 91-537.

———. 1996. *1996 Census of Canada.*

———. 1998a. *1996 Census of Population,* The Nation Series.

———. 1998b. "Aboriginal Population Characteristics: Are We Informed by the Aggregate Picture?" Paper presented at the annual meeting of the Canadian Population Society, Queen's University, Kingston, Ontario, June.

———. 1998c. *The Daily* (13 January). Cat. no. 11-001.

UNESCO. 1996. *Atlas of the World's Languages in Danger of Disappearing,* ed. Stephen A. Wurm. Paris: UNESCO.

Webb, M.L. 1973. "Maternal and Child Health, Indian and Eskimo." *Parliamentary Enquiry* 724. Ottawa.

CHAPTER 8

Aboriginal People in Urban Areas

Evelyn Peters

There have always been Aboriginal people living in urban areas in Canada, though for much of Canada's history since contact, non-Aboriginal Canadians have tended to view the presence of Aboriginal people in urban areas with misgivings. This chapter describes the source of these misgivings and suggests alternative views of Aboriginal people and urban life.

The largest increase in the urban Aboriginal[1] population has occurred since the early 1950s. After 1960, a substantial literature emerged that addressed the implications of this movement to cities. Although attention to the issue had declined by the late 1980s, the urban Aboriginal population had not, and the 1991 census suggested that many cities had substantial numbers of people with Aboriginal origins living in them. Now, public attention seems again to be drawn to urban Aboriginal people. In 1992, the Royal Commission on Aboriginal Peoples identified urban Aboriginal people as an important emphasis in their research. Urban Aboriginal people have been featured in chapters in recent books on Aboriginal people generally (Comeau and Santin, 1990; Frideres, 1993; Richardson, 1994), a bibliography (Kastes, 1993), and a book of "life stories" (Shorten, 1991).

There has been almost no writing by Aboriginal people on the experience of migrating to and living in urban areas. Most of the available literature comes from non-Aboriginal academics, consultants, and researchers. From the beginning, Aboriginal urbanization has been presented as problematic in this literature. The way this "social problem" was defined provided a framework for identifying appropriate policy responses. There is evidence that this framework is increasingly being challenged by Aboriginal people. In this context, it is appropriate to provide a critical assessment of non-Aboriginal writing about Aboriginal urbanization.

The primary object of this chapter is not to explore the situation of Aboriginal people in urban areas. The works cited above are available to interested readers, as is material in the report of the Royal Commission on Aboriginal Peoples (Royal Commission, 1996, pp. 519–621). More-over, I am not an Aboriginal person; I am an academic of Dutch and Ukrainian origins who is not qualified to speak about the urban experience for Aboriginal people. What I do feel qualified to write about, in a critical way, is how I and my peers have conceptualized the situation of urban Aboriginal people, what some of the implications have been, and what are some possible ways forward.[2]

The chapter begins with a brief profile of Aboriginal people and organizations in urban areas. Next, it compares Aboriginal urbanization patterns with cycles of public interest in their situation. The chapter then moves to an exploration of how Aboriginal people in cities have been labelled problematic and how this problem has been characterized. The final sections of the chapter present an alternative approach and identify some ways to make cities better places for Aboriginal people and cultures.

A PROFILE OF CONTEMPORARY URBAN ABORIGINAL PEOPLE

Population Characteristics

A brief profile of the characteristics of Aboriginal people in urban areas cannot possibly do justice to all the important issues facing this population, nor can it depict the diversity of urban Aboriginal populations or of urban areas. The following paragraphs highlight five themes: urbanization rates in 1991; socio-economic, legal, and cultural characteristics; and urban institutions.

In 1991, approximately 320 000 (44.4 percent) of those who identified themselves[3] as Aboriginal people in Canada lived in urban areas (Table 8.1). Urbanization rates varied for different groups of Aboriginal people. A little over 30 percent of registered Indians live in cities. In comparison, the majority of non-registered Indians and Métis live in urban areas. The Inuit are the least urbanized of all the Aboriginal groups.

Until recently, very little statistical information was available on the socio-economic characteristics of urban Aboriginal people across the country. Surveys conducted in 1978 and 1982 by the Institute of Urban Studies in Winnipeg provided information about Aboriginal people in Winnipeg, Saskatoon, and Regina (Clatworthy, 1980; Clatworthy and Hull, 1983), but there was little in the way of more recent information that provided wider geographic coverage. Data from the Aboriginal Peoples Survey (APS)[4] demonstrate that many of the attributes highlighted

TABLE 8.1

Residence of Adjusted[1] Aboriginal Identity Population, 1991

	Total Aboriginal[2]	Registered North American Indian[3]	Non-registered North American Indian[4]	Métis[5]	Inuit
Total	720 600	438 00	112 600	139 400	37 800
On-reserve	254 600 (35.3%)	254 600 (58.1%)	3 600 (3.2%)	4 535 (3.3%)	620 (1.7%)
Off-reserve	466 100 (64.6%)	183 500 (41.9%)	109 000 (96.8%)	134 835 (96.7%)	37 180 (98.3%)
Urban,[6] off-reserve	320 000 (44.4%)	148 500 (33.9%)	77 800 (69.1%)	90 100 (64.6%)	7 900 (20.9%)

[1] A total of 95 000 individuals were added to the APS count to compensate for the population on unenumerated reserves and under-coverage in participating reserve and non-reserve areas.

[2] Because some respondents (approximately 1 percent) gave multiple Aboriginal identities, summing identity categories will result in overcounting. The "Total Aboriginal" category does not double count those giving multiple Aboriginal identities.

[3] The North American Indian population registered according to the Indian Act of Canada. This category *excludes* 4830 North American Indians with registration status not stated in the APS; 17 060 Métis who reported being registered according to the Indian Act (they are counted as Métis); 2080 Inuit who reported being registered according to the Indian Act (they are counted as Inuit); and an estimated 58 000 persons residing on unenumerated Indian reserves or settlements.

[4] Those who identified themselves as North American Indian who were not registered according to the Indian Act.

[5] Those who identified themselves as Métis.

[6] This number does not include urban reserves.

Source: Adapted from Privy Council Office. 1996. "Urban Perspectives." P. 604 in *Perspectives and Realities.* Vol. 4. Report of the Royal Commission on Aboriginal Peoples. Reproduced with the permission of the Minister of Public Works and Government Services Canada, 1999.

for urban Aboriginal people in these prairie cities hold in other urban areas and in recent years. Table 8.2 shows that the urban Aboriginal population tends to be younger than the total urban population, with a higher proportion of women, particularly in the main childbearing years. Unemployment rates are much higher for Aboriginal people than for total metropolitan populations, and many more Aboriginal people have relatively low incomes. Although some Aboriginal people are earning incomes of $40 000 and more, the proportion is much lower than the total metropolitan population. Because of their low incomes, Aboriginal people are more likely to live in poor housing. As other researchers have found, migration rates are similar for Aboriginal and non-Aboriginal people.

It is important to recognize, however, the variation in the characteristics of the Aboriginal population in different urban areas. Table 8.3 compares major Canadian cities with respect to some characteristics of Aboriginal residents. These data are based on the population that identified itself as Aboriginal in the APS. The number of Aboriginal people varies from slightly more than 1000 in Halifax to over 35 000 in Winnipeg.

TABLE 8.2

Socio-Economic Characteristics of People Who Identify Themselves as Aboriginal in Selected Census Metropolitan Areas[1]

	Aboriginal identity population	Total metropolitan population
Total	159 945	16 665 360
Ages 0–14	35.9%	19.8%
Females in 25+ population	57.5%	52.1%
Unemployment rate	23.4%	9.4%
Adults 15+ with total income less than $10 000	48.4%	25.3%
Adults 15+ with total income greater than $40 000	6.4%	19.0%
Residence needs major repairs	12.8%	6.9%
Moved between 1986 and 1991	46.1%	50.4%
Moved in last 12 months	20.4%	17.6%

[1] Data are available for Halifax, Montreal, Ottawa–Hull, Toronto, Winnipeg, Regina, Saskatoon, Calgary, Edmonton, Vancouver, and Victoria.

Sources: Statistics Canada, 1991, *1991 Census*, cat. nos. 93-339 and 93-340, Ottawa: Industry, Science and Technology Canada; Statistics Canada, 1991, *Aboriginal Peoples Survey*, cat. no. 94-327, Ottawa: Industry, Science and Technology Canada.

Aboriginal people comprise the largest proportion of the metropolitan populations of Regina and Saskatoon. Cultural characteristics also vary. Prairie cities contain the largest number of Métis people. They also contain the most people who understand an Aboriginal language. The latter dimension varies from 14.1 percent in Montreal to 61.1 percent in Saskatoon. With respect to socio-economic characteristics, unemployment rates are highest in Saskatoon (32.7 percent) and lowest in Toronto (11.2 percent).

Aboriginal people living in urban areas are subject to a complicated legal regime. According to the APS, Indians registered under the Indian Act of Canada constituted the largest legal category. The federal government

TABLE 8.3

Selected Characteristics of People Who Identify Themselves as Aboriginal in Major Metropolitan Areas,[1] 1991

	Number who identify as Aboriginal	% of city population	% Métis	% who understand Aboriginal language	Unemployment rate	% 15+ who moved since 1986
Halifax	1 185	0.3	—	—	—	38.2
Montreal	6 775	0.4	24.7	14.1[2]	13.1	42.1
Ottawa–Hull	6 915	0.8	20.6	22.2[2]	12.7	47.0
Toronto	14 205	0.2	5.6[2]	25.3[2]	11.2	36.1
Winnipeg	35 150	3.3	21.3	49.1	27.3	44.1
Regina	11 020	4.1	33.8	49.2	25.8	57.8
Saskatoon	11 920	3.8	46.9	61.1	32.7	44.2
Calgary	14 075	0.9	30.4	37.3	18.1	52.5
Edmonton	29 235	2.0	46.2	50.2	28.1	46.1
Vancouver	25 030	0.8	16.3	39.6	29.0	49.4
Victoria	4 435	1.2	7.8[2]	38.5[2]	19.5	40.2

[1] Data are available for Halifax, Montreal, Ottawa–Hull, Toronto, Winnipeg, Regina, Saskatoon, Calgary, Edmonton, Vancouver, and Victoria.

[2] The coefficient of variation of the estimate is between 16.7% and 33.3%. These estimates should be used with caution to support a conclusion.

Sources: Statistics Canada, 1993, *1991 Census*, cat. no. 94-327, Ottawa: Industry, Science and Technology Canada; Statistics Canada, 1991, *Aboriginal Peoples Survey*, cat. nos., 94-327, 89-533, and 89-534, Ottawa: Industry, Science and Technology Canada.

has held that it was responsible only for registered Indians and that these responsibilities were limited to reserve borders (Morse, 1989). Only a few federally funded services are available to registered Indians generally, no matter where they live. The most notable of these are non-insured health benefits and postsecondary educational assistance. The federal government has regarded non-registered Indians and Métis as a provincial responsibility. In 1939, the courts ruled that the Inuit would be considered as Indians for the purposes of clarifying federal jurisdiction.

These categories are further complicated by differences between registration status and band membership. Under Bill C-31, passed in 1985, registration and band membership were separated. After Bill C-31, bands were given the opportunity to draw up and adopt codes governing membership, while registration continues to be governed according to (revised) Indian Act regulations. Band membership involves a variety of rights and privileges with respect to an individual's band of origin, including rights of residency on the reserve. Some urban Aboriginal people are registered but are not band members, while some are band members but are not registered.

The complex amalgam of legal categories that has emerged has created inequalities for and among urban Aboriginal people. Registered Indians living on-reserve have access to federally funded programs not available to urban Indians. Registered Indians in urban areas have access to some federally funded programs that other Aboriginal people do not have. Band members have opportunities to participate in self-government through their bands of origin. These opportunities are denied to Aboriginal people who do not have band membership.[5] Although some urban programs have been established through federal, provincial, and municipal funding, these initiatives are unevenly distributed, with short-term and often limited funding.

The cultural diversity of Aboriginal people in urban areas is not often recognized. Although published data on cultural origins are not available from the Aboriginal Peoples Survey, information about Aboriginal people living in Regina in 1982 is suggestive (Table 8.4). First Nations people living in the city came from 27 reserves, eight treaty areas, at least five First Nations, six provinces, and two countries. Métis people came from five provinces and two countries. Many other cities must demonstrate comparable heterogeneity.

Researchers in the past commented on the paucity of Aboriginal institutions representing or providing services for urban Aboriginal people (Clatworthy and Gunn, 1981; Falconer, 1985, 1990; Frideres, 1984). At present, however, many large urban areas have a considerable number of organizations controlled and staffed by Aboriginal people, whose focus is

TABLE 8.4

Origins of the Aboriginal Population, Regina, Saskatchewan, 1982

First Nations

Reserve origins: 27 reserves in Saskatchewan plus others in other provinces
Treaty area of origin: Treaty numbers 1, 2, 3, 4, 5, 6, 7, and 9
First Nation of origin: Assiniboine, Blackfoot, Cree, Dakota, Ojibwa, and
  possibly others
Provincial origins: British Columbia, Alberta, Saskatchewan, Manitoba,
  Ontario, and Nova Scotia
Countries of origin: Canada and the United States

Métis

Provincial origins: British Columbia, Alberta, Saskatchewan, Manitoba,
  Ontario, and Nova Scotia
Countries of origin: Canada and the United States

Source: E.J. Peters. 1994. "Geographies of Self-Government." Pp. 20–30 in
Implementing Aboriginal Self-Government in Canada, ed. J. Hylton. Saskatoon:
Purich Publishers.

the permanent urban Aboriginal population. Winnipeg appears to be
among urban centres with the most well-developed set of urban Aboriginal institutions (Table 8.5).[6] While some of these organizations have a
very long history, many have been established only in recent years. Collectively, these organizations provide a fairly broad range of services to
Aboriginal people.

Several features of the Winnipeg situation appear to be unique. Unlike
most urban areas with large Aboriginal populations, Winnipeg has two
organizations, the Aboriginal Centre Inc. and the Winnipeg Native Family Economic Development Corporation (WNFED), which have focussed
on community development and attempted to provide interagency links
and networks.[7] The Aboriginal Centre Inc. recently purchased Winnipeg's CPR station in the heart of Winnipeg's core area, with the objective of bringing under one roof a variety of Aboriginal organizations. The
building attempts to provide a critical mass of Aboriginal services, provide a place for Aboriginal activities, and serve as a focal point for the
urban Aboriginal community. WNFED is an umbrella organization created to bring together a number of different projects in order to provide
linkage and a support network within the Aboriginal community. Winnipeg also appears to be unique in that it has Métis, First Nations, and
pan-Aboriginal political organizations functioning simultaneously. Like

TABLE 8.5

Aboriginal Institutions in Winnipeg, 1994

Organization	Primary focus	Year established
A-Bah-Nu-Gee Child Care	Child and family services	1984
Aboriginal Centre Inc.	Social service, community and economic development	1990
Aboriginal Council of Winnipeg	Political	1990
Aboriginal Literacy Foundation	Education	1990
Aiyawin Corporation	Housing	1983
Anishinabe Oway-Ishi	Employment	1989
Anishinabe RESPECT	Employment	1981
Bear Clan Patrol Inc.	Safety	1992
Children of the Earth High School	Education	1991
Indian Family Centre Inc.	Religious/social service	1973
Indian Métis Friendship Centre	Cultural/social service	1959
Iwkewak Justice Society	Justice	1986
Kinew Housing	Housing	1970
Ma Mawi Chi Itata Centre	Child and family services	1984
Manitoba Association for Native Languages	Language education	1984
MMF — Winnipeg Region	Political	n.a.
Native Clan	Inmates	1970
Native Employment Services	Employment	1972
Native United Church	Religious	n.a.
Native Women's Transition Centre	Housing	n.a.
Nee-Gawn-Ah-Kai Day Care Centre	Child care	1986
Neechi Foods Community Store	Economic development	n.a.
Original Women's Network	Women's resource centre	n.a.
Payuk Inter-Trival Housing Co-op	Housing	1985
Three Fires Society	Cultural	1982
Winnipeg Council of First Nations	Political	1991
Winnipeg Native Families Economic Development Corporation	Social service, community and economic development	n.a.

n.a.   Not available or unknown.

Source: S. Clatworthy, J. Hull, and N. Loughran. 1995. "Urban Aboriginal Organizations: Edmonton, Toronto and Winnipeg." Pp. 25–81 in *Self-Government for Aboriginal People in Urban Areas*, ed. E.J. Peters. Kingston, Ont.: Institute of Intergovernmental Relations, Queen's University.

many other Aboriginal political bodies, these organizations are exploring self-governance options (Helgason, 1995).

Urbanization Patterns

It is difficult to build up a reliable historical picture of the movement of Aboriginal people to Canadian cities. Changing definitions of ancestry in census data (Goldman, 1993) make it difficult to compare population numbers over time. The Indian Register kept by the Department of Indian Affairs omits Métis and non-registered Indian people, dates only from 1959, and identifies residence on- or off-reserve, but not in particular cities.[8] Despite problems with finding accurate, comparable data, it appears that Aboriginal urbanization is a comparatively recent phenomenon. In this section, data from the Indian Register, the Aboriginal Peoples Survey, and the census are analyzed to provide a picture of Aboriginal populations in urban areas.

Although early studies show that, even in the 1950s, some Aboriginal people had been relatively long-term residents of cities (Boek and Boek, 1959, p. 20; Davis, 1965, p. 372; Lurie, 1967), overall urbanization rates appear to have been low. No statistical information is available about Métis urbanization trends, but it appears that relatively few registered Indians left their reserves between the turn of the century and the 1950s. In 1959, only 16.9 percent of registered Indians lived off-reserve, with probably an even smaller proportion resident in cities (Table 8.6). In 1981, 29.6 percent of registered Indians lived off-reserve, and by 1996 that proportion had increased to 41.9 percent.

Table 8.7 shows census statistics on the changing number of people with Aboriginal ancestry in major metropolitan centres. Data for the years 1951 to 1981 in this table are based on answers to the census question on ethnic origin or ancestry. Although the data for various years are not directly comparable because of changing definitions and questions on census forms (Goldman, 1993), they present some rough estimates of the size of the urban Aboriginal population. Changes in the census question on ancestry make it impossible to compare 1991 data with data for earlier years.[9] The 1991 statistics are from the Aboriginal Peoples Survey, which asked individuals who reported Aboriginal ancestry in the census whether they identified with an Aboriginal group. If the 1981 method of collecting information about ancestry had been used, these numbers would probably be greater.

In interpreting these statistics, it is important to remember that changes in census statistics on urban Aboriginal populations are not only a function of migration, but also a reflection of changing patterns of

TABLE 8.6

Total and Off-Reserve Registered Indian Population, 1959–1991

	Registered Indian population	Off-reserve Number[2]	Off-reserve Percent	Enfranchisements[1] per five-year period Number	Enfranchisements[1] per five-year period Percent
1959[3]	179 126	30 372	16.9	n/a[4]	
1961	191 709			2077	1.1[5]
1966	224 164	43 746	19.5	3216	1.4
1971	257 619	69 106	26.8	3009	1.2
1976	288 938	79 301	27.4	1094	0.4
1981	323 782	96 290	29.6	40	0.01
1986[6]	415 898	123 642	31.9	14	0.00
1991	511 791	207 032	40.5		
1996	610 874	256 505	41.9		

[1] The Indian Register records only individuals who maintain their registration under the Indian Act. It is possible that a substantial number of Indians gave up their status under the Indian Act, or enfranchised, and moved to cities during this period. However, enfranchisement rates do not bear out this possibility.

[2] Not including those living on Crown land.

[3] Statistics on off-reserve residency began to be collected only in 1959 (Bradley, 1993).

[4] Enfranchisement data are not easily available for these years, however, Department of Indian Affairs records indicate that enfranchisements between 1876 and 1948 totalled about 4000 (Canada, Joint Committee of the Senate and the House of Commons on Indian Affairs, 1960b, *Minutes of Proceedings and Evidence*, Vol. 12: p. 539).

[5] Figures for 1961 and 1966 are estimates based on DIAND's fiscal year; figures for 1971 to 1986 are based on the calendar year.

[6] In 1985, the Indian Act was amended by Bill C-31 to allow the restoration of Indian status to those who had lost it due to discriminatory clauses in the Indian Act. Subsequently enfranchisement was no longer an option.

Sources: Canada, Information Canada, 1974, *Perspective Canada: A Compendium of Social Statistics*, p. 244, Ottawa: Department of Industry, Trade and Commerce; Canada, DIAND, 1967, *Indian Affairs: Facts and Figures*, Ottawa: DIAND; Canada, DIAND, 1994, *Basic Departmental Data*, p. 5, Ottawa: Supply and Services, 1992; J. Powless, DIAND, 1994, personal communication, 12 January; D. Taubman, DIAND, 1998, personal communication.

TABLE 8.7

Aboriginal People in Major Metropolitan Centres, 1951–1991

	1951	1961	1971[1]	1981	1991[2]
Halifax	—	—	—	—	1 185
Montreal	296	507	3215	14 450	6 775[3]
Ottawa–Hull	—	—	—	4 370	6 915
Toronto	805	1196	2990	13 495	14 205
Winnipeg	210	1082	4940	16 575	35 150
Regina	160	539	2860	6 575	11 020
Saskatoon	48	207	1070	4 350	11 920
Calgary	62	335	2265	7 310	14 075
Edmonton	616	995	4260	13 750	29 235
Vancouver	239	530	3000	16 080	25 030
Victoria	—	—	—	2 800	4 435

[1] The 1971 data do not include the Inuit.

[2] Individuals who identified with an Aboriginal group in the Aboriginal Peoples Survey.

[3] The population for the Kahnawake and Kanesatake reserves, which are in the Montreal metropolitan area boundaries, were not enumerated in 1981 or 1991. Population estimates (5218 and 618, respectively) were included in 1981 counts but not included in the 1991 counts.

Source: Statistics Canada, 1993, *Census and Aboriginal Peoples Survey*, cat. no. 94-327, Ottawa: Industry, Science and Technology; Statistics Canada, 1981, DIAND customized data; Canada, Information Canada, 1974, *Perspective Canada: A Compendium of Social Statistics*, p. 244, Ottawa: Minister of Industry.

self-identification as Aboriginal, natural increase, and the addition of Bill C-31 populations,[10] as well as changing definitions of ancestry and methods of data collection. Despite these caveats, it is clear from Table 8.7 that, while the number of people with Aboriginal origins in major cities was very low in 1951,[11] the numbers steadily increased in the following decades. By 1991, several prairie cities had very substantial populations of Aboriginal people, and it is likely that for many cities, the absolute increase between 1981 and 1991 was greater than the increase between 1971 and 1981.

WRITING ABOUT ABORIGINAL URBANIZATION

Changes in the degree of public interest in urban Aboriginal people do not reflect changes in their numbers in cities. Although issues concerning Aboriginal people were very much in the public eye in the late 1800s, they seemed to fade in importance after the turn of the century (Tobias, 1983). As public interest in Aboriginal issues revived in the mid-1900s, federal and provincial governments commissioned an array of studies into the conditions of Aboriginal people (Davis, 1965, p. 519; Hawthorn et al., 1958, p. 84; Hawthorn, 1966–67; Lagasse, 1958). An overriding theme in many of these studies was the depressed social and economic conditions of reserves and rural Métis settlements. As these conditions came to public attention, policy-makers looked to urbanization for at least a partial solution. Even without public policy intervention, rapid population growth on reserves made out-migration seem inevitable.

The prospect of the rapid migration of Aboriginal peoples to cities challenged academics, citizens' groups, and policy-makers to formulate what the "urban experience" meant for migrants and for cities. A large body of literature on the topic, academic and policy-oriented, emerged after the late 1960s and continued to the mid-1970s. A number of studies appeared in the early 1980s, many associated with statistical surveys of Aboriginal people in Winnipeg, Regina, and Saskatoon conducted by the Institute of Urban Studies at the University of Winnipeg. Relatively little was published on urban Aboriginal people after 1985. With the exception of studies commissioned by the Royal Commission on Aboriginal Peoples, little current work is available with respect to urban Aboriginal people, and Kastes's (1993, p. 56) recent overview of the literature on Aboriginal urbanization concluded as follows:

> The literature on urban Aboriginal issues in Canada is sparse, limited in scope, largely dated in relevance. ... Given the significant changes which have occurred in Canada, as well as within the Aboriginal communities themselves since the mid 1980s, the existing literature is of limited use for contemporary policy and program development.

"Large numbers appear threatening," states Larry Krotz (1980, p. 50) in his journalistic account of urban Aboriginal people in prairie cities. However, the interest in urban Aboriginal issues does not appear to be related to numbers. Nor is the decline in interest due to the fact that urban Aboriginal people were being integrated into the economic mainstream in urban areas. These factors suggest that it is not only the objective conditions and numbers of urban Aboriginal people that contribute to public interest in Aboriginal urbanization, but also interpretations of its significance and frameworks of meaning through which Aboriginal peoples' migration to cities was understood. In what follows, I suggest that cycles and themes in writing about urban Aboriginal people reflect ideas about the relationship between Aboriginal culture and urban life.

Constructing Aboriginal Urbanization as a Problem

From the earliest writing on Aboriginal people in cities, their presence was constructed as a problem.[12] Even in the 1950s, when very few Aboriginal people lived in Canadian cities, many employers, municipal governments, and members of the general public viewed Aboriginal migration to cities with apprehension. On the basis of his Manitoba survey, Lagasse (1958, p. 167) concluded that "the belief that an Indian's place is on the reserve is still very strong among the Canadian people." The Saskatchewan government's 1960 submission to the Joint Committee of the Senate and the House of Commons warned that "the day is not far distant when the burgeoning Indian population, now largely confined to reservations, will explode into white communities and present a serious problem indeed" (Canada, 1960c, p. 1083). Buckley's (1992, pp. 72–76) review of attitudes toward Aboriginal employment in northern prairie resource towns in the 1950s and 1960s concluded that, in public opinion, there was no place for Aboriginal people in these communities. Other writers also noted the intense hostility of townspeople in the mid-1900s to Aboriginal residents and visitors (Braroe, 1975; Brody, 1983; Lithman, 1984; Robertson, 1970; Shimpo and Williamson, 1965; Stymeist, 1975).

Although materials from mid-century on demonstrate agreement that migration to cities would create problems for Aboriginal people (Canada, 1960a, p. 369; Canadian Corrections Association, 1967, pp. 7–8; Regina Welfare Council, 1959), there were also worries about the state of cities — about how to maintain property values, keep down welfare rolls, and prevent inner-city decay (Hirabayashi, 1962; Indian-Eskimo Association, 1960; Lagasse, 1958, p. 167).[13] John Melling, former executive director of the Indian–Eskimo Association, chastised federal, provincial, and municipal governments for being concerned about First Nations peoples only when the conditions of inner cities were seen to be threatened. His statement, however, also reflects attitudes toward Aboriginal urbanization at the time:

> One hundred and sixty thousand Indians may wither in their reserves. ... But bring even one-quarter of that number into our towns, or to fester in city tenements and shanty slums ... and that situation is quite intolerable. If the rot can be confined to the lives of Indians alone and if it can remain hidden from the rest of us, that is one thing; if it begins

to affect the lives of others and becomes an open eyesore, that is another thing. (Melling, 1967, p. 72)

Aboriginal people were still conceptualized as a threat to cities in the 1970s. The introduction to a 1977 report for the city of Winnipeg stated:

> [A] major in-migration of generally low skilled, minimally educated ... and relatively impoverished people will serve to exacerbate the increasing expenditure and services demands. Beyond this, native urbanization will pose specific and unique problems and situations for both the City of Winnipeg and native people themselves. (Reiber-Kremers, 1977, p. 1)

The government of Saskatchewan's urban Native initiative in the late 1970s linked urban Aboriginal people and inner-city deterioration (Saskatchewan, 1979). More recently, Kastes (1993, p. 83) argued that the situation of Aboriginal people constituted a serious challenge for prairie cities:

> In recent years, Aboriginal urbanization issues have received little attention from researchers despite the fact that the social, economic and political problems within the urban Aboriginal community represent, by all accounts, one of the most serious and complex set of issues currently affecting urban environments.

Assigning the Source of the Problem

The nature or source of the problem as identified by researchers and policy-makers has changed over time. A common theme in the literature on Aboriginal urbanization before the 1980s was that Aboriginal culture[14] presents a major barrier to successful adjustment to urban society. A 1957 Calgary conference on Aboriginal people in urban areas, organized by the National Commission on the Indian Canadian (later the Indian–Eskimo Association), clearly enunciated this view. Delegates representing churches, labour, government, and community groups concluded as follows:

> Our Indian Canadian is faced or hampered with ... his own personality. The Indian Canadian is different from his fellow Canadians of European descent. ... These differences are from his cultural heritage. ... For instance, his concepts of time, money, social communication, hygiene, usefulness, competition and cooperation are at variance with our own and can prove a stumbling block to successful adjustment. (Canada, 1957, p. 3)

In *Indians in the City*, a book based on his PhD research in Toronto, Nagler wrote:

While urban living is not foreign to most European immigrants, it is a completely new way of life for the Indian. The highly generalized characteristics described as "being Indian" affect the Indian's ability to urbanize. ... Indians thus experience difficulty in adjusting to a new environment because their conceptions of living do not involve punctuality, responsibility, hurry, impersonality, frugality, and the other social practices which are a part of the urban environment." (1970, p. 25)

Zeitoun's (1969) review for the Department of Manpower and Immigration contrasted reserve and urban cultures and identified these differences as underlying the dislocation of urban Indians (Table 8.8). Adaptation to the urban environment, according to Zeitoun and others, required a change in cultural values and orientation.[15]

These views were still current in the late 1970s. A consultant's report (Reiber-Kremers, 1977, p. 2) to the city of Winnipeg, for example, indicated that the problems of Aboriginal people "stem from major cultural differences, lack of familiarity with wage economy participation as well as

TABLE 8.8

Reserve–City Cultural Differences

Reserve characteristics	City characteristics
• Cultural homogenity	• Cultural heterogeneity
• Economic activity requires generalized skills	• Occupational specialization
• Natural environment	• Manufactured environment
• Social life characterized by primary relationships, community, informality, personal relationships	• Social life characterized by class structure, formal relationships, anonymity
• Work is task-oriented; it is one aspect of life and does not confer status; it is independent and unsupervised	• Work is time-oriented, separate from personal life, and the main source of status and satisfaction; it is supervised and directed
• Ties with kin and to the land result in a deep attachment to place and may interfere with geographic mobility	• Nuclear families and occupational specialization result in a weak attachment to place and do not inhibit economic and geographic mobility

Source: L. Zeitoun. 1969. "Canadian Indians at the Crossroads: Some Aspects of Relocation and Urbanization in Canada." Study for the Manpower Utilization Branch, Department of Manpower and Immigration, Ottawa. (Unpublished.)

urban lifestyles." Although some writers challenged these interpretations (for example, Elias, 1975; Lurie, 1967; Price and McCaskill, 1974), the overriding emphasis in the literature of the 1960s and 1970s was on the incompatibility of Aboriginal culture and urban life and the need to abandon cultural values in order to adapt to the urban setting.

The "problem" of Aboriginal urbanization was largely redefined in work after 1980,[16] and explicit mention of issues concerning Aboriginal culture virtually disappeared. Much of the work on urban Aboriginal people during this period framed the issue as a problem of poverty stemming from lack of education and unemployment. Comeau and Santin (1990) focussed primarily on the poverty of urban Aboriginal people. A series of studies based on statistical surveys of Aboriginal people in prairie cities and published by the Institute of Urban Studies in Winnipeg demonstrated low incomes and high levels of unemployment and dependence on transfer payments. Summarizing much of this work, Kastes (1993, p. 78) illustrates that the needs of urban Aboriginal people were seen to derive from their socio-economic status:

> Most studies describing the needs of the urban Aboriginal population develop a common integrated description of needs. They stem from a relative lack of formal education leading to unemployment or low-wage/low-skill jobs, insufficient levels of income, poverty and ultimately dependency on social assistance. The vast majority of needs in much of the urban Aboriginal population related to housing, health care, recreation and child care are not that dissimilar from other disadvantaged groups which make up the urban poor.

The main factors differentiating the urban Aboriginal population from the other urban poor were the services required to adapt to urban life, the degree of their poverty, and the extent of their housing needs (Kastes, 1993, pp. 79–80).

Another approach to typifying the nature of the problem emphasized jurisdictional disputes, identifying the confusion over federal and provincial responsibility for making policy and funding programs for urban Aboriginal people as an important element (Breton and Grant, 1984; Comeau and Santin, 1990, p. 43; Falconer, 1985).[17] Analysts noted the inconsistency in relationships between the federal government and various provinces, the inequities between various groups of Aboriginal people, and the wrangling among governments about policy-making and financial responsibility. In their analysis of government programs for urban Indians in Manitoba, Breton and Grant (1984, pp. ix–xx) warned:

> The past ten years of circular jurisdictional squabbling have permitted the situation of Manitoba's Indians to become progressively worse. If we

have ten more years of inconclusive action, the results, in human terms, will be too disastrous to contemplate.

Another theme was the inability of public service organizations to meet the needs of urban Aboriginal people (Falconer, 1985; Frideres, 1988; Maidman, 1981; Reeves and Frideres, 1981). Frideres (1988) argued that public service organizations failed to adequately serve urban Aboriginal peoples because of their assimilationist objectives, limited target groups, unclear mandates, and uncertain funding. Although Aboriginal organizations were more successful in providing culturally appropriate services, they had relatively little success in "graduating" their clients.

The themes of the 1980s provide an important context for efforts to make urban areas better places for Aboriginal people. However, they do not address the essential question of the relationship between Aboriginal culture and urban life. In fact, the invisibility of Aboriginal culture in this literature suggests that it has no role in urban life — that it is irrelevant. In this context, urban Aboriginal people become just another socio-economically marginalized group in Canadian inner cities, with no distinct rights or needs.

Changing frameworks for interpreting Aboriginal urbanization may explain cycles of public interest in Aboriginal people in cities. When the source of the problem is defined as a cultural mismatch between Aboriginal and urban cultures, a substantial literature emerges that focuses on urban Aboriginal issues. When urban Aboriginal people are viewed primarily as a socio-economically disadvantaged population, their situation can be subsumed under the general literature on urban poverty.

ALTERNATIVE CONCEPTIONS OF ABORIGINAL CULTURE IN URBAN LIFE

The ways in which Aboriginal people have been defined in Western thought have set up a fundamental tension between the idea of Aboriginal culture and the idea of modern civilization (Berkhoffer, 1979; Francis, 1992; Goldie, 1989). Although the geographic implications of these deeply held images have not been well developed, Goldie (1989, pp. 16–17, 165) points out that, in non-Aboriginal writing, "true" Aboriginal culture is seen to belong either to history or to places distant from urban centres. The failure to address, critically, how researchers conceptualize Aboriginal culture in relation to the city helps to reproduce a framework that defines Aboriginal people as problematic and potentially disruptive of city life.[18] In this context, assumptions about the incompatibility between urban and Aboriginal culture persist (Peters, 1996). As the Native Council of Canada recently noted, "There is a strong, sometimes racist, perception that being Aboriginal and being urban are mutually exclusive" (1992, p. 10).

In contrast to views of Aboriginal culture as either incompatible with or irrelevant in an urban environment, Aboriginal people have argued that supporting and enhancing Aboriginal culture is a prerequisite for coping in an urban environment. These perspectives recognize that Aboriginal cultures and the Euro-Canadian cultures that dominate Canadian cities are distinct in many ways, but they insist that Aboriginal cultures can adapt to and flourish in urban areas, and that supporting Aboriginal cultures will enrich cities as well as make them better places for Aboriginal people.

Urban Aboriginal people who spoke to journalist Lynda Shorten in Edmonton (1991) identified the process of regaining their cultural heritage as essential for survival in the city. At the National Round Table on Aboriginal Urban Issues sponsored by the Royal Commission on Aboriginal Peoples, speakers emphasized the importance of maintaining their cultural identities in urban areas and passing them on to their children. Aboriginal participants at a 1994 workshop on urban self-government identified the process of healing from the effects of colonialism on their cultures as a priority for urban residents (Peters, 1995).

In their submissions to the 1992–94 public hearings of the Royal Commission on Aboriginal Peoples, participants stressed the need to enhance Aboriginal cultures in urban areas. Nancy Van Heest, working in a pre-employment program for Aboriginal women in Vancouver, told the commissioners:

> Today we live in the modern world and we find that a lot of our people who come into the urban setting are unable to live in the modern world without their traditional values. So we started a program which we call "Urban Images for First Nations People in the Urban Setting" and what we do is we work in this modern day with modern day people and give them traditional values so that they can continue on with their life in the city.[19]

Urban Aboriginal people spoke to the commissioners of the need for a strong foundation in Aboriginal culture for healing the urban Aboriginal community. In Orillia, Ontario, Harold Orten outlined the relationship between recovering Aboriginal cultures and healing:

> Recovering our identity will contribute to healing ourselves. Our healing will require us to rediscover who we are. We cannot look outside for

our self-image, we need to rededicate ourselves to understanding our traditional ways. In our songs, ceremony, language and relationships lie the instructions and directions for recovery.[20]

In Saskatoon, Margaret King, representative for the Saskatoon Urban Treaty Indians, argued that

> our cultural heritage ... formed the basic elements of individual empowerment, a solid foundation of cultural values and the knowledge of our history and traditions, our basic needs in the development of an individual before he or she becomes a productive member of society. As an assembly we believe in the value of individual self-esteem and will strive to empower our people through the development of culturally appropriate programs and services.[21]

The assault on Aboriginal cultures does not originate only in cities. It is part of the colonial legacy of our country. Yet urban areas present special challenges for the survival of Aboriginal cultures. These challenges come in part because many of the traditional sources of Aboriginal culture — contact with the land, elders, Aboriginal languages, and spiritual ceremonies — are difficult to maintain in cities at present (see Box 8.1). Moreover, Aboriginal people are continuously exposed to perceptions, either consciously or unconsciously held, that cities are not where Aboriginal cultures belong and can flourish (RCAP, 1993a, p. 2). At the public hearings, David Chartrand, then president of the National Association of Friendship Centres, told the commissioners:

> Aboriginal culture in the cities is threatened in much the same way as Canadian culture is threatened by American culture, and it therefore requires a similar commitment to its protection. Our culture is at the heart of our people, and without awareness of Aboriginal history, traditions and ceremonies, we are not whole people, and our communities lose their strength. ... Cultural education also works against the alienation that the cities hold for our people. Social activities bring us together and strengthen the relationship between people in areas where those relationships are an important safety net for people who feel left out by the mainstream.[22]

CHANGING CITIES TO WELCOME ABORIGINAL PEOPLES AND CULTURES

Making cities places where Aboriginal cultures are welcomed and enhanced will require sustained effort. Aboriginal people must be involved

BOX 8.1
Balancing Urban Life and Aboriginal Culture

I Forget Who I Am
Edith Duck

When I go back into urban life
I forget who I am
My spirits wonder
As well as my feelings

When at home in the wilderness
I remember who I am
My spirits become whole and strong
Like the surroundings of Mother Earth
Trees water and rocks

I pray to have a balanced life
Even when I am in the urban
Lifestyle or with nature

I am gifted by my grandfathers, to
Be able to cope and understand
Myself and those around me
To live in both worlds

Some people keep one and lose the other
Urban or nature
I pray for understanding
I receive patience and faith
When I am balanced with my spirits
Some people accept one or have no
Choice with the other

When I go back into urban life
I pray to remember who I am
My spirits provide patience and faith
Like the surroundings of Mother Earth
Trees rocks and water

Source: "I Forget Who I Am," by Edith Duck. 1995. Pp. 40–41 in Joel T.
Maki, ed., *Steal My Rage: New Native Voices*. Vancouver: Douglas &
McIntyre. © Na-Me-Res.

in identifying and putting into place appropriate initiatives. The following, however, puts forward some suggestions to illustrate what it means to change long-standing views about the relationship between Aboriginal cultures and urban places. These include cultural programming, building urban Aboriginal communities, supporting urban self-government, and improving the representation of Aboriginal people in urban areas.

Supporting Cultural Programming and Education

At present, there are many urban Aboriginal institutions that attempt to meet the needs of urban Aboriginal people, including the need to strengthen cultural identity. However, a survey of urban Aboriginal institutions in Winnipeg, Toronto, and Edmonton (Clatworthy et al., 1995) showed that although organizations attempted to meet the cultural needs of their clients by incorporating Aboriginal philosophies and cultures into their structures and program delivery, relatively few had as their primary mission the promotion or support of Aboriginal culture and identity. Moreover, while organizations reported flexibility in delivery style and administrative matters, their activities were highly circumscribed by funding relationships with other parties, mostly non-Aboriginal governments.

Friendship centres, which have existed in Canada's urban centres for over 30 years, have often become the main focus of cultural and social events and activities for Aboriginal people living in cities. In many urban areas, the friendship centre has been the only major voluntary association available to meet the needs of Aboriginal people for social and cultural development. Yet there is only limited funding to friendship centres for activities that support Aboriginal cultures, such as celebrations, access to elders, and language education. The cultural work that friendship centres currently carry out is chronically underfunded and relies heavily on the work of volunteers who are already overcommitted. In the context of the sustained assault on Aboriginal cultures in cities and the poverty of much of the urban Aboriginal population, there is a need for substantial new institutional support to assist Aboriginal people in maintaining and enhancing their cultural identity in urban areas. Teaching Aboriginal languages is one area that needs to be stressed. The Aboriginal Peoples Survey showed that only about 15 percent of urban Aboriginal people could speak their Aboriginal language of origin. Yet 71 percent of Aboriginal people who could not speak an Aboriginal language would like to learn or relearn one. Other priorities include providing space for Aboriginal activities and ceremonies and cultural education for children, youth, and adults.

Building Aboriginal Communities

The evolution of strong Aboriginal communities in urban areas remains largely unfulfilled after 40 years of urbanization. In many cities, Aboriginal people exist as an impoverished minority, without a collective cultural identity. Although there are now many cities with a variety of Aboriginal organizations, they do not reflect and have not been able to create group solidarity and cohesion. A study of Aboriginal organizations in Edmonton, Toronto, and Winnipeg found that only a small portion of the total urban Aboriginal population participates as members in or receives benefits or services from existing organizations (Clatworthy et al., 1995). The study also found that there were relatively few formal and effective inter-organizational structures with a focus on community-building and consolidation.

Community-building through the establishment of networks, institutions, and collective identity can enhance political strength and visibility and provide the support for resilient cultural identities. Community-building can also contribute to economic development and begin to address the pressing poverty of many Aboriginal people living in cities (Rothney, 1992). In this context, some urban Aboriginal people have emphasized the need to engage in a process of healing and consensus- and community-building in urban areas.[23] David Chartrand, then president of the National Association of Friendship Centres, told the Royal Commission on Aboriginal Peoples that the most effective way to solve the problems that Aboriginal people face in the city was to catch them before they start by strengthening individuals' identities and awareness of the urban Aboriginal community.[24]

The challenges to community-building in urban areas are considerable. One challenge comes from the cultural diversity of urban Aboriginal people. In his report for the Native Council of Canada, Morse (1993, p. 88) noted:

> In the urban setting, asking the individual members of the potentially very diverse urban group [sic], each with their own unique identity, traditions, language and culture, to put aside their differences and build a new community is a formidable task. It requires the rejection of the long history of federal intervention, and for the urban Aboriginal population to come to terms with their diversity.

Many people who live in urban areas retain ties with their non-urban communities of origin, and these ties represent an important component of their cultural identities. Moreover, some land-based First Nations communities are currently exploring ways of extending their jurisdiction over members who live in urban areas.

At the same time, urban Aboriginal people need local access to places, people, and activities that support the celebration and enhancement of their cultures. In cities where there are relatively few people from any particular cultural group, these opportunities can exist only through co-operation and collective activities. The challenge for Aboriginal people, then, urban and non-urban, is to explore ways of creating urban communities that will support a variety of cultural origins and, at the same time, protect the ties that some people have with their non-urban communities of origin. These approaches can only be designed by Aboriginal people themselves, and they may vary from place to place.

Another challenge to community-building comes from the extreme poverty of many urban Aboriginal people.[25] Poverty and economic marginalization work against community-building, the very thing that could begin to alleviate that condition. The majority of urban residents do not possess the financial resources to support institutional development. Moreover, many are faced with enormous daily challenges in trying to obtain an adequate standard of living, which leave little time or energy for participation in community-building. These struggles take place in the context of a political environment that does not support urban community-building. As representatives to the Royal Commission on Aboriginal Peoples' National Round Table on Aboriginal Urban Issues pointed out: "any sort of co-operative urban Aboriginal movement has been hamstrung by scarce resources, fragmented populations, unclear mandates, and a lack of ... federal or provincial encouragement and support" (RCAP, 1993a, p. 79). In many cities, then, the processes of urban Aboriginal community-building require the infusion of financial resources from other levels of government. These infusions will lose any effectiveness, however, without the resolution of jurisdictional disputes over responsibilities for urban Aboriginal peoples.

Supporting Self-Government

Until recently, most of the literature on the nature of and possibilities for Aboriginal self-government focussed on land-based populations. Although there was some consideration of urban applications (see Dunn, 1986; Reeves, 1986; Weinstein, 1986), most researchers pointed out the difficulties of implementation off a land base and concentrated on land-base arrangements (see, for example, Penner, 1983; RCAP, 1993b, p. 44).

Urban Aboriginal peoples' demands for self-government contradict the colonial legacy, which views Aboriginal cultures, communities, and values as incompatible with or inappropriate in the urban industrial milieu. Self-government is also essential for the enhancement of Aboriginal cultures in urban areas. In their study of Aboriginal organizations in three major urban centres, Clatworthy et al. (1995) found that the activities of the organizations were highly circumscribed by the interests of funding organizations, which were, for the most part, non-Aboriginal governments. Opekokew (1995) argues that cultural preservation and enhancement occur only when Aboriginal people have control over their institutions.

A number of models of urban self-government for Aboriginal peoples in urban areas have been put forward in recent years. Many First Nations support the extension of jurisdiction of land-based governments to urban citizens (Opekokew, 1995). The Native Council of Canada (now the Congress of Aboriginal Peoples) suggested options, including governance over urban reserves or Aboriginal neighbourhoods, self-determining Aboriginal institutions, and pan-Aboriginal governing bodies in urban areas (Native Council of Canada, 1993). Tizya (1992, p. 8) described an approach where urban residents would fall under the jurisdiction of the First Nation in whose traditional territory the urban centre lies. Métis organizations place governance for urban residents in a structure with urban and rural locals nested in provincial and national organizations (Young, 1995).

The issue is complex. In addition to debates over the scope of an inherent right to self-government in urban areas, some approaches to governance cannot be implemented in conjunction with others, and setting up different structures for each cultural group could result in impossible complexity (Peters, 1994). Yet extending opportunities for self-government is crucial for the large number of Aboriginal people living in urban areas.

Representing Aboriginal Peoples in Urban Landscapes

Initiatives to change public perceptions about the relationship between Aboriginal cultures and urban life are needed in addition to support for community-building, cultural programming, and self-government. These initiatives must occur in a wide variety of areas, and they must be sustained because they are part of changing very deeply held ways people have of organizing their view of the world. In this context, changing presentations of Aboriginal peoples and histories in educational materials and the media would benefit urban Aboriginal people. However, some initiatives that focus specifically on urban landscapes are also needed.

One important strategy in this regard has to do with changing the way Aboriginal people are represented (or not represented) in urban landscapes. Symbols in urban landscapes reflect and reproduce societal values about what is and what is not valued and important. Contemporary urban landscapes offer little to valorize Aboriginal cultures, affirm their relevance to contemporary life, or admit their continuing existence. There is little recognition that most cities are on Aboriginal peoples' traditional territories or that urban development may affect sites that are important for spiritual or historical reasons.[26] There are few attempts at historic preservation of significant sites that bring the Aboriginal heritage of the lands on which urban areas are built to public consciousness. There are few streets, parks, or buildings named after significant Aboriginal people, whether historical or contemporary. Aboriginal heroes do not often appear in monuments dedicated to their memory. Making Aboriginal people and cultures visible in urban landscapes would signal that they have a valued place in contemporary urban areas.

CONCLUSION

Support for the maintenance and enhancement of Aboriginal cultures is not the only challenge facing Aboriginal people in urban areas. Aboriginal people have also stressed other pressing needs. Participants at the Royal Commission on Aboriginal People's National Round Table on Aboriginal Urban Issues identified the need for economic development, more appropriate services, changes in government policies and jurisdiction, and a voice in governance and decision making (RCAP, 1993a). I have focussed on cultural issues in this chapter for two reasons. The first has to do with a long history of denying that Aboriginal cultures have an appropriate place in urban areas — a place that has challenged the identities of many urban Aboriginal people. The second has to do with my sense that valuing and supporting urban Aboriginal cultures in cities would contribute to meeting some of the other needs of urban Aboriginal communities.

More than one-third of the Aboriginal people of Canada live in urban areas. Taking measures to support and enhance their cultures will make cities better places for Aboriginal people and for non-Aboriginal residents.

NOTES

1. By Aboriginal peoples I mean the indigenous peoples of this country, including First Nations peoples, Métis, and Inuit. First Nations peoples are

people who identify themselves as such, including people who are and are not registered under the Indian Act. I use the term "Indian" when I refer to Euro-Canadian constructions of First Nations peoples. Registered Indians are registered under the Indian Act.

2. This chapter takes a social constructionist approach to the issue of Aboriginal urbanization (see Best, 1989; Spector and Kitsuse, 1987). This approach argues that people's sense of what is and what is not a problem is not simply the result of objective conditions, but has also been produced or constructed through social action and events. Typically, the social construction of an issue characterizes it as a certain type of problem. This characterization serves as a framework for identifying appropriate strategies for its management or solution.

3. The census question that collects information on Canadians' ethnic or cultural origins asked, "To which ethnic or cultural group(s) did this person's ancestors belong?" In 1991, a postcensal survey, the Aboriginal Peoples Survey (APS), asked individuals who indicated they had Aboriginal ancestry whether they identified with an Aboriginal group. This "identity" population is smaller than the population that has Aboriginal ancestry or cultural origins.

4. See note 3 for a description of the APS.

5. To date, federal negotiations have been held with bands and groups of bands.

6. This list does not represent all Aboriginal organizations in the city, but those that are managed by Aboriginal people and that are autonomous of other organizations, urban-based, and urban-focussed.

7. In Vancouver, URBAN, an umbrella organization for 54 non-profit societies, provided social services to Aboriginal people in Vancouver until recently.

8. Other limitations include changing definitions (Gerber, 1977, p. 4), the location of a number of reserves in urban centres, and failure to update records regularly (Canada, 1992).

9. Before 1981, only one ethnic origin was captured in the census. In 1981, more than one origin was allowed, but respondents were not encouraged to identify more than one.

10. By 1991, about 87 000 had been added to the registered Indian population, increasing the total population by about 21 percent between 1985 and 1991. A substantial proportion of the peoples added to the Register would have lived in urban areas.

11. There are no published statistics on urban Aboriginal people before 1951.

12. John MacLean, a missionary with a doctorate in history and author of *The Indians of Canada* (1889) and *Canadian Savage Folk* (1896), was considered to be an authority. Describing the Sarcees on a reserve near Calgary, he wrote (1896, p. 18):

> Their close proximity to Calgary is injurious to the morals of the white people and Indians, as the natives of the plains always find the lower stratum of society ready to teach the willing learner lessons of immorality, and degradation is sure to follow any close relationship of Indians with white people in the early stages of their training.

13. Although I recognize that some of the concern may be spillover from events in inner cities in the United States during the 1960s, the definition of Aboriginal urbanization as problematic substantially predates these events, and the themes and explanations are too persistent to be simply a reflection of the U.S. experience.

14. There is little recognition of the diversity of Aboriginal cultures in this literature.

15. These quotations do not represent isolated opinions taken out of context, but reflect a general framework within which writers understood the nature of the urban experience for Aboriginal migrants. See also, for example, Asimi, 1967, p. 94; Bond, 1967; Currie, 1966, p. 14; Indian–Eskimo Association, 1971, p. 6; Melling, 1967; Canada, 1960c, pp. 1034–39; Trudeau, 1969; Vincent, 1971, p. 13; Zentner, 1973, p. xii. At the same time, it is important to note that there were writers who argued that urbanization did not represent a rejection of Aboriginal culture (Lurie, 1967; McCaskill, 1981).

16. Clearly these dates are approximate, and there are works that fit into neither time period nor subject category as I have organized them. Moreover, some of the themes I associate with the post-1980 period were also present before then.

17. Ryan (1975) made similar points earlier.

18. It is important to note that Aboriginal people are not the only group that has been so defined (see Ray, 1992; Sibley, 1981).

19. Nancy Van Heest, Vancouver, B.C., Public Hearing, 2 June 1993, p. 14.

20. Harold Orten, Orillia, Ontario, Public Hearing, 13 May 1993, p. 66.

21. Margaret King, Saskatoon Urban Treaty Indians, Saskatoon, Saskatchewan, Public Hearing, 28 October 1992, pp. 146–47.

22. David Chartrand, President, NAFC, Toronto Public Hearing, 26 June 1992, p. 565.

23. See, for example, presentations by Sylvia Maracle and Wayne Helgason to a workshop on urban self-government (Peters, 1995).

24. David Chartrand, President, NAFC, Toronto Public Hearing, 26 June 1992, p. 565.

25. It is important to emphasize that the economic marginalization of urban Aboriginal people is not of their own making. Rather, it comes from a long history of their exclusion from the mainstream of society.

26. Rosalee Tizya, co-coordinator, Urban Perspectives, Royal Commission on Aboriginal Peoples, made this point at a workshop on self-government for urban Aboriginal peoples held at Queen's University, 25–26 May 1994.

DISCUSSION QUESTIONS

1. What do you know about the culture and traditions of the Aboriginal people living in your city (or the city nearest you)?

2. On which nation's traditional territory is your city (or the city near-est you) located?
3. How are Aboriginal people presented in this city?
4. When you read your newspaper, how do articles present local Abo-riginal people? How often are they featured? How is the relationship between Aboriginal culture and urban life conceptualized?

FURTHER READINGS

Maracle, L. 1992. *Sundogs*. Penticton, B.C.: Theytus Books. Lee Maracle's novel, about an Aboriginal family during the time of the downfall of the Meech Lake accord and the Oka crisis, is one of the few pieces of fiction by an Aboriginal person that is set in an urban area.

Peters, E.J. 1995. *Self-Government for Aboriginal Peoples in Urban Areas*. Kingston, Ont.: Institute of Intergovernmental Relations, Queen's University. This publication represents the proceedings of a workshop on urban self-government held at Queen's University in May 1995. Speakers included Aboriginal people involved in urban political and service organizations and representatives from munic-ipal, provincial, and federal governments. Three background papers explore demographic characteristics of urban Aboriginal people, urban Aboriginal institutions, and models of urban self-govern-ment.

Richardson, B. 1994. "The Aboriginal City." Pp. 227–53 in *People of Terra Nullius: Betrayal and Rebirth in Aboriginal Canada*. Vancouver and Toronto: Douglas & McIntyre. Boyce Richardson reports on his inter-views with urban Aboriginal people, primarily in Winnipeg, highlight-ing a variety of issues that are of contemporary concern to them.

Royal Commission on Aboriginal Peoples (RCAP). 1993. *Aboriginal Peo-ples in Urban Centres: Report of the National Round Table on Aboriginal Urban Issues*. Ottawa: Supply and Services. From 21 to 23 June 1992, the Royal Commission on Aboriginal Peoples hosted a national round table on urban Aboriginal issues in Edmonton. The published pro-ceedings of the round table include a summary of the issues raised; a re-port on the workshops on services, health and wellness, economics, and governance; and a series of short issue papers.

Royal Commission on Aboriginal Peoples (RCAP). 1996. "Urban Perspectives." Pp. 519–621 in *Report of the Royal Commission on Aboriginal Peoples*, Vol. 4, *Perspectives and Realities*. Ottawa: Minister of Supply and Services Canada. This section of the final report of the Royal Commission addresses a variety of issues concerning Aboriginal people in urban areas, including cultural identity, financial responsibilities for services off reserves, service delivery, Aboriginal women, governance, and urban demographic and socio-economic conditions. The Commission makes a number of recommendations to address these issues.

Ryan, J. 1979. *Wall of Words: The Betrayal of the Urban Indian*. Toronto: Peter Martin Associates. This classic book tells the story of the attempts of two Blackfoot men to provide services to First Nations people migrating to the city and documents the federal government's consolidation of its stance that it was responsible only for reserve residents.

REFERENCES

Asimi, A.P. 1967. "The Urban Setting." Pp. 89–96 in *Resolving Conflicts — A Cross-Cultural Approach*. Winnipeg: Department of University Extensions and Adult Education, University of Manitoba.

Berkhoffer, R.F. 1979. *The White Man's Indian: Images of the American Indian from Columbus to the Present*. New York: Vintage.

Best, J. 1989. *Images of Issues: Typifying Contemporary Social Problems*. New York: Aldine de Gruyter.

Boek, W.E. and J.K. Boek. 1959. *The People of Indian Ancestry in Greater Winnipeg*. Winnipeg: Queen's Printer.

Bond, J.J. 1967. *A Report on the Pilot Relocation Project at Elliot Lake, Ontario*. Ottawa: Department of Indian Affairs and Northern Development.

Braroe, W.W. 1975. *Indian and White: Self-Image and Interaction in a Canadian Plains Community*. Stanford, Conn.: Stanford University Press.

Breton, R. and G. Grant. 1984. *The Dynamics of Government Programs for Urban Indians in the Prairie Provinces*. Montreal: The Institute for Research on Public Policy.

Brody, H. 1983. *Maps and Dreams: Indians and the British Columbia Frontier*. New York: Penguin.

Buckley, H. 1992. *From Wooden Ploughs to Welfare: Why Indian Policy Failed in the Prairie Provinces*. Montreal and Kingston, Ont.: McGill-Queen's University Press.

Canada, Department of Indian Affairs and Northern Development (DIAND). 1957. *The Indian News* 2(4): p. 3.

———. 1967. *Indian Affairs: Facts and Figures*. Ottawa: DIAND.

———. 1992. Quantitative Analysis and Socio-Demographic Research. *Basic Departmental Data*. Ottawa: Supply and Services.

Canada, Information Canada. 1974. *Perspective Canada: A Compendium of Social Statistics*. Ottawa: Department of Industry, Trade and Commerce.

Canada, Joint Committee of the Senate and the House of Commons on Indian Affairs. 1960a. Brief of the Indian–Eskimo Association of Canada. *Minutes of Proceedings and Evidence*. Vol. 5: pp. 363–427.

———. 1960b. *Minutes of Proceedings and Evidence*. Vol. 14: pp. 537–42.

———. 1960c. Submission by the Government of Saskatchewan. *Minutes of Proceedings and Evidence*. Vol. 12: pp. 1029–79.

Canadian Corrections Association. 1967. *Indians and the Law*. Ottawa: Canadian Welfare Council.

Clatworthy, S.J. 1980. *The Demographic Composition and Economic Circumstances of Winnipeg's Native Population*. Winnipeg: Institute of Urban Studies, University of Winnipeg.

Clatworthy, S.J. and J.P. Gunn. 1981. *The Economic Circumstances of Native People in Selected Metropolitan Centres in Western Canada*. Winnipeg: Institute of Urban Studies, University of Winnipeg.

Clatworthy, S.J. and J. Hull. 1983. *Native Economic Conditions in Regina and Saskatoon*. Winnipeg: Institute of Urban Studies, University of Winnipeg.

Clatworthy, S., J. Hull, and N. Loughran. 1995. "Urban Aboriginal Organizations: Edmonton, Toronto and Winnipeg." Pp. 25–81 in *Self-Government for Aboriginal People in Urban Areas*, ed. E.J. Peters. Kingston, Ont.: Institute of Intergovernmental Relations, Queen's University.

Comeau, P. and A. Santin. 1990. *The First Canadians: A Profile of Canada's Native People Today*. Toronto: James Lorimer.

Currie, W. 1966. "Urbanization and Indians." Address to the Mid-Canada Development Corridor Conference, Indian–Eskimo Association, Lakehead University, Thunder Bay, Ont.

Davis, A.K. 1965. *Edging into Mainstream: Urban Indians in Saskatchewan*. Bellingham: Western Washington State College.

Duck, Edith. 1995. "I Forget Who I Am." Pp. 40–41 in *Steal My Rage: New Native Voices*, ed. Joel T. Maki. Vancouver: Douglas & McIntyre.

Dunn, M. 1986. *Access to Survival: A Perspective on Aboriginal Self-Government for the Constituency of the Native Council of Canada*. Kingston, Ont.: Institute of Intergovernmental Relations, Queen's University.

Elias, P.D. 1975. *Metropolis and Hinterland in Northern Manitoba*. Winnipeg: Manitoba Museum of Man and Nature.

Falconer, P. 1985. "Urban Indian Needs: Federal Policy Responsibility and Options in the Context of the Talks on Aboriginal Self-Government." Discussion paper (unpublished).

———. 1990. "The Overlooked of the Neglected: Native Single-Mothers in Major Cities on the Prairies." Pp. 188–210 in *The Political Economy of Manito-*

ba, ed. J. Silver and J. Hull. Regina: Canadian Plains Research Centre, University of Regina.

Francis, D. 1992. *The Imaginary Indian: The Image of the Indian in Canadian Culture*. Vancouver: Arsenal Pulp Press.

Frideres, J.S. 1984. "Government Policies and Programs Relating to People of Indian Ancestry in Alberta." Pp. 321–517 in *The Dynamics of Government Programs for Urban Indians in the Prairie Provinces*, ed. R. Breton and G. Grant. Montreal: The Institute for Research on Public Policy.

———. 1988. *Canada's Indians: Contemporary Conflicts*, 3rd ed. Scarborough, Ont.: Prentice-Hall.

———. 1993. *Native Peoples in Canada: Contemporary Conflicts*, 4th ed. Scarborough, Ont.: Prentice-Hall.

Gerber, L.M. 1977. "Trends in Out-Migration from Indian Communities across Canada: A Report for the Task Force on Migrating Native People." PhD thesis, Harvard University.

Goldie, T. 1989. *Fear and Temptation: The Image of the Indigene in Canadian, Australian and New Zealand Literature*. Montreal and Kingston, Ont.: McGill-Queen's University Press.

Goldman, G. 1993. "The Aboriginal Population and the Census: 120 Years of Information — 1871 to 1991." Statistics Canada, Ottawa. (Unpublished.)

Hawthorn, H.B., C. Belshaw, and S. Jamieson. 1958. *The Indians of British Columbia*. Toronto: University of Toronto Press.

Helgason, W. 1995. "Urban Aboriginal Issues, Models and Stakeholders Relative to the Transition to Self-Government." Pp. 131–40 in *Self-Government for Aboriginal Peoples in Urban Areas*, ed. E. Peters. Kingston, Ont.: Institute of Intergovernmental Relations, Queen's University.

Hirabayashi, G.K. 1962. *The Challenge of Assisting the Canadian Aboriginal People to Adjust to Urban Environments: Report of the First Western Canadian Indian–Métis Seminar*. Edmonton: University of Alberta Press.

Indian–Eskimo Association. 1960. "Proceedings of the National Research Seminar on Indians in the City." Queen's University. (Unpublished.)

———. 1971. *Final Report: Indians and the City*. Toronto: Contract with Secretary of State.

Kastes, W.G. 1993. *The Future of Aboriginal Urbanization in Prairie Cities: Select Annotated Bibliography and Literature Review on Urban Aboriginal Issues in the Prairie Provinces*. Winnipeg: Institute of Urban Studies, University of Winnipeg.

Krotz, Larry. 1980. *Urban Indians: The Strangers in Canada's Cities*. Edmonton: Hurtig Publishers.

Lagasse, J.H. 1958. *A Study of the Population of Indian Ancestry in Manitoba: A Social and Economic Study*. Winnipeg: Social and Economic Research Office, Manitoba Department of Agriculture and Immigration.

Lithman, Y.G. 1984. *The Community Apart: A Case Study of a Canadian Indian Reserve Community*. Winnipeg: University of Manitoba Press.

Lurie, N.O. 1967. "The Indian Moves to an Urban Setting." Pp. 73–86 in *Resolving Conflicts — A Cross-Cultural Approach*. Winnipeg: Department of University Extensions and Adult Education, University of Manitoba.

MacLean, J. 1896. *Canadian Savage Folk: The Native Tribes of Canada.* Toronto: William Briggs.

———. 1889. *Indians of Canada: Their Manners and Customs.* Toronto: William Briggs.

Maidman, F. 1981. *Native People in Urban Settings: Problems, Needs and Services.* Toronto: Ontario Task Force on Native People in the Urban Setting.

McCaskill, D.N. 1981. "The Urbanization of Indians in Winnipeg, Toronto, Edmonton and Vancouver: A Comparative Analysis." *Culture* 1(1): pp. 82–89.

Melling, J. 1967. *Right to a Future: The Native Peoples of Canada.* Toronto: T.H. Best Printing Co.

Morse, B. 1989. "Government Obligations, Aboriginal Peoples and Section 91(24)." Pp. 59–92 in *Aboriginal Peoples and Government Responsibility: Exploring Federal and Provincial Roles,* ed. D.C. Hawkes. Ottawa: Carleton University Press.

———. 1993. *A Legal and Jurisdictional Analysis of Urban Self-Government.* Ottawa: Native Council of Canada Royal Commission Intervenor Research Project.

Nagler, M. 1970. *Indians in the City.* Ottawa: Canadian Research Centre for Anthropology, St. Paul University.

Native Council of Canada. 1992. *Decision 1992: Background and Discussion Points for the First Peoples Forum.* Ottawa: NCC.

———. 1993. *The First Peoples Urban Circle: Choices for Self-Determination.* Book 1. Ottawa: NCC.

Opekokew, D. 1995. "Treaty First Nations Perspectives on Self-Government of Aboriginal Peoples in Urban Areas." Pp. 168–72 in *Self-Government for Aboriginal Peoples in Urban Areas,* ed. E. Peters. Kingston, Ont.: Institute of Intergovernmental Relations, Queen's University.

Penner, K. 1983. *Indian Self-Government.* Ottawa: Supply and Services.

Peters, E.J. 1994. "Geographies of Self-Government." In *Implementing Aboriginal Self-Government in Canada,* ed. J. Hylton. Saskatoon: Purich Publishers.

———. 1995. *Self-Government for Aboriginal Peoples in Urban Areas.* Kingston, Ont.: Institute of Intergovernmental Relations, Queen's University.

———. 1996. " 'Urban' and 'Aboriginal': An Impossible Contradiction?" Pp. 47–62 in *City Lives and City Forms: Critical Research and Canadian Urbanism,* ed. J. Caulfield and L. Peake. Toronto: University of Toronto Press.

Powless, J. 1994. Department of Indian Affairs and Northern Development. Personal communication. (12 January).

Price, J.A. and D.N. McCaskill. 1974. "The Urban Integration of Canadian Indians." *Western Canadian Journal of Anthropology* 4(2): pp. 29–45.

Ray, B.K. 1992. "Immigrants in a 'Multicultural' Toronto: Exploring the Contested Social and Housing Geographies of Post-War Italian and Caribbean Immigrants." PhD thesis, Department of Geography, Queen's University.

Reeves, W. 1986. "Native Societies: The Professions as a Model of Self-Determination for Urban Indians." Pp. 342–58 in *Arduous Journey: Canadian Indians and Decolonization,* ed. J.R. Ponting. Toronto: McClelland & Stewart.

Reeves, W. and J. Frideres. 1981. "Government Policy and Indian Urbanization: The Alberta Case." *Canadian Public Policy* 7(4): pp. 584–95.

Regina Welfare Council. 1959. *Our City Indians: Report of a Conference*. Regina: Saskatchewan House.

Reiber-Kremers and Associates. 1977. "A Preliminary Overview of Native Migration into the City of Winnipeg." Discussion paper prepared for the City of Winnipeg, Environmental Planning Department.

Richardson, B. 1994. *People of Terra Nullius: Betrayal and Rebirth in Aboriginal Canada*. Vancouver and Toronto: Douglas & McIntyre.

Robertson, H. 1970. *Reservations Are for Indians*. Toronto: James Lewis & Samuel.

Rothney, R.G. 1992. *Neechi Foods Co-op Ltd.: Lessons in Community Development*. Winnipeg: Winnipeg Family Economic Development Inc.

Royal Commission on Aboriginal Peoples (RCAP). 1993a. *Aboriginal Peoples in Urban Centres: Report of the National Round Table on Aboriginal Urban Issues*. Ottawa: Supply and Services.

———. 1993b. *Partners in Confederation: Aboriginal Peoples, Self-Government, and the Constitution*. Ottawa: Supply and Services.

———. 1996. *Report of the Royal Commission on Aboriginal Peoples*. Vol. 4. *Perspectives and Realities*. Ottawa: Minister of Supply and Services.

Ryan, J. 1975. *Wall of Words: The Betrayal of the Urban Indian*. Toronto: Peter Martin Associates.

Saskatchewan. 1979. *The Dimensions of Indian and Native Urban Poverty in Saskatchewan*. Regina: Social Planning Secretariat.

Shimpo, M. and R. Williamson. 1965. *Socio-Cultural Disintegration among the Fringe Saulteaux*. Saskatoon: Centre for Community Studies, University of Saskatchewan.

Shorten, L. 1991. *Without Reserve: Stories from Urban Natives*. Edmonton: NeWest Press.

Sibley, E. 1981. *Outsiders in Urban Societies*. New York: St. Martin's Press.

Spector, M. and J.I. Kitsuse. 1987. *Constructing Social Problems*. New York: Aldine de Gruyter.

Statistics Canada. 1991a. *1991 Census*. Cat. nos. 93-339 and 93-340. Ottawa: Industry, Science and Technology Canada.

———. 1991b. *Aboriginal Peoples Survey*. Cat. nos. 94-327, 89-535, and 89-534. Ottawa: Industry, Science and Technology Canada.

———. 1993. *Census and Aboriginal Peoples Survey*. Cat. no. 94-327. Ottawa: Industry, Science and Technology Canada.

Stymeist, D. 1975. *Ethnics and Indians*. Toronto: Peter Martin Associates.

Tizya, R. 1992. "Comments on Urban Aboriginals and Self-Government." Pp. 45–52 in *Aboriginal Governments and Power Sharing in Canada*, ed. D. Brown. Kingston, Ont.: Institute of Intergovernmental Relations, Queen's University.

Tobias, J.L. 1983. "Protection, Civilization, Assimilation: An Outline History of Canada's Indian Policy." Pp. 29–38 in *As Long as the Sun Shines and Water*

Flows: A Reader in Canadian Native Studies, ed. A.L. Getty and A.S. Lussier. Vancouver: University of British Columbia Press.

Trudeau, J. 1969. "The Indian in the City." *Kerygma* 3(3): pp. 118–23.

Vincent, D.B. 1971. *The Indian–Métis Urban Probe*. Winnipeg: Indian–Métis Friendship Centre and Institute of Urban Studies, University of Winnipeg.

Weinstein, J. 1986. *Self-Determination Off a Land-Base*. Kingston, Ont.: Institute of Intergovernmental Relations, Queen's University.

Young, D. 1995. "Some Approaches to Urban Aboriginal Governance." Pp. 153–62 in *Self-Government for Aboriginal Peoples in Urban Areas*, ed. E. Peters. Kingston, Ont.: Institute of Intergovernmental Relations, Queen's University.

Zeitoun, L. 1969. "Canadian Indians at the Crossroads: Some Aspects of Relocation and Urbanization in Canada." Study for the Manpower Utilization Branch, Department of Manpower and Immigration, Ottawa. (Unpublished.)

Zentner, H. 1973. *The Indian Identity Crisis*. Calgary: Strayer Publications.

CHAPTER 9

Struggles within the Circle: Violence, Healing, and Health on a First Nations Reserve[1]

Terry Fox and David Long

INTRODUCTION

> Health is the core of the well-being that must lie at the centre of each healthy person and the vitality that must animate healthy communities and cultures. Where there is good health in this sense, it reverberates through every strand of life. (RCAP, 1993b, p. 51)

In this chapter we explore the relationship among violence, healing, and health in the lives of Aboriginal people in Canada. We do so by examining a number of ways in which Aboriginal and non-Aboriginal people have contributed to the health status of Aboriginal individuals, families, and communities in this country. Our story and analysis are grounded in the assumption that health in both individual and collective terms is a gift. Out of its wholeness one can draw an appreciation for life and envision a path of healing. Healing, therefore, might best be understood as a sometimes difficult, even painful, path toward health. As we note, many Aboriginal people who are committed to walking a path of healing often experience fear, anger, frustration, and even despair in relation to the physical, social, and spiritual ills that have long afflicted them and their people. The generalized pictures of Aboriginal family violence and suicide we paint in the initial section of this chapter are punctuated by Terry Fox's disturbing account of life among her people living on the Stoney First Nation reserve in Morley, Alberta. Her story illustrates that for these and many other Aboriginal people in Canada, walking a path of healing is at times a despairing struggle. It also challenges the reader to acknowledge that an important and quite painful step in the healing process involves naming the people, circumstances, and social structures that cultivate violence and perpetuate individual and collective unwellness.

We recognize that Aboriginal people and their supporters have taken a variety of paths over the past 40 years in response to the experiences and living conditions of Aboriginal people in Canada. One of these paths involves violence, and because violence involving Aboriginal people in Canada is in many instances an expression of their anger, frustration, and fear that meaningful social change will not occur, it is important that we examine it in the context of healing and health. Consequently, after presenting our general picture of Aboriginal family violence and suicide in Canada and their place in the lives of the Stoney First Nation, we conclude with a discussion of various "healing initiatives" in the context of some of the obstacles that have stood in the way of healing.

ABORIGINAL FAMILY VIOLENCE

Incidence and Implications

It has only been in the last decade or so that sustained research effort has focussed on Aboriginal family violence in Canada. Thus it is difficult to know just how recent a phenomenon it is, the extent of the violence that occurs in "family" situations, and the extent to which the incidence has increased, remained constant, or decreased over the past 40 years. For many reasons — changing perceptions of what constitutes assault; the economic, physical, and sometimes emotional dependency of women; cultural expectations of loyalty to one's community; fear of reprisal by family or community members; fear of having one's children taken away or one's sole source of support put in jail; lack of awareness of available services; fear of the police, threats, and loss of privacy — family violence tends to remain hidden from public view and from potential sources of support for those involved (Frank, 1993, pp. 15–18). As a result, it is estimated that for the Canadian population, police become aware of family violence in only approximately 50 percent of assaults by a spouse or former spouse (Appleford, 1989, p. 3). A study of family violence in the Northwest Territories estimated that only between 10 and 30 percent of assaults ever come to the attention of social services. For the many more who never seek help, violence is simply a part of their everyday experience (RGNWT, 1986, p. iii). Moreover, the personal, social, and economic costs are extremely difficult to measure (RCAP, 1996b, p. 54). As Sharon Caudron noted in her submission to the Royal Commission on Aboriginal Peoples (RCAP) (1996b, p. 54):

Our children are vastly affected by family violence even when they are not the direct victims. The cost to our children is hidden in their inability to be attentive in school, in feelings of insecurity and low self-esteem, and in acting out behaviour which may manifest itself in many ways, such as vandalism, self-abuse, bullying, and often these children suffer in silence.

It is therefore difficult even to estimate the extent of family violence experienced by the Canadian population as a whole and by Aboriginal people in particular.

Part of the difficulty in trying to understand and address family violence in Canada is that although the "rule of thumb"[2] was outlawed over 100 years ago, many social attitudes, beliefs, and practices regarding female–male relationships remain unchanged. The view that the domination of women by men is legitimate and that physical, emotional, and other expressions of violence are acceptable aspects of interpersonal relationships affects our ability to see many aspects of family violence as a problem. A study carried out by the Solicitor General's office (1985, p. 4) found that women were more likely than men to have been assaulted by their relatives (12 percent vs. 2 percent) or acquaintances (36 percent vs. 25 percent). Moreover, women were victims in 77 percent of family-related assaults, 90 percent of assaults between spouses, 80 percent of assaults between ex-spouses, and 55 percent of assaults involving other relatives. The majority of assaults against both men (98 percent) and women (89 percent) also involved male offenders. MacLeod (1987), among others, notes that the problem of underreporting by victims is compounded by the fact that when victims do not report incidents to the police, community members, friends, and even close relatives are also unlikely to do so. In the Solicitor General's study mentioned above, reporting of incidents by someone other than the victim ranged from 9 percent in assaults involving marital partners to 16 percent in incidents involving acquaintances and 21 percent in assaults by strangers (Solicitor General, 1985, p. 4).

So just how "big" a problem does family violence in Canada appear to be? MacLeod's (1980) "conservative estimate" that every year 10 percent of Canadian women are abused by their spouses or partners was based on a study of the number of women in transition homes, combined with the number of women filing for divorce on the grounds of physical cruelty. In a subsequent study, MacLeod (1987) estimated that almost 1 million women are abused in Canada each year. In 1989, members of the Manitoba Royal Commission on Family Violence heard that one in six women in that province had been abused and that the figure for Aboriginal women was much higher (MAWS, 1989). Another report to the same inquiry stated that spousal homicides account for 40 percent of all homicides in Canada (Indian and Inuit Nurses of Canada, 1991) and that the story for Aboriginal women in Canada is probably worse. Not only is the incidence of family violence involving Aboriginal women believed to be much higher, but the pressure to be loyal to one's spouse and community perpetuates personal and communal silence and lack of change (Frank, 1993, p. 16). In a 1989 study on family violence involving Aboriginal women in Ontario, 42 percent of the respondents indicated that when family violence occurs in their communities, it is not talked about in public. In the same study, only 48 percent of respondents stated that family violence is reported when it occurs, 28 percent stated that it is not reported, and 24 percent said they did not know. In addition, 54 percent of respondents indicated that they thought very few Aboriginal women who experienced family violence actually sought social, medical, or legal help (ONWA, 1989, p. 21). In a report to the RCAP (1993a), a representative of the Child Protection Centre of Winnipeg estimated that while only 10 percent of non-Aboriginal women testify in court against their abusive partners, the number of Aboriginal women willing to take their cases to court is even lower.[3] Frank (1993, p. 18) reports that 65 percent of respondents to a Helping Spirit Lodge survey stated that many Aboriginal women are discouraged from receiving medical treatment because of the fear of reprisal from the abuser or the abuser's family. Moreover, the approximately 65 percent of Aboriginal people who live in rural and remote parts of the country receive neither the information nor the services necessary to understand and address the many problems and issues associated with family violence in their homes and communities (NADC, 1988, p. 8). Thus, in many respects, addressing Aboriginal family violence represents one more struggle against oppression and toward self-understanding and determination (Frank, 1993, p. 7).

Although information is essential to these struggles, care must be taken in both gathering and analyzing our information. Indeed, estimates vary widely as to the extent of victimization among Aboriginal women in Canada. A 1989 study in British Columbia indicated that 86 percent of Aboriginal respondents had experienced family violence (Frank, 1993). In a study carried out by the Ontario Native Women's Association (1989, pp. 18–20), 84 percent of respondents indicated that family violence occurred in their communities, while a further 80 percent indicated that they had personally experienced it.[4] In the same study, 78 percent of respondents indicated that more than one member of their family was regularly abused. A similar study carried out by the Yukon Task Force on

Family Violence (YTFFV) estimated that roughly 700 women in the Yukon are assaulted each year (1985, p. 13). Other research suggests that, overall, one in three Aboriginal women in Canada is abused by her partner (Jamieson, 1987), and 40 percent of respondents to Statistics Canada's Aboriginal Peoples Survey (1993) reported that family violence is a problem in their community.[5] Based on RCMP statistics, the incidence of spousal assaults[6] in the Yukon in 1985 was 526 per 100 000 people, substantially higher than the national average of 130 per 100 000, though substantially lower than the 1 in 6 cited in the Manitoba study. In their report to the YTFFV (1985, p. 15), representatives from the Transition Home in Whitehorse reported that their organization provided shelter to an average of 160 women and 170 children per year. They also noted that 80 percent of their clients had fled violent home situations. According to one study, such statistics suggest that physical abuse has become an "acceptable way of resolving conflict and of getting one's own way" that is being passed from generation to generation in many Aboriginal communities (YTFFV, 1985, p. 4).

Data comprised of personal accounts and summary statistics help us to see family violence as both an intensely isolating, individual experience and a disturbingly social phenomenon. It also challenges us to acknowledge that family violence is as difficult a phenomenon to understand as it is to address. Although measuring rates of victimization and offence is important if we are to understand the pervasiveness of family violence involving Aboriginal people in Canada, such data barely scratches the surface of the physical, emotional, psychological, social, and spiritual pain and suffering involved.

ABORIGINAL SUICIDE

Researchers agree that family violence involves acts of aggression directed outside of oneself (Bachmann, 1993, p. 2). In contrast, suicide is the most extreme expression of violence directed inward. All available data suggest that the suicide rates for Aboriginal people in Canada are significantly higher than comparative rates for non-Aboriginal Canadians. The Canadian age-specific suicide mortality rate (ASSMR) averaged approximately 13 per 100 000 people between 1969 and 1987 (Statistics Canada, 1990, p. 332). Moreover, the ASSMR between 1984 and 1988 for males was over three times the rate for females during that same period, and the 2794 male suicides registered in 1987 represented just over 80 percent of all recorded suicides (Statistics Canada, 1990, p. 99).

For female and male Aboriginal people, the figures are much higher. In 1979, the ASSMR for Aboriginal people was over 2.5 times the national average (Canada, 1987). By the late 1970s, suicide accounted for 10.4 percent of all deaths for First Nations people (Jarvis and Boldt, 1981, p. 10). Between 1983 and 1986, the suicide rate for First Nations people was 34 per 100 000, compared with the national average of just over 14 for the same period (Bobet, 1989, pp. 12–13). The overall rate for First Nations males between 1984 and 1988 was almost three times the rate for non-Aboriginal males. By 1989, the suicide rate for Aboriginal males in Canada aged 20–24 was more than five times the national average for this age group and represented the highest rate for their age group in the world. Although the standardized suicide rate for First Nations females during this time was lower than their male counterparts, their rate was still more than twice that of non-Aboriginal females in Canada. Finally, between 1975 and 1986, 104 of the 144 suicides in the Northwest Territories were committed by Aboriginal people (Westcott et al., 1987, pp. 6–7).

Although the suicide rate for all Aboriginal people in Canada between 1984 and 1988 was almost three times the rate for the Canadian population as a whole, suicide rates of Aboriginal people have slowly declined since the early 1980s. From 1984 to 1988, suicides involving First Nations peoples decreased by 17 percent from the previous four-year period (Muir, 1991, pp. 39–40). In 1990, the suicide rate of 27.4 for registered Indians living on reserves was just over twice the Canadian rate of 13, down from the 3-to-1 ratio in 1981. According to Canada's Minister of Health (Canada, 1988, pp. 74–79), declining suicide rates may reflect better prevention, intervention, and postvention programs in Aboriginal communities and urban settings. Acknowledging that the problem of suicide has reached near-epidemic proportions, especially among Aboriginal youths, also appears to have helped communities and potential victims identify and address their suicide-related "problems" more quickly and affectively. Notwithstanding these developments, suicide rates involving Aboriginal people continue to be much higher than those for the Canadian population as a whole.

It also appears that there is a certain regional pattern to suicide involving First Nations people in this country. Although suicide rates for both males and females declined in most provinces during the 1980s, the Yukon, Saskatchewan, Alberta, and Quebec recorded the highest rates of decline (Muir, 1991, pp. 39–40). There also appears to be a relationship between suicide and the sex of the victim, since rates for First Nation and non-Aboriginal females are notably lower than those for Aboriginal males. Suicides by First Nations females were quite evenly distributed throughout Canada between 1980 and 1988, though again slightly higher rates were recorded in certain prairie and northern regions. Though some have speculated on the reasons for differential suicide rates, it is not clear whether the differences are due to improved medical reporting practices in certain areas, implementation of more successful community awareness and suicide prevention programs, or changes in personal and social conditions of Aboriginal peoples' lives.

For example, it is interesting to note that the suicide rate among the Inuit living in the Northwest Territories was close to Canada's national average in 1971. Traditionally, suicide among the Inuit was a culturally acceptable way of responding to infirmity or the death of one's kin. Consequently, even though the suicide rate among the Inuit was equal to the national average, the Inuit did not view suicide as a serious social problem prior to the 1970s (Pauktuutit, 1990, p. 2). Moreover, prior to 1970 non-Aboriginal people had shown little interest in settling in or even developing northern Canada. However, a global energy crisis in the early 1970s, coupled with the improved technological ability to tap into rich northern oil and natural gas deposits, apparently changed some people's minds. Despite the concerns and warnings of many (Berger, 1977), development of the Mackenzie Valley pipeline went ahead. By 1978, after just eight years of pipeline construction, the suicide rate among the Inuit had risen to 8.5 times the 1970 rate (Canada, 1993). By the early 1980s, Inuit suicide had become a major social problem. Health and Welfare Canada reported that between 1981 and 1985, the Inuit suicide rate was 3.3 times the Canadian rate. The increase continued throughout the 1980s, with the recorded rate in 1988 being almost four times the national average (Canada, 1993).

As noted by many RCAP intervenors, the number of suicides and suicide attempts involving Canada's Aboriginal people continues to be disturbingly high. Over 600 serious suicide attempts have been dealt with by the Sioux Lookout hospital since 1986. Forty-six of the 500 Innu people living in Davis Inlet attempted suicide in 1992. The mayor of Nain reported to the RCAP (1993b) that there were approximately 30 suicide attempts in his community between 1990 and 1992. Social workers in Aboriginal communities estimate that for every suicide that takes place, at least seven people are directly affected. Given that many Aboriginal communities in Canada are relatively small and close-knit, the sense of loss and despair that follows suicide and other expressions of personal and interpersonal violence ripple far beyond the bounds of the immediate family. For both Aboriginal children and adults, escaping the violence "at home" may mean leaving one's community to try to find a place in the larger, colonizing society. As the following account by Terry Fox suggests, there are also many difficulties facing those who do stay and attempt to address the violence "at home."

THE STONEY SAGA[7]

At the foot of the statuesque Canadian Rockies just west of Calgary in Morley, Alberta, lies the incredibly scenic home of the Stoney people (see Figure 9.1). With its mixture of majestic mountains, graceful forests, and rolling hills, the death and despair that live just beneath the surface of Morley's natural beauty can be difficult to detect. Although previously well concealed, many of the ugly realities of the Stoney reserve were recently exposed when a courageous Alberta provincial court judge ordered an investigation into the reserve's internal affairs. A much-publicized scandal followed that helped to expose issues of political corruption, misappropriation of funds, and shocking social conditions on the Stoney reserve.

FIGURE 9.1

The Stoney Indian Reserve

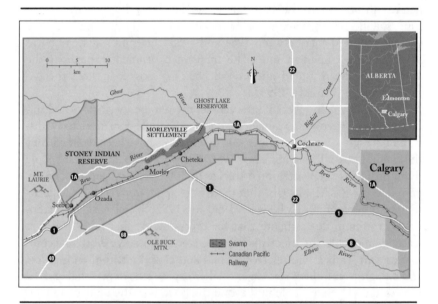

Source: Produced under license from Her Majesty the Queen in Right of Canada, with permission of Natural Resources Canada.

The problems of this reserve are nothing new, nor are they isolated to the Stoney people. In fact, I would say that the majority of First Nations communities are in many ways dysfunctional, unhealthy places to live. Even though colonization, residential schools, and the Indian Act have all contributed to the social problems experienced by Aboriginal people in Canada, the oppressive and corrupt actions of certain Aboriginal leaders also serve to maintain and in some cases worsen conditions. As painful as it is to admit that our own people can and do contribute to problems within our communities, many are beginning to acknowledge that healing is possible only if we identify the people, circumstances, and social structures that perpetuate unhealthiness. And although I present my own community as an example of an unhealthy Aboriginal community, I hope that readers will be able to identify similar problems and signs of hope in other Aboriginal and non-Aboriginal communities in Canada.

The Scandal

The summer of 1997 on the Stoney Reserve was depressing. Many young Stoney people died senseless, violent deaths. Amidst continuous trauma, there was a sense of urgency that something had to change. The public call for change began with a seemingly innocent and quite typical court case involving a Stoney man accused of assaulting his wife. As it turns out, the scandal that emerged from this trial may have paved the way for much-needed change, since it pointed to political corruption as one of the root causes of many social problems on the Stoney reserve.

The scandal began on 26 June 1997 when Judge J.D. Reilly said that he was unable to sentence a Morley man on a spousal abuse charge without knowing what community conditions may have contributed to his behaviour. Judge Reilly wrote that "for many years I have been asking why it is that this reserve which should be so prosperous, has so many poor people, has such a low level of education, has such horrendous social problems, and has such an apparent lack of programs to deal with these problems" (Reilly, 1997, p. 5). He went on to say that

> explanations [of problems on the reserve] include allegations of political corruption that one would associate with the dictatorship of a banana republic. ... Over and over, in the conversations I have with Stoney people ... the finger is pointed at the band's Chief as a significant factor. If [the allegations] are true, he is guilty of self-interest and exploitation of his people that is unbelievable for a so-called democratic community. (Reilly, 1997, p. 6)

After describing the many political injustices and the conditions of the reserve, Judge Reilly ordered the Crown to investigate allegations of political corruption, misappropriation of funds, exploitation of the poor, and poor social conditions (*The Calgary Sun*, 27 June 1997).

Fallout from the Scandal

Judge Reilly's call for an investigation quickly hit the papers and caused a great uproar. The Stoney chief immediately made a public statement denying any wrongdoing and called the judgement "outrageous, inappropriate, false and racist" (*Calgary Herald*, 27 June 1997). After a band councillor informed the press that, contrary to the comments made by the chief to the press, the council's decision had not been unanimous, another council member stated publicly that "the reserve is run like a dictatorship and has no accountability" (*Calgary Herald*, 2 July 1997).

Provincial and federal government responses were disappointing, though perhaps not surprising. Alberta Justice Minister Jon Havelock stated that investigating Aboriginal communities was not within provincial jurisdiction, and that perhaps Judge Reilly had "exceeded his jurisdiction ... [and] as such, we [the province] will be applying to the Court of Queen's Bench for prerogative to quash that order" (*The Calgary Sun*, 28 June 1997). The provincial government soon announced that the matter would be handed over to the federal government (*Calgary Herald*, 1 July 1997). The federal Department of Indian Affairs (DIA) similarly attempted both to minimize the Stoney situation and to minimize any direct responsibility of their department. The DIA refused to investigate the Stoney reserve, saying that it was an "internal matter" and that "the department does not investigate criminal charges" (*Alberta Report*, 28 July 1997). Even though no investigation had taken place, a DIA representative later commented that there "was no evidence of wrongdoings" (*Calgary Herald*, 27 Sept 1997), that "an inquiry into the reserve would only delay a solution of the problem" (*Cochrane This Week*, 2 September 1997), and that "it would not be in the best interest of the Stoneys to air their dirty laundry" (*Calgary Herald*, 7 August 1997).

Due to their concern over possible repercussions, the majority of people within the Stoney community chose not to say anything when the scandal broke out. Some who did speak anonymously to the press said that they feared losing their welfare cheques or their jobs if they spoke up. The Stoney Tribal Administration attempted to ensure the silence of Stoney employees through a memo that warned if anyone passed on information to the media, "they would be fired immediately" (*Calgary Herald*, 25 September 1997). Despite the danger, a courageous few spoke out publicly. Others spoke under the protection of anonymity, including a Stoney woman who stated that all three bands of the Stoney Nation were "infected with corruption" and that many Stoneys wanted "to speak out against nepotism and mismanagement" (*The First Perspective*, August 1997). Other Stoneys remarked, "I think it's good that the judge is saying those things," "I want to see the truth come out. ... I hope [the investigation] goes through for the benefit of my people," and "It's about time someone opened the doors" (*Calgary Herald*, 28 June 1997). Still others were angry about the allegations, including one Stoney man who told a reporter that "It's all lies" (*Calgary Herald*, 28, June 1997). Rumours circulated that outspoken members of the band were being threatened by their own people. One reserve resident reported that "Stoneys are being intimidated into silence by people on the reserve who resist change. They're using fear to keep these people quiet" (*Calgary Herald*, 17 September 1997).

As news of the scandal spread, however, more Stoney people decided to publicly show support for Judge Reilly. Not only did a group of 200 Stoneys call for the resignation of the Stoney chief (*The Calgary Sun*, 28 September 1997), but a petition was started on the reserve in an attempt to force the DIA to conduct an inquiry (*Calgary Herald*, 8 September 1997). In addition, 30 Stoneys rallied outside the Court of Queen's Bench to protest apparent attempts by provincial government representatives to quash Judge Reilly's order. As one Stoney demonstrator said, "[F]inally, we see a decision that was made from the heart by someone who understands the problem and, if it isn't heeded, we'll once again be caught in the middle" (*Calgary Rural Times*, 9 September 1997).

Publicity surrounding the Stoney scandal generated responses from many other First Nations individuals and groups. The Assembly of First Nations' national chief reportedly tried to downplay the Stoneys' troubles. He cast them as normal problems experienced by all governments and asserted that only 2 percent of the 663 bands in Canada had shown significant financial mismanagement (*Calgary Herald*, 15 September 1997). He was further quoted as saying, "I totally disagree with Judge Reilly — intervention is best left up to elected leaders not judicial officials" (*Calgary Herald*, 16 September 1997). In contrast, other First Nations people and groups confirmed that the conditions of the Stoney Reserve exist on many other reserves. For example, a group of Treaty 7 people from the neighbouring Blackfoot, Blood, and Sarcee Nations held a press conference in support of Judge Reilly. Acknowledging that poverty, unemployment, oppression, and lack of accountability of leaders was a reality on their reserves as well, people began saying that similar investigations should occur on all reserves in Canada. Accusing his own leaders of "empire-building" and having "mafia-like control," a member of the Blackfoot Nation thought that Judge Reilly's decision was "full of revolution that may straighten out our lives under the wicked system we live under." A member of the Sarcee Nation similarly commented that "we have been mistreated by our own people," while a man from the Blood Nation stated that his reserve was a "place where poor people are pushed aside" (*The Calgary Sun*, 3 July 1997). On the Hobemma reserve and Elizabeth Métis settlement, members occupied band offices, took their leaders hostage, and demanded investigations (*Calgary Herald*, 6 October 1997). Aboriginal unrest could also be seen on the Sandy Bay Reserve in Manitoba and the Fort Albany Reserve in Ontario. Complaining of nepotism, corruption, and mismanagement of band funds, band members also occupied the band offices in their communities (*Alberta Report*, 15 September 1997).

While the public scandal was spreading, the social problems of the Stoney reserve appeared to get worse. Violence and deaths involving Stoney young people in the form of suicides, murders, and accidents continued to plague the reserve. Newspaper and magazine headlines highlighted the problems: "Human Tragedy Ignored" (*Calgary Herald*, 19 August 1997), "Overdose Blamed for Latest Death" (*Calgary Herald*, 28 September 1997), "No Probe Despite Murder Charge" (*Calgary Herald*, 15 August 1997), and finally, "Six Dead Indians Worth an Inquiry" (*Alberta Report*, 1 September 1997). Sadly, the sixth death was my cousin, Abby Dawn, who was killed by a vehicle while she was walking on the highway. Altogether, eight young Stoneys under 30 years of age died violently in a three-month span.

Faced with all the human tragedy and mounting social and political pressure, the DIA was eventually forced to investigate. The day after Abby's death, Indian Affairs called for "expanded police presence" and announced an investigation into social conditions and plans for a forensic audit going back to 1994 (*Calgary Herald*, 22 August 1997). Court of Queen's Bench Judge LoVecchio partially rejected the provincial plea to quash Reilly's order for an investigation into Stoney tribal conditions, and despite limiting the scope of the investigation, concluded that "the Crown's office must still answer some probing questions about social conditions at Morley" (*The Calgary Sun*, 27 September 1997). Two months later the Crown issued its final report, consisting of "a few paragraphs and minimal statistics" (*The Globe and Mail*, 19 November 1997) concerning domestic abuse, court appearances, incarcerations, unemployment, available social programs, issues of safety, incidence of alcohol and drug abuse, and levels of suicide (*Calgary Herald*, 19 November 1997). Judge Reilly called the report "contemptuous" and "not very helpful" and told the Crown attorney that his office ought to think about laying contempt-of-court charges against the Stoney leaders (*The Globe and Mail*, 19 November 1997). The lawyer representing the Stoney man who had been originally charged with spousal abuse commented that Judge Reilly "has probably done all he can ... [but] I still see a lot of sadness on the reserve" (*The Globe and Mail*, 19 November 1997).

Background

The Stoney Tribe originally belonged to the Great Sioux Nation of the United States but relocated to southern Alberta during the late 1600s. Though Nakoda, they became known as the Stoneys. Along with the Blackfoot, Peigan, Blood, and Sarcee Nations, the Stoneys signed Treaty 7 in 1877. The Stoney people still speak the Nakoda dialect of the Sioux language fluently. The Stoney Nation now has a population of about 3400, with residents living on the three reserves of Morley (the main reserve), Bighorn, and Eden Valley. The three bands that make up the Stoney Nation are the Bearspaw, Chiniki, and Wesley. The fifteen-member Stoney Nation Tribal Council is unique in that it is made up of one chief and four councillors from each of the three bands. Elections for all three bands are held in December every two years.

When campaigns are in full swing, the community goes into a frenzy. It is common knowledge on the reserve that during election time, politicians are busy trying to secure votes by any means possible, while the people busy themselves trying to manipulate politicians for favours in return for their votes. The means by which politicians attempt to obtain votes are many, and these include manipulation and scare tactics. During the 1996 election, for example, a Stoney woman working on a campaign team said she was "instructed to tell people that the band was not ready for the brand of self-government being pushed by Ottawa and the current Wesley Chief. The band would lose its treaty rights ... and pretty soon the reserve would be cut up into acreages, sold to white people and the Stoneys would be evicted from their homes" (*Alberta Report*, 14 July 1997).

Along with intimidation, votes are often secured with money, alcohol, livestock, ranch and rodeo equipment, vehicles, and other material goods. Confirming this, a Stoney man told of how "votes are routinely bought with promises of new vehicles. In return for supporting the candidate, they either get cash ... for a down payment, a job that boosts creditworthiness, an offer from someone to co-sign a loan for them, or a combination of all three" (*Alberta Report*, 14 July 1997). In addition to jobs, handouts, and other financial favours, candidates offer people powerful and prestigious seats on boards and committees.

Similar to other reserves, large clans comprised of extended families often decide who the leaders will be. Judge Reilly stated that "there appears to be a ruling elite which uses large sums of money for itself and gives jobs on the basis of nepotism and political favouritism" (*Calgary Herald*, 29 November 1997). When voting for a candidate, it appears that clan members tend not to be concerned with the well-being and future of the Stoney people, but vote according to which politicians promise financial favours. When their preferred candidate wins, relatives and supporters then "share the spoils" (Reilly, 1997, p. 5). In contrast, those voting against a particular chief are usually punished through discrimination and deprivation because "every aspect of life is controlled by political officials, and if you are not 'connected,' nothing is done for you" (*Calgary Herald*, 27 December 1997).

Economic Issues

When they struck oil and gas in the 1970s and 1980s, the Stoneys quickly became one of the wealthiest Native communities in Canada. At the height of their boom, up to $60 million per year was being generated through gas and oil revenues (*Calgary Herald*, 28 June 1997). Many of the people believe that the future well-being of the Stoney Nation could have been secured if there had been wise investing and a strong commitment to long-term economic development. They also believe that greed, the desire for immediate gratification, and shameful financial mismanagement took their toll. In 1997, even with a budget of $50 million, which included $20 million in government transfers and $13 million in gas and oil revenues (*Calgary Herald*, 27 December 1997), the Stoneys ran up a $5.3 million deficit. In the face of this enormous debt, many Stoneys increasingly asked where their money had gone and who was responsible for their people's debt (*First Perspective*, August 1997).

In addition to the ongoing "mismanagement" of gas and oil revenues, problems were associated with the distribution of per-capita royalties to band members. During the early 1980s, every Stoney received $500 a month in gas and oil royalties. Since all people had to do was wait for their monthly cheque, many felt no need to work. Today, Stoneys receive $60 a month in per-capita distributions. Even though some oil and gas revenues still exist, they are nothing compared with the past wealth. Moreover, poverty and unemployment on the Stoney reserve appear to make the social problems worse. Roughly two-thirds of the reserve's population rely on welfare (*Calgary Herald*, 13 September 1997). Based on

DIA statistics, a single on-reserve person receives only $195 per month in welfare, while those with children receive an additional $55 per child. As a result, many Stoneys feel they will "never escape the cycle of welfare dependency" (*Calgary Herald*, 28 September 1997). A man reported that young Stoney people drink and do drugs because "they haven't got anything else to do. There's no work" (*Calgary Herald*, 28 September 19). Because they have been conditioned by handouts and are faced with largely unsupportive Aboriginal and non-Aboriginal leaders, the majority of Stoneys are virtually helpless to escape their poverty and dependence on others.

The extreme and relentless character of social problems on the Stoney reserve are duplicated on First Nations reserves all across Canada. Unwellness in Native communities is usually manifest in rampant alcohol and drug abuse, one result of which is extremely high rates of premature and unnatural violent deaths. Along with alcoholism, abuse of prescription drugs has become a significant problem for many Stoneys and other Native people. A Stoney social worker estimated that "70 percent of band residents are hooked on drugs" (*Alberta Report*, 14 July 1997). A reserve resident who recently lost two sisters to prescription drug abuse stated that "prescription drugs are easy for anybody to get. Doctors are giving pills away like ... candy to children" (*Calgary Herald*, 9 October 1997). Canada's Auditor General reported that "prescription drug abuse among registered Indians in Alberta was the highest of the country," and of the "262 deaths [in Alberta in 1997], prescription drugs had been a significant factor in 113 of those deaths" (*Calgary Herald*, 9 October 1997). The other frequent form of unnatural death on the Stoney reserve is suicide. Driven by hopelessness and depression, scores of young Stoneys have killed themselves through drug overdose, hanging, self-inflicted gunshot wounds, and slashing their wrists. A more recent method of suicide is walking in front of fast-moving vehicles travelling on the Trans-Canada highway, which runs through the reserve. A 19-year-old Stoney boy, for example, "died instantly when he was struck by a motorhome on a stretch of highway" (*Calgary Herald*, 6 July 1997). He was one of three who died this way during the summer of 1997. A young Stoney man attending this boy's funeral was asked by reporters how many of his own friends had died. "Fifteen," he replied, adding that "some shot themselves, some took pills, some jumped in the river" (*Calgary Herald*, 16 July 1997).

The senseless deaths of so many young Stoneys have been a cause of great concern among many of our band's members. Upon hearing young Stoneys remark that "it's easier to die than to live here" (*Calgary Herald*, 27 December 1997), Morley Band Councillor Tina Fox worried that "we are losing too many young people. We need to deal with what's happening" (*Calgary Herald*, 27 December 1997). Attending burial after burial, one woman said she was "tired of going to all these funerals" (*Calgary Herald*, 6 July 1997), while another saw these endless deaths as "related to our present social conditions" (*Calgary Herald*, 28 September 1997). Sick of all the social problems, another young Stoney man preferred living on the streets of Calgary. He felt that if he stayed on the reserve, it would be "the cause of my death" (*Calgary Herald*, 27 December 1997).

Social Program Issues

A number of programs on the reserve are intended to help deal with the many social problems experienced by reserve residents. These include child welfare, a battered women's shelter, adult and elder care, youth services, the welfare department, and the health centre. Unfortunately, these programs are controlled by people in positions of power. Politicians can stop or sabotage new initiatives or decide who should and shouldn't receive help. In addition, workers who support a certain chief often refuse to help those who support another. For example, one woman who didn't receive her welfare cheques felt she "was being punished by tribal leaders for talking to reporters" (*Calgary Herald*, 1 September 1997). RCMP were recently called to the reserve because violence nearly erupted over welfare cheques not received (*Calgary Herald*, 7 September 1997).

Along with politicians exhausting program finances by providing financial assistance to their supporters, leaders use program funds for their own personal use. For example, one chief took a total of $44 000 in welfare money over a four-month span. When confronted about these substantial payouts in the midst of poverty and hunger, the chief responded by saying that "no one on the reserve is going hungry. [Band members] still get $30 every two weeks in gas and oil royalties" (*Calgary Herald*, 24 December 1997). Following the example set by their corrupt leaders, six welfare workers were found to have "collected welfare payments at the same time as they drew salaries from the band's social service department" (*Times Colonist*, 28 September 1997). Worried that a major financial crisis was developing, band members who also worked in the Social Services office sent a letter to the DIA (*Calgary Herald*, 27 September 1997), which responded that these employees should take any criminal complaints to the RCMP. Not only were the employees fired within five days of writing their letter, Stoney Social Services continued to run a deficit of $500 000.

Another reason why Stoney Social Services cannot deal effectively with social problems is that most of the work force is made up of inadequately trained, uncommitted, politically appointed workers who often "collect pay cheques without doing any work" (*Calgary Herald*, 1 September 1997). Because of the lack of trained Stoney managers, non-Native people are often placed in management positions in which they tend to face much abuse from Stoney workers and politicians. Coupled with the fact that many of these non-Aboriginal managers are afraid of losing their jobs, it should not be surprising that many of the programs within the Stoney and other Native communities are very ineffective.

Educational Issues

The average level of education on the Stoney reserve is currently Grade 7. Even though the education budget for 1997 was $6 million (*Calgary Herald*, 29 November 1997), very few Stoneys attended school. Reasons for this undoubtedly include their dependency, lack of self-confidence, fear of responsibility, and nepotism. Nepotism is not uncommon, and the relatives of chiefs are often placed in the education department in administrative positions. The *Calgary Herald* verified the problem of nepotism when it reported that "four of [the Chief's] children got senior jobs. His daughter, ... was appointed assistant director of education" (27 December 1997). Consequently, students not supporting the chiefs do not have an easy time. Not only are they often rudely treated by staff, their student allowance cheques are often late, their tuition is often not paid, and they are periodically threatened with having their funding cut off.

Although chiefs often publicly claim the need for education, their public claims are contradicted by their behind-the-scenes actions. Numerous Stoneys told Judge Reilly that their chief "deliberately interferes with Stoney education because the less educated his people are, the more he is able to dominate them" (Reilly, 1997, p. 7). After the last election, the "moccasin telegraph" informed members of the community that the newly elected Chiniki chief had been advised by the Stoney chief that keeping people uneducated would enable him to remain chief for a long time. It appears that Stoneys are correct when they claim that "they've had the doors of higher learning slammed in their faces by their own leaders" (*Calgary Herald*, 18 October 1997).

Housing Issues

Nepotism is also evident in the allotment and renovation of housing on reserves. Each year, Stoney politicians are allotted a number of houses to be distributed among the people. There are no set criteria for distribution, so politicians decide who will get housing. As such, houses often go to politicians' relatives. This results in certain single families owning two or three houses while others remain homeless. A recent example of those who are not politically favoured being excluded involved a Stoney couple that had their house burned down by an arsonist. They had been living in their rusted out van for months because they were unable to get emergency housing from the band. When reporters caught up with them, the couple were "preparing, with two comforters, to ride out the winter in the back of their 1986 van" (*Calgary Herald*, 1 September 1997).

Political favouritism also affects the maintenance and renovation of houses. People who show support by voting for certain leaders not only get their houses maintained regularly, some even receive money for extravagant renovations to their homes. In contrast, non-supporters have an extremely difficult time getting support for even minor house repairs. There are many stories of people living for months in houses with flooded basements, ruptured waterlines, broken windows, or linoleum so worn out that floorboards are exposed. One woman who lived in a house with no indoor plumbing, cardboard instead of window panes, holes in the flooring, and crumbling walls stated, "I don't like to live here because of the conditions. But I have no place to go" (*Calgary Herald*, 28 September 1997).

Community and Cultural Issues

Through stories handed down over many generations, it is well known that precontact First Nations had effective infrastructures, upheld traditional values and beliefs, followed customs and traditions, and were in fact very healthy people. However, many things have changed over the years. Many First Nation communities currently find themselves drowning in unwellness, the roots of which can be observed at historical, political, and community levels.

At the historical level, much has been written about the ways in which residential schools contributed to the loss of cultural identity for many Aboriginal people. As one member of the Blackfoot Nation said, "[Y]oung people and their parents are suffering the aftermath of more than 100 years of government efforts, especially through church-run residential schools, to assimilate natives" (*Calgary Herald*, 29 December 1997). Having been students themselves, many of today's Aboriginal leaders did not escape the effects of residential schooling.

At the political level, the Department of Indian Affairs and the Indian Act have long contributed to problems in Native communities. Referring to the situation at Morley, one Aboriginal woman wrote that "the issue is the wicked and corrupt system forced upon our people everywhere by Indian Affairs and the Indian Act" (*Calgary Herald*, 23 October 1997). For example, under the Indian Act chiefs hold virtually all the power and authority. Not only do many people at the bottom of a band's hierarchy suffer at the hands of their chief, but very little help and money flow down to the grass-roots level. Problems of tribal council accountability also stem from the Indian Act. Political corruption and the misappropriation of funds are at least in part possible because DIA's "funding agreements ... require minimal standards ... and little accountability" (*The First Perspective*, July 1997). Furthermore, because Indian Affairs lacks data on band spending, "[B]and leaders believe the chance of being caught is slim in cases of double-dipping" (*Calgary Herald*, 26 November 1997).

At the community level, misinterpretation and misuse of "tribal custom" also create many problems. Under this "custom," many people are left out because leaders tend to look after only their own families (*Calgary Herald*, 26 November 1997). In the past, leaders tried to ensure the well-being of all members of their community. Commenting on the misinterpretation and misapplication of tribal custom, Stoney Elder J.R. Twoyoungmen stated:

> There are two conflicting political philosophies, each called tribal custom. The genuine brand of tribal custom ... passed down by our elders ... carries the gentle wisdom of centuries of life together in community. The other is a concoction by government bureaucracy deaf to the true teachings of our elders ... [that] dictates life in our reserve today. We have all been conned into thinking that the present form of tribal custom is our own, when it is not. The system was cleverly developed by government bureaucracy, filled with European values, given a label to fool people into thinking it was Indian-made. ... Few, if any, tribal values can be found in the government's model. The whole system reeks of colonization. (*Calgary Herald*, 27 October 1997)

Conclusion

In order for the Stoney Nation to free itself of its massive problems, the whole community will need to undergo intensive, holistic healing. Former Stoney Chief Ernest Wesley said that in order for the Stoney community to heal, "we must address individual needs. Once the individual [is healthy], then it will change the family. Once the family is well, then our community becomes well also" (Long and Fox, 1996, p. 257). Along with healing, traditional cultures must be revitalized to achieve community wellness and productivity. This means that Aboriginal people have to relearn to live by our traditional values of respect, caring, humility, honesty, and sharing and perhaps invite the practice of certain customs such as sentencing circles and decision making based on true consensus that were once a part of many

Aboriginal communities. Individual and collective economic dependency must also be reversed if the people of the Stoney Nation and other Native peoples ever hope to achieve a state of wellness. We must be slowly moved away from dependency and toward self-reliance and self-sufficiency. As it is now, virtually everything is given out for free. The unfortunate result of most people in my community not having had to earn anything is that many of us have learned to take much of our lives for granted.

The establishment of strong, harmonious, self-governing communities will also depend on reintroducing traditional leadership. As Ovide Mercredi (1993) noted, "[T]he assessment of a First Nations leader was ultimately based on ... responsibility to treat others according to the traditional values of kindness, respect, sharing and compassion." Having strong leaders depends to a great extent on having political systems that challenge and enable leaders to be accountable to their people. This perhaps needs to begin with power being restored to elders through traditional elder councils and to community members by setting up structures that enable us to contribute meaningfully to the growth and development of our communities.

Some argue that healing will come through self-government. However, it is extremely difficult to comprehend how self-government can function effectively in a community as dysfunctional as the Stoney reserve. The story I have told of my people is meant to illustrate that implementing self-government in this or any other sick Aboriginal community will in all likelihood only perpetuate our suffering. As Mohawk author Brian Maracle (1993, pp. 3 and 233) argues, "[S]elf-government alone will not ... work until we are sober, healthy and happy" and "there is almost an unanimous agreement that any solution will have to be based on cultural and spiritual revival in the native community." I fully agree with those who say that healing must begin. I also agree with Maracle (1993, p. 15) that there is great urgency to our healing efforts since, as he argues, "[W]e have to start somewhere, sometime, if we are ever going to get out of the hellhole we're in. That means we're going to have to face up to the truth. Even if it hurts."

HEALING PERSPECTIVES, POLICIES, AND INITIATIVES

Perspectives on Health and Healing

[T]he wounds of the past run deep. Although many Aboriginal people retain a strong sense of their roots and a positive identity, many others are almost lost to themselves and their people. Perhaps no one is undamaged. (RCAP, 1993b, p. 52)

As Long (1995) suggests, some of the paths taken by Aboriginal people in Canada over the past 40 years have had violent consequences, while others have not. Data presented above also illustrate that Aboriginal people have been disproportionately involved as both victims and offenders in relation to family violence and suicide. In his analysis of the violence and healing picture, Long (1995) argues that many of the violent and non-violent activities involving Aboriginal people have been strategic in nature and that they have also at times led to constructive change in the lives of Aboriginal individuals and communities. In many ways the actions of Aboriginal peoples and their supporters have contributed to the strengthening of Aboriginal identities, the integrity of social and political change efforts, and the belief that healing changes are possible.

It is nonetheless evident to many of those living and working in Aboriginal communities that no single solution will address the needs of all Aboriginal children, women, men, families, and communities (ONWA, 1989, p. 114). Increasingly, there is agreement that "if solutions are going to work, they have to be made by, and within, the community, however that community may be defined" (Frank, 1993, p. 17). Recognizing this, many people working in community and health-related areas have designed programs that are easily adapted to different needs and circumstances (Canada, 1987, pp. 74–79). Social change initiatives are also increasingly taking into account both the history of the communities affected and that those most likely to intervene at the community level will be para-professional and non-professional volunteers, many of whom are Aboriginal people who are sensitive to the cultures of the people they are serving (Council for Yukon Indians, 1992, p. 8).

One of the main reasons offered in support of community-based health programs run by and for Aboriginal people is that "the system" has historically worked against rather than for Aboriginal people. As Dr. Jonathan Sheehan, health practitioner at the Sagkeeng First Nation, told the RCAP (1993b), many potential Native clients fall through the cracks and are denied services to which they are entitled because the provincial and federal health care systems share responsibility for Aboriginal people, and both seem more concerned about saving money than addressing people's needs. Specific concerns relating to the planned devolution of health and other services for Aboriginal peoples have centred around three main questions: (1) who will control the policies, funds, and other resources? (2) what is the underlying agenda of those who control the health, justice, community development, and other budgets for Aboriginal peoples in Canada? and, perhaps most importantly, (3) will those who are most in need have their needs met? Responses to the first two questions provide a sense of the possible directions that policy and program initiatives, and possibly even legislative developments, could take in the future.

There are those who propose that if the immediate and long-term needs of Aboriginal people are to be met, Aboriginal people themselves must have absolute control over the policy agendas and program implementation. In the words of Dr. Chris Durocher of the Yukon Medical Association, "[S]elf-determination for Aboriginal peoples is a prerequisite for healing and the development of wellness — wellness meaning of body, mind and spirit. Control of their cultural rights, land resources, education, justice system and health care delivery must come into the hands of Aboriginal people first" (RCAP, 1993a, p. 52). Central to this Aboriginal self-determination position is the view that the philosophies underlying health, family, justice, social, political, economic, and other agendas need to reflect the traditional worldviews and lived experiences of the Aboriginal people involved. Advocates of this view note that a traditional, holistic Aboriginal approach to healing seeks to integrate the physical, spiritual, mental, and emotional aspects of life. Socio-economic problems such as poverty, unemployment, welfare dependence, and poor housing are thus understood in terms of the direct effects they have on the well-being of individuals, communities, and whole societies (Agenda for First Nation and Inuit Mental Health, 1991). From this perspective,

> abuse and other imbalances of life cannot be healed by attempting to heal isolated Aboriginal individuals apart from their family and their community. To get to the root cause of abuse and neglect, the entire system that allowed it to occur must be restored to balance. This means that the accumulated hurt of generations, carried to our families and our communities, needs to be released through a healing process. (Nechi Institute, 1988, p. 4)

From our perspective, openness to exploring the cultural and structural sources of violence and healing is necessary if accumulated hurts are to be released and signs of hope are to grow.

Cultural and Structural Issues

Reports and testimonies from those who are respectful of spiritual and cultural aspects of Aboriginal life acknowledge the uniqueness of Aboriginal communities and the importance of restoring communal balance and spiritual harmony (YTFFV, 1985, p. 10). Advocates of this perspective on

Aboriginal self-determination also underscore the importance of grass-roots developments in Aboriginal communities and the need for healing individuals and whole communities. The most strident of these recommend that resources and efforts toward change need to be directed primarily toward community-based programs and initiatives (RCAP, 1993a, p. 59). They also assert that respect for traditional Aboriginal approaches to healing is vital and that merely tinkering with parts of a fundamentally flawed socio-political system will not help to alleviate the root causes of violence by and against their people (Nuu-Chah-Nulth Tribal Council, 1989).

Many who are involved in the Aboriginal revitalization movement think that it is essential that the perspectives, insights, and skills of non-Aboriginal people be combined with those of non-Aboriginal people. Especially in relation to healing, these "new traditionalists" maintain that Aboriginal perspectives and practices need to be combined with non-Aboriginal approaches to conflict resolution, group therapy, and community health and development programs (Frank, 1993, p. 17). They believe that combining the perspectives, strategies, and techniques of Aboriginal and non-Aboriginal people will enable Aboriginal people to rediscover and strengthen their identities in community while learning to co-exist with others in the modern world (RCAP, 1996a, p. 12). For example, suggested ways of responding to family violence in Aboriginal communities include greater enforcement of wife assault policy and subsequent use of the criminal justice system; assurances from police that they will in fact respond to calls and take appropriate action; alternative approaches to the justice system (based on traditional values); more transition houses, second-stage housing, and safe homes, as well as easier access for Aboriginal women and children to these facilities; greater access to counselling, both in Aboriginal communities and within mainstream services; enhanced or holistic support services throughout the justice system; increased access to legal aid; cross-cultural training of justice personnel; cultural awareness through public education; development of wife assault intervention models and men's assault prevention programs; and family counselling and mental health teams that are sensitive to the many different experiences and perspectives of Native people (Frank, 1993, p. 17). Given the complexity of bringing together Aboriginal and non-Aboriginal people and perspectives, there seems to be some wisdom in the call by new traditionalists that everyone seek understanding and have patience during this time of transition (RCAP, 1993a, p. 60).

Central to all discussions regarding policy development and implementation is the issue of program effectiveness, with everyone involved in the "healing debates" maintaining that they have the best interests of Aboriginal people in mind. In contrast to those who support the inclusion of Aboriginal perspectives and people in the healing process, others act in ways that suggest they believe Native people are best left out of the dialogue (Boldt, 1993, pp. 18–21). Although advocates of this position state publicly that Aboriginal cultures and traditions are a valid part of the healing process, their policies and practices suggest that they do not support the fundamental, systemic changes advocated by many Aboriginal people and their supporters. Testimonies and reports given over the last 40 years in relation to Aboriginal life in Canada suggest that many non-Aboriginal and Aboriginal people who benefit from supporting the status quo have been able to maintain their positions of power and influence. Much like those mentioned in Terry Fox's saga of life on the Stoney reserve, there still appear to be many Aboriginal and non-Aboriginal people who are willing to stifle meaningful change in the healing process and who, as a result, perpetuate the oppressiveness of colonial structures, policies, and practices.

Although the Department of Indian Affairs and Northern Development and other federal and provincial government departments have often worked with Aboriginal people in developing and initiating "healing-related" policies and programs, the majority of these initiatives have been neither preventive in nature nor arrived at through an inclusive, consensual process (Barnaby, 1992, p. 40). Moreover, it appears that obstacles to healing reflect more than a lack of political will or resources. Rather, there have been and continue to be at least two significant factors that hinder healing. On the one hand, most dialogue and efforts to implement meaningful structural changes continue to be constrained by an underlying paternalistic, bureaucratized perspective that views Aboriginal peoples in Canada as wards of the state who, after well over 200 years of colonial administration, continue to be in need of protection and help (Boldt, 1993, p. 21). Consequently, increasing numbers of Aboriginal people and their supporters have taken the stand that nothing short of violent protest and confrontation will change the perspective of those who want to continue to control the lives of Canada's Aboriginal peoples (Long, 1992). Compounding the problem of bureaucratic paternalism is the unwillingness or inability of many Aboriginal and non-Aboriginal people to admit that they do not like the prospect of change or that they fear reprisal from their colleagues or community members for making honest, dissenting comments (Dyck, 1993, p. 194). Numerous Royal Commission on Aboriginal Peoples intervenors echoed the words of people quoted in Terry Fox's saga, noting that interference by political leaders in Aboriginal communities inhibits healing and meaningful, hopeful change on their reserves. They point out that many Aboriginal people, especially women, have often had to be satisfied with programs and services that at best have served to meet only their most basic needs (Canada, 1990, p. 106), and at worst have ignored the needs of some altogether (Silman, 1987, p. 125).

Efforts to revitalize Aboriginal culture have been accompanied by continued demands for structural changes in a wide variety of areas, including restoring community standards and inclusive forms of representation in decision making, enforcing community safety, and addressing problems with health care, education, criminal justice, and economic development policies (RCAP, 1996b, pp. 75–80). For well over 40 years, one of the key assumptions underlying these demands is that Aboriginal people are best suited to identify and develop policies and programs that serve their needs. Though many government representatives have deemed that such an arrangement is impossible or at best unlikely to occur in the immediate future, Aboriginal people have continued to assert that both those who have suffered and those who have perpetuated violence and illness need to be an integral part of the healing process (RCAP, 1996b, p. 224). Along with major political and legal changes, Aboriginal people and their supporters have therefore also proposed, among other things:

- All Aboriginal people should be invited and enabled to take responsibility for changes that will affect their own lives (RCAP, 1996a, p. 12).
- Aboriginal peoples should have more control over policy development, funding, and program implementation in all areas of their lives (RCAP, 1993b, p. 35).
- National forums should be established to address the myriad issues involved in the areas of physical violence, criminal justice, and community development as they relate to Aboriginal people.
- Expert Advisory Committees should be appointed by the federal government to facilitate discussions, program implementation, and policy changes in all areas where physical violence is a problem.
- The federal government should enact a Child Welfare Act and establish a child welfare system by the year 2000.
- The federal government should establish a mental health policy for Aboriginal peoples by the year 2000 (Canada, 1990, pp. 108–9).
- Prevention, intervention, and postvention policies and programs should take into account the unique experiences and perspectives of the Aboriginal people they are meant to serve (RCAP, 1993b, p. 35).
- Comprehensive education programs in family violence, suicide, and criminal justice should be established for leaders and other members of

Aboriginal communities, as well as for professionals and lay practitioners working with Aboriginal people in these areas (Canada, 1990, p. 108).

• There should be cross-national education programs for non-Aboriginal people in education and work-related areas.

• There should be support for community-based alternatives to the formalized systems of justice, health care, family and child welfare, and economic development that incorporate customary law and traditional practices and, where needed, facilitate healing and reconciliation (RCAP, 1993b, pp. 35–63).

• Social, educational, health, and justice-related services should be implemented for Aboriginal people living in urban areas (RCAP, 1993b, p. 3).

• In formalized settings, more positions should be created, such as Aboriginal court workers and prison elders, that provide culturally sensitive assistance and support to Aboriginal people in those settings (Canada, 1990, p. 109).

• The federal and provincial governments should address all outstanding land claims with integrity and as expeditiously as possible.

• The governments and courts of Canada should work with Aboriginal people in making self-government and self-sufficiency a reality for Aboriginal peoples all across Canada (RCAP, 1993b, p. 41).

As these examples illustrate, the ideas and activities suggested by those concerned for addressing violence and healing are as varied as the people themselves.

Whatever the theoretical reasons for personal illness, interpersonal violence, and unhealthy Aboriginal communities may be, many continue to refuse to accept the status quo. They recognize that healing will fail to materialize to the degree that Aboriginal people lack control over their own lives, families, communities, and Nations. This is because healing implies the revitalization of Aboriginal people's confidence in themselves, their communities, and their cultures, confidence that must be grounded in their everyday lives (RCAP, 1996a, p. 12). Accordingly, they believe that only implementing Aboriginal self-government and restoring Aboriginal traditions will stop the cycles of violence and brokenness and allow for meaningful changes and healing to begin. The often painful truth for many, however, is that self-government, community-based control over health and other services, and traditional beliefs and practices do not, in and of themselves, ensure healing and growth (YTFFV, 1985, p. 318). This is not to deny the importance of community-level programs, for many of them have resulted in positive social change (Canada, 1987,

p. 74). As Terry Fox's Stoney Saga illustrates, however, Aboriginal individuals and communities continue to experience illness and violence whether or not programs are implemented and people are educated about the problems. Although this may appear to paint a bleak picture of Aboriginal violence and unwellness, the determination and vision of many who are committed to walking a path of healing offer some degree of hope. As Halfe (1993, pp. 9–10) notes:

> When the Indigenous people are allowed to dance their journey by reclaiming their visions, their personhood, their families, their societies, and all which they encompass, perhaps then we shall see a decrease in self-destructive behaviour.

Their hope, it appears, rests on the continued revitalization of Aboriginal spirituality, holistic traditions of healing, cultural rebirth, and reconciliation with non-Aboriginal people who share this land. For many, this calls for Aboriginal and non-Aboriginal people in Canada to commit ourselves to walking the sometimes painful path of healing together.

NOTES

1. Terry Fox wrote the "Stoney Saga" section of this chapter, while the surrounding sections were written by David Long.
2. The "rule of thumb" refers to the expectation that husbands were to keep their wives in line by whipping them when necessary, though it was illegal to use a stick that was thicker than the husband's thumb.
3. Presentation to the RCAP in Winnipeg on 10 March 1993.
4. The response rate for the 680 questionnaires was approximately 15 percent. In addition, 127 telephone and 40 personal interviews were conducted. Though the low response rate and non-random sample may lead some to question the findings of this study, the researchers expressed confidence in the reliability of the data.
5. Given the findings of a number of provincial task forces on the incidence of family violence in Aboriginal families and communities, the data from this national survey raise a number of important questions. Three of the more important are: (1) why is the incidence of family violence (at least 80 percent) reported in provincial task force and community-level surveys so high in comparison with the 40 percent of respondents to the RCAP survey who believed family violence is a problem? (2) given the differences between the community-, provincial-, and national-level survey findings, how valid and generalizable are their data? and (3) to what extent should the validity and reliability of data on family violence in Aboriginal families be questioned merely because survey data appear to differ?

6. Assaults were coded as "spousal assaults" only if the victim and the accused were living together at the time of the assault. This coding criterion, developed by Statistics Canada, does not account for the fact that women often report being assaulted well after their relationship with the abuser has formally ended.

7. Born and raised on the Stoney reserve, I have witnessed many injustices and experienced much pain. As such, my aim in this section is to provide a personal, insider's perspective on what I call the "Stoney Saga."

DISCUSSION QUESTIONS

1. How would you make sense of the relationship between European colonization and personal as well as interpersonal violence involving Aboriginal people in Canada?

2. What do you think are currently the most important healing-related issues facing Aboriginal people in Canada? In what ways might these be similar to and different from the healing-related issues facing non-Aboriginal people in this country?

3. How do you think the problems associated with Aboriginal family violence are similar to and different from problems experienced by non-Aboriginals? What about suicide?

4. In what ways do you think the story of the Stoney First Nation is typical of Aboriginal experiences, and in what ways is it unique?

5. What do you think are the most significant personal, cultural, and structural obstacles faced by Aboriginal and non-Aboriginal people who want to bring healing and health to the lives of Canada's Aboriginal peoples?

FURTHER READINGS

Alexei, Sherman. 1994. *The Lone Ranger and Tonto Fistfight in Heaven.* New York: HarperCollins Books. A collection of poignant and disturbingly realistic stories about life and death in Aboriginal communities.

Bachmann, Ronet. 1993. *Death and Violence on the Reservation: Homicide, Family Violence, and Suicide in American Indian Populations.* New York: Auburn House. Detailed theoretical and empirical analysis of three extreme forms of criminal violence on American Indian reservations.

Ontario Native Women's Association (ONWA). 1989. *Breaking Free, A Proposal for Change to Family Violence.* Thunder Bay, Ont.: ONWA. Discussion and analysis of controversial findings from a large-scale study of Native family violence commissioned by the ONWA.

Supernault, Esther. 1993. *A Family Affair.* Edmonton: Native Counselling Services of Alberta. Esther Supernault, an Aboriginal counsellor, outlines her perspective on how Aboriginal individuals, families, and communities can bring about inner and outer healing.

Warry, Wayne. 1998. *Unfinished Dreams: Community Healing and the Reality of Aboriginal Self-Government.* Toronto: University of Toronto Press. Insightful and sensitive analysis of the spiritual, cultural, and political dimensions of healing toward self-government.

REFERENCES

Appleford, Barbara. 1989. *Family Violence Review: Prevention and Treatment of Abusive Behaviour.* Ottawa: Correctional Service Canada.

Assembly of First Nations. 1991. *Agenda for First Nation and Inuit Mental Health.* Ottawa: Assembly of First Nations.

Bachmann, Ronet. 1993. *Death and Violence on the Reservation: Homicide, Family Violence, and Suicide in American Indian Populations.* New York: Auburn House.

Barnaby, Joanne. 1992. "Culture and Sovereignty." Pp. 39–44 in *Nation to Nation: Aboriginal Sovereignty and the Future of Canada,* eds. Diane Englestad and John Bird. Toronto: Anansi Press.

Berger, Justice Thomas R. 1977. *Northern Frontier: Northern Homeland. The Report of the Mackenzie Valley Pipeline Inquiry.* Vol. 1. Ottawa: Supply and Services Canada.

Bobet, Ellen. 1989. "Indian Mortality." *Canadian Social Trends.* Statistics Canada, pp. 1–14.

Boldt, Menno. 1993. *Surviving as Indians: The Challenge of Self-Government.* Toronto: University of Toronto Press.

Canada, Health and Welfare Canada. 1988. *Suicide in Canada: Report of the National Task Force on Suicide in Canada.* Ottawa: Supply and Services.

———. 1989. *Family Violence: A Review of Theoretical and Clinical Literature.* Ottawa: Supply and Services.

———. 1990. *Reading for Solutions: Report of the Special Advisor to the Minister of National Health and Welfare on Child Sexual Abuse in Canada.* Ottawa: Supply and Services.

Canada, Health and Welfare Canada, Medical Services Branch. 1992. *Aboriginal Health in Canada.* Ottawa: Supply and Services.

———. 1993. *Report on Intentional Deaths (Suicides) for Registered Indians in Canada: 1979–1991*. Edmonton: Supply and Services.

Council for Yukon Indians. 1992. "Council for Yukon Indians Family Violence Project." *Transition* 4(4): pp. 1–2.

Dyck, Noel. 1993. "Telling It Like It Is: Some Dilemmas of Fourth World Ethnography and Advocacy." Pp. 192–212 in *Anthropology, Public Policy, and Native Peoples in Canada*, ed. Noel Dyck and James B. Waldram. Montreal and Kingston, Ont.: McGill-Queen's University Press.

Frank, Sharlene. 1993. *Family Violence in Aboriginal Communities: A First Nations Report*. Report to the Government of British Columbia. Victoria: Queen's Printer.

Halfe, Louise. 1993. "Healing from a Native Perspective." *Cognica* 26(1): pp. 7–10.

Indian and Inuit Nurses of Canada. 1991. *National Family Violence Abuse Study/Evaluation*. Toronto: Indian and Inuit Nurses of Canada.

Jamieson, Wanda. 1987. *Aboriginal Male Violence against Aboriginal Women in Canada*. Unpublished MA thesis, Department of Criminology, University of Ottawa.

Jarvis, George K. and Menno Boldt. 1981. *Native Indian Mortality: A Prospective Study*. Edmonton: Department of Indian Affairs and Northern Development.

Long, David. 1992. "Culture, Ideology and Militancy: The Movements of Native Indians in Canada 1969–1992." Pp. 18–34 in *Organizing Dissent: Contemporary Social Movements in Theory and Practice*, ed. William B. Carroll. Toronto: Garamond.

———. 1995. "On Violence and Healing: Aboriginal Experiences." Pp. 40–77 in *Violence in Canada: Socio-Political Perspectives*, ed. Jeffrey Ian Ross. Toronto: Oxford University Press.

Long, David and Terry Fox. 1996. "Circles of Healing: Illness, Healing, and Health among Aboriginal People in Canada." Pp. 239–69 in *Visions of the Heart: Canadian Aboriginal Issues*, ed. David Alan Long and Olive Patricia Dickason. Toronto: Harcourt Brace & Company.

MacLeod, Linda. 1980. *Wife Battering in Canada: The Vicious Circle*. Ottawa: Canadian Advisory Council on the Status of Women.

———. 1987. *Battered but Not Beaten: Preventing Wife-Battering in Canada*. Ottawa: Canadian Advisory Council on the Status of Women.

Manitoba Association of Women's Shelters (MAWS). 1989. *Report to the Manitoba Royal Commission on Family Violence*. Winnipeg: Manitoba Royal Commission on Family Violence.

Maracle, Brian. 1993. *Crazywater*. Toronto: Viking Press.

Mercredi, Ovide and Mary Ellen Turpel. 1993. *In the Rapids: Navigating the Future of First Nations*. Toronto: Viking.

Muir, Bernice. 1991. *Health Status of Canadian Indians and Inuit — 1990*. Ottawa: National Health and Welfare.

The Nechi Institute, The Four Worlds Development Project, The Native Training Institute, and New Direction Training. 1988. *Healing Is Possible: A Joint*

Statement on the Healing of Sexual Abuse in Native Communities. Alkalai Lake, B.C.: The Nechi Institute.

Northern Alberta Development Council (NADC). 1988. *Family Violence in Northern Alberta.* Edmonton: NADC.

Nuu-Chah-Nulth Tribal Council. 1989. *Nuu-Chah-Nulth First Family Proposal.* Vancouver, B.C.: Nuu-Chah-Nulth Tribal Council.

Ontario Native Women's Association (ONWA). 1989. *Breaking Free, A Proposal for Change to Family Violence.* Thunder Bay, Ont.: ONWA.

Pauktuutit, Inuit Women's Association of Canada Newsletter. 1990. *Suvaguuq* 5(1).

Reilly, Judge J.D. 1997. "Judgement on Her Majesty the Queen and Ernest-Vernon Hunter." 26 June. Docket #70015995P10101. Cochrane, Alta.

Report to the Government of the Northwest Territories (RGNWT). 1986. *Choices: A Three Year Program to Address Family Violence in the Northwest Territories.* Yellowknife: Queen's Printer.

Royal Commission on Aboriginal Peoples (RCAP). 1993a. *Public Hearings: Focusing the Dialogue.* Ottawa: Supply and Services.

———. 1993b. *Public Hearings: Overview of the Second Round.* Ottawa: Supply and Services.

———. 1996a. *Looking Forward, Looking Back.* Ottawa: Supply and Services.

———. 1996b. *Restructuring the Relationship.* Ottawa: Supply and Services.

Silman, Janet. 1987. *Enough Is Enough: Aboriginal Women Speak Out.* Toronto: Women's Press.

Statistics Canada. 1990. *Health Reports.* Cat. nos. 82-003, 2, 4, 332. Ottawa: Supply and Services.

———. 1993. *Aboriginal Peoples Survey.* Ottawa: Supply and Services.

Westcott, David, Sharon Freitag, and Luis Barreto. 1987. *Review of Mortality Due to Suicide in the Northwest Territories 1975–1986.* Yellowknife: Government of the Northwest Territories.

Yukon Task Force on Family Violence (YTFFV). 1985. *Report of the Task Force on Family Violence.* Whitehorse: Queen's Printer.

CHAPTER 10

"We Can Heal": Aboriginal Children Today

Suzanne Fournier and Ernie Crey

I believe now is our time. Now is our time. We are starting to be looked at now and I believe we can really make a difference now because we are finally standing up. (Randy Nepoose, Hobbema, Alberta)

INTRODUCTION

First Nations people in Canada agree that the next two decades will belong to Aboriginal youth. Today a strong young generation is struggling to emerge from the dark colonial days into the bright hope of autonomy and self-determination. All across the country, Aboriginal young people are making themselves heard: in schools and universities, in Native politics, at protests over education cutbacks, at community marches to combat child abuse, and in healing circles and sobriety treatment centres.

Young First Nations athletes are cheerfully clashing at basketball games, hockey playoffs, lacrosse tournaments, and canoe races; there are rowers, runners, and hockey players of national renown. Angela Chalmers of Manitoba's Birdtail Sioux First Nation, the first woman in the history of the Commonwealth Games to win both the 1500-metre and the 3000-metre races, in 1990, credits her Aboriginal roots for teaching her patience and perseverance. "Look at my grandmothers, how tough they had to be, and my mother, the discrimination I saw her deal with," says Chalmers today. "I've faced racism too, and I tell the Aboriginal kids I speak to as part of the Native role model program [sponsored by the federal Indian Affairs department] that you can put that anger to good use: in physical exertion, in confidence and passion. Find out what you care about and prove you can excel as well or better than anyone; for the

Source: Excerpt from Stolen from Our Embrace: The Abduction of First Nations Children and the Restoration of Aboriginal Communities, *by Suzanne Fournier and Ernie Crey,* © 1997, *published by Douglas & McIntyre. Reproduced with permission of the publisher.*

community, your family, but above all for yourself. Don't forget, I say when I talk to young Aboriginal kids, because we've been through a lot, we're strong people and we have a deep, deep well of strength to draw on."

At the Splat'sin day-care in Spallumcheen; at Xitolacw school in Mount Currie; inside a kukeli hut or traditional pit-house in Alkali Lake's elementary school; in the Nisga'a school board districts from kindergarten to Grade 12, First Nations children are learning their language and culture along with their math and science. At Keremeos Senior Secondary School, in B.C.'s southern interior, almost all the teens from the Lower and Upper Similkameen bands who enrol also graduate, and some rank among the school's top achievers. An ever-increasing number of Aboriginal youth are going on to university and college and actively seeking careers. They are speaking out in Aboriginal and mainstream media. They are connecting with indigenous people all over the world via the Internet through hundreds of websites, such as the popular Canadian-based Aboriginal Youth Network. And they are flocking by the thousands to the youth conferences held over the past few years everywhere from Inuvik to Regina, Ottawa, Montreal, Halifax, Edmonton, and Vancouver. A young Aboriginal man named Randy Nepoose spoke for all when he declared at a northern youth conference in 1992: "Now is our time."

There have never been, in recorded history, more Aboriginal young people than there are now in Canada. Today, more than 36 percent of the Aboriginal population is under the age of 14, compared to 21 percent of the non-Native population. Another 20 percent of Aboriginal youth is aged 15 to 24. The population of young Aboriginal people will continue to grow until there are almost 200 000 First Nations youths in the 15- to 24-year-old age bracket by the year 2011.

The traditional values that sustained First Nations for thousands of years before contact are emerging as the foundation that will carry Aboriginal nations to recovery and renewal. After five centuries of a cultural and economic war waged primarily against their children, First Nations still believe it is the young who will prove to be the mainstay of the renaissance now under way. The Aboriginal birth rate, in itself a sign of hope, is almost twice that of the rest of Canada. More and more Aboriginal children are being raised by sober parents connected to their culture. Children who require substitute care while their families are in recovery are increasingly cared for by Aboriginal child welfare agencies in all parts of the country. Although Aboriginal children still face immense challenges, there are generations of young people ready to become politically astute future leaders and contributing members of autonomous nations.

Healing Our Children: Issues and Obstacles

The Royal Commission on Aboriginal Peoples emphasized Canada's responsibility to Aboriginal youth in their 1996 report. "Their numbers in the population of today and their role in shaping and leading their communities and nations tomorrow make it essential for governments — Aboriginal and non-Aboriginal alike — to listen to their concerns and act on their priorities," the commissioners wrote. "They are the current generation paying the price of cultural genocide, racism and poverty, suffering the effects of hundreds of years of colonialist public policies. It's as though an earthquake has ruptured their world from one end to another, opening a deep rift that separates them from their past, their history and their culture. They have seen parents and peers fall into this chasm, into patterns of despair, listlessness and self-destruction. They fear for themselves and their future as they stand at the edge. Yet Aboriginal youth can see across this great divide. Their concern about the current crisis is leavened with a vision of a better tomorrow."

Canada stands on the brink of a momentous decision that no national government has yet had the political will to make. First Nations need not only Canada's official acknowledgement of their inherent right to self-government but also adequate resources to allow them to govern in the future and to compensate them for decades of damage inflicted in large part by Canada's misguided and morally tarnished Indian policies. Restitution does not mean more piecemeal government programs, dollars doled out to perpetuate a climate of dependency. As Ovide Mercredi, the former chief of the Assembly of First Nations, declared in 1994, this is a nation of young people that is "moving beyond the psychology of grievance." This is a nation of young people with high expectations, seeking not handouts but empowerment.

Still, the landscape is littered with mines that Aboriginal young people must somehow dodge in order to succeed: systemic racism and higher rates of illness, disease, suicide, substance abuse, school drop-out levels, and unemployment. From the very moment of birth — even in the womb — Aboriginal children face infinitely more challenges than non-Native babies. Higher rates of smoking, alcohol, and polydrug use among Aboriginal mothers compromise the health and survivability of the fetus, as well as the child's long-term future. Almost twice as many Aboriginal babies die in infancy than do other Canadian infants, despite a steady improvement in Aboriginal infant mortality over the last 40 years. In the 1960s in Canada, 60 Aboriginal babies died for every 1000 live births. That improved to 23.7 deaths for every 1000 Aboriginal births by 1980.

Today, the deaths of Aboriginal babies average about 12 to 14 per 1000 births, but that is still far higher than the national mortality rate of about 6 per 1000. Premature births and low birth weight, both of which are far more common in Aboriginal babies, can impair an infant's ability to thrive and may even lead to lifelong health problems. Aboriginal babies are three times more likely to die in the first six months of life from Sudden Infant Death Syndrome.

Poverty is a scourge that stalks Aboriginal children as they grow up. It is a well-documented fact that poor children suffer more health problems of every kind, and Aboriginal children in Canada are among the poorest of the poor. They suffer and even die from Third World conditions that are relatively rare among mainstream Canadian children. Substandard housing conditions, unsafe drinking water, and inadequate sewage treatment can cause serious and sometimes fatal diarrhea, gastroenteritis, and malnutrition. Native children are three times more likely to suffer bronchitis, pneumonia, and croup than are non-Native children. They endure far more chronic ear and respiratory tract infections, and more flu, which can in turn cause serious illnesses like rheumatic fever, according to a 1996 review of Aboriginal health care by Dr. Harriet MacMillan of McMaster University. Deaths from injuries are four times greater for Indian infants than for those in the general population, five times greater for Aboriginal preschoolers and three times greater for Aboriginal teenagers up to 19 years of age. The average life expectancy for Aboriginal children as they reach adulthood is eight years less than the national average.

By almost every measure, Aboriginal children's health and well-being lags far behind that of the mainstream. "Dental decay is almost universally prevalent among Aboriginal children and it may not be improving," says James Leake, who conducted the Oral Health Survey of Canada's Aboriginal Children in 1992. Poor hygiene due to lack of education, inadequate dental care, lack of fluoridated water supplies on-reserve, and the high-sugar junk food diet often associated with poverty are the causes of these high rates of dental decay; all are entirely correctable conditions in an industrialized country like Canada.

Perhaps the most disturbing challenge to the health of Aboriginal young people is the phenomenon of inhalant abuse. The chemicals sniffed are common and accessible: typewriter correction fluid, nail polish remover, felt pens, and, most widely available of all, gasoline. In exchange for a giddy high that makes a child dizzy and numb, a growing body suffers harm ranging from slowed reflexes, double vision, and hallucinations to long-term damage to the brain, kidneys, and liver.

In the B.C. First Nations Solvent Abuse Study, an as-yet-unpublished survey conducted in 1995 by the Community Health Representatives Association of B.C. (CHR), community health nurses reported that the average age of solvent sniffers was 13 and that a fifth of all solvent users were children under 11. Information collected in 166 of B.C.'s 204 Aboriginal communities showed that, of the 235 solvent users identified, 61 percent were under 19 years old, and a majority (70.5 percent) were male. Despite these disturbing figures, the CHR study concluded it had uncovered just the tip of the iceberg; it estimates there could be as many as 2000 chronic solvent abusers in B.C., a staggering number of them young children. "Denial is high in many communities," the study points out. "People do not like to talk about solvent use and in particular do not like to identify users." Solvent use is more chronic and serious in isolated northern regions of the province, the study says, although reserves across the province concurred on what the social problems were that led to sniffing: "Young people not having enough to do, drug dealers in the community, intense rivalry in the community, lack of spiritual/cultural traditions and geographical isolation," as well as serious health issues such as alcohol and drug abuse, diabetes, domestic violence, suicide, and fetal alcohol syndrome. The B.C. study provides alarming proof that hundreds of Aboriginal children are quietly doing permanent damage to their brains and their bodies just to achieve a brief escape from their harsh reality.

The epidemic spectre of suicide also faces Aboriginal children as they reach adolescence. Their sisters, brothers, relatives, and friends are hanging themselves, blowing their heads off with guns, jumping from bridges, and stepping in front of speeding trains. To a young Aboriginal person in Canada, it's like growing up in a war zone with an enemy that attacks from within. Suicide is six times more common for Aboriginal youth than for their non-Aboriginal peers. It is "a blunt and shocking message," the Royal Commission on Aboriginal Peoples warned in *Choosing Life*, its special report on suicide, that "a significant number of Aboriginal people in this country believe they have more reasons to die than to live." Suicides tend to occur in clusters, each death leading to a rebound despair expressed in copycat acts. A spate of suicides can strike an Aboriginal community anywhere in the country, leaving the best and the brightest dead. Pitangikum, a northern Ontario reserve, experienced eight suicides and more than 100 attempts in 1994 alone. At Whitedog, near Kenora, Ontario, four young people died by their own hand in April of 1995 and another in July.

There is no more telling indictment of the future Canada has handed First Nations children than their rejection of life itself. First Nations care-givers say their children are killing themselves in record numbers as an expression of self-hatred induced by the intergenerational assault, in many guises, on the very core of Aboriginal identity. Research confirms that the early separation of a child from family, followed by emotional deprivation, puts him or her at high risk for self-harm. Children who remain with parents and grandparents do not necessarily emerge unscathed; their care-givers may react to trauma they themselves have experienced by lashing out with abuse, violence, and addictive behaviour. Adolescents who have been physically and sexually abused were found in a recent study to be ten times more likely to kill themselves. Alcohol and drug use are also more closely associated with Aboriginal suicide than with suicides in the general population. In a recent B.C. study, 74 percent of Aboriginal people who killed themselves did so while intoxicated, compared with only 36 percent of a comparable sample of non-Native suicides.

Like alcoholism, suicide is a symptom of underlying malaise; denial must be confronted and causes understood before the deaths will stop. The tiny Pacheenacht community on the west coast of Vancouver Island suffered a rash of suicides between 1993 and 1995. The day after Christmas in 1993, a young mother wrote a goodbye letter to her baby daughter, then hung herself from a beam. Another group of Pacheenacht youths were discovered to have struck a suicide pact; all in all, there were five suicides within three years. A scheduled inquest was cancelled because the band feared the rebound effects of more adverse media publicity. Band councillors blamed alcoholism and a complete lack of recreation or career opportunities for young people; the federal government responded by identifying Pacheenacht as one of five "communities in crisis." B.C. Chief Coroner Vincent Cain issued his own inquiry report, citing lack of role models, poor education and employment prospects, low self-esteem, unresolved grief, welfare dependency, alcohol and drug use, poor parenting skills, and loss of cultural identity.

It soon became clear that the solution to the suicide epidemic lay with the Pacheenacht people, however, not with outside "experts." The small community began a concerted drive to provide options for its young people: language and cultural training for the very young; recreation, volunteer, and employment opportunities for older children and young adults. A year later, Pacheenacht youth were hard at work building part of the new Juan de Fuca Marine Trail. The local health centre, rejuvenated by some federal funding, was offering social development and health programs, while the provincial government funded a "Kids at Risk" program that used recreation to teach self-esteem and conflict resolution skills to children of elementary-school age. The Pacheenacht and other First Nations have found that gently introducing their young people to the long-house, powwow dancing, or the big drum — cultural activities that require sobriety and commitment — can bring children back from the brink of despair. There is an urgent need all across the country for suicide-prevention programs like these, with support from all levels of government and even from the private sector, to help First Nations prevent the loss of their most precious resource.

AIDS among young Aboriginal people is also of grave concern. Although there were only 176 confirmed cases of AIDS among Aboriginal Canadians by January of 1997, First Nations leaders speculate those numbers simply illustrate Ottawa's difficulty in collecting statistics in the Aboriginal community. Aboriginal health activists point to conditions that could allow AIDS to spread rapidly, such as the disproportionate number of Aboriginal people in and out of jail, where anal sex and intravenous drug use are common. Aboriginal people also tend to die of AIDS up to twice as fast as non-Natives, as the Vancouver Native Health Society documented in a 1995 study conducted at St. Paul's Hospital in Vancouver. Aboriginal people were admitted to hospital far less frequently and tended to have briefer stays, although this was often due to non-compliance with medical advice. The median age of death for Aboriginal people with AIDS in the study population of 96 people was 29, compared with 41 for non-Native AIDS patients.

The Royal Commission on Aboriginal Peoples was restrained when it suggested in its final report that a very real potential for violence also exists if the urgent needs of First Nations youth, already exacerbated by the wrongs visited upon their parents and grandparents, are shunted aside by government. In almost every large city or town in Canada, young urban Natives face a crisis of rootlessness. Most of Winnipeg's 65 000 Aboriginal people have emigrated from Manitoba's 62 reserves and 120 Métis communities. They may be fleeing poverty or seeking a job, education, or more social contact. Whole families leave the reserve to escape the cronyism and elitism of many elected chiefs and band councils. Teenagers and young adults on their own are also leaving rural reserves in ever-increasing numbers, attracted by the allure of the big city.

Unfortunately, what many people find in an urban setting is more grinding poverty and an environment even more scary and isolating than the one back home. "People come thinking they will have a better life in the city, but they end up trapped," Dave Chartrand of the Manitoba Métis Federation told *Maclean's* magazine. "The kids see what's happened to their parents, and don't see any hope for themselves." Employment prospects for Aboriginal people in the city, particularly youth, are scarcely better than on-reserve. "In this economy, it's more and more difficult for young people," says Wayne Helgason, a Cree from Manitoba's Sandy Bay Reserve who is executive director of the Winnipeg Social Planning Council. "They don't see finding a decent job even if they get an education, and so other forms of activity become their only choice."

In Winnipeg, Aboriginal youth gangs with names like the Manitoba Warriors and Indian Posse have attracted an estimated 800 young, disadvantaged, and angry Natives. Not merely a nuisance, the gangs are involved in criminal activities such as prostitution, assault, armed robbery, drive-by shootings, and even murder. Since the Winnipeg police formed its fifteen-member gang unit in the summer of 1995, they have made 440 gang-related arrests. Native youth gang violence has also spread to other prairie cities, including Regina, which saw 71 gang-related arrests in 1996, and Saskatoon. In Vancouver, although there is little organized Native gang activity, Aboriginal youth dominate the street kids' scene, especially in the poorer Downtown Eastside and east-end neighbourhoods, where young Aboriginal girls have been recruited into prostitution by Latino gangs.

In March 1996, Manitoba's Aboriginal affairs minister David Newman declared himself determined to reduce gang activity by increasing opportunities for young urban Natives through a co-ordinated approach involving all levels of government, community groups, and the private sector. Despite Newman's apparent good intentions, the Conservative provincial government of which he is a member cut funding to the Winnipeg Indian and Métis Friendship Centre by 85 percent that same fiscal year. It was left to five Manitoba Aboriginal organizations and former Manitoba Cree MP Elijah Harper to set in motion a series of youth conferences designed to entice young people away from gangs. In the trenches of Winnipeg's inner city, Aboriginal street workers and an order of Catholic sisters try to deter Aboriginal youth from crime and violence.

CULTURAL, POLITICAL, AND EDUCATIONAL SIGNS OF HEALING AND HOPE

Nonetheless, Aboriginal youth activism, a vital alternative to apathy and violence, has begun to assert itself all over Canada. Both urban and on-reserve Aboriginal communities have been forced to address the urgent crisis facing their youth, pressured by young activists with no particular allegiance to any Aboriginal political organization. "I call them runners, these organizers for the Native Youth Movement, because they'll work with whatever organization can give them access to their members and resources to advance their issues, which are all very real — like education, housing, employment, social, and medical care," says Viola Thomas, president of the United Native Nations, an organization representing off-reserve Aboriginal people in B.C. "A lot of the young people are second- or third-generation urban and a lot have blended Aboriginal heritage, so they don't identify with one particular First Nation or reserve. They're disenfranchised from treaty settlements and status benefits if they don't have a relationship with their home band; and if they're in the city, they are being told they don't have any more rights and benefits than non-Natives. They live with the legacy of generations of grief and pain, parents damaged by residential schools and foster care, but they don't qualify for education or housing assistance, or even counselling. No wonder they're angry."

Tim Fontaine, a young Manitoba Cree organizer and nephew of Assembly of First Nations National Chief Phil Fontaine, explains: "The Native Youth Movement offers the same things to Aboriginal kids that the gangs do — belonging, a sense of family, and empowerment. But we try to make sure we don't fit the profile of the young Aboriginal man who's more likely to go to jail than university in this country. We're not into crime. We're channelling anger into seeking change, and that's really positive. The only thing we can't compete with the gangs on is the money, and that's hard, because almost all of us have grown up in poverty."

The youth wing of the United Native Nations has begun to play a vital role in the B.C. provincial organization and even at meetings of the UNN's national organization, the Congress of Aboriginal Peoples. "Every time we have an important meeting with politicians or Aboriginal leaders, we take a member of our youth group, because this is their future — they're going to have to fight long and hard for what they need," says Viola Thomas.

In the early summer of 1997, a busload of Aboriginal youth urged B.C. cabinet ministers and members of the Legislative Assembly in Victoria to rebuff attempts by the federal government, as it moves to offload its responsibility for health, welfare, and education services, to transfer financial responsibility for off-reserve Aboriginal people, both status and non-status, onto the provinces. The premiers of Manitoba, Saskatchewan, and Alberta had also strongly protested this federal initiative, which could cost the provinces billions of dollars annually, at a first ministers' conference in October of 1996. "When Ottawa decided to say off-reserve, non-status treaty Indians are no longer being funded by the federal government, they broke a fiduciary relationship," said Saskatchewan Premier

Roy Romanow at the time. "That hurt the provinces and it hurt the other First Nations." But by April 1997, when the premiers met again — this time with off-reserve Aboriginal representatives present — cuts to the Canada Health and Social Transfer Agreement were virtually a fait accompli, affecting not only off-reserve Aboriginal people but many other Canadians as well. By mid-1997, urban Aboriginal people and their children were beginning to feel the pinch of the new financial restrictions. Worried that the federal government was returning billings for the care of off-reserve Aboriginal people and advising practitioners to seek reimbursement directly from patients, doctors' offices stopped accepting status Indian cards. Off-reserve Aboriginal people were left with a choice of getting medical coverage under provincial welfare schemes, paying their own premiums, or seeking coverage from their bands, most of which were quietly serving notice to people living away from home that the band could not afford to cover their medical bills.

The attempt to disqualify Aboriginal people from federal benefits based on their place of residence was compared by one First Nations leader to "negotiating by entering the room with a loaded gun." Others likened the move to the pass system that endured until the 1950s; no Indian could leave a reserve without permission from the Indian agent. Viola Thomas of the United Native Nations calls the federal government's actions a human rights violation. "Nowhere does it say in the Canadian constitution or in the Indian Act that Aboriginal rights depend on where you live. As ever, it will be Aboriginal children who are primarily hurt, because they will have no entitlement to federal health and welfare benefits or education dollars unless they have a good connection to an elected band council," says Thomas, a Secwepemc from Kamloops who has lived in Vancouver for most of her adult life. "In B.C., more than one-half of Aboriginal people live off-reserve, and 65 percent of urban Aboriginal families are single-parent, female-headed, living in poverty. Women flee reserves with their children to escape violence, and now the federal government is telling them they have to go back to that same band — to the same powerful male leaders they're afraid of — to get the financial help to which they're legally entitled." Aboriginal "graduates" of foster and adoptive care face the additional Catch-22 of being legally severed from their band of origin but unable to access federal funding except through that same band.

The Royal Commission on Aboriginal Peoples called for a twenty-year commitment to the renewal of the relationship between Canada and First Nations, particularly the 405 200 children and youth under 25 who make up 56 percent of the country's Aboriginal population. In 440 specific recommendations, whose implementation would cost an estimated $1.5 to $2 billion a year in addition to the $6.2 billion spent annually on Aboriginal people, the commission urged Canada to close the gap between mainstream and Aboriginal standards in health, housing, and education. Former federal Indian Affairs minister Ron Irwin promised to study the report, yet publicly disparaged the commission's cost estimates. Irwin and former Assembly of First Nations chief Ovide Mercredi, locked into a long-standing feud, disagreed over the importance of the $58 million report. When Irwin retired from elected office in 1997, he remarked that he didn't see the need for a major restructuring of government relations with Aboriginal people.

With the advent of two new leaders who are bound to dominate national Aboriginal politics in Canada — both of whom have pledged to bring a fresh commitment to negotiation rather than confrontation — hope has recently revived that the commission's thorough research and analysis will not go to waste. Jane Stewart, appointed Indian Affairs minister when Jean Chrétien's Liberal government was re-elected in June 1997, has already called the commission's report a "wonderful framework" and pledged her willingness to discuss its recommendations with Aboriginal groups. As MP for the southern Ontario riding of Brant, which is beside the high-profile Six Nations reserve, Stewart is well-versed in the importance of establishing co-operative relationships with First Nations. "I do really believe this is about a partnership," Stewart told reporters after she was named to the post. "We need a continuation or a new beginning in terms of our relationship with Aboriginal peoples that builds a bright future for us all. I think it begins with consensus and with mutual respect and recognizing the need for us all to treat each other with dignity."

Stewart will soon confront a cordial but formidable counterpart in Aboriginal politics. Phil Fontaine, the new national chief of the Assembly of First Nations, was elected in a hard-fought battle in the early morning hours of 31 July 1997. Fontaine, the former grand chief of the Assembly of Manitoba Chiefs, made it clear at the outset that the relationship between the AFN and the federal government "must be government to government" and stressed the importance on the federal government's side of being "open, accessible and flexible." One of Fontaine's first acts was to speak directly to Prime Minister Jean Chrétien; following their conversation, Fontaine told reporters: "There is a desire on the part of the government to work with us." He also stated his intention to seek unity among the 600 chiefs of the Assembly of First Nations.

Both Fontaine and his closest competitor for national chief, the Musqueam Nation's former chief and treaty negotiator Wendy

Grant-John, are committed to making the future better for Aboriginal youth. "I appreciate the deep frustrations our young people feel and we want to give them an opportunity to set their own path," Fontaine said. "We have to find ways and means of bringing them into the circle."

Although she lost her bid for the position of national chief, Grant-John will continue to play a key role in provincial and national Aboriginal politics. One of her most heartfelt personal and political priorities is to achieve implementation of the Royal Commission's key recommendations while hope and promise are still alive for the 56 percent of the Aboriginal population under the age of 25. "We need to empower our youth by providing strong education and employment options, to overcome with concrete action and goals the growing feeling of hopelessness, the unacceptable levels of suicide, poverty, and other signs of despair," Grant-John says. "Never before in our history can it be more strongly said that our youth is our future. We have got to empower them to succeed."

Nowhere is the future of young Aboriginal people more clearly hanging in the balance than in the field of education. In 1972, the National Indian Brotherhood urged in its landmark paper "Indian Control of Indian Education" that schools should not only educate Aboriginal children to modern standards but also play a central role in the revitalization of Native languages and cultures. To accomplish that, the NIB stated, schools would have to come under First Nations influence and control. The NIB position paper signalled the dawning of a new day in Aboriginal education, but since then it has been a long and difficult struggle to establish Aboriginal-directed education. Aboriginal education bodies have been kept on a short leash with a rudimentary structure of federal funding that supports the basic curriculum but provides few resources for cultural instruction or special needs. The federal government now typically provides education dollars directly to each First Nation, which can choose to set up its own school or reimburse the local school board for children sent to its facilities. By 1993–94, 51 percent of all federally funded schools on-reserve were band-owned and operated. But more than half of all Aboriginal children living on-reserve still have to travel off-reserve to attend schools. Of the 60 percent of all First Nations people in Canada now living off-reserve, 95 percent send their children to conventional schools. In the census year of 1991, 68.7 percent of all Aboriginal students were still in provincial public school systems.

The overall education of Aboriginal children lags far behind that of other Canadian children. Fewer Aboriginal youth complete their studies at any level of the education system. Among Aboriginal youth aged 15 to 24, 68.5 percent have not completed Grade 12. Three times as many

Aboriginal Canadians as non-Natives have less than a Grade 8 education; fewer than 1 percent of Aboriginal Canadians possess a university degree.

Nevertheless, in the years since First Nations made a deliberate decision to be major players in the field of education, there has been significant progress in curriculum development and language and cultural teachings, the development of versatile programs to suit Aboriginal learning and lifestyles, and a general improvement in educational levels attained. In 1981, 63 percent of Aboriginal people older than 15 had completed primary school, while 29 percent had a high-school education. A decade later, 76 percent of Aboriginal people over 15 had completed primary school, and 43 percent had completed high school.

Personal Stories of Healing and Hope

Role models are invaluable to young Aboriginal students battling shaky self-esteem and uncertainty about their goals. In May of 1997, a young woman from Kamloops named Nadine Caron became the first female First Nations medical doctor to graduate in British Columbia. While she was attending medical school at the University of B.C., Nadine's off hours were spent not packing up skis and heading for the slopes but loading her car with microscopes, stethoscopes, preserved fetal pigs, and tissue samples to accompany her talks to schoolchildren on reserves around the province. "I'd let the younger kids try on the stethoscope and see how it worked, or look at some pond water through the microscope, while the high-school kids could try their hand at dissecting the fetal pigs," says Caron, who first attended Simon Fraser University on basketball and soccer scholarships.

Caron, whose heritage is Ojibway and Italian, was determined from a young age to excel at everything she did. "I encourage the kids I talk to to set their sights high — there's such an urgent need for Aboriginal people in science and medicine careers," she says. Now, following in Caron's footsteps, there are two more Aboriginal women in UBC's medical school.

Three young Aboriginal women who began at an early age to address conflicts and pursue their career goals are Rose-Marie Francis, Bessie Austin, and Gaylene Henry. All attended Vancouver high schools, although each of them is a member of a First Nation far from the west-coast city, and all took part in a special graduation ceremony held in June 1997 for First Nations graduates of the Vancouver school system. Rose-Marie

Francis, a 19-year-old Kwakiutl born in Bella Coola but registered to her mother's band, gave the valedictory at the ceremony. Bessie Austin, a 17-year-old Gitksan member of the Frog clan, spoke to Grade 11 students to encourage them to make it all the way to graduation. Gaylene Henry, an 18-year-old born to a Sioux father she knew briefly as a child and a Cree mother from the Ochapowace band southeast of Regina, celebrated her graduation from Vancouver Technical, the city's largest high school, with a well-formed plan for her future.

In the fall of 1997, Francis will follow the lead of her father, Ted, by becoming a student at the Institute for Indigenous Education, which now offers two-year diplomas but soon will offer full university-level degrees. Started in 1995 by the Union of B.C. Indian Chiefs, the institute provides 25 First Nations students at a time with the opportunity to learn about their own history and culture, as well as to pick up conventional subjects. "I want to be a science teacher," says Francis. "I got straight As in biology and I'd love to work with kids. Ultimately, though, I plan to get my doctorate in science." She is passionately interested in Aboriginal politics and in the negotiation of modern-day treaties in British Columbia, particularly since her father is involved in the treaty process as an urban representative of the Sliammon band. "As urban people, we have to stay on top of what's going on in the treaty process, because there is no formal way for us to participate, and yet it's our future that is being negotiated too," Francis points out.

Francis's father has always been the primary care-giver for her and her brother. Because her mother is an unrecovered alcoholic, Francis seldom sees her. "I don't agree with her lifestyle," she says. Both her parents and her grandparents were the products of residential school, and in her early years, Francis lived with the unhappy patterns created by that family history. She recalls the New Year's Eve when, as a child of 4 or 5, she walked up to her father and demanded: "Why do you drink and smoke like that all the time?" Recalls Francis: "He poured his liquor down the sink and threw his smokes in the fire — my mom was screaming at him not to — and from that day on, he never smoked or drank again. He told me years later that he suddenly saw he was choosing booze over his children, and that he couldn't do that ever again." As a single father, Ted Francis often worked several jobs at a time to support his children, while making sure they did well in school.

Francis also has a new concern: day-care. Her first child was to be born just a month before she enters the Institute for Indigenous Education. Her father has invited the child's father, a N'laka'pamux man with whom Francis has been involved for four years, to move in with the family while

Francis finishes her schooling. Grandpa has offered to help look after the baby. But Francis anticipates she will be going to school for a long time. "The first thing I plan to do at the institute is lobby for more student day-care," she says. The prospect of having her own child, at an age young for mainstream society but not unusually so for First Nations, has strengthened Francis's resolve to succeed. "Children are the future, that's what I was raised to understand. I appreciate what I was given in life, despite what both my parents have gone through, and I feel I'm in a much better position to provide for this child and make sure she or he grows up knowing our history."

Gaylene Henry will be 21 at the turn of the millennium, just entering full adulthood, but she has a lot of living planned between now and then. In the summer of 1997 she returned to the Prairies, where she will attend the University of Regina in the fall. "I missed my grandmother, and I missed the prairie, just what it smells like and feels like back home — it took me a long time to get used to the coast," she says. She often visits her Saskatchewan reserve to see her beloved grandmother, who helped to raise Henry. Her grandmother and her grandmother's siblings sometimes talk about their days in residential school, which shocks Henry: "They talk about how they'd get hit with a ruler for talking their language. If somebody tried that with me, I'd hit them right back." Powwow dancing, a prairie tradition, has sprung up on the west coast, so even while Henry lived in Vancouver she was able to keep up her fancy dancing and jingle-dress competition dance.

After moving to Vancouver when she was 10 years old, Henry attended several schools, including the alternative Tumanos program for Aboriginal students at Van Tech. "I got all screwed up in Tumanos because you were allowed to work at your own pace and really fall behind," she says. "My marks were better in the regular school program so I switched back." Henry will take an undergraduate degree in anthropology in Regina. "I want to study all the indigenous people in the world, in Central and South America, New Zealand and Australia, the Maoris and the Aborigines. I want to study their customs and beliefs and history." Then she plans to return to the University of B.C. to study law. "I'm totally determined to get my PhD; if I could, I'd go to school all my life," she says. "If the federal government wants to help First Nations young people, it should support our education, then we'll be able to help ourselves for the rest of our lives."

Henry believes the federal government should support First Nations youth through full funding for postsecondary education and skills and trades training, and provide career counselling, instead of doling out "handouts" to kids who fail. "To me, First Nations kids are given so many opportunities to screw up that they fulfil that expectation — there's a program for everything when you screw up in life. I'm trying to be straight and get educated and I get doors slammed in my face. We need to be empowered and self-determining, and the best way to do that is through education." Friends and family members have attended school drop-out programs for Native kids "where they get money to go to school, and if they skip, they still get the 50 bucks," Henry says disgustedly. "What does that teach anyone about responsibility? We want to be in control of our own destiny, not getting money to fail."

Henry has stuck to her plans even when her family life at times became chaotic, even dangerous. Her mother, Nowela Henry, has been very supportive, but Gaylene has seen other close family members succumb to high unemployment and easy drugs. "With some of my cousins and uncles doing hard drugs, it got so that everything of value to us is gone; anything that wasn't nailed down in our house was stolen and sold," says Henry. In her last winter of high school, Henry sank into a deep depression, and began to drink. She attended school enough to avoid expulsion, but in every spare moment she reached for alcohol. "I finally stopped because my mother was going to commit me to detox and treatment," she says. Henry snapped out of her depression and drinking in time to finish high school with good enough grades to get into university, but the experience frightened her enough to decide to return home, where she feels most comfortable among Cree-speaking peoples.

Bessie Austin, who attended a Vancouver alternative secondary-school program called Total Education, claims she can sum up her cultural knowledge in one sentence: "I'm Gitksan and I'm a member of the Frog clan." All through her school years, in three regions of B.C., Austin was taught very little about Aboriginal culture. Although her grandmother and her great-grandmother are fluent Gitksan speakers, neither of them was with Austin consistently enough to pass the language on to her, a fact she laments. Yet when the three high-school girls begin to talk about traditional Aboriginal values, Austin expresses a well-articulated point of view. "Every time a teacher calls us 'Indians,' I'll put up my hand and say, 'Excuse me, we're Aboriginal or First Nations, or if you must, native Indians, but we are not Indians. The only reason we're called Indians is that Columbus got lost and thought he was in India.'"

Austin's only memory of her father, an American of German and Apache heritage, was of the police coming to deport him when she was 3, "but he was really abusive to my mother and used to hit her around, so she was glad to get rid of him." Bessie's mother, an alcoholic, left Hazelton, B.C., for Vancouver Island with one of Austin's many "stepfathers," leaving her daughter and son with their grandmother, Ina. Ina cared for many children with the help of her own mother, Austin's great-grandmother Eliza, whom Austin called Mamma. Though Austin recalls her Mamma with fondness, her life with her grandmothers came to an abrupt end when she was just 8 years old. Austin and her brother John were apprehended by social workers after it was discovered that an uncle living with them was sexually molesting some of the children in Ina's care, including Austin.

"After that, I bounced from foster home to foster home, but I refused to let go of John; I hollered that he had to go with me no matter what, so we stuck together," says Austin. "All of the foster homes were non-Native, except for once, when we were put with an auntie, but it didn't matter because we kept running away. I wanted to go home although I wasn't sure where home was. I'd go back to Mamma's." During brief periods of sobriety, Austin's mother would reclaim her children from "the welfare." Finally, she moved Bessie and her brother to Vancouver. Austin attended several Vancouver schools, trying to stay awake and learn despite her mother's chaotic, alcoholic lifestyle. "When I was 15, I realized my mother would never look after me properly, that I would never eat healthy with her or be able to finish high school," says Austin. "I went to ASU [the Adolescent Street Unit of what is now the B.C. Ministry for Children and Families] and signed myself into care." This time, Austin was determined to make the system work for her. "I convinced them to let me try 'independent living.' A support worker came around once a week or so and helped me buy groceries and talked to me about school and everything. She was really more like a friend." After a year, Austin convinced the social worker to allow her to live with her boyfriend, a young non-Native tradesman.

Austin plans to be a social worker, or perhaps a letter-carrier; she likes the idea of fresh air, independence, and exercise. There is no trace of self-pity as she talks about her life, nor does she blame her mother. "I am who I am because I want to be here and I want to succeed," she says. "My mother's made her choice to keep drinking. I always nagged her about quitting and then, about four years ago, I just stopped. It's her life." Austin understands her mother's alcoholism even as she rejects it as a choice for herself. "My mother and her family all went to residential school, where they were abused physically, sexually, and emotionally," she says. Yet through all the Gitksan family's travail, Austin has emerged with a strong sense that she is loved. "I'm a strong First Nations person I think because I absolutely have always known that I was loved. As for my grandmothers, especially Eliza, I know she adored me and put me first in everything, because that's the Aboriginal way. I have a great mother who taught me to be truthful and honest. Even though she's an alcoholic, I know my mom loves me with all her soul and heart." Austin believes the key for her generation is to overcome the lingering damage done by residential schools and foster homes: "For me, my goal is to figure out ways to stop it, to stop the abuse and alcohol, to prevent the stuff that happened to me from ever happening to my children."

Gaylene Henry agrees: "When you're raised in residential school or foster homes, you don't get parenting skills. Even our parents who went to public schools had to deal with a lot of racism. There's a lot for our generation to overcome, but we also have a lot more opportunities. I really want my life to be solid and settled so I can give my children the love and the cultural knowledge that I got, but also what I didn't have — safety and security." Both Henry and Austin are emphatic that they won't be ready to think about motherhood for several more years; they have their own urgent needs and goals. Says Austin: "I'm still working on bringing up myself; I just don't have the patience to work with little kids yet." Rose-Marie Francis is joyfully looking forward to the birth of her baby. Her partner has taken training as a counsellor at the Hey-Way-Noqu Healing Circle for Addictions Society in Vancouver, and Francis envisages the couple offering their combined skills to both of their First Nations in turn, without severing ties from the city where they grew up. "I guess we're a First Nations family of the future, because although both of us want to live in our home territory and stay involved there, we both know we have to live in the city to reach our education goals. We really want our child to have the best of both worlds."

To Lorna Williams, the St'at'yemc educator who is the Vancouver School Board's First Nations education specialist, these three young women represent the strong potential of Aboriginal youth. Williams documented the problems Aboriginal schoolchildren face in a 1993 study. Asked what kept them from staying in school in Vancouver, Native students replied: "Ashamed and embarrassed to be Indian," "racism," "alcohol and drug abuse," and "no support from home." Williams, a proponent of establishing an Aboriginal high school within the Vancouver school system, says such schools can be refuges from racism and the sometimes unhelpful attitudes of mainstream educators. Even more important is the positive role that a separate school could play in revitalizing the Aboriginal languages and cultures that were "virtually destroyed" by the educational system.

In the decade that she has worked with the Vancouver School Board, Williams has encouraged First Nations educators, helped to develop a home-school support system, and hired close to twenty school-based First Nations support workers. Five special programs are situated in regular schools to meet the needs of about 150 Aboriginal children. Williams knows all about attitudes that prejudge Aboriginal or immigrant children as "slow" learners. Sent to a residential school when she was only 6, she recalls being placed in a class of 45 students where the teacher assessed Williams and all except two of the other Aboriginal children as mentally retarded. As an adult, Williams has become a linguist, educator, and administrator of renown.

Among Lorna Williams's most far-reaching accomplishments has been her pioneering work with Feuerstein Intensive Enrichment, a mediated learning method. FIE uses the simple "instruments" of shapes, dots, and lines to help children reason both concretely and abstractly without having to puzzle through value-laden lessons. As the instruments become more difficult, the child's brain subtly increases its reasoning power, imperceptibly overcoming emotional and cultural blocks. The method is ideal for children who have suffered a cognitive loss due to trauma or have learning disabilities, language and cultural differences, or behaviour issues. FIE was created by Dr. Reuven Feuerstein, who developed the technique for children of the Jewish diaspora who had survived traumatic and tumultuous live events before they came to Israel. Williams saw instantly the usefulness of such a method to Aboriginal children, who were dealing with staggering events of grief and loss in their own lives. She travelled to Israel to meet with Feuerstein, and over the years, the two educators developed a warm professional relationship, the Jewish elder sometimes coming to Canada to work with Aboriginal children. "It was through Feuerstein and his work that I began to see that I have, as a teacher, a very, very significant and powerful role in the lives of children," says Williams. "The stronger that I can make these children — to understand how to problem-solve, to make decisions, and to understand their actions and behaviour — I can only make them stronger for all the things they have to contend with outside school." Williams has taught FIE to hundreds of teachers all over North America and Europe.

A First Nations graduation ceremony was Williams's brainchild. Although in 1985 only two Aboriginal children graduated from high school in Vancouver, a decade later there were 56. Now each June brings together a whole auditorium of bright, excited First Nations graduates to the ceremony, full of plans for the future.

In late May of 1997 about 800 parents, teachers, and elders gathered at the Walnut Grove Secondary School in Langley, B.C., in another ceremony to honour Aboriginal students, including close to 100 Grade 12 graduates. Among the students who received awards of excellence was 15-year-old Karrmen Crey, Ernie Crey's second-oldest daughter and a Grade 11 student who has topped the honour roll in every year of high school. Karrmen has experienced all the benefits as well as the downside of her Aboriginal heritage. "It is nice to know that I'm a part of a culture so diverse, so elaborate and meticulously beautiful," says Karrmen, who appreciates "perks" such as "government education sponsorship, the cultural experience, and everything therein such as art, language, and history." Karrmen has also witnessed the racism and resentment directed at Aboriginal people over fishing rights, "land claims," and "what people perceive as a free ride for us just because we're Aboriginal." She is happy that she was raised "with full knowledge of my cultural background," but she is primarily focussed on her future, which to her lies in continuing her education. "I like learning and reading and accumulating my resources educationally. I want to keep learning so that my abilities are far-reaching," Karrmen says. "I want to know that I will be able to provide for myself in the future no matter what the circumstances. I was born with an instinct to write, but you can't survive in the woods with a pen and parchment, so I'll need something more substantial than my status card — an education and the ability to provide for myself."

Later in the same ceremony, the Pam Koczapska Award was presented to Lakahahmen community member Kenneth Lancaster, a 26-year-old Sto:lo man who graduated with a biochemistry degree from McGill University in 1995 and plans to enrol in medicine at the University of B.C. Koczapska was a non-Native teacher respected for her long and honourable relationship with the Sto:lo people, and the elders presenting the award also acknowledged the presence in the audience of Ernie Crey, for whom Pam remained a lifelong mentor after she briefly welcomed him to her home as a foster child.

THE FORMAL CHALLENGES TO BRINGING FIRST NATIONS CHILDREN HOME

After centuries of the compulsory surrender of their children to strangers, First Nations all across Canada have made their highest priority acquiring the legal, social, and financial resources to care for their own. The Micmac in Nova Scotia and the Cree of northern Ontario have established sophisticated child and family support systems that depend on professionally trained Aboriginal social workers and have strengthened cultural traditions by seeking extended family support. In Manitoba, control of Aboriginal children was delegated to several Aboriginal agencies in the 1970s, and today more than 90 percent of Aboriginal children needing protection in the province are placed in First Nations homes, most within their own extended family or culture.

Some of the Manitoba agencies have had to battle political interference from elected chiefs and councillors who may have a vested interest in obscuring child protection needs among their immediate family and friends. The Dakota-Ojibway Child and Family Services (DOCFS) agency in southern Manitoba was shaken to its core in 1992 by the death of Lester Desjarlais, a 13-year-old boy who had been tied to a tree and sodomized by a relative of the chief of his community. The perpetrator received more protection than Desjarlais, who committed suicide after he was repeatedly revictimized. A scathing indictment of the DOCFS was delivered by Judge Brian Giesbrecht, who headed a 1993 inquiry into Desjarlais's death. But Giesbrecht was also highly critical of the federal and Manitoba provincial governments, which he said had offloaded an enormous responsibility for Aboriginal social services onto Manitoba First Nations but provided meagre financial resources and virtually no professional support.

In B.C., tripartite negotiations are under way among the federal and provincial governments and at least eleven separate First Nations seeking to administer their own child and family programs. The size of Aboriginal groups represented ranges from an individual band to an entire nation of 25 communities. The groups are at varying stages of negotiation, ranging all the way from a simple protocol that requires provincial social workers and the RCMP to notify a band social worker before entering the reserve for a child apprehension to the complete delegation of the statutory authority to apprehend children and certify foster homes.

Among the first tribal groups in B.C. to set up their own social services agency was the Nuu-chah-nulth Tribal Council, representing fourteen communities on the west coast of Vancouver Island, which in 1985 created the Usma Nuu-chah-nulth Child and Family Services Program. "Traditionally it was everyone's responsibility to protect our children because they were Usma, the most precious one, the cherished ones," notes Usma director Debra Foxcroft, who grew up on the Tseshaht reserve just outside Port Alberni, where the Usma offices are located today. Usma was a mandated agency almost from the outset; its social workers were soon able to apprehend children from homes without having to call in a provincial social worker. This authority, combined with the agency's proactive sexual abuse prevention program and aggressive child protection goals, initially provoked resentment as well as appreciation among its member communities. "It's been very hard for me as a Nuu-chah-nulth woman to work in my own community — there were times when I was threatened to my face at events that were supposed to be traditional feasts or peaceful potlatches," admits Foxcroft. After Usma had been in existence for several years, however, "the community settled down and realized we weren't there to be brown government social workers and take their children away. We put more emphasis on family support and tried to set up committees in each of the member bands to work with us."

Usma has been able to significantly improve the overall well-being of Nuu-chah-nulth children, offering parenting workshops, counselling resources, and sexual abuse prevention programs. It has certified dozens of safe Aboriginal foster homes for children requiring care, and returned many Nuu-chah-nulth children from all over Canada and the United States to their home territory. The agency has been able to place the majority of children in care — about 60 in 1996 — in the homes of extended family members or in another community within the tribal council's mandate.

Even so, Usma has had to defend its child protection actions in at least two ongoing court challenges launched by disgruntled parents and caregivers. Although a brief produced by Usma in 1992 for the provincial legislative review panel declared that "the court system is too adversarial, intimidating and imposing," ironically the agency has had to spend time and money in court defending its own policies. "That's all part of the growing pains," Foxcroft says philosophically.

Among other First Nations proceeding in various phases to child protection authority are the Gitksan and Wet'suwet'en, the Nicola Valley, the N'laka'pamux, the Burns Lake, the Sechelt, the Cowichan, the Squamish Nation, and the Sto:lo Nation. Unique among all the agreements is that of the small Spallumcheen band, which first asserted its right to control its children's destiny in a 1979 band council resolution made under the provisions of the Indian Act; the federal government has declined to challenge the resolution. Although Spallumcheen social workers, with the assistance of the chief and council, now make most key decisions about the community's children, the band has left the mandated child protection function to provincial social workers.

The Sto:lo people, as one of the tribal groups most impacted by close proximity to non-Native settlement, have sought wide-ranging jurisdiction over their children, with a strong conviction that child protection must be culturally based. In the spring of 1994, the Sto:lo issued invitations, first to the community and then to the B.C. social services minister and an array of provincial and federal bureaucrats, to attend information sessions about the Sto:lo child and family services program, known as Xolhmi:lh.

"Xolhmi:lh???" the invitations read. "Say what? How is that pronounced? 'Zolmeet?' 'Ex-ol-mee-l?' 'Hoth-meeth?' 'Ha-clear your throat-
meeth?'" In Halq'emeylem, the Coast Salish language of the Sto:lo, Xolh-
mi:lh — the last pronunciation is the closest — means the special
relationship of caring, respect, and love that exists between a care-giver
and a child. The daytime open house was the public representation of a
private ceremony that had taken place in a Sto:lo longhouse a year earlier, when the talks first began. There, according to Sto:lo custom, the
name Xolhmi:lh was bestowed by Sto:lo leaders upon the honoured members of the community who would uphold the mission of the sacred undertaking: to bring Sto:lo children home and raise them in a safe, loving
environment. The name was given not only to Sto:lo hereditary chiefs
but also to the federal and provincial employees who had helped to negotiate the initial agreement, and to Xolhmi:lh's first executive director,
Dan Ludeman, a non-Native social worker.

After three years of operation, the Xolhmi:lh Child and Family Services
Agency is emerging as a strong and healthy model of First Nations admin-
istration, praised by everyone from former B.C. social services minister Joy
MacPhail to federal Health and Welfare administrators, including Pacific
Region director Paul Kyba. Of 3800 Sto:lo children, of whom about 1500
live on-reserve, there are about 140 children in the care of the agency at
any given time, a ratio of about one in ten. "If that seems high, it's because
Sto:lo people are still in recovery and a lot are still living in poverty," says
Ludeman. "Also, our social workers know the community much better and
are trusted more. The vast majority of children in care are there because of
neglect. Neglect is a function of poverty and the fact that parenting skills
skipped a generation or two with residential schools and foster care." Now,
about 70 percent of the Sto:lo children who require substitute care can be
placed in approximately 80 Sto:lo foster homes; the rest are placed in non-
Native homes scattered throughout the Fraser Valley. The agency receives
funding from the federal government at the same per-diem rate paid to
provincially run foster homes, group homes, or institutions.

The most recent First Nation in Canada to move toward full responsibility for child and family services is the Nisga'a Tribal Council, the first
Aboriginal body in British Columbia to have negotiated an agreement-
in-principle for a modern treaty with the provincial and federal governments. The Nisga'a are also the first nation to sign a delegation agreement
with the B.C. government under the new Child, Family and Community
Service Act enacted in 1996. The signing of the initial child protection
agreement on 13 May 1997 was announced in a joint press release by B.C.
children and families minister Penny Priddy and Nisga'a Tribal Council

president Joseph Gosnell. "This is one of the last stepping stones on the path to Nisga'a autonomy under self-government," said Gosnell. "Our mission is to ensure the physical, mental, emotional, and cultural well-being of all Nisga'a children and to maintain families according to Nisga'a tradition."

Nisga'a authority will be phased in in three stages. First, while the Nisga'a develop skills and resources, they will be responsible only for preventive and support services, including foster homes. In the second phase, they will take on child protection services, including the right to apprehend children. In the third and final phase, the Nisga'a will appoint a director who will have powers and responsibilities equal to the B.C. ministry's own director of child, family, and community services. Once this stage has been achieved, the Nisga'a will be well along the road to the restoration of full self-government in a contemporary context. Ultimately, the Nisga'a — and other First Nations — will be able to write and administer their own child welfare legislation.

In July 1997, the Sto:lo Nation's Xolhmi:lh Child and Family Services achieved a breakthrough in tripartite negotiations with federal and provincial governments by inking an agreement that would allow Aboriginal families of any nation living inside Sto:lo traditional territory to choose to be served by Xolhmi:lh rather than by the B.C. Ministry for Children and Families. "In the vast majority of cases, Aboriginal families prefer an Aboriginal agency, even if it is a different First Nation, because there is a commonality of values and an understanding of the obstacles which parents have to overcome to raise healthy families," says Xolhmi:lh director Dan Ludeman. "This recognizes the right of Aboriginal families to live where they choose, and should they get into difficulties while living away from home and be in need of family support, addiction counselling, or temporary care for their children, they have the option of working within an Aboriginal value system." Ludeman notes Aboriginal people still harbour immense mistrust of the mainstream social services system; even in the face of modest reforms, memories have not faded of "the welfare" and its predatory history.

In the years to come, First Nations in B.C. and across Canada intend to negotiate full jurisdiction over their own children and those of other Aboriginal families living in traditional territory, in a bid to ensure not only cultural integrity but a more efficient and humane means of serving diverse Aboriginal families. In order to properly discharge their responsibilities, First Nations are adamant that they must receive the same funding levels that have been channelled to provincial governments for decades as federal reimbursement for the care of Aboriginal children. Indeed, the resources need to be far greater to repair the devastating effects of Canada's failed Indian policy on Aboriginal families and to bring the health and future prospects of Aboriginal children up to the level enjoyed by other Canadian children. It is here that the funds from redress or restitution are most urgently needed.

A blanket of First Nations jurisdiction covering Aboriginal children all over the country would have been unthinkable in Canada at almost any point in the last several hundred years, since Europeans first began to "cultivate the young plants" of the New World. Yet it is only half a millennium since Aboriginal children were the vital, cherished soul of strong societies that had endured far longer than the European nations who regarded the indigenous peoples as inferior savages. Child-centred traditions never truly vanished within the collective memory of First Nations societies, and many tribes have already begun to recover — and flourish — as they restore their wise child-rearing ways. Aboriginal communities today know they face formidable challenges, but they also know that healthy, intact families are the cornerstone of self-determination. At the heart of the ongoing restoration of Aboriginal communities is their hope for the future: their children.

DISCUSSION QUESTIONS

1. What do you think are important signs of hope in relationships involving Aboriginal children and their families? Why are many of these signs of hope only fairly recent phenomena?
2. What do you think are the most difficult social, economic, educational, and political barriers that hinder Aboriginal youth from living healthy, meaningful, and productive lives?
3. How would you explain the fairly recent groundswell of organizational and political activism involving Aboriginal youth in Canada?
4. Do you think violent political activism is a valid way for Aboriginal youth to bring about meaningful social and political change? Why or why not?

FURTHER READINGS

Armitage, Andrew. 1993. "Family and Child Welfare in First Nation Communities." Pp. 131–71 in *Rethinking Child Welfare in Canada*, ed.

B. Wharf. Toronto: McClelland & Stewart. A critical overview of child welfare issues in Aboriginal communities in Canada. The author identifies three stages of First Nation child welfare between the years 1867 to 1960 (the assimilation phase), 1960 to the late 1970s (the integration phase), and 1980 and beyond (the Aboriginal self-government phase). The article also provides a detailed analysis of the relationships between major issues in First Nation family and child welfare and various forms of community and administrative self-government.

Durst, Doug. 1992. "The Road to Poverty Is Paved with Good Intentions: Social Interventions and Indigenous Peoples." *International Social Work* 35(2): pp. 191–202. A critical examination of the relationship between the social welfare laws, policies, and programs introduced by colonial governments throughout the world and the oppressive experiences of indigenous peoples. The article concludes with a series of recommendations based on a vision of self-government grounded on Aboriginal values and customs.

First Nation's Child and Family Task Force. 1993. *Children First: Our Responsibility.* Winnipeg: First Nation's Child and Family Task Force. The Task Force on First Nations Child and Family Services was established by the Assembly of Manitoba Chiefs, the federal government, and the Manitoba provincial government. The report attempts to identify the structure and process of technical details necessary for implementing a self-government child welfare system for First Nations communities. Its strength is the community planning model it lays out, though the authors unfortunately do not address the model's implementation in the context of broader social, political, and legal issues.

Hungry Wolf, Adolf and Star. 1992. *Children of the Circle.* Skookumchuck, B.C.: Good Medicine Books. A collection of photographs and brief commentaries of Aboriginal people, their camps, and scenes of many traditional activities. According to the authors, the "words are mainly presented for pleasure; the value of each photo speaks for itself." The book is presented to encourage Aboriginal children to keep their tribal cultures alive, "while at the same time showing people of other cultures why Indian childhood is something to be very proud of."

Johnson, Patrick. 1983. *Native Children and the Child Welfare System.* Toronto: Canadian Council on Social Development. A landmark book that had a major impact on the social work profession regarding child welfare services to Aboriginal children by providing an exposé of services offered from the 1960s to the 1980s, a period that witnessed high numbers of Aboriginal children in care. Though its data are somewhat dated, the book's discussion of new directions continues to provide hope by pointing out Aboriginal initiatives to correct the treatment of Aboriginal children and families in Canada.

McKenzie, B., E. Seidl, and N. Bone. 1995. "Child Welfare Standards in First Nations: A Community-Based Study." Pp. 54–65 in *Child Welfare in Canada, Research and Policy Implications*, ed. J. Hudson and B. Galaway. Toronto: Thompson Educational Publishing. A report on a study involving the author's "community-based approach to the development of Aboriginal child welfare standards" in nine First Nations communities in Manitoba. Throughout, the authors raise numerous relevant and sensitive interpretive and cultural issues in a critical yet respectful manner.

REFERENCES

As well as the publications listed below, we consulted newspapers and magazines, including *The Globe and Mail*, the Vancouver *Province*, the Vancouver *Sun*, *The Toronto Star*, the *Winnipeg Free Press*, the Regina *Leader-Post*, *Maclean's*, *Saturday Night*, the Seattle *Post-Intelligencer*, and the *Oregonian*; and broadcast media, including CBC Radio's "Sunday Morning" and "Ideas," and news programs on CBC Radio and Television, BCTV, CKNW, CKVU, and CHEK-TV.

All interviews not credited to acknowledged or published sources are from personal interviews conducted by the authors.

Health Canada. 1995. *A Statistical Report on the Health of First Nations in British Columbia*. Ottawa: Health Canada.
McKee, Christopher. 1996. *Treaty Talks in British Columbia: Negotiating a Mutually Beneficial Future*. Vancouver: University of British Columbia Press.
National Indian Brotherhood. 1972. "Indian Control of Indian Education." Policy paper presented to the Minister of Indian Affairs and Northern Development by the National Indian Brotherhood.
Royal Commission on Aboriginal Peoples (RCAP). 1995. *Choosing Life: Special Report on Suicide among Aboriginal Peoples*. Ottawa: RCAP.
———. 1996a. *Report of the Royal Commission on Aboriginal Peoples*. Vol. 2. Restructuring the Relationship. Ottawa: RCAP.

―――. 1996b. *Report of the Royal Commission on Aboriginal Peoples*. Vol. 4. Perspectives and Realities. Ottawa: RCAP.

―――. 1996c. *Report of the Royal Commission on Aboriginal Peoples*. Vol. 5. Renewal: A Twenty-Year Commitment. Ottawa: RCAP.

Smart, Stephen and Michael Coyle. 1997. *Aboriginal Issues Today: A Legal and Business Guide*. Vancouver: Self-Counsel Press.

Waldram, James B., D. Ann Herring, and T. Kue Young. 1995. *Aboriginal Health in Canada: Historical, Cultural and Epidemiological Perspectives*. Toronto: University of Toronto Press.

CHAPTER 11

Aboriginal Education:
Is There a Way Ahead?

Jan Hare and Jean Barman

Though Aboriginal education has undergone many transitions, the problems and issues that characterized it in the past remain. They have only become more complex as Aboriginal people attempt to implement their own vision of education in a contemporary world. To understand the current issues facing Aboriginal people, we must begin with the history of schooling.

Residential schools represent a horrific, yet important, era in Aboriginal education and Canadian history. Designed to assimilate Aboriginal children into mainstream society and remove any traces of their language and culture, these schools failed dismally. Three factors ensured that residential schools, and their lesser counterpart of federal day schools, would not educate Aboriginal children to participate equitably in society: the government's assumption of Aboriginal peoples' sameness across Canada, inadequate curriculum and teaching, and the lack of federal funding for the operation of schools.

Only in the mid-twentieth century did Aboriginal families acquire other educational options, and only in the past two decades have communities taken charge of schooling on reserves. Measures of educational success can be seen in the increasing number of Aboriginal students graduating from both high school and university. But the legacy of residential schooling endures. Its policies and practices have had a devastating effect on individuals, families, and communities. For many families, negative attitudes toward schools today are grounded in their own experience or that of parents and grandparents who attended these institutions. Others have suffered more severe consequences.

Aboriginal people have begun to speak out about their experiences, as is evident in the growing accounts of residential schooling (AFN, 1994; Bull, 1991; Furniss, 1992; Jaine, 1993; Knockwood, 1992; Chrisjohn and Young, 1997). Their narratives are important to the healing process that is under way in many First Nation communities. It is not only Aboriginal people who must heal themselves; members of the dominant society must also acknowledge this educational disaster as part of a common history.

Aboriginal people have experienced a horrible injustice, but we cannot undo the past. Aboriginal people can no longer afford to look back and place blame outside themselves for the atrocities they experienced and the impact residential schooling has had on their lives. If Aboriginal people are to address the complexity of issues related to education, then they must look inward and forward — inward to themselves to promote healing and wellness, and forward to their own vision of education.

LOOKING BACK

The paternalism that characterizes the relationship between Aboriginal people and the government of Canada fostered a historical belief that Aboriginal people were not only inferior to their non-Aboriginal counterparts, but posed a problem to formulating the Canadian nation. Policymakers sought to "civilize" Aboriginal peoples "so as to cause them to reside in towns, or, in the case of farmers, in settlements of white people, and thus become amalgamated with the general community" (Canada, 1887, p. ixxx). For Aboriginal people to be assimilated into Canadian society, their cultures, languages, and traditions had to be eradicated.

Education was to serve as the vehicle for assimilation. "The Indian problem exists owing to the fact that the Indian is untrained to take his place in the world. Once teach him to do this, and the solution is had" (Canada, 1895, p. xxi). It was believed that Aboriginal people could be assimilated only if they were removed from the influences of their family and community. The essential structures of family and community house the languages, values, and culture, as well as give identity to Native people. Since adults were less malleable, it was children who fell victim to the policy.

The Indian Act allowed the federal government to legally arrange for other bodies to provide education to Aboriginal children, and the government turned responsibility over to the churches. Various religious denominations and missionary groups accepted this responsibility, and residential schools were created for Aboriginal children. Formal education would replace traditional education and eliminate any involvement of the family and community in their children's education.

It was at these schools that the attack on Aboriginal culture began. Children were forbidden to speak their language and received harsh punishment if caught doing so. They were isolated from their parents and siblings, as many attended the schools for ten to twelve months a year and for as many as ten years. Once at school, children were separated by age and gender, rarely having any contact with brothers and sisters. With few care-givers at the schools, it was difficult for children to develop positive adult–child relationships (Frideres, 1988). The loss of language and the erosion of family values, traditions, and parenting skills are two of the paramount effects of residential schooling. But the abuse suffered by children at these schools has had the most serious consequences. In *Breaking the Silence* (1994), the Assembly of First Nations divided Aboriginal children's experience at residential schools into the emotional, mental, physical, and spiritual realms and demonstrated through individual recollections how students were wounded by having their feelings ridiculed, their creativity and independent thinking stifled, their bodily needs ignored or violated, and their ways of life denied.

The learning opportunities that did take place at residential schools focussed on domestic skills and religious indoctrination. Though a basic education was provided, it was to prepare students for participation in the lower fringes of the dominant society (Barman et al., 1986). Federal policy, initiated by government and carried out by church, legitimized and even compelled children to be schooled not for assimilation purposes but for inequality. Their education ensured that students could not participate socially or economically in the dominant society, but also prevented them from returning to their traditional ways of life.

Factors Ensuring Inequality in Education

Assumption of Aboriginal Peoples' Sameness

Of the attributes of residential schools that fostered inequality, the primary one was the assumption of Aboriginal people's sameness. Aboriginal people have always maintained a nation status in their relationship with Canada. "They lived as nations — highly centralized, loosely federated, or small and clan-based — for thousands of years before the arrival of Europeans. ... To this day, Aboriginal people's sense of confidence and well being as individuals remains tied to the strength of their nations" (RCAP, 1996a, pp. x–xi). As nations, Aboriginal peoples possessed enormous variety in their languages, cultures, and traditions. On the Prairies, groups such as the Plains Cree and Blackfoot lived in close harmony with the buffalo and caribou, speaking Sarcee, Assiniboine, or Chipewyan. On the west coast, where the potlatch was a common ceremony, groups such as the Salish or Haida looked to the resources of the sea and forests to maintain themselves. The distinctness of each nation remains today.

The educational practices of Aboriginal groups were just as distinct. The differing conditions under which each community lived would necessitate varied features in education. Miller (1996, p. 16) explains how "subsistence fishers and sealers such as the Inuit in the Arctic north, sedentary agriculturalists such as the Huron (Wendat) and Iroquois, woodlands hunter–gatherers such as the Cree and the Dene, and west-coast fishing and commercial peoples such as the Kwagiulth could not be expected to subscribe to a uniform system of socialization, instruction, and vocational training."

Some Aboriginal peoples were, on their own, making the transition to new forms of schooling. From the time that free non-denominational public schools were legislated shortly after British Columbia became a province in 1871, numerous Aboriginal children enrolled alongside their neighbours (Barman, 1995). Several factors contributed to their being accepted in local schools. In many outlying settlements, Aboriginal children were essential to securing the minimum enrolment necessary for a public school's establishment and survival. The material conditions under which many Aboriginal peoples lived enabled them to be self-sufficient. These characteristics were looked favourably upon by some European settlers and government officials. Aboriginal children's attendance began to be accepted as a matter of course, perhaps because they were often not that different in actions and even appearance from their contemporaries. Aboriginal families in British Columbia and elsewhere demonstrated an independence that would have served them well had federal education policy not assumed Aboriginal peoples' sameness across Canada.

Provisions of the British North America Act made Aboriginal peoples "wards" of the federal government. Through treaties whereby Aboriginal people surrendered occupied lands, the government assumed responsibility for education, health care, and other services. The British North America Act made no attempt to distinguish Aboriginal peoples in all of their diversity and individuality, but simply reduced them to a single dependent condition captured in the word "status."

Federal policy that favoured segregated residential schools for Aboriginal children was intended to help achieve the goal of assimilation of all Aboriginal peoples across Canada. Two types of residential schools were established in the late nineteenth century: boarding schools for younger children and industrial schools for their older siblings. Not only did the latter put greater emphasis on occupational training, but they also tended to be larger and located farther away from students' home reserves (Titley, 1986). Over time, the distinction between the two types of schools broke down, and they all became known as residential schools. Day schools also existed. In the 1900s, 65.9 percent of Aboriginal children were registered at these schools; by the 1940s, the number was still as high as 50.9 percent. Even though more children were going to day schools, these were perceived as less acceptable and to be established only where circumstances did not permit residential schools.

Until the mid-twentieth century, federal policy toward Aboriginal peoples — adults as well as children — refused to acknowledge their distinctiveness between geographical areas or as individuals. They were treated as a single category to be dealt with as expeditiously and economically as possible. The initiative demonstrated by British Columbia's Aboriginal peoples, in political and economic matters as well as in schooling, only served to label them as nuisances for refusing to conform to their given role of dependency (Tennant, 1990). Another narrative might well be constructed today about Canada's Aboriginal peoples had their distinctiveness been recognized and maintained.

Curriculum and Teaching

Various religious denominations, under the guise of rescuing Aboriginal children from their "uncivilized" ways, accepted the responsibility of providing schooling. Both curriculum and teaching were substandard compared with that made available to non-Aboriginal children and, moreover, took place in a harsher environment. The most glaring conditions of residential school that contributed to Aboriginal children's inequitable treatment were the little time they spent in the classroom, the curriculum to which they were exposed, and the quality of instruction that they received from teachers. Aboriginal children were expected to succeed in a system that was clearly paternalistic and represented the self-interest of the church.

Residential schools were established in every province and territory except Prince Edward Island, New Brunswick, and Newfoundland. They registered children from every Aboriginal culture — Indian, Inuit, and Métis — although the federal government assumed no constitutional responsibility for Métis people (RCAP, Vol. 1, 1996b). In 1895 the newly established School Branch of the Department of Indian Affairs laid down a uniform curriculum based on provincial counterparts. Aboriginal students were to move between six "standards" or grades centred around readers similar to those being used in provincial systems (Canada, 1895).

The new curriculum would have boded well for the proclaimed federal goal of assimilating Aboriginal peoples had the children not been expected to somehow get through it in less time each day than was allotted to non-Aboriginal children in provincial schools. In residential schools, usually only half of each day was spent in the classroom, sometimes in segments. At one school, the hours of instruction were 9:00 to 11:30 A.M. and 2:00 to 3:00 P.M. (Gresko, 1986, p. 96). The reports on individual schools included in the annual reports of the Department of Indian Affairs often implied longer hours of instruction, but accounts from individual schools almost always reveal a short time period. Personal testimonies are damning: "We spent very little time in the classroom. We were in the classroom from nine o'clock in the morning until noon. Another shift [of children] came into the classroom at one o'clock in the afternoon and stayed until three" (Manuel and Posluns, 1974, p. 64; Haig-Brown, 1988, p. 61). Regardless of the format, the total was two to four hours per day compared with the five hours or longer that other Canadian children spent on the prescribed curriculum.

Making learning even more difficult was the language barrier between children and teachers. The local Aboriginal languages that most boys and girls brought with them to school were almost always prohibited, even for private conversations between students. One student recounts: "In my first meeting with the brother, he showed me a long black leather strap and told me, through my interpreter, 'If you are ever caught speaking Indian this is what you will get across your hands'" (Manuel and Posluns, 1974, p. 64). Classroom instruction was in English or French, depending on which religious denomination maintained the school. Children, expected to learn in a second language, encountered confusion and fear, hence leading to failure.

Though the government provided limited funding for the schools' maintenance, the church relied on the children for their daily operation. In return for the limited schooling they received, they were expected to carry out the chores that kept the schools running. "We knew we had to do our chores, such as sweeping the dormitory, cleaning the washrooms, in the morning, and go to school half a day" (Baker, 1994, pp. 30–31). This student's daily round grew more onerous as he got older: "Our job was getting tougher. We went to school for half a day. One month you worked in the mornings and the next month you worked in the afternoons. We never went to school full-time until the last year, in grade eight" (Baker, 1994, p. 29). As seasons of the year dictated the need for certain chores to be done, some children did not even go to class. One student recalls:

> The older boys who tended the furnace never went to classes except of course Sunday school. The other boys who were not working in the barn were taken out of school during the coal-shovelling season for weeks at a time until all the coal was put in the bins. Then they returned to classes

only to be called out again. ... Their classroom hours were very irregular and an afternoon session once or twice a week was average. Full-time barn and furnace boys worked fifteen hours a day seven days a week. (Knockwood and Thomas, 1992, pp. 57–58)

These experiences are echoed throughout residential school accounts.

The logic behind the limited time allotted to the formal curriculum was obvious to policy-makers. While it was important for children to be resocialized, it was even more critical that they acquire the practical skills permitting their entry into mainstream society, if only at its very lowest rungs. Assimilation was a desirable goal, but only as long as its achievement did not challenge the status quo. During the second half of each school day, boys learned how to do farm work or some low-status trade such as shoemaking. Girls performed household tasks ranging from potato-peeling to bread-making to dusting to needlework. The Department of Indian Affairs was ensuring the inability of Aboriginal peoples to compete socially or intellectually with their white neighbours, while also attempting to remove any traces of their culture that would ensure their survival within their own communities.

A religious upbringing was considered necessary to the Aboriginal child's transformation, as "all true civilization must be based on moral law. Christianity had to supplant the children's Aboriginal spirituality, which was nothing more than 'pagan'" (RCAP, 1996b, Vol. 1, p. 340). Aboriginal beliefs and rituals were forbidden, and children were instilled with a new faith. Prayer was deeply ingrained in the routines, curriculum, and values to which Aboriginal children were exposed: "We had prayers ten, twenty times a day and when we weren't praying we were changing clothes for prayer. We prayed when we got up, we prayed before breakfast and after breakfast, and we prayed when we got to the classroom and when we were in the classroom. I lost count of how many times a day we prayed" (Monk, 1994, p. 57).

Emphasis on vocational skills and on moral training contributed to the children's academic failure. The gap in illiteracy rates between mainstream Canadian and Aboriginal peoples remained overwhelming, indicating that many Aboriginal children were not being much educated at all. In 1921, by which time residential schools were widespread, about 2 percent of Canadian youth were illiterate, compared with 40 percent of Aboriginal youth. The illiteracy rate for Canadian youth declined to 1 percent over the next decade; the rate for Aboriginal youth also fell, but still stood in 1931 at about 25 percent. An overwhelming majority of Aboriginal children never got beyond Grade 1 or 2. Up to 1920, four out of every five Aboriginal boys and girls attending a federal school across Canada were enrolled in Grade 1, 2, or 3 (Canada, 1921). This did not necessarily mean that they had been in school for so short a time, but more likely that they were simply being kept in the lower grades year after year for the sake of convenience or because the level of instruction was so poor.

Indeed, Aboriginal students were long prohibited by law from going beyond the elementary grades. "There was a rule at that time that Indians could not go past Grade eight. I do not recall many boys staying around long enough to protest the education that was being denied us" (Manuel and Posluns, 1974, p. 66). "We had to stay in school until we were eighteen years of age to go as high as grade eight. And then no high school after" (Hall, 1992, p. 81). An Oblate historian of residential schools summed up the situation in his observation that "the half-day academic program in effect until the middle of this century ensured that the children did not receive an education on par with that given in the public schools" (Lascelles, 1990, p. 83).

By leaving the ongoing operation of the schools to missionary groups, the federal government relieved itself of direct responsibility for providing, paying, or supervising teaching staffs. Most teachers were missionaries principally motivated by a commitment to convert Aboriginal peoples. They were trained to provide religious guidance, not to instruct in the classroom. Edward Ahenakew, a Cree who became an Anglican priest in the early twentieth century, remarked: "The teachers have been too often the poorest type, and those who were good seldom stayed long, for they could always find more congenial work and higher pay elsewhere" (Ahenakew, 1973, pp. 127–28). One Indian agent noted that "the churches do not pay an adequate salary and trained teachers prefer to go to white schools, where social surroundings are always preferable to the isolated location among the Indians" (Canada, 1912, p. 399).

Where individuals' religious commitments conflicted with their role as teacher, the former usually triumphed. A local Indian agent observed in 1912 that "there is a disposition to devote too much time imparting religious instruction to the children as compared with the imparting of secular knowledge, which is perhaps not unnatural when the teachers are employed and selected by various churches" (Canada, 1912, p. 399). Although individual teachers at day schools, as at residential schools, were sometimes sympathetic to the students' plight and so remembered by them, they were generally untrained.

Federal Funding

The third and perhaps most fundamental reason why Aboriginal children received a poor education lay in the residential and day schools' low levels of federal financial support. Even taking into account the volunteers available as a consequence of schools' missionary ties and the labour that the children provided, institutions were severely underfunded compared with their provincial counterparts or even with the bare basics of survival. The per-student subsidy provided by the federal government assumed that much of the teaching would be volunteer, but it was still inadequate to provide a minimum standard of everyday life for students, much less material conditions conducive to learning. The men and women who ran the schools were expected to scramble for donations to ensure the schools' survival, and hence their own livelihoods.

From the beginning, the officials hoped to see residential schools become "self-supporting" by using the students to raise crops, make clothes, and generally do "outside work" (Canada, 1891, p. xiii). This meant that much of the supposed occupational training was, in effect, unpaid brute labour. A male student recalls:

> So I feed the horses, clean the barn, feed the cows and later even milk the cows. I get up at four o'clock in the morning sometimes and go look for them cows. ... I also helped look after the farm, help with the potatoes, and helped cut the hay. I tried to go to school but there was not enough time. I worked most of the time. I went to Alert Bay for school and instead they put me in a job! (Mack, 1993, pp. 22–23)

The need for manual labour cut across the sexes, and many "an Indian girl washed, cooked, cleaned, and mended her way through residential school" (Mitchell and Franklin, 1984, p. 24). "We had to patch. We had to patch the boys' clothes. We had to wash and iron Mondays and Tuesdays. We had to patch and keep on patching till Saturday" (Tappage, 1973, p. 18).

Hunger was a constant recollection of students — hunger not just for attention or affection, but for the basic physical need of food. It was poor or too little food that caused the most everyday distress. "Hunger is both the first and last thing I can remember about that school. I was hungry from the day I went into the school until they took me to the hospital two and a half years later. Not just me. Every Indian pupil smelled of hunger" (Manuel and Posluns, 1974, p. 65). Particularly difficult to understand was children being expected to eat the barest of fare day after day while subjected to the smells and even the sight of school staffs dining far more sumptuously:

> At school it was porridge, porridge, porridge, and if it wasn't that, it was boiled barley or beans, thick slices of bread spread with lard. Weeks went by without a taste of meat or fish. ... A few times I would catch the smell of roasting meat coming from the nuns' dining room, and I couldn't help

myself — I would follow that smell to the very door. Apart from the summers, I believe I was hungry for all seven of the years I was at school. ...
We were on rations more suited for a concentration camp! (John, 1988,
p. 39)

Schools were forced to struggle to make ends meet. Government grants allotted on a per-student basis were expected to cover all the costs of maintaining students, not just food. This included housekeeping expenses, physical upkeep of facilities, salaries for the minority of staff who received wages, and miscellaneous expenses ranging from books to clothing. Compounding the financial difficulties was the schools' religious commitment to service. They accepted more children — often Métis or other non-status children — than were allotted to them by the Department of Indian Affairs, so federal funds had to be stretched over a larger student body than intended. Aboriginal children suffered the consequences of poor nutrition, inadequate clothing for varied weather conditions, exposure to working and living conditions that were deteriorating and could pose a danger, and insufficient resources within the classroom. This was hardly an environment conducive to learning.

Though funding to the schools increased over the years, it always remained below the funding provided to provincial schools. As late as 1947, even as a joint parliamentary committee was finally being established to probe Aboriginal affairs, the federal government was spending $45 a year per Aboriginal student in federal day schools compared with about $200 per student in British Columbia public schools. The government failed in its obligation to provide for the education of Aboriginal children, and "financial problems were one of the major handicaps the schools laboured under for more than half a century" (Lascelles, 1990, p. 83).

LOOKING INWARD

Although residential schools have disappeared from the Canadian landscape in favour of a mix of provincial, private, and First Nations–operated schools, their legacy endures. It hangs heavy in the air, tainting the very concept of schooling. School for many Aboriginal people is much more an object of fear to be avoided than a place of learning. The consequences of residential schools are being lived out in the lives of Aboriginal peoples across Canada:

If I had to pick one area where the federal government, through the Department of Indian Affairs, inflicted the most harm on my people, it would have to be in the field of education. ... At the beginning of the white man's rule, Aboriginal people were confined to reserves, most of them far way from schools. When the government was finally forced to do something about the lack of educational facilities, the solution was a partnership between church and state to set up residential schools. Children were removed from their communities and placed in an alien environment that almost destroyed their culture and their language; we call it cultural genocide. (Monk, 1994, pp. 155–56)

The personal narratives of those who attended residential school and those who have family that attended the schools tell a similar story. Their recollections reveal a dehumanizing experience marked by isolation, hunger, hypocrisy, the demise of Indian culture, and forms of abuse.

Necessary to assimilation was the erosion of culture and language. If not banned outright, both were so disparaged in school that they were among its casualties. Phil Fontaine, Grand Chief of the Assembly of First Nations, remembers this about his residential school experience:

We never learned anything about ourselves, or the history of our people in this country. Everything had to do with the French or English, the discovery and the contact between the Europeans and the "savages." There was never anything that represented a positive reinforcement of who we were, even if we were of mixed ancestry, so we never developed a positive image of ourselves. We were taught to forget who we were and to accept everything about the outside world so we could emulate the non-Indian. (Jaine, 1993, pp. 49–50)

In some cases families themselves were complicit in the disappearance of language and culture in order to protect their children. "Because my parents also attended residential school they didn't see the value in teaching us our language. The Indian Agent told them not to speak to their children in Haida because it would not help them in school" (R. Bell, in Jaine, 1993, p. 10).

The self-fulfilling prophecy inherent in residential schooling came to fruition as Aboriginal men and women who had attended them did largely end up in the bottom ranks of Canadian society. Personal testimonies are revealing: "The residential school system (not just the one I went to — they were the common form of Indian education all across Canada) was the perfect system for instilling a strong sense of inferiority" (Manuel and Posluns, 1974, p. 67). The reasons are not difficult to fathom:

For many of us our most vulnerable and impressionable years, our childhood years, were spent at the residential school where we had always been treated like dirt and made to believe that we weren't as good as other people. … The constant message [was] that because you are Native you are part of a weak, defective race, unworthy of a distinguished place in society. That is the reason you have to be looked after. ... That to me is not raising for success, it is training for self-destruction. (B. Sellers, in Jaine, 1993, p. 131)

I was frustrated about how we were treated, humiliated, and degraded, so I drank and took drugs to numb the frustrations of how my life had turned out. (A. Collison, in Jaine, 1993, p. 39)

A lot of us left residential school as mixed-up human beings, not able to cope with family life. Many of us came out with a huge inferiority complex realizing something was missing, but not knowing what it was. Many searched for love and support in the wrong way. Girls became promiscuous, thinking this was the only way they could feel close to another person. Never having learned to cope with the outside world, many turned to drinking and became alcoholics. (L. Guss, in Jaine, 1993, p. 39)

The forced separation of children from their families and communities, combined with the harsh policies and practices of the residential school, have contributed to disrupting Aboriginal families. Children were socialized in an environment devoid of any of the nurturing that parents provide. Students of different sexes were almost always separated in residential school, and siblings in the same school often could not even speak to each other for months and years on end. As a result, many former students have reported they lack not only the confidence and ability to parent, but also interpersonal relationship skills (AFN, 1994; Bull, 1991; Haig-Brown; 1988; Ing, 1991). "Children learn parenting skills by the way they are parented. ... In the same way that their language use is based on the knowledge they gained before going to school, so their parenting skills must draw on that limited experience" (Haig-Brown, 1988, p. 123).

What cannot go untold in residential school accounts, both personal and scholarly, is the physical and sexual abuse that children endured that has contributed to the dysfunction of Aboriginal families and communities. The strappings, whippings, and beatings doled out as punishment for misbehaviour or at the whims of staff constituted abuse. As Aboriginal peoples try to heal themselves, they disclose the sexual abuse rampant at these schools. In British Columbia and Ontario, numerous criminal charges relating to abuse at these schools have been laid. A former supervisor at the Port Alberni school, operated by the United Church, received a prison sentence for sexually assaulting boys at the school between 1948 and 1968.

The family unit is the centre of Aboriginal society and serves as the primary medium for cultural continuity. Any disruption to the family inevitably results in disruption to the community. Many of the problems endemic to Aboriginal communities, such as family violence, alcoholism, suicide, and poverty, have their roots in assimilation and colonialism, in which residential schools played a major role. Aboriginal peoples now have to look inward to heal themselves.

For almost a century the federal government in Canada sought to control the lives and souls of Aboriginal peoples. Outwardly espousing assimilation through education, the federal government took neither the leadership nor the responsibility to achieve any other goal than preventing Aboriginal peoples from preparing for their own future in both Aboriginal and non-Aboriginal society. Religious denominations acted, from their perspective, from the highest motives, but lives were damaged and destroyed nonetheless. The system failed Aboriginal children and left a legacy reaching well beyond the students who attended the schools.

Residential schooling has had a devastating impact on individuals, families, and communities. A healing process is under way among Aboriginal peoples as they reclaim their dignity and unique place within Canadian society. Returning to traditions has assisted many in this process, and some turn to conventional methods such as therapy. Sadly, some people are simply not ready to address their pain. Others have directed their healing energies toward the government and churches, demanding acknowledgement and accountability for the atrocities they endured and justice and restitution for themselves, their communities, and their people. "Some of our people are calling for a national commission of inquiry. Others want financial compensation for their pain and suffering: they want to go to court. Still others just want to express their grief and pain and have it acknowledged. Some just want to know where their children and family members are buried. There is no one answer to the grief" (E. John, in Fournier and Crey, 1997, p. 73).

Under pressure from Aboriginal groups and the increased media attention, several religious denominations have issued formal apologies. Some denominations have provided funds for healing and wellness initiatives, while others have been reticent to provide financial compensation, forcing Aboriginal peoples to go through legal channels to obtain redress. Though many churches have accepted responsibility for the consequences of residential schooling, they maintain that this responsibility is shared with the government.

The federal government was particularly slow to respond with a formal apology to Aboriginal peoples, long evading the issue of responsibility deliberately to avoid any legal liability. It turned the problem back over to Aboriginal peoples themselves, offering to assist them with modest funds directed at family violence and child abuse initiatives (RCAP, 1996).

There was no direct commitment to initiatives that would assist Aboriginal people suffering from the consequences of residential schooling.

Finally, in response to the Royal Commission on Aboriginal Peoples (1996a), the federal government made a long-awaited apology to Aboriginal peoples:

> Against the backdrop of these historical legacies, it is a remarkable tribute to the strength and endurance of Aboriginal people that they have maintained their historic diversity and identity. The government of Canada today formally expresses to all Aboriginal people in Canada our profound regret for past actions of the federal government which have contributed to these difficult pages in the history of our relationship together. ... The Government of Canada acknowledges the role it played in the development and administration of these schools. Particularly to those individuals who experienced the tragedy of sexual and physical abuse at residential schools, and who have carried this burden believing that in some way they must be responsible, we wish to emphasize that what you experienced was not your fault and should never have happened. To those of you who suffered this tragedy at residential schools, we are deeply sorry. (*The Globe and Mail*, 8 January 1998, p. A19)

With the apology came a commitment of $350 million for healing and wellness strategies addressing the legacy of residential schooling abuse. It would be ludicrous to believe that a lump sum of dollars will eliminate all the issues arising from residential schooling. Each community will need its own contextual response, and no one solution will suffice.

Responsibility for the past does not rest solely with the government and church. Canadian society must also accept responsibility, yet many Canadians remain unaware of Aboriginal history. It is important for Canadians to recognize the tragic events that have shaped the lives of Aboriginal peoples and ensure that these events are never repeated. "Canada and Canadians must realize that they need to consider changing their society so that they can discover ways of living in harmony with the original people of the land" (RCAP, 1996b, Vol. 1, p. 382).

Considerable attention has been given to residential schools in the last decade because these schools represent an important era in Aboriginal history, and history provides an understanding of the issues that confront Aboriginal peoples today. The narratives of students who attended these schools are an essential part of the healing process. We should never close the door on this dark part. Some have not yet begun to heal, and many are unaware of these past events.

At the same time, Aboriginal peoples must move beyond this painful past if they are to confront the issues in Aboriginal education today. Remaining focussed on the legacy of residential schooling prevents Aboriginal peoples from addressing more immediate concerns. Understanding the impact of residential schooling is important to providing a context for current educational problems, but at the same time Aboriginal peoples need to direct their energies to dealing with other issues in education.

Some will argue that moving forward cannot be achieved without addressing the past. This is certainly true and necessary — there should always be forums in which Aboriginal peoples can express their experiences with residential schooling. "The future must include making a place for those who have been affected by the schools to stand in dignity, to remember, to voice their sorrow and anger, and to be listened to with respect" (RCAP, 1996b, Vol. 1, p. 382). The Royal Commission on Aboriginal Peoples proposed that a public inquiry be undertaken to "investigate and document the origins, purposes and effects of residential school policies and practices as they relate to all Aboriginal peoples, with particular attention to the manner and extent of their impact on individuals and families across several generations, on communities, and on Aboriginal society as a whole" (1996b, Vol. 1, p. 383). However, Aboriginal people cannot stop at this point. They must utilize the events of the past to develop unique plans for their own communities that will inform present and future educational practice.

LOOKING FORWARD

It was the concerted effort of Aboriginal peoples that eventually brought an end to residential schooling. The policy of assimilation through segregation changed to assimilation through integration in response to pressure from Aboriginal parents. Beginning in the 1950s, residential schools were slowly phased out, and Aboriginal children began to attend schools within the provincial system alongside their non-Aboriginal counterparts. Coinciding with the policy of integrated schooling was a political attempt by the federal government to dissolve the unique status of Aboriginal peoples, which was represented in the 1969 policy statement known as the White Paper. Under the guise of equality, the government proposed to repeal the Indian Act, phase out the Department of Indian Affairs, and provide Aboriginal peoples with the same services as all other Canadians via the same agencies (Brookes, 1991). Provincial governments were to assume the responsibility for education.

A turning point in Aboriginal education came with the Aboriginal response to the White Paper. Aboriginal groups saw it as simply another means of achieving assimilation. Concerned with preserving their Aboriginal identity and maintaining their unique status and relationship with the federal government, the document *Citizens Plus* (1970) addressed these goals. Within the Red Paper, as it was known, education would remain a federal obligation. Aboriginal groups rejected the notion of integrated education, as it failed to address the needs and aspirations of Aboriginal peoples.

These events served as a catalyst for the foremost goal in Aboriginal education. In 1972 the National Indian Brotherhood presented the educational policy *Indian Control of Indian Education*. The policy's primary concerns were parental involvement in children's education and Aboriginal control of education in both First Nations and provincial schools. Dissatisfied with the current state of education for Aboriginal children, the National Indian Brotherhood highlighted parental responsibility, curriculum, teachers, facilities, and services as areas in dire need of attention and improvement. Overall, the aim of the policy was "to prepare Indian children for total living with the freedom of choice of where to live and work, and to enable Indians to participate fully in their own social, economic, political and education advancement ... achieved without resorting to assimilation" (Brookes, 1991, p. 175). Indian control of Indian education remains at the centre of the education of Aboriginal children. Only Aboriginal peoples can determine their educational needs and be responsible for ensuring that those needs are met with quality education.

Despite the educational goals being articulated by Aboriginal peoples, they continue to face policies and practices that do little to address these goals. The government response to *Indian Control of Indian Education* was to transfer jurisdictional control of education to Aboriginal communities, a move that proved ineffective in enabling Aboriginal communities to govern their own education. Following the implementation of this policy, the Assembly of First Nations undertook a national review of Aboriginal education that focussed on jurisdiction, quality, management, and resourcing. The study, *Tradition and Education, Towards a Vision of Our Future* (1988), revealed that "many of the shortcomings identified in 1972 were still in existence. It pointed out that education programs to which Indians are exposed are predominantly assimilationist in the curriculum, learning materials, pedagogy, learning objectives and the training of teachers and educational administrators" (Kirkness and Bowman, 1992, p. 20). The Royal Commission on Aboriginal Peoples confirms that current education polices fail to realize the goals of Aboriginal education:

> The majority of Aboriginal youth do not complete high school. They leave the school system without requisite skills for employment, and

without the language and cultural knowledge of their people. Rather than nurturing the individual, the schooling experience typically erodes identity and self-worth. Those who continue in Canada's formal school systems told [the commission] of regular encounters with racism, racism expressed not only in interpersonal exchanges but also through the denial of Aboriginal values, perspectives and cultures in the curriculum and the life of the institution. (RCAP, 1996b, Vol. 3, p. 434)

Aboriginal children persevere in educational systems that are paternalistic and racist and do little to address their needs.

Some change is occurring. With the devolution of control to Aboriginal communities, the number of community-controlled schools has increased. Though restricted in their control, communities have been able to address curriculum, language, and resourcing issues. There are also some successes in the urban setting. A study of exemplary schools across Canada observed Joe Duquette High School, an alternative school for Aboriginal youth in Saskatchewan, that provides highly contextualized responses to clearly articulated local needs (Haig-Brown et al., 1997). Carefully directed and monitored by the Aboriginal Parent Council, the school itself is a special program with a central focus on Aboriginal culture, particularly the spiritual dimensions. There is an ongoing balance between a healing focus and academic achievement for the students. "The school is one of exciting possibility which works, in some ways, against all odds — odds which are primarily the result of continuing racist oppression and punishment of the poor" (Haig-Brown et al., 1997, p. 180).

Aboriginal peoples are making gains slowly. Children are staying in school longer and attending postsecondary institutions in greater numbers. The proportion of students living on-reserve who remained in school to Grade 12 has risen from 3 percent in 1960–61 and 15 percent in 1970–71 to 20 percent in 1980–81 and 47 percent in 1990–91 (Canada, 1995, p. 39). About half of the on-reserve elementary students in 1991 reported being taught in part in an Aboriginal language, as did a quarter of all on-reserve secondary students (Statistics Canada, 1993, pp. 66, 70). The number of Aboriginal students undertaking university programs increased 8.6 percent between 1981 and 1991, and Aboriginal teacher education programs have made gains (RCAP, 1996b, Vol. 3, p. 549).

Despite efforts by Aboriginal peoples to implement change through policy, disquiet persists in Aboriginal education. The statistical gains are deceptive: far too many Aboriginal students lag behind non-Aboriginal students, and the conditions under which Aboriginal children were schooled inequitably in the past still exist for the children being educated today. The problems and issues have only become more complex as Aboriginal peoples implement their own vision of education in a contemporary world. The factors that ensured that residential schools would not educate Aboriginal children to participate politically and socially in Aboriginal or non-Aboriginal society — the government's assumption of Aboriginal peoples' sameness across Canada, the curriculum and teachers, and the level of federal funding — continue to hinder today's Aboriginal children.

Assumption of Sameness

The educational needs of Aboriginal peoples are diverse. While some communities are seeking to control their children's education, others send their children to provincial or territorial schools. With the growth of off-reserve populations, provincial schools must respond to the needs of both urban and rural Aboriginal children, which vary. Communities, whose educational budgets are limited, often cannot fund all students wishing to attend college or university. The problem is compounded by priority lists that may prohibit those who previously attended postsecondary institutions from upgrading their skills or obtaining higher degrees. Educational circumstances vary from community to community, as a complex set of social, economic, and political variables affect each community. The issues, then, cannot be addressed with one panacea.

Just as communities are unique with their own set of circumstances, so are the dilemmas and so must be the solutions. Yet governments expect Aboriginal peoples to be in agreement on their educational needs:

> The fact that there are a number of First Nations who have different perspectives on education is not recognized by [provincial and federal] governments. The fact that no clear "Indian" position has been put forward is taken as an indication of confusion and dissent in the Indian community. This gives the government the opportunity to delay substantial negotiations on the basis that there is no one with whom to negotiate. (Pauls, 1996, p. 252)

Governments fail to acknowledge the uniqueness of each Aboriginal community and criticize Aboriginal peoples for not presenting a unified voice in their dealings with government.

Though Aboriginal communities have aligned themselves with Aboriginal organizations to initiate action, the concerns within each community remain distinctive. The economic, social, and political status of each community affects education and must be viewed against these conditions. Treating Aboriginal peoples as a single category to be dealt with as expeditiously and economically as possible has proved disastrous in the past and will continue to do so.

Curriculum and Teachers

Cultural assimilation is no longer a formal part of education policy, yet education systems still fail to accommodate the cultural needs of Aboriginal peoples. By failing to represent the Aboriginal perspective within the curriculum, Canadian public schools continue to expose Aboriginal children to a process of cultural assimilation. "The failure to [recognize Aboriginal culture] sets in motion a culturally insensitive and therefore culturally assimilative system of education that produces feelings of extreme alienation, low self-esteem and an inability to relate to formal education as meaningful or useful" (Canada, 1990, p. 14).

A consistent recommendation in reviews of Aboriginal education (NIB, 1972; AFN, 1988; RCAP, 1996a) has been to develop culturally relevant curricula, but innovations in curriculum development have been slow and inconsistent (RCAP, Vol. 3, 1996b; Satzewich and Wotherspoon, 1993). Provincial school board attempts to include Aboriginal content within the curriculum are, at best, limited or superficial. Too often schools regard an Aboriginal studies unit that lasts a week or two as sufficient for addressing Aboriginal needs or concerns.

In reality, schools need to consider increasing Aboriginal content within existing curriculum, developing more subject areas that encompass an Aboriginal perspective, and making use of the growing Aboriginal resources. The science and math curriculum developed and implemented by Akwesasne, a Mohawk community bordering Ontario, Quebec, and New York state, has been heralded as a model of innovation in Aboriginal education in Canada (RCAP, 1996a). An examination reveals that the whole community was involved in creating a curriculum that is holistic in nature, balances Euro-Canadian and Aboriginal perspectives, is relevant to students' experiences, recognizes elders and spiritual leaders, and operates firmly under Mohawk leadership. These features provide students with a better chance of operating in both Aboriginal and non-Aboriginal society.

For Aboriginal community-controlled schools, locally developed curriculum can be particularly useful, as provincial curriculum may be incompatible with the needs of the community. This means traditional knowledge and skills can become an important facet of the curriculum. "The influence of First Nations peoples on educational curricula over the last two decades has contributed to the quality and quantity of locally developed Native studies curricula ... students now have an opportunity to learn about First Nations cultures, past and present, in a relevant, meaningful way" (Archibald, 1995, pp. 296–97).

School boards can no longer pay lip-service to the educational needs of Aboriginal peoples. They must commit themselves to programming that does more than just give sporadic and isolated attention to Aboriginal issues. A multitude of Aboriginal resources are being developed by Aboriginal peoples for use in the schools. It is the responsibility of educators to be continually infusing Aboriginal history, culture, and language into the curriculum so it permeates into the lives of Aboriginal children. Armed with a strong sense of identity and a quality education in mind, body, and spirit, Aboriginal children will succeed in both Aboriginal and non-Aboriginal society.

Curriculum changes alone, however, will not address the disparity in educational achievement between Aboriginal and non-Aboriginal children. How children learn is as important as what they learn. Cultural discontinuity between home and school environments is varied and complex: educators fail to accommodate different teaching and learning styles, and school boards refuse to legitimize alternative ways of learning and knowing; conflict at home or at school becomes inevitable for Aboriginal children when schools fail to validate traditional forms of knowledge. For example, value is placed on listening and observing in Aboriginal society. Talking for the sake of talking is discouraged, and the power of words is understood. Therefore, Aboriginal children may speak slowly, quietly, and deliberately. Their quietness reflects the emphasis on listening, and much of what they learn is achieved by watching others. Yet, school methods of instruction emphasize speaking over listening, posing questions as a means of inquiry. Verbal skills are highly utilized, neglecting the power of observation. Educators employ instructional methods that are incompatible with Aboriginal ways of learning and knowing, hence contributing to the academic failure of Aboriginal children.

Public school boards that are reluctant to embrace initiatives that would contribute to the success of Aboriginal students must reconsider their policies and practices if Aboriginal children are to be on par with non-Aboriginal children. For example, school boards and districts fail to recognize the important role elders play in the education of Aboriginal children. Elders are held in high esteem for their wisdom and experience, which preserve and maintain cultural traditions, knowledge, and language. They are also teachers who pass on to Aboriginal children the necessary skills and knowledge to ensure cultural continuity. Yet their role is devalued in present education systems, where they are used to give the impression that schools are accommodating the needs of Aboriginal peoples. Students have difficulty attaining accreditation for traditionally based education that is provided by elders, as they are not perceived as "real" teachers, despite their vital role in Aboriginal communities. School boards must find ways to legitimize the incredible resource that elders represent.

With nearly 70 percent of Aboriginal children attending provincial schools, it is more than probable that at one time almost every Aboriginal child will be taught by a non-Aboriginal teacher. It is the lack of cross-cultural awareness that results in serious inadequacies for Aboriginal children. Behaviours and values inherent in Aboriginal culture but misunderstood by non-Aboriginal teachers lead to problems for the Aboriginal child. Evidence of this can be seen with children who do not engage in direct eye contact, but cast their eyes downward as a sign of respect. Frequently and erroneously, non-Aboriginal teachers presume the children are being disrespectful or become suspicious of their behaviour. Continual lateness for class is mistakenly interpreted as irresponsibility, whereas time is relative and subject to flexibility in Aboriginal societies. Teachers make assumptions based on a child's behaviour or adhere to stereotypes that affect their relations with Aboriginal children and parents. Further compounding the problems is teachers' lack of knowledge concerning Aboriginal issues. Conveying inaccurate information about Aboriginal issues does as much harm to Aboriginal children as does simply not addressing Aboriginal concerns at all.

Teacher education programs must equip educators with the skills and knowledge to respectfully address Aboriginal subject matter and instil a sensitivity to the language, culture, and traditions of Aboriginal peoples. Faculties of education are beginning to take steps to include First Nations, gender, and multicultural issues as part of the course content. "First Nations content should be a larger portion of all education students' curriculum. With the changing demographics increasing the numbers of First Nations children coming into schools, all education students need to be better prepared to meet their needs. ... It would be beneficial for [faculty] to research and include First Nations approaches and perspectives in their reading and lectures" (NITEP, 1997, p. 3). Teachers are an important part of children's learning experiences, and much of Aboriginal children's success will depend on them.

Aboriginal peoples are cognizant of the impact educators have on the success of their children. Aboriginal communities and school boards actively recruit and hire Aboriginal teachers. However, Aboriginal teachers are underrepresented in relation to the numbers of Aboriginal children in school. In British Columbia, the low number of Aboriginal teachers available suggests that they have not achieved the critical mass in the schools to affect First Nations education significantly (NITEP, 1997). Some teacher education programs have responded with specific programs for Aboriginal teachers, but appear unable to meet the demands of Aboriginal communities and public schools. If Aboriginal children are to operate within two worlds, curriculum and instructional changes have to be made.

Federal Funding

As was the case historically, issues related to funding Aboriginal education pose the greatest challenge for Aboriginal peoples wanting to ensure that their children obtain a quality education. The funding of Aboriginal education is the responsibility of the federal government as a result of treaties. However, the government refuses to acknowledge education as a treaty right and continues a relationship with Aboriginal peoples based on paternalism. Though the government allows Aboriginal communities to determine their own educational needs, it maintains control over the distribution of funds. That is, communities may decide their own educational budgets and where they would like funds to be allocated, but the federal government oversees the educational expenses and which initiatives will receive funding.

The goal of Aboriginal peoples to determine their own educational needs has been achieved at great expense to many communities. Long subject to outside control over their affairs, Aboriginal peoples had limited, if any, opportunities to develop expertise in managing economic funds on a large scale. In the past, the government always determined policies for budgets and allocated funding. The government's decision to give Aboriginal communities the authority to determine their own expenditures was done without giving them any training in economic management. The lack of foresight by governments and communities has resulted in the mismanagement of funds, which in turn has led to cutbacks in educational programming for some communities, with implications for the quality of education for Aboriginal children in elementary, secondary, and postsecondary schools.

The numerous changes in community circumstances have placed a greater demand on already limited funding for education. Aboriginal peoples who have reclaimed their status through Bill C-31 have increased the number of students seeking educational assistance. The Department of Indian and Northern Affairs at first recognized the strain these claimants would have on community resources and increased education funding to ensure these students would receive support for their education. But in the style that typically characterizes government funding for community initiatives, this commitment was only short-term. After a few years communities were expected to operate with the same amount of funding as they did before Bill C-31, despite even greater numbers of students. The growing number of students who want postsecondary education or vocational training has created tighter restrictions and cutbacks in the length and amount of funding.

Creative educational initiatives have begun to make their mark in meeting the diverse needs of Aboriginal communities. Kenjgenwin-Teg, located on Manitoulin Island in Ontario, serves as an educational training institution offering community-based programming to surrounding Aboriginal communities. It has developed effective partnerships with community schools and postsecondary institutions in providing Aboriginal students with education that is relevant to their needs. Institutions such as this one must also compete for education funding alongside the elementary and secondary schools and other educational initiatives in a community. Communities are thus forced to focus on financial issues, undermining the quality of education to which Aboriginal children are entitled.

Government control over funding prevents Aboriginal communities from making real gains in education. The extent of government control is evidenced in how the government determines which issues related to Aboriginal affairs will receive funding. If the government determines health initiatives will receive capital support, educational proposals must sit dormant as communities place emphasis on health concerns and develop new projects to tap that particular funding source. The government's commitment of funds to healing and wellness strategies related to the legacy of residential school abuse will address essential aspects of community healing, but will not bring immediate attention to the present-day educational dilemmas. Classrooms in need of language assistants or secondary-school students wishing to attend a traditional skills hunting camp will not have access to funds designated to healing and wellness.

The already limited funding prevents Aboriginal communities from operating the level of programming comparable to provincial and private schools, which have separate funds for school operations and administrative infrastructure. The superintendents, office personnel, curriculum and instruction planning branches, career counselling, staff development officers, and other numerous divisions of a school board contribute to the quality of education. This range of roles and tasks must be assumed by Aboriginal communities administering education for their own children. "All is to be accomplished with a limited budget. It is well recognized by

First Nation educators that staff at band-controlled schools must regularly fill no less than three of four roles, while being paid for only one" (Morris and Price, 1991, p. 184).

External control and the serious lack of commitment to long-term funding arrangements by the government has severe consequences for Aboriginal education and contributes to the disparity between Aboriginal and non-Aboriginal children. Aboriginal communities must be able to control funding mechanisms. Education is the responsibility of the federal government, which delegates the Department of Indian and Northern Affairs to oversee Aboriginal concerns. However, numerous government agencies could contribute resources to Aboriginal communities, giving surplus and flexibility to educational budgets. Substantial changes to funding relationships must occur if the specific needs of communities are to be met.

THE WAY AHEAD

Under the control of the federal government Aboriginal peoples long endured an education that was paternalistic, racist, and destructive. But looking to the past to provide solutions only serves to focus on Aboriginal peoples' victimization. Aboriginal peoples must look inward and forward. The experiences of those who attended these schools and others affected indirectly must always be given respect and recognition. It is in this historical context that the complex and conflicting traditions affecting Aboriginal peoples are rooted. Aboriginal peoples must move beyond the residential school era as a way to explain their current educational dilemmas. They must make self-determination their goal as they plan a future for their children that is consistent with their own vision of education.

Despite numerous obstacles, Aboriginal education has made great strides. Increased educational options for Aboriginal children mean children living on-reserve often attend a school that is operated by their own community. Other on-reserve families choose to send their children to provincial or private schools. Most Aboriginal children living in urban settings now attend school alongside non-Aboriginal children as a matter of course. Children in some urban areas also have alternative Aboriginal-oriented facilities available to them. These shifts have contributed to the success Aboriginal children are experiencing at the elementary, secondary, and postsecondary levels.

Yet, as the Royal Commission on Aboriginal Peoples points out: "All these changes are not enough to close the gap between the education obtained by Aboriginal students and that of other Canadians. As the skills requirements of a post-industrial, globalized economy rise, the marginalization, poverty and relative disadvantage of Aboriginal peoples are in danger of increasing unless success can be radically improved" (RCAP, 1996b, Vol. 3, p. 561). The state of Aboriginal education remains bleak, and it must not in any case be viewed as a panacea for addressing Aboriginal concerns. Education is a vital tool that contributes to self-worth and self-determination, but it should also be seen as a means by which Aboriginal peoples can critically examine the broader issues that affect their lives.

DISCUSSION QUESTIONS

1. In what ways did residential schools discourage Aboriginal people from competing socially, economically, and intellectually in the mainstream society?
2. Why have the conditions under which Aboriginal children have been schooled for inequality been allowed to persist?
3. How does the legacy of residential schools affect Aboriginal people who did not themselves attend the schools?
4. How can Aboriginal people achieve self-determination in education given the present constraints?
5. What might Aboriginal peoples' vision of education in the contemporary world look like?

FURTHER READINGS

Assembly of First Nations (AFN). 1994. *Breaking the Silence: An Interpretive Study of Residential School Impact and Healing as Illustrated by the Stories of First Nations Individuals.* Ottawa: AFN. Based on thirteen interviews with former students, this Assembly of First Nations study goes far beyond its small database in its sensitivity to the residential school experience and thoughtful recommendations for "breaking the silence."

Battiste, M. and J. Barman. 1995. *First Nations Education in Canada: The Circle Unfolds.* Vancouver: University of British Columbia Press. Essays by Aboriginal and non-Aboriginal scholars conceptualize Aboriginal education using a sacred medicine wheel model, assess priorities, and offer perspectives on a variety of education issues.

Fournier, S. and E. Crey. 1997. *Stolen from Our Embrace: The Abduction of First Nations Children and the Restoration of Aboriginal Communities.* Vancouver: Douglas & McIntyre. Narratives of Aboriginal people who were subject to the assimilationist practices of residential schools and seizure by social workers are presented, and the growing number of First Nation communities returning to traditional healing methods and initiatives in education and social services are described.

Jaine, L., ed. 1993. *Residential Schools: The Stolen Years.* Saskatoon: Extension Division Press, University of Saskatchewan. This book is a compilation of narratives, poems, and stories that reflect the diversity of voices and responses of those who attended residential schools.

Miller, J.R. 1996. *Shingwauk's Vision: A History of Native Residential Schools.* Toronto: University of Toronto Press. A comprehensive look at the history of residential schools in Canada, this analysis spans three and a half centuries and moves through the various phases that characterize the history of residential schools, beginning with their origin in the early seventeenth century through to the final phase in the 1960s. The interests and perspectives of the government, the church, and Aboriginal people are delineated in each phase.

Sterling, S. 1992. *My Name Is Seepeetza.* Vancouver: Douglas & McIntyre. Shortlisted for the Governor General's award, this charming young people's novel is a fictionalized evocation of the author's years at the Kamloops Residential School.

REFERENCES

Ahenakew, E., ed. R.M. Buck. 1973. *Voices of the Plains Cree.* Toronto: McClelland & Stewart.

Archibald, J. 1995. "Locally Developed Native Studies Curriculum: An Historical and Philosophical Rationale." Pp. 288–312 in *First Nations Education in Canada: The Circle Unfolds,* ed. M. Battiste and J. Barman. Vancouver: University of British Columbia Press.

Assembly of First Nations (AFN). 1988. *Tradition and Education: Towards a Vision of Our Future.* Ottawa: AFN.

———. 1994. *Breaking the Silence: An Interpretive Study of Residential School Impact and Healing as Illustrated by the Stories of First Nations Individuals.* Ottawa: AFN.

Baker, S., ed. V.J. Kirkness. 1994. *Khot-La-Cha: The Autobiography of Chief Simon Baker.* Vancouver: Douglas & McIntyre.

Barman, J. 1995. "Schooled for Inequality: The Education of British Columbia Aboriginal Children." Pp. 57–80 in *Children, Family and Schools in the History of British Columbia*, eds. J. Barman, N. Sutherland, and J.D. Wilson. Calgary: Detselig.

Barman, J., Y. Hébert, and D. McCaskill. eds. 1986. *Indian Education in Canada*, Vol. 1. Vancouver: University of British Columbia Press.

Brookes, S. 1991. "The Persistence of Native Education Policy in Canada." Pp. 163–80 in *The Cultural Maze: Complex Questions on Native Destiny in Western Canada*, ed. J. Friesen. Calgary: Detselig.

Bull, L.R. 1991. "Indian Residential Schooling: The Native Perspective." *Canadian Journal of Native Education* 18 (supplement): pp. 1–64.

Canada, Department of Indian Affairs (DIA). 1891. *Annual Report*. Ottawa: DIA.

———. 1895. *Annual Report*. Ottawa: DIA.

———. 1897. *Annual Report*. Ottawa: DIA.

———. 1912. *Annual Report*. Ottawa: DIA.

Canada, Department of Indian Affairs and Northern Development (DIAND). 1969. *Statement on Indian Policy 1969* (The White Paper). Ottawa: Supply and Services.

———. 1995. *Basic Departmental Data, 1994*. Ottawa: DIAND.

Canada, Dominion Bureau of Statistics. 1921. *Annual Survey of Education*. Ottawa: Dominion Bureau of Statistics.

Canada, House of Commons, Standing Committee on Aboriginal Affairs. 1990. *You Took My Talk: Aboriginal Literacy and Empowerment*. Fourth report of the Standing Committee on Aboriginal Affairs. Ottawa: Queen's Printer.

Chrisjohn, R.D., S.L. Young, and M. Maraun. 1997. *The Circle Game: Shadows and Substance in the Indian Residential School Experience in Canada*. Penticton, B.C.: Theytus.

Evans, A., ed. J.E. Speare. 1992. *The Days of Augusta*. Vancouver: Douglas & McIntyre.

Fournier, S. and E. Crey. 1997. *Stolen from Our Embrace: The Abduction of First Nations Children and the Restoration of Aboriginal Communities*. Vancouver: Douglas & McIntyre.

Frideres, J.S. 1988. *Native Peoples in Canada: Contemporary Conflicts*. Scarborough, Ont.: Prentice-Hall Canada.

Furniss, E. 1992. *Victims of Benevolence: Discipline and Death at the Williams Lake Indian Residential School, 1891–1920*. Williams Lake: Cariboo Tribal Council.

Gresko, J. 1986. "Creating Little Dominions within the Dominion: Early Catholic Indian Schools in Saskatchewan and British Columbia." Pp. 88–109 in *Indian Education in Canada*, Vol. 1, eds. J. Barnam, Y. Hébert, and D. McCaskill. Vancouver: University of British Columbia Press.

Haig-Brown, C. 1988. *Resistance and Renewal: Surviving the Indian Residential School*. Vancouver: Tillicum.

Haig-Brown, C., K.L. Hodgson-Smith, R. Regnier, and J. Archibald. 1997. *Making the Spirit Dance Within: Joe Duquette High School and Aboriginal Community*. Toronto: Our Schools/Our Selves Foundation.

Hall, L. 1992. *The Carrier, My People.* Quesnel, B.C.: L. Hall.

Indian Association of Alberta. 1970. *Citizens Plus.* Edmonton: Indian Association of Alberta.

Ing, R. 1991. "The Effects of Residential Schools on Native Child-Rearing Practices." *Canadian Journal of Native Education* 18 (supplement): 65–118.

Jaine, L., ed. 1993. *Residential Schools: The Stolen Years.* Saskatoon: Extension University Press, University of Saskatchewan.

Kirkness, V. and S.S. Bowman. 1992. *First Nations and Schools: Triumphs and Struggles.* Toronto: Canadian Educational Association.

Knockwood, I. (with G. Thomas). 1992. *Out of the Depths: The Experience of Mi'kmaw Children at the Indian Residential School at Shubenacadie, Nova Scotia.* Lockeport, N.S.: Roseway.

Lascelles, T.A. 1990. *Roman Catholic Indian Residential Schools in British Columbia.* Vancouver: Order of OMI in B.C.

Mack, C. and H. Thommasen, eds. 1993. *Grizzlies & White Guys: The Stories of Clayton Mack.* Madeira Park, B.C.: Harbour Publishing.

Manuel, G. and M. Posluns. 1974. *The Fourth World: An Indian Reality.* Toronto: Collier Macmillan.

Miller, J.R. 1996. *Shingwauk's Vision: A History of Native Residential Schools.* Toronto: University of Toronto Press.

Mitchell, M. and A. Franklin. 1984. "When You Don't Know the Language, Listen to the Silence: An Historical Overview of Native Indian Women in B.C." Pp. 17–35 in *Not Just Pin Money: Selected Essays on the History of Women's Work in British Columbia,* eds. B.K. Latham and R.J. Pazdro. Victoria, B.C.: Camosun College.

Moran, Bridget. 1988. *Stoney Creek Woman: The Story of Mary John.* Vancouver: Tillacum Library.

———. 1994. *Justa: A First Nations Leader.* Vancouver: Arsenal Pulp Press.

Morris, J.S. and R.T. Price. 1991. "Community Educational Control Issues and the Experience of Alexander's Kipohtakaw Education Centre." Pp. 181–98 in *The Cultural Maze: Complex Questions on Native Destiny in Western Canada,* ed. J. Friesen. Calgary: Detselig.

National Indian Brotherhood (NIB). 1972. *Indian Control of Indian Education.* Ottawa: NIB.

Native Indian Teacher Education Program (NITEP). 1997. *Review Committee Report.* Vancouver: University of British Columbia Faculty of Education.

Pauls, S. 1996. "An Examination of the Relationship between First Nations Schools and Departments of Education in Alberta, Saskatchewan, and Manitoba." Unpublished PhD dissertation, University of Alberta, Edmonton.

Royal Commission on Aboriginal Peoples (RCAP). 1996a. *People to People, Nation to Nation: Highlights from the Report of the Royal Commission on Aboriginal Peoples.* Ottawa: RCAP.

———. 1996b. *Report of the Royal Commission on Aboriginal Peoples,* 5 Vols. Ottawa: RCAP.

Satzewich, V. and T. Wotherspoon. 1993. *First Nations: Race, Class, and Gender Relations*. Scarborough, Ont.: Nelson.

Statistics Canada. 1993. *Aboriginal Peoples Survey*. Ottawa: Supply and Services.

Sterling, S. 1992. *My Name Is Seepeetza*. Vancouver: Douglas & McIntyre.

Tennant, P. 1990. *Aboriginal Peoples and Politics: The Indian Land Question in British Columbia, 1849–1989*. Vancouver: University of British Columbia Press.

Titley, E.B. 1986. "Indian Industrial Schools in Western Canada." Pp. 133–53 in *Schools in the West: Essays in Canadian Educational History*, eds. N.M. Sheehan, J.D. Wilson, and D.C. Jones. Calgary: Detselig.

CHAPTER 12

Lessons in Decolonization: Aboriginal Overrepresentation in Canadian Criminal Justice

Patricia A. Monture-Angus[1]

And it was rare for Crees to commit any crimes against one another at that time, even though there were so many people of different tribes, they did not very often commit violent crimes against one another, they lived together peacefully.

—Peter Vandall, Cree Elder, Atahk-akop's Reserve, Sandy Lake, Saskatchewan (quoted in Ahenakew and Wolfant, 1987, p. 47)

INTRODUCTION

The loss of and interference with peaceful existence in many Aboriginal communities has been the subject of many reports, inquiries, academic studies, and research. Much of this work has been funded by government dollars. Unfortunately, the analysis of the "problem" in Aboriginal communities has generally had a distinct and overly narrow focus. The majority of our understanding has been developed without a serious regard for the pattern of colonialism that is clear and pronounced in Aboriginal communities and Aboriginal experiences, including the experience of the criminal justice system. This has serious consequences for Aboriginal peoples.[2]

In some jurisdictions, Aboriginal people account for over half the admissions to correctional institutions. The overrepresentation of Aboriginal people in the system of Canadian criminal justice is all too often seen as an Aboriginal problem — that is, a problem *with* Aboriginal people. In 1983, Don McCaskill observed:

The conventional explanation for this phenomenon views native offenders as members of a pathological community characterized by extensive social and personal problems. The focus is inevitably on the individual offenders. They are seen as simply being unable to adjust successfully to the rigors of contemporary society. They are part of a larger "Indian problem" for which various social service agencies have been created to help Indians meet the standards of the dominant society. The long-range goal is that, in time, with sufficient help, Indians will lose most of their culture, adopt the values of the larger society, become upwardly mobile, and be incorporated into mainstream society. In short, Indians will assimilate. (McCaskill, 1983, p. 289)

Professor McCaskill made this observation nearly two decades ago. Unfortunately, since then, these theoretical presumptions have changed very little, and the belief that Aboriginal people should change to fit the system is still implicit. It is important to question why a system that has so markedly failed Aboriginal peoples (and people) has been allowed to continue to operate in an unjust and colonial manner for so many years and through so many reports and inquiries. In fact, McCaskill's point was made before the majority of justice reports were commissioned.

This failure to take responsibility for the continued perpetuation of colonial relations in current criminal justice practices and policies has not escaped the gaze or understanding of Aboriginal people and our governments. It is a situation that magnifies the contempt that Aboriginal peoples have for a system that is neither fair and just nor responsible. My purpose in agreeing to add my voice to the others in this collection is simple. I choose to name and expose the colonialism present in both Canada's criminal justice system and in the literature about the overrepresentation of Aboriginal people in that system. By naming and exposing, I hope to narrow the gap that exists between the understanding of justice relations in Aboriginal communities and the research communities, including the university.[3]

At the outset, several myths must be exposed for what they are. It is curious to me that non-Aboriginal people always think that Aboriginal peoples have lost their culture. Having your culture interfered with (and even made illegal),[4] does not mean that your culture fails to exist. The response of non-Aboriginal people to Aboriginal people who are skilled at being bicultural (because our survival generally depends on this skill) is misinterpreted. Because I have learned to relate to you on terms that you have defined cannot lend itself to a reasonable construction of Aboriginal culturelessness. Because I can understand non-Aboriginal ways does not necessarily mean I can no longer understand or, worse yet, that I reject Aboriginal ways of doing, thinking, and being. All that can be concluded is that non-Aboriginal people have not been as successful (as a group) at understanding Aboriginal culture as some Aboriginal people have been successful at understanding Canadian culture and ways. This does not mean that Aboriginal people have chosen to assimilate. For the most part, we have not.

The second myth is a component of the larger myth that "Indians were savages." As the opening quote indicates, there were few problems of crime and disorder among Aboriginal populations at the time of contact and for some years after. This reality is well-documented but infrequently given the respect or position in the discourse that it deserves.[5] Any curious mind considering this fact can easily conclude that Aboriginal people had systems to maintain order in our communities. This is true despite the fact that we did not have prisons, punishment, and all the trappings that Canadians recognize as the characteristics of an organized and institutionalized justice system. The crux of the problem is Canada's failure (that is, non-Aboriginal people including policy-makers, researchers, prison administrators, politicians, lawyers, and so on) to own and address the fact that Aboriginal overrepresentation in the justice system is not necessarily the individual failure of particular Aboriginal people but also the impact and vestige of colonialism.

Colonialism is not a difficult concept to understand. It is easily conceptualized:

> Colonialism involves a relationship which leaves one side dependent on the other to define the world. At the individual level, colonialism involves a situation where one individual is forced to relate to another on terms unilaterally defined by the other. The justice system becomes a central institution with which to impose the way of life of the dominant society. (McCaskill, 1983, p. 289)

Recognizing colonialism as a central explanation — if not *the* central explanation — for Aboriginal overrepresentation in the justice system is essential. At the same time, we must recognize that the process of colonization requires colonizers, not just the colonized (Freire, 1996, p. 26). The process of decolonization is not just an Aboriginal responsibility but must also involve the colonizer learning new ways of relating to enclaved peoples. It is very difficult to honour my commitment to live in a decolonized way when I survive in an environment where others (Aboriginal and not) continue to remain committed to the entrenchment of the colonizers' ways. So far my efforts to decolonize my own life and mind have proven to be part of a long and difficult process.

THE MANY JUSTICE REPORTS

The situation of Aboriginal people and Canada's criminal justice systems has been studied by commissions, inquiries, and task forces since 1967. In 1990, the Alberta Cawsey Commission noted:

The real proliferation in reports began in the mid-1980s. ... Seventeen of the twenty-two reports were released between 1984 and 1990 (and note that this does not include the anticipated Blood and Manitoba Inquiry Reports). In 1988 and 1989, alone, 11 reports were published. This suggests that, in the last five to six years, something has occurred to make all levels of Government acutely aware and concerned with Native involvement in the Criminal Justice System. Considering the repetition of recommendations it could be speculated that this "something" is an awareness that earlier recommendations were not implemented, or that current strategies are not effective (but perhaps with a hope that more of the same might be). (Alberta, 1991, p. 4-4)

Since 1991, in addition to the reports that were expected, the Royal Commission on Aboriginal Peoples has published a volume of collected justice papers (RCAP, 1993) and the Law Reform Commission of Canada studied and reported on the impact of the criminal sanction on Aboriginal Peoples (LRCC, 1991). Correctional Service Canada released two reports that considered the situation of Aboriginal people in federal prisons. In 1996, the Royal Commission on Aboriginal Peoples released the report *Bridging the Cultural Divide: A Report on Aboriginal People and Criminal Justice in Canada* (1996a). This report is largely a discussion of the previous justice reports and offers little that is new to the discussion. Obviously the Royal Commissioners felt that "more of the same" might just work! Later in the year, the Royal Commission released its six-volume final report.

The final report of the Royal Commission on Aboriginal Peoples offers little to no discussion of justice issues given the fact that a separate report on justice was issued earlier in the same year. This is unfortunate, as it misconstructs the centrality that justice issues occupy within Aboriginal communities. Justice issues overlap with most if not all issues that Aboriginal communities face, including self-government. Justice, therefore, should have been a central and integrated focus in the final report as well. The commissioners noted that there are four important dimensions of social change in Aboriginal lives and communities: healing, economic opportunity, human resources, and institutional development. Matters of criminal justice have a significant relationship with at least two of the four dimensions, healing and institutional development. Prior to 1996 and the release of this report, at least one healing lodge had already been constructed for federally sentenced women. This healing lodge is an institution under the authority of Correctional Service Canada.

In defining healing, the commissioners state:

Healing is a term used often by Aboriginal people to signify the restoration of physical, social, emotional and spiritual vitality in individuals and social systems. It implies the revitalization of their confidence in themselves, their communities and cultures, confidence that must be grounded in their daily lives.

Healing also has an intercultural meaning. Learning about and acknowledging the errors of the past, making restitution where possible, and correcting distortions of history are essential first steps in the process of healing between Aboriginal and non-Aboriginal people. In Volume 1, we recommended remedies for past injustices and neglect in *residential schools, relocation policies, and the treatment of veterans*. (RCAP, 1996c, p. 12, emphasis added)

Given the rates of overrepresentation of Aboriginal persons in the Canadian criminal justice system, and particularly the rates that demonstrate over-incarceration, I find the exclusion from this last list of matters of criminal justice to be particularly disturbing.

There is a haunting repetition throughout the two decades of reports and the corresponding 1500 recommendations.[6] The Cawsey Commission makes these comments on the trends in the recommendations:

Despite the patterns of recommendations, there have been changes in the type of recommendations made over the years. The Reports between 1967 and 1978 made wide-ranging recommendations that put the Criminal Justice System in a wider societal context. These recommendations included alcohol treatment, diversion, economic development and recreation as crime prevention strategies.

Of the later reports, only *Policing in a Pluralistic Society* (1989) includes such recommendations. Later reports tend to be very Criminal Justice System–specific and frequently focus on only one component, such as the Police (especially the Police), the Courts, or corrections. It should be noted that: 1) only one report deals with Native victims of crime; and, 2) recommendations dealing with specific services are concentrated in certain reports (e.g. the policing studies). In addition to these reports there have been an increasing number of reports on discrimination, education and socioeconomic conditions which may account for the decrease in contextual recommendations in the Criminal Justice reports. (Alberta, 1991, pp. 4–6)

The work of the Cawsey Commission has been the only attempt to rigorously analyze the existing recommendations.[7] The overall conclusion is obvious: the problem cannot be characterized as one of *not* knowing what is happening to Aboriginal people in the justice system, as pointed out clearly in 1991 by the Alberta study.

Of greater concern than the failure to do much in practical or analytical terms with existing recommendations is the pattern in the kinds of recommendations put forward in the studies. As the Cawsey Commission notes, recommendations become more specific over time. The more specific the recommendations become, the more Aboriginal involvement in the criminal justice system as a result of colonial relations is disguised. This shifts the fault to Aboriginal people and nations at the same time as it shifts responsibility away from the system. If in fact colonialism, racism, and discrimination cause the present rates of Aboriginal overrepresentation, as concluded by the Aboriginal Justice Inquiry of Manitoba, then this trend in the recommendations to become more specific (and individualized) conceals the real problem and leaves little hope for real change in the near future.

This is not the only concern that arises from an analysis of the commissioned reviews. In 1993, the Royal Commission on Aboriginal Peoples reviewed eight of the major justice reports and noted that "the extent to which recommendations have been implemented is a matter for concern; certainly the release of an inquiry report has not necessarily signified the beginning of change and amelioration of the problem" (Blackburn, 1993, p. 16). The realization that few reports have been substantially implemented raises a series of questions. This is an area where systematic research of government responses would benefit our understanding.[8] It is not Aboriginal communities that need to be further studied. There are two sides to the justice problems Aboriginal people face, and the truth is that very little is known about why the knowledge we have has not been fully implemented. Rather, our communities need to be resourced so that crime and justice projects can begin or be strengthened. After all, one of the things we do know is that (in the words of Justice Cawsey): "Everything that has worked for natives has come from natives" (RCAP, 1993, p. 12).

The most important realization is that Aboriginal people's struggle with the criminal law sanction is not manifest only in our overrepresentation. Aboriginal struggles with the criminal law sanction in Canada are also not a new phenomenon. They did not begin in 1967 when Canadians began to study the issue as well as label it as a problem; it is a historic relationship that finds its origins in the time of contact (see Kly, 1991; Schuh, 1979; Stonechild, 1986). The historical understanding that is accessible concerning the relationship between Aboriginal peoples and the criminal justice system is at best rudimentary, a result of the fact that the "problem" has been studied from only one location.

Most frequently, discussion about Aboriginal people and the Canadian criminal justice system focusses on two issues, over- and underrepresentation. With these two issues as the focus, there is little hope that systemic change will occur within the system. Remedies to overrepresentation look at individualized ways of decreasing the number of Aboriginal people involved with the system. Diversion programs, fine options, and sentencing circles are three examples of such initiatives. The underrepresentation of Aboriginal people with authority within the system is addressed by equity hiring, which is hoped to increase the numbers of Aboriginal people employed by the system. Both of these kinds of "quick fixes" also rely on cross-cultural education to enhance their successes. All of the energy devoted to these kinds of activities actually diverts attention from the larger structural problems within the system. For example, Aboriginal people have had their internal power to address problems of law and order within their communities directly interfered with by instruments such as the Indian Act. The Royal Commission on Aboriginal Peoples, in one of the small references to justice in the final report, addresses this concern:

> Effective enforcement of *Indian Act* by-laws and the most common criminal offences involves not only laying charges against offenders, but also prosecution, adjudication and sentencing. The current situation with outside police forces refusing to enforce by-laws, the limited criminal justice jurisdiction of *Indian Act* justices of the peace, the forced reliance on provincially and territorially administered courts, and the absence of any authority for bands to correct these anomalies means jurisdiction gaps, confusion over procedures and policies, and the continuing inability of bands to provide effectively for the safety and security of their own members.
>
> Paradoxically, most bands have moved from a position of extremely heavy judicial control of reserve law and order matters to a situation of almost no control, except by outside forces on a sporadic basis. From a position of too much enforcement, they have arrived at one of not enough. This is just one of the legacies of the past, but it is one that has profoundly serious consequences for daily life in most reserve communities. (RCAP, 1996b, pp. 290–91)

Criminal justice experts (who tend to be non-Aboriginal people) minimize the historic relations between Aboriginal people and the state as a source of the problems that Aboriginal people presently face in the existing criminal justice system. This is a significant difference that continues to separate Aboriginal and non-Aboriginal understandings of the problem. As an Aboriginal woman who struggles to understand decolonization, I am aware of the impact of the history of my people in this country. I know that the Royal Canadian Mounted Police (formerly known as the North West Mounted Police) were actively involved in suppressing our traditional forms of government and insisting that we follow the Indian

Act model of non-democratic elected rule. These facts ground my response to the criminal sanction in such a way that I cannot view the Canadian system as a just one.

THE CONTOURS OF OVERREPRESENTATION WITHIN INSTITUTIONS OF CRIMINAL JUSTICE

The overrepresentation of Aboriginal people in the Canadian criminal justice system has been the starting place of every Canadian justice inquiry mandated in the last three decades. In keeping with this well-established preoccupation with documenting the current situation, this paper also considers the statistics. Truly the picture revealed is bleak. No commission or inquiry has managed to fully move beyond this fixation with numbers — even the Royal Commission on Aboriginal Peoples formed almost their entire research agenda on this numerical documentation preoccupation. We all admit there is a problem, but this preoccupation with documentation is a trend that must not continue, as it ensures that no meaningful change can occur. This paper adds the theory of decolonization to the statistical picture that is overwhelmingly available.

It is still difficult to rely on existing data to provide a clear and complete picture of Aboriginal involvement and experience of the justice system.[9] Data collection methods are inconsistent across various components of the justice system. The federal/provincial sharing of criminal jurisdiction also complicates the problem by adding a further level of data inconsistency. National police statistics were abolished three decades ago. In police data, only gender is specified; age, race, and other socio-demographic data are not consistently available (Johnson and Rodgers, 1993, p. 95). In the 1980s Statistics Canada abandoned efforts to collect national court data (Johnson and Rodgers, 1993, p. 96). All of this raises concerns about the reliability of the statistical pictures we have all been insistently drawing. In 1967, the authors of the report *Indians and the Law* experienced difficulties in data collection that they described as follows:

> Since collection of such data by the provincial agencies required special report forms not ordinarily used, the information was difficult to obtain. Indeed, serious difficulties were encountered in practically all agencies because very few differentiate between Indians and non-Indians when recording arrests, court appearances or sentences. Consequently, the statistics are not as complete as would be desirable although they do indicate trends that cannot be ignored. (Laing and Monture, 1967, p. 12)

After almost three decades of looking at the problem of Aboriginal over-representation, the statistical picture remains incomplete. Perhaps this is one of the reasons that researchers remain preoccupied with examining the statistical backdrop. Nonetheless, either situation is a barrier to meaningful change in the experiences of Aboriginal people in Canada's justice system.

It is helpful to understand the patterns that emerge when statistical information is examined. These patterns help us understand the shape of the discrimination that Aboriginal people are exposed to in their current experiences of criminal justice. We know more about federal offenders than we do about provincial offenders or young offenders. It is difficult to make interprovincial comparisons of young offenders and provincial offenders because of differences in record-keeping practices across the provinces. It must be understood that the statistical picture is incomplete and perhaps inaccurate. What is absolute is that Aboriginal people are clearly and dramatically overrepresented in the Canadian justice system. This alone is sufficient evidence to question the justness of that system. Aboriginal overrepresentation is only a window through which the existing system can begin to be examined and understood.

The overrepresentation of Aboriginal people in Canadian prisons is a well-acknowledged fact. In Manitoba, Aboriginal people account for only 12 percent of the population but represent half of the admissions to correction institutions (Manitoba, 1991, p. 85). The overrepresentation of Aboriginal offenders in the federal system is most pronounced in the Prairie region (Alberta, Saskatchewan, and Manitoba). As of November of 1994, Aboriginal inmates accounted for 75 percent of the individuals incarcerated federally in the Prairie region.[10] In the fiscal year 1989–90, the overrepresentation was greatest in the province of Saskatchewan (Correctional Service Canada, 1994a, p. 1). Correctional Service Canada noted in 1998:

> While the proportion of Aboriginal offenders has increased from 10.4% in March 1993 to 12.4% in March 1997, the percentage of Aboriginal employees for this same period has only increased from 2.4% to 3.2%. (p. 13)

In and of itself, the overrepresentation is a disturbing fact. It is, however, a superficial and incomplete portrait of the reality that faces Aboriginal people caught by the Canadian criminal justice system.[11]

The data provided by the Aboriginal Justice Inquiry of Manitoba are an informative place to start looking in detail at the experience of Aboriginal people in the justice system. Data for the other western provinces are not unlike that of Manitoba. The Manitoba report notes in 1989 that

40 percent of the population at Stoney Mountain prison were Aboriginal men.[12] This figure has steadily increased since 1965, when it was noted that Aboriginal men accounted for 22 percent of the federal admissions at the same prison (Manitoba, 1991, pp. 9–10, 101).[13] Despite attempts in the last two decades to address the problem of overrepresentation, there has been no meaningful decrease in the rate of overrepresentation. In fact, the situation has steadily worsened in this federal prison.

In Saskatchewan, the situation is even worse. Aboriginal prisoners account for 55 percent of the population at Saskatchewan Penitentiary. There is reason to question the accuracy of this statistic as "some managers suggest that the official figures ... underestimate the number of Aboriginal inmates in their Institutions" (Correctional Service Canada, 1994a, p. 1). Compare this with the realization that in the 1920s, only 5 percent of all provincial inmates in Saskatchewan were Aboriginal (School of Human Justice, 1991). This is despite a number of well-intentioned attempts to address Aboriginal overrepresentation. The reforms attempted have not been successful if the standard is a decrease in overrepresentation. Reforms may have changed, perhaps even improved, the individual experience of Aboriginal offenders. Improving the individualized experience of Aboriginal offenders (that is, the amount of cultural distance they experience while in the system) does not amount to challenging the structural barriers that are the cause of the overall rates of overrepresentation. The failure of past reforms must be taken seriously and form a basis for the conclusion that a new direction in correctional reform is required.

The statistical evidence that is available clearly indicates that the situation is not going to improve in the next decade. The overrepresentation of Aboriginal youth in Manitoba's provincial institutions is more pronounced than in the federal population. In 1990, "64 percent of the Manitoba Youth Centre population and 78 percent of Agassiz's population were Aboriginal youth" (Manitoba, 1991, p. 10). Provincial offenders in Manitoba are also overrepresented. In 1989, 47 percent of the admissions to Headingley Institution were Aboriginal. The same pattern of increasing disproportional representation in youth and provincial offender populations over the last decade must be noted. The many attempts at amelioration have been failures if the reduction in overrepresentation is the measure of meaningful change.

Those involved in corrections understand that there is a pattern in the progression of individuals from youth to provincial to federal institutions. Since the overrepresentation of Aboriginal people is most pronounced in youth offender populations, and more pronounced in provincial than in federal institutions, there is no relief to be seen from the disproportional representation of Aboriginal people in custodial institutions in the next few years. If youth overrepresentation was notably lower than provincial and federal overrepresentation, there would be some immediate hope for a decrease in overrepresentation in provincial and federal inmate populations in the future. The concern is deepened when it is noted that the portion of the Aboriginal population between the ages of 15 and 24 is greater than that found in the Canadian population. This further evidence predicts that we will see a continued increase in the overrepresentation of Aboriginal people in Canadian prisons, jails, and youth facilities — that is, unless something radically different is done to combat the continued increase in rates of incarceration for Aboriginal people.

The figures presented thus far in the paper largely involve only the overrepresentation of Aboriginal men. Men account for a greater percentage of all adult offenders. On any given day the head count in federal prisons tallies around 18 400 men (Correctional Service Canada, 1994c); women number only 500.[14] The number of individual lives of women *directly* affected by incarceration is far lower than for men. However, the rate of overrepresentation of Aboriginal people in the criminal justice system is most noted among Aboriginal women. In a decade-old Saskatchewan study, it was found that a treaty Indian woman is 131 times more likely, and a Métis woman 28 times more likely, to be incarcerated than a non-Aboriginal woman (Jackson, 1988, p. 3). As these figures are now a decade old and the overrepresentation of Aboriginal women in the Canadian criminal justice system has continued to increase, these figures will now be higher. This is true for both provincially and federally sentenced women, particularly in the Prairie region. In Manitoba, 67 percent of the 1989 admissions to the Portage jail for women were Aboriginal women (Manitoba, 1991, p. 10). In the 1996 Arbour Inquiry, the commissioner notes in her report:

> As of September, 1995, Aboriginal women comprised just over 13% of federally sentenced women overall. However, they comprised 19% of the population of federally sentenced women in prison, and only 7% of federally sentenced women in the community. Seventy-three percent of federally sentenced Aboriginal women were in prison, while only 49% of the non-Aboriginal federally sentenced women were in prison. (Solicitor General, 1996, p. 219)

The impact of incarceration on Aboriginal people must thus include a gendered analysis.

The impact of incarceration on Aboriginal women must be understood through an analysis of the development of correctional policy in Canada.

The system was created to house prisoners, the vast majority of whom were and remain men.[15] Until 1934 when the federal Prison for Women was opened in Kingston, women were housed in prisons alongside men. Women's incarceration was an afterthought in corrections. The system of incarceration in Canada is a system designed and developed for men, by men, and about male crime. Just as women were an afterthought in corrections, so were Aboriginal people. It is equally true that the system of corrections in Canada was designed and developed for white men by white men. Aboriginal women are, therefore, an afterthought within an afterthought (Correctional Service Canada, 1990, pp. 17–18). This situation must be seen to be unacceptable. The Task Force on Federally Sentenced Women, mandated in 1989, was the first to be charged with examining the situation of women in federal prisons. Because of a strong Aboriginal women's lobby, our views were included in this work. The task force report, *Creating Choices* (1990), did not examine the overall situation of women in conflict with the law, but it examined only the situation of women sentenced to federal terms of imprisonment. In this way, the report is narrowly focussed and no clear national picture is available on the way that women experience the full range of criminal justice sanctions.

The figures that document the drastic overrepresentation of Aboriginal people in the Canadian criminal justice system measure only the experience of those who have come into direct contact with the penal system. This particular focus can diminish the overall impact that the criminal justice sanction has on Aboriginal people and our communities. For example, it is known that men are more likely to be federal prisoners (at more than a ratio of 20:1). It is a serious error to conclude that the problem of overrepresentation is borne by our men. Those men are brothers, fathers, husbands, and sons of Aboriginal women. Statistics indicate that in one urban centre, Winnipeg, 43 percent of Aboriginal families are headed by single women compared with 10 percent of non-Aboriginal families (Manitoba, 1991, p. 481). It is unnecessary to wonder where *all* of these men have gone. We know, logically, that some of them are incarcerated. Aboriginal women may not be directly affected by the criminal justice system as frequently as men, but the impact the system has on our lives is equally extreme.

It is not just the fact of overrepresentation and the repercussions felt in our families and communities that must be publicly noted and must evoke concern — the depth of the disparity in the treatment of Aboriginal and non-Aboriginal offenders must also be noted. The Aboriginal Justice Inquiry of Manitoba concluded that every aspect of the criminal justice system is problematic for Aboriginal people (Manitoba, 1991, p. 481). The inquiry conducted a survey and reviewed provincial court records and came to some startling observations. Aboriginal people are more likely to be charged by police for multiple offences. Twenty-two percent of Aboriginal people appearing in court face four or more charges, while for non-Aboriginal people this happens in 13 percent of the cases. Once arrested, Aboriginal people are 1.34 times more likely to be held in jail prior to their court appearances. Once in pretrial custody, Aboriginal people spend 1.5 times longer in custody before their trials. When preparing for court appearances, Aboriginal people see their lawyers less frequently and for less time than do non-Aboriginal people: "Forty-eight percent of Aboriginal people spent less than an hour with their lawyers compared to 46 percent of non-Aboriginal inmates who saw their lawyers for more than 3 hours" (Manitoba, 1991, p. 102).[16] These 1991 findings have been reached by other reviews since then. Although statistics from one jurisdiction cannot be assumed to apply to other areas, there is no information that suggests that the same kinds of difficulties do not face the majority of Aboriginal offenders in other parts of the country. Furthermore, the overrepresentation of Aboriginal people in correctional institutions is clearly and obviously linked to these factors.

In the Manitoba courts, the disparity in treatment of Aboriginal people is also remarkable. Sixty percent of Aboriginal people entered guilty pleas, while only 50 percent of non-Aboriginal people did the same. Aboriginal people received jail terms in 25 percent of the cases, while non-Aboriginal people were jailed in 10 percent of the cases. Aboriginal people receive longer sentences and receive absolute or conditional discharges less frequently (Manitoba, 1991, p. 103). These statistics also enhance our understanding of the patterns of and reasons behind the grave overrepresentation of Aboriginal people in Canadian prisons. There are important systemic patterns within the justice system that contribute to Aboriginal overrepresentation in prisoner populations. Furthermore, Aboriginal overrepresentation is not properly explained by theories of individual Aboriginal pathology.

After documenting the pattern of overrepresentation of Aboriginal people in Canadian prisons, courts, and police contacts, the commissioners of the Aboriginal Justice Inquiry came to this poignant conclusion:

> These statistics are dramatic. There is something inherently wrong with a system which takes such harsh measures against an identifiable minority. It is also improbable that systemic discrimination has not played a major role in bringing this state of affairs into being. (Manitoba, 1991, p. 103)

The recognition that the problem of criminal justice and corrections is in fact systemic has yet to be fully incorporated into the thinking of those

with the power to change correctional relations. An analysis of the reforms to date indicates that the vast majority of reforms have expected
Aboriginal people to change to fit into the system — that is to say, that
most efforts at reform have been individualized as opposed to systemic.
Reforms such as provincial court workers and legal education projects
have been established to assist Aboriginal people in understanding the
foreign system of Canadian laws and justice relations. Why is it that Aboriginal people are expected to change to accommodate the system rather
than the system changing in such a way that Aboriginal people are fundamentally respected by that system? A system of justice that is capable
of singling out any identifiable group to receive special and more exces-
sive contact cannot be seen to be just and fair. However, this situation has
not only existed in Canada since at least 1967, the situation has continued to worsen.

Once incarcerated, Aboriginal offenders continue to receive unequal
treatment. The Aboriginal Justice Inquiry of Manitoba again provides an
interesting window to the shape of the problems within correctional institutions. The inquiry surveyed 258 inmates, 60 Aboriginal and 198 non-
Aboriginal. The Aboriginal inmates reported that they felt Aboriginal
spirituality was not respected in their institution (81 percent). Fewer than
5 percent of these inmates indicated that they had regular access to spiritual activities (Manitoba, 1991, p. 444). In fact, the commissioners of the
inquiry concluded that Aboriginal spirituality is not being encouraged in
institutions but instead is actively discouraged (Manitoba, 1991, p. 445).
Although Correctional Service Canada has made efforts in the last decade
to improve cultural and spiritual services, they still lag behind the need. In
a 1997 research report commissioned by the Correctional Service, 67.9 percent of inmates surveyed indicated that they did not have enough access
to cultural activities (Correctional Service Canada, 1997, p. 35). In the
same report, 40.7 percent of the inmates surveyed that their spiritual needs
were not being met (Correctional Service Canada, 1997, p. 44).

Aboriginal inmates also report that programming in the institutions
is not acceptable. In most cases appropriate programming that addresses their needs is not available.[17] "Yet, if they do not participate in the
programs that are offered, that fact appears on their record and harms
their chances for parole" (Manitoba, 1991, p. 447). Aboriginal offenders are forced to engage in programs that have little personal (cultural)
worth if they wish to have any opportunity to secure a parole. The statistics available on parole indicate that Aboriginal people are less likely to be granted parole. There is a relationship between the services
available in prison to Aboriginal inmates that are culturally sensitive

and the rate of paroles granted to them. In 1998, in its review of the Corrections and Conditional Release Act, Correctional Service Canada summarizes its findings:

> Findings revealed that proportionately, Aboriginal offenders were more likely to be serving their sentence in institutions than in the community on supervision. Aboriginal offenders were also less likely to be released on full parole, more likely to be released on statutory release, and significantly more likely to be referred for detention. When granted parole, they received it later in their sentence and were more likely to be returned to imprisonment for a technical violation of supervision conditions. (Correctional Service Canada, 1998, p. 20)

In 1994, 60 percent of non-Aboriginal offenders were granted parole, while only 44.5 percent of Aboriginal offenders were granted parole. These release rates are an improvement over the 1980 figures, but there is still a long way to go. For several years now, and particularly in the Prairie region, Aboriginal inmates have been able to have elder-assisted parole hearings. Studies indicate that this has not significantly improved the rate of granting of parole to Aboriginal offenders, but parole board members report that these types of hearings have provided Aboriginal inmates with the opportunity to have "hearings that are more relaxed and informal which many find is conducive to openness and sincerity" (Correctional Service Canada, 1994b, pp. 25–26). It is not documented whether Aboriginal offenders agree with this conclusion.

As equally remarkable as the overrepresentation of Aboriginal people as clients in the criminal justice system is the exclusion or underrepresentation of Aboriginal people from any place of authority in the criminal justice system (Manitoba, 1991, p. 663). There are very few Aboriginal lawyers, police officers, court personnel, corrections workers, or parole officers. There is usually no one in our communities employed in the system to turn to if we are confused about what is happening to us in that system. As a result, Aboriginal people view the justice system as a system that belongs to Canada and not to Aboriginal people. We understand that as the clients of that system, we "support" it; in fact, the system is built on the backs of many Aboriginal offenders and their families. Aboriginal people see little if any benefit accruing to our communities from this system. We do not earn our livelihood by involvement in that system — instead, we pay fines and we see dollars and people going out of our communities and know that the benefit goes to the government and Canadians in general (Manitoba, 1991, p. 420). It is little wonder that Aboriginal people have little respect for the Canadian criminal justice system.

The overrepresentation of Aboriginal people in penal institutions, their disparate treatment in prisons, and their chronic underrepresentation in positions of employment within the justice area are merely glimpses of the way in which justice relations have a negative impact on Aboriginal people. Although it would be unfair to stereotype reserves as all having high crime rates, there is a greater statistical likelihood that an individual living on reserve will be victimized by crime.[18] The national crime rate is 92.7 criminal acts per 1000 population. The Department of Indian Affairs reports that the crime rate on reserves is 165.6 per 1000 population — 1.8 times the national average (Manitoba, 1991, p. 87). Even more troubling is the fact that the rate of violent crime is greater on Indian reserves — 3.67 times the national rate (Manitoba, 1991, p. 87). Indian people are more likely to be victims of crime, and the "opportunity" to be a victim of violent crime is even greater. The need to address the difficulties in Canadian criminal justice as it is applied to Aboriginal people is a concern that is much broader than the mere jailing of our citizens. It is a reflection of the life experiences of Aboriginal people and has a negative impact on the quality of life in our communities. The impact of the Canadian criminal justice system and its failure to provide meaningful correctional and criminal justice services to Aboriginal offenders also creates additional burdens on our communities and on victims.

UNDERSTANDING THE COLONIAL IMPACT OF CANADIAN JUSTICE INSTITUTIONS

The situation of over- and underrepresentation must be understood to create the situation where Aboriginal people can have no respect for Canada's system of criminal law and corrections. This is not the fault[19] of Aboriginal people, but must be seen to be a systemic problem that is the responsibility of the Canadian justice system and those who support it. Canadians must also come to understand colonization and, more importantly, decolonization. It is very difficult for Aboriginal people to live in a decolonized manner when the practice of colonialism is still alive and well in Canada. Since 1967 and the release of the report of the Canadian Corrections Association, social scientists, often in partnership with government departments, have searched for the cause of Aboriginal criminality. In the 1967 report, the discussion concluded with a realization "that much of whatever trouble these people were having with the law could be understood only in light of economic conditions, culture patterns, minority group status and other underlying factors" (Laing and

Monture, 1967, p. 9). Since the release of the Donald Marshall Inquiry report in 1989, the factors analyzed to produce an understanding of Aboriginal criminality became individualized. This is troubling. Economic disadvantage, underemployment, substance abuse, and other factors that are used to explain Aboriginal overinvolvement are not the sources of the problem but symptoms of the problems of a society that is structured on discriminatory values, beliefs, and practices that are then applied without consent to Aboriginal nations. The outcome of the individualized analysis of Aboriginal patterns of crime conceals the true relationship.

Commissioners Hamilton and Sinclair note in the *Report of the Aboriginal Justice Inquiry of Manitoba* two immediate answers to the reasons for the shocking overrepresentation of Aboriginal people in the criminal justice system. Either Aboriginal people commit disproportionately more crimes than do non-Aboriginal people, or Aboriginal people are the victims of a discriminatory justice system. They further add:

> We believe that both answers are correct, but not in the simplistic sense that some people might interpret them. We do not believe, for instance, that there is anything about Aboriginal people or their culture that predisposes them to criminal behavior. Instead, we believe that the causes of Aboriginal criminal behavior are rooted in a long history of discrimination and social inequality that has impoverished Aboriginal people and consigned them to the margins of Manitoban society. (Manitoba, 1991, p. 85)

In particular, discrimination in the justice system cannot be simply understood. Discrimination comes in many forms: Aboriginal people experience discrimination in the courts and in jails; in our communities, we have a greater statistical likelihood of being victimized; and we recognize familiar patterns of exclusion in the lack of opportunity to be employed within the justice system. The two causes of Aboriginal overrepresentation expressed by the Manitoba commissioners lead to several logical conclusions about reforming the justice system.

I have never been an advocate of reform of the existing system as being a full and complete remedy. This became a hardened opinion during my years as a volunteer in the Kingston area penitentiaries.[20] This lesson is reaffirmed every time I consider the government-sponsored justice reports. It saddens me to think that it is even a necessary remedy, but it is. Reform of the existing system is most necessary. Many Aboriginal prisoners are currently serving sentences in Canada's prisons and jails. These are relatives and friends on whom I cannot turn my back. I am very much convinced that even if the existing system was reformed in such a way that Aboriginal people were proportionately represented and received equal treatment, Aboriginal people would still continue to report that they perceive the Canadian criminal justice system as unfair.

Another factor affects the perception of Aboriginal people that they are treated unfairly by the existing system, a factor that has largely been ignored in the academic literature and multiple reports but that I have heard mentioned by many Aboriginal people. This forgotten factor is history. There is a long history of the criminal law sanction being used to control, oppress, and force the assimilation of Aboriginal peoples. This is carefully remembered by some Aboriginal people. There are a number of examples of the problematic nature of the historical relationship.

Examining the introduction of alcohol to Aboriginal populations provides an important example of the way that an understanding of historical relations must complement present-day understandings. The abuse of alcohol has been demonstrated to influence the participation in criminal activity. This is true across most categories of offences and is particularly true for Aboriginal offenders. Alcohol was introduced into Aboriginal nations by European traders who learned they could accumulate great profits when they relied on alcohol as a trade commodity. For the Cypress Hills area (southern Saskatchewan) it has been reported that

> The trading of whiskey could boost a trader's profits substantially. In 1854 a clear profit of 45 percent could be made on trading a $9.67 gun for $416.00 worth of buffalo robes. Proof alcohol cost the trader $3.25 to $6.00 a gallon — diluted and spiced up it could bring up to $50.00 in hides. In one rate of exchange, two robes were traded for one large glass of "rot-gut" whiskey. (Hildebrandt and Hubner, 1994, p. 36)[21]

Today, the history of Aboriginal peoples' introduction to alcohol consumption is forgotten. It is within this relationship that one of the seeds of Aboriginal overrepresentation in the criminal justice system is firmly rooted.

The Aboriginal Justice Inquiry of Manitoba was the first Canadian report to develop a consistent focus on the effect of racism, individual and systemic, in the overrepresentation of Aboriginal people within the criminal justice system. This focus on racism and criminal sanction extends back in time to the period of contact. In their own words, the commissioners explain:

> Historically, the justice system has discriminated against Aboriginal people by providing legal sanction for their oppression. This oppression of previous generations forced Aboriginal people into their current state of social and economic distress. Now, a seemingly neutral justice system discriminates against current generations of Aboriginal people by applying

laws which have an adverse impact on people of lower socio-economic status. This is no less racial discrimination; it is merely "laundered" racial discrimination. It is untenable to say that discrimination which builds upon the effects of racial discrimination is not racial discrimination itself. Past injustices cannot be ignored or built upon. (Manitoba, 1991, p. 109)

The work of the Aboriginal Justice Inquiry introduced a new level of analysis to an old question. The question of Aboriginal overinvolvement in all relations of criminal justice in Canada is analyzed at a systemic level. Racism is understood to be the central factor.

Racism is in fact an incomplete explanation of what is happening in the Canadian criminal justice system. Racism does not emphasize enough the historical relationships that appear when the overrepresentation of Aboriginal people in Canadian jails is placed in context. In fact, colonialism is also a necessary component of the explanation. The Canadian justice system is now the central institution that reinforces colonial relationships with Aboriginal people. In many ways, the system of incarceration has taken the place that residential schools once occupied. This fact must influence the way that any reformation of Canadian criminal justice systems proceeds.

Beyond the individual and systemic discrimination that can be measured by disproportional rates of over- and underrepresentation, beyond the context that is exposed when history is remembered, is the shocking fact that the branches of the criminal justice system in Canada continue to this day to operate in a way that oppresses the mechanisms and practices of social control in Aboriginal communities. This third factor obviously continues to create the situation where rates of Aboriginal overrepresentation will continue to increase. And yet, it is barely noted in the literature. It has not been the topic of any extensive research program.

WALKING TOWARD THE FUTURE

When I think about reforming the Canadian criminal justice system, I often find myself reflecting on my experiences of the struggle that individuals have faced to keep out of prison. Learning to walk on this side of the prison wall has been difficult for many people with whom I have shared small parts of this experience. Little in the way of programming within the prison system has prepared them for the journey that they face outside. Little is known in a scholarly sense about what works in the "aftercare" field. I know of no rigorous studies of this issue. Few resources are devoted to providing post-incarceration services and programs.

I am not totally dismayed by the situation of Aboriginal people in the Canadian criminal justice system, as there are sources of hope on the horizon. Perhaps the most promising, other than the faith I have in my people, are the new provisions of the Corrections and Conditions Release Act. Section 81 of this legislation allows for the release of an Aboriginal offender to the Aboriginal community. Both Aboriginal offender and Aboriginal community are broadly defined. This section allows for the possibility that Aboriginal communities can gain "care and custody" of Aboriginal prisoners prior to their parole release dates. Subject to the minister's approval and adequate levels of both funding and support, Aboriginal communities can now step forward creatively to bring our people home. This is a broad section that does not step on the hope that things will someday change. Unfortunately, more could be done with this section to speed up the realization of the potential it holds.

The question of how we keep our people out of the justice system has become central in my thoughts on criminal justice and Aboriginal peoples. Intuitively I know the answer. Caring and connection keeps people out. This does not surprise me, because I understand that the vast majority of Aboriginal law is nothing more than rules about kinship and caring. Aboriginal law is relational-based. The question of how we keep our people out is the question I wish to leave you with.

NOTES

1. Mohawk Nation, Grand River Territory, currently residing at the Thunderchild First Nation, Saskatchewan. Associate Professor, Department of Native Studies, University of Saskatchewan. This article is written for my brothers and sisters in iron cages. It is written with prayer that meaningful change is not far away.
2. In recent articles I have chosen to adopt constitutionally prescribed language. "Aboriginal peoples" include the Indian (status and not), Inuit, and Métis. I intend this language to include all Indigenous peoples of the territory now known as Canada.
3. In the refereeing process that is part of the standard practice of academic scholarship, I received some feedback from "colleagues" that I can only describe as hateful. This situation nearly caused me to withdraw this chapter from this text. It has resulted in the withdrawal of one section of the paper.

    In writing this paper and in choosing to distinguish between Aboriginal and non-Aboriginal researchers, policy-makers, scholars, and so on, I meant no disrespect to "white" people. However, the truth of the matter is that if we cannot even acknowledge that there are differences in Indigenous and "white" knowledge systems and practices, then it will remain impossible to overcome colonialism. Colonial relations cannot be addressed until we all understand the detail of this situation for both the colonized and the colonizer. This is the primary reason why this paper distinguishes between Aboriginal and non-Aboriginal people.

For now, I am unwilling to share the preliminary analysis of several scholars' work as examples of the way non-Aboriginal scholars disappear the colonial legacy embedded in Aboriginal overrepresentation and the manner in which one scholar has bastardized and fundamentally misunderstood the sacred ways of Aboriginal people (at least as I was taught). There will again come a time when I carry the strength to speak fully to these issues. In this publication, because of the complicity of those involved in the publishing process, I choose silence.

4. For example, in 1886, section 114 of the Indian Act provided for a term of imprisonment not to exceed six months (and not less than two months) for anyone engaging in the "festival" known as the Potlatch or the dance known as the Tamanawas. A similar provision existed in subsequent Indian Acts until the 1951 amendments. Since it was first enacted, the section was broadened to include many other Indian ceremonies and dances.

5. See the work of William B. Newell (Ta-io-wah-ron-ha-gai), *Crime and Justice among the Iroquois Nations* (1965) and L.F.S. Upton, *Micmacs and Colonists: Indian–White Relations in the Maritimes, 1713–1867* (1979).

6. No systematic and detailed analysis of these recommendations has ever been undertaken and made accessible. The Royal Commission on Aboriginal Peoples disappointingly did not attempt such a project, even though it was well within their mandate and their resources. Rather, every study commissioned replicates the ones that came before. Part of this is a problem of the multiple jurisdictions involved in criminal justice matters and the fragmentation of services, from prevention to policing to corrections.

7. The Cawsey Commission notes that the top ten recommendations are (in no particular order):

> cross-cultural training for non-Native staff; employ more Native staff; have more community-based programs in corrections; have more community-based alternatives in sentencing; have more special assistance to Native offenders; have more Native community involvement in planning, decision-making and service delivery; have more Native advisory groups at all levels; have more recognition of Native culture and law in Criminal Justice System service delivery; emphasize crime prevention programs; and, self-determination must be considered in planning and operation of the Criminal Justice System. (pp. 4–7).

This report also notes that there "has been very little focus at the front-end of the system." Little attention has been paid to victim services and prevention.

8. A recent paper by Professor Russell Barsh (1996), "Anthropology and Indian Hating," discusses this very problem with the preoccupation with studying

Aboriginal people to the exclusion of those who did (and do) the colonizing. An important collateral issue, how do "white" scholars situate themselves in their work, is discussed by Professor Denise McConney in "Dear Wynonah (First Daughter)" (1996).

9. The most complete picture available is found in the Aboriginal Justice Inquiry of Manitoba, which focuses on justice relations and experiences in the province of Manitoba only. No comprehensive national picture is available.

10. As of 31 March 1997, Correctional Service Canada reports this figure to be 64 percent in the Prairie region (Correctional Service Canada, 1998, p. 22), a decrease of 11 percent from the 1994 figures cited. The report does not note this decrease, nor is any explanation put forward. It seems appropriate to note the problems with relying on self-report data that were mentioned earlier in this chapter.

11. I believe justice to be a much larger relation than just one involving the criminal law sanction. This paper will, however, focus on the consequences of Aboriginal overrepresentation in the existing justice system. Discussions of the broader meaning of justice can be found in Patricia A. Monture-Okanee, "Aboriginal Peoples and Canadian Criminal Justice: Myths and Revolution" (1994) and "The Roles and Responsibilities of Aboriginal Women: Reclaiming Justice" (1992).

12. Stoney Mountain is a federal penitentiary operated by Correctional Service Canada. It houses prisoners who are serving sentences of longer than two years. Provincial prisons (discussed in the next paragraph of the text) are prisoners who are serving sentences of less than two years. Youth offenders are under the age of 18.

13. It must be noted that these statistics are subject to criticism. Part of the increase in the overrepresentation may be due to the fact that it has become more acceptable to admit Aboriginal ancestry. Federal data rely solely on self-report figures.

14. These numbers were provided to the members of the Task Force on Federally Sentenced Women. Also note that between the years 1989–90 and 1994–95, the federal prison population has grown quickly, increasing by 22 percent. This figure is twice the historic average (Canada, 1996, pp. 1 and 4).

15. For fuller discussions on the situation of women in conflict with the law, see Elizabeth Comack, *Women in Trouble* (1996) and Karlene Faith, *Unruly Women* (1993).

16. Part of this phenomenon may be explained by the greater number of guilty pleas that Aboriginal people enter.

17. The Aboriginal inmates indicated what kinds of programs they would like to see in the Manitoba institutions. The most desired program was educational or vocational (43 percent). The next most desired were programs involving spirituality and culture (29 percent). Also in demand were life-skills programs (14 percent) and "alcohol and drug dependency, stress management, crafts, parenting, marital counseling and Native languages" (Manitoba, 1991, p. 449).

18. Figures such as these are available for registered Indians only.
19. I do not believe that assigning blame is necessarily part of the solution to the problems that exist in the justice system.
20. I lived in the Kingston area from 1983 to 1988. I was actively involved in the prisons during those years and have maintained many of the friendships I made there after I left the area. My involvement with the Task Force on Federally Sentenced Women also reinforced this view.
21. Similar figures and the tale of a trader can be found in Mary Weekes, *The Last Buffalo Hunter* (1994).

DISCUSSION QUESTIONS

1. What knowledge is gained from the many justice reports commissioned in the last decade?
2. Why is it essential to include the perspective of Aboriginal people in an analysis of overrepresentation within the criminal justice system?
3. What inequalities do Aboriginal people face in the Canadian criminal justice system?
4. Why have reforms to the criminal justice system in the last decade not been fully successful?
5. What "reforms" do you believe would be more successful?

FURTHER READINGS

Gosse, Richard, James Youngblood Henderson, and Roger Carter, eds. 1994. *Continuing Poundmaker and Riel's Quest: Presentations Made at a Conference on Aboriginal Peoples and Justice.* Saskatoon: Purich Publishing. This collection of papers is the most recent publication on Aboriginal peoples and the Canadian justice system. It is also unique in that it combines the views of correctional workers, politicians responsible for running correctional systems, and Aboriginal peoples.

Monture-Angus, Patricia. 1995. *Thunder in My Soul: A Mohawk Woman Speaks.* Halifax: Fernwood. This book does not focus solely on issues of criminal justice but also on the perspectives of one Aboriginal woman academic. The book contains papers on justice from a holistic (or Aboriginal) perspective, child welfare, education, and feminism. This text will help readers understand some specific justice concerns and provide a larger context in which to consider these issues.

Royal Commission on Aboriginal Peoples (RCAP). 1996. *Bridging the Cultural Divide: A Report on Aboriginal People and Criminal Justice in Canada.* Ottawa: Supply and Services. In 1996, the Royal Commission brought together a group of Aboriginal people and a number of non-Aboriginal people involved in various components of the criminal justice system to discuss the direction in which the commission could take its work. The people brought together were lawyers, academics, justice employees, and politicians. This text canvasses several issues that surround the establishment of Aboriginal justice systems from a range of perspectives.

Solicitor General. 1996. *Report of the Commission of Inquiry into Certain Events at the Prison for Women in Kingston.* The Honourable Louise Arbour, Commissioner. Ottawa: Public Works and Government Services Canada. Lana Fox and Fran Sugar. 1989–1990. "Nistum Peyako Seht'wawin Iskwewak: Breaking Chains." *Canadian Journal of Women and the Law* 3(2): 465–82. The report of the Solicitor General and the research paper compiled for the Task Force on Federally Sentenced Women examine the situation of women in federal prisons with particular attention to the overrepresentation of Aboriginal women.

Solomon, Arthur. 1990. *Songs for the People: Teachings on the Natural Way.* Toronto: NC Press Limited. And 1994. *Eating Bitterness: A Vision Beyond the Prison Walls.* Toronto: NC Press. Dr. Solomon was one of the first elders to visit on a regular basis with federal prisoners in the Ontario region. He was both a teacher and activist for the rights of Aboriginal prisoners. His two books contain many reflections on his experiences.

REFERENCES

Ahenakew, Freda and H.C. Wolfart, eds. 1987. *Waskahikaniwiyiniw — Acimowina* (Stories of the House People). Winnipeg: University of Manitoba Press.

Alberta. 1991. *Report of the Task Force on the Criminal Justice System and Its Impact on the Indian and Métis People of Alberta.* Vol. III. *Working Papers and Bibliography.* Edmonton: Solicitor General.

Barsh, Russel. 1996. "Anthropology and Indian Hating." *Native Studies Review* 11(2): pp. 3–22.

Blackburn, Carole. 1993. "Aboriginal Justice Inquiries, Task Forces and Commissions: An Update." Pp. 15–41 in *Aboriginal Peoples and the Justice System,* Royal Commission on Aboriginal Peoples. Ottawa: Supply and Services.

Canada. 1996. *Corrections Population Growth*. Report for the Federal/Provincial/ Territorial Ministers Responsible for Justice. Ottawa: Supply and Services.

Comack, Elizabeth. 1996. *Women in Trouble: Connecting Women's Law Violations to Their Histories of Abuse*. Halifax: Fernwood Publishing.

Correctional Service Canada. 1990. *Creating Choices: The Report of the Task Force on Federally Sentenced Women*. Ottawa: Correctional Service Canada.

———. 1994a. "Aboriginal Issues," internal CSC Newsletter. (n.d.)

———. 1994b. *Care and Custody of Aboriginal Offenders*. Ottawa: Solicitor General.

———. 1994c. *Inmate Profile* (29 June). Ottawa: Correctional Service Canada.

———. 1997. *Aboriginal Offender Survey: Case Files and Interview Sample*. Ottawa: Correctional Service Canada.

———. 1998. *CCRA 5 Year Review: Aboriginal Offenders*. Working Group on the Review of the Corrections and Conditional Release Act. Ottawa: Supply and Services.

Faith, Karlene. 1993. *Unruly Women: The Politics of Confinement and Resistance*. Vancouver: Press Gang Publishers.

Freire, Paulo. 1996. *Pegagogy of the Oppressed*, trans. Myra Bergman Ramos. New York: Continuum.

Gosse, Richard, James Youngblood Henderson, and Roger Carter, eds. 1994. *Continuing Poundmaker and Riel's Quest: Presentations Made at a Conference on Aboriginal Peoples and Justice*. Saskatoon: Purich Publishing.

Hildebrandt, Walter and Brian Hubner. 1994. *The Cypress Hills: The Land and Its People*. Saskatoon: Purich Publishing.

Jackson, Michael. 1988. *Locking up Natives in Canada: Report of the Canadian Bar Association Committee on Imprisonment and Release*. Toronto: Canadian Bar Association.

Johnson, Holly and Karen Rodgers. 1993. "A Statistical Overview of Women and Crime in Canada." Pp. 95–116 in *In Conflict with the Law: Women and the Canadian Justice System*, ed. Ellen Adelburg and Claudia Currie. Vancouver: Press Gang Publisher.

Kly, Yussuf. 1991. "Aboriginal Canadians, the Anti-Social Contract, and Higher Crime Rates." Pp. 81–94 in *Criminal Justice: Sentencing Issues and Reform*, eds. Les Samuelson and Bernard Schissel. Toronto: Garamond Press.

Laing, Arthur and Gilbert C. Monture. 1967. *Indians and the Law*. Ottawa: Canadian Corrections Association.

LaPrairie, Carol. 1995. "Seen but Not Heard: Native People in Four Canadian Inner Cities." *Journal of Human Justice* 6(2): pp. 30–45.

Law Reform Commission of Canada (LRCC). 1991. *Aboriginal Peoples and Criminal Justice*. Report 34. Ottawa: LRCC.

Manitoba. 1991. *Report of the Aboriginal Justice Inquiry of Manitoba: The Justice System and Aboriginal People*. Vol. 1. A.C. Hamilton and C.M. Sinclair, Commissioners. Winnipeg: Queen's Printer.

McCaskill, Don. 1983. "Native People and the Justice System." Pp. 288–98 in *As Long as the Sun Shines and Water Flows: A Reader in Canadian Native Studies*, eds. Ian A.L. Getty and Antoine S. Lussier. Vancouver: University of British Columbia Press.

McConney, Denise. 1996. "Dear Wynonah (First Daughter)." *Native Studies Review* 11(2): pp. 116–24.

Monture-Angus, Patricia. 1995. *Thunder in My Soul: A Mohawk Woman Speaks.* Halifax: Fernwood Publishing.

Monture-Okanee, Patricia. 1992. "The Roles and Responsibilities of Aboriginal Women: Reclaiming Justice." *Saskatchewan Law Review* 56(2): pp. 237–66.

———. 1994. "Aboriginal Peoples and Canadian Criminal Justice: Myths and Revolution." Pp. 222–32 in *Continuing Poundmaker and Riel's Quest: Presentations Made at a Conference on Aboriginal Peoples and Justice,* eds. Richard Gosse, James Youngblood Henderson, and Roger Carter. Saskatoon: Purich Publishing.

Newell, William B. (Ta-io-wah-ron-ha-gai). 1995. *Crime and Justice among the Iroquois Nations.* Montreal: Caughnawaga Historical Society.

Royal Commission on Aboriginal Peoples (RCAP). 1993. *Aboriginal Peoples and the Justice System: Report of the National Round Table on Aboriginal Justice Issues.* Ottawa: RCAP.

———. 1996a. *Bridging the Cultural Divide: A Report on Aboriginal People and Criminal Justice in Canada.* Ottawa: Supply and Services.

———. 1996b. *Report of the Royal Commission on Aboriginal Peoples.* Vol. 1. *Looking Forward, Looking Back.* Ottawa: RCAP.

———. 1996c. *Report of the Royal Commission on Aboriginal Peoples.* Vol. 5. *Renewal: A Twenty-Year Commitment.* Ottawa: RCAP.

School of Human Justice, University of Regina. 1991. Brief submitted to the Saskatchewan Indian and Métis Justice Review Committee.

Schuh, Cornelia. 1979. "Justice on the Northern Frontier: Early Murder Trials of Native Accused." *Criminal Law Quarterly* 22: pp. 74–111.

Solicitor General. 1996. *Report of the Commission of Inquiry into Certain Events at the Prison for Women in Kingston.* The Honourable Louise Arbour, Commissioner. Ottawa: Public Works and Government Services Canada.

Stonechild, Blair. 1986. "The Uprising of 1885: Its Impacts on Federal/Indian Relations in Western Canada." *Saskatchewan Indian Federated College Journal* 2(2): pp. 81–96.

Upton, L.F.S. 1979. *Micmacs and Colonists: Indian–White Relations in the Maritimes, 1713–1867.* Vancouver: University of British Columbia Press.

Waldram, James B. 1997. *The Way of the Pipe: Aboriginal Spirituality and Symbolic Healing in Canadian Prisons.* Peterborough: Broadview Press.

Weekes, Mary. 1994. *The Last Buffalo Hunter.* Saskatoon: Fifth House Publishers.

CHAPTER 13

The Precarious Movements of Aboriginal Peoples and Their Supporters: A Case Study of the Lubicon First Nation Coalition

David Long

INTRODUCTION

Canada has long been regarded throughout the world as a land of peace, hope, and prosperity (RCAP, 1996, p. 107). Contrary to this idealistic image, the history of Aboriginal–state relations in Canada suggests that our country is less than deserving of the title "peaceable kingdom."[1] Even though appreciation of regional and socio-cultural differences has long been a hallmark of the Canadian landscape, the considerable distances that separate most of Canada's 600 or so Aboriginal communities from other Aboriginal and non-Aboriginal communities, as well as their myriad cultural and structural arrangements, have contributed to geographical and social isolation for a large majority of Aboriginal people in Canada. Consequently, it might seem surprising to find meaningful similarities of experience and perspective among Aboriginal peoples in this country. That certain fundamental similarities do exist is less surprising when we acknowledge that from the time European explorers claimed the land of Canada "in the name of their King," every Aboriginal person living in Canada has lived in a colonial context. Some people assert that dwelling on this country's colonialist past will hinder Aboriginal and non-Aboriginal people from cultivating a renewed and hopeful vision for the future. Others argue that ignoring the relationship between the past and the present will result in our being plagued by the mistakes and problems of the past. My view is that examining the connections between past and present circumstances involving Aboriginal peoples, their supporters, and their opponents is important for a number of reasons. For one, it helps us to see current expressions of organized dissent involving Aboriginal peoples and their supporters in a larger historical context. Equally important, it invites "observers" to walk in the shoes of Aboriginal people and their supporters who, over the past 40 or so years, have fundamentally challenged this country's image as a peaceable kingdom.

Throughout Canada's history, organized dissent involving Aboriginal peoples and their supporters has taken the form of court challenges, lobbying efforts, and protests of various sizes, types, and intensities (Long, 1995, pp. 45–50). Although there appears to have been minimal public support for Aboriginal interests throughout much of Canada's history, things changed in this regard toward the end of the 1960s. During this time, a groundswell of dissent involving Aboriginal and non-Aboriginal people was expressed in various strategic ways against what some termed the "unjust fate" shared by a majority of Aboriginal people in Canada (Long, 1993, pp. 15–16).

One of the more recent and striking expressions of the Aboriginal movement in Canada has involved national and international coalition support on behalf of the Lubicon First Nation. Briefly, the coalition emerged in late 1991 after a Toronto-based group called the Friends of the Lubicon (FOL) informed representatives of Diashowa Canada Company Ltd. of their intention to initiate a public boycott campaign of Diashowa products until the company expressed "a clear, firm and public commitment to not cut and not purchase any wood cut on unceded Lubicon territory until after a settlement of Lubicon land rights and negotiation of a harvesting agreement that takes into account Lubicon wildlife and environmental concerns."[2] The FOL also sent letters urging various organizations and businesses to honour the boycott in support of the Lubicon, who are based in Alberta. Within days the FOL had sent out a press release announcing both that there would be a demonstration on 14 November outside Diashowa's Toronto office and that a boycott of companies using Diashowa's products was imminent. After roughly four years of the FOL's "successfully" organized boycott, Diashowa filed a lawsuit, asking for an injunction to "restrain permanently the consumer boycott activities of the defendant Friends of the Lubicon and some of its individual supporters" (MacPherson, 1998, p. 1). On 14 April 1998, Ontario Court of Justice Judge J. MacPherson ruled in favour of the defendants by refusing to grant the injunction. Diashowa subsequently issued a press release stating that the company would not cut trees on land claimed by the Lubicon until their land claim dispute with the government was resolved.

Documented activities involving the FOL and a diverse collection of other Lubicon supporters illustrate how quickly a broad base of counter-hegemonic support can grow. Nonetheless, close examination of different perspectives and interests among Aboriginal peoples and between Aboriginal peoples and their non-Aboriginal supporters and opponents suggests why it is often difficult for social movement activists and organizations to maintain momentum and act together. In the following analysis, we will see that although the appreciation for and mobilization of people's differences has brought strength and vitality to the activities of Aboriginal social movement supporters in general and Lubicon coalition members in particular, differences from within and challenges from without also contribute to uncertainty, the potential for dissent, and possibly the emergence of new forms of hegemonic control. Although Diashowa has apparently agreed to suspend the harvesting of trees on Lubicon-claimed land until the land-claim dispute is resolved, the following analysis also shows that even long-term agreement between Diashowa and the Lubicon will not ensure that the problems related to logging practices on Lubicon-claimed land will cease.

My general concern is to understand the ways in which hegemonic and counter-hegemonic agents' perspectives and interactions give shape and movement to the Aboriginal movement in Canada. My specific concern in this chapter is to examine how spiritual, cultural, economic, and political differences and similarities interact in relation to the Lubicon Lake First Nation coalition in Canada. Understanding the ebb and flow of coalition and social movement activities means taking into account the pressures on the participants from the past as well as the present, and from within as well as from without. As many of the chapters in this book attest, countless people, circumstances, and events have brought Aboriginal–state relations to where they are currently. Consequently, we begin our case study of the Lubicon coalition with a brief description of the emergence of the Aboriginal peoples' movement in the 1960s.

RECENT MOVEMENT WITHIN ABORIGINAL–STATE RELATIONS

Similar to other social movements, the emergence and growth of the Aboriginal peoples' movement in Canada during the 1960s was facilitated by the recruitment of a wide variety of people that cultivated a broad base of support, effective mobilizing of scarce resources, and diligence at addressing divisions that threatened to fragment movement solidarity and delay or prevent potential successes (Long, 1993, pp. 5–6, 15–16; 1992, pp. 127–28). Although effective organizational strategies have contributed to the growth of this movement in Canada since the early 1960s, the unique experiences and perspectives of Aboriginal peoples have been central to the directions their movements have taken over time. Current ideas and activities of those involved are therefore both an outgrowth of seeds sown in the past and a sign of creative adaptability during the past four decades. The militancy of certain factions within the Aboriginal movement has precedent in Aboriginal warrior societies of the past (Thompson, 1992, p. 175); the nurturing of formal alliances and grass-roots public support with non-Aboriginal peoples and the professionalization of movement activities illustrate the ability of movement supporters to adapt to current, often volatile social contexts (Fort Good Hope Community Council, 1992; Long, 1993, p. 16); and the concern of many Aboriginal women to be protected by the Charter of Rights and Freedoms, at least until agreement can be reached among Aboriginal peoples on the meaning of traditional ways and the implications of self-government, reflects the belief of some Aboriginal people that the past can be honoured without losing a critical perspective on current experiences, conditions, and aspirations (Hammersmith, 1992).

Bureaucratization of Aboriginal–State Relations

Although little sustained political activity and organized interest and pressure were aimed at bringing about change in Aboriginal–state relations during the 1950s and early 1960s, a number of developments in the 1960s were important catalysts for the resurgence of both violent and non-violent efforts at social change on the part of Aboriginal people and their supporters. One was the establishment of the National Indian Brotherhood (NIB) in 1968 as the first national organization run by and for Canada's First Nation peoples. Although it appears that the organization's turbulent history was largely a result of disagreements over funding and agendas (Ponting, 1986, pp. 40–41), NIB board member Harold Cardinal (who was also president of the Indian Association of Alberta) noted that the creation of the NIB was a turning point for Aboriginal peoples in Canada (Cardinal, 1969, p. 107). Unlike provincially based Indian associations, the NIB was the national, autonomous social movement organization needed by movement supporters for sustained mobilization. Along with serving as the national clearing house for information on developments involving Aboriginal peoples, the NIB embodied a new development in the history of the organization and mobilization of Aboriginal peoples in Canada. As a national organization, the NIB facilitated both the sharing and development of ideas as well as the strategic organization of movement activities. In short, the Aboriginal-run NIB expressed as well as cultivated a new sense of unity and organized purpose among Aboriginal people and their supporters across Canada.

The second major focal point for the organized mobilization of Aboriginal interests and movement identity at this time was the introduction of the 1969 White Paper, *Statement on Indian Policy*, by the Minister of Indian Affairs, Jean Chrétien, which sought to end the federal government's responsibility for Aboriginal peoples and issues. For many Aboriginal peoples in Canada, the White Paper symbolized the many problems associated with colonization. A large number of Aboriginal leaders from across Canada were motivated[3] to immediately and categorically reject what they termed the genocidal[4] implications of the White Paper, and in 1970 they adopted the Indian Association of Alberta's position paper, *Citizens Plus*, as their alternative vision of the state. As an outspoken representative of two of the most recognized Aboriginal organizations in the country, Harold Cardinal was both hopeful and wary of developments surrounding the NIB and the government's White Paper. On the one hand, he viewed the NIB and other such organizations as vital to strengthening Aboriginal identity in Canada. On the other hand, he was compelled to warn state representatives that failure of the NIB and other similar organizations, especially if Canadian governments were at fault, could result in Aboriginal peoples "taking the dangerous and explosive path travelled by the Black militants of the United States."

> We can and we have watched black riots in the United States and we can and we have pondered their lessons. Our people have seen the methods used by other groups in similar situations, and we have measured their successes — and failures. We are learning from others about the forces that can be assembled in a democratic society to protect oppressed minorities. These things, too, are our classrooms now and our textbooks. And we are learning our lessons well. (Cardinal, 1969, pp. 107–8)

In the wake of the failed Indian policy of 1969, the attitudes and activities among Aboriginal peoples and their supporters began to reflect a growing self-confidence. Along with the emergence and growth of state-supported Aboriginal organizations, there was an increase in popular support for organized grass-roots activities such as the Native People's Caravan; the often unpredictable and controversial though communally well-supported actions of the Canadian chapters of the American Indian Movement (AIM) (Long, 1992, pp. 129–30); and numerous community-based protests (Ashini, 1992; Braul, 1992).

Post-1970s Lobbies and Protests

Numerous violent political incidents involving AIM and other Aboriginal organizations during the 1970s and 1980s seemed to fulfil Cardinal's prophecy. It is important to note, however, that most of these incidents were strategically planned: they were not the spontaneous, unexpected occurrences that media and state representatives often made them out to be (York and Pindera, 1992, pp. 414–18). In fact, Aboriginal people often initiated such action only after exhausting other more legitimate means of attempting to bring about change (Gabriel, 1992, p. 171; Penashue, 1992).

By the mid-1970s the idealistic radicalism that had blossomed in the late 1960s and early 1970s had begun to wane. In its stead was an emerging bureaucratic revolution, evidenced by Aboriginal people and their supporters developing more socially and politically astute tactics and strategies that took seriously the practices and interests of those being lobbied. This "professionalization" of Aboriginal leaders, supporters, and organizations during the 1970s further revolutionized Aboriginal–non-Aboriginal relations. From the perspective of many Canadian politicians and Indian Affairs bureaucrats, changes in Aboriginal organizations from an issue-oriented to a more bureaucratic, institutionally based structure provided those organizations with a degree of bureaucratic credibility (Frideres, 1988, p. 282).

However, the compromises that often accompany bureaucratization also led to growing frustration among Aboriginal people and their supporters, who had been trying to bring about radical political and social change (Thompson, 1992). Increased frustration and aggression toward the state were especially apparent during the 1970s and early 1980s as increasing numbers of articulate, outspoken Aboriginal women and men graduated from Canadian and American universities.[5] Armed with a rediscovered respect for the spiritual and cultural dimensions of their peoples' traditions and histories, many of these formally educated young leaders joined with others in blending and alternating legitimate and illegitimate organizational goals and techniques (Frideres, 1988, p. 269). Supporters of Aboriginal rights could now be expected to intersperse their peaceful lobbying, negotiating, and demonstrating activities with violent political action. Although the targets of their non-violent and violent actions have varied — including logging and other private companies, the military, non-Aboriginal communities, and at times factions within their own communities — the primary concern of these and other Aboriginal movement supporters over the past 40 years has been to challenge the policies and practices used by state representatives to gain Aboriginal consent to state rule (Thompson, 1992, pp. 174–75).

Challenging the state has been both difficult and costly for Aboriginal peoples and their supporters, due in large part to what has become a culturally and structurally ingrained process and state of internal colonization. Representatives of the Canadian state have adopted a variety of policies and practices that have contributed to internal colonization, including publicly supporting Aboriginal sovereignty by negotiating treaties with First Nations peoples while at the same time assuming the fundamental principle of Crown sovereignty (Boldt, 1993, p. 5); isolating Aboriginal people socially and geographically on reserves (Dickason, 1993, p. 257); conducting socio-cultural indoctrination through residential schooling and subsequent political co-optation of key Aboriginal leaders (Hammersmith, 1992, p. 55); and widening the division between bands and tribes by sponsoring competitive, specialized funding programs for community development projects and research into specific tribal histories for land-claims arguments (Frideres, 1988, p. 286). According to Gabriel (1992, p. 166), Aboriginal peoples in Canada have not had meaningful control of their lands, funds, business interactions, or educational, social, community, and local-government activities for well over a century. Although the federal government's stated goal for its Aboriginal wards has long been full and equal participation in Canadian society, it appears that the politics of segregation enshrined in the Indian Acts of 1876 and 1951 continued to result in the political, legal, cultural, and social marginality of Canada's Aboriginal peoples (Erasmus, 1989, p. 295). It is in the face of deeply ingrained colonialist perspectives and practices that Aboriginal peoples have continued to organize against the policies, legislation, and practices of European colonization (Long, 1995, p. 48).

The most widely publicized action by Aboriginal peoples in the past 40 years was the Oka crisis.[6] During the summer of 1990, the Mohawks of Kanasetaké engaged in an armed stand-off with the Canadian military on the grounds that extending a local golf course onto their land would break an agreement between the government of Quebec and the Mohawk people. This confrontation received unprecedented national and international attention (York and Pindera, 1992). But it was by no means the only occasion in Canada on which police or army personnel were dispatched to quell potential Aboriginal uprisings (Long, 1992, p. 127). Recent examples of such conflict include the 30-day armed stand-off in fall 1995 near Gustafsen Lake, B.C., between the RCMP and about 30 Shuswap Indians fighting for land that the Shuswap claim is sacred Aboriginal land. Around the same time, an RCMP officer shot and killed a 17-year-old Aboriginal youth involved in a blockade in Ipperwash Provincial Park, Ontario.[7]

These and many other examples illustrate the preparedness of Aboriginal people and their supporters to engage in counter-hegemonic activity.

Various expressions of social and political activism also highlight the tension that has characterized Aboriginal–state relations since the arrival of the European explorers. In response to increased activism involving Aboriginal peoples and their supporters, the RCMP described the Aboriginal movement in 1974 as the single greatest threat to national security. Although this may now be viewed as a rather gross overstatement, what the RCMP does appear to have understood was that those with relatively little power can and do resort to both violence and non-violence in attempts to bring about change (Gurr, 1970, pp. 210–12). By contrast, others, including Prime Minister Trudeau, dismissed the early militant outbursts as insignificant actions by a small and desperate group of extremists (York, 1989, p. 251). While the Trudeau assessment may have contained a grain of truth — certainly many such incidents did reflect a degree of desperation — a more critical interpretation would view the social and political activism of Aboriginal peoples and their supporters as strategic means of defending Aboriginal rights and bringing to light the economic, legal, and political injustices that most Aboriginal people in Canada experience every day of their lives (Thompson, 1992, p. 174).

THE LUBICON COALITION

Historical Context of Coalition Support

One segment of the Aboriginal movement that has not taken a violent counter-hegemonic path has been the (now international) coalition in support of the Lubicon Lake First Nation. According to John Goddard (1991), the dispute between members of the Lubicon Lake First Nation and federal and provincial government representatives is one of the longest standing land-rights disputes in Canadian history. For a variety of reasons, the Lubicon were not included in an 1899 treaty signed by the federal government and numerous other Cree bands in northern and central Alberta. As a result, the Lubicon were essentially ignored by government representatives until band status was granted to them in 1940. Although the government of Alberta agreed to provide about 65 square kilometres of land for a reserve at that time, the land was never transferred to the Lubicon (see Figure 13.1). During the 1940s, Malcolm McCrimmon of Indian Affairs removed more than 700 people from the treaty lists of northern Alberta. This resulted in the elimination of those peoples' rights as Indians and served to cut "official" Lubicon band membership almost in half.[8] Furthermore, oil exploration and production in

FIGURE 13.1
The Lubicon Land Dispute

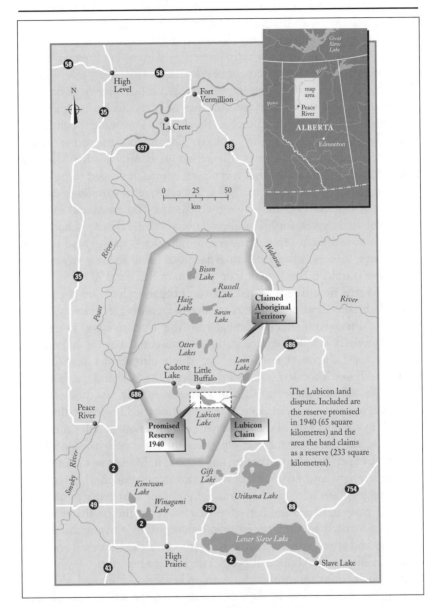

Sources: "Lubicon Claim Exaggerated," *Edmonton Journal*, 8 November 1991; *Calgary Herald*/Paul Van Ginkel, 1988.

the area began in the late 1950s. In the early 1960s, residents of a Lubicon community in Marten River were moved to nearby Cadotte Lake to allow oil companies to begin drilling. Although many residents were reportedly unhappy with the move, Marten River was bulldozed before the people were able to return home (Goddard, 1991).

In 1977, the passing of retroactive legislation by Premier Peter Lougheed enabled the government of Alberta to win a court case against the Lubicon, who were still attempting to fight oil development on land they claimed was theirs. Despite warnings of "genocidal consequences" from the World Council of Churches, the Alberta government continued to challenge the claims of the Lubicon. This included ignoring, along with their federal counterparts, the report of Federal Justice Minister Davie Fulton, which stated that a generous approach needed to be taken to settle such a "grave injustice."[9] The federal government did eventually offer the Lubicon $45 million, which the Lubicon countered in 1988 with a detailed request for $70 million. Lubicon Chief Bernard Ominayak met with government representatives on numerous occasions to resolve the dispute, although these meetings failed to bring about a satisfactory resolution (Lubicon Settlement Commission of Review, 1993).

During this time international attention began to focus on the plight of the Lubicon. Coalition support for the Lubicon began growing in response to a massive publicity campaign by the Toronto-based Friends of the Lubicon (FOL). The campaign raised awareness that the harvesting of trees on Lubicon-claimed land by the multinational corporation Daishowa Forest Products was destroying both the land and the Lubicon way of life. While support for the Lubicon grew rapidly, coalition support did not emerge in a vacuum. One way of viewing the Lubicon coalition is to see it as a microcosm of the movement of indigenous peoples throughout the world, a movement that embodies the spirit and vision of those who have experienced colonization and oppose it. Moreover, understanding the strength and character of coalition support for the Lubicon requires taking into account how and why potential supporters identify with the people, ideas, and activities that make up the coalition in the first place, which in turn necessitates examining the overarching perspectives and specific interests that have informed the historical and cultural movements of Aboriginal peoples and their supporters.

Although countless conflicts have arisen between Aboriginal and non-Aboriginal people since the days of first contact, the willingness of people to align themselves with the Lubicon coalition has not depended primarily on supporters having a clear understanding of the place of Aboriginal peoples in Canadian history. Even those unfamiliar with the specific history and circumstances of Aboriginal people in general, and the Lubicon in particular, are probably aware of the presence of dissatisfied Aboriginal peoples in Canada during the past few decades. The growing awareness throughout Canada of Aboriginal issues is both a reflection and result of media coverage of Aboriginal issues and activities, regardless of whether people agree with the actions of Elijah Harper, the Mohawks of Kanesetaké, protesters at Ipperwash and Gustaffson Lake, and others. But unfortunately for Aboriginal people in Canada, mass media coverage of Aboriginal issues and activities, according to Marc Grenier (1992, p. 274) "has probably operated more as a steadfast obstacle to ... mutual cultural acceptance and co-operation."

Ironically, one of the difficulties facing those who want to mobilize support for the Lubicon and other Aboriginal peoples is that a majority of Canadians recognize that Aboriginal issues now touch all areas of Canadian life. It appears that increased awareness of the complexity of Aboriginal issues and interests, rather than spurring more interest and involvement, may result in reducing grass-roots coalition support. As Peter Hamel (1994, p. 35) notes, it is much harder to mobilize people around the constitution than it is to mobilize them around a pipeline or a dam. Apathy on the part of many non-Aboriginal people in Canada toward Aboriginal issues also suggests that colonial attitudes die hard. The problem, however, cannot be reduced to media manipulation of Aboriginal issues or racially motivated apathy on the part of non-Aboriginal Canadians. Although many continue to ignore or oppose the interests of Aboriginal peoples, others actively support them. Clearly, factors other than how the media frames certain issues and events or the attitudes people hold toward their own or others' racial/ethnic heritage contribute to support for the counter-hegemonic visions and activities of Aboriginal peoples and their supporters. One important factor that has contributed to the strength and growth of the Lubicon coalition is its international reach.

International Context of Coalition Support

Although the boycott organized against Daishowa by the FOL emerged within Canada, international support for the Lubicon suggests the existence of similar coalitions and "parent" movements elsewhere (Jhappan, 1992, pp. 73, 80). The two global, socio-historical movements that played a fundamental role in the growth of the coalition are the indigenous peoples and environmental movements. Although coalition supporters and opponents living outside of Canada may have little or no direct contact with the Lubicon, they are informed by global awareness and activity networks that seek to redress the myriad problems associated with colonialism and environmental degradation. The theoretical and political significance of these global movements is that they provide two master frames of reference used by Aboriginal and non-Aboriginal people in relation to the plight of the Lubicon. Some of the more prominent, internationally based Lubicon coalition organizations that are part of the worldwide indigenous peoples' movement are the Coordinated Indigenous Affairs Working Groups (Belgium), National Christian Council (Japan), Innu Support Groups (Netherlands), Munich Society for Endangered Peoples (Germany), Plains Indian Cultural Survival School (United States), Working Circle for North American Indians (Vienna), and Survival International (London). Coalition organizations with an environmental agenda include the German Green Party, Rainforest Action Network (Europe), Friends of the Earth (United States), Iwerliewen (Luxembourg), Big Mountain Action Group (Germany), Synesthetics, Inc. (United States), Bund (Germany), and Greenpeace (United States and international bases). Although coalition support obviously ebbs and flows, well over 100 separate organizations have supported the Lubicon over the past ten years.

Certain differences in perspective and interest among coalition members would appear to make it difficult for co-ordinating groups like the FOL to build and uphold a common sense of purpose and identity for the coalition. Hunt, Benford, and Snow (1994, p. 186) assert that social movement actors tend to cluster around relatively stable, socially constructed identity fields: protagonists support movement values, beliefs, goals, and practices; antagonists oppose the efforts of protagonists; and audiences are uncommitted or neutral observers. Since, as Gusfield (1994, pp. 64–65) notes, the "ties that bind or separate" coalition antagonists, protagonists, and observers are quite precarious and fluid, understanding the strength and the character of the coalition depends on a closer examination of how and why people actually support or oppose it.

Supporters' Perspectives on Coalition Involvement

Problems associated with colonialism and the efforts by Aboriginal people and their supporters to address them are often understood in primarily political and legal terms. For example, Sally Weaver (1981) argues that it is essential to acknowledge the special status of the original occupants of a territory if we hope to restore the political and legal rights and entitlements of Aboriginal peoples. Accordingly, she asserts that the most critical issues associated with Aboriginal rights pertain to establishing separate political and legal jurisdiction and a land base. Many Lubicon coalition supporters view the problems of the Lubicon within this type of political and legal framework, and much activity by federal and Alberta government representatives has focussed on challenging the political and legal interests of the Lubicon. However, Lubicon supporters who view things from within this perspective do not necessarily understand or even identify with the fundamental concerns and claims of the Lubicon. Although focussing on political, legal, and even land issues is vital, other coalition supporters claim that the essence of Lubicon identity and Lubicon land-rights claims rests on the spiritual and cultural dimensions of "being" Lubicon.

In contrast to those who focus on the political and legal dimensions of social movement ideologies and activities, Alain Touraine (1981) has argued that hegemonic and counter-hegemonic conflict is fundamentally a conflict between alternate visions of the state. In this respect, Aboriginal people have developed an alternative vision for their place in Canada by defining their political and legal concerns and activities in spiritual terms (Long, 1992). Generally, many Aboriginal people acknowledge that a balanced life is one that honours the laws of both the spiritual and physical dimensions of reality (Bopp et al., 1984, p. 27). As Stan McKay (1992, p. 30) notes: "The vision that moves us in the struggle toward Aboriginal sovereignty is integral to our spirituality. The elders speak to us of our need for balance between the physical and spiritual aspects of our being. They would caution our political leaders not to become so caught up in the struggle for power that they compromise the spiritual heritage that shaped our being."

McKay's comments suggest that coalition supporters' ability to understand the concerns of the Lubicon depends on their ability to understand and acknowledge that the vision of political and legal sovereignty for the Lubicon is part of a larger spiritual vision. Comments and activities by supporters representing the Oblate Missionary Society, the United Church of Canada, the Aboriginal Rights Coalition, the Edmonton Interchurch Committee for Aboriginal Rights, the Society for Endangered Peoples, Catholic Action for Native America, and many other similar organizations suggest that awareness of the relationship between the spiritual and the political is central to the vision of those whose view of human life transcends physical and cultural dimensions. In a letter to Prime Minister Brian Mulroney, representatives from Catholic Action for Native America stated: "It is unfortunate that ... the government of Canada ... refuses to accept the legal and moral implications of the fact that the Lubicon nation has never ceded any of its ancestral territory."[10]

These and other such groups view the pursuit of justice for the Lubicon as the spiritual tie that binds many coalition members.

Numerous visions of and for social change in relation to the Lubicon situation are also very pragmatic and concrete. For example, a 1993 press release from the Rainforest Action Network (RAN) warned: "If the Alberta government doesn't significantly modify existing agreements with Diashowa and Al-Pac — which is majority-owned by Mitsubishi — we will at the request of provincial environmental groups call for a worldwide boycott of tourism in this province until changes are made which could begin as early as 1994." RAN support for the Lubicon in the form of an Alberta tourism boycott was based on their concern over the enormous area covered by logging agreements (about one-third of the province), the fragile ecosystem in the province with its shallow soil and short growing season, Al-Pac's expansion of pulp and paper production, and the pace of logging. Unlike those concerned with protecting the political, legal, or spiritual interests of the Lubicon, the focus of RAN and similar groups was to fight against abuse of the environment and to "help groups develop non-destructive, sustainable alternatives that will provide Albertans with jobs while protecting their beautiful, vital and fragile world."

Inviting difference is thus an important aspect of coalition activity. This supports the view of Antonio Melucci (1989, p. 18), who notes that neither social movements nor the many coalitions that comprise them are concrete, homogeneous entities. In fact, Melucci argues that the appearance of a unity of identity and purpose within social movements is more a social science construction than a reality for movement participants. Just as there are beliefs and practices that serve to unify coalition supporters, so too there are beliefs, interests, and practices that potentially divide them.

Relationships between Framing Perspectives and Specific Interests

Given their historical and socio-cultural differences, it is difficult to identify precisely what ties Lubicon coalition supporters together. A first step in attempting to do so involves distinguishing between the overarching perspectives and concrete interests of those involved. Generally, Lubicon coalition members believe that the Lubicon deserve to be treated in a just manner by governments in Canada and that government representatives should do their part in settling the Lubicon land claims. However, coalition supporters such as the Society for Endangered Peoples, Innu Support Groups, Austrian Society for Endangered Peoples, Working Circle for North American Indians, Assembly of First Nations, Aboriginal Rights

Coalition, Native Women's Association of Canada, and National Association of Japanese Canadians view the government's "abuse of this small group of Aboriginal people [as] an outright violation of nationally and internationally accepted human rights principles."[11]

Other coalition members emphasize that the injustice experienced by the Lubicon reflects that hegemonic agents are more concerned with economic gain than respecting the relationship between humans and their natural environments. Such environmentally focussed groups as the Rainforest Action Network, Earthkeepers, Greenpeace, Friends of the Earth, Iwerliewen, Big Mountain Action Group, Synesthetics, Friends of Athabascan Environmental Association, Northern Light, and Environment Probe assert that the physical environment ought to be respected and nurtured. Although these supporters of the Lubicon coalition also share a desire to protect the environment from what they regard as the destructive log-harvesting practices of Daishowa, their primary interest is to "protect and preserve wildlife and the natural environment."[12] Outside of their involvement in the Lubicon coalition, many of these groups and organizations engage in international lobbying efforts to establish parks and animal sanctuaries. In contrast, the Lubicon have stated that their main concern and hope is to negotiate a land-claim settlement with the provincial government of Alberta and the federal government of Canada that would essentially allow them to do as they wish with their land. On more than one occasion, Lubicon representatives have stated their intention to negotiate business agreements with companies such as Diashowa and Al-Pac once their land-claim dispute is resolved. Thus, although environmentally concerned coalition members currently support the Lubicon, it is not difficult to envision a future clash between these same environmentalists and the Lubicon over the appropriate use of land if and when a land-claim settlement is reached.

As Berger and Luckmann (1967) note, overarching meaning systems are often comprised of discrete beliefs. These overarching systems, which they term "plausibility structures," are malleable systems of belief and practice that enable collectivities like the Lubicon and their coalition supporters to make sense of the Lubicon situation in broad, everyday terms. The Lubicon-focussed plausibility structure that coalition supporters operate within is informed by religious, environmental, business, philosophical, and economic interests and perspectives. While one could argue that differences in perspective and purpose are the lifeblood of a given coalition or social movement, such differences also contribute to the precarious nature of the identities and activities of those involved.

The "Problem" of Difference

Representatives of the Edmonton Interchurch Committee on Aboriginal Rights, Aboriginal Rights Coalition, Assembly of First Nations, and Native Women's Association of Canada view what happens politically and legally to the Lubicon in spiritual terms.[13] Environmental groups such as Friends of the Earth, Bund, Greenpeace, and Big Mountain Action Group often use similar language, although their primary concern is to convey the message that humans must learn to respect the natural environment. In contrast, businesses such as Roots Canada, Knechtel's Grocery Wholesaling, and The Body Shop assert that Daishowa's logging practices are unacceptable because they contribute to the degradation of the environment, which also occurs at the expense of the Lubicon's well-being. In a somewhat different vein, organizations such as Kentucky Fried Chicken, Maison Du Fromage, the YWCA, and NOW magazine supported the coalition boycott of Daishowa paper products because of the corporation's apparent concern with making money at the expense of basic human rights.

Somewhat different interests were reflected in the willingness of businesses that joined the coalition boycott in order to prevent similar boycotts from being organized against their businesses. In November 1991, for example, the Toronto-based Pizza Pizza chain initially refused to "take sides" in the Lubicon dispute. Representatives of the company stated that they were convinced that Diashowa was negotiating with the Lubicon and the government of Alberta in good faith. During their subsequent three months of discussion with FOL boycott organizers, Pizza Pizza was a target of the boycott. Although the company eventually joined the Lubicon coalition by honouring the boycott of Daishowa, the changing tone and content of letters from the company's president to FOL representatives indicate that its interest in doing so was primarily an economically motivated business decision.[14]

That there can be major differences among coalition members has important implications for understanding coalition activity. Although supporters of the Lubicon coalition have many different perspectives on and interests in being involved, such differences may or may not contribute to weakening coalition activity. Nonetheless, failure to take the diversity of coalition and movement supporters into account can lead to distorted, even mythical pictures of coalitions and of the larger movements of which they are a part. Since even the smallest coalitions give expression to a diversity of beliefs, perspectives, and interests that are themselves open to challenge and change, counter-hegemonic coalitions and the larger social movements that encompass them are inherently fragile.

Coalitions and movements are highly complex phenomena that reflect the coming together and movement of diverse groups of people. In this regard the crystallization of beliefs, sentiments, and activities into what we have referred to as the Lubicon coalition is much more than a collection of people fighting against injustice: both the Lubicon coalition and the larger Aboriginal social movement fundamentally represent the dynamic movements of diverse people who have decided to contend for their alternate visions of the state. That counter-hegemonic agents agree on certain fundamental issues and interests does not guarantee success, for equally fundamental concerns and interests can easily become sources of division and conflict. Indeed, the often successful application of divide-and-conquer tactics by coalition and movement opponents (Frideres, 1988, p. 286) attests to their understanding that support for counter-hegemonic coalitions and movements is a precarious phenomenon.

Even though hegemonic forces may appear monolithic, they are similarly comprised of individuals and groups holding many different beliefs, perspectives, interests, and goals. Because coalition and movement antagonists undoubtedly have different reasons for supporting the status quo, their apparent unity is as subject to the same sources of disruption and change that threaten the coalitions and social movements they oppose. In short, although social movements appear to be a case of "us against them," unity of vision and activity involving supporters or opponents of large-scale social change is a precarious phenomenon. Predicting the directions that hegemonic or counter-hegemonic activities will take in relation to the Aboriginal peoples movement in Canada is thereby difficult for a number of reasons, including the subtlety and diversity of social action; disagreements within hegemonic and counter-hegemonic camps over beliefs, perspectives, tactics, and goals; and the frequent lack of predictable, concrete public support for hegemonic or counter-hegemonic ideas and activities.

CONCLUSION

Aboriginal peoples in Canada have been socially and politically active for thousands of years. The countless expressions of counter-hegemonic activity involving Aboriginal peoples and their supporters over the past 40 or so years are thus properly seen as much more than idiosyncratic, knee-jerk reactions to isolated experiences of government or corporate colonialism. For a variety of reasons, Aboriginal peoples in Canada continue to choose different paths of resistance to state-induced hegemony. The development of a militant agenda that expressed itself in an often violent manner during the 1970s and into the 1980s was for many Aboriginal people a matter of survival (York, 1989, pp. 260–61). During the 1990s, violent confrontations between Natives and state representatives at Oka, Gustafsen Lake, and Ipperwash Provincial Park illustrate that militant expressions of counter-hegemonic activity are likely to continue. Clearly, such militancy is in contrast to the more diplomatic resistance exhibited by Native M.P. Elijah Harper in his stand against the Meech Lake Accord in 1991.

In general, the Lubicon coalition and the Aboriginal movement involve the actions and reactions of those wanting to challenge ideas, policies, laws, and organized activities that perpetuate what they view as injustice against Aboriginal people in Canada. As we have seen, similarities and differences among coalition and social movement protagonists and antagonists are important to the success or failure of social movements and coalitions. Protagonists and antagonists potentially hold many different perspectives on the purpose of human life and why they support or oppose a specific social movement, they become involved in counter-hegemonic or hegemonic activities for a wide variety of reasons, and they often have very different interests at stake in the success or failure of a given social movement.

Social movements and the many coalitions that give them definition and "movement" must therefore be understood as historical phenomena in which countless factors interact. Understanding why coalitions and larger social movements exist, fail, or succeed depends on understanding them in historical context and in terms of their particular social make-up and interpersonal dynamics. Making sense of the Aboriginal social movement in Canada thus means placing it in the context of the complex history of Aboriginal–white relations both before and after Confederation, of the unique overarching perspectives and specific interests of the people involved, and of how protagonists and antagonists are linked to those who support or oppose the more global indigenous peoples and environmental protection movements.

Mobilizing and maintaining large-scale support for alternative visions of the state is a complex, precarious task. One ever-present difficulty faced by social movement supporters is taking into account the challenge of hegemonic and apathetic forces from without, as well as potential sources of division and conflict from within. Given the profound differences in the perspectives and interests of Native social movement supporters in general and Lubicon coalition members in particular, active support for the Lubicon and other Aboriginal peoples will undoubtedly wane with the settling of their land claims. Diminution of active support for Aboriginal peoples will also likely occur as other Aboriginal concerns and interests are addressed to the satisfaction of those involved.

The diminution or potential dissolving of support for the Lubicon and other Aboriginal peoples raises the important question of how the relationships between social systems, social movements, coalitions, and individual social actors in an increasingly globalizing network of counter-hegemonic activity ought to be understood and addressed. In a world in which active support for alternate visions of the state can apparently emerge as quickly as it can disappear, understanding the "big picture" of coalition and social movement activity requires taking into account their highly complex and thoroughly precarious character. Indeed, the challenge to understand this and other "big pictures" holds for all who want both to prevent the violence and confrontation that has characterized much of Canada's past and to work toward a common, peaceful, and just vision for the country's future. In brief, healing past wounds and building a vision of hope for all people who live in Canada will occur to the extent that people express a willingness to honour the particular visions of their hearts that seek understanding, celebrate diversity, and embrace the pursuit of justice.

NOTES

1. See Ted Robert Gurr's description of the "peaceable kingdom" thesis in Gurr (1995, pp. viii–x).
2. Excerpt of letter from Friends of the Lubicon representative Kevin Thomas to Diashowa Canada Company Ltd. President Mr. Tom Hamaoka, 6 November 1991.
3. Hunt, Benford, and Snow (1994, pp. 1231–32) view such occurrences in terms of motivational framing, a process that involves stabilizing and articulating Aboriginal and other social movement identities. The consequence of this process, which involves social movement supporters constructing and internalizing common motives and identities, is that social movement supporters become motivated to act collectively.
4. Genocide has long been defined as the systematic killing or extermination of a whole people or nation. During the 1960s, cultural genocide was used to describe the profoundly destructive socio-cultural consequences of European colonization in relation to the lives of Aboriginal peoples in Canada.
5. Ironically, most of the leaders of the Pan-Indian (political) movements that rose to prominence during the 1970s and early 1980s were the products of state-sponsored and church-run residential schools (Tennant, 1990, pp. 81, 139–40).
6. Equally important as Oka, Clayoquot Sound, Ipperwash, and elsewhere is how and why the mainstream media selectively cover news involving

Aboriginal peoples and issues. See, for example, Grenier's (1992, pp. 273–99) critical analysis of media framing of "the Oka crisis."

7. That the Grand Chief of the Assembly of First Nations, Ovide Mercredi, met with the Shuswap to encourage and support them to resolve their dispute with police peacefully, and that the Shuswap afforded Mercredi a cold reception, illustrates that Aboriginal people can and do disagree over strategies and tactics to effect change. Although Mercredi agreed with the Shuswap that Aboriginal peoples in Canada have long experienced injustice, his statement to them and to the media was that "I disagree with the use of violence as a means of getting justice" (*The Edmonton Journal*, 25 August 1995, p. A3). In an interview on CBC's 11 September 1995 "Journal Newsmagazine," Mercredi clarified his position. He stated that while he supports peaceful negotiation, politicians and others in Canada need to be aware that the escalation of violence by militant Aboriginal people is understandable and warranted if state representatives continue to refuse to take the concerns of Aboriginal people seriously.

8. This was clearly in the government's interest, because the amount of land and money offered by the government to settle Aboriginal land-rights disputes was (and continues to be) tied directly to the number of band members on the band membership list.

9. The provincial government's position was supported by an Alberta judge, who ruled against the claim filed by the Lubicon Lake First Nation that their way of life was being destroyed. The reason given by the judge for his ruling was that current and proposed development of Lubicon-claimed land affected only a few individuals.

10. Letter, 14 January 1993.

11. Letter, National Association of Japanese Canadians to Prime Minister Brian Mulroney, 10 May 1993.

12. Letter, Big Mountain Action Group to Daishowa, 16 April 1993.

13. We must be careful not to oversimplify the workings of the Lubicon (or any other) coalition by suggesting that all those with spiritual (or other) perspectives share the same material visions and interests. As Hamel (1994, pp. 22–23) notes, religiously based coalitions are not exempt from experiencing intense conflict and debate from within over concrete interests and goals.

14. Press release, Friends of the Lubicon, 28 January 1992.

DISCUSSION QUESTIONS

1. What different reasons do Aboriginal people give for the relationship between the colonization of Aboriginal peoples in Canada and the current Aboriginal peoples movements in this country?

2. How do you view the relationship between the socio-economic conditions of life for Aboriginal people and the Aboriginal peoples movement? Do you think socio-economic conditions are the main determining factor in life satisfaction? Why or why not? What

might be some other factors that contribute to people being satisfied with life?

3. In trying to make sense of the Lubicon Coalition, how do you see the relationships between what supporters believe, how they view what is important in life, and what their specific interests are?

4. What do you think holds social movement supporters and opponents together in the face of their sometimes highly divergent perspectives, experiences, and interests?

FURTHER READINGS

Cornell, Stephen. 1988. *The Return of the Native: American Indian Political Resurgence*. New York: Oxford University Press. A sweeping analysis of Native American social and political activism.

Engelstad, Diane and John Bird, eds. 1992. *Nation to Nation: Aboriginal Sovereignty and the Future of Canada*. Toronto: Anansi. Wide variety of thoughtful articles by Aboriginal and non-Aboriginal writers on points of agreement and tension between Aboriginal and non-Aboriginal people in Canada.

Goddard, John. 1991. *Last Stand of the Lubicon Cree*. Toronto: Stoddart. A challenging and insightful journalistic case study of what can happen when the interests of Aboriginal people and Canadian government representatives collide.

Kelly, M.T. 1987. *A Dream Like Mine*. Toronto: Stoddart. A haunting allegory of Aboriginal and non-Aboriginal worlds clashing in violent, unpredictable ways.

Silman, Janet. 1987. *Enough Is Enough: Aboriginal Women Speak Out*. Toronto: Women's Press. Thoughtfully narrated discussion of the struggles and victories of women involved with the Tobique Women's Political Action Group. Splendid example of oral history research and writing.

REFERENCES

Ashini, Napes. 1992. "Nitassinan: Caribou and F-16s," Pp. 120–29 in *Nation to Nation: Aboriginal Sovereignty and the Future of Canada*, ed. Diane Engelstad and John Bird. Toronto: Anansi Press.

Berger, Peter and Thomas Luckmann. 1967. *The Social Construction of Reality*. Garden City, NY: Doubleday.

Boldt, Menno. 1993. *Surviving as Indians: The Challenge of Self-Government*. Toronto: University of Toronto Press.

Bopp, Judie, Michael Bopp, Lee Brown, and Phil Lane (compilers). 1984. *The Sacred Tree*. Lethbridge, Alta.: Four Worlds Development Publishers.

Braul, Waldemar. 1992. "Ingenika Point: No More Riverboats," Pp. 147–58 in *Nation to Nation: Aboriginal Sovereignty and the Future of Canada*, ed. Diane Engelstad and John Bird. Toronto: Anansi Press.

Canada, Department of Indian Affairs and Northern Development (DIAND). 1969. *Statement on Indian Policy, 1969* (The White Paper). Ottawa: Supply and Services.

Cardinal, Harold. 1969. *The Unjust Society*. Edmonton: Hurtig.

Dickason, Olive Patricia. 1993. *Canada's First Nations: A History of Founding People from the Earliest Times*. Toronto: McClelland & Stewart.

Erasmus, George. 1989. "Epilogue." Pp. 295–302 in *Drum Beat: Anger and Renewal in Indian Country*, ed. Boyce Richardson. Toronto: Summerhill Press.

Fort Good Hope Community Council. 1992. "Regaining Control at Fort Good Hope." Pp. 133–46 in *Nation to Nation: Aboriginal Sovereignty and the Future of Canada*, eds. Diane Engelstad and John Bird. Toronto: Anansi Press.

Frideres, James. 1988. *Native Peoples in Canada: Contemporary Conflicts*, 3rd. ed. Scarborough, Ont.: Prentice-Hall.

Gabriel, Ellen. 1992. "Kanesatake: The Summer of 1990." Pp. 165–72 in *Nation to Nation: Aboriginal Sovereignty and the Future of Canada*, ed. Diane Engelstad and John Bird. Toronto: Anansi Press.

Goddard, John. 1991. *Last Stand of the Lubicon Cree*. Toronto: Stoddart.

Grenier, Marc. 1992. "The Centrality of Conflict in Native Indian Coverage by the Montreal *Gazette*: War Zoning the Oka Incident." Pp. 273–99 in *Critical Studies of Canadian Mass Media*, ed. Marc Grenier. Toronto: Butterworths.

Gurr, Ted Robert. 1970. *Why Men Rebel*. Princeton, N.J: Princeton University Press.

———. 1995. "Foreword." Pp. viii–xvii in *Violence in Canada: Sociopolitical Perspectives*, ed. Jeffrey Ian Ross. Don Mills, Ont.: Oxford University Press.

Gusfield, Joseph R. 1994. "The Reflexivity of Social Movements: Collective Behavior and Mass Society Theory Revisited." Pp. 58–78 in *New Social Movements: From Ideology to Identity*, ed. Enrique Larana, Hank Johnston, and Joseph R. Gusfield. Philadelphia: Temple University Press.

Hamel, Peter. 1994. "The Aboriginal Rights Coalition." Pp. 16–36 in *Coalitions for Justice: The Story of Canada's Interchurch Coalitions*, ed. Christopher Lind and Joe Mihevc. Ottawa: Novalis.

Hammersmith, Bernice. 1992. "Aboriginal Women and Self-Government." Pp. 53–59 in *Nation to Nation: Aboriginal Sovereignty and the Future of Canada*, ed. Diane Engelstad and John Bird. Toronto: Anansi Press.

Hunt, Scott A., Robert D. Benford, and David A. Snow. 1994. "Identity Fields: Framing Processes and the Social Construction of Movement Identities."

Pp. 185–208 in *New Social Movements: From Ideology to Identity*, ed. Enrique Larana, Hank Johnston, and Joseph R. Gusfield. Philadelphia: Temple University Press.

Indian Association of Alberta. 1970. *Citizens Plus*. Edmonton: Indian Association of Alberta.

Jhappan, C. Radha. 1992. "Global Community? Supra-National Strategies of Canada's Aboriginal Peoples." *Journal of Indigenous Studies* 3(1) (Winter): 59–97.

Long, David. 1992. "Culture, Ideology and Militancy: The Movement of Indians in Canada 1969–1991." Pp. 118–34 in *Organizing Dissent: Contemporary Social Movements in Theory and Practice*, ed. W. Carroll. Toronto: Garamond.

———. 1993. "Oldness and Newness in the Movement of Canada's Native Peoples." Paper presented to the Society for Socialist Studies, Learned Societies Conference. Ottawa: Carleton University.

———. 1995. "On Violence and Healing: Aboriginal Experiences, 1969–1994." Pp. 40–77 in *Violence in Canada: Sociopolitical Perspectives*, ed. Jeffrey Ian Ross. Don Mills, Ont.: Oxford University Press.

Lubicon Settlement Commission. 1993. *Final Report*. Edmonton, Alta.: Lubicon Settlement Commission.

Macpherson, Judge J. 1998. "Judgement on Daishowa and Friends of the Lubicon, Kevin Thomas, Ed Bianchi, Stephen Kenda, Jane Doe, John Doe, and Persons Unknown." 14 April. Court file no. 95-CQ-59797. Toronto, Ont.

McKay, Stan. 1992. "Calling Creation into Our Family." Pp. 28–34 in *Nation to Nation: Aboriginal Sovereignty and the Future of Canada*, ed. Diane Engelstad and John Bird. Toronto: Anansi Press.

Melucci, Antonio. 1989. *Nomads of the Present: Social Movements and Individual Needs in Contemporary Society*. Philadelphia: Temple University Press.

Penashue, Peter. 1992. "Nitassinan: Nation to Nation." Pp. 129–32 in *Nation to Nation: Aboriginal Sovereignty and the Future of Canada*, ed. Diane Engelstad and John Bird. Toronto: Anansi Press.

Ponting, J. Rick, ed. 1986. *Arduous Journey: Canadian Indians and Decolonization*. Toronto: Butterworths.

Royal Commission on Aboriginal Peoples (RCAP). 1996. *Restructuring the Relationship*. Ottawa: Supply and Services.

Silman, Janet. 1987. *Enough Is Enough: Aboriginal Women Speak Out*. Toronto: Women's Press.

Tennant, Paul. 1990. *Aboriginal People and Politics: The Indian Land Question in British Columbia, 1849–1989*. Vancouver: University of British Columbia Press.

Thompson, Loran. 1992. "Fighting Back." Pp. 173–78 in *Nation to Nation: Aboriginal Sovereignty and the Future of Canada*, ed. Diane Engelstad and John Bird. Toronto: Anansi Press.

Touraine, Alain. 1981. *The Voice and the Eye: An Analysis of Social Movements*. Trans. Alan Duff. Cambridge: Cambridge University Press.

Weaver, Sally. 1981. *Making Canadian Indian Policy*. Toronto: University of Toronto Press.

York, Geoffrey. 1989. *The Dispossessed: Life and Death in Native Canada*. London: Vintage Press.

York, Geoffrey and Loreen Pindera. 1992. *The People of the Pines*. Toronto: Little, Brown and Company (Canada).

CHAPTER 14

Aboriginal Peoples' Vision of the Future: Interweaving Traditional Knowledge and New Technologies

Simon Brascoupé

In the past century, the locus of Aboriginal peoples' economic activity has shifted from the primary sector to the service sector. In some regions, this transformation occurred in only the past quarter-century. The end result is that Aboriginal peoples in Canada have been pushed to the margins economically and socially. Will this continue to be the pattern for the future? Can we put an end to this trend?

Since the 1970s, Aboriginal peoples' political and economic influence has been growing in Canada. This new, although limited, autonomy provides Aboriginal peoples with an opportunity to build a new economic, cultural, and social sustainable future. This chapter argues that through education, training, planning, and traditional knowledge, Aboriginal peoples can expand upon an economical and environmental strategy that consists of seven elements:

1. education based on science, technology, and traditional knowledge
2. training directed toward the environment, leading-edge technology, and resource management
3. developing traditional knowledge institutions controlled by Aboriginal peoples
4. policy and development support for Aboriginal environmental employment strategies
5. resource planning based on traditional knowledge and supportive technologies such as remote sensing and geographic information systems (GIS)
6. developing partnerships between Aboriginal communities, universities, colleges, and governments
7. short-term education, training, and internship programs supported by federal and provincial governments to attract Aboriginal peoples into key sectors of environmental fields, including business, resource management, research, and science

Change for the coming generations of Aboriginal peoples is likely to be just as dramatic as the change from the fur trade to the industrial age. This time, though, there appears to be a number of favourable conditions for Aboriginal peoples. First, they have greater political autonomy (self-government and land claims) and therefore are able to negotiate for greater control over their lives and resources. Second, in the current restructuring of the world economy, with its emphasis on resolving the environmental crisis, there is a place for traditional ecological knowledge and perspective. Third, society demands more environmentally sound solutions to production and development, opening the door for Aboriginal knowledge–based resource and environmental solutions. Fourth, there is a growing awareness that a serious national environmental strategy can create employment and growth.

It is now important that Aboriginal peoples regain control over their economy and traditional territories through a strategy that includes sustainable resource harvesting, restoring the environment, land claims, traditional knowledge, and new technologies. There are several sectors in which this strategy would be perfect for Aboriginal peoples to pursue development in the future. Tourism, forestry, business, and new technologies are the main ones reviewed in this chapter.

Communities need to address several barriers in their planning to realize this strategy:

1. lack of understanding of the traditional economy and traditional knowledge of Aboriginal peoples
2. lack of models for strengthening traditional economies as a viable alternative to the present exploitative models of economic development
3. lack of understanding of how to link traditional environmental knowledge and science

Removing the barriers will involve research and education directed at improving Canadians' understanding of Aboriginal peoples' wide use of the environment and resources, as well as validating indigenous knowledge and traditional areas of work such as fishing, hunting, and trapping.

LEARNING FROM ABORIGINAL PEOPLES

This section argues that the world will have to change its basic value system to save the planet. This is not to say that westerners should become like Aboriginal peoples. But Western society needs to learn from indigenous peoples about respecting and living harmoniously with Mother Earth and return to their own religious and spiritual teachings, with their own ancient systems of knowledge, customs, and practices that respect Mother Earth. This process of reflection has emerged into a dialogue between Western society and Aboriginal peoples in the past three decades.

Without a fundamental and profound change in our value systems, culture, and social relations, the survival of human beings is threatened. Evidence of this abounds. Václav Havel, playwright, human rights campaigner, and former president of the Czech Republic (formerly Czechoslovakia), identifies overpopulation, AIDS, the greenhouse effect, holes in the ozone layer, depletion of biodiversity (e.g., fisheries, trees, and medicines), nuclear terrorism, commercial television culture, racism, and the growing threat of regional wars as some of the threats we face at the close of the twentieth century.

Parents may find it disquieting that we have to keep our children out of direct sunlight to prevent skin cancer, but even more worrying is the unknown impact of clear-cutting, fisheries depletion, pollutants, and garbage disposal. Increasing the awareness of and care for the environment by all people, all over the world, is our greatest challenge.

The Seventh Generation

One Aboriginal people's teaching that is having an impact on the world is the Seventh Generation philosophy/prediction. Simply put, it refers to how indigenous peoples make decisions with the Seventh Generation in mind. The present generation is responsible for leaving future generations with a continuous cycle of resources and a habitable and safe environment. This contrasts with Western planners, who once thought they were morally responsible only for a planning period, usually five years.

Aboriginal culture is endowed with a rich diversity of teachings, rituals, and ceremonies that continuously remind us of our responsibility to Mother Earth. When I was 10 years old, I had a garden next to our house on the Tuscarora Indian Nation. It was quite dry, and so I had to water my growing plants every day. I asked my grandmother if she knew of a way I could make it rain. She said I could go and sing in my garden. It did not matter what song I sang, but it would help. I did as she said. I do not remember if it rained, but remember becoming closer to my garden that summer.

Years later when I was doing research, I found there was a song Seneca women sang to Mother Earth apologizing for disturbing her skin, explaining that they needed to cultivate to survive. I have since experienced and learned that indigenous peoples all around the world have this sacred relationship with Mother Earth. This respect, honouring, and

responsibility according to our teaching extends to the Seventh Generation. In the words of Oren Lyons, faithkeeper of the Onondaga Nation:

> In our way of life, in our government, with every decision we make, we
> always keep in mind the Seventh Generation to come. It's our job to see
> that the people coming ahead, the generations still unborn, have a world
> no worse than ours — and hopefully better. When we walk upon Mother
> Earth we always plant our feet carefully because we know the faces of
> our future generations are looking up at us from beneath the ground. We
> never forget them. (Wall and Arden, 1990, p. 68)

The Seventh Generation teaching is also a prophecy that predicts that
the world one day will come to indigenous peoples to relearn how to live
in harmony with the Earth. The prophecy says there will be a time when
the air will make a person's eyes water, a time when the water will be un-
drinkable. It describes large black snakes, which our elders have interpreted as roads, that stretch across the land. The World Commission on
Environment and Development, also known as the Bruntland Commission (WCED, 1987), saw the importance of indigenous teachings and recommended that indigenous peoples be consulted to learn how to live sustainably with the Earth. Indigenous peoples have laws or original
instructions given to them by the Creator. The first principle, "natural
law," identifies the relational quality of all life:

> Our ancestors developed ways and means of relating to each other and
> to the land, based upon simple and pragmatic understanding of their
> presence on this earth. If they failed to consider what the environment
> had to offer, how much it could give, and at what times it was prepared
> to this — they would simply die. This basic law held for every living thing
> on the earth. All living creatures had to be cognizant of the structure of
> the day, the cycle of the seasons, and their effects on all other living mat-
> ter. (Clarkson et al., 1992, p. 4)

We have been instructed by the Creator to live in harmony with nature.
If we pollute and misuse the water for example, we will not be given a
fine, we threaten our own existence. Oren Lyons, Onondaga Nation
Faithkeeper, says:

> Natural law prevails everywhere. It supersedes Man's law. If you violate
> it, you get hit. There's no judge and jury, there's no lawyers or courts,
> you can't buy or dodge or beg your way out of it. If you violate this
> Natural law you're going to get hit and get hit hard. One of the Natural
> laws is that you've got to keep things pure. Especially the water. Keeping
> the water pure is one of the first laws of life. If you destroy the water, you
> destroy life. (Wall and Arden, 1990, p. 66)

Aboriginal spirituality also plays an important role in living sustainably. Day-to-day spirituality, based on the principle of respect, can balance our desire for more material things and fill our spiritual void. At the United Nations Conference on Environment and Development (UNCED) in June 1992, Oren Lyons, the Onondaga Faithkeeper, discussed spirituality. He asked what we do after we have said our prayers, given our thanks, and completed our rituals and ceremonies. He answered that caring for each other is our highest calling. He said helping each other is a shortcut to spirituality. Thus, spirituality is about our personal and daily relationship with the environment and our community.

Having respect for each other and the land and showing our humanity are powerful instruments of peace. When Aboriginal peoples first meet someone, they are interested in a person's humanity. Václav Havel is interested in somewhat the same issue — he is aware of how dehumanizing the world can be and how we are sacrificing our spirit because we have lost our balance. He thinks that human beings must have a new face, a new way of being in the postmodern world.

> A politician [leader] must become a person again, someone who trusts not only a scientific representation and analysis of the world, but also in the world itself. He must believe not only in sociological statistics, but in real people. He must trust not only an objective interpretation of reality, but also his own soul, not only an adopted ideology, but also his own thoughts; not only the summary reports he receives each morning, but also his own feelings. Soul, individual spirituality, first hand personal insights into things, the courage to be himself and go the way his conscience points, humility in the face of the mysterious order of Being, confidence in its natural direction and, above all, trust in his own subjectivity as his principal link with the subjectivity of the world — these, in my view, are the qualities that politicians of the future should cultivate. (Havel, 1992a)

Havel goes on to say in *Summer Meditations* (1992), "[W]e must build a state on intellectual and spiritual values." He describes a state that has its own history, its own specificity:

> Building an intellectual and spiritual state — a state based on ideas — does not mean building an ideological state. Indeed, an ideological state cannot be intellectual or spiritual. A state based on ideas is precisely the opposite; it is meant to extricate human beings from the straitjacket of ideological interpretations, and to rehabilitate them as subjects of individual conscience, of individual thinking backed up by experience, of individual responsibility, and with love for their neighbours that is anything but abstract. (Havel, 1992b, p. 128)

Society must learn not only to respect the Earth but to love Mother Earth as loving children love their parents. We have accepted a second-rate system based on cynicism and mistrust of people. Even Adam Smith, the original economist, said that a society built on altruism is superior to a market system based on self-interest. We need new systems and leaders who can instil a sense of ownership and responsibility for each other and our institutions. Aboriginal peoples have much that can be learned by Western society of what is possible. Havel says that

> A state based on ideas should be no more and no less than a guarantee of freedom and security for people who know that the state and its institutions can stand behind them only if they themselves take responsibility for the state — that is, if they see it as their own project and their own home, as something they need not fear, as something they can without shame love, because they have built it for themselves. (Havel, 1992b, p. 128)

Values are not simply what we value in our lives, friends, community, and spiritual life. All societies have environmental or Earth-based values. Western society has placed a lot of attention on social and economic values with the result that there is an imbalance with environmental values. Today's environmental problems are not just about the scale of industrialization but are also about perspective, strategy, and long-term planning. Interestingly, we live in a time when Western society is recognizing Aboriginal peoples' environmental knowledge and values.

Aboriginal peoples are also undergoing a deep and profound spiritual renaissance. This renaissance is not of a material nature but is a spiritual renaissance, a retrieving and reviving of our original covenant with the Creator. We are reaffirming our relationship and stewardship with our Mother the Earth. While we are inspired and directed to do this for our children and ourselves, we also realize that many, if not all, of our elders have fallen asleep, forgotten, or have never known our rightful spiritual heritage. Therefore, it is up to those of us who have, in whatever measure, the teachings, philosophy, and traditions, including the rituals, to work for their revival and continuance (Wall and Arden, 1990, p. 50).

At the heart of the renaissance is a deep reflection on indigenous values and the need for healing between Western society and indigenous peoples. Indigenous values are based on a deep respect for the environment, natural law, and everyday spirituality. These could provide a base for insight and direction for the environmental, technological, and demographic issues. At the heart of this renaissance is a new paradigm requiring an overhaul of values, ideas, norms, and actions.

INDIGENOUS TRADITIONS AND WORLD RELIGIONS

The Seventh Generation prophecy also teaches us that the peoples of the four directions need to find peace to achieve harmony with nature. All the world's major religions have teachings on living harmoniously with the Earth.

In 1986, religious leaders of the Buddhist, Christian, Hindu, Jewish, and Muslim religions made the five declarations of Assisi. The declarations "speak of values and ethics which challenge many of the assumptions which secular conservation has held to be true — such as the anthropocentric nature of conservation" (Assisi, 1986, p. 1). The following highlights parts of the declarations from each of the five religions.

Buddhist: His Holiness the Dalai Lama

Our ancestors have left us a world rich in its natural resources and capable of fulfilling our needs. This is a fact. It was believed in the past that the natural resources of the Earth were unlimited, no matter how much they were exploited. But we know today that without understanding and care these resources are not inexhaustible. It is not difficult to understand and bear the exploitation done in the past out of ignorance, but now that we are aware of the dangerous factors, it is very important to examine our responsibilities and our commitment to values, and think of the kind of world we are to bequeath to future generations. (Assisi, 1986, pp. 6–7)

Christian: St. Gregory of Nazianzen

God set man upon earth as a kind of second world, a microcosm; another kind of angel, a worshipper of blended nature. ... He was king of all upon earth, but subject to heaven; earthly and heavenly; transient, yet mortal; belonging both to the visible and to the intelligible order; midway between greatness and lowliness. (Assisi, 1986, p. 11)

Hindu: Mahabharata

[E]ven if there is only one tree full of flowers and fruits in a village, that place becomes worthy of worship and respect. (Assisi, 1986, p. 18)

Hinduism believes in the all encompassing sovereignty of the divine, manifesting itself in a graded scale of evolution. The human race, though at the top of the evolutionary pyramid at present, is not seen as something apart from the earth and its multitudinous lifeforms. The Atharava Veda has the magnificent Hymn to the Earth which is redolent with ecological and environmental values. (Assisi, 1986, p. 17)

Muslim

The classical Muslim jurist, Izz ad-din ibn Abd as-Salam ... formulated the bill of legal rights of animals in the thirteenth century. Similarly, numerous other jurists and scholars developed legislation to safeguard water resources, prevent over-grazing, conserve forests, limit growth of cities, protect cultural property and so on. (Assisi, 1986, p. 24)

Judaism: Kabbalistic Teaching

[A]s Adam named all God's creatures, he helped define their essence. Adam swore to live in harmony with those whom he had named. Thus, at the very beginning of time, man accepted responsibility before God for all of creation. (Assisi, 1986, p. 29)

The religious teachings, original instructions, and contemporary indigenous peoples all have a common and deep respect for Mother Earth. With growing populations, inefficient and polluting technologies, and real dangers to human survival, we are in urgent need of a dialogue between peoples. Indigenous peoples believe we are entering a new era of peace. This is an opportunity to learn how to live with one another and respect one another's diversity. Some believe that the first step (Clarkson et al., 1992, p. iii) is for Western society to listen and learn from indigenous peoples. Indigenous peoples need to speak for themselves to break through Western images and stereotypes, such as the image of the noble savage. We must also find a balance among our notions of progress, spirituality, and technology. Culture results from the interaction among people, land, production, and reproduction, and in developing systems that are in harmony with the Earth and each other. Indigenous peoples have learned that there is a connection between our basic values and how we choose to use technology for production. Therefore, it is possible to eliminate pollution and poverty while maintaining a comfortable standard of living.

ABORIGINAL ECONOMIES AND CHANGE

The traditional economy of Aboriginal peoples in Canada was not one but many economies of the arctic, coastal, prairie, forest, and subarctic. Since time immemorial, ancient peoples developed sustainable systems in a variety of environments. Aboriginal peoples were hunters, gatherers, fishers, horticulturists, healers, midwives, faithkeepers, storytellers, transporters, traders, scientists, leaders, and protectors.

During the fur trade era, Aboriginal families adapted their economic and social systems to become trappers, hunters, fishers, traders, guides, educators, and transporters.[1] Trapping focussed on small fur-bearing animals instead of larger game, thus changing the peoples' economic and social systems. The modern North American economy emerged from the fur trade and the labour of thousands of Aboriginal hunters, trappers, and traders. The fur trade, which began with the first explorers, was a major economic force until the middle of the nineteenth century, when it declined rapidly in the face of growing American agriculture and industrialization. From its beginning to its decline, the fur trade depended on Indian hunters and trappers. They knew the land, understood the behaviour of the animals, and possessed the skills and technology to harvest them (Weatherford, 1991, pp. 77–78).

With the decline of the fur trade, the growth of agriculture, and the expansion of logging, mining, and fishing, Aboriginal peoples found themselves on a collision course with Euro-Canadians in a competition over resources. The myth is that Aboriginal peoples did not have the capacity for or could not adjust to the new economy. In reality, however, most were pushed to the margins. Studies of Aboriginal farming (Buckley, 1992; Carter, 1993), for example, indicate that Indians were indeed successful at farming, but were set back by Indian policy. Helen Buckley, in *From Wooden Ploughs to Welfare: Why Indian Policy Failed in the Prairie Provinces*, writes:

> This promising beginning does not fit the popular image of hunters who were unable to adapt to farming. It also raises a new question as to why the farming ultimately failed, having made a good start. But the answers are not long in coming for, as early as the late 1880s, farm policy moved into a new phase. This new policy, together with the continuing scarcity of equipment and working capital, defeated the efforts of the [Indian] farmers themselves. (Buckley, 1992, p. 52)

Similar tragedies associated with competition over fishing are described by Boyce Richardson in *People of Terra Nullius* (1993). He writes that within a decade of passing the federal Fisheries Act in 1868, "commercial fish companies selling into the United States were permitted to operate on Lake of the Woods, and began a devastation of the sturgeon population that must rank as one of the worst ecological disasters in our history" (Richardson, 1993, p. 203). This phenomenon was in sharp contrast to the pre-existing sustainable fishery managed by the Ojibway.

For many decades, the Ojibway had maintained the harvest of sturgeon at between 250 000 and 400 000 pounds a year. In the first half of the 1880s, the commercial companies more than doubled the take to an average 864 000 pounds a year, and in the last part of that decade to 1 250 000 pounds.

Naturally, the Ojibway fishery began to collapse. In 1894, Manitou and Long Sault, the essential centres of the Ojibway economy, reported no fish, while great scarcity was reported from every other lake invaded by the commercial fishermen. In contrast, the lakes where Ojibway remained in control — Wabuskang, Lac Seul, Wagigoon, Shoal Lake, Whitefish Bay — continued to report large catches (Richardson, 1993, p. 203). Aboriginal peoples lost control of their sustainable economic systems because colonial policies gradually eroded Aboriginal access and control over their resources.

The shift from the traditional Aboriginal economies to low-end employment in resource harvesting activities, known as the primary sector, happened over a millennium with marked changes after the 1950s. A survey in the sixties of Aboriginal employment shows that the shift to the primary sector took place well into the sixties. The report completed by Hawthorn et al., A Survey of the Contemporary Indians of Canada (1966), clearly demonstrates the reliance of Indians living on reserves on employment in the primary (renewal and non-renewable resource) sector. The 1966 data from selected Indian reserves across Canada indicates that nearly 80 percent of employment was in the primary sector.

However, by 1990 the Aboriginal employment situation had dramatically changed, reflecting larger societal and global changes. Employment both on- and off-reserve has shifted from dependence on the primary sector of the economy to the service sector. In less than three decades, the dominance of agriculture, forestry, fishing, trapping, and mining has given way to the service sector. The trend is similar for the Canadian economy, but not nearly as significant as for the Aboriginal economy.

There has been an equally dramatic shift in the past century for Aboriginal families living a traditional lifestyle by trapping, gathering, and living off the land. Within this time period, Aboriginal peoples shifted further into the primary sector of the labour market in agriculture, forestry, fishing, and trapping. The most recent shift has been into the service sector. Another important trend is the migration of Aboriginal peoples to urban centres. Presently, approximately 75 percent of Aboriginal peoples live off-reserve in urban environments.

The employment data illustrate the shift from the primary sector to the service sector today. In 1966, nearly 80 percent of the employment on-reserve was in the primary sector, whereas today 80 percent is in the service sector (see Tables 14.1 and 14.2).

Nevertheless, many Aboriginal peoples continue to live in their traditional ways on the land. They have been successful in sustainable fishing and agriculture and have adjusted to changes in the economy, but exter-

TABLE 14.1

Survey of Indian Employment in 35 Bands across Canada, 1966

Industry or occupation	Percentage of total jobs
Primary sector	
Forestry	
On-reserve	7.4
Off-reserve	3.6
Fishing	4.6
Trapping	14.0
Guiding	2.2
Food gathering (including making wild hay)	13.4
Handicrafts	4.1
Proprietor farm	3.7
Unskilled, casual, and farm labour[1]	27.2
Total	**80.2**
Tertiary (service) sector	
Proprietor, non-farm	2.3
Professional and technical	0.65
Clerical	2.6
Skilled[2]	14.0
Total	**19.55**

[1] In a number of the completed questionnaires, farm labour was included in the broad category of "unskilled and casual." Only 95 were clearly defined as farm labour (not shown here).

[2] A number of relatively well-paid, semi-skilled workers, such as loggers in British Columbia, truck drivers, and steadily employed factory workers, were included under "skilled" in this table, rather than under "unskilled, casual, and farm labour" or (in the case of loggers) "forestry," as provided in the Indian Affairs Branch Questionnaire.

Source: Adapted from H.B. Hawthorn et al., eds. 1966. *A Survey of the Contemporary Indians of Canada: A Report on Economic, Political, Educational Needs and Policies.* Vol. I. DIAND Publication No. Q5-0603-020-EE-A-18. Ottawa: Indians Affairs.

nal policies have interfered with their approaches to development. These barriers to traditional development approaches are today inhibiting the

TABLE 14.2

Aboriginal Employment by Industry, 1991

On-reserve		Off-reserve	
Primary sector		*Primary sector*	
Agriculture	1 510	Agriculture	5 295
Forestry and logging	2 220	Forestry and logging	5 195
Fishing and trapping	1 255	Fishing and trapping	1 825
Mining, quarries, and oil wells	685	Mining, quarries, and oil wells	5 585
Total	5 670	Total	17 900
Secondary sector		*Secondary sector*	
Manufacturing	2 845	Manufacturing	29 520
Total	2 845	Total	29 520
Tertiary sector		*Tertiary sector*	
Construction	4 020	Construction	15 130
Transportation, communication, and other	2 225	Transportation, communication, and other	17 515
Trade	2 485	Trade	30 640
Finance, insurance, and real estate	310	Finance, insurance, and real estate	7 380
Community, business, and personal services	3 785	Community, business, and personal services	44 055
Public administration and defence	19 090	Public administration and defence	51 440
Total	31 915 (79%)	Total	166 160 (78%)
Total all industries	40 430	Total all industries	213 580

Source: Adapted from Statistics Canada. 1995. "Profile of Canada's Aboriginal Population." *1991 Census.* Cat. no. 94-325. Ottawa: Minister of Industry.

potential for Aboriginal innovation in production, environmental management, and employment creation. The current unemployment situation in Aboriginal communities will be substantially improved when Aboriginal peoples regain control over their lives and implement development strategies that use traditional knowledge and new technologies.

ABORIGINAL SUSTAINABLE DEVELOPMENT

A number of Aboriginal communities are employing traditional knowledge and new technologies to initiate new ways of achieving sustainable development. They are effectively using consensus decision making, elders' advice, participative community-based development, partnerships with stakeholders, and capacity building for holistic ecosystem management. This section presents some examples.

The Traditional Dene Environmental Knowledge Pilot Project is based at the Dene Cultural Institute in Hay River, Northwest Territories. It was established in 1987 to preserve and promote Dene culture through research and education. Because of its link to culture and the land, traditional environmental knowledge is the focus of the project, which has been a major contributor to methods of documenting knowledge, community participation, training, and partnering with other institutions. The project has been instrumental in promoting the integration of traditional environmental knowledge with Western science in managing resources.

The Inuit Circumpolar Conference has been instrumental in promoting the use of indigenous knowledge in environmental problem solving. In a speech to the 1992 preparatory meeting to the U.N. Conference on Environment and Development (UNCED), Mary Simon, then president of the ICC, called on UNCED to recognize "that various levels of support will be required from governments to ensure that the traditional knowledge held by indigenous peoples survives to take its rightful place as an important knowledge system" (Simon, 1992).

The Porcupine Caribou Management Board has been responsible for caribou conservation and management in the Yukon and Northwest Territories since 1985. Issues dealt with are hunting on the Dempster Highway, antler sales, chemical contamination, trade and barter of caribou meat, and industrial disturbance. This effective co-management organization includes Gwich'in, Inuvialuit, and three government jurisdictions and operates on the Native principle of consensus management. The Porcupine Caribou Management Board is often referred to as a model for similar joint management organizations.

The Kluskus and Ulkatcho bands, in the interior of British Columbia, developed plans for holistic forestry because of their concerns that current allowable cuts are two to three times the sustainable rate. As an alternative to these practices, the bands have applied for a holistic tree farm licence that would involve traditional practices, local economies, and indefinite forest conservation. Their strategy includes a complete field-based inventory, zoning for land use, alternative timber extraction (e.g., selective logging), and value-added manufacturing.

The Shuswap Nation Tribal Council has established an institute to develop plans for habitat restoration on a regional scale that would integrate forestry, mining, and agriculture. The council will share information with indigenous communities and other interested parties.

These development initiatives are founded on the belief that sustainable development will spawn prosperity, strengthen culture, and generate employment. The major institutional innovation is that Aboriginal peoples are taking control of development, sharing decision making, and building on traditional knowledge. The other factor for success is the involvement of many stakeholders in the process. These are but a few examples of sustainable development strategies being used by Aboriginal peoples.

ABORIGINAL EMPLOYMENT PLANNING

Improving and managing the environment results in increased employment. Paul Hawken, in *The Ecology of Commerce* (1993), argues that environmentalists who do not talk jobs are not really serious. Since the early eighties, researchers have maintained that environmental protection will create jobs. This has been true for the Clean Air Act in the United States and where communities have developed comprehensive employment strategies around protecting nature, such as in the case of the spotted owl. Thus, the widespread belief that protecting the environment will result in the loss of jobs appears false. Of course, for these new strategies to function appropriately, they must be comprehensive (focussing on all present and future opportunities), be effectively networked and co-ordinated, and involve partners or stakeholders.

For Aboriginal peoples, the best opportunities for future jobs will be linked to the environment, self-government, small business, and natural resources. Of course, Aboriginal employment will be shaped by the economy, but the nature and the extent of growth will be determined by the Aboriginal community's ability to control the process. Aboriginal peoples have also been interested in competing in international markets based on their traditional knowledge, sustainable practices, and experience. Aboriginal peoples have learned that they must control and manage their own resources and economies.

Aboriginal peoples need a new model that links resource management, education and training, and strategic planning. Education and training must prepare Aboriginal peoples for a future built on traditional environmental knowledge and information technology. Finally, Aboriginal communities need to support an economic development strategy that builds on all the economic potentials of the community and allows economic self-sufficiency, sustainable development, and self-government.

The strategic plan must not only be environmentally sustainable, but must also support cultural, social, economic, and political sustainability. This can only be done when a community is building its future vision on knowing where they have come from based on their own values and culture. To achieve this objective, Aboriginal economic development must have the following goals:

1. To become an active player in the regional economy, focussing on restoring natural resources based on traditional ecological knowledge and new technologies. Two main target areas are forestry projects, with priority placed on sustainable resource harvesting and multi-use strategies, and cultural tourism, with priority placed on projects that involve indigenous knowledge, help strengthen local culture, and educate non-Aboriginals.
2. To develop and research indigenous ecological knowledge related to the environment, resource management, and subsistence systems.
3. To develop a human resource strategy focussing on the following areas: information technology, resource management and sustainable production, business development and entrepreneurship, subsistence hunting and gathering, and administration and services.
4. To support the formation of local enterprises to provide local goods and services (e.g., retail, personal services, and government services), to reduce economic leakages, and to increase employment and wealth in Aboriginal communities.
5. To develop a development strategy that will facilitate managing natural resources in traditional territories and strengthen the traditional economy based on indigenous knowledge and restoring the resource base.
6. To develop partnerships with postsecondary institutions to provide environmental, technological, administrative, managerial, and entrepreneurial education and training based on lifelong learning, capacity building, and skill development.
7. To develop the technical and manufacturing capacities in new and emerging environmental fields. Development in computing, telecommunications, and remote sensing technologies must occur early in order to generate large economic and employment gains in the future. This involves research into softer manufacturing techniques, particularly in the computer and communications industries, that eliminate waste and pollution.
8. To develop community-based participative planning mechanisms to ensure the strategy reflects community needs, aspirations, and long-term objectives and strengthens culture and traditional economies.

9. To continue to develop the community's ability to access capital to finance business and business development.

Today, Aboriginal economic development strategies need to be comprehensive in scope to capture all available opportunities. In the past decades, communities around the world tried, often in vain, to attract that one large industry that would solve all their economic ills. Communities now realize that this approach has failed. In order for local economies to grow, they must utilize all opportunities and create capacity in industries that support a regional industrial strategy. The following briefly summarizes the broad opportunities and discusses them in the context of self-reliance, self-government, and preparing Aboriginal peoples for the future.

A resource-based development strategy should focus on wise use, employment, technology, multiple use, traditional knowledge, and commercial opportunities. Several Aboriginal communities that have based their economic strategy on these factors have demonstrated significant growth in their economy and employment (Blanchet-Cohen, 1996). Aboriginal peoples' most powerful economic tools are the bringing together of traditional knowledge and information technologies in new models of sustainable resource management. The Aboriginal employment and economic strategies can be divided into six sectors: resource management, tourism, traditional economy, emerging industries, business development, and First Nations governance.

Resources

Forestry is arguably the most significant economic opportunity for the future of Aboriginal peoples and their territories in the woodlands. Many Aboriginal peoples live in the forest regions of Canada and possess the traditional knowledge to manage them. They could participate in resource industries by adopting sustainable management systems, restoring the environment, and developing new industrial standards. The resource strategy could include restoration plans and sustainable yield harvesting that would also permit multiple use of forests. A mixed-use strategy combines sustainable forestry with hunting, tourism, recreation, and gathering. For sustainable resource planning and management, Aboriginal peoples can use their traditional environmental knowledge and combine it with new technologies, such as geographic information systems (GIS), to develop databases and planning instruments. As discussed above, a number of Aboriginal communities are already applying traditional knowledge in this way. In order to increase

Aboriginal peoples' participation, training programs must be in place and linked to business development plans for this sector at the regional level. This strategy will work in the woodlands, arctic, and coastal regions of Canada.

Tourism

As a growth area of the Canadian economy, tourism is another promising economic sector for Aboriginal peoples. Tourism offers unique opportunities for employment based on traditional knowledge and ways and for educating Canadians and foreign tourists about traditional environmental practices and values. Ecotourism and cultural tourism are most likely to interest tourists who seek new experiences and are interested in the natural environment. Plenty of employment opportunities in tourism services and operations can generate significant jobs for Aboriginal people, including tourism operations, visitor centres, museums, travel agencies, services, lodges, and restaurants.

Strengthening Traditional Economy

Training should be developed to meet the needs of resource management, new technologies, processing and marketing of natural resources, resource inventories, and adoption of new technologies such as remote sensing for sustainable resource management. The basis of training would be the collection and documentation of traditional knowledge. A pilot program could be established to collect such knowledge and determine its applications to employment and business development. Traditional knowledge could be integrated with other plans, such as sustainable forestry management. Finally, Aboriginal peoples have identified the need for training in hunting, fishing, trapping, and other traditional knowledge areas.

Emerging Industries

The service sector is gradually being dominated by energy-saving information technologies. The information highway promises to save energy by reducing the need to travel (local, national, and international). Internet communications systems, e-mail, and computer conferencing promise to be efficient and effective tools for Aboriginal planning, dialogue, and communication. For example, Cultural Survival Canada is developing an Internet system for indigenous peoples to undertake biological diversity research, planning, and information sharing. The system will be available worldwide and is becoming a significant development tool for sharing information, experience, and knowledge. In this and many other ways, the shape of our work life will be dramatically affected by information technologies in the next decades. Although there are risks in information technology that cannot be ignored, it could also have a democratizing effect where communities control information. For example, Aboriginal firms such as the First Nations Technological Institute in Deseronto, Ontario, are tapping into the high-growth potential of the new technologies sector, particularly in the area of governance and services.

In order for Aboriginal peoples to benefit from the new technologies, they need adequate training and education. Developing capacity in technology, computers, and the software industries is a long-term goal, yet implementation must begin immediately.

Business Development

The provision of local goods and services for local and First Nations markets could generate many new jobs and wealth in the Aboriginal economy in the medium term. The number of Aboriginal businesses could double in the next decade from the present 20 000 without worry of saturating local markets. Money circulating within Aboriginal communities has a "multiplier" effect that generates further jobs and business opportunities. All indications are strong that supporting business development is a good investment in job generation and economic self-sufficiency. This is a rapidly emerging area because Aboriginal peoples have developed strong capacities in development, management, and business.

Aboriginal Services and Administration

At present, Aboriginal government is the major source of stable full-time employment. As government programs and services are further devolved to Aboriginal government, more employment and training will be required. New fields are emerging, such as accounting, bookkeeping, project management, administration, data processing, and computer technologies. Many Aboriginal peoples have had the foresight to seek training in the growing field of public administration and management. Aboriginal communities should develop long-term capacity-building and training plans. In addition, plans to use energy-conserving electronic systems and software would not only protect the environment, but prepare Aboriginal employees for the future economy.

CONCLUSION

In the future, all employment will be determined by our social and technological responses to environmental crises. Environmental challenges will affect production, natural resource extraction, and consumption. Production methods that produce waste and pollution will not be tolerated by society. Traditional ways teach us to use everything and always return benefits to nature. Institutions and new commercial relationships, such as fair trade, must replace transactions that exploit producers and the environment. It is noteworthy that producers and companies with a social conscience are emerging; corporate leaders are learning that efficient production produces no waste and pollution and does not exploit people. This is a winning market strategy for the next century.

In a sense, Aboriginal peoples are completing a circle. After being hunters, fishers, ecologists, and storytellers, they are now major players in resource restoration and sustainable resource harvesting. Aboriginal peoples in Canada are also playing a greater role in nation building. They are gradually regaining control and management of large tracts of territories. Aboriginal peoples can become major players in the natural resource sector by transforming it into a sustainable sector based on traditional knowledge and information technology. The challenge is planning for this transformation and having the vision to confront the obstacles.

The new economy will have to be rooted in traditional knowledge combined with new and emerging technologies. Already there are examples of this occurring. The Dene Cultural Centre has demonstrated vision in applying traditional knowledge to new areas of resource management. The First Nations Technical Institute has shown how new technology can dramatically increase employment for Aboriginal peoples.

This future employment cannot occur without the commitment of Aboriginal peoples, government, the private sector, and educational institutions to develop employment based on sustainable development.

NOTE

1. Thomas D. Lonner identifies several economic activities, as follows: hunting, fishing, gathering, farming, herding, crafting, trading, toolmaking, transportation, skill training, storage, energy development, and so on, in "Subsistence as an Economic System in Alaska" (1986).

Discussion Questions

1. How can traditional Aboriginal values be applied in economic and resource development planning? For example, how can "respect for nature" inform resource management decisions?
2. What is the link between future employment, environment, new technology, and sustainable development? How can we develop plans that pull all these elements together?
3. How can the barriers to sustainable development be overcome? The barriers include lack of knowledge about traditional economies and how to strengthen them and the link between traditional and scientific knowledge.
4. What can industrialized societies learn from indigenous peoples about the environment and sustainable development?
5. How can Aboriginal communities develop strong, self-reliant, and self-sufficient economies?
6. How can Aboriginal peoples capitalize on economic opportunities in new and emerging industries?

Further Readings

Clarkson, Linda, Vern Morrissette, and Gabriel Regallet. 1992. *Our Responsibility to the Seventh Generation*. Winnipeg: International Institute for Sustainable Development. This is an excellent introduction to Aboriginal teachings and thinking about the environment and development. The report offers a critique of development and shows how indigenous peoples have been victims of modernization. The text provides recommendations on how to achieve sustainable development.

Hawken, Paul. 1993. *The Ecology of Commerce: A Declaration of Sustainability*. New York: Harper Business. If you want a vision of the future for business, read this book. Hawken writes that the present "green" businesses are just the tip of the iceberg for the future of business. This is an inspiring book with insights on the future of enterprise.

Inter Press Service, comp. 1993. *Story Earth: Native Voices on the Environment*. San Francisco: Mercury House. This book gives voice to traditional cultures and their vision of Mother Earth. Understanding traditional peoples is difficult, and understanding traditional peoples' concerns about development is even more complex. This book is full of insight about indigenous peoples' teachings, reaction to development, and lessons for sustainable living.

Royal Commission on Aboriginal Peoples (RCAP). 1993. *Sharing the Harvest: The Road to Self-Reliance, Report of the National Round Table on Aboriginal Economic Development and Resources*. Ottawa: RCAP. This book provides an excellent overview of current thinking on development and natural resource models and strategies. The subjects cover the components of a comprehensive development strategy for Aboriginal communities. The text also describes innovative models for community and private enterprise.

Sachs, Wolfgang, ed. 1992. *The Development Dictionary: A Guide to Knowledge as Power*. London: Zed Books. This is an excellent reference for those interested in critical analysis of twentieth-century ideas on development, aid, and progress. The editor has constructed a concise collection of short chapters to resemble a learned dictionary. This book will help clarify key ideas that are central to the themes in the other Further Readings recommended for this chapter.

World Commission on Environment and Development. 1987. *Our Common Future*. Oxford and New York: Oxford University Press. *Our Common Future* is a classic, also known as the *Bruntland Commission Report*, that pointed the way for the Earth Summit in 1992. The WCED was set up as an independent body in 1983 by the United Nations to re-examine critical environment and development problems on the planet. The report compelled nations to act together to put the world on a sustainable path.

REFERENCES

Arden, Harvey and Steve Wall. 1990. *Wisdomkeepers: Meetings with Native American Spiritual Elders*. Hillsboro, Ore.: Beyond Words Publishing.

The Assisi Declarations: Messages on Man and Nature from Buddhism, Christianity, Hinduism, Islam and Judaism. 1986. Basilica di S. Francesco, Assisi, Italy, World Wide Fund for Nature (WWF). (29 September).

Blanchet-Cohen, Natasha. 1996. *Strategies for a Living Earth: Examples from Canadian Aboriginal Communities*. Biodiversity Associates Report, No. 2. Ottawa: Environment Canada.

Buckley, Helen. 1992. *From Wooden Ploughs to Welfare: Why Indian Policy Failed in the Prairie Provinces*. Montreal: McGill-Queen's University Press.

Carter, Sarah. 1993. *Lost Harvests: Prairie Indian Reserve Farmers and Government Policy*. Montreal: McGill-Queen's University Press.

Clarkson, Linda, Vern Morrissette, and Gabriel Regallet. 1992. *Our Responsibility to the Seventh Generation: Indigenous Peoples and Sustainable Development*. Winnipeg: International Institute for Sustainable Development.

Havel, Václav. 1992a. "Speech at the World Economic Forum." 4 February 1992. Davos, Switzerland.

———. 1992b. *Summer Meditations*. Trans. Paul Wilson. Toronto: Alfred A. Knopf.

Hawken, Paul. 1993. *The Ecology of Commerce: A Declaration of Sustainability*. New York: Harper Business.

Hawthorn, H.B., H.A.C. Cairns, and M.A. Tremblay. 1966. *A Survey of the Contemporary Indians of Canada: A Report on Economic, Political, Educational Needs and Policies*. 2 Vols. Ottawa: Indian Affairs. (October).

Lonner, Thomas D. 1986. "Subsistence as an Economic System in Alaska: Theoretical Observations and Management Implications." Pp. 15–27 in *Contemporary Alaskan Native Economies*, ed. Steven J. Langdon. Lanham, MD: University Press of America.

Richardson, Boyce. 1993. *People of Terra Nullius: Betrayal and Rebirth in Aboriginal Canada*. Vancouver: Douglas & McIntyre.

Weatherford, Jack. 1991. *Native Roots: How the Indians Enriched America*. New York: Fawcett Columbine.

World Commission on Environment and Development (WCED). 1987. *Our Common Future*. Oxford and New York: Oxford University Press.

GLOSSARY

Glossaries are comprised of particular definitions of terms specified by the author(s) of a given text. It is therefore important to recognize that each definition contained in this (or any other) glossary reflects the particular perspective and focus of its contributor.

ABORIGINAL IDENTITY POPULATION: Persons who identify with one or more Aboriginal groups (e.g., North American Indian, Métis, and/or Inuit).

ABORIGINAL ORIGIN OR ANCESTRY POPULATION: Persons who identify with the ethnic or cultural origins of one or more ancestral Aboriginal groups (e.g., North American Indian, Métis, and/or Inuit).

ABORIGINAL PEOPLES (ALSO INDIGENOUS PEOPLES): Refers to the descendants of the original occupants of the land. Aboriginal peoples remain a fundamentally autonomous and self-determining political community who continue to possess a special relationship with the colonizers, together with the rights and entitlements that flow from their unique relational status. Legal categories for Aboriginal poeples in Canada include registered or status Indians, Métis, Inuit, and non-status Indians. However, many Aboriginal people prefer to identify themselves by their cultural community of origin (e.g., Gwitchin, Cree, Métis, Nisga'a).

ABORIGINAL PEOPLES SURVEY (APS): Statistics Canada conducted this post-censal survey in 1991. The sample of approximately 180 000 persons were asked if they identified with their Aboriginal origins or were registered Indians. Survey results, therefore, reflect the responses of individuals who identify themselves as Aboriginal people, in contrast to census data comprised of responses from individuals who have Aboriginal ancestry but may or may not identify themselves as Aboriginal.

ABORIGINAL REVITALIZATION: Growing support for Aboriginal spirituality and cultural traditions in a wide variety of modern social and political contexts.

ABORIGINAL RIGHTS (ALSO INDIGENOUS RIGHTS): By virtue of their status as the descendants of the original occupants, Aboriginal peoples possess both inherent and collective claims (rights) over those jurisdictions related to land, identity, and political voice that have never been extinguished but continue to serve as a basis for entitlement and engagement.

ABORIGINAL SELF-GOVERNMENT: The ideal of parity among Aboriginal, provincial, and federal political authorities and powers.

ABORIGINALITY (ALSO INDIGENEITY): A nominalization of the adjective "Aboriginal" in the same way that "ethnicity" nominalizes the adjective "ethnic." Aboriginality refers to a shared awareness of original occupancy as a catalyst for challenging the status quo with respect to who gets what and why.

AGING (OF A POPULATION): An increase in the number of old people as a percentage of the total population.

ALBERTA MÉTIS SETTLEMENTS ACCORD: An agreement between the Métis Settlements Councils and the Alberta provincial government that was formally legislated in November 1990. The agreement established Métis land ownership rights (fee simple ownership of 1.28 million acres) and a reorganized form of governance for the Métis of the eight Alberta settlements. The Alberta government also agreed to pay $310 million over seventeen years and to establish the Transition Commission, which consisted of a membership tribunal, a revenue trust fund, and other groups, to work with provincial government and settlement representatives to assist in implementation and maintenance.

AMERICAN INDIAN MOVEMENT (AIM): Organization initiated and controlled by American Indian people dedicated to grassroots, social, and political revitalization of Indian people.

AMERINDIAN: One of the terms by which Europeans refer to the Aboriginal peoples of the Americas and the Caribbean. It is a variation of "Indian," the name given to the people by Christopher Columbus, who thought he had landed in the Asiatic Indies. "Amerindian" is used in some scholarly circles to distinguish the original people of the Americas from those of India.

ASSEMBLY OF FIRST NATIONS (AFN): National organization established in 1982 to represent the perspectives and interests of status Indians in Canada.

ASSIMILATION: Process through which a dominant group seeks to undermine the cultural distinctiveness of a subordinate group by subjecting them to the rules, values, and sanctions of the dominant group and then absorbing the "decultured" minority into the mainstream.

BAND COUNCIL: Elected body of representatives, including a chief and band councillors, that is responsible for administering the affairs of a First Nation band.

BAND COUNCILLOR: Member of a First Nation band elected every two years by fellow band members to develop band-related policies and administer community resources.

BAND MEMBERS: First Nations people who belong to a particular band. Before 1985 all registered Indians belonged to a band. Since Bill C-31 was passed in 1985, status and band membership have been separated and bands have been given jurisdiction over band membership. Only band members have the right to live on the reserve held in trust for a band, run for band council, vote in band elections, or participate in decision making about how band resources are to be dispersed.

BICULTURALISM: Two nations with two distinct cultures existing within the context of a single, overarching political–legal framework.

BILINGUALISM: Government policy that grants equal official status to two distinct languages.

BILL C-31: In June 1985, Parliament enacted a series of amendments to the Indian Act known as Bill C-31: Act to Amend the Indian Act. The legislation brought the Indian Act into line with the provisions of the Canadian Charter of Rights and Freedoms. The three principles that guided the amendments were the removal of sex discrimination, restoring Indian status and membership to women, and increasing the control Indian bands have over their own affairs.

BUREAUCRATIC PATERNALISM: Formalized, ideologically grounded relationship between superordinate and subordinate peoples that controls all aspects of subordinate people's lives.

CHARTER OF RIGHTS AND FREEDOMS: The Charter adopted when the Canadian Constitution Act, 1982, terminated the United Kingdom's imperial rule over Canada. The Charter protects certain fundamental rights and freedoms of Canadian citizens, such as equality before the law.

CLANS: Extended family groups related by blood or marriage.

COLONIAL WARS: A series of wars between Europeans and Indians, between French and English, and finally between English and Americans that marked the colonization of Canada. These began with the French–Iroquois War in 1609 and concluded with the War of 1812 between British and Americans, in which Canada participated as a British colony.

COLONIZATION: The establishment of imperial rule over foreign territories and peoples through economic, social, and political policies. Colonizing policies and practices are often informed by racist and ethnocentric beliefs and attitudes.

COMPREHENSIVE LAND CLAIMS: Process of clarifying Aboriginal peoples' legal relationship with the land as a basis for cultural renewal, economic development, and political control.

CONSTITUTIONALISM: The political and moral framework (or first principles) that governs a society or country and provides a blueprint for defining internal relationships among the governed.

CONSTRUCTIVE ENGAGEMENT: The process by which central authorities such as the Crown and Aboriginal peoples establish a non-dominating, co-determining relationship in a spirit of co-operative co-existence.

CO-OPTATION: Process through which socially, organizationally, or politically powerless people come to support the perspectives of those who have power and control over them.

COUNCIL OF ELDERS: A group that provides direction to the Assembly of First Nations by developing the rules and procedures for members and overseeing the individual and collective activities of AFN members.

COUNTER-HEGEMONY: Ideas and practices designed to challenge or subvert processes and structures that support those in positions of power and dominance.

CROWN SOVEREIGNTY: The power and right of a monarch to rule over people and resources in a given territory.

CULTURAL GENOCIDE: Destruction of a people's cultural ways and means, often through colonial policies, legislation, and practices.

CURRICULUM: Content, sequence, and scope of material taught in schools.

DECOLONIZATION: Process of restructuring relations between indigenous and colonizing peoples, often through efforts to establish Aboriginal right to ownership of land and control by Aboriginal people over social and economic development.

DEPARTMENT OF INDIAN AFFAIRS AND NORTHERN DEVELOPMENT (DIAND): Federal government department established in 1966. Also referred to as the Department of Indian Affairs (DIA), the Department of Indian and Northern Affairs (DINA), and Indian and Northern Affairs Canada (INAC). Previous Indian Affairs branches resided in the Secretary of State, Department of the Interior, Department of Health and Welfare, and Department of Citizenship and Immigration.

DEVOLUTION: Colonial governmental policies and practices designed to decrease governmental responsibility and simultaneously increase indigenous peoples' responsibility for administering their own affairs.

DUALISM: The view that the world consists of fundamental entities. In the case of human existence, it is the view that human life comprises two distinct entities: the soul and the body.

ETHNIC MOBILITY: The movements of people caused by voluntary or externally imposed changes in ethnic group affiliation.

ETHNICITY: A characteristic that can describe the ancestral origins of an individual or can be a more subjective attribute that is based on factors such as identity and cultural behaviour.

ETHNOCENTRISM: The view that a people's cultural and institutional ways are superior to those of other peoples.

ETHNOHISTORY: Use of written historical materials or a people's oral literature or memory to reconstruct a people's cultural history.

FIDUCIARY: A trust relationship in which responsibility is assumed for looking after the best interests of an individual, group, or thing. Canada's federal government is in a fiduciary relationship with its Aboriginal peoples.

FIRST NATION: A term that came into common usage in the 1970s to replace the word "Indian," which many people found offensive. Although the term First Nation is widely used, no legal definition of it exists. Among its uses, the term "First Nations peoples" refers to the Indian people in Canada, both status and non-status. Many Indian people have also adopted the term "First Nation" to replace the word "band" in the name of their community.

FOURTH WORLD: Concept describing the phenomenon that emerges as a people develop customs and practices that wed them uniquely to their own land.

GLOBAL CULTURAL PATHOLOGY: Set of perspectives, attitudes, and actions that are contributing to the destruction of the earth's ecology.

HEGEMONY: Ideological as well as political processes and structures through which one class or people achieves domination over others.

HOLISM: The perspective that the inner and outer states of existence are profoundly connected and that the purpose of all of life is harmony and balance between all aspects and dimensions of reality.

HOLISTIC HEALING: The view that healing involves the harmonious restoration of physical, psychological, emotional, and spiritual dimensions of human life.

HOME LANGUAGE POPULATION: Those people whose language spoken most often at home is an Aboriginal language.

INDEX OF CONTINUITY: Measures language continuity, or vitality, by comparing the number of those who speak a given language at home to the number who learned that language as their mother tongue. A ratio of less than 100 indicates some decline in the strength of the language (i.e., for every 100 people with an Aboriginal mother tongue, there are fewer than 100 in the overall population who use it at home). The lower the score, the greater the decline or erosion.

INDIAN ACT INDIAN: Any male person of Indian blood reputed to belong to a particular band, any child of such a person, or any woman who is or was lawfully married to such a person.

INDIAN ACTS (1876, 1951): Bodies of federal legislation that specified who, legally, was an Indian; what Indian peoples were entitled to under the government's legal obligation; who could qualify for enfranchisement; what could be done with Indian lands and resources; and how Indian peoples were to be governed (through Indian agents and elected band councils).

INDIAN CONTROL OF INDIAN EDUCATION: Policy initiated by the National Indian Brotherhood in 1972 that sought to shift control of First Nations education into the hands of First Nations people, including increasing the involvement of Aboriginal parents in the education of their children.

INDIAN REGISTER: A list of all Indians registered according to the Indian Act. The Register carries information about the name, date of birth, gender, marital status, and place of residence (on- or off-reserve) of all registered Indians. The Indian Register was centralized in 1951; previously, individual Indian agents were responsible for lists of individuals eligible for registration.

INDIAN RESERVE: Land, the legal title to which is vested in the Crown, that has been set apart for the use and benefit of an Indian band and is subject to the terms of the Indian Act.

INDIGENIZATION: Process through which colonial laws, policies, and organizational practices are reformulated according to indigenous peoples' perspectives and interests.

INDIGENOUS: People who were born in or are natural to a specified territory or land.

INDIGENOUS PEOPLES' MOVEMENT: Global effort dedicated to protecting the rights of indigenous people by seeking to redress injustices committed against them and ensuring their social, economic, and political well-being.

INDIGENOUS SOVEREIGNTY: Sovereignty based on the principles that (a) Aboriginal peoples are sovereign in their own right regardless of formal recognition, (b) Aboriginal peoples possess a right of sovereignty if not necessarily the right to sovereignty, and (c) Crown sovereignty can be shared by way of multiple yet joint jurisdictions.

INDOCTRINATION: Process through which individuals are socialized to see and act in exclusive, narrowly defined ways.

INFANT MORTALITY RATE: Mortality of children less than a year old expressed as the number of deaths per 1000 live births.

INTERNAL COLONIALISM: Context and process through which one ethnic group or coalition rules the affairs of others living within the state; there is territorial separation of the subordinate ethnic groups in "homelands," "Native reserves," and the like; land tenure rights for subordinate groups are different from those of members of the dominant group; an internal "government within the government" is established by the dominant group to rule the subordinate groups; unique legal status is granted to the subordinate group and its members, who are then considered to have a corporate status that takes precedence over their individual status; members of the ruling ethnic groups are considered individuals in the eyes of the state; and economic inequality is ensured since subordinate peoples are relegated to positions of dependency and inferiority in the division of labour and the relations of production.

INTERNAL MIGRATION: Movement of population between communities and regions within Canada. Migrants are defined as movers who lived in a different community five years ago; non-migrants include movers who lived in a different residence five years ago but in the same community, as well as those who did not move.

INUIT: Relatively recent Aboriginal immigrants who share genetic similarities with certain Asian peoples and are the majority inhabitants of Canada's northern regions.

INUKTITUT: The language of the Inuit across the Canadian Arctic.

JURISDICTION: The right of authority to have final say or control over a territory, its inhabitants, and activities within that domain. Implies some degree of non-interference from external authorities.

KINSHIP: Relationship by blood or marriage. In precontact days, kinship was the universal basis for the social and political organization of Aboriginal societies, and it is still a powerful influence in those societies today.

KNOWLEDGE OR ABILITY POPULATION: Those people who speak an Aboriginal language well enough to conduct a conversation.

LAND CLAIMS: Process of negotiating agreements that specify the rights of occupation in relation to a particular territory, as well as arrangements among governments, private enterprises, and Aboriginal peoples to control the resources available on lands or other places often designated sacred by Aboriginal groups.

LIFE EXPECTANCY: A statistical measure that indicates the average years of life remaining for a person at a specified age if the current age-specific mortality rates prevail for the remainder of that person's life.

MARGINALITY: Personal experiences and social designation of those with subordinate social, economic, and political status.

MEDIAN AGE: An age "x," such that exactly half of the population is older than x and the other half is younger than x.

MÉTIS: Individuals who identify themselves as being Métis. The history of the Métis is complex, but many people who identify with this Aboriginal group trace their origins to Indian and non-Indian parentage. Distinct Métis and "mixed-blood" cultures emerged in various areas of Canada, the community at

Red River probably being the most well-known. In 1982 the repatriated Canadian constitution identified the Métis as being one of the three Aboriginal groups in Canada.

MOTHER TONGUE POPULATION: Those people whose first language learned at home, and still understood, is an Aboriginal language.

MYSTICISM: The belief that becoming and being are grounded in one's relationship to all immanent and transcendent aspects or dimensions of reality.

NATION: Refers to a people whose shared awareness of their history, culture, and homeland provides a catalyst for collective action to preserve or enhance self-determination over their lives, destiny, and life chances.

NATIONAL INDIAN BROTHERHOOD (NIB): National organization established in 1968 by Aboriginal people to represent the perspectives and interests of status Indians.

NATION-STATE: A nation is a people sharing a distinctive culture and usually associated with a particular territory under one government; a state can be an independent nation or a group of nations sharing the same government. The term "nation" refers primarily to peoples and cultures, while "state" refers primarily to political autonomy.

NATIVE COUNCIL OF CANADA (NCC): National organization established in 1968 by Aboriginal people to represent the perspectives and interests of the Métis and non-status Indians.

NATIVE WOMEN'S ASSOCIATION OF CANADA (NWAC): National organization established in 1973 by Aboriginal women to represent the perspectives and interests of non-status Indian, status Indian, Métis, and Inuit women.

NATURAL INCREASE: A change, either positive or negative, in population size over a given period as a result of the difference between the number of births and deaths.

NEPOTISM: Practice in which those in positions of power use their position to provide social, political, or material benefits primarily to their own relatives or close friends.

NEW TRADITIONALISTS: Aboriginal people committed to combining traditional Aboriginal and modern Western ways of thinking and acting.

NEW WORLD: The term that Europeans applied to the western hemisphere (the Americas), which they had not been aware existed until the voyage of Columbus in 1492.

NON-STATUS INDIAN: An Indian person who is not registered as an Indian under the Indian Act. This may be because his or her ancestors were never registered or because he or she lost Indian status under former provisions of the Indian Act.

NUMBERED TREATIES: In Canada, refers to the treaties signed with the Amerindians in the west and north, by which the prairies were opened for European settlement and the north for mining. The series began with Treaty One, signed at Lower Fort Garry, Manitoba, in 1871, covering the Manitoba nucleus, and concluded with Treaty Eleven, signed in 1921 at various posts in the Mackenzie District and covering the Northwest Territories north of Great Slave Lake.

NUNAVUT: Canada's third territory stretching from Hudson Bay to the northernmost parts of Ellesmere Island. Under the terms of the Nunavut land claim settlement agreement, signed on 25 May 1993, the government of Nunavut has powers like those of other territorial governments, established and maintained in the context of a very close working relationship with the federal government. The basic land claim settlement gives the Inuit outright ownership of about 18 percent of the land — 353 610 square kilometres, including 36 257 square kilometres of subsurface mineral rights. The remaining 82 percent of Nunavut remains Crown land, although the Inuit keep the right to hunt, fish, and trap throughout the territory. The federal government also agreed to pay $1.15 billion, which will be put toward economic development and social revival.

OFF-RESERVE: A term used to describe people, services, or objects that are not part of a reserve but relate to First Nations.

OKA: The scene of a major confrontation in 1990 between Mohawks and Quebeckers over land. Roots of the conflict go back to 1717, when Louis XV of France granted a seigneury to the Seminary of St. Sulpice on the Ottawa River where it meets the St. Lawrence, about 30 kilometres west of Montreal, on condition that it be used for an Amerindian mission. As far as the Mohawks were concerned, this had always been their land, a point that they unsuccessfully tried to assert in 1781, after the British conquest of New France, when the British upheld the legality of the seminary's title. The situation became more hostile over the years as the seminary sold off sections of the grant and the town of Oka developed. The dispute finally boiled over in 1990 when the town of Oka announced its intention to expand a golf course into the disputed area. The Mohawks responded by barricading the location; in the ensuing confrontation, a policeman was killed. In the end, Ottawa responded to Quebec's appeal by sending in the army to settle the situation.

ON/OFF-RESERVE MIGRATION: Movement between places of residence on-reserve and off-reserve (e.g., urban census metropolitan areas, urban non-census metropolitan areas, and rural) within a region and between regions, that involves a permanent change of residence.

ORGANIZED DISSENT: Strategically organized social activity focussed on challenging status quo arrangements and practices.

PATERNALISM: A "father knows best" ideology that views those who maintain power and control over the affairs of others as legitimately deserving their authority and power, and that has served to perpetuate inequality and the oppression of Aboriginal people in Canada.

PATRIARCHY: A social system marked by the supremacy of the father, the reckoning of descent and inheritance according to male lineage, and the dependent legal status of wives and children.

PEDAGOGY: Art/science of teaching based on one's perspective of how and why humans learn.

PLAUSIBILITY STRUCTURE: Organized set of beliefs and practices that explain and legitimize a particular way of thinking about one's place in the world and one's relationship to other human beings.

POPULATION GROWTH: A change, either positive or negative, in population size over a given period.

POPULATION PYRAMID: A special type of bar chart that shows the distribution of a population by age and sex.

POSTCOLONIALISM: Deconstructing analysis or critique of the social ideas, policies, everyday practices, and organizational structures that perpetuate the subordination of indigenous and other marginalized peoples. In Canada, the worst forms of colonialism have been addressed, though systemic aspects of colonialism such as Crown authority have yet to be explored or explained. A postcolonizing constitutionalism promotes the idea of Aboriginal models of self-determination over land, identity, and political voice.

POWER BROKERS: Describes the roles played by the chief and council members on some First Nations reserves, since they have the power to determine who receives the limited band resources, such as band employment opportunities, educational funding, occupational training, housing, housing repairs, and other band-administered benefits and services.

PRECONTACT: In the Americas, the period before the arrival of Europeans.

PREHISTORIC, PROTO-HISTORIC: "Prehistoric" is a general term referring to the period before written histories, while "proto-historic" is more specific, referring to the time immediately before the advent of written history. In Canada, both of these terms refer to the period immediately preceding the arrival of Europeans. Prehistory depends on an interdisciplinary approach for its body of knowledge, drawing upon such areas as geology, archaeology, anthropology, linguistics, oral traditions, and the arts.

PRIMORDIAL EXPERIENCE: The connection of elders (as well as shamans and others) to the pervasive, all-encompassing reality of the life force that reveals to them the oneness of all that has been, is, and is to come.

PROPRIETARY RIGHTS: Exclusive ownership to property of any nature.

RACISM: Assumption that psychocultural traits and capacities are determined by biological race, coupled with the belief in the inherent superiority of a particular race and the right of its people to dominate others.

RATE: The frequency of demographic events (births, deaths, migration, etc.) in a population in a specified time period. Rates tell how frequently an event is occurring. Crude rates are rates computed for an entire population. Specific rates are rates computed for a specified subgroup — usually the population at risk of having the event occur. Thus, rates can be age-specific, sex-specific, and so on.

RATIO: The relation of one population subgroup to another subgroup in the same population; that is, one subgroup divided by another.

RESERVE: Land set aside by the federal government for the use and occupancy of an Indian group or band.

RESIDENTIAL SCHOOLS: Government-established facilities, often run by religious groups, that housed Aboriginal children for the purpose of providing them with a European education for almost a century and began to be phased out in the 1950s.

RESOLUTION 18: A resolution introduced by Premier Peter Lougheed of Alberta in 1982 that represented a formal commitment by the government to negotiate a renewed relationship between the province and the eight Métis settlements in Alberta. It eventually led to the Métis Settlements Accord and to land ownership for the Métis.

RESOURCE MOBILIZATION: Process through which individuals and organizations bring human and material resources together to achieve collective goals.

SAVAGE: Not cultivated, tamed, or domesticated; that which frightens easily. In the case of humans, a person who lives away from society, without law or fixed abode; one who is rude or fierce. In old French, *sauvage* signified a forest habitat; by extension, it came to mean living according to nature, in a manner closer to that of wild animals than to that of humans.

SELF-DETERMINATION: Essentially a political and politicized assertion about autonomy and control, this refers to the right of a people to exercise control over political, cultural, economic, and social issues that are of concern to them.

SELF-GOVERNMENT: Predicated on the premise that a people have the authority to create and maintain the organizational structures necessary to administer the daily affairs of their community.

SEX RATIO: Ratio of males to females in a given population, usually expressed as the number of males per 100 females.

SHAMAN: Intermediaries to the spirit world. Include individual men and women who, due to dreams, visions, illness, or some inborn sensitivity or need, directly experience the presence of spirits and therefore may receive sacred knowledge or possess special power to guide and cure others.

SOCIAL INFRASTRUCTURE: Groups, organizations, policies, legislation, and practices established to address the diverse cultural, health, justice, and education needs of individuals living in a given community.

SOCIAL MOVEMENT IDEOLOGY: Set of beliefs that inform the experiences as well as legitimize the actions of a diverse body of people committed to reorganizing society or any of its major components.

SOVEREIGN RIGHTS: The rights of supreme authority, which are not limited by external authority or influences.

SPECIFIC LAND CLAIMS: Land claims based on perceived violations by federal authorities of their treaty obligations.

STANDARDIZED DEATH RATE: For total Aboriginal population, standardized death rate shows what the Aboriginal death rate would be if it had the same age structure as the overall Canadian population with Aboriginal age-specific death rates.

STATE: A set of politically dominant institutions that has a monopoly on the legitimate use of violence and is formally comprised of the legislature, executive, central and local administration, judiciary, police, and armed forces.

STATUS: The relative position of a person on a publicly recognized scale or hierarchy of social worth.

STATUS INDIAN: An Indian person who is registered under the Indian Act.

STRUCTURAL SUPREMACY: The hierarchical structure of European society at the time of contact between First Nations and European peoples.

SUZERAINTY: Paramount authority over a locally autonomous region.

TOTAL FERTILITY RATE: The sum of the age-specific fertility rates during a given year. It indicates the average number of children that a woman would have if the current age-specific fertility rates prevail over her reproductive period.

TRADITION: Any human practice, belief, institution, or artifact that is regarded as the common inheritance of a social group.

TREATIES: Agreements between two parties for such purposes as peace and friendship, the transfer of land, or establishing terms for trade. In Canada before the Proclamation of 1763, most treaties fell into the peace and friendship category; afterwards, the transfer of land became a principal feature.

UNEMPLOYMENT RATE: Percentage of the total labour force (individuals 15 or older) who were, during the week prior to enumeration, (a) without work, actively looked for work in the past four weeks, and were available for work; or (b) were on layoff and expected to return to their job and were available for work; or (c) had definite arrangements to start a new job in four weeks or less and were available for work.

WELFARE DEPENDENCY: An apparently inescapable cycle of poverty in which individuals and communities become dependent on regular government handouts.

WHITE PAPER (1969): Federal government policy designed to phase out federal responsibilities toward First Nations people and to eventually remove the special status of Indian peoples in Canada.

WISDOM: A holistic understanding of what is true, right, and lasting.

WOMEN'S ISSUES: Issues of concern to Aboriginal women including, to name a few of the more prominent ones, child care, housing, education, family violence, social programs, spirituality, political representation, and legal status.

WORLDVIEW: The view of the world and everything in it as part of the cosmos that is the basis for spiritual and, by extension, cultural formulations.

CONTRIBUTORS

JEAN BARMAN is a professor in the Department of Educational Studies at the University of British Columbia. She is co-editor of *Indian Education in Canada*, 2 vols. (UBC Press, 1986–87) and *First Nations Education in Canada: The Circle Unfolds* (UBC Press, 1995) and author of *The West beyond the West: A History of British Columbia* (University of Toronto Press, 1991, rev. 1996). She co-edits *BC Studies: The British Columbian Quarterly.*

SIMON BRASCOUPÉ, an Algonquin/Mohawk, is a Lecturer in the Department of Native Studies at Trent University in Peterborough, Ontario, and an Adjunct Research Professor at Carleton University. He has a BA and MA from State University in New York at Buffalo, where he is presently completing a PhD. He has extensive national and international experience in environmental issues, traditional knowledge, and the application of TEK and science-based knowledge to resource management and environmental assessment. At Trent University, where he is also on the Indigenous Knowledge PhD Council, his courses focus on traditional knowledge and culture, Aboriginal management theory, and resource management.

JOSEPH E. COUTURE is an Alberta Métis of Cree ancestry. His PhD training and experience are in the areas of Native development, psychology, and education at all levels. His work experience includes teaching, addictions counselling, community development, and research. He has been apprenticed to elders since 1971.

ERNIE CREY is a member of the Sto:lo First Nation in British Columbia's Fraser River Valley. Over the years he has been an Aboriginal activist, social worker, and advocate addressing a wide variety of issue areas in his work with the B.C. Association of Non-Status Indians and the Company of Young Canadians, as vice-president and then acting president of the United Native Nations, and more recently as fisheries manager for the Sto:lo Nation.

OLIVE PATRICIA DICKASON is Professor Emeritus of History at the University of Alberta and Adjunct Professor at the University of Ottawa. She is the author of several books, including *Canada's First Nations: A History of Founding Peoples*, *The Myth of the Savage*, and *Indian Arts in Canada* (all published in English and French). Before she began her career as a scholar, she was a journalist for the Regina *Leader-Post*, the *Winnipeg Free Press*, the Montreal *Gazette*, and *The Globe and Mail*, Toronto. She holds honorary degrees from several universities and is a Fellow of Ryerson Polytechnic University, Toronto. A member of the Order of Canada and recipient of the Canada Medal 125, she holds an Aboriginal Lifetime Achievement Award from the National Aboriginal Achievement Foundation, Toronto, and in 1992 was named Métis Woman of the Year by the Women of the Métis Nation of Alberta.

AUGIE FLERAS is an Associate Professor in the Department of Sociology at the University of Waterloo. His primary interests reside in the field of race, ethnic, and Aboriginal relations, with particular emphasis on Aboriginal–state renewal in Canada and Aotearoa (New Zealand), multiculturalism, and society-building, and the concept of institutional accommodation. He has spent three years in New Zealand at the University of Canterbury pursuing his interests in the ongoing reconstruction of Maori–Crown relations, with a particular focus on their implications for Canada. He has published widely in the areas of race, ethnic, and Aboriginal relations and intends to continue with current research on the topic of media–minority relations and the politics of representation.

SUZANNE FOURNIER, who is of Aboriginal ancestry, was raised in the rural foothills of Alberta near the Stoney Reserve just west of Calgary. In her long-time work as a journalist for the Vancouver *Province*, she has worked with and written countless articles about Aboriginal people.

TERRY FOX is Nakoda-Sioux and a member of the Stoney Nation of Morley, Alberta. She currently resides on the west coast with her son. Terry has a Bachelor of Arts in First Nation Studies and is currently working on her Masters degree in Public Administration at the University of Victoria. She strongly believes that due to the various effects of long-term oppression, Native communities need to undergo healing prior to implementating Native self-government. Much of her writing reflects this belief.

JAN HARE is an Anishinaabe member of the Mchi'ging (West Bay) First Nation in Ontario. As a PhD candidate at the University of British Columbia, she is focussing her research on Aboriginal literacy. Her exposure to the diversity of First Nations in Canada has provided a strong foundation for her commitment to issues concerning Aboriginal people.

DAVID LONG, who is of Anglo-Celtic descent, resides with his partner and their four children in Edmonton, Alberta. He is currently Associate Professor of Sociology at The King's University College. Along with the disciplinary and interdisciplinary writing and speaking he has done in exploring relations involving Aboriginal and non-Aboriginal peoples in Canada, he continues to be involved in academic and non-academic dialogue with those interested in examining contemporary issues that involve such areas as religion and spirituality, science and technology, pedagogy, gender, and deviance. His commitment to a just and interdisciplinary vision for academic writing is reflected in his wide variety of research collaborations and writing projects.

PETER MCFARLANE is a Montreal-based freelance writer. His most recent book is *Brotherhood to Nationhood: George Manuel and the Making of the Modern Indian Movement.*

PATRICIA MONTURE-ANGUS was born to the Mohawks at Six Nations (near Brantford, Ontario). She currently resides at the Thunderchild First Nation with her partner, children, and several foster children. She has taught in Canadian universities for the last decade and is also an activist lobbying for the rights of Aboriginal people, including women and prisoners.

MARY JANE NORRIS is a senior research manager with the Department of Indian and Northern Affairs. At the time of writing she was a senior analyst with Statistics Canada. She has written on Aboriginal languages and demography, including migration and population projections. Her interest in Aboriginal issues stems in part from her Aboriginal ancestry, with family roots in the Algonquin First Nation of Golden Lake, in the Ottawa Valley.

EVELYN PETERS is an Associate Professor at Queen's University, Kingston, Ontario, teaching in the areas of urban and social geography. Her research and publications are in the areas of Aboriginal self-government, the demographic characteristics of urban Aboriginal peoples, and the ways in which Aboriginal urbanization has been conceptualized in non-Aboriginal literature.

CORA J. VOYAGEUR is an Assistant Professor at the University of Calgary. Her research and publications investigate the Aboriginal experience in Canada, including education, economic development, social stratification, and women's issues. Her dissertation explored the impact of the 1986 Employment Equity Act on Aboriginal people in Canada. She is a member of the Athabasca Chipewyan First Nation from Fort Chipewyan, Alberta.

DENIS WALL has a PhD in Intercultural Education from the University of Alberta. His main research interests have been in educational and management decision making and in Canadian Aboriginal issues. He has taught Canadian Aboriginal issues in Sociology for Concordia University College and for the School of Native Studies at the University of Alberta. He has conducted research and consultancies internationally and in a number of Canadian provinces.

APPENDIX

Treaty No. 6 and the Nisga'a Final Agreement

TREATY MAKING OLD AND NEW

A treaty is a formal agreement between two or more peoples containing terms of relations involving trade, peace, political alliance, and the like. Consequently, even though each treaty in Canada's history is unique, all reflect a patterning of expectations and conditions of relations. As George Stanley (1988, p. 11) notes, Canada's treaties all designate an area of "reserve lands" to be ceded; mention the names of chiefs and other spokespersons in positions of leadership or political authority; specify any monetary considerations to be paid; specify that any such payments take the form of annuities or "interest money" to be paid to each member of the signatory band; reserve the rights of the state government to acquire any reserve land required for roads, railways, or other public works; specify means by which reserve residents can generate their own livelihood on reserve lands; and state conditions of provision for various other services that seek to ensure the physical, educational, economic, and social well-being of reserve residents.

Although on first reading the terms of many of Canada's early treaties appear to be quite simple and straightforward, there nonetheless continue to be serious points of contention between Aboriginal and state representatives over the meaning and implications of aspects of these treaties. For example, despite the fact that the Indian Act of 1876 states that the government accepted responsibility to "prevent, mitigate, and control the spread of diseases on reserves ..., to provide medical treatment and health service for Indians, to provide compulsory hospitalization and treatment for infectious diseases ..., and to provide for sanitary conditions ... on reserves," there continues to be much dispute and disagreement over the meaning and implications of the "medicine chest clause" contained in Treaty 6 (Young, 1984, p. 258).

Moreover, there are obvious differences between older treaties and the much more recent Nisga'a Treaty. The sheer volume and complexity of the Nisga'a Agreement are evidence of significant changes in the meaning and process of treaty-making in latter twentieth-century Canada. As noted throughout *Visions of the Heart*, some of the more important developments contributing to the "modernization" of Aboriginal issues and activities — including treaty-making — include the increased politicization and bureaucratization of Aboriginal–state relations, changes in decision-making processes and structures among Aboriginal peoples, publicly expressed disagreement among Aboriginal people over how to think about and act in relation to a wide variety of issues, and increased media coverage and public awareness of Aboriginal issues.

In this appendix, we are able to include the full text of Treaty 6, though space limitations prevent the inclusion of the full 250-page Nisga'a Treaty. Our hope, nonetheless, is to provoke discussion around a number of issues and questions by including certain sections in our abridged version of the Nisga'a Treaty. For example, while many sections of the treaty indicate Nisga'a sovereignty in relation to their land and many cultural, legal, political, and economic aspects of Nisga'a life, numerous sections also specify that the treaty is subsumed under the Constitution Act of Canada. Moreover, the content and language of the treaty provide evidence of the bureaucratized complexity of Nisga'a society and of relations between the Nisga'a and various levels and branches of state government; implicitly and explicitly stated responsibilities for development, management and use of natural resources in Nisga'a territory; and the organization, promotion, and delivery of services by and for those living on Nisga'a land.

While social scientists and others can now look back and see evidence in Treaty 6 of what could be termed the "culturally genocidal paternalism" that informed the attitudes and actions of Crown and state signatories, the conditions and implications of Nisga'a–state relations appear to be much less clear. Perhaps we might say that this issue indicates both the ongoing dilemma and hope faced by those wanting to establish treaty relations in a postcolonial context; it highlights the many challenges facing those who are committed to the idea of geographically, socially, politically, and economically marginalized people becoming sovereign partners within a mutually respectful, supportive, and interdependent relationship.

TREATY NO. 6[1]

Articles of a treaty made and concluded near Carlton on the 23rd day of August and on the 28th day of said month, respectively, and near Fort Pitt on the 9th day of September, in the year of Our Lord one thousand eight hundred and seventy-six, between Her Most Gracious Majesty the Queen of Great Britain and Ireland, by Her Commissioners, the Honourable Alexander Morris, Lieutenant-Governor of the Province of Manitoba and the North-west Territories, and the Honourable James McKay, and the Honourable William Joseph Christie, of the one part, and the Plain and Wood Cree and the other Tribes of Indians, inhabitants of the country within the limits hereinafter defined and described by their Chiefs, chosen and named as hereinafter mentioned, of the other part.

Source: Indian Affairs and Northern Development. 1964. IAND Pub. no. QS-0574-000-EE-A-1, Cat. no. R33-0664. Ottawa: Queen's Printer.

Whereas the Indians inhabiting the said country have, pursuant to an appointment made by the said Commissioners, been convened at meetings at Fort Carlton, Fort Pitt and Battle River, to deliberate upon certain matters of interest to Her Most Gracious Majesty, of the one part, and the said Indians of the other.

And whereas the said Indians have been notified and informed by Her Majesty's said Commissioners that it is the desire of Her Majesty to open up for settlement, immigration and such other purposes as to Her Majesty may seem meet, a tract of country bounded and described as hereinafter mentioned, and to obtain the consent thereto of Her Indian subjects inhabiting the said tract, and to make a treaty and arrange with them, so that there may be peace and good will between them and Her Majesty, and that they may know and be assured of what allowance they are to count upon and receive from Her Majesty's bounty and benevolence.

And whereas the Indians of the said tract, duly convened in council, as aforesaid, and being requested by Her Majesty's said Commissioners to name certain Chiefs and Headmen, who should be authorized on their behalf to conduct such negotiations and sign any treaty to be founded thereon, and to become responsible for Her Majesty for their faithful performance by their respective Bands of such obligations as shall be assumed by them, the said Indians have thereupon named for that purpose, that is to say, representing the Indians who make the treaty at Carlton, the several Chiefs and Councillors who have subscribed hereto, and representing the Indians who make the treaty at Fort Pitt, the several Chiefs and Councillors who have subscribed hereto.

And thereupon, in open council, the different Bands having presented their Chiefs to the said Commissioners as the Chiefs and Headmen, for the purposes aforesaid, of the respective Bands of Indians inhabiting the said district hereinafter described.

And whereas, the said Commissioners then and there received and acknowledged the persons so presented as Chiefs and Headmen, for the purposes aforesaid, of the respective Bands of Indians inhabiting the said district hereinafter described.

And whereas, the said Commissioners have proceeded to negotiate a treaty with the said Indians, and the same has been finally agreed upon and concluded, and follows, that is to say:

The Plain and Wood Cree Tribes of Indians, and all the other Indians inhabiting the district hereinafter described and defined, do hereby cede, release, surrender and yield up to the Government of the Dominion of Canada, for Her Majesty the Queen and Her successors forever, all their rights, titles and privileges, whatsoever, to the lands included within the following limits, that is to say:

Commencing at the mouth of the river emptying in to the north-west angle of Cumberland Lake; thence westerly up the said river to its source; thence on a straight line in a westerly direction to the head of Green Lake; thence northerly to the elbow in the Beaver River; thence down the said river northerly to a point twenty miles from the said elbow; thence in a westerly direction, keeping on a line generally parallel with the said Beaver River (above the elbow), and about twenty miles distant therefrom, to the source of the said river; thence northerly to the north-easterly point of the south shore of Red Deer Lake, continuing westerly along the said shore to the western limit thereof; and thence due west to the Athabasca River; thence up the said river, against the stream, to the Jaspar House, in the Rocky Mountains; thence on a course south-easterly, following the easterly range of the mountains to the source of the main branch of the Red Deer River; thence down the said river, with the stream, to the junction therewith of the outlet of the river, being the outlet of the Buffalo Lake; thence due east twenty miles; thence on a straight line south-eastwardly to the mouth of the said Red Deer River on the south branch of the Saskatchewan River; thence eastwardly and northwardly, following on the boundaries of the tracts conceded by the several treaties numbered four and five to the place of beginning.

And also, all their rights, titles and privileges whatsoever to all other lands wherever situated in the North-west Territories, or in any other Province or portion of Her Majesty's Dominions, situated and being within the Dominion of Canada.

The tract comprised within the lines above described embracing an area of 121 000 square miles, be the same more or less.

To have and to hold the same to Her Majesty the Queen and Her successors forever.

And Her Majesty the Queen hereby agrees and undertakes to lay aside reserves for farming lands, due respect being had to the lands at present cultivated by the said Indians, and other reserves for the benefit of the said Indians, to be administered and dealt with for them by Her Majesty's Government of the Dominion of Canada; provided, all such reserves shall not exceed in all one square mile for each family of five, or in that proportion for larger or smaller families, in manner following, that is to say: that the Chief Superintendent of Indian Affairs shall depute and send a suitable person to determine and set apart the reserves for each band, after consulting with the Indians thereof as to the locality which may be found to be most suitable for them.

Provided, however, that Her Majesty reserves the right to deal with any settlers within the bounds of any lands reserved for any Band as She shall deem fit, and also that the aforesaid reserves of land, or any interest therein, may be sold or otherwise disposed of by Her Majesty's Government for the use and benefit of the said Indians entitled thereto, with their consent first had and obtained; and with a view to show the satisfaction of Her Majesty with the behaviour and good conduct of Her Indians, She hereby, through Her Commissioners, makes them a present of twelve dollars for each man, woman and child belonging to the Bands here represented, in extinguishment of all claims heretofore preferred.

And further, Her Majesty agrees to maintain schools for instruction in such reserves hereby made as to Her Government of the Dominion of Canada may seem advisable, whenever the Indians of the reserve shall desire it.

Her Majesty further agrees with Her said Indians that within the boundary of Indian reserves, until otherwise determined by Her Government of the Dominion of Canada, no intoxicating liquor shall be allowed to be introduced or sold, and all laws now in force, or hereafter to be enacted, to preserve Her Indian subjects inhabiting the reserves or living elsewhere within Her North-west Territories from the evil influence of the use of intoxicating liquors, shall be strictly enforced.

Her Majesty further agrees with Her said Indians that they, the said Indians, shall have right to pursue their avocations of hunting and fishing throughout the tract surrendered as hereinbefore described, subject to such regulations as may from time to time be made by Her Government of Her Dominion of Canada, and saving and excepting such tracts as may from time to time be required or taken up for settlement, mining, lumbering or other purposes by Her said Government of the Dominion of Canada, or by any of the subjects thereof duly authorized therefor by the said Government.

It is further agreed between Her Majesty and Her said Indians, that such sections of the reserves above indicated as may at any time be required for public works or buildings, of what nature soever, may be appropriated for that purpose by Her Majesty's Government of the Dominion of Canada, due compensation being made for the value of any improvements thereon.

And further, that Her Majesty's Commissioners shall, as soon as possible after the execution of this treaty, cause to be taken an accurate census of all the Indians inhabiting the tract above described, distributing them in families, and shall, in every year ensuing the date hereof, at some period in each year, to be duly notified to the Indians, and at a place or places to be appointed for that purpose within the territory ceded, pay to each Indian person the sum of $5 per head yearly.

It is further agreed between Her Majesty and the said Indians, that the sum of $1500.00 per annum shall be yearly and every year expended by her Majesty in the purchase of ammunition, and twine nets, for the use of the said Indians, in manner following, that is to say: In the reasonable discretion, as regards the distribution thereof among the Indians inhabiting the several reserves, or otherwise, included herein, of Her Majesty's Indian Agent having the supervision of this treaty.

It is further agreed between Her Majesty and the said Indians, that the following articles shall be supplied to any Band of the said Indians who are now cultivating the soil, or who shall hereafter commence to cultivate the land, that is to say: Four hoes for every family actually cultivating; also, two spades per family as aforesaid; one plough for every three families, as aforesaid; one harrow for every three families, as aforesaid; two scythes and one whetstone, and two hay forks and two reaping hooks, for every family as aforesaid, and also two axes; and also one crosscut saw, one hand-saw, one pit-saw, the necessary files, one grindstone and one auger for each Band; and also for each Chief for the use of his Band, one chest of ordinary carpenter's tools; also, for each Band, enough of wheat, barley, potatoes and oats to plant the land actually broken up for cultivating by such band; also for each Band four oxen, one bull and six cows; also, one boar and two sows, and one hand-mill when any Band shall raise sufficient grain therefor. All the aforesaid articles to be given once for all for the encouragement of the practice of agriculture among the Indians.

It is further agreed between Her Majesty and the said Indians, that each Chief, duly recognized as such, shall receive an annual salary of twenty-five dollars per annum; and each subordinate officer, not exceeding four for each Band, shall receive fifteen dollars per annum; and each such Chief and subordinate officer, as aforesaid, shall also receive once every three years, a suitable suit of clothing, and each Chief shall receive, in recognition of the closing of the treaty, a suitable flag and medal, and also as soon as convenient, one horse, harness and waggon.

That in the event hereafter of the Indians comprised within this treaty being overtaken by any pestilence, or by a general famine, the Queen being satisfied and certified thereof by Her Indian Agent or Agents, will grant to the Indians assistance of such character and to such extent as Her Chief Superintendent of Indian Affairs shall deem necessary and sufficient to relieve the Indians from the calamity that shall have befallen them.

That during the next three years, after two or more of the reserves hereby agreed to be set apart to the Indians shall have been agreed upon and surveyed, there shall be granted to the Indians included under the Chiefs adhering to the treaty at Carlton, each spring, the sum of one thousand dollars, to be expended for them by Her Majesty's Indian Agents, in the purchase of provisions for the use of such of the Band as are actually settled on the reserves and are engaged in cultivating the soil, to assist them in such cultivation.

That a medicine chest shall be kept at the house of each Indian Agent for the use and benefit of the Indians at the direction of such agent.

That with regard to the Indians included under the Chiefs adhering to the treaty at Fort Pitt, and to those Chiefs within the treaty limits who may hereafter give their adhesion thereto (exclusively, however, of the Indians of the Carlton region), there shall, during three years, after two or more reserves shall have been agreed upon and surveyed be distributed each spring among the Bands cultivating the soil on such reserves, by Her Majesty's Chief Indian Agent for this treaty, in his discretion, a sum not exceeding one thousand dollars, in the purchase of provisions for the use of such members of the band as are actually settled on the reserves and engaged in the cultivation of the soil, to assist and encourage them in such cultivation.

That in lieu of waggons, if they desire it and declare their option to that effect, there shall be given to each of the Chiefs adhering hereto at Fort Pitt or elsewhere hereafter (exclusively of those in the Carlton district), in recognition of this treaty, as soon as the same can be conveniently transported, two carts with iron bushings and tires.

And the undersigned Chiefs on their own behalf and on behalf of all other Indians inhabiting the tract within ceded, do hereby solemnly promise and engage to strictly observe this treaty, and also to conduct and behave themselves as good and loyal subjects of Her Majesty the Queen.

They promise and engage that they will in all respects obey and abide by the law, and they will maintain peace and good order between each other, and also between themselves and other tribes of Indians, and between themselves and others of Her Majesty's subjects, whether Indians or whites, now inhabiting or hereafter to inhabit any part of the said ceded tracts, and that they will not molest the person or property of any inhabitant of such ceded tracts, or the property of Her Majesty the Queen, or interfere with or trouble any person passing or travelling through the said tracts, or any part thereof, and that they will aid and assist the officers of Her Majesty in bringing to justice and punishment any Indian offending against the stipulations of this treaty, or infringing the laws in force in the country so ceded.

THE NISGA'A FINAL AGREEMENT

Preamble

WHEREAS the Nisga'a Nation has lived in the Nass Area since time immemorial;

WHEREAS the Nisga'a Nation is an aboriginal people of Canada;

WHEREAS section 35 of the *Constitution Act, 1982* recognizes and affirms the existing aboriginal and treaty rights of the aboriginal peoples of Canada, which the Courts have stated include aboriginal title;

WHEREAS the Nisga'a Nation has never entered into a treaty with Canada or British Columbia;

WHEREAS the Nisga'a Nation has sought a just and equitable settlement of the land question since the arrival of the British Crown, including the preparation of the Nisga'a Petition to His Majesty's Privy Council, dated 21 May, 1913, and the conduct of the litigation that led to the decision of the Supreme Court of Canada in *Calder v. the Attorney-General of British Columbia* in 1973, and this Agreement is intended to be the just and equitable settlement of the land question;

WHEREAS Canadian courts have stated that the reconciliation between the prior presence of aboriginal peoples and the assertion of sovereignty by the Crown is best achieved through negotiation and agreement, rather than through litigation or conflict;

WHEREAS the Parties intend that this Agreement will result in this reconciliation and establish a new relationship among them;

WHEREAS this Agreement sets out Nisga'a section 35 rights inside and outside of the area that is identified in this Agreement as Nisga'a Lands;

Source: Canada, British Columbia, and Nisga'a Nation, Nisga'a Final Agreement. Ottawa: Queen's Printer, 1998.

WHEREAS the Parties acknowledge the ongoing importance to the Nisga'a Nation of the *Simgigat* and *Sigidimhaanak* (hereditary chiefs and matriarchs) continuing to tell their *Adaawak* (oral histories) relating to their *Ango'oskw* (family hunting, fishing, and gathering territories) in accordance with the *Ayuuk* (Nisga'a traditional laws and practices);

WHEREAS the Parties intend their relationship to be based on a new approach to mutual recognition and sharing, and to achieve this mutual recognition and sharing by agreeing on rights, rather than by the extinguishment of rights; and

WHEREAS the Parties intend that this Agreement will provide certainty with respect to Nisga'a ownership and use of lands and resources, and the relationship of federal, provincial and Nisga'a laws, within the Nass Area;

NOW THEREFORE THE PARTIES AGREE AS FOLLOWS:

Chapter 2: General Provisions

Nature of Agreement

1. This Agreement is a treaty and a land claims agreement within the meaning of sections 25 and 35 of the *Constitution Act, 1982*.

Representation and Warranty

5. The Nisga'a Nation represents and warrants to Canada and British Columbia that, in respect of the matters dealt with in this Agreement, it has the authority to enter, and it enters, into this Agreement on behalf of all the persons who have any aboriginal rights, including aboriginal title, in Canada, or any claims to those rights, based on their identity as Nisga'a.
6. Canada and British Columbia represent and warrant to the Nisga'a Nation that, in respect of the matters dealt with in this Agreement, they have the authority to enter into this Agreement within their respective authorities.

Nisga'a Culture and Language

7. Nisga'a citizens have the right to practice the Nisga'a culture, and to use the Nisga'a language, in a manner consistent with this Agreement.

Constitution of Canada

8. This Agreement does not alter the Constitution of Canada, including:
   a. the distribution of powers between Canada and British Columbia;
   b. the identity of the Nisga'a Nation as an aboriginal people of Canada within the meaning of the *Constitution Act, 1982*; and
   c. sections 25 and 35 of the *Constitution Act, 1982*.

9. The *Canadian Charter of Rights and Freedoms* applies to the Nisga'a Government in respect of all matters within its authority, bearing in mind the free and democratic nature of Nisga'a Government as set out in this Agreement.

Other Rights, Benefits, and Programs

15. Nisga'a citizens who are Canadian citizens or permanent residents of Canada continue to be entitled to all of the rights and benefits of other Canadian citizens or permanent residents of Canada, applicable to them from time to time.
18. Subject to the *Indian Act* Transition Chapter and paragraphs 5 and 6 of the Taxation Chapter, the *Indian Act* has no application to the Nisga'a Nation, Nisga'a Villages, Nisga'a Institutions, or Nisga'a citizens as of the effective date, except for the purpose of determining whether an individual is an "Indian."

Full and Final Settlement

22. This Agreement constitutes the full land final settlement in respect of the aboriginal rights, including aboriginal title, in Canada of the Nisga'a Nation.

Other Aboriginal People

35. If Canada or British Columbia enters into a treaty or a land claims agreement, within the meaning of sections 25 and 35 of the *Constitution Act, 1982*, with another aboriginal people, and that treaty or land claims agreement adversely affects Nisga'a section 35 right as set out in this Agreement:
    a. Canada or British Columbia, or both, as the case may be, will provide the Nisga'a Nation with additional or replacement rights or other appropriate remedies;
    b. at the request of the Nisga'a Nation, the Parties will negotiate an attempt to reach agreement on the provision of those additional or replacement rights or other appropriate remedies; and
    c. if the Parties are unable to reach agreement on the provision of the additional or replacement rights or other appropriate remedies, the provision of those additional or replacement rights or remedies will be determined in accordance with Stage Three of the Dispute Resolution Chapter.

Conflict and Inconsistency

53. If a Nisga'a law has an incidental impact on a subject matter in respect of which Nisga'a Government does not have jurisdiction to make laws, and there is an inconsistency or conflict between that incidental impact and a federal or provincial law in respect of that subject matter, the federal or provincial law prevails to the extent of the inconsistency or conflict.

Chapter 3: Lands

Nisga'a Lands

General

1. On the effective date, Nisga'a Lands consist of all lands, including islands, within the boundaries set out in Appendix A except submerged lands, the Gingietl Creek Ecological Reserve, the Nisga'a Highway corridor, and the lands within the boundaries set out in Appendix B: ...

2. On the effective date, Nisga'a Lands comprise 1992 square kilometres, more or less, of land in the lower Nass Valley, ...

Ownership of Nisga'a Lands

3. On the effective date, the Nisga'a Nation owns Nisga'a Lands in fee simple, being the largest estate known in law. This estate is not subject to any condition, proviso, restriction, exception, or reservation set out in the *Land Act*, or any comparable limitation under any federal or provincial law. No estate or interest in Nisga'a Lands can be expropriated except as permitted by, and in accordance with, this Agreement.

Designations of Nisga'a Lands

16. Nisga'a Lands comprise Nisga'a Public Lands, Nisga'a Private Lands, and Nisga'a Village Lands.

Mineral Resources

19. For greater certainty, in accordance with paragraph 3, on the effective date the Nisga'a Nation owns all mineral resources on or under Nisga'a Lands.

20. Nisga'a Lisims Governments has the exclusive authority to determine, collect, and administer any fees, rent, royalties, or other charges in respect of mineral resources on or under Nisga'a Lands.

Federal Acquisition of Interests in Nisga'a Lands and Nisga'a Fee Simple Lands

General

73. Canada acknowledges that it is of fundamental importance to maintain the size and integrity of Nisga'a Lands and Nisga'a Fee Simple Lands, and therefore, as a general principle, estates or interests in Nisga'a Lands, or Nisga'a Fee Simple Lands, will not be expropriated under federal legislation.

Heritage Sites and Key Geographic Features

95. On the effective date, British Columbia will designate as provincial heritage sites the sites of cultural and historic significance outside Nisga'a Lands that are set out in Appendix F-1. The Parties acknowledge that those sites may

have cultural or historic significance to persons or groups other than the Nisg̲a'a Nation.

Parks and Ecological Reserve

102. The Nisg̲a'a Nation has the right to participate in the planning, management, and development of the Park and the Ecological Reserve in accordance with this Agreement.

Water Volumes

Nisg̲a'a Water Reservation

122. On the effective date, British Columbia will establish a Nisg̲a'a water reservation, in favour of the Nisg̲a'a Nation, of 300 000 cubic decametres of water per year from:
a. the Nass River; and
b. other streams wholly or partially within Nisg̲a'a Lands for domestic, industrial, and agricultural purposes.

Chapter 5: Forest Resources

Ownership of Resources

3. On the effective date, the Nisg̲a'a Nation owns all forest resources on Nisg̲a'a Lands.

Applicable Laws and Standards

Forest Practices and Standards

6. Nisg̲a'a Lisims Government will make laws in respect of the management of timber resources on Nisg̲a'a Lands, that will take effect on the effective date.

8. Laws made under paragraph 6 will include forest standards that meet or exceed forest standards established under forest practices legislation applicable to Crown land, and will include forest standards in respect of the following subject areas if these subject areas are addressed in forest practices legislation:
a. riparian management;
b. cut block design distribution;
c. road construction, maintenance and deactivation;
d. reforestation;
e. soil conservation;
f. biodiversity;
g. hazard abatement, fire preparedness and initial fire suppression;
h. silvicultural systems and logging methods; and
i. forest health.

Chapter 6: Access

Nisga'a Public Lands

Nisga'a Rights and Obligations

1. Except as notified by this Agreement, the Nisga'a Nation, as owner of Nisga'a Lands, has the same rights and obligations in respect of public access to Nisga'a Lands as other owners of estates in fee simple have in respect of public access to their land, and in respect of Nisga'a Public Lands, the Nisga'a Nation has liabilities similar to those of the Crown in respect of unoccupied Crown land.

Reasonable Public Access

2. Nisga'a Lisims Government will allow reasonable public access to and onto Nisga'a Public Lands for temporary non-commercial and recreational uses, ...
3. Nisga'a Lisims Government may make laws in accordance with the Nisga'a Government Chapter regulating public access to and onto Nisga'a Public Lands, ...

Chapter 8: Fisheries

General

Nisga'a Fish Entitlements

1. Nisga'a citizens have the right to harvest fish and aquatic plants in accordance with this Agreement, subject to:
   a. measures that are necessary for conservation; and
   b. legislation enacted for the purposes of public health or public safety.
6. Nisga'a Lisims Government may authorize persons other than Nisga'a citizens to harvest fish or aquatic plants in Nisga'a fisheries, in accordance with this Agreement, the Harvest Agreement and Nisga'a annual fishing plans. This authority is not intended to alter the application of federal and provincial laws of general application in respect of foreign fishing vessels in Canadian waters.

Trade and Barter

9. Subject to Nisga'a laws, Nisga'a citizens have the right to trade or barter among themselves or with other aboriginal people any fish and aquatic plants harvested in Nisga'a fisheries.

Lisims Fisheries Conservation Trust

Establishment

96. As soon as practicable after the effective date, Canada and the Nisga'a Nation will establish a trust to be known as the Lisims Fisheries Conservation Trust, and will undertake all actions required to register the trust as a charity for the purposes of the *Income Tax Act*.

International Arrangements

115. Canada will consult with the Nisg̲a'a Nation with respect to the formulation of Canada's positions in relation to international discussions or negotiations that may significantly affect fisheries resources referred to in this Agreement.

Chapter 9: Wildlife and Migratory Birds

General

Nisg̲a'a Wildlife Entitlements
1. Nisg̲a'a citizens have the right to harvest wildlife throughout the Nass Wildlife Area in accordance with this Agreement subject to:
   a. measures that are necessary for conservation; and
   b. legislation enacted for the purposes of public health or public safety.

Licences, Fees, Charges, and Royalties
10. Canada and British Columbia will not require Nisg̲a'a citizens:
   a. to have federal or provincial licences; or
   b. to pay fees, charges, or royalties ... .

Wildlife Management

Responsibilities of the Parties
35. Subject to this Agreement, the Minister is responsible for wildlife.
36. The Minister will manage all wildlife harvesting within the Nass Wildlife Area in a manner consistent with any total allowable harvest and harvest objectives established under this Agreement.
37. Nisg̲a'a Lisims Government may make laws that are in respect of the Nisg̲a'a Nation's rights and obligations on respect of wildlife and migratory birds under, and that are consistent with, this Agreement and that are not inconsistent with the annual management plans ...

Wildlife Committee
45. On the effective date, the Parties will establish a Wildlife Committee to facilitate wildlife management within the Nass Wildlife Area.

Chapter 10: Environmental Assessment and Protection

Environmental Protection

11. Except as otherwise set out in this Agreement, Nisg̲a'a Lisims Government may make laws in respect of environmental protection on Nisg̲a'a Lands, including discharges into streams within Nisg̲a'a Lands. In the event of a conflict between a Nisg̲a'a law under this paragraph and a federal or provincial law, the federal or provincial law will prevail to the extent of the conflict.

Chapter 11: Nisga'a Government

Self-Government

1. The Nisga'a Nation has the right to self-government, and the authority to make laws, as set out in this Agreement.

Recognition of Nisga'a Lisims Government and Nisga'a Village Governments

2. Nisga'a Lisims Government and Nisga'a Village Governments, as provided for under the Nisga'a Constitution, are the governments of the Nisga'a Nation and the Nisga'a Villages, respectively.
3. Except as may otherwise be agreed to by the relevant Parties in respect of particular matters, Nisga'a Lisims Government is responsible for intergovernmental relations between the Nisga'a Nation on the one hand, and Canada or British Columbia, or both, on the other hand.
4. The exercise of Nisga'a Government jurisdiction and authority set out in this Agreement will evolve over time.

Legal Status and Capacity

5. The Nisga'a Nation, and each Nisga'a Village, is a separate and distinct legal entity, with the capacity, rights, powers, and privileges of a natural person, including to:
   a. enter into contracts and agreements;
   b. acquire and hold property or an interest in property, and sell or otherwise dispose of that property or interest;
   c. raise, spend, invest, or borrow money;
   d. sue and be sued; and
   e. do other things ancillary to the exercise of its rights, powers and privileges.
6. The rights, powers, and privileges of the Nisga'a Nation, and of each Nisga'a Village, will be exercised in accordance with:
   a. this Agreement;
   b. the Nisga'a Constitution; and
   c. Nisga'a laws.
7. The Nisga'a Nation will act through its Nisga'a Lisims Government in exercising its rights, powers, and privileges and in carrying out its duties, functions, and obligations.
8. Each Nisga'a Village will act through its Nisga'a Village Government in exercising its rights, powers, and privileges and in carrying out its duties, functions, and obligation.

Nisga'a Constitution

9. The Nisga'a Nation will have a Nisga'a Constitution, consistent with this Agreement, which will ...

k. require that Nisga'a Government be democratically accountable to Nisga'a citizens, ...

o. recognize and protect rights and freedoms of Nisga'a citizens, ...

Nisga'a Government Structure

12. Each Nisga'a Village Government consists of elected members as set out in the Nisga'a Constitution.

14. Nisga'a Lisims Government consists of the following members as set out in the Nisga'a Constitution:
    a. at least three officers elected by the Nisga'a Nation in a general election;
    b. the elected members of the Nisga'a Village Governments; and
    c. at least one representative elected by the Nisga'a citizens of each Nisga'a Urban Local.

Relations with Individuals Who Are Not Nisga'a Citizens

19. Nisga'a Government will consult with individuals who are ordinarily resident within Nisga'a Lands and who are not Nisga'a citizens about Nisga'a Government decisions that directly and significantly affect them.

20. Nisga'a Government will provide that individuals who are ordinarily resident within Nisga'a Lands and who are not Nisga'a citizens may participate in a Nisga'a Public Institution, if the activities of that Nisga'a Public Institution directly and significantly affect them.

Legislative Jurisdiction and Authority

Nisga'a Government

34. Nisga'a Lisims Government may make laws in respect of the administration, management and operation of Nisga'a Government, including:
    a. the establishment of Nisga'a Public Institutions, including their respective powers, duties, composition, and membership;
    b. powers, duties, responsibilities, remuneration, and indemnification of members, officials, employees, and appointees of Nisga'a Institutions;
    c. the establishment of Nisga'a Corporations, but the registration or incorporation of Nisga'a Corporations must be under federal or provincial laws;
    d. the delegation of Nisga'a Government authority, but the authority to make laws may be delegated only to a Nisga'a Institution;
    e. financial administration of the Nisga'a Nation, Nisga'a Villages, and Nisga'a Institutions; and
    f. elections, by-elections, and referenda.

35. Each Nisga'a Village Government may make laws in respect of the administration, management, and operation of that Nisga'a Village Government, including:
    a. the establishment of Nisga'a Public Institutions of that Nisga'a Village Government, including their respective powers, duties, composition, and membership;

b. powers, duties, responsibilities, remuneration, and indemnification of members, officials, employees, and appointees of Nisga'a Public Institutions referred to in subparagraph (a); and

c. the delegation of the Nisga'a Village Government's authority, but the authority to make laws may be delegated only to a Nisga'a Institution.

36. In the event of an inconsistency or conflict between a Nisga'a law under paragraphs 34 or 35 and a federal or provincial law, the Nisga'a law prevails to the extent of the inconsistency or conflict.

Culture and Language

41. Nisga'a Lisims Government may make laws to preserve, promote, and develop Nisga'a culture and Nisga'a language, including laws to authorize or accredit the use, reproduction, and representation of Nisga'a cultural symbols and practices, and the teaching of Nisga'a language.

43. In the event of an inconsistency or conflict between a Nisga'a law under paragraph 41 and a federal or provincial law, the Nisga'a law prevails to the extent of the inconsistency or conflict.

Public Order, Peace, and Safety

59. Nisga'a Lisims Government may make laws in respect of the regulation, control, or prohibition of any actions, activities, or undertakings on Nisga'a Lands, or on submerged lands within Nisga'a Lands, other than actions, activities, or undertakings on submerged lands that are authorized by the Crown, that constitute, or may constitute, a nuisance, a trespass, a danger to public health, or a threat to public order, peace, or safety.

60. A Nisga'a Village Government may make laws in respect of the regulation, control, or prohibition of any actions, activities, or undertakings on the Nisga'a Village Lands of that Nisga'a Village, or on submerged lands within those Nisga'a Village Lands, other than actions, activities, or undertakings on those submerged lands that are authorized by the Crown, that constitute, or may constitute, a nuisance, a trespass, a danger to public health, or a threat to public order, peace, or safety.

61. For greater certainty, Nisga'a Government authority does not include authority in respect of criminal law.

Social Services

78. Nisga'a Lisims Government may make laws in respect of the provision of social services by Nisga'a Government to Nisga'a citizens, other than the licensing and regulation of facility-based services off Nisga'a Lands.

Health Services

82. Nisga'a Lisims Government may make laws in respect of health services on Nisga'a Lands.

Adoption

96. Nisga'a Lisims Government may make laws in respect of the adoption of Nisga'a children.

Pre-school to Grade 12 Education

100. Nisga'a Lisims Government may make laws in respect of pre-school to grade 12 education on Nisga'a Lands of Nisga'a citizens, including the teaching of Nisga'a language and culture ...

Post-Secondary Education

103. Nisga'a Lisims Government may make laws in respect of post-secondary education within Nisga'a Lands ...

Chapter 12: Administration of Justice

Police Services

General

1. If Nisga'a Lisims Government decides to provide policing within Nisga'a Lands, it may do so by:
    a. making laws for a Nisga'a Police Board and a Nisga'a Police Service under paragraph 3;
    b. entering into agreements under which some or all of the policing will be provided by the provincial police service or other police services; or
    c. both (a) and (b).

Nisga'a Police Service

13. A member of the Nisga'a Police Service:
    a. has the powers, duties, privileges, liabilities and responsibilities of a peace officer according to law;
    b. has the immunity from personal liability provided to the police officers under provincial law; and
    c. has the authority throughout British Columbia while carrying out the powers, duties, privileges, and responsibilities that a police constable or peace officer is entitled or required to exercise or carry out according to law.

Nisga'a Court

General

30. Nisga'a Lisims Government may make laws to provide for the constitution, maintenance, and organization of a Nisga'a Court for the better administration of Nisga'a laws.

Chapter 14: Capital Transfer and Negotiation Loan Repayment

Capital Transfer

1. Subject to paragraph 4, Canada and British Columbia will each pay their respective capital transfer amounts to the Nisga'a Nation, in accordance with Schedule A.

Negotiation Loan Repayment

2. Subject to paragraph 3, the Nisga'a Nation will pay loan repayment amounts to Canada in accordance with Schedule B.

Chapter 15: Fiscal Relations

Own Source Revenue Administration

21. Nisga'a Lisims Government may make laws that impose an obligation on the Nisga'a Nation, Nisga'a Villages, Nisga'a settlement trusts, or Nisga'a government corporations, in respect of the determination, adjustment, payment, or collection of amounts, to enable the Nisga'a Nation to recover from those entities amounts in respect of Nisga'a Nation own source revenue capacity.

Chapter 16: Taxation

Direct Taxation

1. Nisga'a Lisims Government may make laws in respect of direct taxation of Nisga'a citizens on Nisga'a Lands in order to raise revenue for Nisga'a Nation or Nisga'a Village purposes.
2. Nisga'a Lisims Government powers provided for in paragraph 1 will not limit the powers of Canada or British Columbia to impose or levy tax or make laws in respect of taxation.

Chapter 17: Cultural Artifacts and Heritage

General

1. The Parties recognize the integral role of Nisga'a artifacts in the continuation of Nisga'a culture, values, and traditions.
2. The Parties recognize the Nisga'a Nation's traditional and sacred connection with Nisga'a artifacts, regardless of whether those artifacts are held by the Nisga'a Nation, a Nisga'a Village, a Nisga'a Corporation, a Nisga'a citizen, the Canadian Museum of Civilization, or the Royal British Columbia Museum.

Protection of Heritage Sites

36. Nisga'a Government will develop processes to manage heritage sites on Nisga'a Lands in order to preserve the heritage values associated with those sites from proposed land and resource activities that may affect those sites.

Human Remains

43. Subject to federal and provincial laws, any human remains of individuals of Nisga'a ancestry that are removed from a heritage site will be delivered to the Nisga'a Nation.

Chapter 19: Dispute Resolution

General

2. In this Chapter, and in each Appendix, a Party is deemed to be directly engaged in a disagreement if another Party, acting reasonably, gives the first Party written notice requiring it to participate in a process described in this Chapter to resolve the disagreement.

Disagreements to Go through Stages

11. The Parties desire and expect that most disagreements will be resolved by informal discussions between or among the Parties, without the necessity of invoking this Chapter.
12. Except as otherwise provided, disagreements not resolved informally will progress, until resolved, through the following stages:
    a. Stage One: formal, unassisted efforts to reach agreement between or among the Parties, in collaborative negotiations under Appendix M-1;
    b. Stage Two: structured efforts to reach agreement between or among the Parties with the assistance of a neutral, who has no authority to resolve the dispute, in a facilitated process under Appendix M-2, M-3, M-4, or M-5 as applicable; and
    c. Stage Three: final adjudication in arbitral proceedings under Appendix M-6, or in judicial proceedings.

Chapter 20: Eligibility and Enrolment

Eligibility Criteria

1. An individual is eligible to be enrolled under this Agreement if that individual is:
   a. of Nisga'a ancestry and their mother was born into one of the Nisga'a tribes;
   b. a descendant of an individual described in subparagraphs 1(a) or 1(c);

c. an adopted child of an individual described in subparagraphs 1(a) or 1(b); or

d. an aboriginal individual who is married to someone described in sub-paragraphs 1(a), (b), or (c) and has been adopted by one of the four Nisga'a tribes in accordance with *Ayuukhl* Nisga'a, that is, the individual had been accepted by a Nisga'a tribe, as a member of that tribe, in the presence of witnesses from the other Nisga'a tribes at a settlement or stone moving feast.

Enrolment Committee

8. The Enrolment Committee is a committee established by the General Executive Board of the Nisga'a Tribal Council and governed by enrolment rules adopted by the General Executive Board of the Nisga'a Tribal Council.

9. The Enrolment Committee comprises eight Nisga'a individuals, as follows:

a. two members from the *Laxsgiik* (Eagle) tribe, as selected by that tribe;

b. two members from the *Gisk'aast* (Killer whale) tribe, as selected by that tribe;

c. two members from the *Ganada* (Raven) tribe, as selected by that tribe;

d. two members from the *Laxgibuu* (Wolf) tribe, as selected by that tribe each of whom must understand *Ayuukhl* Nisga'a, Nisga'a culture, Nisga'a ancestry, Nisga'a tribes, and Nisga'a community institutions, and must reside in a Nisga'a village.

Chapter 21: Implementation

1. On the effective date, the Parties will establish an Implementation Plan to guide the Parties on the implementation of this Agreement.

2. The Implementation Plan will be for a term of 10 years, commencing on the effective date.

3. The Implementation Plan:

a. identifies obligations and activities arising from this Agreement;

b. identifies the manner in which the Parties anticipate fulfilling those obligations and undertaking those activities;

c. contains guidelines for the operation of the Implementation Committee established under this Chapter;

d. includes a communication strategy in respect of the implementation and content of this Agreement;

e. provides for the preparation of annual reports on the implementation of this Agreement; and

f. addresses other matters agreed to by the Parties.

Chapter 22: Ratification

Ratification by the Nisga'a Nation

2. Ratification of this Agreement by the Nisga'a Nation requires:
   a. debate at an assembly of the Nisga'a Nation called to consider this Agreement and to determine whether to refer it to a referendum;
   b. proposal at that assembly of a motion to refer this Agreement to a referendum;
   c. adoption of that notion by a simple majority of those voting on that motion;
   d. conduct, by the Ratification Committee, of the referendum referred to in paragraph 5; and
   e. that in the referendum, a simple majority of eligible voters vote in favour of entering into this Agreement.
3. All votes cast in a referendum under this Chapter will be by secret ballot.

Ratification by Canada

10. Ratification of this Agreement by Canada requires:
    a. that this Agreement be signed by a Minister of the Crown authorized by the Governor in Council; and
    b. the enactment of federal settlement legislation giving effect to this Agreement.

Ratification by British Columbia

11. Ratification of this Agreement by British Columbia requires:
    a. that this Agreement be signed by a Minister of the Crown authorized by the Lieutenant Governor in Council; and
    b. the enactment of this provincial settlement legislation giving effect to this Agreement.

Adoption of the Nisga'a Constitution

12. Adoption of the Nisga'a Constitution requires the support of at least 70% of those eligible voters who vote in a referendum on the Nisga'a Constitution.

NOTE

1. Copy of Treaty No. 6 between Her Majesty the Queen and the Plain and Wood Cree Indians and Other Tribes of Indians at Fort Carlton, Fort Pitt and Battle River with Adhesions.

REFERENCES

Stanley, George F.G. 1988. "As Long as the Sun Shines and the Water Flows: An Historical Comment." Pp. 1–26 in *As Long as the Sun Shines and the Water Flows*, eds. Ian A.L. Getty and Antoine S. Lussier. Vancouver: University of British Columbia Press.

Young, T. Kue. 1984. "Indian Health Services in Canada: A Socio-Historical Perspective." *Social Science and Medicine* 18(3): pp. 257–64.

INDEX